ESSENTIALS OF MARKETING RESEARCH

THIRD EDITION

William G. Zikmund
Oklahoma State University

Barry J. Babin
University of Southern Mississippi

THOMSON

SOUTH-WESTERN

Australia · Brazil · Canada · Mexico · Singapore · Spain · United Kingdom · United States

THOMSON

SOUTH-WESTERN

Essentials of Marketing Research, Third Edition
William G. Zikmund, Barry J. Babin

VP/Editorial Director:
Jack W. Calhoun

Publisher:
Neil Marquardt

Developmental Editor:
Ohlinger Publishing Services

Marketing Manager:
Nicole C. Moore

Content Project Manager:
Robert Dreas

Marketing Communications Manager:
Sarah Greber

Manager Editorial Media:
John Barans

Technology Project Manager:
Pam Wallace

Sr. 1st Print Buyer:
Diane Gibbons

Production House:
Interactive Composition Corporation

Printer:
Courier Corp.
Kendallville, Indiana

Art Director:
Stacy Jenkins Shirley

Internal and Cover Designer:
Craig Ramsdell

Cover Images:
® Getty Images/Taxi/James Porto

Photography Manager:
Deanna Ettinger

Photo Researcher:
Susan Van Etten

Library of Congress Control Number:
2006908266

For more information about our products,
contact us at:
Thomson Learning Academic Resource
Center
1-800-423-0563

Thomson Higher Education
5191 Natorp Boulevard
Mason, OH 45040
USA

To my family and friends.

BRIEF CONTENTS

CONTENTS

CONTENTS

PART 2
DESIGNING RESEARCH STUDIES

PART 3
MEASUREMENT

PART 4
SAMPLING AND STATISTICAL THEORY

PART 5
ANALYSIS AND REPORTING

PART 6
COMPREHENSIVE CASES WITH COMPUTERIZED DATABASES

PREFACE

PREFACE

Why a needle in a haystack on the cover? This image presents a graphic analogy to the research process from many perspectives. How do you find the needle? Where do you start? Clearly, it would be helpful if you could discover better places to start searching and better techniques to help direct the search.

Similarly, imagine trying to find a single piece of market information from the Internet. Like the needle, this information may well be hidden beneath piles and piles of irrelevant stuff! Or how about trying to find a key piece of market information that may be hidden in the mind of a consumer or some employee who isn't consciously aware of all his or her reasons for some preference or some behavior and, consequently, can't identify or talk about it? How do you go about finding this information that could be so crucial to making a good market decision?

Searching for the needle is very much like searching for answers to market problems. Both can be very well hidden. And both need to be discovered for you to succeed.

Using an X-ray monitor would be a great way to find the needle. But your real-world success is probably more dependent on the ability to wield an effective research process than an X-ray monitor. And that's where this text comes in: *Essentials of Marketing Research* equips students with the knowledge and skills involved in this basic research process that will simplify and provide more accuracy to their search for market intelligence.

Chapter 3 introduces this process, which includes six stages. Researchers must first work together with decision makers to decide why they are looking for that metaphorical needle; the next two stages plot out the way to go about finding the needle. Next are two stages that focus on the actual search for the needle. The process concludes when the market researcher communicates the benefits of finding "pointed" information that can help mend problems or create something really new and special to the decision maker. Success in this process usually merits the researcher a reward that is a bit more valuable than that needle!

New to Essentials of Marketing Research

To ensure that students are able to conduct market research with an understanding of the latest theories and techniques avalable to them, this third edition is substantially revised and updated. Certainly, the field of marketing research is dynamic both in terms of the demands placed on it by business and in terms of the technological advances that provide more tools for the researcher's toolbox.

The Internet is revolutionizing information systems, ways of gathering secondary data, survey processes, sampling, questionnaire design, qualitative analysis, and communication of results. Practically every chapter includes significant coverage of Internet-related topics, and most chapters also include review questions and activities that get students involved with the Internet in a relevant way.

In addition to greater currency and attention given to the Internet, other key features added to the third edition include

- All New Chapter Vignettes—each chapter opens with a story relevant to the material featured in that particular chapter. Some of these vignettes involve famous brands and companies, so the reader may well be familiar with some of the topics. Other vignettes involve "slice of life" stories describing a business person's struggle to make smart decisions and demonstrate how research is intertwined with this struggle. Most chapters refer back to the vignette multiple times to provide a running example through the chapter.

- A Simplified Approach and Style—the boxed material, chapter objectives, and end-of-case materials are now presented in a simplified form that allows greater focus on the truly important information. Boxed materials are now in the form of Research Snapshots that cover ethical angles of research, provide illustrations of research in practice, and offer relevant tips or detailed examples. The chapter learning objectives give an important coherence and structure to the chapters that culminate with the end-of-chapter materials.

    This deliberate approach has been taken to emphasize significant content material and issues, which will reinforce positive student learning outcomes. Moreover, this simplified approach continues into the analytical chapters, which now deemphaisize statistical theory and detail and focus more on practical statistical application.

- Increased Coverage on International Business Issues—the examples and illustrations make much greater use of international business. Readers of this book may end up working outside the United States or Canada. The increased international examples will increase awareness of research issues beyond North America and open up domestic students to global dynamics. This is a particularly important addition to the text since cultural and language barriers often present challenges for the researcher.

- New Case Materials—nearly all chapters include at least one new end-of-chapter case; two new end-of-book cases have also been added. Many of the revised and new end-of-chapter materials focus on Internet issues or ethical issues associated with marketing research. New and updated video cases provide great opportunities to get into real-world business situations that involve marketing research.

- Greater Attention to Qualitative Research—more and more companies are benefiting from qualitative research. In response to this important phenomenon, Chapter 5 is essentially a new chapter that focuses much more directly on qualitative research philosophies and methodologies. In addition, the ways that technological advances, including advancing Internet technologies, are affecting qualitative research are provided significant coverage. The end-of-chapter materials as well as an end-of-book case provide more attention to qualitative research applications.

Organization of the Book

The organization of the third edition of *Essentials of Marketing Research* follows the logic of the marketing research process. The book is organized into six parts. Each part presents the basic research concepts for one of the stages in the research process and discusses how these concepts relate to decisions about conducting specific projects.

Part 1: Introduction begins the book by discussing the scope of marketing research. An overview of problem definition and the entire marketing research process is provided. The interplay between research and business is emphasized throughout this discussion. Research is not equally important among all firms. The way that the importance and scope of research varies with the type of business orientation that characterizes some company is illustrated. An overview of computerized data management and information systems and an explanation of how all of this is changing due to the Internet follows. Without high ethical standards, no business is good. Thus, the introductory materials also include an emphasis on business ethics and the special ethical problems associated with marketing research.

Part 2: Designing Research Studies covers essentials that provide a starting place to studying business problems. In this context, Part 2 discusses the need for exploratory research and secondary data collection. Research proposals are covered in some detail, and the reader is encouraged to see these as the written agreement that helps put the decision maker and the researcher on the same page.

Chapter 5 emphasizes qualitative research applications. One role played by qualitative research is helping to separate business problem symptoms from true issues that can be attacked with marketing research. However, qualitative research is a topic extending far beyond problem definition by allowing greater potential for discovery and greater potential for deeper and potentially more meaningful explanations.

Part 2 includes a detailed discussion of secondary data and emphasizes its increasing importance in an increasingly data rich world. This part also examines some topics most closely associated with marketing research. For example, the chapters describe issues related to planning, conducting and administering surveys. Surveys remain a mainstay for collecting consumer and employee opinion. Part 2 concludes with material dealing specifically with market experiments. As such, this part emphasizes test marketing, which to many is synonymous with marketing research.

Part 3: Measurement is critical to research. This part of the text discusses the basics of measurement theory. Two chapters offer practical explanations of measurement and questionnaire design. Key topics include descriptions of the different levels of scale measurement and how this affects the interpretation of results.

Part 4: Sampling and Statistical Theory examines sampling designs and sample size. These chapters explain the difference between a population and a sample. The reasons why sampling is needed and why it can be used to confidently allow predictions about larger numbers of people are covered. The fieldwork process also is discussed, including the importance of supervision of the work that goes on in the field.

Part 5: Analysis and Reporting covers important processes necessary in translating raw data into market intelligence. Included among these topics, the data must be edited and coded. The coded data are then ready for analysis. Some of the most commonly used methods for analyzing data also are presented. For instance, basic descriptive statistics are discussed as ways of portraying key results like central tendency. Inferential statistics also are discussed, including often-used univariate and bivariate approaches such as t-tests.

Part 6: Comprehensive Cases with Computerized Databases make up the last section of the book. These cases provide materials to challenge students to apply and integrate concepts learned. Instructors will find that these cases provide some flexibility either to expand or simplify the assignment to suit the demands of varying course assignments. The two cases provide more variety and include some that involve analysis of internal marketing problems as well as an opportunity to use qualitative research. When quantitative data are included, they can be easily analyzed with basic statistical tools like SPSS. Excel files are also included with the same data. These files can be read directly by statistical programs like SAS or other programs.

Superior Pedegogy

More than other marketing research textbooks, the third edition of *Essentials of Marketing Research* addresses students' need to comprehend all aspects of the marketing research process. The following features facilitate learning throughout the book:

- **Learning Outcomes.** Each chapter begins with a concise list of learning objectives that emphasize the major areas of competency the student should achieve before proceeding to the next chapter. Chapter material is clearly linked to the learning objectives, and the end-of-chapter materials emphasize questions and activities relevant to these key competencies.
- **Opening Chapter Vignettes.** The opening vignettes describe marketing research challenges in actual businesses. They frame the material that follows and provide context to the subject matter. Instructors and students are invited to extend these stories with updated current events or with war stories of their own.

- **Research Snapshots.** All of the boxed materials now share a common title, Research Snapshots. The boxes explore marketing research processes in a variety of modern business situations, ranging from natural disasters to international food. The boxes also illustrate some research techniques and applications in a step-by-step fashion.

- **Writing Style.** An accessible, interesting writing style continues as a hallmark of this book. With a careful balance between theory and practice and a sprinkling of interesting examples and anecdotes, the writing style clarifies and simplifies the market research process. In addition, the text offers a comprehensive treatment of important and current topics.

- **Statistical Approach.** A short review of statistical theory in Chapter 13 provides students with an overview of the basic aspects of statistics. Because this text stresses managerial applications more than statistical theory, students are given some basic tools to perform common data analysis. More sophisticated data analysis approaches are left for further reference. Thus, the readers can learn how to test simple hypotheses involving differences between means or relationships among variables. Cross-tabulation, t-tests, ANOVA, and regression are covered in sufficient depth to allow a student to use these techniques.

  In addition, easy-to-follow, click-through sequences can walk a student through a few of the most basic approaches to producing statistical results.

- **Key Terms.** Learning the vocabulary of marketing research is essential to understanding the topic, and *Essentials of Marketing Research* facilitates this with key terms. First, key concepts are boldfaced and completely defined when they first appear in the textbook. Second, all key terms and concepts are listed at the end of each chapter, and many terms are highlighted in a marginal glossary. Third, a glossary summarizing all key terms and definitions appears at the end of the book for handy reference. A glossary of frequently used symbols is also included.

- **Ethics Questions.** Identified by a special icon, ETHICS, ethics questions are included in most chapters. Among the compelling issues students are asked to explore is redefining the right to privacy in light of new technology. The ethical issues also provide a great opportunity for building critical thinking skills.

- **Internet Questions.** Internet questions also are identified by a special 'NET. Nearly all chapters include multiple questions and research activities that illustrate advances in Internet applications common to marketing research.

- **Research Activities.** The end-of-chapter materials include a few real-world research activities intended to provide actual research experience for the student. Most provide an opportunity for the student to gain experience with multiple content areas. Some involve ethical aspects of research, and some involve Internet usage.

- **Cases.** Extensive cases and video cases taken from real-life situations illustrate marketing research concepts and build knowledge and research skills. These cases offer students the opportunity to participate actively in the decision-making process, one of the most effective forms of learning. The video cases portray actual research activities for brands and companies, such as Fisher-Price, Wine.com, Krispy Kreme, Federal Express, and Goya Foods. Five additional cases at the end of the text provide students with real-life opportunities to apply the knowledge and skills they have learned from multiple areas of the text.

Comprehensive Instructor Resources

It is important for any text to develop comprehensive supplemental materials to support instructors in their vital teaching function. Because of this pedagogical philosophy, the extensive learning package provided with *Essentials of Marketing Research* includes a Test Bank, a computerized Test Bank (ExamView Testing Software), a comprehensive Instructor's Manual and Transparency Masters, PowerPoint presentation slides, data sets for several cases, and online marketing resources (available on the web at www.thomsonedu.com/marketing/zikmund).

- The Instructor's Resource CD-ROM (ISBN: 0-324-32206-2) contains valuable instructor resources on one easy-to-use CD-ROM: the Test Bank, ExamView Testing Software, the Instructor's Manual, PowerPoint presentation slides, and data sets for cases.

- The Test Bank (ISBN: 0-324-54798-6), originally written by Thomas Quirk of Webster University, has been carefully rewritten to provide a variety of questions covering every major concept in the textbook. All the questions have been scrutinized to eliminate ambiguity and to provide varying levels of difficulty. Each question is identified with a page number from the textbook where the answer may be located.
- ExamView is an easy-to-use automated testing program that allows instructors to create exams by using provided questions, modifying questions, or adding new questions.
- The Instructor's Manual with Transparency Masters (ISBN: 0-324-54800-1), prepared by Laurie Babin of The University of Southern Mississippi, were designed to ease lecture preparation by offering detailed and comprehensive lecture outlines, solutions to all assignments, and transparency masters. The solution to each case and video case includes the objectives of the case, a brief summary of the case, and recommended questions and solutions. The Instructor's Manual is available both on the Instructor's Resource CD-ROM and at www.thomsonedu.com/marketing/zikmund on the instructor's portion of the website.
- PowerPoint Presentation Slides, prepared by Charlie T. Cook, Jr. of the University of West Alabama, summarize and illustrate key concepts in each chapter. These slides are available both on the Instructor's Resource CD-ROM and at www.thomsonedu.com/marketing/zikmund, where they can be downloaded.
- Data are provided that match several end-of-chapter exercises and different case analyses. The data are provided both in Excel files, allowing great flexibility to be used with many programs, and in SPSS files, which are ready to use with either the student or full version of SPSS. Students may download the data sets at www.thomsonedu.com/marketing/zikmund by clicking on the textbook and then on "Data Sets." Data sets are also available on the Instructor's Resource CD-ROM.
- The Video DVD (ISBN: 0-324-54801-X) consists of eight chapter video cases. Brand new video cases correspond with new video segments. The video cases guide students through marketing research issues faced by a variety of well-known companies, such as Mercedes-Benz, Krispy Kreme, and the successful e-commerce business Wine.com. Discussion questions related to the video cases are included in the Instructor's Manual.
- Web Resources at www.thomsonedu.com/marketing/zikmund provide the latest information about what's new and what's cool in marketing research. The site features links to other research-related sites, tips about using the supplemental video library, and much more.

Resources for Students

To promote learning and competency, it is also important to provide students with well-crafted resources. In addition to covering the latest information technology (described above), the third edition includes the following student resources:

- The Dedicated Website www.thomsonedu.com/marketing/zikmund, developed especially for the new edition, includes chapter quizzes that allow students to test and retest their knowledge of chapter concepts. Each chapter has a quiz to encourage retesting. In addition, the website features downloadable flash cards of key terms, the very best online marketing research resources available, and much more.
- SPSS (ISBN: 0-324-40771-8) brings affordable, professional statistical analysis and modeling tools to a student's own PC. SPSS 15.0 for Windows Student Version includes an easy-to-use interface and comprehensive online help that lets students learn statistics, not software. SPSS 15.0 is available as an optional bundle with the new edition.

Acknowledgments

Certainly, no list of acknowledgments will be complete. So many people have assisted in this project. Chief among these would be to the late Bill Zikmund for carrying the weight of this project for the two previous editions, I am privileged to be able to carry the project along into hopefully many more editions as the premier marketing research text. Also, thanks go to some of my team here at the University. My graduate assistants Melanie Gardner and Christina Chung have helped with research for this text and helped share some of the workload on other endeavors freeing up time for me to spend on this project. Thanks also to Janice Prescott and Betty Dickerson for helping to manage my crazy schedule. My family also has had to put up with less elaborate dinners and many evenings and weekends working around my writing time. Also, thanks go to all the great faculty who mentored me during my days in the Ph.D. program at LSU. Most notable among these are Joseph F. Hair, Jr. and the late William R. Darden.

Special thanks go to all the good people at Thomson Business and Economics who helped make this project possible. Thanks to my publisher, Neil Marquardt, for motivating the whole team to stay on schedule. Thanks to Nicole Moore for creative inspirations and marketing support. Also, a special thanks to Joanne Vickers and Erin Curtis at Ohlinger Publishing Services. They provided tremendous support through the writing and production process, including assistance with proofing, permissions, photos, and exhibits. Thanks also to Karen Hill for assistance with research and editing.

Many colleagues contributed ideas for this book. They made many suggestions that greatly enhanced this book. For their insightful reviews of the manuscript for the third or previous editions of *Essentials of Marketing Research*, I would like to thank the following:

Karen Goncalves
Nichols College

Carol Bienstock
Radford University

Steven V. Cates
Averett University

Stephanie Noble
The University of Mississippi

Bob Lauman
Webster University

Natalie Wood
St. Joseph's University

Robert Jaross
Florida International University

Terry Paul
The Ohio State University

Mike Parent
Utah State University

Stephen Batory
Bloomsburg University

Michael R. Hyman
New Mexico State University

Rick Saucier
St. John's University

Xin Zhao
University of Utah

Gerald Albaum
University of Oregon

William Bearden
University of South Carolina

Joseph A. Bellizzi
Arizona State University–West

James A. Brunner
University of Toledo

F. Anthony Bushman
San Francisco State University

Thomas Buzas
Eastern Michigan University

Roy F. Cabaniss
Huston-Tillotson College

Michael d'Amico
University of Akron

Ron Eggers
Barton College

H. Harry Friedman
City University of New York–Brooklyn

Ron Goldsmith
Florida State University

Larry Goldstein
Iona College

David Gourley
Arizona State University

Jim Grimm
Illinois State University

Al Gross
Robert Morris College

Don Heinz
University of Wisconsin

Craig Hollingshead
Texas A&M University–Kingsville

Victor Howe
University of Kentucky

Roy Howell
Texas Tech University

Rhea Ingram
Columbus State University–Georgia

P. K. Kannan
University of Maryland

Susan Kleine
Arizona State University

David B. Klenosky
Purdue University

C. S. Kohli
California State University–Fullerton

Jerome L. Langer
Assumption College

James H. Leigh
Texas A&M University

Larry Lowe
Bryant College

Karl Mann
Tennessee Technological University

Charles R. Martin
Wichita State University

Marlys Mason
Oklahoma State University

Tom K. Massey
University of Missouri–Kansas City

Sanjay Mishra
University of Kansas

G. M. Naidu
University of Wisconsin–Whitewater

Charles Prohaska
Central Connecticut State University

Alan Sawyer
University of Florida

Robert Schaffer
California State University–Pomona

Leon G. Schiffman
City University of New York–Baruch

K. Sivakumar
Lehigh University

Mark Speece
Central Washington University

Harlan Spotts
Western New England College

Wilbur W. Stanton
Old Dominion University

Bruce L. Stern
Portland State University

James L. Taylor
University of Alabama

Gail Tom
California State University–Sacramento

Deborah Utter
Boston College

David Wheeler
Suffolk University

Richard Wilcox
Carthage College

Margaret Wright
University of Colorado

Clifford E. Young
University of Colorado–Denver

William Lee Ziegler
Bethune-Cookman College

Thanks also to all of the students who have inspired me and reinforced the fact that I made a great career decision about two decades ago. Thanks also to my close colleagues Mitch Griffin, Dave Ortinau, and Jim Boles for their continued support and insight.

Barry J. Babin
October 2006

In Remembrance

William G. Zikmund (1943-2002)

A native of the Chicago area, William G. Zikmund was a professor of marketing at Oklahoma State University and died shortly after completing the previous edition. He received a Ph.D. in business administration with a concentration in marketing from the University of Colorado.

Before beginning his academic career, Professor Zikmund worked in marketing research for Conway/Millikin Company (a marketing research supplier) and Remington Arms Company (an extensive user of marketing research). Professor Zikmund also served as a marketing research consultant to several business and nonprofit organizations. During his academic career, Professor Zikmund published dozens of articles and papers in a diverse group of scholarly journals ranging from the *Journal of Marketing* to the *Accounting Review* to the *Journal of Applied Psychology*. In addition to *Essentials of Marketing Research*, Professor Zikmund authored *Exploring of Marketing Research*, *Business Research Methods*, *Marketing*, *Effective Marketing*, and a work of fiction, *A Corporate Bestiary*.

Professor Zikmund was a member of several professional organizations, including the American Marketing Association, the Academy of Marketing Science, the Association for Consumer Research, the Society for Marketing Advances, the Marketing Educators' Association, and the Association of Collegiate Marketing Educators. He served on the editorial review boards of the *Journal of Marketing Education, Marketing Education Review, Journal of the Academy of Marketing Science*, and *Journal of Business Research*.

Part 1
Introduction

©PHIL KNOTT/PYMCA/JUPITER IMAGES

CHAPTER 1
THE ROLE OF MARKETING RESEARCH

After studying this chapter, you should be able to

1. Explain why marketing research is essential to business success
2. Define marketing research
3. Identify the difference between applied and basic research
4. Explain how marketing research is relevant to product, pricing, promotion, and distribution decisions
5. Discuss how marketing research helps the firm develop and implement strategy
6. Identify the situations that call for market research and those that don't
7. Describe how technology and internationalization are affecting the way research is conducted and used

Chapter Vignette: "If It Quacks Like a Duck?"

"If you're hurt and you miss work": This is the tag line for one of the most popular U.S. advertising campaigns—for AFLAC Insurance. The tag line is accompanied by the familiar Peking duck constantly reminding people with a loud "AFFLLAACKK!!" Recent polls show that the AFLAC duck has become one of America's favorite icons, coming in second only to the Mars M&Ms. But how has the duck's favorable fan status affected AFLAC's business performance? Certainly, AFLAC's marketing strategy goes beyond creating the most popular duck since Donald!

PR NEWSFOTO AFLAC

Through its thirty year history, AFLAC, like other firms, has faced important decisions about how to create brand awareness, how to build consumer knowledge of the brand, and how to build sales and loyalty. Leading up to these decisions, the firm must first assess its current situation and its brand awareness relative to its competitors. Approximately two dozen AFLAC duck commercials ago, research revealed that most consumers were unaware of AFLAC. The vast majority of consumers would not list AFLAC when prompted to name insurance companies. Instead, names like Allstate, State Farm, and Prudential proved more familiar. Not surprisingly, these companies enjoyed greater market share. Based on this research, AFLAC decided to invest in a national television campaign to build awareness of the brand name—"AFFLLAAACCK!!" The phonic similarity to "QUACK" proved successful.

Today, AFLAC has built great awareness of its name, but this hasn't necessarily translated into business success. Despite the tag line, fewer than 30 percent of consumers who recognize the name know that AFLAC specializes in supplemental disability insurance. This accounts for over three-fourths of AFLAC's nearly $14 billion dollar annual revenue. Thus, while the initial research suggested the need for building awareness, their more recent research is addressing difficulties in creating the right "knowledge" of AFLAC. What communication medium is best for building knowledge? Can knowledge be built in the same way as awareness? Will knowledge lead to increased intentions to do business with AFLAC? What role does personal selling play in building knowledge? All of these are questions that should be answered. Marketing research will be directed toward answering these questions. The answers will then be used to try and erase the knowledge deficit faced by AFLAC. If the answers are half as effective as those that lead to the AFLAC duck, the company should enjoy tremendous success. Thus, for AFLAC, as for many firms, marketing research is an important tool in shaping business strategy.[1]

Introduction

The recent history of AFLAC demonstrates the need for information in making informed decisions addressing key issues faced by all competitive businesses. Research can provide that information. Without it, business decisions involving product promotion, distribution, pricing, and the product design itself are made in the dark.

We open with an example illustrating how business decisions require intelligence and how research can provide that intelligence. The following focuses specifically on how marketing research encourages innovation in the form of new products or improvements in existing goods and services. Imagine yourself in the role of brand manager as you read this example and think about the information needs you may have in trying to build success for your brand.

Jelly Belly brand sells fifty varieties of jelly beans, with the number growing every year. Some flavors came from suggestions of visitors to Jelly Belly's website. In return for filling out an interactive questionnaire, visitors had samples sent to them. Jelly Belly received a great response to this offer. Researchers categorized the suggestions, grouping them by similar flavors. Some suggestions were put back on the Web so that people could vote for the flavor they most wanted to see introduced. The company received some really off-the-wall flavor ideas. Among the strangest are flavors such as Dill Pickle, Taco, Persimmon Pudding, Blackened Plantain, and Cream of Wheat.[2]

Jelly Belly brand's market research has capitalized on consumers' desires to produce fifty varieties of jelly beans as well as recipes on how to create snacks with them.

More recently, Jelly Belly is trying to capitalize on consumers' desires to have a healthy snack without giving up tasty treats. Survey research suggests that consumers would respond favorably to food and drink products containing additives that will make them more healthy and/or energetic.[3] As a result, Jelly Belly has introduced "Sport Beans." Sport Beans contain added enzymes, carbohydrates, and vitamins all designed to provide added energy and alertness. In addition, following up on the Harry Potter craze, Jelly Belly's research suggested that kids would indeed go for *vomit, booger,* or *earthworm* flavored beans,

among other similarly interesting flavors. So, the decision was made to launch Bertie Botts Every Flavor Beans in Canada and the United States. More research is needed before deciding to launch this product internationally.

This example illustrates the need for information in making informed business decisions. Jelly Belly provides consumers with the incentive of free samples of jelly beans in return for ideas about desirable new bean flavors. This research illustrates how marketing research can be used to test consumers' reactions to new product concepts. However, this is only the tip of the iceberg when it comes to the types of marketing research that are conducted every day. This chapter introduces basic concepts of marketing research and describes how research can play a crucial role in successful marketing and business success in general.

The Nature of Marketing Research

In its essence, business is very simple. Companies need to produce benefits that people want to buy! That means that consumers must view the company as providing valuable bundles of benefits. There are many factors that can affect this value, and successful companies are those that understand the value equation. With this in mind, there are several key questions, the answers to which help provide this understanding.

1. *What do we sell?*
   This includes not only the benefits that are easily seen, but also the more emotional benefits such as the comfort and relaxation of enjoying a cup of gourmet coffee in a pleasant atmosphere or the novelty of trying a booger jelly bean.

2. *How do consumers view our company?*
   All too often, companies define themselves too narrowly, based only on the physical *product* they sell. A key question involves whom the customers will do business with if they do not choose your company. For instance, how is Starbucks viewed relative to its competitors? Who are the competitors? Does Starbucks compete more directly with Maxwell House, Seattle Drip, or something completely outside the coffee arena like a local lounge? Are we viewed more or less favorably relative to the competition?

3. *What does our company/product mean?*
   What knowledge do people have of the company and its products? Do they know how to use them? Do they know all the different needs the company can address? What does our packaging and promotion communicate to consumers? The opening chapter vignette described AFLAC's problem in creating consumer knowledge now that it has consumer awareness.

4. *What do consumers desire?*
   How can the company make the lives of its customers better, and how can it do this in a way that is not easily duplicated by another firm? Part of this lies in uncovering the things that customers truly desire, but which they can often not put into words.

Answering these questions requires information. Marketing research's function is to supply information that helps answer these questions, thereby leading to more informed and more successful business decision making. With useful information, decisions can be made with less risk.

It's been said that "every business issue ultimately boils down to an information problem":[4] Can the right information be delivered? Research thus seeks to deliver accurate and precise information that can make marketing strategy and management more effective.[5] Marketing research attempts to supply accurate information that reduces the uncertainty in decision making. Very often, decisions are made with little information for various reasons, including insufficient time to conduct research or management's belief that enough is already known. Relying on seat-of-the-pants decision making—decision making without research—is like betting on a long shot at the racetrack because the horse's name is appealing. Occasionally there are successes, but in the long run intuition without research leads to losses. Marketing research helps decision makers shift from intuitive information gathering to systematic and objective investigating.

Marketing Research Defined

Marketing research is the application of the scientific method in searching for the truth about marketing phenomena. These activities include defining marketing opportunities and problems, generating and evaluating marketing ideas, monitoring performance, and understanding the marketing process. Marketing research is more than conducting surveys.[6] This process includes idea and theory development, problem definition, searching for and collecting information, analyzing data, and communicating the findings and their implications.

This definition suggests that marketing research information is not intuitive or haphazardly gathered. Literally, *research* (re-search) means "to search again." The term connotes patient study and scientific investigation wherein the researcher takes another, more careful look at the data to discover all that is known about the subject. Ultimately, all findings are tied back to marketing theory.

The definition also emphasizes, through reference to the scientific method, that any information generated should be accurate and objective. The researcher should be personally detached and free of bias attempting to find truth. Research isn't performed to support preconceived ideas but to test them. If bias enters into the research process, the value of the research is considerably reduced. We will discuss this further in a subsequent chapter.

Clearly, our definition makes it clear that marketing research is relevant to all aspects of the marketing mix. Research can facilitate managerial decision making in all aspects of the firm's marketing mix: product, pricing, promotion, and distribution. By providing the necessary information on which to base marketing mix decisions, marketing research can decrease the risk of making a wrong decision in each area.

Finally, this definition of marketing research is limited by one's definition of *marketing*. Although research in the marketing area of a for-profit corporation like AFLAC clearly is marketing research, marketing research also includes efforts that assist nonprofit organizations such as the American Heart Association, the San Diego Zoo, the Boston Pops Orchestra, or a parochial school. Each of these organizations exists to satisfy social needs, and each requires marketing skills to produce and distribute its products and services. The federal government also performs many functions that are similar, if not identical, to those of for-profit business organizations. Governments can use research in much the same way as managers at Starbucks or General Motors. For instance, the FDA is an important user of marketing research, employing it to address the way people view and use various food and drugs. One such study commissioned and funded research to address the question of how consumers used the risk summaries that are included with all drugs sold in the United States.[7] This book explores marketing research as it applies to all organizations and institutions engaging in some form of marketing activity.

Applied and Basic Marketing Research

One useful way to describe research is based on the specificity of its purpose. **Applied marketing research** is conducted to address a specific marketing decision for a specific firm or organization. The opening vignette describes a situation in which AFLAC may use applied marketing research to decide how to best create knowledge of its supplemental disability insurance products.

Basic marketing research is conducted without a specific decision in mind, and it usually does not address the needs of a specific organization. It attempts to expand the limits of marketing knowledge in general, and as such it is not aimed at solving a particular pragmatic problem. Basic research can be used to test the validity of a general marketing theory (one that applies to all of marketing) or to learn more about some market phenomenon. For instance, a great deal of basic marketing research addresses the ways in which retail atmosphere influences consumers' emotions and behavior.[8] From such research, we can learn how much the physical place creates value for consumers relative to the actual product consumed. This basic research does not examine the problem from any single retail or service provider's perspective. However, Starbucks' management may become aware of such research and use it to design applied research studies examining questions about its store designs. Thus, the two types of research are not completely independent.

Marketing research
The application of the scientific method in searching for the truth about marketing phenomena. These activities include defining marketing opportunities and problems, generating and evaluating marketing ideas, monitoring performance, and understanding the marketing process.

Applied marketing research
Research conducted to address a specific marketing decision for a specific firm or organization.

Basic marketing research
Research conducted without a specific decision in mind that usually does not address the needs of a specific organization. It attempts to expand the limits of marketing knowledge in general and is not aimed at solving a particular pragmatic problem.

RESEARCHSNAPSHOT

Good Fat and Bad Fat

American consumers can be seen every day scouring nutrition labels. Most likely, the item they show the most interest in recently is the amount of fat. The Food and Drug Administration (FDA) is concerned that consumers get information that is not only accurate, but that also conveys the proper message to achieve a healthy diet. But all fat is not created equal. In particular, dieticians warn of the dangers associated with excess amounts of trans-fats; diet nutrition labels break fats into saturated and unsaturated fats. Among numerous factors that complicate the interpretation of the nutrition label, trans-fat (hydrogenated) is technically a nonsaturated fat, but it acts more like a saturated fat when consumed. So, where should it be placed? The FDA cannot address this problem intelligently without marketing research addressing questions like.

1. If trans-fats are listed as a saturated fat, would consumers' beliefs about

their consumption become more negative?

2. If the saturated fat amount includes a specific line indicating the amount of "saturated fat" that is really trans-fat, would consumers become more confused about their diet?

3. If all amounts of fat are given equal prominence on the label, will consumer attitudes toward the different types of fats be the same?

Making this even more complicated is the fact that some consumer segments, such as teenagers in this case, may actually use the nutrition labels to select the brands that are least nutritious rather than most nutritious. So, they may actually seek out the one with the worst proportion of trans-fats!

Sources: "Health Labels Are in the Eye of the Beholder," *Food Management*, 40 (January), 80. Hunter, B.T. (2003), "Labeling Transfat Is Tricky," *Consumers' Research Magazine*, 86 (July), 8–10.

©SUSAN VAN ETTEN

Sometimes researchers use different terms to represent the same distinction. Some reserve the term *marketing* research to refer to basic research. Then, the term *market* research is used to capture applied research addressing the needs of a firm within a particular market. While the distinction is very useful in describing research, there are very few aspects of research that apply to only basic or only applied research. The focus of this text is more on applied research—studies that are undertaken to answer questions about specific problems or to make decisions about particular courses of action or policies. In addition, we will use the term *marketing research* more generally to refer to either type of research. Applied research is emphasized in this text because most students will be oriented toward the day-to-day practice of marketing management, and most students and researchers will be exposed to short-term, problem-solving research conducted for businesses or nonprofit organizations.

The Scientific Method

The scientific method
The way researchers go about using knowledge and evidence to reach objective conclusions about the real world.

All marketing research, whether basic or applied, involves the scientific method. **The scientific method** is the way researchers go about using knowledge and evidence to reach objective conclusions about the real world. The scientific method is the same in social sciences such as marketing and in physical sciences such as physics. In this case, it is the way we come to understand marketing phenomena.

Exhibit 1.1 briefly illustrates the scientific method. In the scientific method, there are multiple routes to developing ideas. When the ideas can be stated in researchable terms, we reach the hypothesis stage. The next step involves testing the hypothesis against empirical evidence (facts from observation or experimentation). The results either support a hypothesis or do not support a hypothesis. From these results, new knowledge is acquired.

In basic research, testing these prior conceptions or hypotheses and then making inferences and conclusions about the phenomena leads to the establishment of general laws about the phenomena. Use of the scientific method in applied research ensures objectivity in gathering facts and testing creative ideas for alternative marketing strategies. The essence of research, whether basic or applied, lies in the scientific method. Much of this book deals with scientific methodology. Thus, the techniques of basic and applied research differ largely in degree rather than in substance.

EXHIBIT 1.1
A Summary of the Scientific Method

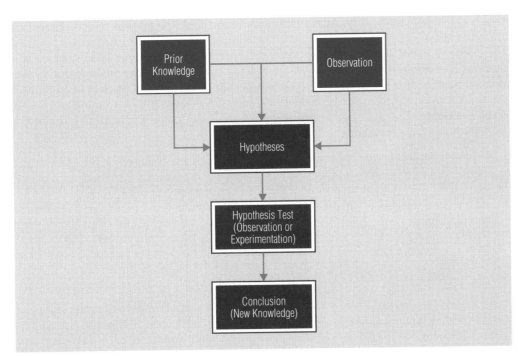

The Marketing Concept

In all of business strategy, there are only a few business orientations (see Exhibit 1.2). A firm can be **product-oriented**. A product-oriented firm prioritizes decision making in a way that empha-sizes technical superiority in the product. Thus, input from technicians and experts in the field is very important in making critical decisions. A firm can be **production-oriented**. Production orientation means that the firm prioritizes efficiency and effectiveness of the production processes in making decisions. Here, input from engineers and accounting becomes important as the firm seeks to drive costs down. Production-oriented firms are usually very large firms

Product-oriented
Describes a firm that prioritizes decision making in a way that emphasizes technical superiority in the product.

Production-oriented
Describes a firm that prioritizes efficiency and effectiveness of the production processes in making decisions.

EXHIBIT 1.2 Business Marketing Orientations

Product-Oriented Firm

Prioritizes decision making that emphasizes the physical product design, trendiness, or technical superiority

Example

The fashion industry makes clothes in styles and sizes that few can adopt.

Little consumer research

Production-Oriented Firm

Prioritizes efficiency and effectiveness of the production processes in making decisions

Example

U.S. auto industry's assembly-line process is intent on reducing costs of production as low as possible.

Little consumer research

Marketing-Oriented Firm

Focuses on how the firm provides value to customers

Example

Well known hotel chains are designed to address the needs of travelers, particularly business travelers.

Much consumer research

Marketing concept
A central idea in modern marketing thinking that focuses on how the firm provides value to customers more than on the physical product or production process.

Marketing orientation
The corporate culture existing for firms adopting the marketing concept. It emphasizes customer orientation, long-term profitability over short-term profits, and a cross-functional perspective.

Customer-oriented
Describes a firm in which all decisions are made with a conscious awareness of their effect on the consumer.

TOTHEPOINT

The aim of marketing is to know your customer so well that when your prospects are confronted with your product, it fits them so exactly that it sells itself.

—Peter Drucker

manufacturing products in very large quantities. In both of these orientations, marketing research may take a backseat.

In contrast, marketing research is a primary tool enabling implementation of a marketing orientation.[9] The **marketing concept** is a central idea in modern marketing thinking that focuses more on how the firm provides value to customers than on the physical product or production process. It has evolved over time as product- and production-oriented firms respond to changes in the competitive and economic environments. When a firm adopts the marketing concept, it develops **marketing orientation**. It calls on management to

1. Be **customer-oriented**—meaning that all firm decisions are made with a conscious awareness of their effect on the consumer
2. Emphasize long-run profitability rather than short-term profits or sales volume
3. Adopt a cross-functional perspective, meaning that marketing is integrated across other business functions

Customer Orientation

According to the marketing concept, the consumer is at the center of the operation, the pivot point about which the business moves to achieve the balanced best interests of all concerned. According to this philosophy, the firm creates products and services with consumers' needs in mind. Many marketing theorists and marketing managers believe that the creation of value for consumers is the justification for a firm's existence. Therefore, unlike the other two orientations, marketing research addressing consumer desires, beliefs, and attitudes becomes essential.

Yoplait Go-Gurt, yogurt packaged in a three-sided tube designed to fit in kids' lunchboxes, had more than $100 million in sales its first year on the market. The development of Go-Gurt clearly illustrates a consumer orientation. The company's consumer research about eating regular yogurt at school showed that moms and kids in their "tweens" wanted convenience and portability. Some brands, like Colombo Spoon in a Snap, offered the convenience of having a utensil as part of the packaging/delivery system. However, from what Yoplait marketers learned about consumers, they thought kids would eat more yogurts if they could "lose the spoon" and eat yogurt anywhere, anytime. Moms and kids participating in a taste test were invited to sample different brand-on-the-go packaging shapes—long tubes, thin tubes, fat tubes, and other shapes—without being told how to handle the packaging. One of the company's researchers said, "It was funny to see the moms fidget around, then daintily pour the product onto a spoon, then into their mouths. The kids instantly jumped on it. They knew what to do."[10] Squeezing Go-Gurt from the tube was a big plus. The kids loved the fact that the packaging gave them permission to play with their food, something parents always tell them not to do. Go-Gurt is a fun, convenient product that allows consumers the freedom to eat whenever and wherever they want. Yoplait realized that knowledge of consumers' needs, coupled with product research and development, leads to successful marketing strategies and that industry leadership—indeed, corporate survival—depends on satisfying consumers.

Long-Run Profitability

Customer orientation does not mean slavery to consumers' every fleeting whim. Implicit in the marketing concept is the assumption of the continuity of the firm. Thus, the firm must eventually experience profitability to survive (see Exhibit 1.3). As popular as Starbucks is, it would probably be even more popular if the average price for a cup of coffee was thirty cents instead of three dollars. However, the production costs of the coffee and the labor costs associated with maintaining the Starbucks atmosphere greatly exceed that figure. Thus, Starbucks would likely have failed had it attempted to satisfy the desire for low prices. In contrast to a production orientation, Starbucks succeeds with perhaps the highest cost profile of all national coffee chains.

The second aspect of the marketing concept argues against profitless volume or sales volume for the sake of volume alone. Sometimes, the best decision for a customer and the best decision in

EXHIBIT 1.3
Long-Run Profitability

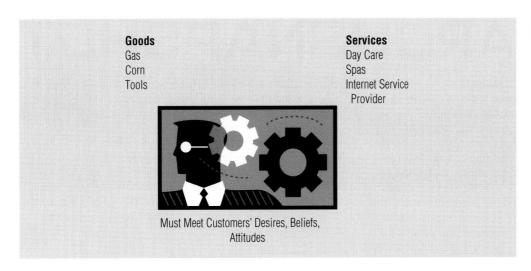

Goods
Gas
Corn
Tools

Services
Day Care
Spas
Internet Service
   Provider

Must Meet Customers' Desires, Beliefs,
Attitudes

the long run for the firm is the sale that is not made. For instance, a parts supplier might be able to mislead a customer about the relative quality of the parts he or she sells and make an immediate sale. However, when the parts begin to fail sooner than expected, it is fairly certain the customer will not do business with this firm again. If instead the salesperson for the supplier had been honest and suggested another supplier, he or she may be able to find another opportunity to do business with that firm.

A Cross-Functional Effort

Marketing personnel do not work in a vacuum, isolated from other company activities. The actions of people in areas such as production, credit, and research and development may affect an organization's marketing efforts. Similarly, the work of marketers will affect activities in other departments. Problems are almost certain to arise from lack of an integrated, company-wide effort. The marketing concept stresses a cross-functional perspective to achieve consumer orientation and long-term profitability.

Problems occur when the marketing department views focusing on consumer needs as its sole responsibility. Indeed, other functional areas' goals may conflict with customer satisfaction or long-term profitability. For instance, the engineering department may want long lead times for product design, with simplicity and economy as major design goals. Marketing, however, may prefer short lead times and more complex designs with custom components and optional features for multiple models. The finance department may want fixed budgets, strict spending justifications, and prices that cover costs, whereas the marketing department may seek flexible budgets, liberal spending rationales, and below-cost prices to develop markets quickly.

Similar differences in outlook may be found in other functional areas of the organization, and these may be sources of serious conflicts. When a firm lacks organizational procedures for communicating marketing information and coordinating marketing efforts, the effectiveness of its marketing programs will suffer. Marketing research findings produce some of the most crucial marketing information; thus, such research is management's key tool for finding out what customers want and how best to satisfy their needs. It is vital, then, that management conducts marketing research, that researchers produce valid and reliable results, and that those results be communicated to decision makers so that they can help shape the firm's marketing strategy.

Marketing-oriented firms visualize a chain of customers within the production/delivery system.[11] An accountant who prepares a report for a sales manager should view the manager as a customer who will use the information to make decisions that will benefit external customers who buy the company's products. Every employee should contribute to quality improvement and providing value to customers.

RESEARCHSNAPSHOT

Harley-Davidson Goes Abroad

Before Harley-Davidson goes overseas, it must perform considerable research on that market. It may find that consumers in some countries, such as France or Italy, have a strong preference for more economical and practical motor bikes. There, people may prefer a Vespa Wasp to a Harley Hog! Other times, they may find that consumers have a favorable attitude toward Harley-Davidson and that it could even be a product viewed as very prestigious. Harley recently considered doing business in India based on trend analysis showing a booming economy. Favorable consumer opinion and a booming economy were insufficient to justify distributing Harleys in India. The problem? Luxury imports would be subject to very high duties which would make them cost-prohibitive to nearly all Indian consumers. Thus, although research on the market was largely positive, Harley's research on the political operating environment eventually determined its decision. Instead, Harley may direct its effort more toward the U.S. women's market for bikes. Research shows that motorcycle ownership among U.S. women has nearly doubled since 1990 to approximately 10 percent. Product research suggests that Harley may need to design smaller and sportier bikes to satisfy this market's desires.

©MICHAEL NEWMAN/PHOTOEDIT

Sources: Asia-Africa Intelligence Wire (2005), "Harley Davidson Rules Out India Foray for Near Future" (September 2), Akron Beacon Journal (2005), "Women Kick It Into Gear" (May 22).

Keeping Customers and Building Relationships

Relationship marketing
Communicates the idea that a major goal of marketing is to build long-term relationships with the customers contributing to their success.

Marketers often talk about getting customers, but keeping customers is equally important. Effective marketers work to build long-term relationships with their customers. The term **relationship marketing** communicates the idea that a major goal of marketing is to build long-term relationships with the customers contributing to their success. Once an exchange is made, effective marketing stresses managing the relationships that will bring about additional exchanges. Effective marketers view making a sale not as the end of a process but as the start of the organization's relationship with a customer. Satisfied customers will return to a company that has treated them well if they need to purchase the same product in the future. If they need a related item, satisfied customers know the first place to look.

Total quality management is a business philosophy that has much in common with the marketing concept. It embodies the belief that the management process must focus on integrating customer-driven quality throughout the organization. The philosophy underlying the implementation of total quality management was clearly articulated by a Burger King executive: "The customer is the vital key to our success. We are now looking at our business through the customers' eyes and measuring our performance against their expectations, not ours."[12] A company that employs a total quality strategy must evaluate itself through the eyes of the customer.

Chapter 7 discusses the measurement of quality, customer satisfaction, and value in detail. Throughout this book, however, we will explain how marketing research can help a company achieve the goal of creating valuable experiences for customers.

Marketing Research: A Means for Implementing the Marketing Concept

Home building used to be a business completely dominated by local construction contractors. If a customer wanted a home that would provide maximum satisfaction, a custom home at a custom price was the only option. Today, there is another option. Several home builders are going national. In doing so, they have implemented market-driven design processes that integrate research into the home designs. The research tracks consumers' actual living patterns to build homes with maximum livability. Thus, rather than "wasting space" on things like hallways that add little or even distract from a home's livability, that space is cannibalized, allowing more space allocated to the places where families really "live." In addition, research shows that consumers will make use of outdoor living areas if they are properly designed. Thus, the homes often include covered porches or lanais in place of less used indoor space like a formal living room.[13]

David Weekley also directs considerable attention to service after the sale. Research indicates that after-sale service could be a significant source of referrals. As a result, each David Weekley home comes with a ten-year warranty. Before any appliances are placed in Weekley homes, they must be proven to be durable enough to have a good chance of lasting the length of the warranty. Consistent with the research, over 30 percent

Fun in the snow depends on weather trends, equipment, and clothing—all subjects for a market researcher.

of Weekley home owners refer new customers to the company. Thus, David Weekley has been tremendously successful with this model and offers both affordability and a custom feel. It is now the nation's largest home building firm.[14]

Marketing research can also help prevent commercialization of products that are not consumer-oriented. Sometimes ideas that look like technological breakthroughs in the laboratory fall flat when presented to consumers. For example, a powdered pain reliever was supposed to be a soothing remedy because it was to be mixed with milk. It did not soothe customers, however. Research showed that the public thought this great step forward was actually a step backward in convenience. Someone forgot to consider the consumer benefit.

By improving efficiency, research also facilitates profitability. For instance, during the introduction of a new product, accurate forecasting of the product's potential sales volume is an essential basis for estimating its profitability. A firm considering the introduction of a cat snack that contains hairball medicine might rely on a test market experiment to determine the optimal price for this new concept. Extensive testing should be done to ensure that the marketing program is fine-tuned to maximize the firm's profitability while satisfying consumers.

Analysis of data may also be a form of marketing research that can increase efficiency. Marketing representatives from Exxon Chemical Company used laptop computers to present a complex set of calculations to sales prospects to show them the advantage of Exxon products over competitors' products. Such analysis of research data improves the salesperson's batting average and the firm's efficiency.

Because of the importance of integrating company efforts, a marketing researcher must be knowledgeable not only about marketing research but about the entire spectrum of marketing activities.

The Managerial Value of Marketing Research for Strategic Decision Making

Effective marketing management requires research. DirectTV, the direct-broadcast satellite television service, uses marketing research to determine which kinds of programming to add to its lineup of channels. A company executive says, "Research has driven every aspect of our business decisions."[15] At Ford Motor Company, research is so fundamental that the company hardly makes any significant decision without the benefit of some kind of marketing research. The prime managerial value of marketing research comes from the reduced uncertainty that results from information and facilitates decision making about marketing strategies and tactics to achieve an organization's strategic goals.

Developing and implementing a marketing strategy involves four stages:

1. Identifying and evaluating market opportunities
2. Analyzing market segments and selecting target markets
3. Planning and implementing a marketing mix that will provide value to customers and meet organizational objectives
4. Analyzing firm performance

Identifying and Evaluating Opportunities

One job that marketing research can perform is monitoring the competitive environment for signals indicating a business opportunity. A mere description of some social or economic activity, such as trends in consumer purchasing behavior, may help managers recognize problems and identify opportunities for enriching marketing efforts. In some cases, this research can motivate a firm to take action to address consumer desires in a way that is beneficial to both the customers and to the firm.

At times, evaluating opportunities may involve something as mundane as tracking weather trends. Consumers have a physical need to maintain some degree of physical comfort. Thus, changes in the temperature patterns may create business opportunities for utility companies, appliance companies, and even beverage companies as more consumers will select a hot beverage like hot chocolate when the weather is cold and dreary. Companies can also adjust their logistic distribution patterns based on the weather. When Hurricane Katrina hit the Gulf Coast of the United States, several chainsaw companies (such as Poulan) and companies that manufacture generators (such as Honda) began directing inventory toward those areas even before the hurricane actually struck. As a result, many home supply stores like Home Depot and Lowe's were able to maintain inventories of these vital products despite an increase in demand of over 1,000 percent! Thus, the misfortune of a hurricane created a business opportunity that also provided real value to consumers. In this case, the businesses and the consumers all benefited from the fact that firms scan the environment for trends.

The purpose of a research study on running shoes was to investigate the occasions or situations associated with product use—that is, when individuals wore running shoes. The researchers found that most owners of running shoes wore the shoes while walking, not running. Also, most of this walking was part of a normal daily activity like shopping or commuting to work. Many of the people who wore running shoes for routine activities considered the shoes an alternative to other casual shoes. This research ultimately led to a shift in design and production toward walking shoes designed for comfortable, everyday walking and casual wear.[16]

Market opportunities may be evaluated using many performance criteria. For example, the performance criterion of market demand typically is estimated using marketing research techniques. Estimates of market potential or predictions about future environmental conditions allow managers to evaluate opportunities. Accurate sales forecasts are among the most useful pieces of planning information a marketing manager can have. Complete accuracy in forecasting the future is not possible, because change is constantly occurring in the marketing environment. Nevertheless, objective forecasts of demand or changing environments may be the foundations on which marketing strategies are built.

Analyzing and Selecting Target Markets

Geo-demographics
Refers to information describing the demographic profile of consumers in a particular geographic region.

The second stage of marketing strategy development is to analyze market segments and select target markets. Marketing research is a major source of information for determining which characteristics of market segments distinguish them from the overall market. Such research can help "locate" or describe a market segment in terms of demographic and characteristics. Geo-demographics can be important to study and track in this effort. **Geo-demographics** refers to information describing the demographic profile of consumers in a particular geographic region. The company may learn that consumers in a particular postal code within a region tend to be middle-aged, have multiple children over the age of twelve, and have college degrees and white-collar jobs. Once the company knows the geo-demographics of a market segment, it can effectively communicate with those customers by choosing media that reach that particular profile. For example, *Architectural Digest* is a magazine that is read predominantly by consumers with very high social status in the most exclusive zip codes in the United States.

Planning and Implementing a Marketing Mix

Using the information obtained in the two previous stages, marketing managers plan and execute a marketing-mix strategy. Marketing research may be needed to support specific decisions about any aspect of the marketing mix. For instance, the research can evaluate an alternative course of action. For example, advertising research might investigate whether an actress like Julia Roberts or a singer like Mariah Carey would make a better spokesperson for a specific brand of hair coloring. Research might be conducted involving test ads with each celebrity examining questions such as whether or not attitudes toward the brand are higher for Julia or for Mariah and how much each celebrity is liked, but also, perhaps not as obviously, how much credibility each celebrity would have based on the beliefs consumers have about whether or not each would really use the product.

It is essential that an overall research plan involve all elements of marketing strategy. In other words, once the research identifies a target market and media that can be used in promotion, it needs to determine what benefits are required to create value for the customers, what price is most appropriate and, not to be overlooked, what channels of distribution will best reach the consumer. The integration of all of this research leads to effective brand management.[17] The following examples highlight selected types of research that might be conducted for each element of the marketing mix.

■ PRODUCT RESEARCH

Product research takes many forms and includes studies designed to evaluate and develop new products and to learn how to adapt existing product lines. Concept testing exposes potential customers to a new product idea to judge the acceptance and feasibility of the concept. Product testing reveals a product prototype's strengths and weaknesses or determines whether a finished product performs better than competing brands or according to expectations. Brand-name evaluation studies investigate whether a name is appropriate for a product. Package testing assesses size, color, shape, ease of use, and other attributes of a package. Product research encompasses all applications of marketing research that seek to develop product attributes that will add value for consumers.

Before Cheetos became the first major brand of American snack food to be made and marketed in China, product taste tests revealed that traditional cheese-flavored corn puffs Cheetos did not appeal to Chinese consumers. So the company conducted consumer research with 600 different flavors to learn which flavors would be most appealing. Among the flavors Chinese consumers tested and disliked were ranch dressing, nacho, Italian pizza, Hawaiian barbecue, peanut satay, North Sea crab, chili prawn, coconut milk curry, smoked octopus, caramel, and cuttlefish. Research did show that consumers liked some flavors. So, when Cheetos were introduced in China, they came in two flavors: savory American cream and zesty Japanese steak.[18] So, the result was essentially cheeseless Cheetos.

■ PRICING RESEARCH

In many ways, pricing research represents typical marketing research. Many test markets address the question of how consumers will respond to a product offering two different prices. **Pricing** involves finding the amount of monetary sacrifice that best represents the value customers perceive in a product after considering various market constraints. Most organizations conduct pricing research. Starbucks may seem expensive now, but if the price doubled, would Starbucks lose many customers? At AFLAC, how much are consumers willing to pay each month for every one dollar

Pricing
Involves finding the amount of monetary sacrifice that best represents the value customers perceive in a product after considering various market constraints.

of supplementary disability insurance? Pricing research also investigates the way people respond to pricing tactics. How do consumers respond to price reductions in one form or another? How much are people willing to pay for some critical product attribute? Do consumers view prices and/or quantity discounts as fair in a given category?[19] Do price gaps among national brands, regional brands, and private labels exist?[20] Most importantly, research also addresses the way consumers determine perceived value.

Pricing research addresses consumer quality perceptions by its very nature. A great deal of research addresses consumer reactions to low prices and documents the fact that, in quite a few instances, prices can actually be too low. In other words, sales can actually decrease with lower prices instead of increasing.[21]

Recently, Wal-Mart test marketed a Starbucks-type coffee shop called Medina's Kicks.[22] A Kicks coffee shop was set up in a Texas Wal-Mart store. They are testing prices relative to the nearby Starbucks. At prices 25 percent below Starbucks, sales remain relatively low while Starbucks remains popular. By lowering the price, they may also have lowered the perceived product quality. By raising the price, might quality perceptions improve and get consumers to think the coffee may be more similar to Starbucks? These are typical pricing questions.

DISTRIBUTION RESEARCH

Marketing channel
A network of interdependent institutions that perform the logistics necessary for consumption to occur.

Distribution involves the marketing channels that will physically "distribute" products from a producer to a consumer. A **marketing channel** is a network of interdependent institutions that perform the logistics necessary for consumption to occur. Some channels are very short and involve only a producer and a consumer, and some are very long, involving much transportation, wholesale, and retail firms. It may be somewhat obvious why the term **supply chain** is sometimes used to refer to a channel of distribution. Distribution is necessary to remove the separations between buyers and sellers.

Supply chain
Another term for a channel of distribution, meaning the link between suppliers and customers.

Distribution research is typified by studies aimed at selecting retail sites or warehouse locations. A survey of retailers or wholesalers may be conducted because the actions of one channel member can greatly affect the performance of other channel members. Distribution research often is needed to gain knowledge about retailers' and wholesalers' operations and to learn their reactions to a manufacturer's marketing policies. It may also be used to examine the effect of just-in-time ordering systems or exclusive distribution on product quality. Research focused on developing and improving the efficiency of marketing channels is extremely important.

Golden Books traditionally distributed its small hardcover children's books with golden spines to book retailers like Waldenbooks or B. Dalton Booksellers. When it researched where its customers would prefer to purchase Golden Books, the company learned that mass merchandisers, grocery stores, and drug stores would be just as popular as the upscale stores as distribution channels. Today, publishing companies like Golden Books face the possibility of new and shorter marketing channels that would allow home delivery via the Internet. Not only does this mean reduced time from production to consumption, but it also allows the books to come alive through interactivity. Should Golden Books abandon its more traditional marketing channels and focus its resources on this new delivery option?

PROMOTION RESEARCH

Promotion
The communication function of the firm responsible for informing and persuading buyers.

Promotion is the communication function of the firm responsible for informing and persuading buyers. **Promotion research** investigates the effectiveness of advertising, premiums, coupons, sampling, discounts, public relations, and other sales promotions. However, among all of these, firms spend more time, money, and effort on advertising research.

Promotion research
Investigates the effectiveness of advertising, premiums, coupons, sampling, discounts, public relations, and other sales promotions.

The marketing research findings of Zales, a large jewelry retailer, helped in the creation of advertising with large, one-word headlines that simply asked, "Confused?," "Nervous?," or "Lost?" The advertisements overtly acknowledged the considerable emotional and financial risks that consumers face in jewelry purchases. Research had shown that typical consumers felt unable to determine the relative quality of various jewelry items, believed jewelry purchases were expensive, and needed reassurance about their purchases, especially because they often purchased jewelry for someone else. This promotion helped communicate an effective message of empathy with the consumer.

Similarly, a business in transition must effectively communicate its meaning. As AT&T's business shifts from that of a pure long-distance provider into that of a distanceless cable, Internet, and wireless communication specialist, it is trying to make sure its image changes too. But research showed its brand name still conjured up the image of an old-fashioned telephone company.[23] Marketing research also indicates great familiarity with the blue-and-white striped globe that served as AT&T's logo. A survey found 75 percent unaided recognition among the broad consumer market, 77 percent recognition among 18- to 24-year-olds, and 80 percent recognition among "high-value, active networkers"—consumers spending seventy-five dollars or more per month on long-distance and wireless services. Because of this high level of recognition, AT&T produced numerous TV commercials featuring an animation of the logo bouncing around, giving fun, high-intensity demonstrations of the various ways the company is transforming itself in the broadband-enabled world, accompanied by voice-over explanations of these new services. Future research may even consider placing the logo on iPod sites or even as a product placement in video games as a way of further transforming AT&T's image from "Ma Bell" into a modern technology service provider.[24]

Media research helps businesses make decisions about whether television, newspapers, magazines, or other media alternatives are best suited to convey the intended message. Choices among media alternatives may be based on research that shows the proportion of consumers in each market segment that a particular advertising vehicle can reach.

THE INTEGRATED MARKETING MIX

Marketing today focuses increasingly on the fact that different promotional decisions should not be made in isolation. Instead, the concept of **integrated marketing communication** is adopted, meaning that all promotional efforts (advertising, public relations, personal selling, event marketing, and so forth) should be coordinated to communicate a consistent image. Likewise, more generally marketing firms realize that the elements of the marketing mix itself must work together. For instance, a change in price can affect the quality of the product, which may also influence decisions about distribution. From a research standpoint, the **integrated marketing mix** means that research studies often investigate effects of various combinations of marketing mix elements on important outcomes like sales and image. Research suggests that consumer-oriented firms are particularly oriented toward integrating all aspects of their marketing into a single message.[25]

Best Buy, a U.S.-based electronic and appliance retailer, recently showed the success of integrating sales and service with promotion. You'll find a Geek in every Best Buy. The Geeks are technology experts (i.e., "computer geeks") that provide knowledgeable sales advice and technical service. To be a Geek, you have to look like a Geek! Their attire is carefully coordinated: white socks with black shoes, black pants that are just a little too short, a white sport shirt, and a narrow black tie. Today, the Geeks have become prominent in Best Buy television ads, and they even provide in-home set-up and technical service. The Geeks are transforming Best Buy in the minds of consumers.[26] Companies that integrate the use of consistent spokespeople, such as the Geeks, across marketing elements enjoy more favorable brand images among consumers and are better able to communicate relevant information.[27]

Integrated marketing communication
Means that all promotional efforts (advertising, public relations, personal selling, event marketing, and so forth) should be coordinated to communicate a consistent image.

Integrated marketing mix
The effects of various combinations of marketing-mix elements on important outcomes.

Best Buy has re-invented the traditional Geek image and made it work for them.

©ASSOCIATED PRESS/AP

RESEARCHSNAPSHOT

Swifter or Swiffer?

Procter & Gamble (P&G) performs a great deal of consumer research. When P&G set out on a research project aimed at designing a better mop, meaning a better mopping experience, consumers' reactions were interpreted as indicating that they didn't want any mop at all. They didn't want to mop! Mopping was too time-consuming, boring, and messy. They wanted to throw away their mops. The result? A mop you throw away! We know it today as a Swiffer. The chemically treated cloths pick up dirt like a magnet and then can be neatly and easily discarded. This same research led to disposable replacements for cleaning cloths and for toilet brushes. Thus, research examining how current products can be improved led to key product developments. All of these products continue to perform very well for P&G.

Sources: Ellison, Sarah (2005), "Studying Messy Habits to Sweep Up a Market," The Wall Street Journal (July 14), B1–B4; Neff, Jack (2005), "Swiffer by Another Name," Advertising Age, 76 (15), 11.

Analyzing Marketing Performance

After a marketing strategy has been implemented, marketing research may serve to inform managers whether planned activities were properly executed and are accomplishing what they were expected to achieve. In other words, marketing research may be conducted to obtain feedback for evaluation and control of marketing programs. This aspect of marketing research is especially important for successful **total value management**, which attempts to manage the entire process by which a consumer receives benefits from a company.

Performance-monitoring research refers to research that regularly, sometimes routinely, provides feedback for evaluation and control of marketing activity. For example, most firms continuously monitor wholesale and retail activity to ensure early detection of sales declines and other anomalies. In the grocery and drug industries, sales research may use Universal Product Codes (UPCs) on packages read by electronic cash registers and computerized checkout counts to provide valuable market-share information to store and brand managers interested in the retail sales volumes of their products. Market-share analysis and sales analysis are the most common forms of performance-monitoring research. Almost every organization compares its current sales with previous sales and with competitors' sales. However, analyzing marketing performance is not limited to the investigation of sales figures.

Marketing metrics refer to quantitative ways of monitoring and measuring marketing performance. Research is needed to determine marketing metrics that allow a firm to know whether the resources invested in marketing activities have met their quantitative business goals. Marketing metrics allow the firm to assess the return on investment (ROI) associated with marketing activities. Performance monitoring research conducted by the ACNielsen firm suggests that only 18 percent of television commercials return a positive ROI for the companies advertised.[28]

When analysis of marketing performance indicates that things are not going as planned, marketing research may be required to explain why something went wrong. Detailed information about specific mistakes or failures is frequently sought. If a general problem area is identified, breaking down industry sales volume and a firm's sales volume into different geographical areas may explain specific problems. Exploring problems in greater depth may indicate which managerial judgments were erroneous.

Total value management
Trying to manage and monitor the entire process by which consumers receive benefits from a company.

Performance-monitoring research
Refers to research that regularly, sometimes routinely, provides feedback for evaluation and control of marketing activity.

Marketing metrics
Quantitative ways of monitoring and measuring marketing performance.

When Is Marketing Research Needed?

The need to make intelligent, informed decisions ultimately motivates marketing research. Not every decision requires marketing research. Thus, when confronting a key decision, a marketing manager must initially decide whether or not to conduct marketing research. The determination of the need for marketing research centers on (1) time constraints, (2) the availability of data, (3) the nature of the decision to be made, and (4) the value of the research information in relation to costs.

Time Constraints

Systematic research takes time. In many instances management believes that a decision must be made immediately, allowing no time for research. Decisions sometimes are made without adequate information or thorough understanding of market situations. Although making decisions without researching a situation is not ideal, sometimes the urgency of a situation precludes the use of research. The urgency with which managers want to make decisions often conflicts with the marketing researchers' desire for rigor in following the scientific method.

Availability of Data

Often managers already possess enough information to make sound decisions without additional marketing research. When they lack adequate information, however, research must be considered. This means that data need to be collected from an appropriate source. If a potential source of data exists, managers will want to know how much it will cost to get the data.

If the data cannot be obtained, or it cannot be obtained in a timely fashion, this particular research project should not be conducted. For example, many African nations have never conducted a population census. Organizations engaged in international business often find that data about business activity or population characteristics that are readily available in the United States are nonexistent or sparse in developing countries. Imagine the problems facing marketing researchers who wish to investigate market potential in places like Uzbekistan, Yugoslavian Macedonia, and Rwanda.

Nature of the Decision

The value of marketing research will depend on the nature of the managerial decision to be made. A routine tactical decision that does not require a substantial investment may not seem to warrant a substantial expenditure for marketing research. For example, a computer company must update its operator's instruction manual when it makes minor product modifications. The research cost of determining the proper wording to use in the updated manual is likely to be too high for such a minor decision. The nature of the decision is not totally independent of the next issue to be considered: the benefits versus the costs of the research. In general, however, the more strategically or tactically important the decision, the more likely it is that research will be conducted.

Benefits versus Costs

There are both costs and benefits to conducting marketing research. Earlier we discussed some of the managerial benefits of marketing research. Of course, conducting research to obtain these benefits requires an expenditure of money. In any decision-making situation, managers must identify alternative courses of action and then weigh the value of each alternative against its cost. Marketing research can be thought of as an investment alternative. When deciding whether to make a decision without research or to postpone the decision in order to conduct research, managers should ask three questions:

1. Will the payoff or rate of return be worth the investment?
2. Will the information gained by marketing research improve the quality of the marketing decision enough to warrant the expenditure?
3. Is the proposed research expenditure the best use of the available funds?

For example, *TV-Cable Week* was not test-marketed before its launch. Although the magazine had articles and stories about television personalities and events, its main feature was program listings, channel by channel, showing the exact programs a particular subscriber could receive. To produce a custom magazine for each individual cable television system in the country required

EXHIBIT 1.4 Determining When to Conduct Marketing Research

Time Constraints		Availability of Data		Nature of the Decision		Benefits versus Costs		
Is sufficient time available before a decision will be made?	Yes →	Can the decision be made with what is already known?	Yes →	Is the decision of considerable strategic or tactical importance?	Yes →	Does the value of the research information exceed the cost of conducting research?	Yes →	Conduct Marketing Research
No ↓		No ↓		No ↓		No ↓		
			Do Not Conduct Marketing Research					

developing a costly computer system. Because that development necessitated a substantial expenditure, one that could not be scaled down for research, conducting research was judged to be an unwise investment. The value of the research information was not positive because its cost exceeded its benefits. Unfortunately, pricing and distribution problems became so compelling after the magazine was launched that the product was a marketing failure. Nevertheless, without the luxury of hindsight, managers made a reasonable decision not to conduct research. They analyzed the cost of the information (that is, the cost of test-marketing) relative to the potential benefits of the information. Exhibit 1.4 outlines the criteria for determining when to conduct marketing research.

Marketing Research in the Twenty-First Century

Marketing research, like all business activity, continues to change. Changes in communication technologies and the trend toward an ever more global marketplace have played a large role in many of these changes.

Communication Technologies

Virtually everyone is "connected" today. Increasingly, many people are "connected" nearly all the time. Within the lifetime of the typical undergraduate college senior, the way information is exchanged, stored, and gathered has been revolutionized completely. Today, the amount of information formally contained in an entire library can rest easily in a single personal computer.

The speed with which information can be exchanged has also increased tremendously. During the 1970s, exchanging information overnight from anywhere in the continental United States was heralded as a near miracle of modern technology. Today, we can exchange information from nearly anywhere in the world to nearly anywhere in the world almost instantly. Internet connections are now wireless, so one doesn't have to be tethered to a wall to access the World Wide Web. Our mobile phones and handheld data devices can be used not only to converse, but also as a means of communication that can even involve marketing research data. In many cases, technology also has made it possible to store or collect data for lower costs than in the past. Electronic communications are usually less costly than regular mail—and certainly less costly than a face-to-face interview—and cost about the same amount no matter how far away a respondent is from a researcher. Thus, the expressions "time is collapsing" and "distance is disappearing" capture the tremendous revolution in the speed and reach of our communication technologies.

Changes in computer technology have made for easier data collection and data analysis. As we discuss in a later chapter, many consumer household panels now exist and can be accessed via the Internet. Thus, there is less need for the time and expense associated with regular mail survey approaches. Furthermore, the computing power necessary to solve complicated statistical problems

RESEARCHSNAPSHOT

"Jacques" Daniels

Sales of U.S. distilled spirits have declined over the last 10 to 15 years as more Americans turn to wine or beer as their beverage of choice. As a result, companies like Bacardi and Brown-Forman, producers of Jack Daniels, have pursued market development strategies involving increased efforts to expand into international markets. The Brown-Forman marketing budget for international ventures includes a significant allocation for marketing research. By doing research before launching the product, Brown-Forman can learn product usage patterns within a particular culture. Some of the findings from this research indicate

1. Japanese consumers use Jack Daniels (JD) as a dinner beverage. A party of four or five consumers in a restaurant will order and drink a bottle of "JD" with their meal.
2. Australian consumers mostly consume distilled spirits in their homes. Also in contrast to Japanese consumers, Australians prefer to mix JD with soft drinks or other mixers. As a result of this research, JD launched a mixture called "Jack and Cola" sold in 12 ounce bottles all around Australia. The product has been very successful.
3. British distilled spirit consumers also like mixed drinks, but they usually partake in bars and restaurants.
4. In China and India, consumers more often chose counterfeit or "knock-offs" to save money. Thus, innovative research approaches have addressed questions related to the way the black market works and how they can better educate consumers about the differences between the real thing and the knock-offs.

The result is that of all Jack Daniels sold is now sold outside of the United States.

Sources: Swibel, Mathew (2005), "How Distiller Brown-Forman Gets Rich by Exploiting the Greenback's Fall—and Pushing Its Brands Abroad," Forbes, 175 (8), 152–155.

©SUSAN VAN ETTEN

is now easily accessible. Again, as recently as the 1970s, such computer applications required expensive mainframe computers found only in very large corporations, major universities, and large governmental/military institutions. Researchers could expect to wait hours or even longer to get results from a statistical program involving 200 respondents. Today, even the most basic laptop computers can solve complicated statistical problems involving thousands of data points in practically a nanosecond.

Global Marketing Research

Marketing research has become increasingly global as more and more firms take advantage of markets that have few, if any, geographic boundaries. Some companies have extensive international marketing research operations. Upjohn conducts marketing research in 160 different countries. ACNielsen International, known for its television ratings, is the world's largest marketing research company. Two-thirds of its business comes from outside the United States.[29] Starbucks can now be found in nearly every developed country on the earth. AFLAC offers its products on multiple continents.

Companies that conduct business in foreign countries must understand the nature of those particular markets and judge whether they require customized marketing strategies. For example, although the fifteen nations of the European Union share a single formal market, marketing research shows that Europeans do not share identical tastes for many consumer products. Marketing researchers have found no such thing as a typical European consumer; language, religion, climate, and centuries of tradition divide the nations of the European Union. Scantel Research, a British firm that advises companies on color preferences, found inexplicable differences in Europeans' preferences in medicines. The French prefer to pop purple pills, but the English and Dutch favor white ones. Consumers in all three countries dislike bright red capsules, which are big sellers in the United States. This example illustrates that companies that do business in Europe must research throughout Europe to adapt to local customs and buying habits.[30]

Even companies that produce brands that are icons in their own country are now doing research internationally. The Real World Research box discusses how Brown-Forman, the parent company of Jack Daniels (the classic American "Sour Mash" or Bourbon Whiskey), are now interviewing consumers in the far corners of the world.[31] The internationalization of research places greater demands on marketing researchers and heightens the need for research tools that allow us to **cross-validate** research results, meaning that the empirical findings from one culture also exist and behave similarly in another culture. The development and application of these international research tools are an important topic in basic marketing research.[32]

Cross-validate
To verify that the empircal findings from one culture also exist and behave similarly in another culture.

Summary

There were seven learning objectives in this chapter. After reading the chapter, the student should be competent in each area described by a learning objective.

1. Explain why marketing research is essential to business success. While many business decisions are made "by the seat of the pants" or based on a manager's intuition, this type of decision making carries with it a large amount of risk. By first researching an issue and gathering intelligence on customers, competitors, and the market, a company can make a more informed decision. The result is less risky decision making.

Marketing research is the intelligence-gathering function in business. The intelligence includes information about customers, competitors, economic trends, employees, and other factors that affect marketing success. This intelligence assists in decisions ranging from long-range planning to near-term tactical decisions.

2. Define marketing research. Marketing research is the application of the scientific method in searching for truth about marketing phenomena. The research must be conducted systematically, not haphazardly. It must be objective to avoid the distorting effects of personal bias. Marketing research can be rigorous, but the rigor is always traded off against the resource and time constraints that go with a particular business decision.

3. Identify the difference between applied and basic research. Applied marketing research seeks to facilitate managerial decision making. Basic or pure research seeks to increase knowledge of theories and concepts. Both are important. Applied research is more often the topic in this text.

4. Explain how marketing research is relevant to product, pricing, promotion, and distribution decisions. Businesses can make more accurate decisions about the marketing mix by using marketing research results. The chapter provides examples of studies involving each dimension of the marketing mix. Thus, marketing research is useful in a tactical sense.

5. Discuss how marketing research helps the firm develop and implement strategy. Marketing research is a means of implementing the marketing concept, the most central idea in marketing. The marketing concept says that a firm must be oriented both toward consumer satisfaction and toward long-run profitability (rather than toward short-run sales volume). Organizations need to focus both on creating and on keeping customers. Marketing research can help implement the marketing concept by identifying consumers' problems and needs, improving efficiency, and evaluating the effectiveness of marketing strategies and tactics.

The development and implementation of a marketing strategy consist of four stages: (1) identifying and evaluating opportunities, (2) analyzing market segments and selecting target markets, (3) planning and implementing a marketing mix that will provide value to customers and meet the objectives of the organization, and (4) analyzing firm performance. Marketing research helps in each stage by providing information for strategic decision making.

6. Identify the situations that call for market research and those that don't. Marketing managers determine whether marketing research should be conducted based on (1) time constraints, (2) availability of data, (3) the nature of the decision to be made, and (4) the benefit of the research information versus its cost.

7. Describe how technology and internationalization are affecting the way research is conducted and used. Technology has changed almost every aspect of marketing research. Modern computer and communications technology makes data collection, study design, data analysis, data reporting, and practically all other aspects of research easier and better. Furthermore, as more companies do business outside their own borders, companies are doing research in an international marketplace. This places a greater emphasis on research that can assess the degree to which research tools can be applied and interpreted the same way in difference cultures. Thus, research techniques often must cross-validate results.

Key Terms and Concepts

Marketing research
Applied marketing research
Basic marketing research
The scientific method
Product-oriented
Production-oriented
Marketing concept
Marketing orientation

Customer-oriented
Relationship marketing
Geo-demographics
Pricing
Marketing channel
Supply chain
Promotion
Promotion research

Integrated marketing communication
Integrated marketing mix
Total value management
Performance-monitoring research
Marketing metrics
Cross-validate

Questions for Review and Critical Thinking

1. Is it possible to make sound marketing decisions without marketing research? What advantages does research offer to the decision maker over seat-of-the-pants decision making?
2. Define a marketing orientation and a product orientation. Under which strategic orientation is there a greater need for marketing research?
3. Name some products that logically might have been developed with the help of marketing research.
4. Define *marketing research* and describe its task.
5. Which of the following organizations are likely to use marketing research? Why? How?
   a. Manufacturer of breakfast cereals
   b. Manufacturer of nuts, bolts, and other fasteners
   c. The Federal Trade Commission
   d. A hospital
   e. A company that publishes marketing textbooks
6. An automobile manufacturer is conducting research in an attempt to predict the type of car design consumers will desire in the year 2020. Is this basic or applied research? Explain.
7. What is the definition of an *integrated marketing mix?* How might this affect the research a firm conducts?
8. Comment on the following statements:
   a. Marketing managers are paid to take chances with decisions. Marketing researchers are paid to reduce the risk of making those decisions.
   b. A marketing strategy can be no better than the information on which it is formulated.
   c. The purpose of research is to solve marketing problems.
9. List the conditions that help a researcher decide when marketing research should or should not be conducted.
10. How have technology and internationalization affected marketing research?
11. **'NET** How do you believe the Internet has facilitated research? Try to use the Internet to find the total annual sales for Starbucks and for AFLAC. You can use the *Business Resource Center* tools that accompany the text to help with this.
12. What types of tools does the marketing researcher use more given the ever increasing internationalization of marketing?

Research Activities

1. **'NET** Suppose you own a jewelry store in Denton, Texas. You are considering opening a second store just like your current store. You are undecided on whether to locate the new store in another location in Denton, Texas, or in Birmingham, Alabama. Why would you decide to have some marketing research done before making the decision? Should the research be conducted? Go to http://www.census.gov. Do you think any of this information would be useful in the research?
2. Visit the Business Resource Center (via the Internet). Use it to find recent examples of news articles involving the use of marketing research in making decisions about each element of the marketing mix.
3. Using the Business Resource Center, find an article illustrating an example of an applied marketing research study involving some aspect of technology. How does it differ from a basic research study also focusing on a similar aspect of technology?

Video Case 1.1 Krispy Kreme

Krispy Kreme began as a storefront business in 1937 when Vernon Rudolph bought a secret raised-doughnut recipe from a French chef. Since then, hundreds of the signature green-roofed shops have sprung up across the United States. Krispy Kreme would even like to expand into countries like Canada, Spain, Japan, Great Britain, and Australia.

The company credits its success to quality products, clean stores, and good relationships with customers in the community. No one seems able to define specifically what makes the Krispy Kreme doughnut taste so much better than any other brand, but everyone agrees that it has something to do with "the hot donut experience." Company marketing managers explain that their bottom-line focus in every store is on what they do best: offer good donuts and good coffee. Their product, they maintain, crosses all socioeconomic and geographical boundaries, and they don't bombard their customers with any other messages.

Krispy Kreme stores are more than just clean. The "donut theater" allows customers to watch donuts being made through glass windows; they can even see the baked donuts going through what the company has termed the "glazing waterfall." All of this invites customers into the production experience and assures them of a quality product.

Krispy Kreme also works hard to develop relationships with its customers and to be a positive force in communities where stores are located. It has helped to raise millions for fundraising events by generously donating donuts to charitable projects; in fact, it was one of the first companies in the United States to get involved in fundraising. Community-relationship programs are specifically family-oriented. For example, they encourage kids to get good grades; students who bring in good report cards receive a free donut for every A grade they earn. The company sponsors local sports teams. It invites groups of children to take tours of its sites, which can include the kids making their own donuts.

Questions

1. To succeed in the global market, what market research should Krispy Kreme undertake?
2. What market research activities does Krispy Kreme engage in to determine where to build a site?
3. Krispy Kreme is currently facing criticism from low-carb diet practitioners that have lowered sales. How can market research help it deal with this problem?

Video Case 1.2 Ben & Jerry's

Ben & Jerry's Homemade, Inc., the Vermont-based manufacturer of ice cream, frozen yogurt, and sorbet, was founded in 1978 in a renovated gas station in Burlington, Vermont, by childhood friends Ben Cohen and Jerry Greenfield, with a $12,000 investment ($4,000 of which was borrowed).[33] They soon became popular for their innovative flavors, made from fresh Vermont milk and cream. The company currently distributes ice cream, low-fat ice cream, frozen yogurt, sorbet, and novelty products nationwide, as well as in selected foreign countries, in supermarkets, grocery stores, convenience stores, franchised Ben & Jerry's scoop shops, restaurants, and other venues.

Ben & Jerry's product strategy is to differentiate its superpremium brand from other ice cream brands. The brand image reflects high quality, uniqueness, and a bit of amusement. Its all-natural flavors have unique names. For example, "Chubby Hubby" has chunks of chocolate-covered, peanut-butter-filled pretzels in a rich vanilla malt ice cream with deep ripples of fudge and peanut butter. Other names in the company's line of ice creams include Cherry Garcia, Bovinity Divinity, Dilbert Totally Nuts, New York Super Fudge Chunk, Chunky Monkey, and From Russia with Buzz.

The new product development process and flavor naming process are a top priority at Ben & Jerry's. For example, Phish Food ice cream was developed as a unique product with a fun name associated with the band Phish. Ben Cohen had been a neighbor of members of Phish since the band's early years as favorites on the local music scene. When Ben & Jerry's suggested mixing up a Phish ice cream to celebrate their shared Vermont roots, the band agreed. So Ben & Jerry's concocted a chocolate ice cream with chewy marshmallow nougat, a thick caramel swirl, and a school of fudge fish in every pint. Most marshmallow variegates disappear into nothingness. The company took great pains to make sure that the marshmallow was the way it was meant to be. With Phish Food you can see, taste, and feel the white streaks of marshmallow. The Phish Food package is a departure from traditional Ben & Jerry's graphics. The pint container is designed with images from Phish's concert light show, featuring Phish band members Trey Anastasio, Mike Gordon, Jon Fishman, and Page McConnell on the pint lid along with Ben and Jerry.

Question

What role does marketing research play in new product development and brand name development for a company like Ben & Jerry's?

CHAPTER 2
INFORMATION SYSTEMS AND KNOWLEDGE MANAGEMENT

After studying this chapter, you should be able to

1. Distinguish between the concepts of data, information, and intelligence
2. Describe the four characteristics that explain the usefulness of data
3. Identify the purpose of research in assisting marketing operations
4. Explain what a decision support system is and what it does
5. Distinguish an Intranet from the Internet

Chapter Vignette: Data for Doughnuts!

Who makes the best doughnut in America? Which doughnut firm does the best marketing? These are two different questions to some extent. There is more to selling doughnuts than making a great doughnut.

Krispy Kreme is the market-share leader among U.S. doughnut firms, operating hundreds of stores in practically every state in the nation; it also has operations in several foreign countries, including South Korea! Although consumers may first think of the neon-laced doughnut shops when they think of Krispy Kreme, the fact is that the bulk of Krispy Kreme's revenue is generated from doughnut sales outside of its own stores. Krispy Kremes can be found in thousands of convenience and grocery stores and at practically every super store in the United States. Thus, there is a great deal of data to keep track of in terms of where doughnuts are delivered and where they are sold. Collecting these data manually would involve thousands of phone calls each time the data were needed. Clearly, this would be a labor intensive process, particularly considering that the decisions made based on these data include many day-to-day operational decisions.

While Krispy Kreme could develop systems and hardware that could track all of these data in real time, it opted to outsource this effort to a company that specializes in tracking, recording, and storing retail sales data. For Krispy Kreme, this proves more cost effective than purchasing and maintaining the technology to complete this task themselves. The data feed into software systems known as decision support systems, which allow Krispy Kreme to adjust production schedules to meet demand, adjust pricing, manage billing processes, and even track inventory-shrinkage trends. Thus, if a store's employees or customers are indulging in the Krispy Kremes without purchasing them, the system lets the executives at Krispy Kreme know. Furthermore, when Krispy Kreme needs additional data, the

©ASSOCIATED PRESS/AP

information provider may very well already have the data available in a data warehouse. Thus, the data provide knowledge that greatly assists Krispy Kreme marketing managers in day-to-day operational matters.[1]

Introduction

Krispy Kreme's use of an outside firm to manage its information illustrates the sometimes sophisticated way in which modern marketing firms integrate data into their decision processes. Many of the decisions that used to be made with guesswork are now supplemented with "intelligence" either automatically delivered by some computer software or drawn from a data warehouse.

Doughnut companies aren't alone in this effort. Imagine all the information that passes through a single Home Depot store each day. Every customer transaction, every empty shelf, every employee's work schedule—right down to the schedule to clean restrooms—creates potentially valuable information that can be used by researchers and decision makers. Considering that Home Depot operates thousands of stores, obviously, Home Depot needs a data depot!

Like Krispy Kreme, Home Depot has outsourced the storage and management of data inventories. In this case, IBM manages the data, allowing it to be integrated into management strategy and tactics. Data from cash registers, time clocks, shelf counts, and much more are all compiled, analyzed, and either fed automatically into management systems or supplied in the form of a research report. In a way, this type of marketing research is automatic![2]

This chapter discusses knowledge management and the role decision support systems play in helping firms make informed marketing decisions. The chapter also introduces the concept of global information systems and sources of data that exist beyond the walls of any business. Modern data technology allows businesses to more easily integrate research into marketing strategy and operations.

Information, Data, and Intelligence

Data
Facts or recorded measures of certain phenomena (things).

Information
Data formatted (structured) to support decision making or define the relationship between two facts.

Market intelligence
The subset of data and information that actually has some explanatory power enabling effective decisions to be made.

In everyday language, terms like *information* and *data* are often used interchangeably. Researchers use these terms in specific ways that emphasize how useful each can be. **Data** are simply facts or recorded measures of certain phenomena (things or events). **Information** is data formatted (structured) to support decision making or define the relationship between two facts. **Market intelligence** is the subset of data and information that actually has some explanatory power enabling effective decisions to be made. So, there is more data than information, and more information than intelligence.

Think again about the thousands upon thousands of unsummarized facts recorded by Home Depot each day. Each time a product is scanned at checkout, that fact is recorded and becomes data. Each customer's transactions are simultaneously entered into the store's computerized inventory system. The inventory system structures the data in such a way that a stocking report can be generated and orders for that store can be placed. Thus, the automated inventory system turns data into information. Further, the information from each store's sales and inventory records may be harvested by analysts tracking sales trends. The analysts may analyze the trends and prepare reports that help Home Depot buyers get the right products into each store or even to suggest places for new Home Depot locations. Thus, the analyst has now completed the transformation of data into intelligence. Exhibit 2.1 helps to illustrate the distinction between data, information, and intelligence.

The Characteristics of Valuable Information

Not all data are valuable to decision makers. Useful data become information and help a marketing manager make decisions. Useful data can also become intelligence. Four characteristics help determine how useful data may be: relevance, quality, timeliness, and completeness.

EXHIBIT 2.1
Data, Information, Intelligence

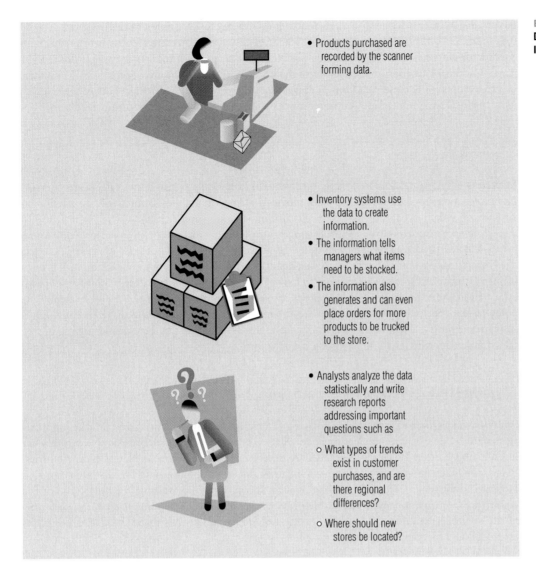

- Products purchased are recorded by the scanner forming data.

- Inventory systems use the data to create information.
- The information tells managers what items need to be stocked.
- The information also generates and can even place orders for more products to be trucked to the store.

- Analysts analyze the data statistically and write research reports addressing important questions such as
  - What types of trends exist in customer purchases, and are there regional differences?
  - Where should new stores be located?

Relevance

Relevance is the characteristics of data reflecting how pertinent these particular facts are to the situation at hand. Put another way, the facts are logically connected to the situation. Unfortunately, irrelevant data and information often creep into decision making. One particularly useful way to distinguish relevance from irrelevance is to think about how things change. Relevant data are facts about things that can be changed, and if they are changed, it will materially alter the situation. So, this simple question becomes important:

Will a change in the data coincide with a change in some important outcome?

American consumers' dietary trends are relevant to Krispy Kreme. If American diets become more health-conscious, then it can be expected that sales of doughnuts will be affected. This may lead Krispy Kreme to rethink its product offering. However, information on French consumers' wine preference is probably irrelevant since it is difficult to think how a change in wine preferences will affect U.S. doughnut preferences.

Quality

Data quality is the degree to which data represent the true situation. High-quality data are accurate, valid, and reliable. High-quality data represent reality faithfully. If a consumer were to replace

Relevance
The characteristics of data reflecting how pertinent these particular facts are to the situation at hand.

Data quality
The degree to which data represent the true situation.

Timeliness
Means that the data are current enough to still be relevant.

Information completeness
Having the right amount of information.

the product UPC from one drill at Home Depot with one from a different drill, not only would the consumer be acting unethically, but it would also mean that the data collected at the checkout counter would be inaccurate. Therefore, to the extent that the cash register is not actually recording the products that consumers take out of the stores, its quality is lowered. Sometimes, researchers will try to obtain the same data from multiple data sources as one check on its quality.[3] Data quality is a critical issue in marketing research, and it will be discussed throughout this text.

Timeliness

Marketing is a dynamic field in which out-of-date information can lead to poor decisions. Marketing information must be timely—that is, provided at the right time. Computerized information systems can record events and dispense relevant information soon after the event. A great deal of marketing information becomes available almost at the moment that a transaction occurs. Timeliness means that the data are current enough to still be relevant.

Computer technology has redefined standards for timely information. For example, if a marketing executive at Home Depot wishes to know the sales volume of any store worldwide, detailed information about any of thousands of products can be instantly determined. At Home Depot, the point-of-sale checkout system uses UPC scanners and satellite communications to link individual stores to the headquarters' computer system, from which managers can retrieve and analyze up-to-the-minute sales data on all merchandise in each store.

Completeness

Information completeness refers to having the right amount of information. Marketing managers must have sufficient information about all aspects of their decisions. For example, a researcher investigating Eastern European markets may plan to analyze four former Soviet-bloc countries. Population statistics and information on inflation rates may be available on all four countries. However, information about disposable personal income may be available for only three of the countries. If information about disposable personal income or other economic characteristics cannot be obtained, the information is incomplete. Often incomplete information leads decision makers to conduct marketing research.

Global Information Systems

Global information system
An organized collection of computer hardware, software, data, and personnel designed to capture, store, update, manipulate, analyze, and immediately display information about worldwide business activity.

Increased global competition and technological advances in interactive media have given rise to global information systems. A global information system is an organized collection of computer hardware, software, data, and personnel designed to capture, store, update, manipulate, analyze, and immediately display information about worldwide business activities. A global information system is a tool for providing past, present, and projected information on internal operations and external activity. Using satellite communications, high-speed microcomputers, electronic data interchanges, fiber optics, data storage devices, and other technological advances in interactive media, global information systems are changing the nature of business.

Consider a simple example. At any moment, United Parcel Service (UPS) can track the status of any shipment around the world. UPS drivers use handheld electronic clipboards called delivery information acquisition devices (DIADs) to record appropriate data about each pickup or delivery. The data are then entered into the company's main computer for record-keeping and analysis. A satellite telecommunications system allows UPS to track any shipment for a customer.

RFID stands for radio frequency identification. It is a new technology that places a tiny chip, which can be woven onto a fabric, onto virtually any product, allowing it to be tracked anywhere in the world. This can provide great insight into the different distribution channels around the world and, potentially, to the different ways consumers acquire and use products. The U.S. military

RESEARCHSNAPSHOT

RFID Technology Gets Cheaper—Marketing Knowledge Grows

Radio frequency identification (RFID) tags have been used by large organizations for several years now. The U.S. military makes great use of RFIDs in tracking the whereabouts of virtually all kinds of products both big and small. Logistics officers can instantly track the whereabouts of Humvees and MREs (Meals Ready to Eat). Information from the tag is transmitted to computer servers and then directly into a GTN (Global Tracking Network). Equipment and supplies can then be ordered and dispatched to needed locations with a minimum of human contact. Product consumption (ammunition, food, water, computer printers, and so forth) can also be tracked in real time. The Marines can know in real time if personnel in a desert use more food and water than personnel in a jungle.

Wal-Mart is pushing suppliers to adopt the technology. Not only can Wal-Mart use them in logistical operations, but the potential exists to "go into" consumers' homes and track how much and the way consumers actually consume products. Potentially, decision support systems (DSS) could tie ordering to customer consumption. However, the costs of RFIDs make it impractial for many suppliers.

Alien Technology Corporation recently announced a drop in the price of RFID tags. Now, when a company orders a million or more, the unit cost for an RFID is 12.9¢. Although this is a "basic" RFID tag, it still can store 96 bits of information. Analysts predict that the price of RFID tags will continue to drop. By 2008, the cost may drop to about 5¢, at which point the use of RFID technology in marketing research and business operations should soar.

Sources: Clark, Don (2005), "Alien Cuts Radio ID Tag Price to Spur Adoption by Retailiners," The Wall Street Journal (September 12), D4; Fergueson, R.B. (2004), "Marines Deploy RFID," e-Week, 21 (November 15), 37.

COURTESY, DIVISION OF PUBLIC AFFAIRS, UNITED STATES MARINE CORPS, DEPARTMENT OF DEFENSE, USA

uses RFID technology to assist in its logistics, and Wal-Mart is one of the leading proponents of the technology as it can greatly assist in its global information system.[4]

With so much diverse information available in a global information system, organizations have found it necessary to determine what data, information, and knowledge are most useful to particular business units.

Decision Support Systems

A marketing **decision support system (DSS)** is a system that helps decision makers confront problems through direct interaction with computerized databases and analytical software programs. The purpose of a decision support system is to store data and transform them into organized information that is easily accessible to marketing managers. Doing so saves managers countless hours so that decisions that might take days or even weeks otherwise can be made in minutes using a DSS.

Modern decision support systems greatly facilitate **customer relationship management (CRM)**. A CRM system is the part of the DSS that addresses exchanges between the firm and its customers. It brings together information about customers, including sales data, market trends, marketing promotions and the way consumers respond to them, customer preferences, and more. A CRM system describes customer relationships in sufficient detail so that managers, salespeople, customer service representatives, and perhaps the customers themselves can access information directly, match customer needs with satisfying product offerings, remind customers of service requirements, and know what other products a customer has purchased.

Casinos track regular customers' behavior via "player's cards" that are swiped each time a consumer conducts a transaction. This information is fed automatically into a CRM system that creates tailor made promotional packages. The promotion may be unique to a specific customer's preferences as tracked by their own pattern of behavior. You may notice when visiting certain websites that they seem to be able to predict your behavior.

Decision support system (DSS)
A computer-based system that helps decision makers confront problems through direct interaction with databases and analytical software programs.

Customer relationship management (CRM)
Part of the DSS that addresses exchanges between the firm and its customers.

EXHIBIT 2.2
Decision Support System

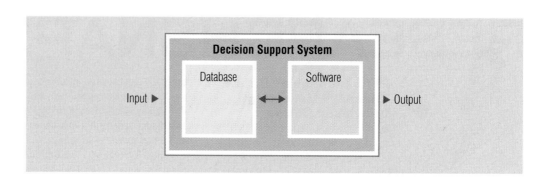

Exhibit 2.2 illustrates a decision support system. Raw, unsummarized data are input to the DSS. Data collected in marketing research projects are a major source of this input, but the data may be purchased or collected by accountants, sales managers, production managers, or company employees other than marketing researchers. Effective marketers spend a great deal of time and effort collecting information for input into the decision support system. Useful information is the output of a DSS. A decision support system requires both databases and software. For firms operating across national borders, the DSS becomes part of its global information system.

Databases and Data Warehousing

Database
A collection of raw data arranged logically and organized in a form that can be stored and processed by a computer.

A **database** is a collection of raw data arranged logically and organized in a form that can be stored and processed by a computer. A customer mailing list is one type of database. Population characteristics may be recorded by state, county, and city in another database. Modern computer technology makes both the storage and the retrieval of this information easy and convenient. The population data needed to do a retail site analysis may have meant days, possibly weeks, in a library. Today, the information is just a few clicks away.

Data warehousing
The process allowing important day-to-day operational data to be stored and organized for simplified access.

Data warehouse
The multitiered computer storehouse of current and historical data.

Data warehousing is the process allowing important day-to-day operational data to be stored and organized for simplified access. More specifically, a **data warehouse** is the multitiered computer storehouse of current and historical data. Data warehouse management requires that the detailed data from operational systems be extracted, transformed, placed into logical partitions (for example daily data, weekly data, etc.), and stored in a consistent manner. Organizations with data warehouses may integrate databases from both inside and outside the company. Managing a data warehouse effectively requires considerable computing power and expertise. As a result, data warehouse companies exist that provide this service for companies in return for a fee.[5] Data warehousing allows for sophisticated analysis, such as data mining, discussed in Chapter 6.

Input Management

How does data end up in a data warehouse where it can be used by a decision support system? In other words, how is the input managed? Input includes all the numerical, text, voice, and image data that enter the DSS. Systematic accumulation of pertinent, timely, and accurate data is essential to the success of a decision support system.

DSS managers, systems analysts, and programmers are responsible for the decision support system as a whole, but many functions within an organization provide input data. Marketing researchers, accountants, corporate librarians, sales personnel, production managers, and many others within the organization help to collect data and provide input for the DSS. Input data can also come from external sources.

Exhibit 2.3 shows five major sources of data input: internal records, proprietary marketing research, salesperson input, behavioral tracking, and outside vendors and external distributors of data. Each source can provide valuable input.

EXHIBIT 2.3 Five Major Sources of Marketing Input for Decision Support Systems

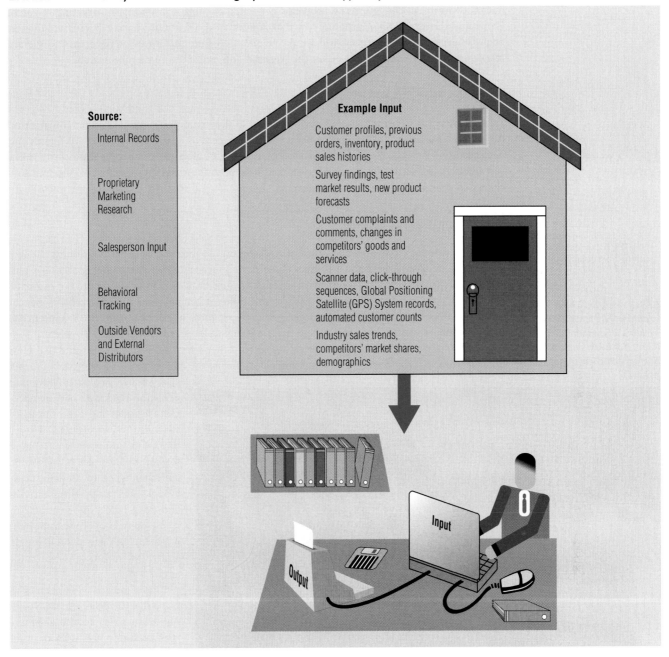

INTERNAL RECORDS

Internal records, such as accounting reports of sales and inventory figures, provide considerable data that may become useful information for marketing managers. An effective data collection system establishes orderly procedures to ensure that data about costs, shipments, inventory, sales, and other aspects of regular operations are routinely collected and entered into the computer.

PROPRIETARY MARKETING RESEARCH

Marketing research has already been defined as a broad set of procedures and methods. To clarify the DSS concept, consider a narrower view of marketing research. Proprietary marketing research emphasizes the company's gathering of new data. Few proprietary marketing research

Proprietary marketing research
The gathering of new data to investigate specific problems.

procedures and methods are conducted regularly or continuously. Instead, research projects conducted to study specific company problems generate data; this is proprietary marketing research. Providing managers with nonroutine data that otherwise would not be available is a major function of proprietary marketing research. Earlier, we discussed four categories of research. Proprietary marketing research may involve either the "testing" and/or "issues" types of research.

■ SALESPERSON INPUT

Salespeople work in firms' external environments, so they commonly provide essential marketing data. Sales representatives' reports frequently alert managers to changes in competitors' prices and new product offerings. It also may involve the types of complaints salespeople are hearing from customers. As trends become evident, this data may become marketing intelligence, leading to a change in product design or service delivery.

■ BEHAVIORAL TRACKING

Scanner data
The accumulated records resulting from point of sale data recordings.

GPS devices, like those used in automobile navigation systems, allow management to track delivery personnel or even actual customer behavior.

Modern technology provides new ways of tracking human behavior. Global positioning satellite (GPS) systems allow management to track the whereabouts of delivery personnel at all times. This is the same system that provides directions through an automobile's navigation system. For example, if your delivery person takes a quick break for nine holes of golf or decides to stop at Neil's Bar for a couple of beers mid-afternoon, management can spot these as deviations from the appropriate delivery route are noted. Thus, it can help track which employees are doing their jobs well.

Technology also allows firms to track actual customer behavior. While it's possible that GPS tracking data of customers is also sometimes possible, as the photograph suggests, the Internet also greatly facilitates customer behavior tracking. For instance, Google tracks the "click-through" sequence of customers. Therefore, if a customer is searching for information on refrigerators, and then goes to BestBuy.com, Google can track this behavior and use the information to let BestBuy know how important it is to advertise on Google and even automate pricing for advertisers.[6]

Purchase behavior can also be tracked at the point of sale. **Scanner data** refers to the accumulated records resulting from point of sale data recordings. In other words, each time products are scanned at a checkout counter, the information can be stored. The term *single-source* data refers to a system's ability to gather several types of interrelated data, such as type of purchase, use of a sales promotion, or advertising frequency data, from a single source in a format that will facilitate integration, comparison, and analysis.

RESEARCHSNAPSHOT

Staying Home at Home Depot

The DSS of any organization is no better than the quality of the data input to its data warehouse. How can firms make sure that the input remains relevant and retains a "high-touch" component in a "high-tech" world?

Home Depot has always tried to make sure its executives "stay in touch" by requiring them to spend a substantial amount of time on the sales floor of a Home Depot store, which means that one of the folks in the bright orange apron helping you choose the right flush valve may well be a six-figure executive. Thus, the people who decide what should go into the data warehouse and how the DSS will use it maintain an appreciation for the types of decisions faced by Home Depot store managers each and every day. Home Depot even asks outside suppliers who may be involved in information technology (IT) design to spend a few

days in an actual Home Depot store. Thus, as Home Depot implements key innovations in its data networks, the people helping it to do so understand what the information needs of employees really are. Even Home Depot's outside directors meet with middle managers and conduct store visits so that they can provide more meaningful advice to senior executives. Part of this advice concerns the data needs of Home Depot managers.

Do you think such a plan would be similarly successful for a company like Krispy Kreme?

Sources: Alberts, Brad (2001), "Home Depot's Special Projects Support Team Powers Information Management for Business Needs," Journal of Organizational Excellence, 21 (Winter), 3–15; Lublin, Joanne (2005), "Home Depot Board Gains Insight from Trenches," The Wall Street Journal (October 10), B3.

■ OUTSIDE VENDORS AND EXTERNAL DISTRIBUTORS

Outside vendors and external distributors market information as their products. Many organizations specialize in the collection and publication of high-quality information. One outside vendor, the ACNielsen Company, provides television program ratings, audience counts, and information about the demographic composition of television viewer groups. Other vendors specialize in the distribution of information. Public libraries have always purchased information, traditionally in the form of books, and they have served as distributors of this information.

Media representatives often provide useful demographic and lifestyle data about their audiences. *Advertising Age, The Wall Street Journal, Sales and Marketing Management,* and other trade- and business-oriented publications are important sources of information. These publications keep managers up-to-date about the economy, competitors' activities, and other aspects of the marketing environment.

Companies called *data specialists* record and store certain marketing information. Computer technology has changed the way many of these organizations supply data, favoring the development of computerized databases.

Computerized Data Archives

Historically, collections of organized and readily retrievable data were available in printed form at libraries. The *Statistical Abstract of the United States,* which is filled with tables of statistical facts, is a typical example. In recent years, the *Statistical Abstract* has become available electronically. Users can purchase it via CD-ROM or access it via the Internet. The entire 2000 census as well as projections through the current year is available in print, CD-ROM, and via the Internet at http://www.census.gov. More and more data are available in digitized form every day.

Numerous computerized search and retrieval systems and electronic databases are available as subscription services or in libraries. Just as a student can query the school library to find information for a term paper without leaving home, data acquisition for businesses has also become far more convenient in recent years. Today, business people access online information search and retrieval services, such as Dow Jones News Retrieval and Bloomberg Financial Markets, without leaving their offices. In fact, some information services can be accessed from remote locations via digital wireless devices.

Modern library patrons can command a computer to search indexes and retrieve databases from a range of vendors. Just as wholesalers collect goods from manufacturers and offer them for sale to retailers who then provide them to consumers, many information firms serve as data wholesalers. **Data wholesalers** put together consortia of data sources into packages that are offered to municipal, corporate, and university libraries for a fee. Information consumers then access the data through these libraries. Some of the better known *databases* include Wilson Business Center, Hoovers, PROQUEST, INFOTRAC, DIALOG (Dialog Information Services, Inc.), LEXIS-NEXIS, and Dow Jones News Retrieval Services. These databases provide all types of information, including recent news stories and data tables charting statistical trends.

DIALOG, for example, maintains more than 600 databases. A typical database may have a million or more records, each consisting of a one- or two-paragraph abstract that summarizes the major points of a published article along with bibliographic information. One of the DIALOG databases, ABI/INFORM, abstracts significant articles in more than 1,000 current business and management journals. Many computerized archives provide full-text downloads of published articles about companies and various research topics.

Exhibit 2.4 illustrates the services provided by two popular vendors of information services that electronically index numerous databases. For a more extensive listing, see the *Gale Directory of Databases.*[7]

Several types of databases from outside vendors and external distributors are so fundamental to decision support systems that they deserve further explanation. The following sections discuss statistical databases, financial databases, and video databases in slightly more detail.

■ STATISTICAL DATABASES

Statistical databases contain numerical data for market analysis and forecasting. Often demographic, sales, and other relevant marketing variables are recorded by geographical area. Geographic information systems use these *geographical databases* and powerful software to prepare computer

Data wholesalers
Companies that put together consortia of data sources into packages that are offered to municipal, corporate, and university libraries for a fee.

EXHIBIT 2.4 Vendors of Information Services and Electronic Indexing

Vendors	Selected Databases	Type of Data
DIALOG	ABI/INFORM	Summaries and citations from over 1,000 academic management, marketing, and general business journals with full text of more than 500 of these publications
	ASI (American Statistics Index)	Abstracts and indexes of federal government statistical publications
	PROMT (The Predicast Overview of Markets and Technologies)	Summaries and full text from 1,000 U.S. and international business and trade journals, industry newsletters, newspapers, and market research studies; information about industries and companies, including the products and technologies they develop and the markets in which they compete
	Investext	Full text of over 2 million company, industry, and geographic research reports written by analysts at more than 600 leading investment banks, brokerage houses, and consulting firms worldwide
Dow Jones News Retrieval	Business Newsstand	Articles from *New York Times, Los Angeles Times, Washington Post*, and other leading newspapers and magazines
	Historical Market Data Center	Historical data on securities, dividends, and exchange rates
	Web Center	Information obtained from searches of corporate, industry, government, and news websites

maps of relevant variables. Companies such as Claritas, Urban Decision Systems, and CACI all offer geographic/demographic databases that are widely used in industry.

One source for these huge data warehouses is scanner data. Substituting mechanized record-keeping like optical scanners for human record-keeping results in greater accuracy and more rapid feedback about store activity.

One weakness of scanner data is that not all points of sale have scanner technology. For instance, many convenience stores lack scanner technology, as do most vending machines. Thus, those purchases go unrecorded. The Universal Product Code, or UPC, contains information on the category of goods, the manufacturer, and product identification based on size, flavor, color, and so on. This is what the optical scanner actually reads. If a large percentage of a brand's sales occur in environments without the ability to read the UPC code, the marketer should be aware that the scanner data may not be representative.

▦ FINANCIAL DATABASES

Competitors' and customers' financial data, such as income statements and balance sheets, may interest managers. These are easy to access in financial databases. CompuStat publishes an extensive financial database on thousands of companies, broken down by industry and other criteria. To illustrate the depth of this pool of information, CompuStat's Global Advantage offers extensive data on 6,650 companies in more than thirty countries in Europe, the Pacific Rim, and North America.

▦ VIDEO DATABASES

Video databases and streaming media are having a major impact on the marketing of many goods and services. For example, movie studios provide clips of upcoming films and advertising agencies put television commercials on the Internet (see http://www. adcritic.com). McDonald's maintains a digital archive of television commercials and other video footage to share with its franchisers around the world. The video database enables franchisers and their advertising agencies to create local advertising without filming the same types of scenes already archived. Just imagine the value of digital video databases to advertising agencies' decision support systems.

Electronic data interchange (EDI)
Type of exchange that occurs when one company's computer system is integrated with another company's system.

Statistical information has its limitations. When a product is sold in an environment that cannot read scanner data, important information about that product is not available for marketing analysis and forecasting.

Networks and Electronic Data Interchange

Individual personal computers can be connected through networks to other computers. Networking involves linking two or more computers to share data and software.

Electronic data interchange (EDI) systems integrate one company's computer system directly with another company's system. Much of the input to a company's decision support system may come through networks from other companies' computers. Companies such as Computer Technology Corporation and Microelectronics market data services that allow corporations to exchange business information with suppliers or customers. For example, every evening Wal-Mart transmits millions of characters of data about the day's sales to its apparel suppliers. Wrangler, a supplier of blue jeans, for instance, shares the data and a model that interprets the data. Wrangler also shares software applications that act to replenish stock in Wal-Mart stores. This DSS lets Wrangler's managers know when to send specific quantities of specific sizes and colors of jeans to specific stores from specific warehouses. The result is a learning loop that lowers inventory costs and leads to fewer stockouts.

For more information about Sensible Snacking, please visit www.nabiscoworld/sensiblesnacking.com.

NABISCO WORLD.COM

Hot Games... Cool Prizes!

See NabiscoWorld.com for details.

CHIPS AHOY! REDUCED FAT CHOCOLATE CHIP COOKIES

BRAND SEAL

0 447310 7

©SUSAN VAN ETTEN

The Internet and Research

In the 1980s, the mainframe computing power of the 1960s, which was available primarily in large universities, government agencies, and very large companies, was transformed into something that could go on nearly every businessperson's desktop. The personal computer (PC) and simple operating systems like DOS and eventually Windows revolutionized many business applications by making computing power relatively inexpensive and convenient. Today, the widespread usage of the Internet is perhaps the single biggest change agent in marketing research. Since most readers are no doubt experienced in using the Internet, we highlight a few terms and facts about the Internet that are especially useful in understanding marketing research.

In the following pages we discuss the World Wide Web and how to use the Internet for research. However, keep in mind that the Internet is constantly changing. The description of the Internet, especially home page addresses, may be out of date by the time this book is published. Be aware that the Internet of today will not be the Internet of tomorrow.

What Exactly Is the Internet?

Internet
A worldwide network of
computers that allows users
access to information from
distant sources.

The **Internet** is a worldwide network of computers that allows users access to data, information, and feedback from distant sources. It functions as the world's largest public library, proving access to a seemingly endless range of data. Many people believe the Internet is the most important communications medium since television.

The Internet began in the 1960s as an experimental connection between computers at Stanford University, the University of California at Santa Barbara, the University of California at Los Angeles, and the University of Utah, in conjunction with the Department of Defense.[8] The Department of Defense was involved because it wanted to develop a communications network that could survive nuclear war. The Internet gradually grew into a nationwide network of connected computers, and now it is a worldwide network often referred to as the "information superhighway."

The Internet has no central computer; instead, each message sent bears an address code that lets a sender forward a message to a desired destination from any computer linked to the Net. Many benefits of the Internet arise because the Internet is a collection of thousands of small networks, both domestic and foreign, rather than a single computer operation.

Host
Where the content for a
particular website physically
resides and is accessed.

A domain is typically a company name, institutional name, or organizational name associated with a host computer. A **host** is where the content for a particular website physically resides and is accessed. For example, *Forbes* magazine's Internet edition is located at http://forbes.com. The "com" indicates this domain is a commercial site. George State University can be virtually reached at http://www.gsu.edu. Educational sites end in "edu." The United States Marine Corps can be found at http://www.marines.mil, and many government sites, such as the U.S. House of Representatives, end with "gov," as in http://www.house.gov. Many nonprofit organizations end in "org," as in http://www.ams-web.org, the web home for the Academy of Marketing Science. Web addresses outside the United States often end in abbreviations for their country such as "ca," "de," or "uk" for Canada, Germany (Deutschland), and the United Kingdom, respectively.

Navigating the Internet

**World Wide Web
(WWW)**
A portion of the Internet that is
a system of computer servers
that organize information into
documents called web pages.

The **World Wide Web (WWW)** refers specifically to that portion of the Internet made up of servers that support a retrieval system that organizes information into documents called web pages. World Wide Web documents, which may include graphic images, video clips, and sound clips, are formatted in programming languages, such as HTML (HyperText Markup Language) and XML (Extensible Markup Language) that allow for displaying, linking, and sharing of information on the Internet.

Content providers
Parties that furnish information
on the World Wide Web.

Parties that furnish information on the World Wide Web are called **content providers**. Content providers maintain websites. A website consists of one or more web pages with related information about a particular topic; for example, a university website might include pages about its mission, courses, and faculty (see http://www.gsu.edu, for example). The introductory page or opening screen is called the home page because it provides basic information about the purpose of the document along with a menu of selections or links that lead to other screens with more specific information. Thus, each page can have connections, or hyperlinks, to other pages, which may be on any computer connected to the Internet. People using the World Wide Web may be viewing information that is stored on a host computer or on a machine halfway around the world.

Most web browsers also allow the user to enter a **Uniform Resource Locator (URL)** into the program. The URL is really just a website address that web browsers recognize. Many websites allow any user or visitor access without previous approval. However, many commercial sites require that the user have a valid account and password before access is granted.

One of the most basic research tools available via the Internet is a search engine. A **search engine** is a computerized directory that allows anyone to search the World Wide Web for information based on a keyword search. A **keyword search** takes place as the search engine searches through millions of web pages for documents containing the keywords. Some of the most comprehensive and accurate search engines are:

Yahoo!	http://www.yahoo.com
Google	http://www.google.com
Hotbot	http://www.hotbot.com
Go network	http://www.go.com
Excite	http://www.excite.com
Lycos	http://www.lycos.com
Ask Jeeves	http://www.ask.com
WebCrawler	http://www.webcrawler.com

Google revolutionized search engines by changing the way the search was actually conducted. It searches based on a mathematical theory known as *graph theory*.[9] Google greatly improved the accuracy and usefulness of the search results obtained from a keyword search.

Interactive Media and Environmental Scanning

The Internet is an **interactive medium** because users click commands and often get customized responses. So the user and equipment can have a continuing conversation. Two or more individuals who communicate one-to-one via e-mail using an Internet service provider are also using interactive media. So are individuals who communicate with many senders and receivers via bulletin boards or chat rooms. Because of its vastness, the Internet is an especially useful source for scanning many types of environmental changes. **Environmental scanning** entails all information gathering designed to detect changes in the external operating environment of the firm. These things are usually beyond the control of the firm, but they still can have a significant impact on firm performance.

Ford Motor Company maintains an Internet-based relationship marketing program that, among other things, helps the automaker scan its environment using the Internet. Its dealer website creates a centralized communication service linking dealers via an Internet connection. Its buyer website allows prospective buyers to visit a virtual showroom and to get price quotes and financial information. Its owner website allows an owner who registers and supplies pertinent vehicle information to get free e-mail and other ownership perks. A perk might be a free Hertz upgrade or an autographed photo of one of the Ford-sponsored NASCAR drivers. In return, Ford collects data at all levels, which allow managers to scan for trends and apply what they learn at a local level.

Information Technology

Data and information can be delivered to consumers or other end users via either **pull technology** or **push technology**. Conventionally, consumers request information from a web page and the browser then determines a response. Thus, the consumer is essentially asking for the data. In this case, it is said to be pulled through the channel. The opposite of pull is push. Push technology sends data to a user's computer without a request being made. In other words, software is used to guess what information might be interesting to consumers based on the pattern of previous responses.

Smart information delivery (known by a variety of technical names, including *push phase technology*) allows a website, such as the Yahoo portal, to become a one-on-one medium for each individual user. Today's information technology uses "smart agents" or "intelligent agents" to

Uniform Resource Locator (URL)
A website address that web browsers recognize.

Search engine
A computerized directory that allows anyone to search the World Wide Web for information using a keyword search.

Keyword search
Takes place as the search engine searches through millions of web pages for documents containing the keywords.

Interactive medium
A medium, such as the Internet, that a person can use to communicate with and interact with other users.

Environmental scanning
Entails all information gathering designed to detect changes in the external operating environment of the firm.

Pull technology
Consumers request information from a web page and the browser then determines a response; the consumer is essentially asking for the data.

Push technology
Sends data to a user's computer without a request being made; software is used to guess what information might be interesting to consumers based on the pattern of previous responses.

The iPod offers one example of how modern technology makes it possible to store and deliver information. Various models can capture, store, and deliver hundreds of songs to their owners.

Smart agent software
Software capable of learning an Internet user's preferences and automatically searching out information in selected websites and then distributing it.

Cookies
Small computer files that a content provider can save onto the computer of someone who visits its website.

Intranet
A company's private data network that uses Internet standards and technology.

deliver customized content to a viewer's desktop. **Smart agent software** is capable of learning an Internet user's preferences and automatically searching out information and distributing the information to a user's computer. My Yahoo! and MyExcite are portal services that personalize web pages. Users can get stock quotes relevant to their portfolios, news about favorite sports teams, local weather, and other personalized information. Users can customize the sections of the service they want delivered. With push technology, pertinent content is delivered to the viewer's desktop without the user having to do the searching.

Cookies, in computer terminology, are small computer files that record a user's web usage history. If a person looks up a weather report by keying in a zip code into a personalized web page, the fact that the user visited the website and the zip code entered are recorded in the cookie. This is a clue that tells where the person lives (or maybe where he or she may be planning to visit). Websites can then direct information to that consumer based on information in the cookie. So, someone in College Station, Texas, may receive pop-up ads for restaurants in College Station. Information technology is having a major impact on the nature of marketing research. We will explore this topic in several places throughout this book.

Intranets

An **Intranet** is a company's private data network that uses Internet standards and technology.[10] The information on an Intranet—data, graphics, video, and voice—is available only inside the organization or to those individuals whom the organization deems as appropriate participants. Thus, a key difference between the Internet and an Intranet is that security software programs, or "firewalls," are installed to limit access to only those employees authorized to enter the system. Intranets then serve as secure knowledge portals that contain substantial amounts of organizational memory and can integrate it with information from outside sources. The challenge in designing an Intranet is making sure that it is capable of delivering relevant data to decision makers. Research suggests that relevance is a key in getting knowledge workers to actually make use of company Intranets.[11]

The Intranet can be extended to include key consumers as a source of valuable research. Their participation in the Intranet can lead to new product developments. Texas Instruments has successfully established an Intranet that integrated communications between customers and researchers leading to the introduction and modification of its calculators.[12] An Intranet lets authorized users, possibly including key customers, look at product drawings, employee newsletters, sales figures, and other kinds of company information.

Summary

1. Distinguish between the concepts of data, information, and intelligence. Increased global competition and technological advances in interactive media have spurred development of global information systems. A global information system is an organized collection of computer hardware, software, data, and personnel designed to capture, store, update, manipulate, analyze, and immediately display information about worldwide business activity.

From a research perspective, there is a difference between data, information, and intelligence. Data are simply facts or recorded measures of certain phenomena (things); information is data formatted (structured) to support decision making or define the relationship between two facts. Market intelligence is the subset of data and information that actually has some explanatory power enabling effective decisions to be made.

2. Describe the four characteristics that explain the usefulness of data. The usefulness of data to management can be described based on four characteristics: relevance, quality, timeliness, and completeness. Relevant data have the characteristic of pertinence to the situation at hand. The information is useful. The quality of information is the degree to which data represent the true situation. High-quality data are accurate, valid, and reliable. High-quality data represent reality faithfully and present a good picture of reality. Timely information is obtained at the right time. Computerized information systems can record events and present information soon after a transaction takes place, improving timeliness. Complete information is the right quantity of information. Marketing managers must have sufficient information to relate all aspects of their decisions together.

3. Identify the purpose of research in assisting marketing operations. A computer-based marketing decision support system helps decision makers confront problems through direct interactions with databases and analytical models. A DSS stores data and transforms them into organized information that is easily accessible to marketing managers.

4. Explain what a decision support system is and what it does. A database is a collection of raw data arranged logically and organized in a form that can be stored and processed by a computer. Marketing data come from four major sources: internal records, proprietary marketing research, marketing intelligence, and outside vendors and external distributors. Each source can provide valuable input. Because most companies compile and store many different databases, they often develop data warehousing systems. Data warehousing is the process allowing important day-to-day operational data to be stored and organized for simplified access. More specifically, a data warehouse is the multitiered computer storehouse of current and historical data. Data warehouse management requires that the detailed data from operational systems be extracted, transformed, and stored (warehoused) so that the various database tables from both inside and outside the company are consistent. All of this feeds into the decision support system that automates or assists business decision making.

Numerous database search and retrieval systems are available by subscription or in libraries. Computer-assisted database searching has made the collection of external data faster and easier. Marketers refer to many different types of databases.

Although personal computers work independently, they can connect to other computers in networks to share data and software. Electronic data interchange (EDI) allows one company's computer system to join directly to another company's system.

5. Distinguish an Intranet from the Internet. The Internet is a worldwide network of computers that allows users access to information and documents from distant sources. It is a combination of a worldwide communication system and the world's largest public library. The World Wide Web is a system of thousands of interconnected pages, or documents, that can be easily accessed with web browsers and search engines.

An Intranet is a company's private data network that uses Internet standards and technology. The information on an Intranet—data, graphics, video, and voice—is available only inside the organization. Thus, a key difference between the Internet and an Intranet is that "firewalls," or security software programs, are installed to limit access to only those employees authorized to enter the system.

A company uses Internet features to build its own Intranet. Groupware and other technology can facilitate the transfer of data, information, and knowledge. In organizations that practice knowledge management, Intranets function to make the knowledge of company experts more accessible throughout their organizations.

Key Terms and Concepts

Data
Information
Market intelligence
Relevance
Data quality
Timeliness
Information completeness
Global information system
Decision support system (DSS)
Customer relationship management (CRM)
Database

Data warehousing
Data warehouse
Proprietary marketing research
Scanner data
Data wholesalers
Electronic data interchange (EDI)
Internet
Host
World Wide Web (WWW)
Content provider
Uniform Resource Locator (URL)

Search engine
Keyword search
Interactive medium
Environmental scanning
Pull technology
Push technology
Smart agent software
Cookies
Intranet

Questions for Review and Critical Thinking

1. What is the difference between data, information, and intelligence?
2. What are the characteristics of useful information?
3. What is the key question distinguishing relevant data from irrelevant data?
4. What types of databases might be found in the following organizations?
   a. Holiday Inn
   b. A major university athletic department
   c. Anheuser-Busch
5. What type of operational questions could a delivery firm like FedEx expect to automate with the company's decision support system?
6. What makes a decision support system successful?
7. What is data warehousing?
8. **'NET** How does data warehousing assist decision making? Visit http://www.kbb.com. While there, choose two cars that you might consider buying and compare them. Which do you like the best? What would you do now? What are at least three pieces of data that should be stored in a data warehouse somewhere based on your interaction with *Kelly Blue Book?*
9. **'NET** Give three examples of computerized databases that are available at your college or university library.
10. **'NET** What is the difference between the Internet and an Intranet?
11. Suppose a retail firm is interested in studying the effect of lighting on customer purchase behavior. Which of the following pieces of information is the least relevant and why?
    a. Amount of natural light in the store
    b. The compensation system for store salespeople
    c. The color of the walls in the store
    d. The type of lighting: fluorescent or incandescent
12. **'NET** Imagine the data collected by eBay each day. List at least five types of data that are collected through the daily operations. Describe each in terms of it illustrating data, information, or intelligence. Make sure you list at least one of each.
13. How could New Balance, a maker of athletic shoes, use RFID technology to collect data?
14. **'NET** The Spider's Apprentice is a website that provides many useful tips about using search engines. Go to http://www.monash.com/spidap.html, then click on The Spider's Apprentice to learn the ins and outs of search engines.

Research Activities

1. **'NET** To learn more about data warehousing, go to http://www.datawarehousing.org.
2. **'NET** Use the Internet to see if you can find information to answer the following questions:
   a. What is the weather in Denver today?
   b. What are four restaurants in the French Quarter in New Orleans?
   c. What is the population of Brazil?

Case 2.1 Harvard Cooperative Society

From his office window overlooking the main floor of the Harvard Cooperative Society, CEO Jerry Murphy can glance down and see customers shopping.[13] They make their way through the narrow aisles of the crowded department store, picking up a sweatshirt here, trying on a baseball cap there, checking out the endless array of merchandise that bears the Harvard University insignia.

Watching Murphy, you can well imagine the Coop's founders, who started the store in 1882, peering through the tiny window-panes to keep an eye on the shop floor. Was the Harvard Square store attracting steady traffic? Were the college students buying enough books and supplies for the Coop to make a profit? Back then, it was tough to answer those questions precisely. The owners had to watch and wait, relying only on their gut feelings to know how things were going from minute to minute.

Now, more than a hundred years later, Murphy can tell you, down to the last stock-keeping unit, how he's doing at any given moment. His window on the business is the PC that sits on his desk.

All day long it delivers up-to-the-minute, easy-to-read electronic reports on what's selling and what's not, which items are running low in inventory and which have fallen short of forecast. In a matter of seconds, the computer can report gross margins for any product or supplier, and Murphy can decide whether the margins are fat enough to justify keeping the supplier or product on board. "We were in the 1800s, and we had to move ahead," he says of the $55 million business.

Questions

1. What is a decision support system? What advantages does a decision support system have for a business like the Harvard Cooperative Society?
2. How would the decision support system of a business like the Harvard Cooperative Society differ from that of a major corporation?
3. Briefly outline the components of the Harvard Cooperative Society's decision support system.

Video Case 2.2 Wine.com

Wine.com advertises itself as the "world's largest wine store." With over 14,000 fine wines in its website inventory, it probably is.

The company was launched in the nineties as an e-commerce venture by Peter Granoff, one of the nation's leading wine experts, with over twenty years of wine-selling experience, and Robert Olson, an expert in the computer industry. The two were talking over a glass of wine about recent trends in the wine industry that threatened both small producers and consumers when they had a brainstorm about how to get a broad variety of fine wines into the retail market. They took their initial program to a couple of wineries and asked if the producers thought their idea would work.

With positive feedback, they "went live," first building their site and then advertising it in appropriate channels both online and offline. Wine.com is one of the first merchants to get started as a purely e-commerce business. A positive aspect of web selling is that it collapses the geography of the retail base, but a challenging reality for this product is that it has a narrow market segment—adults who drink wine and are willing to spend time in choosing the wine they drink.

Granoff explains that marketing initiatives are the important key to branding their company on and off the web. The company has a multimillion dollar advertising campaign. It maintains active affiliate programs with other online products and other e-commerce ventures like Amazon.com. It advertises extensively on television and radio and in print media like *Food & Wine* and *The Wall Street Journal*.

Wine itself has a "passionate customer base," and the company does its best to find the best wines for its customers. Experts review hundreds of samples of wine each month. Wine.com educates consumers about fine wines, helps them find the perfect bottle of wine for a reasonable price, and then delivers the wine directly to their doorsteps. The website is designed to put people at ease and to de-mystify the process of selecting a wine. The wine retailer also retains a full-time customer-support staff that provides the individual attention that customers would expect in a brick-and-mortar wine shop. Customers can contact the company online, through e-mail, and by phone. When customers put in an order, they immediately receive an automated confirmation of their order.

Granoff identifies the metrics that are the best indicators of Wine.com's success: a branding proposition that is working, a customer acquisition model that is working, retention rates that are where they need to be, and a high-visibility public relations and advertising program.

The costs and complexity of the infrastructure in an e-commerce wine business are challenging. Their revenues are ramping between 300 to 500 percent every year, so Wine.com must rethink their fundamental business processes every four to six months. "The speed of the ramp, more than anything else, cuts across everything that we do," says Granoff. And it's the speed of the ramp "that is so exciting."

Questions

1. What suggestions might you have for Wine.com's customer relationship management?
2. In the future, Wine.com wants to expand to Australia, Asia, South Africa, and countries in Europe. How could a global information system help the company?

Video Case 2.3 IBM: Enterprise Resource Planning

By centralizing information and making it more widely available, IBM's ERP (Enterprise Resource Planning) system has the potential to make companies much more competitive and responsive.[14] Here is what IBM says about ERP:

ERP solutions are effective at streamlining business processes that cut across the functional areas of your business. ERP brings together fragmented operations, often replacing a multiplicity of legacy systems. By sharing common information across an integrated set of application modules, ERP can speed up transactions. For instance, ERP can consolidate financial records, allowing you to close the books faster and more accurately.

ERP can help you better manage your inventory, driving dramatic cost savings. ERP can map customer orders to your production plans, helping to improve the cycle time to respond to customer demand. And ERP can help eliminate process duplication, wait times, and information errors, yielding productivity improvements for your professionals. In addition, the regimen of an ERP implementation forces you to look at how you run your business—your processes, practices, and procedures. ERP implementations are a great

opportunity to institutionalize a number of changes, many of which you may have been considering for some time.

While ERP is very good at driving improvements, its focus is inward, within your own enterprise. However, if your company's top challenges involve relationships with your customers or trading partnerships with your suppliers, you may want to consider other solutions—either implemented individually or together with an ERP solution. Also, given the time it takes to fully deploy an ERP solution, you may want to consider a phased approach that includes these additional areas. This will ensure that the solution you implement meets your needs for the coming years, not just your immediate problem.

IBM offers industry expertise to know what it takes to differentiate your business. Plus, IBM offers solution expertise spanning ERP, e-commerce, supply chain, customer relationship management, business intelligence, and more, to help you decide the combination that's best for your business.

Question

Different companies use different terminology for global information systems and decision support systems. After viewing the video, explain how IBM's ERP system parallels the book's definition and explanation of global information systems and decision support systems.

CHAPTER 3
THE MARKETING RESEARCH PROCESS: AN OVERVIEW

After studying this chapter, you should be able to

1. Classify marketing research into one of three types
2. List the major phases of the marketing research process
3. Distinguish between the concepts of theory and hypothesis
4. Explain the difference between a research project and a research program

Chapter Vignette: The Changing Educational Market

Students seeking a higher education today enjoy many more choices than did their parents. Universities offer new degree programs in varied and specific fields, including areas like sports marketing and gaming management. However, it isn't simply the fields of study that may be new, but also the manner of study. Options for nontraditional students who have difficulty attending day classes or devoting years of study to obtaining a degree have grown exponentially. The University of Phoenix, Strayer University, and Nova Southeast typify institutions that specialize in catering to those seeking a nontraditional degree pro-

gram. These competitive pressures have led even the most traditional universities to rethink the traditional "sage on the stage" approach and conventional academic calendars.

The market for the MBA degree is particularly competitive. Students pursue their MBA either traditionally, in weekend-only programs, at night school, online, or in some combination. Over a quarter of a million U.S. students alone attend MBA classes of one form or another at any given time. In urban areas, such as the Dallas-Fort Worth, Texas, area, there are sometimes a dozen or more institutions offering an MBA. In smaller communities, too, universities are facing decisions about their MBA offerings:

- How much should they adapt to the changing market?
- Should they offer courses online?
- If so, who are they competing with?
- Should they offer a weekend program?
- Should they offer classes in multiple locations?
- Is demand sufficient? That is, are there enough potential students to make this financially feasible?
- Is there a potential perceived product-quality difference between a traditional and a nontraditional MBA program?
- Can they better accomplish the university mission with an online MBA program?

The competitive MBA market typifies the landscape of many marketing firms. Clearly, universities could benefit from marketing research addressing some of these key questions. Each university maintains its own academic standard while still trying to attract enough students to make its MBA program feasible. The competitive landscape is filled with both potential opportunities and potential problems. Decisions made by university faculty and administrators will determine how successfully each school deals with the changing marketplace.

Introduction

This chapter focuses on the relationship between business decisions and marketing research. Business success is determined directly by the quality of decisions made by key personnel. Researchers contribute to decision making in several key ways:

1. Helping to better define the current situation
2. Defining the firm—determining how consumers, competitors, and employees view the firm
3. Providing ideas for product improvements or possible new product development
4. Testing ideas that will assist in implementing the marketing-mix strategy for the firm
5. Examining how correct a certain marketing theory is in a given situation

The chapter introduces the types of research that allow researchers to provide input to key decision makers. The chapter also discusses stages in the marketing research process.

Information Reduces Uncertainty

Marketing research provides information to reduce uncertainty. It helps focus decision making. Sometimes marketing researchers know exactly what their marketing problems are and design careful studies to test specific hypotheses. For example, a soft-drink company introducing a new vanilla cola might want to know whether a gold or a silver label would make the packaging more effective. This problem is fully defined, and an experiment may be designed to answer the marketing question with little preliminary investigation.

In more ambiguous circumstances, management may be totally unaware that a marketing problem exists. For example, suppose McDonald's managers notice that Mo's Burgers, a competitor in the Japanese market, has introduced Mo's Roast Katsu Burger, a roast pork cutlet drenched in traditional Japanese katsu sauce and topped with shredded cabbage. The managers may understand little about Japanese consumers' feelings about this menu item. In this case, some exploratory research will yield insights into the nature of this problem.

To understand the variety of research activity, it is beneficial to categorize the types of marketing research.

Types of Marketing Research

Marketing research can reduce uncertainty and focus decision making. Sometimes marketing researchers know exactly what marketing problems are faced and can design careful studies to test specific hypotheses. A university may face a problem with an out-of-date curriculum. Awareness of this problem could be based on input from employers, students, and alumni. The problem could even be contributing to low enrollment. How should the faculty and administration decide to address this problem? They may devise a careful test examining which of three new curricula can be implemented to improve this perception. This type of research is problem oriented and seems relatively unambiguous. The marketing research may culminate with researchers preparing a report suggesting the relative effect of each alternative curriculum on enrollment. The decision should follow relatively directly from the research.

Alternatively, the company may be scanning the environment for opportunities. For example, a small undergraduate university in a mid-sized Colorado town may consider adding an online MBA program. University administrators may have little idea as to how this would affect the image of their school among current students, employers, alumni, or faculty. They also may not know exactly what programs would be most desired by its current or potential customer bases. Some preliminary research may be necessary to gain insights into the nature of such a situation. Otherwise, the situation may remain too ambiguous to make more than a seat-of-the-pants decision. Marketing research is almost certainly needed.

Marketing research can be classified on the basis of either technique or purpose. Experiments, surveys, and observational studies are just a few common research techniques. Classifying research by its purpose shows how the nature of a decision situation influences the research methodology. The following section introduces the three types of marketing research:

1. Exploratory
2. Descriptive
3. Causal

Matching the particular decision situation with the right type of research is important to obtaining useful research results.

Exploratory Research

Exploratory research
Conducted to clarify ambiguous situations or discover ideas that may be potential business opportunities.

Exploratory research is conducted to clarify ambiguous situations or to discover ideas that may be potential business opportunities. Exploratory research is *not* intended to provide conclusive evidence from which to determine a particular course of action. In this sense, exploratory research is not an end unto itself. Usually exploratory research is conducted with the expectation that more research will yet be needed to provide more conclusive evidence. Using exploratory research can sometimes also make the difference in determining the usefulness of other related research. Rushing into detailed surveys before it is clear exactly what decisions need to be made can waste time, money, and effort by providing irrelevant information.

Exploratory research is particularly useful in new product development.[1] Sony and Honda have each been instrumental in developing robot technology.[2] Making a functional robot that can move around, perform basic tasks, carry out instructions, and even carry on a conversation isn't really a problem. What Sony and Honda have to research is what market opportunities may exist based on robot technology. Research can allow consumers to interact with robots as a form of exploratory research. The results suggest that consumers interact much more when the robot has human qualities, including the ability to walk on two legs. Researchers noticed that people will actually talk to the robot (which can understand basic oral commands) more when it has human qualities. In addition, consumers do seem entertained by a walking, talking, dancing robot. Thus, this has allowed each company to form more specific research questions focusing on the relative value of a robot as an entertainment device or as a security guard.

In our university example, exploratory research is perhaps needed to help identify concerns about nontraditional course delivery for business classes. This exploratory research should include open-ended interviews with faculty, students, and alumni. By doing so, researchers can develop specific hypotheses that test the relative attractiveness of alternative curricula to students and the effect of online instruction on job satisfaction and on alumni quality perceptions.[3] These hypotheses may be tested by either or both of the remaining two research types.

Descriptive Research

Descriptive research
Describes characteristics of objects, people, groups, organizations, or environments. Descriptive research tries to "paint a picture" of a given situation.

The major purpose of **descriptive research**, as the name implies, describes characteristics of objects, people, groups, organizations, or environments. Put more simply, descriptive research tries to "paint a picture" of a given situation. Marketing managers frequently need to determine who purchases a product, portray the size of the market, identify competitors' actions, and so on. Descriptive research addresses *who, what, when, where,* and *how* questions.

Descriptive research often helps describe market segments. For example, marketing researchers used simple descriptive surveys to describe consumers who are heavy consumers (buy a lot) of organic food products. The resulting report showed that these consumers tend to live in coastal cities with populations over 500,000, with the majority residing on the West Coast. The most frequent buyers of organic foods are affluent men and women ages 45–54 (36 percent) and 18–34 (35 percent).[4] Interestingly, consumers who buy organic foods are not very brand oriented—81 percent of them cannot name a single organic brand. Research such as this helps high-quality supermarkets such as Whole Foods make location decisions. Over half of Whole Foods food products are organic.

Similarly, the university considering the addition of an online MBA program might benefit from descriptive research describing the market and potential customers. Online customers are not

RESEARCHSNAPSHOT

Cute, Funny, or Sexy? What Makes a Mascot Tick?

Has the Pillsbury Doughboy ever changed? How old should the Brawny (paper towel) man be? What should the M&Ms characters be named? These questions all have many possible answers. In truth, a lot of research goes into these kinds of questions. It often begins with exploratory research. For instance, focus groups involving female consumers revealed a considerable amount of intimate discussion about the Brawny man. Thus, it seemed that a sexy Brawny man would yield a better response than a humorous or intelligent Brawny man.

Mr. Peanut, the icon for Planters peanuts, has actually changed very little since his introduction in the 1920s. He looks good for his age. Again, exploratory research suggests generally positive comments about Mr. Peanut, so only minor changes

in the color scheme have been introduced. A few years ago, exploratory research led to some further tests of a Mr. Peanut in Bermuda shorts, but the tests proved overwhelmingly negative, sending Planters back to a more original peanut!

Similarly, simple exploratory research simply asked a few consumers for their reactions to the Mars M&M characters. Mars was interested in discovering names for the characters. They found that most consumers simply referred to them by their colors. This piece of information became useful in shaping future research and marketing strategy.

Sources: Voight, Joan (2003), "Mascot Makeover: The Risky Business of Tampering with Brand Icons," Adweek (July 7), 20–26. Elliot, Stuart (2004), "Updating a Venerable Character, or Tarnishing a Sterling Reputation?" The New York Times (March 19), C5.

PR NEWSWIRE GEORGIA PACIFIC

identical to the traditional MBA student. They tend to be older than the average 24-year-old traditional student, instead averaging about 30 years of age. Also, they tend to live in rural communities, be more introverted, and expect a higher workload than traditional students. Another key statistic is that the dropout rate for online students is significantly higher than for traditional MBA students. Nearly 14 percent of online students drop before completing a course, as compared to 7.2 percent for traditional in-class students. For this and other reasons, online students are much more costly to serve.[5]

Accuracy is critically important in descriptive research. Overestimating the demand for a university's MBA offering by even a few students can mean the difference between a program sustaining itself or being a drain on already scarce resources. For instance, if a cohort group of twenty-five students is predicted, but only fifteen students actually sign up, the program will likely not generate enough revenue to sustain itself. Therefore, it is easy to see that descriptive research forecasting sales revenue and costs or describing consumer attitudes, satisfaction, and commitment must be accurate or decision making will suffer.

Unlike exploratory research, descriptive studies are conducted with a considerable understanding of the situation being studied. This understanding, which may have been developed in part from exploratory research, directs the study toward specific issues. Later, we will discuss the role of research questions and hypotheses. These statements help greatly in

Descriptive research about consumers who buy organic food has paid off for the Whole Foods chain of stores.

©ASSOCIATED PRESS/THE OAKLAND PRESS

RESEARCHSNAPSHOT

Whines for Wines

Greg Norman is best known for performance on the golf course. However, he is actually one of the most successful business people to come out of sports. Among his many ventures, Greg Norman is a well-respected vintner. Norman Estates gained fame in the wine trade with Australian wines that offered considerable quality at a fair price. More recently, Norman Estates is expanding its portfolio by purchasing vineyard properties and production capacity in California.

As Norman Estates and other wineries consider diversifying production beyond their traditional boundaries, descriptive research can be vital in making these key decisions.

©THE IMAGE BANK/GETTY IMAGES

Descriptive research describes what wine consumers like to drink in terms of where the wine is from and where the consumers are located. Consumers around the world form geographic segments with preferences for wines from certain areas. American consumers, for instance, have contributed to the growing slump in French wine sales by switching increasingly from French wines to Australian- and American-made wines. In particular, French wines at low and moderate prices have suffered, whereas higher-price French wine sales remain steady. In addition, wine sales in the United States and in the United Kingdom are relatively strong compared to wine sales in France and Germany.

All of these descriptive results may lead Greg Norman to a better understanding of the international wine market and therefore make better decisions about where to grow and produce wine. Do you think the choice to expand to California rather than France seems like a good decision?

Sources: Orth, U.R., M.M. Wolf, and T. Dodd (2005), "Dimensions of Wine Region Equity and Their Impact on Consumer Preferences," Journal of Product and Brand Management," 14 (2), 88–97. Conibear, Helena (2005), "World-wide Consumption Trends," AIM-Digest, http://www.aim-digest.com/gateway/pages/trends/articles/trends.htm (accessed November 24, 2005).

designing and implementing a descriptive study. Without these, the researcher would have little or no idea of what questions to ask.

Survey research typifies a descriptive study. Many surveys try to answer questions such as "Why are brand A's sales lower than brand B's sales?" In other words, descriptive surveys can provide a diagnosis. **Diagnostic analysis** seeks to diagnose reasons for market outcomes and focuses specifically on the beliefs and feelings consumers have about and toward competing products. A research study trying to diagnose slumping French wine sales might ask consumers their beliefs about the taste of French, Australian, and American wines. The results might indicate a deficiency in taste, suggesting that consumers do not believe French wines taste as fruity as do the others. Such descriptive research can sometimes provide an explanation by diagnosing differences among competitors, but it does not provide direct evidence of causality.

Diagnostic analysis
Seeks to diagnose reasons for market outcomes and focuses specifically on the beliefs and feelings consumers have about and toward competing products.

Causal Research

If a decision maker knows what causes important outcomes like sales and employee satisfaction, then he or she can shape firm decisions in a positive way. Causal inferences are very powerful because they lead to greater control. **Causal research** allows causal inferences to be made. Causal research explains how one event, a cause, brings about another event, an effect. Causes make effects happen. Rain causes grass to get wet. Rain is the cause and wet grass is the effect.

Exploratory and/or descriptive research usually precedes causal research. In causal studies, researchers typically have a good understanding of the phenomena being studied. Because of this, the research can make an educated prediction about the cause-and-effect relationships that will be tested. Although greater knowledge of the situation is a good thing, knowledge doesn't come without a price. Causal research designs can take a long time to implement. Also, they often involve intricate designs that can be very expensive. Thus, even though managers may often want the assurance that causal inferences can bring, they are not always willing to spend the time and money it takes to get them.

Causal research
Allows causal inferences to be made. That is, it seeks to identify cause-and-effect relationships. When something *causes* an effect, it means it brings it about or makes it happen. The effect is the outcome.

CAUSALITY

Ideally, managers want to know how a change in one event (say, using a new product logo) will change another event of interest, like sales. Causal research attempts to establish that when we do one thing, another thing will follow. A **causal inference** is just such a conclusion. While we use the term "cause" all the time in everyday language, scientifically establishing something as a cause is not so easy. A causal inference can only be supported when very specific causal evidence exists. Three critical pieces of causal evidence are

1. Temporal sequence
2. Concomitant variance
3. Nonspurious association

Causal inference
A conclusion that when one thing happens, another specific thing will follow.

Temporal Sequence

Temporal sequence deals with the time order of events. In other words, having an *appropriate causal order of events,* or temporal sequence, is one criterion for causality. The cause must occur before the effect. It would be difficult for a restaurant manager to blame a decrease in sales on a new chef if the drop in sales occurred before the new chef arrived. If advertising causes sales, the advertising must appear before the change in sales.

Temporal sequence
One of three criteria for causality. It deals with the time order of events. The cause must occur before the effect.

Concomitant Variation

Concomitant variation occurs when two events "covary," meaning they vary systematically. In causal terms, concomitant variation means that when a change in the cause occurs, a change in the outcome also is observed. Correlation, which we discuss in a later chapter, is often used to represent concomitant variation. Causality cannot possibly exist when there is no systematic variation between the variables. For example, if a retail store never changes its employees' vacation policy, then the vacation policy cannot possibly be responsible for a change in customer satisfaction. There is no correlation between the two events. On the other hand, if two events vary together, one event may be causing the other. If a university increases its number of online MBA course offerings and experiences a decrease in enrollment in its traditional in-class MBA offerings, the online course offerings may be causing the decrease. But the systematic variation alone doesn't guarantee it.

Concomitant variation
One of three criteria for causality. It occurs when two events *covary,* meaning they vary systematically.

Nonspurious Association

Nonspurious association means any covariation between a cause and an effect is true and not simply due to some other variable. A spurious association is one that is not true. Often, a causal inference cannot be made even though the other two conditions exist, because both the cause and the effect have some common cause; that is, both may be influenced by a third variable. For instance, a city worker notices an alarming trend. On days when a large number of ice cream cones are sold at Virginia Beach, more people drown. So, when ice cream sales go up, so does drowning. Should the city decide to ban ice cream? This would be silly because the concomitant variation observed between ice cream consumption and drowning is spurious. On days when the beach is particularly crowded, more ice cream is sold and more people drown. So, the number of people at the beach, being associated with both, may cause both.

In summary, causal research should do all of the following:

1. Establish the appropriate causal order or sequence of events
2. Measure the concomitant variation between the presumed cause and the presumed effect
3. Examine the possibility of spuriousness by considering the presence of alternative plausible causal factors

Nonspurious association
One of three criteria for causality. It means any covariation between a cause and an effect is true and not simply due to some other variable.

UNCERTAINTY INFLUENCES THE TYPE OF RESEARCH

The uncertainty of the research problem is related to the type of research project. As Exhibit 3.1 illustrates on the next page, exploratory research is conducted during the early stages of decision

EXHIBIT 3.1 **Types of Marketing Research**

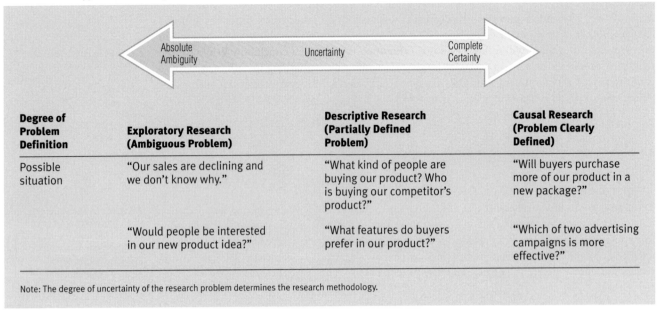

Degree of Problem Definition	Exploratory Research (Ambiguous Problem)	Descriptive Research (Partially Defined Problem)	Causal Research (Problem Clearly Defined)
Possible situation	"Our sales are declining and we don't know why."	"What kind of people are buying our product? Who is buying our competitor's product?"	"Will buyers purchase more of our product in a new package?"
	"Would people be interested in our new product idea?"	"What features do buyers prefer in our product?"	"Which of two advertising campaigns is more effective?"

Note: The degree of uncertainty of the research problem determines the research methodology.

making when the decision situation is ambiguous and management is very uncertain about the nature of the problem. When management is aware of the problem but lacks some knowledge, descriptive research is usually conducted. Causal research requires sharply defined problems.

Stages in the Research Process

Marketing research, like other forms of scientific inquiry, involves a sequence of highly interrelated activities. The stages of the research process overlap continuously, and it is somewhat of an oversimplification to state that every research project has exactly the same ordered sequence of activities. Nevertheless, marketing research often follows a general pattern. The stages are

1. Defining the research objectives
2. Planning the research design
3. Planning a sample
4. Collecting the data
5. Analyzing the data
6. Formulating the conclusions and preparing the report

Exhibit 3.2 portrays these six stages as a cyclical or circular-flow process. The circular-flow concept is used because conclusions from research studies can generate new ideas and knowledge that can lead to further investigation. Thus, there is a connection between *conclusions and reporting* and *defining the research objectives*. Notice also, though, that management is in the center of the process. The research objectives cannot be properly defined without managerial input. After all, it is the manager who ultimately has to make the decision. The manager is the one who will often ask for additional research.

In practice, the stages overlap somewhat from a timing perspective. Later stages sometimes can be completed before earlier ones. Sometimes the earlier stages of research influence the design of the later stages.

Alternatives in the Research Process

The researcher must choose among a number of alternatives during each stage of the research process. The research process can be compared to a map. It is important to remember that there is

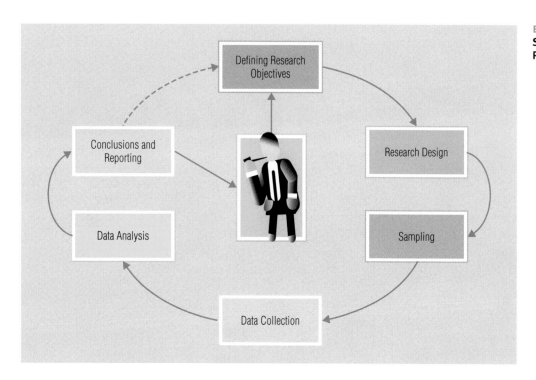

EXHIBIT 3.2
Stages of the Research Process

no single right or best path for all journeys. The road one takes depends on where one wants to go and the resources (money, time, labor, and so on) available for the trip. The map analogy is useful for the marketing researcher because there are several paths that can be followed at each stage. When there are severe time constraints, the quickest path may be most appropriate. When money and human resources are plentiful, the appropriate path may be quite different.

The following sections briefly describe the six stages of the research process. (Each stage is discussed in greater depth in later chapters.) Exhibit 3.3 shows the decisions that researchers must make in each stage. This discussion of the research process begins with defining research objectives because most research projects are initiated to remedy managers' uncertainty about some aspect of the firm's marketing program.

Defining the Research Objectives

Exhibit 3.3 on the next page shows that the research process begins with **research objectives** that are the result of problem discovery and definition. Research objectives are the goals to be achieved by conducting research. In consulting, the term **deliverables** is often used to describe the objectives to a research client. The genesis of the research objectives lies in the type of decision situation faced. The objectives may involve exploring some new product within a new market. Alternatively, they may involve testing the effect of some policy change on service quality. Different types of objectives lead to different types of research designs.

In applied or market research, the objectives cannot be listed until there is an understanding of the decision situation. This understanding must be shared between the actual decision maker and the lead researcher. We often describe this understanding as a problem statement. In general usage, the word *problem* suggests that something has gone wrong. This isn't always the case in the context of market research. The research objective may be to simply clarify a situation, define an opportunity, or monitor and evaluate current operations. Research objectives cannot be developed until managers and researchers have agreed on the actual business "problem" that will be addressed by the research. Thus, they set out to "discover" this problem through a series of interviews and through a document called a research proposal.

This process here is more oriented toward *discovery* than *confirmation*. Managers and researchers alike may not have a clear-cut understanding of the situation at the outset of the research process. Managers may only be able to list symptoms that could indicate a problem. Sales may be declining,

Research objectives
The goals to be achieved by conducting research.

Deliverables
The term used often in consulting or applied market research to describe the objectives.

EXHIBIT 3.3 **Flowchart of the Marketing Research Process**

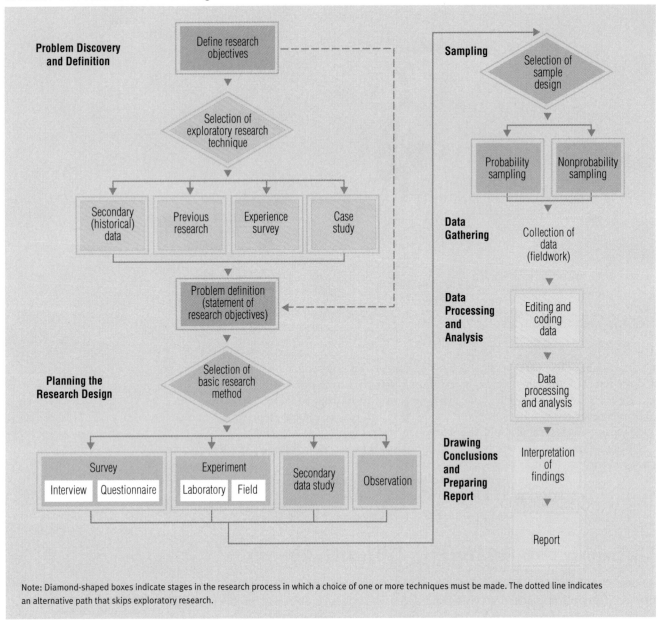

Note: Diamond-shaped boxes indicate stages in the research process in which a choice of one or more techniques must be made. The dotted line indicates an alternative path that skips exploratory research.

but management may not know the exact nature of the problem. Thus, the problem statement often is made only in general terms; what is to be investigated is not yet specifically identified.

▪ DEFINING THE MANAGERIAL DECISION SITUATION

In marketing research, the adage "a problem well defined is a problem half solved" is worth remembering. This adage emphasizes that an orderly definition of the research problem lends a sense of direction to the investigation. Careful attention to problem definition allows the researcher to set the proper research objectives. If the purpose of the research is clear, the chances of collecting necessary and relevant information and not collecting surplus information will be much greater.

Albert Einstein noted that "the formulation of a problem is often more essential than its solution."[6] This is good advice for marketing managers. Managers naturally concentrate on finding the right answer rather than asking the right question. They also want one solution quickly rather than having to spend time considering many possible solutions. Properly defining a problem can be more difficult than solving it. In marketing research, if data are collected before the nature of the marketing problem is carefully thought out, they probably will not allow useful results.

Marketing research must have clear objectives and definite designs. Unfortunately, little or no planning goes into the formulation of many research problems. Consider the case of the Ha-Pah-Shu-Tse brand of Indian fried bread mix (the name "Ha-Pah-Shu-Tse" comes from the Pawnee word for red corn). The owner of the company, Mr. Ha-Pah-Shu-Tse, thought that his product, one of the few Native American food products available in the United States, was not selling because it was not widely advertised. He wanted a management consulting group to conduct some research concerning advertising themes. However, the management consultants pointed out to the Ha-Pah-Shu-Tse family that using the family name on the bread mix might be a foremost source of concern. They suggested that consumer behavior research to investigate the brand image might be a better initial starting point, rather than advertising copy research. Family management agreed.

Defining the decision situation must precede the research objectives. Frequently, the marketing researcher will not be involved until line management has discovered that some information about a particular aspect of the marketing mix is needed. Even at this point, the exact nature of the situation may be poorly defined. Once a problem area has been discovered, the marketing researcher and management together can begin the process of precisely defining it.

Frequently, research is conducted without a clear definition of the research's objectives. Too many researchers forget that the best place to begin a research project is at the end—meaning that one must keep in mind what precisely are the research goals. Knowing what is to be accomplished determines the research process. An error or omission in problem objectives is likely to be a costly mistake that cannot be corrected in later stages of the process.

USING EXPLORATORY RESEARCH TO REACH DECISIONS

Exploratory research can be used to help identify the decisions that need to be made. The preliminary activities undertaken can yield results that place the situation into a more easily researched context. Exploratory research can progressively narrow the scope of the research topic and help transform ambiguous problems into well-defined ones that yield specific research objectives. By investigating any existing studies on the subject, talking with knowledgeable individuals, and informally investigating the situation, the researcher can progressively sharpen the concepts. After such exploration, the researcher should know exactly which data to collect during the formal phases of the project and how to conduct the project. Exhibit 3.3 indicates that managers and researchers must decide whether to use one or more exploratory research techniques. As Exhibit 3.3 indicates, this stage is optional.

The library contains a wealth of information. Studies forming a literature review can be found in the library.

The marketing researcher can employ techniques from four basic categories to obtain insights and gain a clearer idea of the problem: previous research, pilot studies, experience surveys, and case studies. These are discussed in detail in Chapter 6. This section will briefly discuss previous research and focus group interviews, the most popular type of pilot study.

Previous Research

As a general rule, researchers should first investigate previous research to see whether or not others may have addressed the same research problems previously to gain a better understanding of the area. Previous research reports should be searched within the company's archives. In addition, some firms specialize in providing various types of research reports, such as economic forecasts. The *Census of Population* and the *Survey of Current Business* are each examples of previous research conducted by an outside source.

Literature review
A directed search of published works, including periodicals and books, that discusses theory and presents empirical results relevant to the topic at hand.

Previous research may also exist in the public domain. A **literature review** is a directed search of published works, including periodicals and books, that discusses theory and presents empirical results that are relevant to the topic at hand. A literature survey is common in applied market research studies, but it is a fundamental requirement of a basic (i.e., marketing) research report. Literature reviews are conducted using traditional library research tools. The Internet and modern electronic search engines available through most university libraries have made literature reviews simpler and faster to perform.

Suppose, for example, that a bank is interested in determining the best site for additional automated teller machines. A logical first step would be to investigate the factors that bankers in other parts of the country consider important. By reading articles in banking journals, management might quickly discover that the best locations are inside supermarkets located in residential areas where people are young, highly educated, and earning higher-than-average incomes. These data might lead the bank to investigate census information to determine where in the city such people live. Reviewing and building on the work already compiled by others is an economical starting point for most research.

Pilot Studies

Almost all consumers take a test drive before buying a car. A pilot study serves a similar purpose for the researcher. A **pilot study** is a small-scale research project that collects data from respondents similar to those who will be used in the full study. It can serve as a guide for a larger study or examine specific aspects of the research to see if the selected procedures will actually work as intended. Pilot studies are critical in refining measures and reducing the risk that the full study will be fatally flawed. This is particularly true for experimental research because an experiment depends critically on valid manipulation of experimental variables.[7] Pilot studies also often are useful in fine-tuning research objectives. Pilot studies are sometimes referred to as pretests. A **pretest** is a very descriptive term indicating a small-scale study in which the results are only preliminary and intended only to assist in design of a subsequent study.

Focus group interviews are sometimes used as a pilot study. A **focus group** interview brings together six to twelve people in a loosely structured format. The technique is based on the assumption that individuals are more willing to talk about things when they are able to do so within a group-discussion format. Focus group respondents sometimes feed on each other's comments to develop ideas that would be difficult to express in a different interview format.

Pilot study
A small-scale research project that collects data from respondents similar to those to be used in the full study.

Pretest
A small-scale study in which the results are only preliminary and intended only to assist in design of a subsequent study.

Focus group
A small group discussion about some research topic led by a moderator who guides discussion among the participants.

For example, suppose a consultant is hired by Carrefour to research the way consumers react to sales promotions. Carrefour is second in size only to Wal-Mart, operating nearly 11,000 stores in twenty-nine countries. Carrefour began in France over forty-five years ago and pioneered the discount hypermarket format. More specifically, the researcher may be asked to help management decide whether or not the size of promotions should vary with national culture. In other words, the basic research question is whether or not culture influences consumer perceptions of sales promotions.[8] A pretest may be needed to examine whether or not differences in currency might interfere with these perceptions, or whether or not the different terms that refer to promotions and discounts can be translated into the languages of each culture. For example, is a discount expressed in Korean won interpreted the same way as a discount expressed in euros? Each euro equals about $1.28, whereas a single dollar is worth about 960 won.[9]

Exploratory research need not always follow a structured design. Because the purpose of exploratory research is to gain insights and discover new ideas, researchers may use considerable creativity and flexibility. Some companies perform exploratory research routinely as part of a formal environmental scanning process. If the conclusions made during this stage suggest marketing opportunities, the researcher is in a position to begin planning a formal, quantitative research project.

STATING RESEARCH OBJECTIVES

After identifying and clarifying the problem, with or without exploratory research, the researcher must formally state the research objectives. This statement delineates the type of research that is needed and what intelligence may result that would allow the decision maker to make informed choices. The statement of research objectives culminates the process of clarifying the managerial decision into something actionable.

RESEARCHSNAPSHOT

Nothing So Practical as Theory?

Theory and marketing practice do come together. First, students learn theory in their formal education. Business professors consider it good practice to blend theory and practice in their teaching. Business professionals use these theories to help shape their thinking about different business situations.

Neurology, psychobiology, anthropology, economics, and social psychology all offer relevant theories that can help explain marketing problems. Recently, structuration theory has been proposed as a way of explaining marketing communication outcomes. The theory suggests that more focus should be placed on the communication exchanges between buyers and sellers and that if one can understand the goals of the buyer and seller involved in a communication interaction, then the outcome of the interaction can be predicted. Studies using theory of this type may assist electronic communication design in better placements of pop-up ads and hyperlinks, and can also assist face-to-face sales exchanges in better predicting when a consumer is actually ready to buy.

©MICHAEL NEWMAN/PHOTOEDIT

Sources: Green, Paul E. (2004), "Theory, Practice Both Have Key MR Roles," Marketing News, 38 (September 15), 40–44. Schultz, Don (2005), "Accepted Industry Truths Not Always Acceptable," Marketing News, 39 (October 15), 6. Stewart, D. T. (2005), "Traditional Ad Research Overlooks Interactions," Marketing News, 39 (November 15), 26–29.

A written decision statement expresses the business situation to the researcher. The research objectives try to directly address the decision statement or statements, as the case may be. As such, the research objectives represent a contract of sorts that commits the researcher to producing the needed research. This is why they are expressed as deliverables in applied market research. Research objectives drive the rest of the research process. Indeed, before proceeding, the researcher and managers must agree that the objectives are appropriate and will produce relevant information.

■ IDENTIFICATION OF KEY VARIABLES

A crucial aspect of problem definition is the identification of key variables. The term *variable* is important in research. A **variable** is anything that varies or changes in value. Because a variable represents a quality that can exhibit differences in value, usually in magnitude or strength, it may be said that a variable generally is anything that may assume different numerical or categorical values. For example, attitudes toward airlines may be a variable ranging from positive to negative. Each attribute of airlines' services, such as safety, seat comfort, and baggage handling is a variable.

In statistical analysis, a variable is identified by a symbol, such as X. Categories or numerical values may then be associated with this symbol. Gender may be categorized as male or female; thus, gender is a **categorical** or **classificatory variable**, since it has a limited number of distinct values. On the other hand, sales volume may encompass an infinite range of numbers; it is a **continuous variable**, one that can have an infinite number of values.

In causal research, the terms *dependent variable* and *independent variable* are frequently used. A **dependent variable** is a criterion or a variable that is to be predicted or explained. An **independent variable** is a variable that is expected to influence the dependent variable. For example, average sales compensation may be a dependent variable that is influenced or predicted by an independent variable such as number of years of experience. These terms are discussed in greater detail in the chapters on experimentation and data analysis.

■ WHAT IS A THEORY?

Ultimately, theory plays a role in determining the appropriate research objectives. A **theory** is a formal, logical explanation of some events that includes predictions of how things relate to one another. A theory is built through a process of reviewing previous findings of similar studies, simple logical deduction, and knowledge of applicable theoretical areas. For example, if a web designer is trying to decide what color the background of a web page should be, the researcher may first consult previous studies examining the effects of color on package design and retail store design. He or she may also

Variable
Anything that varies or changes from one instance to another; a variable represents differences in value, usually in magnitude, strength and/or direction.

Categorical variable
A variable that indicates membership in some group.

Classificatory variable
Another term for a categorical variable because it classifies units into categories.

Continuous variable
A variable that can take on a range of values that correspond to some quantitative amount.

Dependent variable
A process outcome or a variable that is predicted and/or explained by other variables.

Independent variable
A variable that is expected to influence the dependent variable in some way.

Theory
A formal, logical explanation of some events that includes predictions of how things relate to one another.

find theories that deal with the wavelength of different colors or theories that explain retail atmospherics. This may lead to specific predictions that predict blue as a good background color.[10]

While someone may think that theory is only relevant to academic or basic marketing research, theory plays a role in understanding practical research as well. Before setting research objectives, the researcher must be able to describe the business situation in some coherent way. Without this type of explanation, the researcher would have little idea of where to start. Ultimately, the logical explanation helps the researcher know what variables need to be included in the study and how they may relate to one another.

◼ WHAT IS A HYPOTHESIS?

Hypothesis
A formal statement explaining some outcome.

A **hypothesis** is a formal statement explaining some outcome. Hypotheses (pl.) must be testable. In other words, when one states a hypothesis, it should be written as a proposition. For example, using our opening vignette as an example, the researcher may use theoretical reasoning to develop the following hypothesis:

H1: The more hours per week a prospective student works, the more favorable the attitude toward online MBA class offerings.

In its simplest form, a hypothesis is a guess. A sales manager may hypothesize that the salespeople who are highest in product knowledge will be the most productive. An advertising manager may hypothesize that if consumers' attitudes toward a product change in a positive direction, there will be an increase in consumption of the product.

Empirical testing
Means that something has been examined against reality using data. When the data are consistent with a hypothesis, we say the hypothesis is *supported*.

We often apply statistics to data to empirically test hypotheses. **Empirical testing** means that something has been examined against reality using data. When the data are consistent with a hypothesis, we say the hypothesis is *supported*. When the data are inconsistent with a hypothesis, we say the hypothesis is *not supported*. We are often tempted to say that we prove a hypothesis when the data conform to the prediction; this isn't really true. Because our result is based on statistics, there is always the possibility that our conclusion is wrong. Now, at times we can be very, very confident in our conclusion, but from an absolute perspective, statistics cannot prove a hypothesis is true.

Exhibit 3.4 illustrates how decision statements are linked to research objectives that are, in turn, linked to research hypotheses. Although the first two objectives each have one hypothesis, notice that the third has two. In reality, most research projects will involve more than one research objective, and each of these may often involve more than one hypothesis. Think about how you might go about trying to test the hypothesis listed in Exhibit 3.4.

◼ PLANNING THE RESEARCH DESIGN

Research design
A master plan that specifies the methods and procedures for collecting and analyzing the needed information.

After the researcher has formulated the research problem, he or she must develop the research design as part of the research design stage. A **research design** is a master plan that specifies the methods and procedures for collecting and analyzing the needed information. A research design

EXHIBIT 3.4
Example Decision Statements, Research Objectives, and Research Hypotheses

Decision Statement:	Research Objectives:	Hypotheses:
What should be the retail price for product X?	Forecast sales for product X at three different prices.	Sales will be higher at $5.00 than at $4.00 or at $6.99.
What things should we invest in to improve our service quality?	Identify the top factors that contribute to customers' service quality perceptions.	Cleanliness is related positively to customers' service quality perceptions.
Should we invest in a training program to reduce role conflict among our employees?	Determine how much role conflict influences employee job satisfaction.	Crowding is related negatively to customers' service quality perceptions.
		Role conflict is related positively to job satisfaction.

provides a framework or plan of action for the research. Objectives of the study determined during the early stages of research are included in the design to ensure that the information collected is appropriate for solving the problem. The researcher also must determine the sources of information, the design technique (survey or experiment, for example), the sampling methodology, and the schedule and cost of the research.

Selection of the Basic Research Method

Here again, the researcher must make a decision. Exhibit 3.3 shows four basic design techniques for descriptive and causal research: surveys, experiments, secondary data, and observation. The objectives of the study, the available data sources, the urgency of the decision, and the cost of obtaining the data will determine which method should be chosen. The managerial aspects of selecting the research design will be considered later.

▦ SURVEYS

The most common method of generating primary data is the survey. Most people have seen the results of political surveys by Gallup or Harris Online, and some have been respondents (members of a sample who supply answers) to marketing research questionnaires. A **survey** is a research technique in which a sample is interviewed in some form or their behavior is observed and described in some way. The term *surveyor* is most often reserved for civil engineers who describe some piece of property using a transit. Similarly, marketing researchers describe some market segment using a questionnaire. The task of writing a list of questions and designing the format of the printed or written questionnaire is an essential aspect of the development of a survey research design.

> **Survey**
> A research technique in which a sample is interviewed in some form or their behavior is observed and described in some way.

  Research investigators may choose to contact respondents by telephone or mail, on the Internet, or in person. An advertiser spending nearly $2.5 million for thirty seconds of commercial time during the Super Bowl may telephone people to quickly gather information concerning their responses to the advertising. A forklift manufacturer trying to determine a cause for low sales in the wholesale grocery industry might choose a mail questionnaire because the appropriate executives are hard to reach by telephone. A manufacturer of a birth control device for men might determine the need for a versatile survey method wherein an interviewer can ask a variety of personal questions in a flexible format. While personal interviews are expensive, they are valuable because investigators can use visual aids and supplement the interviews with observations. Each of these survey methods has advantages and disadvantages. A researcher's task is to find the most appropriate way to collect the needed information.

▦ EXPERIMENTS

Marketing experiments hold the greatest potential for establishing cause-and-effect relationships. Experimentation allows investigation of changes in one variable, such as sales, while manipulating one or two other variables, perhaps price or advertising, under controlled conditions. Ideally, experimental control provides a basis for isolating causal factors by eliminating outside, or exogenous, influences. Thus, the experiment controls conditions so that one or more variables can be manipulated to test a hypothesis.

  Test marketing is a frequently used form of marketing experimentation. Chelsea, Anheuser-Busch's unsuccessful "not-so-soft soft drink," illustrates the usefulness of marketing experiments. Anheuser-Busch first introduced Chelsea as a drink with a slight alcoholic content—about 0.4 percent—that was a socially acceptable alternative to beer for adults who did not want to get intoxicated. During an experiment to test market the "not-so-soft soft drink" and the "not-so sweet" concept, a Virginia nurses' association and some religious groups strongly criticized the company and the new product. These critics suggested that Anheuser-Busch had introduced a product that might encourage children to become beer drinkers. They contended that Chelsea was packaged like beer and looked, foamed, and poured like it. The criticism led the brewery to suspend production, advertising, and promotion of the drink. Later it reintroduced the product as a soft drink with only "a trace of alcohol" as a "natural alternative" to soft drinks, with not-so-sweet and stylish attributes. Similar problems occurred in the second experiment. This experiment pointed out to Anheuser-Busch that an extraneous variable, alcohol level, caused an inadvertent miscommunication: Consumers confused the original Chelsea with beer.

■ SECONDARY DATA FOR DESCRIPTIVE AND QUANTITATIVE ANALYSIS

Like exploratory research studies, descriptive and causal studies use previously collected data. Although the terms *secondary* and *historical* are interchangeable, we will use the term *secondary data*. An example of a secondary data study is the use of a mathematical model to predict sales on the basis of past sales or a correlation with related variables. Manufacturers of color printers for personal computers may find that sales are highly correlated with discretionary personal income. To predict future market potential, projections of disposable personal income may be acquired from the government or a university. This information can be manipulated mathematically to forecast sales. Formal secondary data studies have benefits and limitations similar to those of exploratory studies that use secondary data, but generally the quantitative analysis of secondary data is more sophisticated.

■ OBSERVATION

The objective of many research projects is merely to record what can be observed—for example, the number of automobiles that pass by a proposed site for a gas station. This can be mechanically recorded or observed by humans. Research personnel known as *mystery shoppers* may act as customers to observe actions of sales personnel or do comparative shopping to learn prices at competing outlets. A mystery shopper is paid to pretend to be a customer and gather data about the way employees behave and the way they are treated in general. How often are store policies followed? How often are they treated courteously? Mystery shoppers can be valuable sources for observational data.

The main advantage of the observation technique is that it records behavior without relying on reports from respondents. Observational data are often collected unobtrusively and passively without a respondent's direct participation. For instance, the ACNielsen Company uses a "people meter" attached to television sets to record the programs being watched by each household member. This eliminates the possible bias of respondents stating that they watched the president's State of the Union address rather than a situation comedy on another station.

Observation is more complex than mere "nose counting," and the task is more difficult than the inexperienced researcher would imagine. Several things of interest, such as attitudes, opinions, motivations, and other intangible states of mind, simply cannot be observed.

■ THE "BEST" RESEARCH DESIGN

It is argued that no single best research design exists. Because of this, the researcher often has several alternatives that can accomplish the stated research objectives. Consider the researcher who must forecast sales for the upcoming year. Some commonly used forecasting methods are surveying executive opinion, collecting sales force composite opinions, surveying user expectations, projecting trends, and analyzing market factors. Any one of these may yield a reliable forecast.

The ability to select the most appropriate research design develops with experience. Inexperienced researchers often jump to the conclusion that a survey methodology is usually the best design because they are most comfortable with this method. When Chicago's Museum of Science and Industry wanted to determine the relative popularity of its exhibits, it could have conducted a survey. Instead, a creative researcher familiar with other research designs suggested a far less expensive alternative: an unobtrusive observation technique. The researcher suggested that the museum merely keep track of the frequency with which the floor tiles in front of the various exhibits had to be replaced, indicating where the heaviest traffic occurred. When this was done, the museum found that the chick-hatching exhibit was the most popular. This method provided the same results as a survey but at a much lower cost.

After determining the proper design, the researcher moves on to the next stage: planning the sample.

Sampling

Although the sampling plan is outlined in the research design, the sampling stage is a distinct phase of the research process. For convenience, however, we will treat the sample planning and the actual sample generation processes together in this section.

If you take your first bite of a steak and conclude that it needs salt, you have just conducted a sample. **Sampling** involves any procedure that draws conclusions based on measurements of a portion of the population. In other words, a sample is a subset from a larger population. If certain statistical procedures are followed, a researcher need not select every item in a population, since the results of a good sample should have the same characteristics as the population as a whole. Of course, when errors are made, samples do not give reliable estimates of the population.

Sampling
Involves any procedure that draws conclusions based on measurements of a portion of the population.

A famous example of error due to sampling is the 1936 *Literary Digest* fiasco. The magazine conducted a survey and predicted that Republican Alf Landon would win over Democrat Franklin D. Roosevelt by a landslide in that year's presidential election. This prediction was wrong—and the error was due to sample selection. The postmortems showed that *Literary Digest* had sampled its readers as well as telephone subscribers. In 1936, these people were not a representative cross section of voters, because a disproportionate number of them were Republicans.

More recently, early "exit polls" led many to believe that John Kerry would win the 2004 U.S. presidential election.[11] The "exit polls" were performed early on election day and done mostly in highly urban areas in the Northeast, areas that are predominantly Democratic. The resulting sample of voters responding to the early exit polls did not represent the entire U.S. population, and Kerry lost to Bush by over 3 million votes, or about 3 percent of all votes cast. Thus, the accuracy of predictions from research depends on getting a sample that really matches the population.

The first sampling question to ask is, who is to be sampled? The answer to this primary question requires the identification of a *target population*. Defining this population and determining the sampling units may not be so easy. If, for example, a savings and loan association surveys people who already have accounts for answers to image questions, the selected sampling units will not represent *potential* customers. Specifying the target population is a crucial aspect of the sampling plan.

The next sampling issue concerns sample size. How big should the sample be? Although management may wish to examine every potential buyer of a product or service, doing so may be unnecessary as well as unrealistic. Typically, larger samples are more precise than smaller ones, but proper probability sampling can allow a small proportion of the total population to give a reliable measure of the whole.

The final sampling decision is how to select the sampling units. Simple random sampling may be the best-known type, in which every unit in the population has an equal and known chance of being selected. However, this is only one type of sampling. For example, a cluster-sampling procedure may reduce costs and make data-gathering procedures more efficient. If members of the population are found in close geographical clusters, a sampling procedure that selects area clusters rather than individual units in the population will reduce costs. Rather than selecting 1,000 individuals throughout the United States, a more economical approach is to first select twenty-five counties and then sample within those counties. This will substantially reduce travel, hiring, and training costs. In determining the appropriate sampling plan, the researcher will have to select the most appropriate sampling procedure for meeting the established study objectives. A later chapter provides a discussion of sampling.

Gathering Data

The data-gathering stage begins once the sampling plan has been formalized. Data gathering is the process of gathering or collecting information. Data may be gathered by human observers or interviewers, or they may be recorded by machines, as in the case of scanner data.

Obviously, the many research techniques involve many methods of gathering data. Surveys require direct participation by research respondents. This may involve filling out a questionnaire or interacting with an interviewer. In this sense, they are obtrusive. An **unobtrusive method** of data gathering is one in which the subjects do not have to be disturbed for data to be collected. They may even be unaware that research is going on at all. For instance, a simple count of motorists driving

Unobtrusive methods
Methods in which research respondents do not have to be disturbed for data to be gathered.

past a proposed franchising location is one kind of data-gathering method. However the data are collected, it is important to minimize errors in the process. For example, the data gathering should be consistent in all geographical areas. If an interviewer phrases questions incorrectly or records a respondent's statements inaccurately (not verbatim), major data collection errors will result.

Processing and Analyzing Data

▨ EDITING AND CODING

After the fieldwork has been completed, the data must be converted into a format that will answer the marketing manager's questions. This is part of the data processing and analysis stage. Here, the information content will be mined from the raw data. Data processing generally begins with editing and coding the data. Editing involves checking the data collection forms for omissions, legibility, and consistency in classification. The editing process corrects problems such as interviewer errors (an answer recorded on the wrong portion of a questionnaire, for example) before the data are transferred to the computer.

Before data can be tabulated, meaningful categories and character symbols must be established for groups of responses. The rules for interpreting, categorizing, recording, and transferring the data to the data storage media are called codes. This coding process facilitates computer or hand tabulation. If computer analysis is to be used, the data are entered into the computer and verified. Computer-assisted (online) interviewing is an example of the impact of technological change on the research process. Telephone interviewers, seated at computer terminals, read survey questions displayed on the monitor. The interviewer asks the questions and then types in the respondents' answers. Thus, answers are collected and processed into the computer at the same time, eliminating intermediate steps that could introduce errors.

▨ DATA ANALYSIS

Data analysis
The application of reasoning to understand the data that have been gathered.

Data analysis is the application of reasoning to understand the data that have been gathered. In its simplest form, analysis may involve determining consistent patterns and summarizing the relevant details revealed in the investigation. The appropriate analytical technique for data analysis will be determined by management's information requirements, the characteristics of the research design, and the nature of the data gathered. Statistical analysis may range from portraying a simple frequency distribution to more complex multivariate-analysis approaches, such as multiple regression. Later chapters will discuss the most popular techniques for statistical analysis.

Drawing Conclusions and Preparing a Report

One of the most important jobs that a researcher performs is communicating the research results. This is the final stage of the research project, but it is far from the least important. The conclusions and report preparation stage consists of interpreting the research results, describing the implications and drawing the appropriate conclusions for managerial decisions. These conclusions should fulfill the deliverables promised in the research proposal. In addition, it's important that the researcher consider the varying abilities of people to understand the research results. The report shouldn't be written the same way to a group of PhDs as it would be to a group of line managers.

All too many applied market research reports are overly complicated statements of technical aspects and sophisticated research methods. Frequently, management is not interested in detailed reporting of the research design and statistical findings, but wishes only a summary of the findings. If the findings of the research remain unread on the marketing manager's desk, the study will have been useless. The importance of effective communication cannot be overemphasized. Research is only as good as its applications. Exhibit 3.5 illustrates a short research proposal for the Internal Revenue Service that explored public attitudes toward a variety of tax-related issues.

Now that we have outlined the research process, note that the order of topics in this book follows the flowchart of the research process presented in Exhibit 3.3. Keep this flowchart in mind while reading later chapters.

EXHIBIT 3.5 **An Abbreviated Version of a Research Proposal for the IRS**

Current Situation

Public perception of the IRS appears to be extremely negative. The IRS is the brunt of jokes, and the public avoids contact with any IRS entity. As a result, taxpayers are more inclined to cheat on their returns and many services provided by the IRS to assist taxpayers in preparing their tax returns and to help them understand ways they can avoid paying unnecessary taxes and penalties go unused. In addition, negative attitude lessens the Service's ability to effectively lobby for policy changes. The key decision faced by the IRS due to this situation can be stated as,

What steps could be taken to effectively improve consumer perceptions of the IRS and help design more user-friendly services?

Purpose of the Research

The general purpose of the study is to determine the taxpaying public's perceptions of the role of the IRS in administering the tax laws. In defining the limits of this study, the IRS identified the study areas to be addressed. A careful review of those areas led to the identification of the following specific research objectives:

1. To identify the extent to which taxpayers cheat on their returns, their reasons for doing so, and approaches that can be taken to deter this kind of behavior
2. To determine taxpayers' experience and level of satisfaction with various IRS services
3. To determine what services taxpayers need
4. To develop an accurate profile of taxpayers' behavior relative to the preparation of their income tax returns
5. To assess taxpayers' knowledge and opinions about various tax laws and procedures

Research Design

The survey research method will be the basic research design. Each respondent will be interviewed in his or her home. The personal interviews are generally expected to last between 35 and 45 minutes, although the length will vary depending on the previous tax-related experiences of the respondent. For example, if a respondent has never been audited, questions on audit experience will not be addressed. Or, if a respondent has never contacted the IRS for assistance, certain questions concerning reactions to IRS services will be skipped.

Some sample questions that will be asked are

Did you or your spouse prepare your federal tax return for (year)?

☐ **Self**
☐ **Spouse**
☐ **Someone else**

Did the federal income tax package you received in the mail contain all the forms necessary for you to fill out your return?

☐ **Yes**
☐ **No**
☐ **Didn't receive one in the mail**
☐ **Don't know**

If you were calling the IRS for assistance and no one was able to help you immediately, would you rather get a busy signal or be asked to wait on hold?

☐ **Busy signal**
☐ **Wait on hold**
☐ **Neither**
☐ **Don't know**

During the interview a self-administered questionnaire will be given to the taxpayer to ask certain sensitive questions, such as

Have you ever claimed a dependent on your tax return that you weren't really entitled to?

☐ **Yes**
☐ **No**

Sample Design

A survey of approximately 5,000 individuals located in 50 counties throughout the country will provide the database for this study. The sample will be selected on a probability basis from all households in the continental United States.

Eligible respondents will be adults over the age of 18. Within each household an effort will be made to interview the individual who is most familiar with completing the federal tax forms. When there is more than one taxpayer in the household, a random process will be used to select the taxpayer to be interviewed.

Data Gathering

The fieldworkers of a consulting organization will conduct the interviews.

Data Processing and Analysis

Standard editing and coding procedures will be utilized. Simple tabulation and cross-tabulations will be utilized to analyze the data.

Report Preparation

A written report will be prepared, and an oral presentation of the findings will be made by the research analyst at the convenience of the IRS.

Budget and Time Schedule

Any complete research proposal should include a schedule of how long it will take to conduct each stage of the research and a statement of itemized costs.

The Research Program Strategy

Our discussion of the marketing research process began with the assumption that the researcher wished to collect data to achieve a specific marketing objective. When the researcher has only one or a small number of research objectives that can be addressed in a single study, that study is referred

Research project
A single study that addresses
one or a small number of
research objectives.

to as a **research project**. We have emphasized the researcher's need to select specific techniques for solving one-dimensional problems, such as identifying market segments, selecting the best packaging design, or test-marketing a new product.

However, if you think about a firm's marketing-mix activity in a given period of time (such as a year), you'll realize that marketing research is not a one-shot activity—it is a continuous process. An exploratory research study may be followed by a survey, or a researcher may conduct a specific research project for each aspect of the marketing mix. If a new product is being developed, the different types of research might include market potential studies to identify the size and characteristics of the market, product usage testing to record consumers' reactions to prototype products, brand name and packaging research to determine the product's symbolic connotations, and test-marketing the new product. Thus, when numerous related studies come together to address issues about a single company, we refer to this as a **research program**. Because research is a continuous process, management should view marketing research at a strategic planning level. The *program strategy* refers to a firm's overall plan to use marketing research. It is a planning activity that places a series of marketing research projects in the context of the company's marketing plan.

Research program
Numerous related studies that
come together to address
multiple, related research
objectives.

The marketing research program strategy can be likened to a term insurance policy. Conducting marketing research minimizes risk and increases certainty. Each research project can be seen as a series of term insurance policies that makes the marketing manager's job a bit safer.

Summary

1. Classify marketing research into one of three types. Exploratory, descriptive, and causal research are three major types of marketing research projects. The clarity with which the decision situation is defined determines whether exploratory, descriptive, or causal research is most appropriate. When the decision is very ambiguous, or the interest is on discovering ideas, exploratory research is most appropriate. Descriptive research attempts to paint a picture of the given situation by describing characteristics of objects, people, or organizations. Causal research identifies cause-and-effect relationships or, in other words, what change in "Y" will occur when there is some change in "X"? Three conditions must be satisfied to establish evidence of causality: 1) temporal sequence—the cause must occur before the effect; 2) concomitant variation—a change in the cause is associated with a change in the effect; and 3) nonspurious association—the cause is true and not eliminated by the introduction of another potential cause.

2. List the major phases of the marketing research process. The six major phases of the research process are: 1) defining the research objectives, 2) planning the research design, 3) sampling, 4) data gathering, 5) data processing and analysis, and 6) drawing conclusions and report preparation. Each stage involves several activities or steps. For instance, in planning the research design, the researchers must decide which type of study will be done and, if needed, recruit participants and design and develop experimental stimuli. Quite often research projects are conducted together as parts of a research program. Such programs can involve successive projects that monitor an established product or a group of projects undertaken for a proposed new product to determine the optimal form of various parts of the marketing mix.

3. Distinguish between the concepts of theory and hypothesis. A *hypothesis* is a formal statement explaining some outcome. It is stated in a way that it is testable. A *theory* is a formal, logical explanation of some events that includes predictions of how things relate to one another. A theory is built through a process of reviewing previous findings of similar studies, simple logical deduction, and knowledge of applicable theoretical areas. The explanations in a theory are often in the form of hypotheses. They are extremely useful in research because they give the research an idea of what to expect prior to testing. As such, they also help to identify the variables that need to be included in the study.

4. Explain the difference between a research project and a research program. A *research project* addresses one of a small number of research objectives that can be addressed in a single study. In contrast, a *research program* represents a series of studies addressing multiple research objectives. Many marketing activities require an ongoing research task of some type.

Key Terms and Concepts

Exploratory research
Descriptive research
Diagnostic analysis
Causal research
Causal inference
Temporal sequence
Concomitant variation
Nonspurious association
Research objectives
Deliverables

Literature review
Pilot study
Pretest
Focus group
Variable
Categorical variable
Classificatory variable
Continuous variable
Dependent variable
Independent variable

Theory
Hypothesis
Empirical testing
Research design
Survey
Sampling
Unobtrusive methods
Data analysis
Research project
Research program

Questions for Review and Critical Thinking

1. List five ways that marketing research can contribute to effective business decision making.
2. What are the three types of marketing research? Indicate which type each item in the list below illustrates. Explain your answers.
   a. Establishing the relationship between advertising and sales in the beer industry
   b. Identifying target market demographics for a shopping center located in Omaha, Nebraska
   c. Estimating the 5-year sales potential for CAT-scan machines in the Ark-La-Tex (Arkansas, Louisiana, and Texas) region of the United States
   d. Testing the effect of the inside temperature of a clothing store on sales of outerwear
   e. Discovering the ways that people who live in apartments actually use vacuum cleaners, and identifying cleaning tasks for which they do not use a vacuum
3. Describe the type of research evidence that allows one to infer causality.
4. Do the stages in the research process seem to follow the scientific method?
5. Why is the "define research objectives" stage of the research process probably the most important?
6. Suppose Auchan (http://www.auchan.fr), a hypermarket chain based out of France, was considering opening three hypermarkets in the Midwestern United States. What role would theory play in designing a research study to track how the shopping habits of consumers from the United States differ from those in

France and from those in Japan? What kind of hypothesis might be examined in a study of this topic?

7. Define *research project* and *research program*. Referring to the question immediately above, do you think a research project or a research program is needed to provide useful input to the Auchan decision makers?
8. What type of research design would you recommend in the situations below? For each applied market research project, what might be an example of a "deliverable"?
   a. The manufacturer and marketer of flight simulators and other pilot training equipment wish to forecast sales volume for the next five years.
   b. A local chapter of the American Lung Association wishes to identify the demographic characteristics of individuals who donate more than $500 per year.
   c. A major petroleum company is concerned with the increased costs of marketing regular leaded gasoline and is considering dropping this product.
   d. A food company researcher wishes to know what types of food are carried in brown-bag lunches to learn if the company can capitalize on this phenomenon.
   e. A researcher wishes to identify who plays bingo.
9. What purpose does the research proposal serve?
10. Comment on the following statements:
    a. "The best marketing researchers are prepared to rethink and rewrite their proposals."
    b. "Management is generally interested in detailed reporting of the research design and statistical findings."

Research Activities

1. **'NET** Look up information about the online MBA programs at the University of Phoenix (http://www.phoenix.edu/online_learning). Compare it to the traditional MBA program at your university. Suppose each was looking to expand the numbers of students in their programs; how might the research design differ for each?
2. **'NET** Use a web browser to go to the Gallup Organization's home page (http://www.gallup.com). The Gallup home page changes regularly. However, it should provide an opportunity to read the results of a recent poll. For example, a poll might break

down Americans' sympathies toward Israel or the Palestinians based on numerous individual characteristics such as political affiliation or religious involvement. After reading the results of a Gallup poll of this type, learn how polls are conducted. You may need to click on the Frequently Asked Questions list (FAQ) to find this information. List the various stages of the research process and how they were (or were not) followed in Gallup's project.

3. Any significant business decision requires input from a research project. Write a brief essay either defending this statement or refuting it.

Video Case 3.1 Black Forest Motors/Mercedes-Benz

Mercedes-Benz entered the United States market in the late 1950s and dominated the foreign luxury car scene during the 1970s and 1980s until other luxury cars like Lexus and Infiniti appeared on stage. Their sales then began to drop substantially—other car companies could offer comparable products for lesser prices. At this point, Mercedes knew it faced a real challenge.

Robert Wilshaw, market manager of the Chicago Region of Mercedes-Benz of North America, affirms that the company met this challenge squarely. New company strategies led to the development of a customer-value triad that highlights perceived goods quality, perceived service quality, and value-based prices.

Mercedes was always regarded as the leader in engineering and design, but their engineers were given two new guidelines. Rule 1 states, "Build the best car in the world," and Rule 2 adds, "Build a more affordable car without breaking rule number one."

Dealerships are a key element in Mercedes' quest to provide quality service. Black Forest Motors in northern Michigan is the premier dealership in this geographic area. Robert S. Chan, the principal, sums up his dealership's relationship with his customer base: "To our customers, we are Mercedes-Benz." This means offering customers "a no-excuses product . . . [a car] that is as perfect as man can make a machine." But it also means offering high-quality, reliably consistent service that keeps customers coming back. When interviewed, Chan's customers confirm the organization's commitment to "world-class service."

Noting that, in today's market, economics can be as important as engineering, Wilshaw says that Mercedes has proved that it can now build a premier product that can be priced lower than those of their competitors, and they have driven this message into the marketplace. He adds that the company's price-sensitive strategies have maximized perceived customer value and led to successful new product introductions, which, in turn, have continued to increase overall customer satisfaction.

Question

1. What market research should be done to develop a program that could persuade more customers in the luxury car market to buy Mercedes-Benz? Define the problem and explain the types of research that would be necessary to develop such a program.

Video Case 3.2 Fisher-Price Rescue Heroes

Fisher-Price's action-figure collection Rescue Heroes, as well as the CBS television show with the same name, is popular with boys ages three and older. The Rescue Heroes characters' mission is to help and rescue with courage, perseverance, resourcefulness, and nonviolent problem solving. The product line consists of action figures (such as Jake Justice Police Officer, Wendy Waters Firefighter, and Rocky Canyon Mountain Ranger), vehicles (for example, Rescue Heroes Quick Response Helicopter), and command centers. Additional details about the characters may be found online at http://www.fisher-price.com/us/rescueheroes/.

Fisher-Price uses marketing research extensively in its new product development process. Rescue Heroes went from an identified need to a commercial product line with the help of a multistage research program. Through exploratory research, the company learned that there was a gap in toys available for preschool and early elementary school boys. Little boys liked the idea of the action figures that their older brothers and friends played with, but those toys were difficult for them to understand and handle. The findings led Fisher-Price to coin the term KAGO—"Kids Are Getting Older"—meaning younger children want more grown-up toys.

Research with mothers indicated their toy preferences. The mothers liked the idea of imaginative play with action figures, but they clearly did not want their young children playing with toys that had violent overtones. As a result of these research findings and creative thinking, Fisher-Price came up with the idea of age-appropriate action figures. After much marketing research, the company learned that young boys had trouble with the figures toppling over. The product concept was refined so that the new action figures would have wide feet for stability.

During the marketing research process, Fisher-Price's researchers conduct focus group interviews to test new toy concepts. They interview both kids and moms in search of ideas for toys that have play value—the tangible features and intangible allure that entice a child to interact with and have fun with a toy. Fisher-Price tried versions of the action-figure line in its play laboratory, a large nursery overflowing with toys that is different from ordinary nurseries because there is a wall of one-way mirrors and microphones dangle from the ceiling so that researchers can observe how children are using the toys.

Fisher-Price also conducted extensive in-home testing around the country. After the boys played with the toys at home, researchers interviewed the parents about price and asked if they would buy the toys.

Questions

1. Using the flowchart in Exhibit 3.3, outline the steps in the research process that you would recommend that Fisher-Price take in evaluating an idea for a new toy.
2. What type of outcome might Fisher-Price expect from its exploratory research efforts?
3. Describe the program strategy for Rescue Heroes. How did the early research projects influence subsequent research objectives?

CHAPTER 4
THE HUMAN SIDE OF MARKETING RESEARCH:
ORGANIZATIONAL AND ETHICAL ISSUES

After studying this chapter, you should be able to

1. Identify when research should be conducted externally and when it should be done internally
2. Discuss the types of jobs, job responsibilities, and career paths available within the marketing research industry
3. Define ethics and understand how it applies to marketing research
4. Explain and appreciate the rights and obligations of a) research respondents—particularly children, b) marketing researchers, and c) research clients or sponsors
5. Avoid a conflict of interest in performing marketing research

Chapter Vignette: Researching Online Auctions—Do's and Don'ts Are Not Always Clear

Auctions are certainly not new. However, auctions are no longer relegated to estate sales, livestock yards, or art sales; eBay and competing websites have brought the consumer auction to the masses. Consumers can bid on practically any product imaginable. The NCAA BCS Football Championship Game is sold out each year. But you can always bid for tickets on eBay. A lucky owner of tickets for this game can sell tickets to the highest bidder. In 2004, loyal Louisiana State University Tiger fans were willing to bid and pay more than $600 for a ticket with a face value of about $60.

©ASSOCIATED PRESS/AP

Recently, there has been considerable interest in understanding why consumers have flocked to online auctions in such large numbers.[1] The research can help web designers and online auction companies decide how to design their sites to enhance the experience for consumers. When questioned, consumers often talk about how they can get a good price by participating in an auction, or they can get something they might not be able to otherwise. However, could it be that emotional reasons involved in competing to "win" the auctions are equally as important?

When consumers are unable or unwilling to voice their emotional or psychological reasons for behavior, some researchers have turned to hypnosis. Hypnosis relaxes the inhibitions of consumers and can get them to behave in a manner that may more accurately reflect their true thoughts, emotions, and behavior.[2] A researcher may consider using hypnosis to study online auctions. Research participants could be recruited and asked to participate in a real online auction on eBay. Half of the participants will participate in the auction while a researcher looks on. The other half will do the same thing, but only after being induced into a hypnotic state by a member of the research team.

When preparing the report, the researcher notices that, indeed, those in the hypnotic state reported experiencing more emotions and more feelings of competitiveness than did other participants. Hypnotized respondents also placed more bids, purchased more goods, and had higher average price offers than did the others. Although the results appear to be valuable to the client, the researcher is beginning to have some reservations about the research approach used. Is the use of hypnosis ever ethical marketing research?[3] If so, would this situation qualify as one in which there are no ethical issues in the use of hypnosis? Questions like these continue to plague the researcher. Compounding this problem is the fact that the research client wanted the research report completed by yesterday. The researcher suspects that the company already has a tactical plan for redesigning their web operations. It isn't clear that the research results would ever be used anyway.

Who Does the Research?

TOTHEPOINT

To manage a business is to manage its future; and to manage the future is to manage information.

—Marion Harper

The vignette described above involves one company hiring an outside company to provide results from a research project. Although this is very typical, many companies have their own employees perform research projects and research programs. Thus, research is sometimes performed in-house, meaning that employees of the company that will benefit from the research project actually perform the research. In other cases, the research is performed by an **outside agency**, meaning that the company that will benefit from the research results hires an independent, outside firm to perform a research project.

While it would seem that **in-house research** would usually be of higher quality because of the increased knowledge of the researchers conducting the studies, there are several reasons why employees of the firm may not always be the best people to do the job. When the firm facing a decision encounters one of the following situations, they should consider having the research performed by an outside agency:

- An outside agency often can provide a fresh perspective. Creativity is often hindered by too much knowledge. When a firm is seeking new ideas, particularly in discovery-oriented research, an outsider is not constrained by the groupthink that often affects a company employee. In other words, employees who spend so much time together in their day-to-day work activities begin to act and think alike to a large degree. History is filled with stories of products that remained unsuccessful commercially for years until someone from outside the company discovered a useful application. The technology for a microwave oven was invented in the 1940s by a company called Raytheon. Raytheon worked on radar systems for the Allied military in World War II. Not until someone from another company, Amana, tested the concept of using microwaves in a kitchen appliance did it become a commercial success.
- An outside agency often can be more objective. When a firm is facing a particularly sensitive situation that may even impact a large number of jobs within the company, it may be difficult for researchers to be objective. Alternatively, if a particular chief executive within the firm is in love with some new idea, researchers may feel a great deal of pressure to present results that are supportive of the concept. In these cases, outside researchers may be a good choice. Since they don't have to work for the company and interact with the players involved on a daily basis, they are less concerned about presenting results that may not be truly welcome.
- An outside agency may have special expertise. When a firm needs research requiring a particular expertise that some outside agency specializes in, it may be a good idea to use that firm to conduct the research. For example, if a company is searching for new ideas about how to use its website, an online focus group interview may be needed. While this is a skill that may not be prevalent within the company, there are several research firms that specialize in this particular type of research. Thus, the outside agency may have greater competency in this specific area.

Likewise, there are conditions that make in-house research more attractive as well, as in the following situations:

- If the research project needs to be completed very quickly, chances are that in-house researchers can get started more quickly and get quicker access to internal resources that can help get the project done in short order.
- If the research project will require the close collaboration of many other employees from diverse areas of the organization, then in-house research may be preferable. The in-house research firms can usually gain cooperation and can more quickly ascertain just who needs to be interviewed and where those people can be found.

- A third reason for doing a project in-house has to do with economy. In-house research can almost always be done more cheaply than that done by an outside research firm.
- If secrecy is a major concern, then the research is best done in-house. Even though the outside firm might be trusted, it may take slightly less care in disguising its research efforts. Thus, other companies may pick up on signals in the marketplace that suggest the area of research for a firm.

This chapter focuses on the human side of research. We first discuss the internal working of a research unit within a large company. We then turn to the different types of options that exist when dealing with an outside agency. All of this is wrapped up by a discussion of the many ways in which ethics and research come together.

Organizational Structure of Marketing Research

According to the American Marketing Association, 76 percent of organizations reported having formal marketing research departments. Consumer products companies, manufacturers, and retailers are most likely to have an in-house marketing research department.[4] Larger companies also are more likely to have marketing research departments.

The placement of marketing research within a firm's organizational structure and the structure of the research department itself vary substantially, depending on the firm's acceptance of the marketing concept and its stage of marketing research sophistication. A marketing research department can easily become isolated with poor organizational placement. Researchers may lack a voice in executive committees when they have no continuous relationship with marketing management. This can occur when the research department is positioned at an inappropriately low level. Given the critically important nature of the intelligence coming out of a research department, it should be placed relatively high in the organizational structure to ensure that senior management is well informed. Research departments should also be linked with a broad spectrum of other units within the organization. Thus, they should be positioned to provide credible information both upstream and downstream within the marketing organization.

Research departments that perform a staff function must wait for management to request assistance. Often the term "client" is used by the research department to refer to line management for whom services are being performed. The research department responds to clients' requests and is responsible for the design and execution of all research. A research department should function like an internal consulting organization that develops action-oriented, data-based recommendations.

Director of marketing research
This person provides leadership in research efforts and integrates all staff-level research activities into one effort. The director plans, executes, and controls the firm's marketing research function.

When market research departments grow, they begin to specialize by product or business unit. This happened in the Marriot Corporation, which now has a specific director of marketing research for its lodging facilities.

Marketing Research Jobs

Marketing research organizations themselves consist of layers of employees. Each employee has certain specific functions to perform based on his or her area of expertise and experience. A look at these jobs not only describes the potential structure of a research organization, but it also provides insight into the types of careers available in marketing research. The **director of marketing research** provides leadership in research efforts and integrates all staff-level research activities. The director of marketing research plans, executes, and controls the

©JEFF GREENBERG/PHOTOEDIT

RESEARCHSNAPSHOT

Marketing Research Pays

Marketing research can pay! Careers in marketing research can be very lucrative. This is particularly true if one has the right attributes. These attributes include being a good people person as well as having good quantitative skills and a good education. The fastest career tracks in marketing research are for those with at least a master's degree.

The prospects of finding a job remain good. Marketing researchers have long been in greater demand than the supply can address. The salaries also can be very lucrative. The 2002 U.S. Department of Labor Salary Survey suggests that marketing research analysts' salaries are generally between $40,000 and $80,000. These are for actual research analysts and not research directors. Beginning research employees, with little or no experience, generally enter the firm as a survey researcher. Those salaries are considerably less, generally between $20,000 and $40,000. However, they require no significant work experience.

Job opportunities in marketing research exist outside the United States as well. The salaries also are lucrative in other countries. The chart below shows salaries for non-managerial marketing research positions in the United States, Australia, Japan, and the United Kingdom. For

©PHOTODISC/GETTY IMAGES

comparison purposes, salaries for non-managerial sales employees also are provided. The salaries are expressed in thousands of U.S. dollars and reflect the latest available statistics. As can be seen, research jobs compare very favorably. In addition, researchers that move into research director positions see a substantial increase in pay. Perhaps you'll give marketing research a try?

Common Currency ($)	Australia	U.K.	Japan	United States
Sales Market Analysts				
High	44.78	122.81	82.82	55.00
Low	33.58	61.40	41.41	35.00
Marketing Research				
High	55.97	78.95	82.82	76.30
Low	48.51	43.86	49.69	38.76

Sources: Enright, A. (2005), "Carve Out a Niche," Marketing News (November 15), 17; Fellman, M.W. (1998), "Survey: Employment Levels Critically Low in MR Industry," Marketing News, 322 (June 8), 12; U.S. Department of Labor (2006), "Wages, Benefits, and Earnings," http://www.bls.gov/bls/wages.htm. Accessed May 2, 2006. Robert Walters (2006), "Market Research Search Results," http://www.robertwalters.com. Accessed January 20, 2006.

---

marketing research function. This person typically serves on executive committees that identify competitive opportunities and formulate marketing strategies for the organization. The director's responsibility is to provide the research point of view on these strategic issues. In many cases, the director serves as an internal consultant to the organization about consumer behavior and strategic business issues.[5]

Research analyst
A person responsible for client contact, project design, preparation of proposals, selection of research suppliers, and supervision of data collection, analysis, and reporting activities.

A **research analyst** is responsible for client contact, project design, preparation of proposals, selection of research suppliers, and supervision of data collection, analysis, and reporting activities. Normally, the research analyst is responsible for several projects simultaneously covering a wide spectrum of the firm's organizational activities. He or she works with product or division management and makes recommendations based on analysis of collected data.

Research assistants
Research employees who provide technical assistance with questionnaire design, data analyses, and similar activities.

Research assistants (or associates) provide technical assistance with questionnaire design, data analyses, and so forth. Another common name for this position is *junior analyst*. The **manager of decision support systems** supervises the collection and analysis of sales, inventory, and other periodic customer relationship management (CRM) data. Sales forecasts for product lines usually are developed using analytical and quantitative techniques. Sales information is provided to satisfy the planning, analysis, and control needs of decision makers. The manager of decision support systems may be assisted by a **forecast analyst** who provides technical assistance, such as running computer programs and manipulating data to forecast sales.

Manager of decision support systems
Employee who supervises the collection and analysis of sales, inventory, and other periodic customer relationship management (CRM) data.

Forecast analyst
Employee who provides technical assistance such as running computer programs and manipulating data to generate a sales forecast.

Personnel within a planning department may perform the marketing research function in a mid-sized firm with between 100 and 500 employees. At times, they may outsource some research functions. The planner may design research studies and then contract with outside firms that supply research services such as interviewing or data processing. They can combine the input from these outside agencies with their own work to write research reports.

As marketing research departments grow, they tend to specialize by product or strategic business unit. Major firms can be thought of as those with over 500 employees. Marriott Corporation has a director of marketing research for lodging (for example, Marriott Hotels and Resorts, Courtyard by

EXHIBIT 4.1 **Organization of the Marketing Research Department in a Large Firm**

Director
Marketing
Research

Manager
Market/
New
Product
Research

Manager
Customer
Satisfaction
and
Total
Quality

Manager
Marketing
Research

Manager
Decision
Support
Systems

Supervisor
Product
Research

Supervisor
Product
Research

Supervisor
Customer
Satisfaction
Research

Supervisor
Employee
Research[a]

Supervisor
Marketing
Practice
Research[b]

Supervisor
Promotion
Research[c]

Supervisor
Fundamental
Research[d]/
Environmental
Research

Supervisor
Marketing
Statistics

Supervisor
Marketing
Information
from
Syndicated
Services

(by product groupings)

[a]Conducts research to improve total quality management in production.
[b]Conducts research that cuts across product lines or involves competitive marketing practices or characteristics of customer groups.
[c]Conducts research that cuts across product lines to measure the effectiveness of promotional activities.
[d]Conducts research aimed at gaining a basic understanding of various elements of the marketing process.

Marriott, and Fairfield Inn) and a director of marketing research for contract services and restaurants (for example, Roy Rogers, Big Boy, and Senior Living Services). Each business unit's research director reports to the vice president of corporate marketing services. Many large organizations have managers of customer quality research who specialize in conducting surveys to measure consumers' satisfaction with product quality.

Exhibit 4.1 illustrates the organization of a major firm's marketing research department. Within this organization, the centralized marketing research department conducts research for all the division's product groups. This is typical of a large research department that conducts much of its own research, including fieldwork. The director of marketing research reports to the vice president of marketing.

TO THE POINT

The longer the title, the less important the job.

—George McGovern

Cross-Functional Teams

Marketing orientation was discussed in Chapter 1. In a truly marketing-oriented organization, all employees are involved in the intelligence-gathering and dissemination process. Therefore, employees from different areas of the organization are more likely to communicate and act on marketing information in marketing-oriented firms.

Thus, employees are more likely to discuss market information between different functional areas in a marketing-oriented firm. **Cross-functional teams** are composed of individuals from various functional areas such as engineering, production, finance, and marketing who share a common purpose. Cross-functional teams help organizations focus on a core business process, such as customer service or new-product development. Working in teams reduces the tendency for employees to focus single-mindedly on an isolated functional activity. Cross-functional teams

Cross-functional teams
Employee teams composed of individuals from various functional areas such as engineering, production, finance, and marketing who share a common purpose.

help employees increase customer value since communication about their specific desires and opinions are better communicated across the firm.

At trendsetting organizations, many marketing research directors are members of cross-functional teams. New-product development, for example, may be done by a cross-functional team of engineers, finance executives, production personnel, marketing managers, and marketing researchers who take an integrated approach to solve a problem or exploit opportunities. In the old days, marketing research may not have been involved in developing new products until long after many key decisions about product specifications and manufacturing had been made. Now marketing researchers' input is part of an integrated team effort. Researchers act both as business consultants and as providers of technical services. Researchers working in teams are more likely to understand the broad purpose of their research and less likely to focus exclusively on research methodology.

The effective cross-functional team is a good illustration of the marketing concept in action. It reflects an effort to satisfy customers by using all the organization's resources. Cross-functional teams are having a dramatic impact on views of the role of marketing research within the organization.

Research Suppliers and Contractors

Research suppliers
Commercial providers of marketing research services.

As mentioned in the beginning of the chapter, there are times when it makes good sense to obtain marketing research from an outside organization. In these cases, marketing managers must interact with **research suppliers**, who are commercial providers of marketing research services. Marketing research is carried out by firms that may be variously classified as marketing research consulting companies, such as Burke or Market Facts, Inc.; advertising agencies, such as J. Walter Thompson; suppliers of syndicated research services, such as Roper Starch Worldwide; as well as interviewing agencies, universities, and government agencies.

Syndicated Service

Syndicated service
A marketing research supplier that provides standardized information for many clients in return for a fee.

No matter how large a firm's marketing research department is, some projects are too expensive to perform in-house. A **syndicated service** is a marketing research supplier that provides standardized information for many clients in return for a fee. They are a sort of supermarket for standardized research results. For example, J. D. Power and Associates sells research about customers' ratings of automobile quality and their reasons for satisfaction. Most automobile manufacturers and their advertising agencies subscribe to this syndicated service because the company provides important industry-wide information it gathers from a national sample of thousands of car buyers. By specializing in this type of customer satisfaction research, J. D. Power gains certain economies of scale.

Syndicated services can provide expensive information economically to numerous clients because the information is not specific to one client but interests many. Such suppliers offer standardized information to measure media audiences, wholesale and retail distribution data, and other forms of data.

Standardized Research Services

Standardized research service
Companies that develop a unique methodology for investigating a business specialty area.

Standardized research service companies develop a unique methodology for investigating a business specialty area. Several research firms, such as Retail Forward (http://www.retailforward.com), provide location services for retail firms. Research suppliers such as these conduct studies for multiple, individual clients using the same methods.

ACNielsen (http://www.acnielsen.com) collects information throughout the new-product development process, from initial concept screening through test-marketing. The BASES system can evaluate initiatives relative to other products in the competitive environment. For example, a client can compare its Day-After Recall scores with average scores for a product category.

Even when a firm could perform the research task in-house, research suppliers may be able to conduct the project at a lower cost, faster, and relatively more objectively. A company that wishes to quickly evaluate a new advertising strategy may find an ad agency's research department is able to provide technical expertise on copy development research that is not available within the company itself. Researchers may be well advised to seek outside help with research when conducting research in a foreign country in which the necessary human resources and knowledge to effectively collect data are lacking.

Limited Research Service Companies and Custom Research

Limited-service research suppliers specialize in particular research activities, such as syndicated service, field interviewing, data warehousing, or data processing. Full-service research suppliers sometimes contract these companies for ad hoc marketing research projects. The client usually controls these marketing research agencies or management consulting firms, but the research supplier handles most of the operating details of **custom research** projects. These are projects that are tailored specifically to a client's unique needs. A custom research supplier may employ individuals with titles that imply relationships with clients, such as *account executive* or *account group manager*, as well as functional specialists with titles such as *statistician, librarian, director of field services, director of tabulation and data processing*, and *interviewer*.

ACNielsen, IMS Health, Information Resources, VNU, NFO World Group, The Kantar Group, and Westat are among the top U.S. research suppliers. Most of these firms provide a variety of services ranging from design activities to fieldwork. Their services are not covered in detail here because they are discussed throughout the book.

In many cases the marketing research manager's job is primarily administrative: hiring interviewing services, data-processing services, and so on. When it is necessary to hire outside research suppliers or contractors, the marketing researcher must be able to evaluate such specialized services. An analogy is the make-or-buy decision in the factory: The researcher can hire a research service to conduct the project or conduct the project with in-house personnel.

"Doing research in a foreign country is often better done by an outside agency with resources in those places."

Custom research
Research projects that are tailored specifically to a client's unique needs.

Ethical Issues in Marketing Research

As in all human interactions, ethical issues exist in marketing research. Our earlier discussion of organizational politics and the use of pseudo-research to bolster one's position within the organization introduced a situation where ethics can come into play. This book considers various ethical issues concerning fair business dealings, proper research techniques, and appropriate use of research results in other chapters. The remainder of this chapter addresses society's and managers' concerns about the ethical implications of marketing research.

Ethical Questions Are Philosophical Questions

Ethical questions are philosophical questions. There are several philosophical theories that address how one develops a moral philosophy and how behavior is affected by morals. These include theories about cognitive moral development, the bases for ethical behavioral intentions, and opposing moral values.[6] While ethics remains a somewhat elusive topic, what is clear is that not everyone involved in business, or in fact involved in any human behavior, comes to the table with the same ethical standards or orientations.[7]

Marketing ethics
The application of morals to behavior related to the exchange environment.

Moral standards
Principles that reflect beliefs about what is ethical and what is unethical.

Ethical dilemma
Refers to a situation in which one chooses from alternative courses of actions, each with different ethical implications.

Relativism
A term that reflects the degree to which one rejects moral standards in favor of the acceptability of some action. This way of thinking rejects absolute principles in favor of situation-based evaluations.

Idealism
A term that reflects the degree to which one bases one's morality on moral standards.

Marketing ethics is the application of morals to behavior related to the exchange environment. Generally, good ethics conforms to the notion of "right," and a lack of ethics conforms to the notion of "wrong." Highly ethical behavior can be characterized as being fair, just, and acceptable.[8] Ethical values can be highly influenced by one's moral standards. **Moral standards** are principles that reflect beliefs about what is ethical and what is unethical. More simply, they can be thought of as rules distinguishing right from wrong. The Golden Rule, "Do unto others as you would have them do unto you," is one such ethical principle.

An **ethical dilemma** simply refers to a situation in which one chooses from alternative courses of actions, each with different ethical implications. Each individual develops a philosophy or way of thinking that is applied to resolve the dilemmas they face. Many people use moral standards to guide their actions when confronted with an ethical dilemma. Others adapt an ethical orientation that rejects absolute principles. Their ethics are based more on the social or cultural acceptability of behavior. If it conforms to social or cultural norms, then it is ethical. From a moral theory standpoint, idealism is a term that reflects the degree to which one accepts moral standards as a guide for behavior. **Relativism** is a term that reflects the degree to which one rejects moral standards in favor of the acceptability of some action. This way of thinking rejects absolute principles in favor of situation-based evaluations. Thus, an action that is judged ethical in one situation can be deemed unethical in another. In contrast, **idealism** is a term that reflects the degree to which one bases one's morality on moral standards. Someone who is an ethical idealist will try to apply ethical principles like the golden rule in all ethical dilimmas.

For example, a student may face an ethical dilemma when taking a test. Another student may arrange to exchange multiple choice responses to a test via electronic text messages. This represents an ethical dilemma because there are alternative courses of action each with differing moral implications. An ethical idealist may apply a rule that cheating is always wrong and therefore would not be likely to participate in the behavior. An ethical relativist may instead argue that the behavior is acceptable because a lot of the other students will be doing the same. In other words, the consensus is that this sort of cheating is acceptable, so this student would be likely to go ahead and participate in the behavior. Marketing researchers, marketing managers, and even consumers face ethical dilemmas practically every day. The following sections describe how this can occur.

General Rights and Obligations of Concerned Parties

Everyone involved in marketing research can face an ethical dilemma. For this discussion, we can divide those involved in research into three parties:

1. The people actually performing the research, who can also be thought of as the "doers"
2. The research client, sponsor, or the management team requesting the research, who can be thought of as "users" of marketing research
3. The research participants, meaning the actual research respondents or subjects

Each party has certain rights and obligations toward the other parties. Exhibit 4.2 diagrams these relationships.

Like the rest of business, research works best when all parties act ethically. Each party depends on the other to do so. A client depends on the researcher to be honest in presenting research results. The researcher depends on the client to be honest in presenting the reasons for doing the research and in describing the business situation. Each is also dependent on the research participant's honesty in answering questions during a research study. Thus, each is morally obligated toward the other. Likewise, each also has certain rights. The following section elaborates on the obligations and rights of each party.

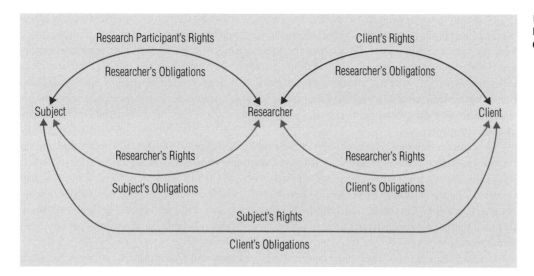

EXHIBIT 4.2
Interaction of Rights and Obligations

Rights and Obligations of the Research Participant

Most marketing research is conducted with the research participant's consent. In other words, the participation is active. Traditional survey research requires that a respondent voluntarily answer questions in one way or another. This may involve answering questions on the phone, responding to an e-mail request, or even sending a completed questionnaire by regular mail. In these cases, **informed consent** means that the individual understands what the researcher wants him or her to do and consents to the research study. In other cases, research participants may not be aware that they are being monitored in some way. For instance, a research firm may monitor superstore purchases via an electronic scanner. The information may assist in understanding how customers respond to promotions. However, no consent is provided since the participant is participating passively. The ethical responsibilities vary depending on whether participation is active or passive.

Informed consent
When an individual understands what the researcher wants him or her to do and consents to the research study.

▧ THE OBLIGATION TO BE TRUTHFUL

When someone willingly consents to participate actively, it is generally expected that he or she will provide truthful answers. Honest cooperation is the main obligation of the research participant. In return for being truthful, the subject has the right to expect confidentiality. **Confidentiality** means that information involved in the research will not be shared with others. When the respondent truly believes that confidentiality will be maintained, then it becomes much easier to respond truthfully, even about potentially sensitive topics.

Confidentiality
The information involved in research will not be shared with others.

▧ PARTICIPANT'S RIGHT TO PRIVACY

Active Research

Americans relish their privacy. Hence, the right to privacy is an important issue in marketing research. This issue involves the participant's freedom to choose whether to comply with the investigator's request. Traditionally, researchers have assumed that individuals make an informed choice. However, critics have argued that the old, the poor, the poorly educated, and other underprivileged individuals may be unaware of their right to choose. They have further argued that an interviewer may begin with some vague explanation of a survey's purpose, initially ask questions that are relatively innocuous, and then move to questions of a highly personal nature. The interviewer should provide the respondent with an opportunity to forgo participation if they wish.

Generally, interviewing firms practice common courtesy by trying not to interview late in the evening or at other inconvenient times. However, the computerized random phone number interview has stimulated increased debate over the privacy issue. As a practical matter, respondents may feel more relaxed about privacy issues if they know who is conducting the survey. Thus, it is generally recommended that field interviewers indicate that they are legitimate researchers and name the company they work for as soon as someone answers the phone. For in-person surveys, interviewers should wear official name tags and provide identification giving their name and the names of their companies.

Research companies should adhere to the principles of the "Do Not Call" policy and should respect consumers' "Internet privacy." **Do Not Call legislation** restricts any telemarketing effort from calling consumers who either register with a no-call list in their state or who request not to be called. Legislators aimed these laws at sales-related calls. However, legislation in several states, including California, Louisiana, and Rhode Island, has extended this legislation to apply to "those that seek marketing information." Thus, the legislation effectively protects consumers' privacy from researchers as well as salespeople.[9]

Companies using the Internet to do marketing research also face legislative changes. Much of this legislation is aimed at making sure consumers are properly notified about the collection of data and to whom it will be distributed. Researchers should make sure that consumers are given a clear and easy way either to consent to participation in active research or to easily opt out. Furthermore, companies should ensure that the information consumers send via the Internet is secure.[10]

Passive Research

Passive research involves different types of privacy issues. Generally, it is believed that unobtrusive observation of public behavior in places such as stores, airports, and museums is not a serious invasion of privacy. This belief is based on the fact that the consumers are indeed anonymous in that they are never identified by name nor is any attempt made to identify them. They are "faces in the crowd." As long as the behavior observed is typical of behavior commonly conducted in public, then there is no invasion of privacy. In contrast, recording behavior that is not typically conducted in public would be a violation of privacy. For example, hidden cameras recording people (without consent) taking showers at a health club, even if ultimately intended to gather information to help improve the shower experience, would be considered inappropriate.

Technology has also created new ways of collecting data passively that have privacy implications. Researchers are very interested in consumers' online behavior. For instance, the paths that consumers take while browsing the Internet can be extremely useful in understanding what kinds of information are most valued by consumers. Much of this information can be harvested and entered into a data warehouse. Researchers sometimes have legitimate reasons to use this data, which can improve consumers' ability to make wise decisions. In these cases, the researcher should gain the consumers' consent in some form before harvesting information from their web usage patterns. Furthermore, if the information will be shared with other companies, a specific consent agreement is needed. This can come in the form of a question to which consumers respond yes or no.

Not all of these attempts are legitimate. Most readers have probably encountered spyware on their home computer. **Spyware** is software that is placed on your computer without consent or knowledge while using the Internet. This software then tracks your usage and sends the information back through the Internet to the source. Then, based on these usage patterns, the user will receive push technology advertising, usually in the form of pop-up ads. Sometimes, the user will receive so many pop-up ads that the computer becomes unusable. The use of spyware is illegitimate because it is done without consent and therefore violates the right to privacy and confidentiality.

Legislators are increasingly turning their attention to privacy issues in data collection. When children are involved, researchers have a special obligation to insure their safety. COPPA, the Children's Online Privacy Protection Act, was enacted into U.S. federal law on April 12, 2000. It defines a child as anyone under the age of thirteen. Anyone engaging in contact with a child through the Internet is obligated to obtain parental consent and notification before any personal information or identification can be provided by a child. Therefore, a researcher collecting a child's name, phone number, or e-mail address without parental consent is violating the law. While the law and ethics do not always correspond, in this case, it is probably pretty clear that a child's personal

Do Not Call legislation
Restricts any telemarketing effort from calling consumers who either register with a no-call list or who request not to be called.

Spyware
Software placed on a computer without consent or knowledge of the user.

RESEARCHSNAPSHOT

Is It Right, or Is It Wrong?

Sometimes, the application of research procedures to research participants can present significant ethical issues that cannot be easily dismissed by a single researcher alone. This is where a peer review process takes place. A Human Subjects Research Committee consists of a panel of researchers (and sometimes a legal authority) who carefully review the proposed procedures to identify any obvious or non-obvious ethical or legal issues. In fact, any research supported by U.S. federal funds must be subject to a peer review of this type. The peer review process for grants is described at this website: http://grants.nih.gov/ grants/peer/peer.htm.

Most business research is innocuous and affords little opportunity for substantial physical or psychological trauma. However, companies involved in food marketing, dietary supplements or programs, and exercise physiology and pharmaceuticals, among others, do conduct consumer research with such possibilities. Academic researchers also sometimes conduct research with significant risks for participants. Consider research examining how some dietary supplement might make exercise more enjoyable, thus creating a better overall health and psychological effect. Clearly, a peer review by knowledgeable researchers is needed before proceeding with such research.

As it isn't possible to completely eliminate risk from research, a human subjects review is a good safety net. Deaths have been attributed to lack of or the breakdown of the human subjects review. Some of these have brought negative publicity to well-known universities including the University of Pennsylvania and Johns Hopkins University. At other times, the risk to research participants is not obvious. For example, recently several researchers were interested in surveying through personal interviews victims of Hurricane Katrina. The results of the research may help public entities better serve victims, allow companies to respond with more appropriate goods and services, and help build psychological theory about how consumers make decisions under conditions of high personal trauma and stress. However, is it ethical to survey participants standing in the rubble of their home? Is it ethical to survey participants who are in the process of searching for or burying relatives that did not survive the disaster? Clearly, a thorough review of the procedures involved in such situations is called for.

Corporate human subjects committees are also becoming common. These reviews also consider the possibility of legal problems with experimental or survey procedures. In addition, as technology blurs the line between research and sales, they also should review the ethics of "research" that may somehow blend with sales. In addition, research conducted on animals also needs a critical review.

Sources: Glenn, David (2005), "Lost (and Found) in the Flood," Chronicle of Higher Education, 52 (10/7), A14–A19; Putney, S.B. and S. Gruskin (2002), "Time, Place and Consciousness: Three Dimensions of Meaning for U.S. Institutional Review Boards," American Journal of Public Health, 92 (July), 1067–1071.

information shouldn't be collected. The Research Snapshot box further explains how conducting research with children is ethically complex.

▩ DECEPTION IN RESEARCH DESIGNS AND THE RIGHT TO BE INFORMED

Experimental Designs

Experimental manipulations often involve some degree of deception. In fact, without some deception, a researcher would never know if a research subject was responding to the actual manipulation or to their perception of the experimental variable.

Imagine two consumers, each participating in a study of the effect of a new herbal supplement on hypertension. One consumer receives a packet containing the citrus-flavored supplement, which is meant to be mixed in water and drunk with breakfast. The other also receives a packet, but in this case the packet contains a mixture that will simply color the water and provide a citrus flavor. The second consumer also believes he or she is drinking the actual supplement. In this way, the psychological effect is the same on both consumers, and any actual difference in hypertension must be due to the actual herbs contained in the supplement. Interestingly, experimental subjects often display some placebo effect, in which the mere belief that some treatment has been applied causes some effect.

This type of deception can be considered ethical. Primarily, researchers conducting an experiment must generally (1) gain the willful cooperation of the research subject and (2) fully explain the actual experimental variables applied following the experiment's completion.

Descriptive Research

Researchers sometimes will even withhold the actual research questions from respondents in simple descriptive research. A distinction can thus be made between deception and discreet silence. For instance, sometimes providing the actual research question to respondents is simply providing them more information than they need to give a valid response. A researcher may ask questions about the perceived price of a product when his or her real interest is in how consumers form quality impressions.

Research aimed at marketing employees also sometimes involves deception. For instance, employees are sometimes passive respondents in observational research involving a mystery shopper. **Mystery shoppers** are employees of a research firm that are paid to "pretend" to be actual shoppers. A mystery shopper would rarely identify him or herself as anything other than a customer. However, since most employees perform their jobs in public, and perform behaviors that are easily observable, research using mystery shoppers is not considered an invasion of an employee's privacy.

Mystery shoppers
Employees of a research firm that are paid to pretend to be actual shoppers.

PROTECTION FROM HARM

Researchers should do everything they can to make sure that research participants are not harmed by participating in research. Most marketing research does not expose participants to any harm. However, the researcher should consider every possibility. For example, if the research involves tasting food or drink, the possibility exists that a research participant could have a severe allergic reaction. Similarly, researchers studying retail and workplace atmospherics often manipulate odors by injecting certain scents into the air.[11]

Other times, research may involve some potential psychological harm. This may come in the form of stress or in the form of some experimental treatment that questions some strongly held conviction.

Human subjects review committee
Carefully reviews proposed research design to try to make sure that no harm can come to any research participant.

Many research companies and practically all universities now maintain a **human subjects review committee**. This is a committee that carefully reviews a proposed research design to try to make sure that no harm can come to any research participant. A side benefit of this committee is that it can also review the procedures to make sure no legal problems are created by implementing the particular design.

Rights and Obligations of the Researcher

Marketing research firms and marketing research departments should practice good business ethics. Researchers are often the focus of discussions of business ethics because of the necessity that they interact with the public. Several professional organizations have written and adopted codes of ethics for their researchers, including the American Marketing Association, the European Society for Opinion and Market Research, and the Marketing Research Society.[12]

In addition, the researchers have rights. In particular, once a research consulting firm is hired to conduct some research, they have the right to cooperation from the sponsoring client. In addition, the researchers have the right to be paid for the work they do as long as it is done professionally. Sometimes, the client may not like the results. But not liking the results is no basis for not paying. In addition, the client should pay the researcher in full and in a timely manner.

THE PURPOSE OF RESEARCH IS RESEARCH

Mixing Sales and Research

Consumers sometimes agree to participate in an interview that is purported to be pure research, but it eventually becomes obvious that the interview is really a sales pitch in disguise. This is unprofessional at best and fraudulent at worst. The Federal Trade Commission (FTC) has indicated that it is illegal to use any plan, scheme, or ruse that misrepresents the true status of a person seeking admission to a prospect's home, office, or other establishment. No research firm or basic marketing researcher should engage in any sales attempts. Applied market researchers working for the sponsoring company should also avoid overtly mixing research and sales. However, the line is becoming less clear with increasing technology.

OBJECTIVITY

The need for objective scientific investigation to ensure accuracy is stressed throughout this book. Researchers should maintain high standards to be certain that their data are accurate. Furthermore, they must not intentionally try to prove a particular point for political purposes.

■ MISREPRESENTATION OF RESEARCH

It should go without saying, but research results should not be misrepresented. This means, for instance, that the statistical accuracy of a test should be stated precisely and the meaning of findings should not be understated or overstated. Both the researcher and the client share this obligation. There are many ways that research results can be reported in a less than full and honest way. For example, a researcher may present results showing a relationship between advertising spending and sales. However, the researcher may also discover that this relationship disappears when the primary competitors' prices are taken into account. In other words, the relationship between advertising spending and sales is made spurious by the competitors' prices (see Chapter 3). Thus, it would be questionable to say the least to report a finding suggesting that sales could be increased by increasing ad spending without also mentioning the spurious nature of this finding.

Honesty in Presenting Results and Reporting Errors

Misrepresentation can also occur in the way results are presented. For instance, charts can be created that make a very small difference appear very big. Likewise, they can be altered to make a meaningful difference seem small. Exhibit 4.3 illustrates this effect. Each chart presents exactly the same data. The data represent consumer responses to service quality ratings and satisfaction ratings.

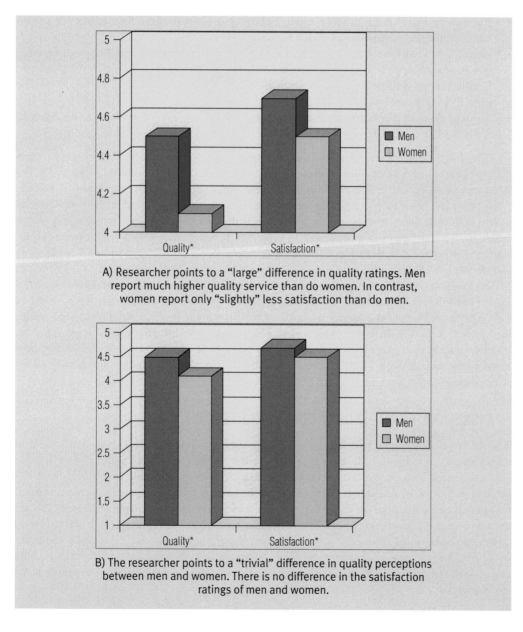

EXHIBIT 4.3
How Results Can Be Misrepresented in a Report or Presentation

A) Researcher points to a "large" difference in quality ratings. Men report much higher quality service than do women. In contrast, women report only "slightly" less satisfaction than do men.

B) The researcher points to a "trivial" difference in quality perceptions between men and women. There is no difference in the satisfaction ratings of men and women.

Both quality and satisfaction are collected on a 5-point strongly-disagree-to-strongly-agree scale. In frame A, the chart appears to show meaningful differences between men and women, particularly for the service-quality rating. However, notice that the scale range is shown as 4 to 5. In frame B, the researcher presents the same data but shows the full scale range (1 to 5). Now, the differences are reported as trivial.

Likewise, any major error that has occurred during the course of the study should not be kept secret from management or the sponsor. Hiding errors or variations from the proper procedures tends to distort or shade the results.

CONFIDENTIALITY

Confidentiality comes into play in several ways. The marketing researcher often is obligated to protect the confidentiality of both the research sponsor and the research participant. In fact, business clients value marketing researchers' confidentiality more than any other attribute of a research firm.[13] Imagine a researcher conducting a test-market for a new high-tech Apple iPod device that allows interactive video. Just after conducting the research, the same researcher is contacted by Samsung. Samsung, which has yet to develop video capability, wants research that addresses whether or not there is a market for iPod video of any type. The researcher is now in a difficult position. Certainly, an ethical dilemma exists presenting multiple choices to the researcher, including

- Agreeing to do the research for Samsung and using some results from the Apple study to prepare a report and recommendation for Samsung
- Agreeing to sell the new concept to Samsung without doing any additional research. In other words, provide Apple's company secrets to Samsung
- Conducting an entirely new project for Samsung without revealing any of the results or ideas from the Apple study
- Turning down the chance to do the study without revealing any information about Apple to Samsung

Which is the best choice? Obviously, both of the first two options violate the principle of maintaining client confidentiality. Thus, both are unethical. The third choice, conducting an entirely new study, may be an option. However, it may prove nearly impossible to do the entire project as if the Apply study had never been done. Even with the best of intentions, the researcher may inadvertently violate confidentiality with Apple. The last choice is the best option from a moral standpoint. It avoids any potential **conflict of interest**. In other words, actions that would best serve one client, Samsung, would be detrimental to another client, Apple. Generally, it is best to avoid working for two direct competitors.

Conflict of interest
Occurs when one researcher works for two competing companies.

Likewise, the researcher must also predict any confidentiality agreement with research participants. For instance, a researcher conducting a descriptive research survey may have identified each participant's e-mail address in the course of conducting the research. After seeing the results, the client may ask for the e-mail addresses as a logical prospect list. However, as long as the researcher assured each participant's confidentiality, the e-mail addresses cannot ethically be provided to the firm. Indeed, a commitment of confidentiality also helps build trust among survey respondents.[14]

DISSEMINATION OF FAULTY CONCLUSIONS

The American Marketing Association's marketing research Code of Ethics states that "a user of research shall not knowingly disseminate conclusions from a given research project or service that are inconsistent with or not warranted by the data." A dramatic example of a violation of this principle occurred in an advertisement of a cigarette smoker study. The advertisement compared two brands and stated that "of those expressing a preference, over 65 percent preferred" the advertised brand to a competing brand. The misleading portion of this reported result was that most of the respondents did *not* express a preference; they indicated that both brands tasted about the same. Thus, only a very small percentage of those studied actually revealed a preference, and the results were somewhat misleading. Such shading of results violates the obligation to report accurate findings.

Rights and Obligations of the Client Sponsor (User)

ETHICAL BEHAVIOR BETWEEN BUYER AND SELLER

The general business ethics expected between a purchasing agent and a sales representative should hold in a marketing research situation. For example, if a purchasing agent has already decided to purchase a product from a friend, it would be unethical for that person to solicit competitive bids from others because they have no chance of being accepted. Similarly, a client seeking research should only seek bids from firms that have a legitimate chance of actually doing the work. In addition, any section on the ethical obligation of a research client would be remiss not to mention that the user is obligated to pay the provider the agreed upon wage and pay within the agreed upon time.

AN OPEN RELATIONSHIP WITH RESEARCH SUPPLIERS

The client sponsor has the obligation to encourage the research supplier to objectively seek out the truth. To encourage this objectivity, a full and open statement of the decision situation, a full disclosure of constraints in time and money, and any other insights that assist the researcher should be provided. This means that the researcher will be provided adequate access to key decision makers. These decision makers should agree to openly and honestly discuss matters related to the situation. Finally, this means that the client is open to actually using the research results. Time is simply too valuable to ask a researcher to perform a project when the results will not be used.

AN OPEN RELATIONSHIP WITH INTERESTED PARTIES

Conclusions should be based on data—not conjecture. Users should not knowingly disseminate conclusions from a research project in a manner that twists them into a position that cannot be supported by the data. Twisting the results in a self-serving manner or to support some political position poses serious ethical questions. A user may also be tempted to misrepresent results while trying to close a sale. Obviously, this is also morally inappropriate.

Advocacy research—research undertaken to support a specific claim in a legal action or to represent some advocacy group—puts a client in a unique situation. Researchers often conduct advocacy research in their role as an expert witness. For instance, a researcher may be deposed to present evidence showing that a "knock-off" brand diminishes the value of a better known name brand. In conventional research, attributes such as sample size, profile of people actually interviewed, and number of questions asked are weighed against cost in traditional research. However, a court's opinion on whether research results are reliable may be based exclusively on any one specific research aspect. Thus, the slightest variation from technically correct procedures may be magnified by an attorney until a standard marketing research project no longer appears adequate in a judge's eyes. How open should the client be in the courtroom?

Advocacy research
Research undertaken to support a specific claim in a legal action or represent some advocacy group.

The ethics of advocacy research presents a number of serious issues that can lead to an ethical dilemma:

- Lawyers' first responsibility is to represent their clients. Therefore, they might not be interested as much in the truth as they are in evidence that supports their client's position. Presenting accurate research results may harm the client.
- A researcher should be objective. However, he or she runs the risk of conducting research that does not support the desired position. In this case, the lawyer may ask the researcher if the results can somehow be interpreted in another manner.
- Should the lawyer (in this case a user of research) ask the researcher to take the stand and present an inaccurate picture of the results?

Ethically, the attorney should certainly not put the researcher on the stand and encourage an act of perjury. The attorney may hope to ask specific questions that are so limited that taken alone, they may appear to support the client. However, this is risky because the opposing attorney likely also has an expert witness that can suggest questions for cross-examination. Returning to our branding example, if the research does not support an infringement of the known brand's name, then the brand name's attorney should probably not have the researcher take the stand.

Advocacy researchers do not necessarily bias results intentionally. However, attorneys rarely submit advocacy research evidence that does not support their clients' positions.

The question of advocacy research is one of objectivity: Can the researcher seek out the truth when the sponsoring client wishes to support its position at a trial? The ethical question stems from a conflict between legal ethics and research ethics. Although the courts have set judicial standards for marketing research methodology, perhaps only the client and individual researcher can resolve this question.

Privacy

People believe the collection and distribution of personal information without their knowledge is a serious violation of their privacy. The privacy rights of research participants create a privacy obligation on the part of the research client. Suppose a database marketing company is offering a mailing list compiled by screening millions of households to obtain brand usage information. The information would be extremely valuable to your firm, but you suspect those individuals who filled out the information forms were misled into thinking they were participating in a survey. Would it be ethical to purchase the mailing list? If respondents have been deceived about the purpose of a survey and their names subsequently are sold as part of a user mailing list, this practice is certainly unethical. The client and the research supplier have the obligation to maintain respondents' privacy.

Privacy on the Internet

Privacy on the Internet is a controversial issue. A number of groups question whether website questionnaires, registration forms, and other means of collecting personal information will be kept confidential. Many marketers argue that their organizations don't need to know who the user is because the individual's name is not important for their purposes. However, they do want to know certain information (such as demographic characteristics or product usage) associated with an anonymous profile. For instance, a web advertiser could reach a targeted audience without having access to identifying information. Of course, unethical companies may violate anonymity guidelines. Research shows that consumers are sensitive to confidentiality notices before providing information via a website. Over 80 percent of consumers report looking for specific privacy notices before they will exchange information electronically. In addition, over half believe that companies do not do enough to ensure the privacy of personal information.[15] Thus, research users should not disclose private information without permission from the consumers who provided that information.

A Final Note on Ethics

Certainly, there are researchers who would twist results for a client or who would fabricate results for personal gain. However, these are not professionals. When one is professional, one realizes that one's actions not only have implications for oneself but also for one's field. Indeed, just a few unscrupulous researchers can give the field a bad name. Thus, researchers should maintain the highest integrity in their work to protect our industry. Research participants should also play their role, or else the data they provide will not lead to better products for all consumers. Finally, the research users must also follow good professional ethics in their treatment of researchers and research results. When all three parties participate with integrity, consumers in general, and society overall, gain the most benefit from professional marketing research.

Summary

1. Identify when research should be conducted externally and when it should be done internally. The company that needs the research is not always the best company to actually perform the research. Sometimes it is better to use an outside supplier of some form. An outside agency is better when a fresh perspective is needed, when it would be difficult for inside researchers to be objective, and when the outside firm has some special expertise. In contrast, it is better to do the research in-house when it needs to be done very quickly, when the project requires close collaboration of many employees within the company, when the budget for the project is limited, and when secrecy is a major concern. The decision to go outside or stay inside for research depends on these particular issues.

2. Discuss the types of jobs, job responsibilities, and career paths available within the marketing research industry. A marketing research function may be organized in any number of ways depending on a firm's size, business, and stage of research sophistication. Marketing research managers must remember they are managers, not just researchers.

Marketing research offers many career opportunities. Entry-level jobs may involve simple tasks such as data entry or performing survey research. A research analyst may be the next step on the career path. This position may involve project design, preparation of proposals, data analysis, and interpretation. Whereas there are several intermediate positions that differ depending on whether one works for a small or large firm, the director of marketing research is the chief information officer in charge of marketing information systems and research projects. The director plans, executes, and controls the marketing research function.

3. Define ethics and understand how it applies to marketing research. Marketing ethics is the application of morals to behavior related to the exchange environment. Generally, good ethics conforms to the notion of "right" and a lack of ethics conforms to the notion of "wrong." Those involved in marketing research face numerous ethical dilemmas. Researchers serve clients or, put another way, the doers of research serve the users. It is often easy for a doer to compromise professional standards in an effort to please the user. After all, the user pays the bills. Given the large number of ethical dilemmas involved in research, ethics is highly applicable to marketing research.

4. Explain and appreciate the rights and obligations of a) research respondents—particularly children, b) marketing researchers, and c) research clients or sponsors. Each party involved in research has certain rights and obligations. These are generally interdependent in the sense that one party's right often leads to an obligation for another party. While the rights and obligations of all three parties are important, the obligation of the researcher to protect research participants is particularly important. Experimental manipulations can sometimes expose subjects to some form of harm or involve them in a ruse. The researcher must be willing to fully inform the subjects of the true purpose of the research during a debriefing. The researcher must also avoid subjecting participants to undue physical or psychological trauma. In addition, it should be reasonably easy to return an experimental subject to his or her original, pre-experiment condition.

5. Avoid a conflict of interest in performing marketing research. A conflict of interest occurs when a researcher is faced with doing something to benefit one client at the expense of another client. One good way to avoid a conflict of interest is to avoid getting involved with multiple projects involving competing firms.

Key Terms and Concepts

Outside agency
In-house research
Director of marketing research
Research analyst
Research assistants
Manager of decision support systems
Forecast analyst
Cross-functional teams
Research suppliers

Syndicated service
Standardized research service
Custom research
Marketing ethics
Moral standards
Ethical dilemma
Relativism
Idealism
Informed consent

Confidentiality
Do Not Call legislation
Spyware
Mystery shoppers
Human subjects review committee
Conflict of interest
Advocacy research

Questions for Review and Critical Thinking

1. What are the conditions that make in-house research preferable? What are the conditions that make outside research preferable?
2. Read a recent news article from *The Wall Street Journal* or other key source that deals with a new-product introduction. Would you think it would be better for that firm to do research in-house or to use an outside agency? Explain.
3. What might the organizational structure of the research department be like for the following organizations?
   a. A large advertising agency
   b. A founder-owned company that operates a 20-unit restaurant chain
   c. Your university
   d. An industrial marketer with four product divisions
   e. A large consumer products company
4. **ETHICS** What are marketing ethics? How are marketing ethics relevant to research?
5. **ETHICS** What is the difference between ethical relativism and ethical idealism? How might a person with an idealist ethical philosophy and a person with a relativist ethical philosophy differ with respect to including a sales pitch at the end of a research survey?
6. **ETHICS** What obligations does a researcher have with respect to confidentiality?
7. How should a marketing researcher help top management better understand the functions and limitations of research?
8. **ETHICS** List at least one research obligation for researcher participants (respondents), marketing researchers, and research clients (sponsors)?
9. **ETHICS** What is a conflict of interest in a research context? How can such conflicts of interest be avoided?
10. **ETHICS** What key questions help resolve the question of whether or not research participants serving as subjects in an experiment are treated ethically?
11. Identify a research supplier in your area and determine what syndicated services and other functions are available to clients.
12. **'NET** Use the Internet to find at least five marketing research firms that perform survey research. List and describe each firm briefly.
13. What actions might the marketing research industry take to convince the public that marketing research is a legitimate activity and that firms that misrepresent their intentions and distort findings to achieve their aims are not true marketing research companies?
14. **ETHICS** Comment on the ethics of the following situations:
   a. A food warehouse club advertises "savings up to 30 percent" after a survey showed a range of savings from 2 to 30 percent below average prices for selected items.
   b. A radio station broadcasts the following message during a syndicated rating service's rating period: "Please fill out your diary (which lists what media the consumer has been watching or listening to)."
   c. A sewing machine retailer advertises a market test and indicates that the regular price will be cut to one-half for three days only.
   d. A researcher tells a potential respondent that an interview will last ten minutes rather than the thirty minutes he or she actually anticipates.
   e. A respondent tells an interviewer that she wishes to cooperate with the survey, but her time is valuable and, therefore, she expects to be paid for the interview.
   f. When you visit your favorite sports team's home page on the web, you are asked to fill out a registration questionnaire before you enter the site. The team then sells your information (team allegiance, age, address, and so on) to a company that markets sports memorabilia via catalogs and direct mail.
15. **ETHICS** Comment on the following interview:

Interviewer:	*Good afternoon, sir. My name is Mrs. Johnson, and I am with Counseling Services. We are conducting a survey concerning Memorial Park. Do you own a funeral plot? Please answer yes or no.*
Respondent:	*(pauses)*
Interviewer:	*You do not own a funeral plot, do you?*
Respondent:	*No.*
Interviewer:	*Would you mind if I sent you a letter concerning Memorial Park? Please answer yes or no.*
Respondent:	*No.*
Interviewer:	*Would you please give me your address?*

16. **ETHICS** Try to participate in a survey at a survey website such as http://www.mysurvey.com or http://www.themsrgroup.com. Write a short essay response about your experience with particular attention paid to how the sites have protections in place to prevent children from providing personal information.

Research Activities

1. Find the mission statement of Burke, Inc. (http://www.burke.com). What career opportunities exist at Burke? Would you consider it a small, mid-sized, or large firm?
2. **'NET – ETHICS** One purpose of the United Kingdom's Market Research Society is to set and enforce the ethical standards to be observed by research practitioners. Go to its website at http://www.marketresearch.org.uk. Click on its code of conduct and evaluate it in light of the AMA's code.

Case 4.1 Global Eating

Barton Boomer, director of marketing research for a large research firm, has a bachelor's degree in marketing from Michigan State University. He joined the firm nine years ago after a one-year stint as a marketing research trainee at the corporate headquarters of a western packing cor-poration. Barton has a wife and two children. He earns $60,000 a year and owns a home in the suburbs. He is typical of a marketing research analyst. He is asked to interview an executive with a local restaurant chain, Eats-R-Wee. Eats-R-Wee is expanding internation-ally. The two logical choices for expansion are either to expand first to other nations that have values similar to those in the market area of Eats-R-Wee or to expand to the nearest geographical neighbor. During the initial interviews, Mr. Big, Vice President of Operations for Eats-R-Wee, makes several points to Barton.

- "Barton, we are all set to move across the border to Ontario and begin our international expansion with our neighbor to the north, Canada. Can you provide some research that will support this position?"
- "Barton, we are in a hurry. We can't sit on our hands for weeks waiting to make this decision. We need a comprehensive research project completed by the end of the month."
- "We are interested in how our competitors will react. Have you ever done research for them?
- "Don't worry about the fee; we'll pay you top money for a 'good' report."

Marla Madam, Barton's Director of Marketing Research, encourages Barton to get back in touch with Mr. Big and tell him that the project will get underway right away.

Question

Critique this situation with respect to Barton's job. What recommen-dations would you have for him? Should the company get involved with the research? Explain your answers.

Case 4.2 Big Brother Is Watching?

Technology is making our behavior more and more difficult to keep secret. Right at this very moment, there is probably some way that your location can be tracked in a way that researchers could use the information. Do you have your mobile phone with you? Is there an RFID tag in your shirt, your backpack, or some other personal item? Are you in your car, and does it have a GPS (Global Positioning Satellite) device? All of these are ways that your location and movements might be tracked.

For instance, rental cars can be tracked using GPS. Suppose a research firm contracts with an insurance firm to study the way people drive when using a rental car. A customer's every movement is then tracked. So, if the customer stops at a fast-food restaurant, the researcher knows. If the customer goes to the movie when he or she should be on a sales call, the researcher knows. If the customer is speeding, the researcher knows.

Clearly, modern technology is making confidentiality more and more difficult to maintain. While legitimate uses of this type of tech-nology may assist in easing traffic patterns and providing better loca-tions for service stations, shopping developments, and other retailers, at what point does the collection of such information become a concern? When would you become concerned about having your whereabouts constantly tracked?

Question

Suppose a GIS research firm is approached by the state legislature and asked to provide data about vehicle movement within the state for all cars with a satellite tracking mechanism. Based on the move-ment of the cars over a certain time, the police can decide when a car was speeding. They intend on using this data to send speeding tickets to those who moved too far, too fast. If you are the research firm, would you supply the data? Discuss the ethical implications of the decision.

Part 2
Designing
Research Studies

©STOCKBYTE PLATINUM/GETTY IMAGES

CHAPTER 5
QUALITATIVE AND EXPLORATORY RESEARCH TOOLS

After studying this chapter, you should be able to

1. Understand the differences between qualitative research and quantitative research
2. Understand the role of qualitative research in exploratory research designs
3. Describe the four basic categories of exploratory research
4. Prepare a focus group interview outline
5. Recognize technological advances in the application of qualitative research approaches
6. Recognize common qualitative research tools and know the advantages and limitations of their use
7. Know the risks associated with acting on only exploratory results

Chapter Vignette: What's in the Van?

Is this shoe too cool? That was really the question asked by VF Corporation when they acquired Vans, the company that makes the shoe shown here.[1] Vans traditionally are synonymous with skateboarding and skateboard culture. Readers that are unfamiliar with skateboarding may well have never heard of the company. However, a reader that is part of the skateboard culture is probably looking down at his or her Vans right now!

Former Vans CEO Gary Schoenfield points out that a decade before the acquisition (a $396 million deal), Vans was practically a dead brand.[2] However, the last ten years has seen a revival in skateboard interest and Vans has remained the number one skateboard shoe provider. Now, the incoming management team has been given the task of deciding how to raise Vans sales to $500 million per year.

Where will the growth come from? Should the company define itself as a "skateboard footwear" company, a "lifestyle" company, or as the icon for the skate culture? Answering this question will require a deeper interpretation of the meaning of the "Van."

Skateboarding is a dynamic activity. A study by Board-Trac suggests that today over one in four skateboarders is female, as opposed to fewer than one in ten as recently as 2000.[3] So, what exactly is in the mind and heart of a "boarder"? Two important research questions involve "What is the meaning of a pair of Vans?" and "What things define the skateboarding experience?"

Questions like these call for qualitative research methods.[4] Not just any researcher is "fit" for this job. One way to collect this data is to hire young, energetic research employees to become "boarders" and immerse themselves into the culture.

They may have to "Kasper" like a "flatland techer" while probing for meaning among the discussion and activities of the other boarders. Here, Vans may find that their brand helps identify a boarder and make them feel unique in some ways. If so, Vans may want to investigate increasing their product line beyond shoes and simple apparel.

Depth interviews of Vans wearers in which people describe in detail why they wear Vans will also be useful. Vans shouldn't be surprised if they find a significant portion of their shoes are

©SUSAN VAN ETTEN

sold to people like Mr. Samuel Teel, a retired attorney from Toledo, Ohio. Sam is completely unaware of the connection between Vans and skateboarding. He likes them because he doesn't have to bend to tie his shoes! Maybe there are some secondary segments that could bring growth to Vans. But marketing to them could complicate things—who knows?

What Is Qualitative Research?

Describing a Qualitative Approach

Chemists sometimes use the term *qualitative analysis* to mean research that determines what some compound is made of. In other words, the focus is on the inner meaning of the chemical—its *qualities*. As the word implies, qualitative research is interested more in *qualities* than quantities. Therefore, qualitative research is not about applying specific numbers to measure variables or using statistical procedures to numerically specify a relationship's strength.

Qualitative marketing research is research that addresses marketing objectives through techniques that allow the researcher to provide elaborate interpretations of market phenomena without depending on numerical measurement. Its focus is on discovering true inner meanings and new insights. Qualitative research is very widely applied in practice. There are many research firms that specialize in qualitative research.

Qualitative research is less structured than most quantitative approaches. It does not rely on self-response questionnaires containing structured response formats. Instead, it is more **researcher-dependent** in that the researcher must extract meaning from unstructured responses, such as text from a recorded interview or a collage representing the meaning of some experience, such as skateboarding. The researcher interprets the data to extract its meaning and converts it to information.

◼ USING A QUALITATIVE APPROACH

Mechanics can't use a hammer to fix everything that is broken. Instead, the mechanic has a toolbox from which a tool is matched to a problem. Marketing research is the same. The researcher has many tools available and the research design should try to match the best tool to the research objective. Also, just as a mechanic is probably not an expert with every tool, each researcher usually has special expertise with a small number of tools. Not every researcher has expertise with tools that would comprise qualitative research.

Generally, the less specific the research objective, the more likely that qualitative research tools will be appropriate. Also, when the emphasis is on a deeper understanding of motivations or on developing novel concepts, qualitative research is very appropriate. The following list represents common situations that often call for qualitative research:[5]

1. When it is difficult to develop specific and actionable decision statements or research objectives. For instance, if after several interviews with the research client the researcher still can't determine what needs to be measured, then qualitative research approaches may help with problem definition. Perhaps several previous studies of the same topic have not proven particularly useful.
2. When the research objective is to learn how consumers use a product in its natural setting or to learn how to express some concept in colloquial terms. A survey can probably ask many useful questions, but watching how someone actually experiences a product will usually be more insightful. Qualitative research produces many product improvement ideas.
3. When a fresh approach to studying some problem is needed. This is particularly the case when quantitative research has been less than satisfying. Qualitative tools can yield unique insights, many of which may lead to new product ideas.

Each situation also describes a situation that may require an exploratory orientation. In Chapter 3, we defined exploratory research as appropriate in ambiguous situations or when new insight is needed. We also indicated that exploratory research approaches are sometimes needed just to reach the appropriate decision statement and research objectives. While equating qualitative research

Qualitative marketing research
Research that addresses marketing objectives through techniques that allow the researcher to provide elaborate interpretations of market phenomena without depending on numerical measurement; its focus is on discovering true inner meanings and new insights.

Researcher-dependent
Research in which the researcher must extract meaning from unstructured responses such as text from a recorded interview or a collage representing the meaning of some experience.

with exploratory research is an oversimplification, the application of qualitative tools can help clear up ambiguity and provide innovative ideas.

Qualitative "versus" Quantitative Approaches

Quantitative marketing research can be defined as marketing research that addresses research objectives through empirical assessments that involve numerical measurement and analysis approaches. Qualitative research is more apt to stand on its own in the sense that it requires less interpretation. For example, quantitative research is quite appropriate when a research objective involves a managerial action standard. For example, a salad dressing company considered changing its recipe.[6] The new recipe was tested with a sample of consumers. Each consumer rated the product using numeric scales. Management established a rule that a majority of consumers rating the new product higher than the old product would have to be established with 90 percent confidence before replacing the old formula. A project like this can involve both quantitative measurement in the form of numeric rating scales and quantitative analysis in the form of applied statistical procedures.

Exhibit 5.1 illustrates some differences between qualitative and quantitative research. Certainly, these are generalities and exceptions may apply. However, it covers some of the key distinctions.

Quantitative researchers direct a considerable amount of activity toward measuring concepts with scales that either directly or indirectly provide numeric values. The numeric values can then be used in statistical computations and hypothesis testing. As will be described in detail later, this process involves comparing numbers in some way. In contrast, qualitative researchers are more interested in observing, listening, and interpreting. As such, the researcher is intimately involved in the research process and in constructing the results. For these reasons, qualitative research is said to

Quantitative marketing research
Marketing research that addresses research objectives through empirical assessments that involve numerical measurement and analysis.

EXHIBIT 5.1

Comparing Qualitative and Quantitative Research

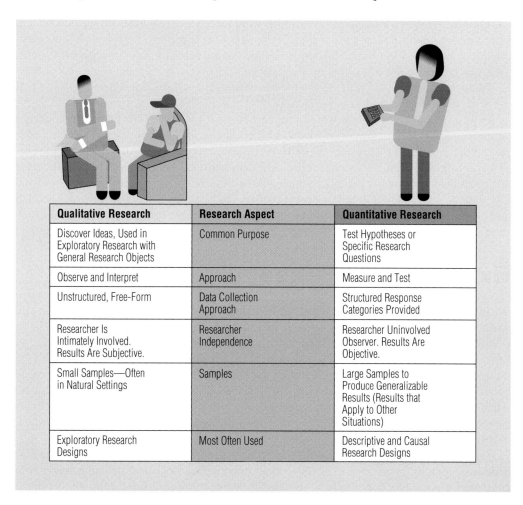

Qualitative Research	Research Aspect	Quantitative Research
Discover Ideas, Used in Exploratory Research with General Research Objects	Common Purpose	Test Hypotheses or Specific Research Questions
Observe and Interpret	Approach	Measure and Test
Unstructured, Free-Form	Data Collection Approach	Structured Response Categories Provided
Researcher Is Intimately Involved. Results Are Subjective.	Researcher Independence	Researcher Uninvolved Observer. Results Are Objective.
Small Samples—Often in Natural Settings	Samples	Large Samples to Produce Generalizable Results (Results that Apply to Other Situations)
Exploratory Research Designs	Most Often Used	Descriptive and Causal Research Designs

RESEARCHSNAPSHOT

Surprises at P&G!

With literally thousands of products to manage, Procter & Gamble (P&G) finds itself having to conduct qualitative research almost daily. P&G doesn't introduce a product that hasn't been reviewed from nearly every possible angle. Likewise, before taking a product to a new country, P&G has probably combined qualitative research techniques to discover potential problems or opportunities for marketing the product. So we can be sure that a product modification like Tide Kick or a laundry detergent made just for the French market, Le Croix Plus, has been "focus grouped."

At times, P&G seeks outside help for its research. Such was the case when P&G wanted a study of its marketing problems. The researchers selected began by applying qualitative research techniques including depth interviews, observational techniques (shadowing), and focus groups on P&G managers and marketing employees. These interviews gave the researchers the idea that perhaps P&G was suffering more from a management problem than from a marketing problem. It helped form a general research question that asked whether any marketing problems were really due to low morale among the marketing employees. After a lot of qualitative interviews with dozens and dozens of P&G employees, a quantitative study followed up these findings and supported this idea and led to suggestions for improving marketing morale!

Sources: Nelson, Emily (2002), "Focus Groupies: P&G Keeps Cincinnati Busy with All Its Studies," The Wall Street Journal—Eastern Edition, 239 (1/24), A1; Stengel, J.R., A.L. Dixon, and C.T. Allen (2003), "Listening Begins at Home," Harvard Business Review (November), 106–116.

Subjective
Results are researcher-dependent, meaning different researchers may reach different conclusions based on the same interview.

be more **subjective**, meaning that the results are researcher-dependent. Different researchers may reach different conclusions based on the same interview. In contrast, when a survey respondent provides a commitment score on a quantitative scale, it is thought to be more objective because the number will be the same no matter what researcher is involved in the analysis.

Qualitative research seldom involves samples with hundreds of respondents. Instead, a handful of consumers are usually the source of qualitative data. This is perfectly acceptable in discovery-oriented research. All ideas would still have to be tested before being adopted. Does a smaller sample mean that qualitative research is cheaper than qualitative? Perhaps not. Although fewer respondents have to be interviewed, the greater researcher involvement in both the data collection and analysis can drive up the costs of qualitative research.

Given the close relationship between qualitative research and exploratory designs, it should not be surprising that qualitative research is most often used in exploratory designs. Small samples, interpretive procedures that require subjective judgments, and the unstructured interview format all make traditional hypothesis testing difficult with qualitative research. Thus, these procedures are not best suited for drawing definitive conclusions such as results from causal designs involving experiments. These disadvantages for drawing inferences, however, become advantages when the goal is to draw out potential explanations because the researcher spends more time with each respondent and is able to explore much more ground due to the flexibility of the procedures.

Exploratory Research

When researchers have limited experience or knowledge about a research issue, exploratory research is a useful step. Exploratory research, which often involves qualitative methods, can be an essential first step to a more rigorous, conclusive, confirmatory study by reducing the chance of beginning with an inadequate, incorrect, or misleading set of research objectives.

Qualitative data
Data that are not characterized by numbers, and instead are textual, visual, or oral; focus is on stories, visual portrayals, meaningful characterizations, interpretations, and other expressive descriptions.

Quantitative data
Represent phenomena by assigning numbers in an ordered and meaningful way.

Most exploratory research designs produce **qualitative data**. These data are not characterized by numbers and instead are textual, visual, or oral. The focus of qualitative research is not on numbers but on stories, visual portrayals, meaningful characterizations, interpretations, and other expressive descriptions. Exploratory designs do not usually produce **quantitative data**, which represent phenomena by assigning numbers in an ordered and meaningful way.

For example, a quantitative researcher may search for numbers that indicate economic trends. This may lead to hypothesis tests concerning how much the economy influences movie consumption. An exploratory researcher is more likely to adopt a qualitative approach that might involve trying to develop a deeper understanding of how families are impacted by changing economic times and why people suffering economically spend scarce resources on movie consumption. This may lead to the development of a hypothesis, but would not test one.

Some types of qualitative studies can be conducted very quickly. Others take a very long time. For example, a single focus group analysis involving a large bottling company's sales force can likely be conducted and interpreted in a matter of days. This would provide faster results than most descriptive or causal designs. However, other types of qualitative research, such as a participant-observer study aimed at understanding skateboarding, could take months to complete. A qualitative approach can but does not necessarily save time.

Why Conduct Exploratory Research?

The purpose of exploratory research is intertwined with the need for a clear and precise statement of the recognized problem. Researchers conduct exploratory research for two interrelated purposes: (1) idea generation and (2) concept testing.

IDEA GENERATION

Exploratory research plays a big role in new product development, including developing and screening new product ideas. Exploratory research is particularly useful in idea generation and screening by producing multiple ideas and then narrowing the choices down to a small number of alternatives. In this process, exploratory research may indicate that some new product ideas are unworkable.

Qualitative research can generate ideas for new products, advertising copy, promotional ideas, and product improvements in numerous ways. Researchers using qualitative approaches can ask consumers to describe their product experiences in great detail. This data can reveal the consumer needs that a product can truly address. For example, a consumer may be asked to describe their dog food experiences. When a customer is asked what he or she wants in a dog food, the reply likely will be "Something that is good for the dog." Once the consumer is encouraged to continue, however, we may learn that the dog food "smells bad in the refrigerator" and "is messy to clean up." Thus, the interview reveals needs related to dog food that are not entirely centered on the dog.

Technology can also assist in this effort. For example, automobile marketers have consumers design their dream cars using computerized design systems similar to those used by automotive designers. This exploratory research might generate ideas that would never have occurred to the firm's own designers.[7]

CONCEPT TESTING

Research's main role in idea screening is concept testing. **Concept testing** is a frequently performed type of exploratory research representing many similar research procedures all having the same purpose: to screen new, revised, or repositioned ideas. Although the term *testing* is used, concept testing approaches are largely qualitative. Typically, respondents are presented with a written statement, pictorial representation, or some other idea description form and asked for comments. The questions almost always include whether the idea is likeable, whether it would be useful, and whether it seems new. Respondents are provided an opportunity to elaborate on the idea orally, in writing, or through some visual communication. Concept testing allows an initial evaluation prior to the commitment of any additional research and development, manufacturing, or other company resources. Perhaps just as importantly, the qualitative analysis of respondent comments provides themes that can be used to improve the product.

Concept testing processes work best when they not only identify ideas with the most potential, but they also lead to important refinements. Beiersdorf, the German company that produces Nivea skin care products (http://www.beiersdorf.com, http://www.nivea.com), like all consumer product firms, is constantly developing and screening new product ideas. One idea included a blemish-hiding skin crème that worked by reflecting light from the blemish, causing it to "disappear." During concept testing, most consumers were interested but asked questions about its moisturizing abilities. As a result, the product was introduced by emphasizing both its ability to hide blemishes and to moisturize the skin.[8]

TOTHEPOINT

The cure for boredom is curiosity. There is no cure for curiosity.

—Dorothy Parker

Concept testing
A frequently performed type of exploratory research representing many similar research procedures all having the same purpose: to screen new, revised, or repositioned ideas.

Likewise, if Vans introduces snowboarding and biking products as a way of increasing sales revenues, those products will have to undergo concept screening. Will consumers respond favorably to the ideas of a Vans Cushioned Snowboard or Vans Biking Shoes? What does the Vans idea mean to snowboarders or bikers? Clearly, concept testing including probing interview techniques will be helpful in this effort.

Categories of Exploratory Research

There are many techniques for investigating undefined research problems. Several of the most popular qualitative techniques are discussed in the next section. However, the purpose, rather than the technique, determines whether a study is exploratory, descriptive, or causal. For example, telephone surveys (discussed in Chapter 6) are sometimes used for exploratory purposes, although they are used mainly for descriptive research. The versatile qualitative techniques discussed in this chapter tend to be used primarily, but not exclusively, for exploratory purposes.

A manager may choose from four general categories of exploratory research methods: (1) experience surveys, (2) secondary data analysis, (3) case studies, and (4) pilot studies. Each category provides various alternative ways to gather information. Exhibit 5.2 lists characteristics of some common exploratory research techniques.

EXHIBIT 5.2 **Common Qualitative Research Tools**

Tool	Description	Key Advantages	Key Disadvantages
Focus Group Interviews	Small group discussions led by a trained moderator	• Can be done quickly • Gain multiple perspectives • Flexibility	• Results dependent on moderator • Results do not generalize to larger population • Difficult to use for sensitive topics • Expensive
Depth Interviews	One-on-one, probing interview between a trained researcher and a respondent	• Gain considerable insight from each individual • Good for understanding unusual behaviors	• Results dependent on researcher's interpretation • Results not meant to generalize • Very expensive
Word Association/ Sentence Completion	Records the first thoughts that come to a consumer in response to some stimulus	• Economical • Can be done quickly	• Lack the flexibility that is likely to produce truly creative or novel explanations
Observation	Recorded notes describing observed events	• Can be unobtrusive • Can yield actual behavior patterns	• Can be very expensive with participant-observer series
Collages	Respondent assembles pictures that represent their thoughts/feelings	• Flexible enough to allow novel insights	• Highly dependent on the researcher's interpretation of the collage
Thematic Apperception/ Cartoon Tests	Researcher provides an ambiguous picture and respondent tells about the story	• Projective, allows to get at sensitive issues • Flexible	• Highly dependent on the researcher's interpretation

Experience Surveys

If management decides that an idea is worthwhile, a decision maker may spend some time personally analyzing the situation. In attempting to gain insight into the problems at hand, researchers may discuss the concepts with top executives and knowledgeable individuals, both inside and outside the company, who have had personal experience in the field. These conversations constitute an informal **experience survey**.

People who are knowledgeable about the area to be investigated often are willing to share their experiences with others (competitors excluded, of course). For example, a firm that is ready to launch a new product may discuss the general nature of the product with some of its key retailers and wholesalers. Members of the company's sales force also may be valuable sources of information. The purpose of such discussions is to exhaust the information available from relatively inexpensive sources before gathering expensive primary data. While the interviews with knowledgeable individuals may reveal nothing conclusive, they may help define the problem more formally.

Exploratory research during situation analysis may be quite informal. Input from knowledgeable people both inside and outside the company may come merely from informal conversations. To simply get ideas about the problem, the marketing manager, rather than the research department, may conduct an experience survey. An experience survey may consist of a small number of interviews with some carefully selected people. Some formal questions may be asked, but the respondents generally will be allowed to discuss the questions with few constraints. Knowledgeable people who are articulate on a particular subject should be selected; the researcher is not trying to establish a representative probability sample. The purpose is to help formulate the problem and clarify concepts rather than to develop conclusive evidence.

Experience survey
An exploratory research technique in which individuals who are knowledgeable about a particular research problem are questioned.

TOTHEPOINT

I never predict. I just look out the window and see what is visible—but not yet seen.

—Peter Drucker

Secondary Data Analysis

Another economical and quick source of background information is trade literature. Searching through such material is exploratory research with secondary data. Basic theoretical research rarely is conducted without extensive reviews of the literature or reviews of similar research reports.

Using secondary data may be equally important in applied research. Suppose the brand manager of a company that manufactures dental hygiene products is contacted by an inventor of a tongue cleaner. The inventor states that her stainless steel device cleans the tongue deposits that cause bad breath. Shortly thereafter, the brand manager finds information in the library that explains the practice of tongue cleaning: It began centuries ago and is a common practice among certain Asian people. If the problem had concerned an existing product, the manager's situational analysis might have begun with an analysis of sales records by region and by customer or some other source of internal data.

Investigating data that have been compiled for some purpose other than the project at hand, such as accounting records or trade association data, is one of the most frequent forms of exploratory research. Because this is also a technique for conclusive research (both descriptive and causal research), a separate chapter is devoted to the investigation of secondary sources.

Case Studies

Case studies simply refer to the documented history of a particular person, group, organization, or event. Typically, a case study may describe consumers' acceptance or rejection of a particular product. Alternatively, case studies may describe the events of a specific company introducing a new product or dealing with some management crisis. Textbook cases typify this kind of case study. Clinical interviews of individual consumers can represent a case study. These may focus on their experiences with certain brands or products.

Case studies are commonly applied in business. For instance, case studies of brands that sell "luxury" products helped provide insight into what makes up a prestigious brand. A marketing researcher carefully conducted case studies (no pun intended) of higher end wine labels (such as Penfold's Grange) including the methods of production and marketing. This analysis suggested that a key ingredient to a prestige brand may well be authenticity. When consumers know something is authentic, they attach more esteem to that product or brand.[9]

Case studies
The documented history of a particular person, group, organization, or event.

RESEARCHSNAPSHOT

It's Like Riding a Bike!

Schwinn has long relied on observational research in their exploratory research studies. Here is a description of a case study documented from observational techniques:

We had a very successful dealer on the West Coast. So it occurred to me that we'd go out and find out how he's doing it. So we go out. The guy's got a nice store out in Van Nuys. We sit in the back room and we listen. The first customers come in, a man and a woman with a boy about nine or ten years old. The dad says, "Which one is it?" The son says, "This one over here." Dad looks at it. He says to the clerk, "How much is it?" The clerk says, "$179.95." The father says, "Okay, we'll take it." It blew the whole bit [there were no magic sales approaches]. Suddenly it dawned on us that it's not what they say, it's the atmosphere of the store. Here was not Joe's old, dirty bike shop — it was a beautiful store on the main street. A big sign was in front, "Valley Cyclery," inside [were] fluorescent lights, carpeting on the floor, stereo music, air-conditioning, and a beautiful display of bicycles. It was like a magnet. People came in. So, we've tried to introduce that idea to other dealers. Put a bigger investment into your store and see what happens. Some of them did, and it happened [sales improved].

More recently, researchers documented with photographs the way that most people use their bicycles. Although the vast majority of bikes available for sale are multispeed racing or mountain bikes, even a cursory observation of the photos suggested that most people clearly do not race on their bikes nor use them off-road. As a result, Schwinn reintroduced the Cruiser with much success. The Cruiser is the 1950ish touring bike with the big cushioned seat and fenders. Observation is like riding a bike — once you learn, you shouldn't ever forget!

Sources: Burch, Ray (1973), "Marketing Research: Why It Works, Why It Doesn't Work," speech to the Chicago Chapter of the American Marketing Association, 1973, reprinted with permission of the Chicago Chapter of the American Marketing Association; Curry, A. and M. Silver (2004), "One Speed Is Enough," U.S. News and World Report, 136 (May 10), 67–68.

©ROYALTY-FREE/CORBIS

Qualitative research reveals that products that are perceived as "authentic" offer more value for consumers.

©PHOTO CUISINE/CORBIS

Case studies often overlap with one of the other categories of qualitative research. The Research Snapshot box above illustrates how observation was useful in discovering insights leading to important marketing changes.

A primary advantage of the case study is that an entire organization or entity can be investigated in depth with meticulous attention to detail. This highly focused attention enables the researcher to carefully study the order of events as they occur or to concentrate on identifying the relationships among functions, individuals, or entities. Conducting a case study often requires the cooperation of the party whose history is being studied. This freedom to search for whatever data an investigator deems important makes the success of any case study highly dependent on the alertness, creativity, intelligence, and motivation of the individual performing the case analysis.

Pilot Studies

The term *pilot study* covers a number of diverse research techniques. Within the context of exploratory research, the term indicates that some aspect of the research (e.g., fieldwork) will be on a small scale. Thus, a **pilot study** is a research project that involves sampling but relaxes the rigorous standards used to obtain precise quantitative estimates from large representative samples.

In one kind of pilot study, researchers or managers try to experience what consumers experience to gain inexpensive and valuable insights. Without indicating their real positions with the company, researchers or managers may wait on customers, ride in repair trucks, and answer telephones. For example, the chairperson of Avis occasionally gets in line with airport customers waiting for cars or works behind the counter to get customer reactions. This form of pilot study may yield true comprehension of the situation to be investigated.

A pilot study generates primary data, but usually for qualitative analysis. This characteristic distinguishes pilot studies from research that gathers background information using secondary data. Some researchers refer to pilot studies that generate qualitative information as *qualitative research*. The primary data usually come from consumers or other subjects of ultimate concern rather than from knowledgeable experts or case situations. This distinguishes pilot studies from experience surveys and case studies. Major categories of pilot studies include focus group interviews, depth interviews, and projective techniques.

Pilot study
A collective term for any small-scale exploratory research project that uses sampling but does not apply rigorous standards.

FOCUS GROUP INTERVIEWS

The focus group interview is so widely used that many advertising and research agencies do nothing but focus group interviews. In that sense, it is wrongly synonymous with qualitative research. A **focus group interview** is an unstructured, free-flowing interview with a small group of people, usually between six and ten. Focus groups are led by a trained moderator who follows a flexible format encouraging dialogue among respondents. Common focus group topics include employee programs, brand meanings, problems with products, advertising themes, or new-product concepts.

The group meets at a central location at a designated time. Participants may range from consumers talking about hair coloring, petroleum engineers talking about problems in the "oil patch," children talking about toys, or employees talking about their jobs. A moderator begins by providing some opening statement to broadly steer discussion in the intended direction. Ideally, discussion topics emerge at the group's initiative, not the moderator's. Moderators should avoid direct questioning unless absolutely necessary.

Focus group interview
An unstructured, free-flowing interview with a small group of around six to ten people. Focus groups are led by a trained moderator who follows a flexible format encouraging dialogue among respondents.

Advantages of Focus Group Interviews

Focus groups allow people to discuss their true feelings, anxieties, and frustrations, as well as the depth of their convictions, in their own words. While other approaches may also do much the same, focus groups offer several advantages:

1. Relatively fast
2. Easy to execute
3. Allow respondents to piggyback off each other's ideas
4. Provide multiple perspectives
5. Flexibility to allow more detailed descriptions
6. High degree of scrutiny

Speed and Ease

In an emergency situation, three or four group sessions can be conducted, analyzed, and reported in a week or so. The large number of research firms that conduct focus group interviews makes it easy to find someone to conduct the research. Practically every state in the United States contains multiple research firms that have their own focus group facilities. Companies with large research departments likely have at least one qualified focus group moderator so that they need not outsource the focus group.

Piggybacking and Multiple Perspectives

Furthermore, the group approach may produce thoughts that would

Focus group facilities typically include a comfortable room for respondents, recording equipment, and a viewing room via a two-way mirror.

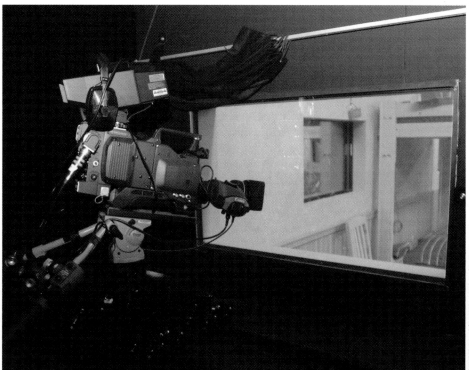

©CHRIS DAVIS/GAMMA-LIAISON/GETTY IMAGES

not be produced otherwise. The interplay between respondents allows them to `piggyback` off of each other's ideas. In other words, one respondent stimulates thought among the others and, as this process continues, increasingly creative insights are possible. A comment by one individual often triggers a chain of responses from the other participants. The social nature of the focus group also helps bring out multiple views as each person shares a particular perspective.

Flexibility

The flexibility of focus group interviews is advantageous, especially when compared with the more structured and rigid survey format. Numerous topics can be discussed and many insights can be gained, particularly with regard to the variations in consumer behavior in different situations. Responses that would be unlikely to emerge in a survey often come out in group interviews: "*If* it is one of the three brands I sometimes use and *if* it is on sale, I buy it; otherwise, I buy my regular brand" or "*If* the day is hot and I have to serve the whole neighborhood, I make Kool-Aid; otherwise, I give them Dr Pepper or Coke."

If a researcher is investigating a target group to determine who consumes a particular beverage or why a consumer purchases a certain brand, situational factors must be included in any interpretations of respondent comments. For instance, in the situation above, the fact that a particular beverage is consumed must be noted. It would be inappropriate to say that Kool-Aid is preferred in general. The proper interpretation is situation-specific. On a hot day the whole neighborhood gets Kool-Aid. When the weather isn't hot, the kids may get nothing, or if only a few kids are around, they may get lucky and get Dr Pepper. Thus, Kool-Aid can be interpreted as appropriate for satisfying large numbers of hot kids while Dr Pepper is a treat for a select few.

Scrutiny

A focus group interview allows closer scrutiny in several ways. First, the session can be observed by several people, as it is usually conducted in a room containing a two-way mirror. The respondents and moderator are on one side, and an invited audience that may include both researchers and decision makers is on the other. If the decision makers are located in another city or country, the session may be shown via a live video hookup. Either through live video or a two-way mirror, some check on the eventual interpretations is provided through the ability to actually watch the research being conducted. Second, focus group sessions are generally recorded on audio or videotape. Later, detailed examination of the recorded session can offer additional insight and help clear up disagreements about what happened.

Group Composition

The ideal size of the focus group is six to ten people. If the group is too small, one or two members may intimidate the others. Groups that are too large may not allow for adequate participation by each group member.

Homogeneous groups seem to work best because they allow researchers to concentrate on consumers with similar lifestyles, experiences, and communication skills. The session does not become rife with too many arguments and different viewpoints stemming from diverse backgrounds. The respondents should all be members of a unique and identifiable culture. Vans may benefit from a focus group interview comprised only of skateboard enthusiasts. Perhaps participants can be recruited from a local skate park.

When the Centers for Disease Control and Prevention tested public service announcements about AIDS through focus groups, it discovered that single-race groups and racially diverse groups reacted differently. By conducting separate focus groups, the organization was able to gain important insights about which creative strategies were most appropriate for targeted versus broad audiences.

For example, a typical homogeneous group might be made up of married, full-time homemakers with children at home. The researcher may find that including first-time mothers in a group with women who have three or four children reduces the new mothers' participation. Instead of giving their opinion, they become more interested in listening to the more experienced mothers for advice. Although they may differ in their opinions, they defer to the more experienced mothers.

Therefore, researchers may consider interviewing first-time mothers and experienced mothers in separate groups.

Researchers who wish to collect information from different types of people should conduct several focus groups. A diverse overall sample may be obtained by using different groups even though each group is homogeneous. Although each group is homogenous, by using four groups, researchers obtain opinions from a wide degree of respondents. Similarly, a rule of thumb is that four focus group sessions, each in a different city, can satisfy exploratory research needs dealing with common consumer product or possible employee development issues.

Environmental Conditions

A focus group session may typically take place at the research agency in a room specifically designed for this purpose. Research suppliers that specialize in conducting focus groups operate from commercial facilities that have videotape cameras in observation rooms behind two-way mirrors and microphone systems connected to tape recorders and speakers to allow greater scrutiny, as discussed above. Refreshments are provided to help create a more relaxed atmosphere conducive to a free exchange of ideas. More open and intimate reports of personal experiences and sentiments can be obtained under these conditions.

The Focus Group Moderator

Exhibit 5.3 is a partial transcript of a focus group interview. Notice how the **moderator** ensures that everyone gets a chance to speak and the way he or she contributes to the discussion.

A good moderator must possess several qualities. The moderator must develop rapport with the group to promote interaction among all participants. The moderator should be someone who is really interested in people, who listens carefully to what others have to say, and who gains people's confidence and makes them feel relaxed and eager to talk.

The moderator must try not to interject his or her own opinions. Good moderators usually say less rather than more. They can stimulate productive discussion with generalized follow-ups such

Moderator
A person who leads a focus group interview and ensures that everyone gets a chance to speak and contribute to the discussion.

EXHIBIT 5.3 **What Happens in a Focus Group**

"My company is interested in finding out how people feel about different products and services," the moderator tells the semicircle of women. "In this group situation, what we're doing is exploring how you feel. Today we're interested in talking about restaurants and eating out."

The women have been told that someone "from a market research company" is listening to them, but they don't know which franchiser is the sponsor.

When the moderator displays the first card on the easel beside her, a card reading "McDonald's, Jack in the Box, Carl's Jr., Burger King, Wendy's," she asks, "What do you think of these restaurants?"

"The only one I really enjoy going to is Carl's Jr.," says Anne, a bright-faced woman in her early twenties who wears athletic shorts and flip-flops. "I don't know what Burger King does to their hamburgers, but I always get indigestion."

"You get indigestion at Burger King?" the moderator asks solicitously.

Anne nods. "It looks great when they bring it to you, but as soon as I start eating it, and especially when I finish, I get this awful feeling. . . ."

"I think it looks great on TV," says Nancy, whose hair has been frosted with two colors, for a total of three. "The lettuce is so crispy, you know—"

"Oh yeah, and it's these huge hamburgers," says Laura.

"But then you get it and it's all crushed together," Anne says ruefully.

"I think the worst is Jack in the Box," says Victoria, a very thin woman who lives in Reseda, near a block that she contends houses one of every food franchise in the world. "The meat doesn't taste like meat. It tastes . . . low-grade. Fatty. The last time I ate there—I had a coupon for it and we were close by and this friend of mine hadn't tried it—" she explains quickly, "it was terrible. I've heard that Wendy's—I haven't been there yet, but everybody who goes there thinks it's terrific."

"Really?" Nancy looks a little funny at Victoria. "Wendy's?"

"I've been there," Anne says. "It's terrible."

"Is it terrible?" Victoria asks sheepishly, retreating from the group's conclusion that she's been taking restaurant advice from a pack of cretins out there in Reseda.

"Oh, my daughter is the hamburger addict of the world, and she couldn't finish it," Nancy says. "It ran all down—it was so greasy—"

"I like Burger King," says Marlene, who has had nine children during her 25-year marriage, "and I like Carl's Jr." She smiles nicely, relishing the impending heresy: "McDonald's I could vomit from." The women laugh. "I like Jack in the Box Super Tacos."

"Charlie Hass on Advertising," New West Magazine, November 5, 1979, pp. 32–39.

as, "Tell us more about that incident" or "How are your experiences similar or different from the one you just heard?" The moderator must be particularly careful not to ask leading questions such as, "You do like cornflakes, don't you?" The moderator must also be able to control discussion without being overbearing. The moderator's role is also to focus the discussion on the areas of concern. When a topic is no longer generating fresh ideas, the effective moderator changes the flow of discussion.

Planning the Focus Group Outline

Discussion guide
A focus group outline that includes written introductory comments informing the group about the focus group purpose and rules and then outlines topics or questions to be addressed in the group session.

Focus group researchers use a discussion guide to help control the interview and guide the discussion into product areas. A **discussion guide** includes written introductory comments informing the group about the focus group purpose and rules and then outlines topics or questions to be addressed in the group session. Thus, the discussion guide serves as the focus group outline. Some discussion guides will have only a few phrases in the entire document. Others may be more detailed. The amount of content depends on the nature and experience of the researcher and the complexity of the topic. Exhibit 5.4 offers an example of a discussion guide for a focus group interview planned by a cancer center that wanted to warn the public about the effects of the sun.

EXHIBIT 5.4 Discussion Guide for a Focus Group Interview

Thank you very much for agreeing to help out with this research. We call this a focus group; let me explain how it works, and then please let me know if something isn't clear.

This is a discussion, as though you were sitting around just talking. You can disagree with each other, or just comment. We do ask that just one person talk at a time, because we tape-record the session to save me from having to take notes. Nothing you say will be associated with you or your church—this is just an easy way for us to get some people together.

The subject is health risk warnings. Some of you may remember seeing a chart in a newspaper that gives a pollen count or a pollution count. And you've heard on the radio sometimes a hurricane watch or warning. You've seen warnings on cigarette packages or cigarette advertising, even if you don't smoke. And today we're going to talk about warnings about the sun. Before we start, does anybody have a question?

1. OK, let's go around and talk about how often you spend time in the sun, and what you're likely to be doing. (FOR PARENTS): What about your kids—do you like them to be out in the sun?
2. OK, can you think of any reason that somebody would give you a warning about exposure to the sun?

(PROBE: IS ANY SUN EXPOSURE BAD, OR ONLY A CERTAIN DEGREE OF EXPOSURE, AND IF SO, WHAT IS IT? OR IS THE SUN GOOD FOR YOU?)

3. What if we had a way to measure the rays of the sun that are associated with skin problems, so that you could find out which times of the day or which days are especially dangerous? How could, say, a radio station tell you that information in a way that would be useful?
4. Now let me ask you about specific ways to measure danger. Suppose somebody said, "We monitored the sun's rays at noon, and a typical fair-skinned person with

unprotected skin will burn after 40 minutes of direct exposure." What would you think?

5. Now let me ask you about another way to say the same kind of thing. Suppose somebody said, "The sun's rays at noon today measured 10 times the 8 A.M. baseline level of danger." What would you think?
6. OK, now suppose that you heard the same degree of danger expressed this way: "The sun's rays at noon today measured 8 on a sun danger scale that ranges from 1 to 10." What would you think?
7. What if the danger scale wasn't in numbers, but words? Suppose you heard, "The sun's rays at noon showed a moderate danger reading," or "The sun's rays showed a high danger reading." What would you think?
8. And here's another possibility: What if you heard, "Here's the sun danger reading at noon today—the unprotected skin of a typical fair-skinned person will age the equivalent of 1 hour in a 10-minute period."
9. OK, what if somebody said today is a day to wear long sleeves and a hat, or today is a day you need sunscreen and long sleeves? What would you think?
10. OK, here's my last question. There are really three things you can do about sun danger: You can spend less time in the sun, you can go out at less dangerous times of day, like before 10 in the morning or after 4 in the afternoon, and you can cover your skin by wearing a hat or long sleeves, or using protective sunscreen lotion. Thinking about yourself listening to the radio, what kind of announcement would make you likely to do one or more of those things? (PARENTS: WHAT WOULD MAKE YOU BE SURE THAT YOUR CHILD WAS PROTECTED?)
11. And what would you be most likely to do to protect yourself? (YOUR CHILD?)
12. Before we break up, is there anything else you think would be useful for M. D. Anderson's people to know? Do you have any questions about any aspect of this interview?

OK, thank you very much for your help.

Betsy D. Gelb and Michael P. Eriksen, "Market Research May Help Prevent Cancer," Marketing Research, September 1991, p. 46. Published by American Marketing Association. Reprinted with permission.

In general, the following steps should be used to conduct an effective focus group discussion guide:

1. Welcome and introductions should take place first.
2. Begin the interview with a broad icebreaker that does not reveal too many specifics about the interview. Sometimes, this may even involve respondents providing some written story or their reaction to some stimulus like a photograph, film, product, or advertisement.
3. Questions become increasingly more specific as the interview proceeds. However, the moderator will notice that a good interview will cover the specific question topics before they have to be asked. This is preferable as respondents are clearly not forced to react to the specific issue. Results are much better when an issue just emerges naturally.
4. If there is a very specific objective to be accomplished, such as explaining why a respondent would either buy or not buy a product, that question should probably be saved for last.
5. A debriefing statement should provide respondents with the actual focus group objectives and answer any questions they may have. This is also a final shot to gain some insight from the group.

Focus Groups as Diagnostic Tools

Focus groups are perhaps the predominant means by which marketing researchers implement exploratory research designs. Focus groups also can be helpful in later stages of a research project, particularly when the findings from surveys or other quantitative techniques raise more questions than they answer. Managers who are puzzled about the meaning of survey research results may use focus groups to better understand what consumer surveys indicate. In such a situation, the focus group supplies diagnostic help after quantitative research has been conducted. Focus groups are also excellent diagnostic tools for spotting problems with ideas. For instance, an initial concept is presented to the group and then they are allowed to comment on it in detail. This usually leads to lengthy lists of potential product problems and some ideas for overcoming them.

Videoconferencing and Streaming Media

The videoconferencing industry has grown dramatically in recent years. As our ability to communicate via telecommunications and videoconferencing links has improved in quality, the number of companies using these systems to conduct focus groups has increased. With videoconference focus groups, marketing managers can stay home and watch on television rather than having to take a trip to a focus group facility.

Focus Vision Network of New York is a marketing research company that provides videoconferencing equipment and services. The Focus Vision system is modular, allowing for easy movement and an ability to capture each group member close up. The system operates via a remote keypad that allows observers in a far-off location to pan the focus group room or zoom in on a particular participant. Managers viewing at remote locations can even send the moderator messages during the interview. For example, while new product names were being tested in one focus group, an observant manager contacted the moderator with an idea and the moderator then asked respondents for a reaction to the new name on the spot.[10]

Streaming media consist of multimedia content such as audio or video that is made available in real time over the Internet or a corporate Intranet. This new technology for digital media delivery allows researchers to "broadcast" focus groups that can be viewed online. Offsite managers view the focus group using a media player like Microsoft Media Player. Like videoconferencing, this saves a trip to a focus group facility. Traditionally, the quality of streaming video has been far lower than videoconferencing. However, the quality difference is fast disappearing as streaming technology improves.

Interactive Media and Online Focus Groups

Internet applications of qualitative exploratory research are growing rapidly and involve both formal and informal applications. Formally, the term **online focus group** refers to a qualitative research effort in which a group of individuals provides unstructured comments by entering their

Streaming media
Consist of multimedia content such as audio or video that is made available in real time over the Internet or a corporate Intranet.

Online focus group
A qualitative research effort in which a group of individuals provides unstructured comments by entering their remarks into an electronic Internet display board of some type.

remarks into an electronic Internet display board of some type. Participants use a keyboard and mouse to make their remarks during a chat-room session or in the form of a blog. Because respondents enter their comments into the computer, transcripts of verbatim responses are available immediately after the group session. Online groups can be quick and cost-efficient. However, because there is less interaction between participants, group synergy and snowballing of ideas may be diminished.

Several companies have established a form of informal, "continuous" focus group by establishing an Internet blog for that purpose.[11] We might call this technique a **focus blog** when the intention is to mine the site for business research purposes. General Motors, American Express, and Lego all have used ideas harvested from their focus blogs. The Lego blog can be found at http://www.bricksonthebrain.com. While online focus group respondents are generally paid $100 or more to show up and participate for ninety minutes, bloggers and online focus group respondents often participate for absolutely no fee at all! Thus, technology provides some cost advantages over traditional focus group approaches.[12]

Online versus Face-to-Face Focus Group Techniques

A research company can facilitate a formal online focus group by setting up a private, electronic chat room for that purpose. Participants in formal and informal online focus groups feel that their anonymity is very secure. Often respondents will say things in this environment that they would never say otherwise. For example, a lingerie company was able to get insights into how it could design sexy products for larger women. Online, these women freely discussed what it would take "to feel better about being naked."[13] One can hardly imagine how difficult such a discussion might be face to face. Increased anonymity can be a major advantage for a company investigating sensitive or embarrassing issues.

Because participants do not have to be together in the same room at a research facility, the number of participants in online focus groups can be larger than in traditional focus groups. Twenty-five participants or more is not uncommon for the simultaneous chat-room format. Participants can be at widely separated locations, even in different time zones, because the Internet does not have geographical restrictions. Of course, a major disadvantage is that often the researcher does not exercise as much control in precisely who participates. In other words, a person could very easily not match the desired profile or even answer screening questions in a misleading way simply to participate.

A major drawback with online focus groups is that moderators cannot see body language and facial expressions (bewilderment, excitement, interest, and so forth). Thus, they cannot fully interpret how people are reacting. Also, moderators' ability to probe and ask additional questions on the spot is reduced in online focus groups. Research that requires focus group members to actually touch something (such as a new easy-opening packaging design) or taste something is not generally suitable for an online format.

Disadvantages of Focus Groups

Focus groups offer many advantages. Like practically every other research technique, the focus group has some limitations and disadvantages too. Problems with focus groups include those discussed below.

First, focus groups require objective, sensitive, and effective moderators. It is very difficult for a moderator to remain completely objective about most topics. In large research firms, the moderator may be provided only enough information to effectively conduct the interview, no more. The focus group interview shouldn't reduce to only the moderator's opinion. Also, without a good moderator, one or two participants may dominate a session, yielding results that are really the opinion of one or two people, not the group. The moderator has to try very hard to make sure that all respondents feel comfortable giving their opinions and even a timid respondent's opinion is given due consideration. While many people, even some with little or no background to do so, conduct focus groups, good moderators become effective through a combination of good people skills (which cannot be taught), training (in qualitative research), and experience.

Second, some unique sampling problems arise with focus groups. Researchers often select focus group participants because they have similar backgrounds and experiences or because screening indicates that the participants are more articulate or gregarious than the typical consumer. Such

Focus blog
A type of informal, "continuous" focus group established as an Internet blog for the purpose of collecting qualitative data from participant comments.

TOTHEPOINT

Necessity, mother of invention.

—William Wycherley

participants may not be representative of the entire target market. Thus, focus group results are not intended to be representative of a larger population.

Third, although not so much an issue with online formats where respondents can remain anonymous, traditional face-to-face focus groups may not be useful for discussing sensitive topics. A focus group is a social setting and usually involves people with little to no familiarity with each other. Therefore, issues that people normally do not like to discuss in public may also prove difficult to discuss in a focus group.

Fourth, focus groups do cost a considerable amount of money, particularly when they are not conducted by someone employed by the company desiring the focus group. As research projects go, there are many more expensive approaches, including a full-blown mail survey using a national random sample. This may costs thousands of dollars to conduct and thousands of dollars to analyze and disseminate.

DEPTH INTERVIEWS

An alternative to a focus group is a depth interview. A **depth interview** is a one-on-one interview between a professional researcher and a research respondent. Depth interviews are much the same as a psychological, clinical interview, but with a different purpose. The researcher asks many questions and follows up each answer with probes for additional elaboration. An excerpt from a depth interview is given in Exhibit 5.5.

Like focus group moderators, the interviewer's role is critical in a depth interview. He or she must be a highly skilled individual who can encourage the respondent to talk freely without influencing the direction of the conversation. Probing questions are critical.

Laddering is a term used for a particular approach to probing, asking respondents to compare differences between brands at different levels. What usually results is that the first distinctions are attribute-level distinctions, the second are benefit-level distinctions, and the third are at the value or motivation level. Laddering can then distinguish two brands of skateboarding shoes based on a) the materials they are made of, b) the comfort they provide, and c) the excitement they create.

Each depth interview may last more than an hour. Thus, it is a time-consuming process if multiple interviews are conducted. Not only does the interview have to be conducted, but each

Depth interview
A one-on-one interview between a professional researcher and a research respondent conducted about some relevant business or social topic.

Laddering
A particular approach to probing, asking respondents to compare differences between brands at different levels that produces distinctions at the attribute level, the benefit level, and the value or motivation level.

EXHIBIT 5.5 **Excerpt from a Depth Interview**

An interviewer (I) talks with Marsha (M) about furniture purchases. Marsha indirectly indicates she delegates the buying responsibility to a trusted antique dealer. She has already said that she and her husband would write the dealer telling him the piece they wanted (e.g., bureau, table). The dealer would then locate a piece that he considered appropriate and would ship it to Marsha from his shop in another state.

M: . . . We never actually shopped for furniture since we state what we want and (the antique dealer) picks it out and sends it to us. So we never have to go looking through stores and shops and things.

I: You depend on his (the antique dealer's) judgment?

M: Uh, huh. And, uh, he happens to have the sort of taste that we like and he knows what our taste is and always finds something that we're happy with.

I: You'd rather do that than do the shopping?

M: Oh, much rather, because it saves so much time and it would be so confusing for me to go through stores and stores looking for things, looking for furniture. This is so easy that I just am very fortunate.

I: Do you feel that he's a better judge than . . .

M: Much better.

I: Than you are?

M: Yes, and that way I feel confident that what I have is very, very nice because he picked it out and I would be doubtful if I picked it out. I have confidence in him, (the antique dealer) knows everything about antiques, I think. If he tells me something, why I know it's true—no matter what I think. I know he is the one that's right.

This excerpt is most revealing of the way in which Marsha could increase her feeling of confidence by relying on the judgment of another person, particularly a person she trusted. Marsha tells us quite plainly that she would be doubtful (i.e., uncertain) about her own judgment, but she "knows" (i.e., is certain) that the antique dealer is a good judge, "no matter what I think." The dealer once sent a chair that, on first inspection, did not appeal to Marsha. She decided, however, that she must be wrong, and the dealer right, and grew to like the chair very much.

From Donald F. Cox, Ed. *Risk Taking and Information Handling in Consumer Behavior* (Boston: Division of Research, Harvard Business School, © 1967), pp. 65–66. Reprinted with permission.

interview produces about the same amount of text as does a focus group interview. This has to be analyzed and interpreted by the researcher. A third major issue stems from the necessity of recording both surface reactions and subconscious motivations of the respondent. Analysis and interpretation of such data are highly subjective, and it is difficult to settle on a true interpretation.

Depth interviews provide more insight into a particular individual than do focus groups. In addition, since the setting isn't really social, respondents are more likely to discuss sensitive topics than are those in a focus group. Depth interviews are particularly advantageous when some unique or unusual behavior is being studied. For instance, depth interviews have been usefully applied to reveal characteristics of adolescent behavior, ranging from the ways they get what they want from their parents to shopping, smoking, and shoplifting.[14]

Depth interviews are similar to focus groups in many ways. The costs are similar if only one to two interviews are conducted. However, if a dozen or more interviews are included in a report, the costs are higher than focus group interviews due to the increased interviewing and analysis time.

▓ PROJECTIVE TECHNIQUES

There is an old story about asking a man why he purchased a Mercedes. When asked directly why he purchased a Mercedes, he responds that the car holds its value and does not depreciate much, that it gets better gas mileage than you'd expect, or that it has a comfortable ride. If you ask the same person why a neighbor purchased a Mercedes, he may well answer, "Oh, that status seeker!" This story illustrates that individuals may be more likely to give true answers (consciously or unconsciously) to disguised questions. Projective techniques seek to discover an individual's true attitudes, motivations, defensive reactions, and characteristic ways of responding.

The assumption underlying these methods lies in Oscar Wilde's observation: "A man is least himself when he talks in his own person; when he is given a mask he will tell the truth." In other words, advocates of projective techniques assume that when directly questioned, respondents do not express their true feelings because they are embarrassed about answers that reflect negatively on their self-concepts; they wish to please the interviewer with the "right" answer, or they cannot reveal unconscious feelings of which they are unaware. However, if respondents are presented with unstructured, ambiguous stimuli, such as cartoons or inkblots, and are allowed considerable freedom to respond, they will express their true feelings.

Projective technique
An indirect means of questioning that enables a respondent to project beliefs and feelings onto a third party or an inanimate object or into a task situation.

A **projective technique** is an indirect means of questioning that enables respondents to project beliefs and feelings onto a third party, onto an inanimate object, or into a task situation. Respondents are not required to provide answers in any structured format. They are encouraged to describe a situation in their own words with little prompting by the interviewer. Individuals are expected to interpret the situation within the context of their own experiences, attitudes, and personalities and to express opinions and emotions that may be hidden from others and possibly from themselves. The most common projective techniques in marketing research are word association tests, sentence completion methods, third-person techniques, and thematic apperception tests.

▓ FREE-ASSOCIATION/SENTENCE COMPLETION METHOD

Free-association techniques
Record respondents' first (top-of-mind) cognitive reactions to some stimulus.

Free-association techniques simply record a respondent's first cognitive reactions (top-of-mind) to some stimulus. The Rorschach or inkblot test typifies the free-association method. Respondents view an ambiguous figure and are asked to say the first thing that comes to their mind. Free-association techniques allow researchers to map a respondent's thoughts or memory.

The sentence completion method is based on free-association principles. Respondents simply are required to complete a few partial sentences with the first word or phrase that comes to mind. For example:

People who drink beer are _____.
A man who drinks a dark beer is _____.
Imported beer is most liked by _____.
The woman in the commercial _____.

RESEARCHSNAPSHOT

Let the Computer Do Your Reading!

Computerized qualitative analysis is now commonly used. Two commonly used programs are Atlas-Ti and NVivo. These can save a lot of time by helping to identify themes and connections within text. In fact, today's programs can even assist in interpreting videotapes and photographs for meaning.

Computerized analysis of depth interviews with service providers and their customers revealed interesting key themes dealing with the friendship or bond that forms between them. Some of the themes that emerged included the feeling that meetings were more like get-togethers with a friend, the feeling that the service provider wants to give something back to a client, and the belief that one can share one's true thoughts and feelings with a client. On the not-so-positive side, a theme that also emerged was that sometimes the friendships are not mutual.

Comments like, "I thought she would never leave" or "Won't he give me a break?" would be consistent with that theme.

There are many software programs that can assist with basic qualitative interpretation. Some are available as freeware. AnSWR is available from the U.S. Centers for Disease Control (http://www.cdc.gov/hiv/software/answr.htm), as is EZ-Text (http://www.cdc.gov/hiv/software/ez-text.htm). Transana will read video and audio tape data and is available from the Wisconsin Center for Education Research (http://www.transana.org). Commercial programs will normally have a student or trial version available free of charge or at reduced rates.

Source: Journal of Marketing by Bolton, Ruth N. Copyright 1999 by Am Marketing Assn. (AMA) (CHIC) in the format Textbook via Copyright Clearance Center.

©PHOTODISC/GETTY IMAGES

Answers to sentence-completion questions tend to be more extensive than responses to word-association tests. Although the responses lack the ability to probe for meaning as in other qualitative techniques, they are very effective in finding out what is on a respondent's mind. They can also do so in a quick and very cost-effective manner. Free-association and sentence-completion tasks are sometimes used in conjunction with other approaches. For instance, they can sometimes be used as effective icebreakers in focus group interviews.

Observation

Throughout this chapter, we have described how observation can be a very important qualitative tool. The participant-observer approach typifies how observation can be used to explore various issues. Meaning is extracted from field notes. **Field notes** are the researcher's descriptions of what actually happens in the field. These notes then become the text from which meaning is extracted.

Observation may also take place in visual form. Researchers may observe consumers in their home, as mentioned above, or try to gain knowledge from photographic records of one type or another. Observation can either be very inexpensive, such as when a research associate sits and simply observes behavior, or it can be very expensive, as in most participant-observer studies. Observational research is keenly advantageous for gaining insight into things that respondents cannot or will not verbalize.

Field notes
The researcher's descriptions of what actually happens in the field; these notes then become the text from which meaning is extracted.

Collages

Marketing researchers sometimes have respondents prepare a collage to represent their experience with some good, service, or brand. The collages are then analyzed for meaning much in the same manner as text dialogues are analyzed. Computer software can even be applied to help develop potential grounded theories from the visual representations.

Harley-Davidson commissioned research in which collages depicting feelings about Harley-Davidson were compared based on whether the respondent was a Harley owner or an owner of a competitor's brand. The collages of "Hog" owners revealed themes of artwork and the freedom of the great outdoors. These themes did not emerge in the non-Hog groups. This led to confirmatory research which helped Harley continue its growth, appealing more specifically to its diverse market segments.[15]

Like sentence completion and word association, collages are often used within some other approach, such as a focus group or a depth interview. Collages offer the advantage of flexibility but are also very much subject to the researcher's interpretations.

■ THEMATIC APPERCEPTION TEST (TAT)

Thematic apperception test (TAT)
A test that presents subjects with an ambiguous picture(s) in which consumers and products are the center of attention; the investigator asks the subject to tell what is happening in the picture(s) now and what might happen next.

A **thematic apperception test (TAT)** presents subjects with an ambiguous picture(s) in which consumers and products are the center of attention. The investigator asks the subject to tell what is happening in the picture(s) now and what might happen next. Hence, themes (*thematic*) are elicited on the basis of the perceptual-interpretive (*apperception*) use of the pictures. The researcher then analyzes the contents of the stories that the subjects relate.

The picture or cartoon stimulus must be sufficiently interesting to encourage discussion but ambiguous enough not to disclose the nature of the research project. Clues should not be given to the character's positive or negative predisposition. A pretest of a TAT investigating why men might purchase chainsaws used a picture of a man looking at a very large tree. The research respondents were homeowners and weekend woodcutters. They almost unanimously said that they would get professional help from a tree surgeon to deal with this situation. Thus, early in pretesting, the researchers found out that the picture was not sufficiently ambiguous. The tree was too large and did not allow respondents to identify with the tree-cutting task. If subjects are to project their own views into the situation, the environmental setting should be a well-defined, familiar problem, but the solution should be ambiguous.

Frequently, the TAT consists of a series of pictures with some continuity so that stories may be constructed in a variety of settings. The first picture might portray two people discussing a product in a supermarket; in the second picture, a person might be preparing the product in the kitchen; the final picture might show the product being served at the dinner table. A TAT might include several ambiguous pictures of a skateboarder and then show him or her heading to the store. This might reveal ideas about the brands and products that fit the role of skateboarder.

Picture frustration
A version of the TAT using a cartoon drawing in which the respondent suggests a dialogue in which the characters might engage.

A **picture frustration** version of the TAT uses a cartoon drawing in which the respondent suggests a dialogue in which the characters might engage. Exhibit 5.6 is a purposely ambiguous illustration of an everyday occurrence. The two office workers are shown in a situation and the respondent is asked what the woman might be talking about. This setting could be used for discussions about products, packaging, the display of merchandise, store personnel, and so on.

EXHIBIT 5.6
Picture Frustration Version of TAT

Exploratory Research in Science and in Practice

Misuses of Exploratory and Qualitative Research

Any research tool can be misapplied. Exploratory research cannot take the place of conclusive, confirmatory research. Thus, since many qualitative tools are best applied in exploratory design, they are likewise limited in the ability to draw conclusive inferences—test hypotheses. One of the biggest drawbacks is the subjectivity that comes along with "interpretation." In fact, sometimes the term *interpretive* research is used synonymously with qualitative research. When only one researcher interprets the meaning of what a single person said in a depth interview or similar technique, one should be very cautious before major marketing decisions are made based on these results. Is the result replicable, meaning the same conclusion would be reached based on another researcher's interpretation?

Indeed, some qualitative methodologies were generally frowned upon for years based on a few early and public misapplications during what became known as the "motivational research" era. While many of the ideas produced during this time had some merit, as can sometimes be the case, too few researchers did too much interpretation of too few respondents. Compounding this, marketers were quick to act on the results, believing that the results peeked inside one's subliminal consciousness and therefore held some type of extra power. Thus, often the research was flawed based on poor interpretation, and the decision process was flawed because the deciders acted prematurely. Projective techniques and depth interviews were frequently used in the late 1950s and early 1960s, producing some interesting and occasionally bizarre reasons for consumers' purchasing behavior:

- A woman is very serious when she bakes a cake because unconsciously she is going through the symbolic act of giving birth.
- A man buys a convertible as a substitute mistress and a safer (and potentially cheaper) way of committing adultery.
- Men who wear suspenders are reacting to an unresolved castration complex.[16]

About two decades later, researchers for McCann-Erickson advertising agency interviewed low-income women using a form of TAT involving story completion regarding attitudes toward insecticides. Themes noted included:

- The joy of victory over roaches (watching them die or seeing them dead)
- Using the roach as a metaphor through which women can vicariously take out their hostility of men (women generally referred to roaches as "he" instead of "she" in their stories)[17]

Certainly, some useful findings resulted. Even today, we have the Pillsbury Doughboy as evidence that useful ideas were produced. In many of these cases, interpretations were either misleading or too ambitious (taken too far). However, many companies became frustrated when decisions based upon motivational research approaches proved poor. Thus, marketing researchers moved away from qualitative tools during the late 1960s and 1970s. Today, however, qualitative tools have won acceptance once again as researchers realize they have greater power in discovering insights that would be difficult to capture in typical survey research (which is limited as an exploratory tool).

Replicable
When the same conclusion is reached based on another researcher's interpretation.

Summary

1. Understand the differences between qualitative research and quantitative research. The chapter emphasized that any argument about the overall superiority of qualitative versus quantitative research is misplaced. Rather, each approach has advantages and disadvantages that make it appropriate in certain situations. The most noticeable difference is the relative absence of numbers in qualitative research. Qualitative research relies more on researchers' subjective interpretations of text or other visual material. In contrast, the numbers produced in quantitative research are objective in the sense that they don't change simply because someone else computed them. Qualitative research involves small samples while quantitative research usually uses large samples. Qualitative procedures are generally more flexible and produce deeper and more elaborate explanations than quantitative research.

2. Understand the role of qualitative research in exploratory research designs. The high degree of flexibility that goes along with most qualitative techniques makes them very useful in exploratory research designs. Therefore, exploratory research designs most often involve some qualitative research technique.

3. Describe the four basic categories of exploratory research. The four basic categories of exploratory research are experience surveys, secondary data analysis, case studies, and pilot studies. Major categories of pilot studies include focus group interviews, depth interviews, and projective techniques such as the Thematic Apperception Test. Each of these categories provides various ways to gather information for qualitative analysis.

4. Prepare a focus group interview outline. A focus group outline should begin with introductory comments followed by a very general opening question that does not lead the respondent. More specific questions should be listed until a blunt question directly pertaining to the study objective is included. It should conclude with debriefing comments and a chance for question-and-answers with respondents.

5. Recognize technological advances in the application of qualitative research approaches. Videoconferencing and online chat rooms are more economical ways of trying to do much the same as traditional focus group interviews. Some companies have even established a focus blog that is a source for continuous commentary on a company. While they are certainly cost advantageous, there is less control over who participates.

6. Recognize common qualitative research tools and know the advantages and limitations of their use. The most common qualitative research tools include the focus group interview and the depth interview. The focus group has some cost advantage per respondent because it would take ten times as long to conduct the interview portion(s) of a series of depth interviews compared to one focus group. However, the depth interview is more appropriate for discussing sensitive topics.

7. Know the risks associated with acting on only exploratory results. Companies do make decisions using only exploratory research. There are several explanations for this behavior. The researcher's job is to make sure that decision makers understand the increased risk that comes along with basing a decision only on exploratory research results.

Key Terms

Qualitative marketing research	Pilot study	Laddering
Researcher-dependent	Focus group interview	Projective technique
Quantitative marketing research	Piggyback	Free-association techniques
Subjective	Moderator	Field notes
Qualitative data	Discussion guide	Thematic apperception test (TAT)
Quantitative data	Streaming media	Picture frustration
Concept testing	Online focus group	Replicable
Experience survey	Focus blog	
Case studies	Depth interview	

Questions for Review and Critical Thinking

1. Define *qualitative* and *quantitative* research. Compare and contrast the two approaches.
2. Why do exploratory research designs rely so much on qualitative research techniques?
3. What are the basic categories of exploratory research?
4. What benefits can be gathered from case studies? What dangers, if any, do they present? In what situations are they most useful?
5. What is the function of a focus group? What are its advantages and disadvantages?
6. If a researcher wanted to conduct a focus group with teenagers, what special considerations might be necessary?

7. What type of exploratory research would you suggest in the following situations?
   a. A product manager suggests development of a non-tobacco cigarette blended from wheat, cocoa, and citrus.
   b. A research project has the purpose of evaluating potential brand names for a new insecticide.
   c. A manager must determine the best site for a convenience store in an urban area.
   d. An advertiser wishes to identify the symbolism associated with cigar smoking.

8. What are the key differences between a focus group interview and a depth interview?

9. **'NET** Visit some websites for large companies like Honda, Qantas Airlines, Target, Tesco, and Marriott. Is there any evidence that they are using their Internet sites in some way to conduct a continuous online focus blog or intermittent online focus groups?

10. What is *laddering?* How might it be used in trying to understand which fast-food restaurant customers prefer?

11. Comment on the following remark by a marketing consultant: "Qualitative exploration is a tool of marketing research and a stimulant to thinking. In and by itself, however, it does not constitute market research."

12. **ETHICS** A researcher tells a manager of a wine company that he has some "cool focus group results" suggesting that respondents like the idea of a screw-cap to top wine bottles. Even before the decision maker sees the report, the manager begins purchasing screw-caps and the new bottling equipment. Comment on this situation.

13. A packaged goods manufacturer receives many thousands of customer letters a year. Some are complaints, some are compliments. They cover a broad range of topics. Are these letters a possible source for exploratory research? Why or why not?

Research Activities

1. **'NET** How might the following organizations use an Internet chat room for exploratory research?
   a. A zoo
   b. A computer software manufacturer
   c. A video game manufacturer

2. Go back to the opening vignette. What if Vans approached you to do a focus group interview that explored the idea of offering casual attire (off-board) aimed at their primary segment (skateboarders) and offering casual attire for male retirees like Samuel Teel? How would you recommend the focus group(s) proceed? Prepare a focus group outline(s) to accomplish this task.

3. Interview two people about their exercise behavior. In one interview, try to use a semi-structured approach by preparing questions ahead of time and trying to have the respondent complete answers for these questions. With the other, try a conversational approach. What are the main themes that emerge in each? Which approach do you think was more insightful? Do you think there were any "sensitive" topics that a respondent was not completely forthcoming about?

Case 5.1 Disaster and Consumer Value

After September 11, 2001, U.S. consumers showed a desire to tone down their consumer activities. They ordered simpler foods in restaurants and spent more time at home. Therefore, a lot of marketing campaigns began emphasizing down-home themes.[18]

At some point after a disaster, it is time to get back to business. But major catastrophic events are likely to leave permanent changes on consumers and employees in those areas. Suppose you are approached by the owner of several delicatessens and full-service wine stores in the Gulf Coast area. It is January 2006, and they want to get back to business. But they are uncertain about whether they should simply maintain the same positioning they had previous to Hurricane Katrina and Hurricane Rita. They would like to have a report from you within eighty days.

1. How could each classification of qualitative research be used here?
2. What qualitative research tool(s) would you recommend be used and why?
3. Where would you conduct any interviews and with whom would you conduct them?
4. **ETHICS** Are there ethical issues that you should be sensitive to in this process? Explain.
5. What issues would arise in conducting a focus group interview in this situation?
6. Prepare a focus group outline.

Video Case 5.2 Goya

"If it is Goya, it has to be good." This is the motto created by the founder of Goya in 1936 when he and his wife emigrated from Spain to New York in to order to establish a food products company that would serve the numbers of Spanish immigrants to the United States. It also describes the current philosophy of a company that is known for its wide assortment of Latin/Hispanic food products, ranging from beans and rice to condiments to beverages to salsa to cooking oils. Robert Unanue, the founder's grandson, is the president of this preeminent Hispanic family-owned business.

Joe Perez, vice president of purchasing, attributes the success of Goya to the fact that it consistently offers a quality product at a fair price to all of its consumers. He notes that Goya makes over 1,200 different food products that appeal to Hispanics and Latinos in North America as well as people in South American countries, such as Peru, Colombia, and Uruguay, and Caribbean countries, such as Cuba, Costa Rica, and Puerto Rico. As another company official notes, the Hispanic market is very diverse.

Consequently, Goya's marketing efforts are sensitive to both the similarities and differences among these populations. As Andy Nenoya, executive vice president and chief of operations, says, the company works at the "micro-market" level. One result is that Goya uses "standard neutral Spanish terms" that every consumer in every country can understand. Another result of marketing research is that the company provides products for every generation of consumer, from the older generation who, for example, might prefer a bulk bag of dry beans, to the younger generations, who prefer frozen and canned products because of various competing commitments in their lives and limited time for food preparation.

Beginning in the late 1970s and early 1980s, Goya also started the "Americanization" of their products into the mainstream U.S. food market. This involves a reeducation of the population to convince them that Goya products work well in such meal-time staples as spaghetti and beef stew and, on their own, offer an interesting diversity to meal choices. The company does not want to compromise the integrity of their products, but they do want U.S. consumers to be aware that their products are low in fat and cholesterol and have a variety of flavors that make food more interesting and enjoyable.

Their efforts have been successful in all market segments, and Goya is experiencing continuous growth. "Nobody has the breadth of products that we have or the distribution throughout the country that we have," affirms Nenoya.

Questions

1. Any exploratory research endeavors should take into account the wide diversity of consumers for Goya products. Identify the relevant factors that might be similar among this consumer population and the factors that might identify relevant differences in this population.

2. What information would a Goya focus group composed of non-Hispanic individuals in the United States want to learn?

Video Case 5.3 Edward Jones

 Edward Jones is one of the largest investment firms in the United States, with over 4,000 branch offices in this country, Canada, and the United Kingdom. It is the only major brokerage firm that exclusively targets individual investors and small businesses, and it has nearly 6 million clients.

Edward Jones' philosophy is to offer personalized services to individual clients starting with a one-on-one interview. During the interview, investment representatives seek to identify each client's specific goals for investing. Richard G. Miller, one such representative, says that he needs to thoroughly understand what a client wants before he can build an investment strategy for that person. His initial conversation starts with, "Hey, how are you?" Gregory L. Starry, another representative, confirms the Edward Jones philosophy: "Most of my day is spent talking with and meeting clients [rather than placing stock trades]."

Only after learning these goals do the representatives design an investment strategy that will provide a client with income, growth, and safety. Each client's goals also evolve over time. Young people are focused on earning enough money to make a down payment on their first home or to buy a car. Clients in the thirty-five to forty-five age range are concerned about getting their children through school and about their own retirement. Those in retirement want to make sure that they have an adequate income level. Miller notes, "It's not the timing in the market, but the time in the market" that will help clients achieve their goals.

Questions

1. Many people in minority groups, including African Americans, Hispanic Americans, Asian Americans, and Native Americans, do not invest. What exploratory research should Edward Jones do to develop the minority market?

2. Another group with low investment activity includes those who stopped their education at the high school level. What factors should Edward Jones representatives consider in designing focus groups with these potential clients?

CHAPTER 6
SECONDARY DATA RESEARCH IN A DIGITAL AGE

After studying this chapter, you should be able to

1. Discuss the advantages and disadvantages of secondary data
2. Define objectives and types of secondary data analysis conducted by marketing managers
3. Understand the nature of model building with secondary data
4. Describe the concept of data mining
5. Identify various internal and proprietary sources of secondary data
6. Give examples of various external sources of secondary data
7. Describe the impact of single-source data and globalization on secondary data research

Chapter Vignette: Pentagon Recruits with Databases

In a nation with an all-volunteer military, finding recruits is an ongoing need. The project is especially challenging in wartime, when more service members are necessary but the costs of serving are too daunting for many citizens. One way that the Department of Defense meets this challenge is by reviewing data that exist in a variety of sources. Its Joint Advertising, Market Research & Studies (JAMRS) project operates over a dozen research initiatives that make data available to military recruiters in all branches of the U.S. armed services.[1] Some involve data collection, but many apply already-existing data (secondary data) to the task of recruitment.

One of these efforts is a service called Population Representation (Pop Rep). For the past three decades, JAMRS has been gathering data on applicants and service members, including their age, race or ethnicity, gender, marital status, and education level. Recruiters can visit the JAMRS website to obtain reports showing which characteristics are associated with particular areas of service and performance levels. This information can help them target candidates for recruitment.

©SONDA DAWES/THE IMAGE WORKS

JAMRS also pays for data from third-party research firms. For example, it uses the PRIZM market segmentation data gathered and sold by Claritas, a marketing research firm. The PRIZM data describe the purchasing and media behavior of many market segments. Recruiters can use the data to identify the activities of potential recruits that live in their region—for example, to identify the magazines they read. This information can help local recruiters or branches of the military target messages likely to appeal to particular groups of young men and women. Many people know that recruits are most likely to come from households with lower-middle incomes or below in rural areas and small towns. However, the PRIZM data go much deeper, showing, for example, that U.S. Army recruits often come from households that listen to Spanish-language radio and that prospective Marines tend to read *Outdoor Life* and enjoy fishing and hunting.

Another JAMRS service is called its Recruit Market Information System (RMIS). This web-based computer application allows recruiting professionals to search a database that combines the Pentagon's own data about recruits and additional data purchased to aid recruiters. For example, recruiters can look up population statistics and the number of contracts signed by new recruits to determine geographic areas in which recruitment is strong. The military also uses data from schools, including names, ages, grades, and e-mail addresses of students aged sixteen to twenty-five.

For the Defense Department, recruiting would no doubt be far more difficult and far less effective without access to secondary data, in this case, data gathered for purposes other than military recruitment. But the data are useful only with careful analysis and interpretation. This chapter discusses how to conduct research with secondary data in a digital age. An appendix listing sources of secondary data is available on this book's website at http://www.thomsonedu.com/marketing/zikmund. Many sources can also be found using Internet search engines.

Secondary Data Research

Research projects often begin with **secondary data**, which are gathered and recorded by someone else prior to (and for purposes other than) the current project. Secondary data usually are historical and already assembled. They require no access to respondents or subjects.

Advantages

The primary advantage of secondary data is their availability. Obtaining secondary data is almost always faster and less expensive than acquiring primary data. This is particularly true when researchers use electronic retrieval to access data stored digitally. In many situations, collecting secondary data is instantaneous.

Consider the money and time saved by researchers who obtained updated population estimates for a town during the interim between the 2000 and 2010 censuses. Instead of doing the fieldwork themselves, researchers could acquire estimates from a firm dealing in demographic information or from sources such as Claritas or PCensus. As in this example, the use of secondary data eliminates many of the activities normally associated with primary data collection, such as sampling and data processing.

Secondary data are essential in instances when data cannot be obtained using primary data collection procedures. For example, a manufacturer of farm implements could not duplicate the information in the *Census of Agriculture* because much of the information there (for example, amount of taxes paid) might not be accessible to a private firm.

TOTHEPOINT

If I have seen farther than others, it is because I have stood on the shoulders of giants.

—Isaac Newton

Disadvantages

An inherent disadvantage of secondary data is that they were not designed specifically to meet the researchers' needs. Thus, researchers must ask how pertinent the data are to their particular project. To evaluate secondary data, researchers should ask questions such as these:

- Is the subject matter consistent with our problem definition?
- Do the data apply to the population of interest?
- Do the data apply to the time period of interest?
- Do the secondary data appear in the correct units of measurement?
- Do the data cover the subject of interest in adequate detail?

Even when secondary information is available, it can be inadequate. Consider the following typical situations:

- A researcher interested in forklift trucks finds that the secondary data on the subject are included in a broader, less pertinent category encompassing all industrial trucks and tractors. Furthermore, the data were collected five years earlier.
- An investigator who wishes to study individuals earning more than $100,000 per year finds the top category in a secondary study reported at $75,000 or more per year.
- A brewery that wishes to compare its per-barrel advertising expenditures with those of competitors finds that the units of measurement differ because some report point-of-purchase expenditures with advertising and others do not.
- Data from a previous warranty card study show where consumers prefer to purchase the product but provide no reasons why.

The most common reasons why secondary data do not adequately satisfy research needs are (1) outdated information, (2) variation in definition of terms, (3) different units of measurement, and (4) lack of information to verify the data's accuracy. Furthermore, in our rapidly changing environment, information quickly becomes outdated. Because the purpose of most studies is to predict the future, secondary data must be timely to be useful.

Every primary researcher has the right to define the terms or concepts under investigation to satisfy the purpose of his or her primary investigation. This practice provides little solace, however, to the investigator of the African-American market who finds secondary data reported as "percent nonwhite." Variances in terms or variable classifications should be scrutinized to determine whether differences are important. The populations of interest must be described in comparable terms. Researchers frequently encounter secondary data that report on a population of interest that is similar but not directly comparable to their population of interest. For example, Arbitron reports its television audience estimates by geographical areas known as ADIs (Areas of Dominant Influence). An ADI is a geographic area consisting of all counties in which the home market commercial television stations receive a preponderance of total viewing hours. This unique population of interest is used exclusively to report television audiences. The geographic areas used in the census of population, such as Metropolitan Statistical Areas, are not comparable to ADIs.

Units of measurement may cause problems if they do not conform exactly to a researcher's needs. For example, lumber shipments in millions of board-feet are quite different from billions of ton-miles of lumber shipped on freight cars. Head-of-household income is not the same unit of measure as total family income. Often the objective of the original primary study may dictate that the data be summarized, rounded, or reported. When that happens, even if the original units of measurement were comparable, aggregated or adjusted units of measurement are not suitable in the secondary study.

When secondary data are reported in a format that does not exactly meet the researcher's needs, data conversion may be necessary. **Data conversion** (also called *data transformation*) is the process of changing the original form of data to a format more suitable for achieving a stated research objective. For example, sales for food products may be reported in pounds, cases, or dollars. An estimate of dollars per pound may be used to convert dollar volume data to pounds or another suitable format.

Data conversion
The process of changing the original form of the data to a format suitable to achieve the research objective; also called data transformation.

Another disadvantage of secondary data is that the user has no control over their accuracy. Although timely and pertinent secondary data may fit the researcher's requirements, the data could be inaccurate. Research conducted by other persons may be biased to support the vested interest of the source. For example, media often publish data from surveys to identify the characteristics of their subscribers or viewers, but they will most likely exclude derogatory data from their reports. If the possibility of bias exists, the secondary data should not be used.

Investigators are naturally more prone to accept data from reliable sources such as the U.S. government. Nevertheless, the researcher must assess the reputation of the organization that gathers the data and critically assess the research design to determine whether the research was correctly implemented. Unfortunately, such evaluation may be impossible without full information that explains how the original research was conducted.

Researchers should verify the accuracy of the data whenever possible. **Cross-checks** of data from multiple sources—that is, comparison of the data from one source with data from

Cross-checks
The comparison of data from one source with data from another source to determine the similarity of independent projects.

EXHIBIT 6.1
Evaluating Secondary Data

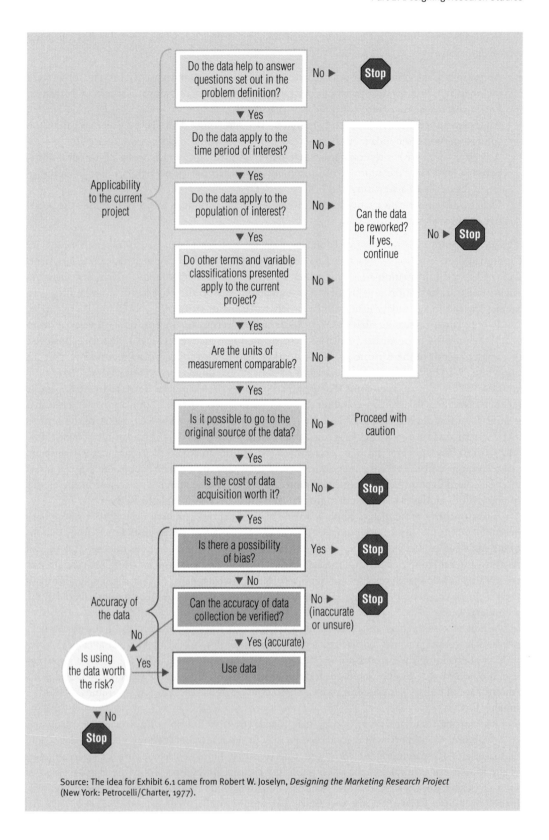

Source: The idea for Exhibit 6.1 came from Robert W. Joselyn, *Designing the Marketing Research Project* (New York: Petrocelli/Charter, 1977).

another—should be made to determine the similarity of independent projects. When the data are not consistent, researchers should attempt to identify reasons for the differences or to determine which data are most likely to be correct. If the accuracy of the data cannot be established, the researcher must determine whether using the data is worth the risk. Exhibit 6.1 illustrates a series of questions that should be asked to evaluate secondary data before they are used.

Broad Objective	Specific Research Example
Fact-finding	Identifying consumption patterns Tracking trends
Model building	Estimating market potential Forecasting sales Selecting trade areas and sites
Database marketing	Enhancing customer databases Developing prospect lists

EXHIBIT 6.2
Common Research Objectives for Secondary-Data Studies

Typical Objectives for Secondary-Data Research Designs

It would be impossible to identify all the purposes of marketing research using secondary data. However, some common marketing problems that can be addressed with secondary research designs are useful. Exhibit 6.2 shows three general categories of research objectives: fact-finding, model building, and database marketing.

Fact-Finding

The simplest form of secondary-data research is fact-finding. A restaurant serving breakfast might be interested in knowing what new products are likely to entice consumers. Secondary data available from National Eating Trends, a service of the NPD Group, show that the most potential may be in menu items customers can eat on the go.[2] According to data from the survey of eating trends, take-out breakfasts have doubled over the past few years, and they have continued to surpass dine-in breakfast sales for over a decade. These trends make smoothies and breakfast sandwiches sound like a good bet for a breakfast menu. Also, NPD found that 41 percent of breakfast sandwiches are consumed by people in their cars and 24 percent of people polled take them to work. These findings suggest that the sandwiches should be easy to handle. But what to put on the biscuit or bun? Another research firm, Market Facts, says almost half of consumers say they would pay extra for cheese. These simple facts would interest a researcher who was investigating the market for take-out breakfasts. Fact-finding can serve more complex purposes as well.

Secondary-data research supports the fact that breakfast sandwiches are at the top of the menu.

RESEARCHSNAPSHOT

New Trends—Music for Mobile Phones

Until a few years ago, selling music involved recordings on CDs, but marketing researchers have lately been tracking the newer practice of selling tunes to serve as ringtones. According to business-news sources, consumers spent $4 billion on ringtones in 2004. Strategy Analytics, a marketing research firm, forecasted that mobile music would generate $9 billion in sales by 2010. So far, the most popular song category is hip-hop, but videogame themes and movie themes also sell well.

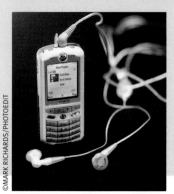

Ringtones are profitable for music sellers. Almost one-third of the ringtones sold in 2004 were song clips known as mastertones or true tones, and consumers were paying more for ringtones ($2.49) than for an entire song downloaded to an MP3 player. The music companies, such as Sony and EMI, get royalties of up to 50 percent for mastertones. In this environment, Sony BMG skipped the traditional approach of CD singles and MTV videos when Cassidy released an album in 2005; instead, the company made a 25-second sample of Cassidy's song "I'm a Hustla" and released it as a ringtone. Coldplay's song "Speed of Sound" was available as a ringtone from Cingular before the album went on sale.

Predicting trends for a new product is difficult. In the case of ringtones, the landscape may quickly shift as mobile-phone makers introduce models that play entire songs. Paying $2.49 for a ringtone will seem too expensive when consumers can play a whole song on their phone for less money.

Sources: Based on Matthew Maier, "Digital Entertainment: Can Cell Phones Save the Music Business?" Business 2.0, September 2005, downloaded from InfoTrac at http://www.galenet.com; Sue Marek, "Ringing in the New Year," Wireless Week, January 1, 2006, http://www.galenet.com; "Music Marketing Gets Digital Tune-Up," Financial Express, January 28, 2006, http://www.galenet.com; and "Top Polyphonic Ringtones of 2005," Wireless Week, January 15, 2006, http://www.galenet.com.

■ IDENTIFICATION OF CONSUMER BEHAVIOR FOR A PRODUCT CATEGORY

A typical objective for a secondary research study might be to uncover all available information about consumption patterns for a particular product category or to identify demographic trends that affect an industry. For example, a company called Servigistics offers software that will scan a company's own parts inventory data and compare it with marketing objectives and competitors' prices to evaluate whether the company should adjust prices for its parts. Kia Motors tried using this service in place of the usual method of marking up cost by a set fraction. By considering secondary data including internal inventory data and external data about competitors' prices, it was able to make service parts a more profitable segment of its business.[3] This example illustrates the wealth of factual information about consumption and behavior patterns that can be obtained by carefully collecting and analyzing secondary data.

■ TREND ANALYSIS

Market tracking
The observation and analysis of trends in industry volume and brand share over time.

Marketers watch for trends in the marketplace and the environment. **Market tracking** is the observation and analysis of trends in industry volume and brand share over time. Scanner research services and other organizations provide facts about sales volume to support this work.

Almost every large consumer goods company routinely investigates brand and product category sales volume using secondary data. This type of analysis typically involves comparisons with competitors' sales or with the company's own sales in comparable time periods. It also involves industry comparisons among different geographic areas.

■ ENVIRONMENTAL SCANNING

In many instances, the purpose of fact-finding is simply to study the environment to identify trends. Environmental scanning entails information gathering and fact-finding designed to detect indications of environmental changes in their initial stages of development. As mentioned in Chapter 2, the Internet can be used for environmental scanning; however, there are other means, such as periodic review of contemporary publications and reports. For example, environmental scanning has shown many marketers that consumer demand in China is skyrocketing. In the case of beauty products such as cosmetics, Chinese authorities in the early 1990s stopped discouraging the use of makeup, and sales of these products took off—hitting $524 million in 2005 and expected to grow by over one-third, reaching $705 million by 2009. Marketers including Procter & Gamble, L'Oréal, and Shiseido have captured a sizable share of this market by realizing the potential and developing products to get into the market early.[4]

A number of online information services, such as Factiva and LexisNexis, routinely collect news stories about industries, product lines, and other topics of interest that have been specified by the researcher. As we mentioned in Chapter 2, push technology is an Internet information technology that automatically delivers content to the researcher's or manager's desktop. Push technology uses "electronic smart agents," custom software that filters, sorts, prioritizes, and stores information for later viewing.[5] This service frees the researcher from doing the searching. The true value of push technology is that the researcher who is scanning the environment can specify the kinds of news and information he or she wants, have it delivered to his or her computer quickly, and view it at leisure.

Model Building

The second general objective for secondary research, model building, is more complicated than simple fact-finding. Model building involves specifying relationships between two or more variables, perhaps extending to the development of descriptive or predictive equations. Models need not include complicated mathematics, though. In fact, decision makers often prefer simple models that everyone can readily understand over complex models that are difficult to comprehend. For example, market share is company sales divided by industry sales. Although some may not think of this simple calculation as a model, it represents a mathematical model of a basic relationship.

We will illustrate model building by discussing three common objectives that can be satisfied with secondary research: estimating market potential, forecasting sales, and selecting sites.

Model building
The use of secondary data to help specify relationships between two or more variables; can involve the development of descriptive or predictive equations.

ESTIMATING MARKET POTENTIAL FOR GEOGRAPHIC AREAS

Marketers often estimate market potential using secondary data. In many cases exact figures may be published by a trade association or another source. However, when the desired information is unavailable, the researcher may estimate market potential by transforming secondary data from two or more sources. For example, managers may find secondary data about market potential for a country or other large geographic area, but this information may not be broken down into smaller geographical areas, such as by metropolitan area, or in terms unique to the company, such as sales territory. In this type of situation, researchers often need to make projections for the geographic area of interest.

An extended example will help explain how secondary data can be used to calculate market potential. Suppose a brewing company is looking for opportunities to expand sales by exporting or investing in other countries. Managers decide to begin by estimating market potential for the Czech Republic, Germany, Japan, and Spain. Secondary research uncovered data for per capita beer consumption and population projections for the year 2005. The data for the four countries appear in Exhibit 6.3 on the next page.

To calculate market potential for the Czech Republic in 2010, multiply that country's population in the year 2010 by its per capita beer consumption:

$$10,158,000 \ people \times 157 \ liters/person = 1,594,806,000 \ liters$$

In the Czech Republic, the market potential for beer is 1,594,806,000 liters. To get a sense of the expected sales volume, the marketer would have to multiply this amount by the price per liter at which beer typically sells in the Czech Republic. As Exhibit 6.3 reveals, Japan's population is much higher, so its market potential is greater, even though the average Czech drinks much more beer.

Of course, the calculated market potential for each country in Exhibit 6.3 is a rough estimate. One obvious problem is that not everyone in a country will be of beer-drinking age. If the

EXHIBIT 6.3
Market Potential for Beer in Four Countries

Country	(1) Population Projection for 2010 (thousands)	(2) Annual per Capita Beer Consumption (liters)	(3) Market Potential Estimate (k liters)
Czech Republic	10,158	157	1,594,806
Germany	82,701	125	10,337,625
Japan	128,457	51	6,551,307
Spain	43,993	80	3,519,440

Source: Population data from Population Division of the Department of Economic and Social Affairs of the United Nations Secretariat, World Population Prospects: The 2004 Revision and World Urbanization Prospects; The 2003 Revision, http://esa.un.org/unpp, accessed February 9, 2006. Consumption data from "Spanish Beer Producers Face Flatter Times," http://just-drinks.com, March 1, 2005, downloaded from Business & Company Resource Center, http://galenet.galegroup.com; and "China Ranked Largest Beer Consumer in 2004," Kyodo News International, December 15, 2005, http://galenet.galegroup.com.

marketer can get statistics for each country's projected *adult* population, the estimate will be closer. Also, the marketer will want to consider whether each country is experiencing growth or decline in the demand for beer to estimate whether consumption habits are likely to be different in 2010. For example, beer consumption is barely growing in Europe and Japan, but it is expanding in Latin America (at about 4 percent a year) and even faster in China (by at least 6 percent a year).[6] Perhaps this information will cause the marketer to investigate market potential in additional countries where more growth is expected.

FORECASTING SALES

Marketing managers need information about the future. They need to know what company sales will be next year and in future time periods. Sales forecasting is the process of predicting sales totals over a specific time period.

Accurate sales forecasts, especially for products in mature, stable markets, frequently come from secondary-data research that identifies trends and extrapolates past performance into the future. Marketing researchers often use internal company sales records to project sales. A rudimentary model would multiply past sales volume by an expected growth rate. A researcher might investigate a secondary source and find that industry sales are expected to grow by 10 percent; multiplying company sales volume by 10 percent would give a basic sales forecast.

Exhibit 6.4 illustrates trend projection using a moving average projection of growth rates. Average ticket prices for a major-league baseball game are secondary data from Team Marketing Report (http://www.teammarketing.com/fci.cfm). The moving average is the sum of growth rates for the past three years divided by 3 (number of years). The resulting number is a forecast of the percentage increase in ticket price for the coming year. Using the three-year average growth rate of 4.5 percent for the 2003, 2004, and 2005 sales periods, we can forecast the average ticket price for 2006 as follows:

$$\$21.17 + (\$21.17 \times .045) = \$22.12$$

Moving average forecasting is best suited to a static competitive environment. More dynamic situations make other sales forecasting techniques more appropriate.

Statistical trend analysis using secondary data can be much more advanced than this simple example. Many statistical techniques build forecasting models using secondary data. This chapter emphasizes secondary-data research rather than statistical analysis. Chapter 14 and Chapter 15 explain more sophisticated statistical model-building techniques for forecasting sales.

EXHIBIT 6.4
**Sales Forecast Using
Secondary Data and Moving
Averages**

Year	Average Ticket Price ($)	Percentage Rate of Growth (Decline) from Previous Year	3-Year Moving Average Rate of Growth (Decline)
1994	10.45	—	—
1995	10.65	+1.9	—
1996	11.20	+5.1	—
1997	12.36	+10.4	+5.8
1998	13.59	+10.0	+8.5
1999	14.91	+9.7	+10.0
2000	16.67	+11.9	+10.5
2001	18.99	+13.9	+11.8
2002	18.30	+3.8	+9.9
2003	19.01	+3.4	+7.0
2004	19.82	+3.9	+3.7
2005	21.17	+6.3	+4.5

Forecast of average ticket price for 2006: $21.17 + ($21.17 × .045) = $22.12

ANALYSIS OF TRADE AREAS AND SITES

Marketing managers examine trade areas and use **site analysis techniques** to select the best locations for retail or wholesale operations. Secondary-data research helps managers make these site selection decisions. Some organizations, especially franchisers, have developed special computer software based on analytical models to select sites for retail outlets. The researcher must obtain the appropriate secondary data for analysis with the computer software.

The **index of retail saturation** offers one way to investigate retail sites and to describe the relationship between retail demand and supply.[7] It is easy to calculate once the appropriate secondary data are obtained:

$$\text{Index of retail saturation} = \frac{\text{Local market potential (demand)}}{\text{Local market retailing space}}$$

For example, Exhibit 6.5 on the next page shows the relevant secondary data for shoe store sales in a five-mile radius surrounding a Florida shopping center. These types of data can be purchased from vendors of market information such as Urban Decision Systems. First, to estimate local market potential (demand), we multiply population by annual per capita shoe sales. This estimate, line 3 in Exhibit 6.5, goes in the numerator to calculate the index of retail saturation:

$$\text{Index of retail saturation} = \frac{\$14,249,000}{94,000} = 152$$

The retailer can compare this index figure with those of other areas to determine which sites have the greatest market potential with the least amount of retail competition. An index value above 200 is considered to indicate exceptional opportunities.

Site analysis techniques
Techniques that use secondary data to select the best location for retail or wholesale operations.

Index of retail saturation
A calculation that describes the relationship between retail demand and supply.

EXHIBIT 6.5
Secondary Data for Calculating an Index of Retail Saturation

1. Population	261,785
2. Annual per capita shoe sales	$54.43
3. Local market potential (line 1 × line 2)	$14,249,000
4. Square feet of retail space used to sell shoes	94,000 sq. ft.
5. Index of retail saturation (line 3/line 4)	152

Data Mining

Large corporations' decision support systems often contain millions or even hundreds of millions of records of data. These complex data volumes are too large to be understood by managers. Consider, for example, Capital One, a consumer lending company with nearly 50 million customer accounts, including credit cards and auto loans. Suppose the company collects data on customer purchases, and each customer makes five transactions in a month, or sixty per year. With 50 million customers and decades of data (the company was founded in 1988), it's easy to see how record counts quickly grow beyond the comfort zone for most humans.[8]

Two points about data volume are important to keep in mind. First, relevant marketing data are often in independent and unrelated files. Second, the number of distinct pieces of information each data record contains is often large. When the number of distinct pieces of information contained in each data record and data volume grow too large, end users don't have the capacity to make sense of it all. Data mining helps clarify the underlying meaning of the data.

The term **data mining** refers to the use of powerful computers to dig through volumes of data to discover patterns about an organization's customers and products. It is a broad term that applies to many different forms of analysis. For example, **neural networks** are a form of artificial intelligence in which a computer is programmed to mimic the way that human brains process information. One computer expert put it this way:

A neural network learns pretty much the way a human being does. Suppose you say "big" and show a child an elephant, and then you say "small" and show her a poodle. You repeat this process with a house and a giraffe as examples of "big" and then a grain of sand and an ant as examples of "small." Pretty soon she will figure it out and tell you that a truck is "big" and a needle is "small." Neural networks can similarly generalize by looking at examples.[9]

Market-basket analysis is a form of data mining that analyzes anonymous point-of-sale transaction databases to identify coinciding purchases or relationships between products purchased and other retail shopping information.[10] Consider this example about patterns in customer purchases: Osco Drugs mined its databases provided by checkout scanners and found that when men go to its drugstores to buy diapers in the evening between 6:00 p.m. and 8:00 p.m., they sometimes walk out with a six-pack of beer as well. Knowing this behavioral pattern, supermarket managers may consider laying out their stores so that these items are closer together.[11]

A data-mining application of interest to marketers is known as **customer discovery**, which involves mining data to look for patterns identifying who is likely to be a valuable customer. For example, a larger provider of business services wanted to sell a new product to its existing customers, but it knew that only some of them would be interested. The company had to adapt each product offering to each customer's individual needs, so it wanted to save money by identifying the best prospects. It contracted with a research provider called DataMind to mine its data on sales, responses to marketing, and customer service to look for the customers most likely to be interested in the new product. DataMind assigned each of the company's customers an index number indicating their expected interest level, and the selling effort was much more efficient as a result.[12]

When a company knows the identity of the customer who makes repeated purchases from the same organization, an analysis can be made of sequences of purchases. The use of data mining to detect sequence patterns is a popular application among direct marketers, such as catalog retailers.

Data mining
The use of powerful computers to dig through volumes of data to discover patterns about an organization's customers and products; applies to many different forms of analysis.

Neural network
A form of artificial intelligence in which a computer is programmed to mimic the way that human brains process information.

Market-basket analysis
A form of data mining that analyzes anonymous point-of-sale transaction databases to identify coinciding purchases or relationships between products purchased and other retail shopping information.

Customer discovery
Involves mining data to look for patterns identifying who is likely to be a valuable customer.

RESEARCHSNAPSHOT

Mining Data from Blogs

One way to find out what people are thinking these days is to read what they are posting on their blogs. But with tens of millions of blogs available on the Internet, there is no way to read them all. One solution: data-mining software designed for the blogosphere.

Umbria Communications, based in Boulder, Colorado, offers a program called Buzz Report, which searches 13 million blogs, looking for messages related to particular products and trends. Marketers can buy the service to find out what people are saying about their new products, or they can explore unmet needs in areas they might consider serving. Not only does Buzz Report identify relevant blogs, but it also has a language processor that can identify positive and negative messages and analyze word choices and spelling to estimate the writer's age range and sex. The company's CEO, Howard Kaushansky, says the program can even recognize sarcasm.

Most of Umbria's clients are large makers of consumer products, including Sprint and Electronic Arts. U.S. Cellular used Buzz Report to learn that teenage users of cell phones are particularly worried about using more than their allotted minutes, fearing that parents would take the extra amount from their allowance. Such knowledge is useful for developing new service plans and marketing messages.

Sources: Based on Bridget Finn, "Consumer Research: Mining Blogs for Marketing Insight," Business 2.0, September 2005, downloaded from InfoTrac at http://www.galenet.com; Justin Martin, "Blogging for Dollars," Fortune, December 12, 2005, http://www.galenet.com.

A catalog merchant has information for each customer, revealing the sets of products that the customer buys in every purchase order. A sequence detection function can then be used to discover the set of purchases that frequently precedes the purchase of, say, a microwave oven. As another example, a sequence of insurance claims could lead to the identification of frequently occurring medical procedures performed on patients, which in turn could be used to detect cases of medical fraud.

Data mining requires sophisticated computer resources, and it is expensive. That's why companies like DataMind, IBM, Oracle, Information Builders, and Acxiom Corporation offer data-mining services. Customers send the databases they want analyzed and let the data-mining company do the "number crunching."

Database Marketing and Customer Relationship Management

As we have already mentioned, a CRM (customer relationship management) system is a decision support system that manages the interactions between an organization and its customers. A CRM maintains customer databases containing customers' names, addresses, phone numbers, past purchases, responses to past promotional offers, and other relevant data such as demographic and financial data. **Database marketing** is the practice of using CRM databases to develop one-to-one relationships and precisely targeted promotional efforts with individual customers. For example, a fruit catalog company CRM contains a database of previous customers, including what purchases they made during the Christmas holidays. Each year the company sends last year's gift list to customers to help them send the same gifts to their friends and relatives.

Because database marketing requires vast amounts of CRM data compiled from numerous sources, secondary data are often acquired for the exclusive purpose of developing or enhancing databases. The transaction record, which often lists the item purchased, the price paid, customer name, address, and zip code, is the building block for many databases. This may be supplemented with data customers provide directly, such as data on a warranty card, and by secondary data purchased from third parties. For example, credit services may sell databases about applications for loans, credit card payment history, and other financial data. Several companies, such as Donnelley Marketing (with its BusinessContentFile and ConsumerContentFile services) and Claritas (with

Database marketing
The use of customer databases to promote one-to-one relationships with customers and create precisely targeted promotions.

PRIZM), collect primary data and then sell demographic data that can be related to small geographic areas, such as those with a certain zip code. (Remember that when the vendor collects the data, they are primary data, but when the database marketer incorporates the data into his or her database, they are secondary data.)

Now that some of the purposes of secondary-data analysis have been addressed, we turn to a discussion of the sources of secondary data.

Sources of Secondary Data

Chapter 2 classified secondary data as either internal to the organization or external. Modern information technology makes this distinction seem somewhat simplistic. Some accounting documents are indisputably internal records of the organization. Researchers in another organization cannot have access to them. Clearly, a book published by the federal government and located at a public library is external to the company. However, in today's world of electronic data interchange, the data that appear in a book published by the federal government may also be purchased from an online information vendor for instantaneous access and subsequently stored in a company's decision support system.

Internal data should be defined as data that originated in the organization, or data created, recorded, or generated by the organization. **Internal and proprietary data** is perhaps a more descriptive term.

> **Internal and proprietary data**
> Secondary data that originate inside the organization.

Sources of Internal and Proprietary Data

Most organizations routinely gather, record, and store internal data to help them solve future problems. An organization's accounting system can usually provide a wealth of information. Routine documents such as sales invoices allow external financial reporting, which in turn can be a source of data for further analysis. If the data are properly coded into a modular database in the accounting system, the researcher may be able to conduct more detailed analysis using the decision support system. Sales information can be broken down by account or by product and region; information related to orders received, back orders, and unfilled orders can be identified; sales can be forecast on the basis of past data. Other useful sources of internal data include salespeople's call reports, customer complaints, service records, warranty card returns, and other records.

Researchers frequently aggregate or disaggregate internal data. For example, a computer service firm used internal secondary data to analyze sales over the previous three years, categorizing business by industry, product, purchase level, and so on. The company discovered that 60 percent of its customers represented only 2 percent of its business and that nearly all of these customers came through telephone directory advertising. This simple investigation of internal records showed that, in effect, the firm was paying to attract customers it did not want.

Internet technology is making it easier to research internal and proprietary data. Often companies set up Intranets so that employees can use web tools to store and share data within the organization. And just as Google's search software lets people search the entire World Wide Web, Google is offering the enterprise search, which is essentially the same technology in a version that searches a corporate Intranet. The enterprise search considers not only how often a particular document has been viewed but also the history of the user's past search patterns, such as how often that user has looked at particular documents and for how long. In addition, other companies have purchased specialized software, such as Autonomy, which searches internal sources plus such external sources as news government websites.[13]

> **External data**
> Data created, recorded, or generated by an entity other than the researcher's organization.

External Data: The Distribution System

External data are generated or recorded by an entity other than the researcher's organization. The government, newspapers and journals, trade associations, and other organizations create or produce

EXHIBIT 6.6
**Information as a Product and
Its Distribution Channels**

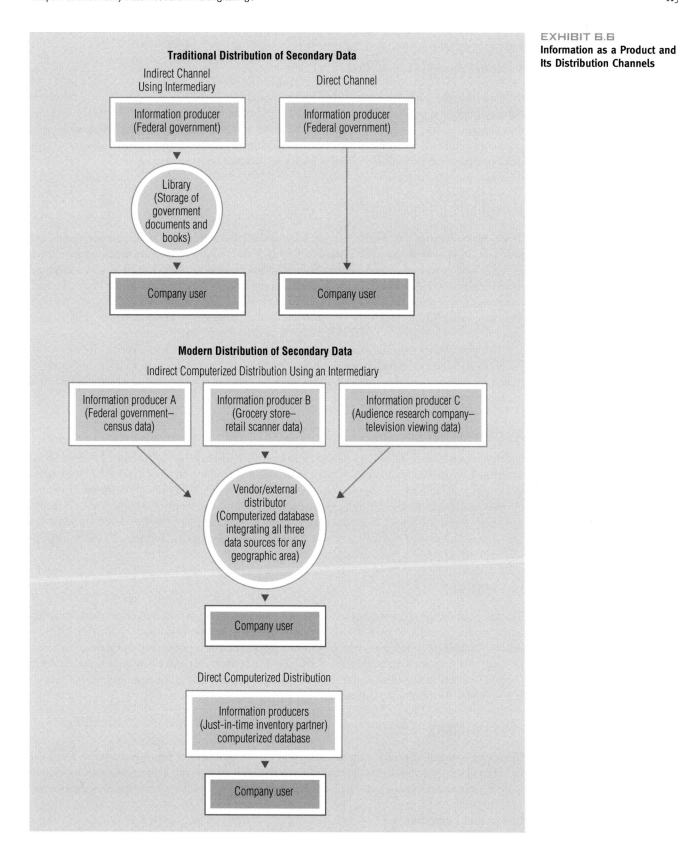

information. Traditionally, this information has been in published form, perhaps available from a public library, trade association, or government agency. Today, however, computerized data archives and electronic data interchange make external data as accessible as internal data. Exhibit 6.6 illustrates some traditional and some modern ways of distributing information.

Information as a Product and Its Distribution Channels

Because secondary data have value, they can be bought and sold like other products. And just as bottles of perfume or plumbers' wrenches may be distributed in many ways, secondary data also flow through various channels of distribution. Many users, such as the Fortune 500 corporations, purchase documents and computerized census data directly from the government. However, many small companies get census data from a library or another intermediary or vendor of secondary information.

LIBRARIES

Traditionally, libraries' vast storehouses of information have served as a bridge between users and producers of secondary data. The library staff deals directly with the creators of information, such as the federal government, and intermediate distributors of information, such as abstracting and indexing services. The user need only locate the appropriate secondary data on the library shelves. Libraries provide collections of books, journals, newspapers, and so on for reading and reference. They also stock many bibliographies, abstracts, guides, directories, and indexes, as well as offer access to basic databases.

The word *library* typically connotes a public or university facility. However, many major corporations and government agencies also have libraries. A corporate librarian's advice on sources of industry information or the United Nations librarian's help in finding statistics about international markets can be invaluable.

THE INTERNET

Today, of course, much secondary data is conveniently available over the Internet. Its creation has added an international dimension to the acquisition of secondary data. For example, Library Spot, at http://www.libraryspot.com, provides links to online libraries, including law libraries, medical libraries, and music libraries. Its reference desk features links to calendars, dictionaries, encyclopedias, maps, and other sources typically found at a traditional library's reference desk.

Chapter 2 discussed how to access and use the Internet. Exhibit 6.7 lists some of the more popular Internet addresses where secondary data may be found.

VENDORS

The information age offers many channels besides libraries through which to access data. Many external producers make secondary data available directly from the organizations that produce the data or through intermediaries, which are often called *vendors*. Vendors such as Factiva now allow managers to access thousands of external databases via desktop computers and telecommunications systems. Hoovers (http://www.hoovers.com) specializes in providing information about thousands of companies' financial situations and operations.

PRODUCERS

Classifying external secondary data by the nature of the producer of information yields five basic sources: publishers of books and periodicals, government sources, media sources, trade association sources, and commercial sources. The following section discusses each type of secondary data source.

Books and Periodicals

Some researchers consider books and periodicals found in a library to be the quintessential secondary data source. A researcher who finds books on a topic of interest obviously is off to a good start.

Professional journals, such as the *Journal of Marketing, Journal of Marketing Research, Journal of the Academy of Marketing Science, The Journal of Business Research, Journal of Advertising Research, American Demographics,* and *The Public Opinion Quarterly,* as well as commercial business periodicals such as *The Wall Street Journal, Fortune,* and *BusinessWeek,* contain much useful material. *Sales and Marketing*

TOTHEPOINT

The man who does not read good books has no advantage over the man who cannot read them.

—Mark Twain

EXHIBIT 6.7 **Selected Internet Sites for Secondary Data**

Name	Description	URL
Yahoo!	Portal that serves as a gateway to all kinds of sites on the Web.	http://www.yahoo.com
CEOexpress	The 80/20 rule applied to the Internet. A series of links designed by a busy executive for busy executives.	http://www.ceoexpress.com
The New York Public Library Home Page	Library resources and links available online.	http://www.nypl.org
Census Bureau	Demographic information from the U.S. Census Bureau.	http://www.census.gov
Statistical Abstract of the United States	Highlights from the primary reference book for government statistics.	http://www.census.gov/statab/www
STAT-USA/Internet	A comprehensive source of U.S. government information that focuses on economic, financial, and trade data.	http://www.stat-usa.gov/
Advertising Age magazine	Provides content on marketing media, advertising, and public relations.	http://www.adage.com
Inc.com	*Inc.* magazine's resources for growing a small business.	http://www.inc.com
The Wall Street Journal Online	Provides a continually updated view of business news around the world.	http://online.wsj.com
CNN Money	Provides business news, information on managing a business and managing money, and other business data.	http://money.cnn.com
NAICS—North American Industry Classification System	Describes the new classification system that replaced the SIC system.	http://www.census.gov/epcd/www/naics.html
MapQuest	Allows users to enter an address and zip code and see a map.	http://www.mapquest.com
Brint.com: The BizTech Network	Business and technology portal and global network for e-business, information, technology, and knowledge management.	http://www.brint.com

Management's Survey of Buying Power is a particularly useful source of information about markets. To locate data in periodicals, indexing services such as the *ABI/INFORM and Business Periodicals Index* and *The Wall Street Journal Index* are very useful. Guides to data sources also are helpful. For example, *American Statistical Index and Business Information Sources* is a very valuable source. Most university libraries provide access to at least some of these databases. Some can also be accessed through the Business Resource Center (http://www.thomson.com).

Government Sources

Government agencies produce data prolifically. Most of the data published by the federal government can be counted on for accuracy and quality of investigation. Most students are familiar with the U.S. *Census of Population,* which provides a wealth of data.

The *Census of Population* is only one of many resources that the government provides. Banks and savings and loan companies rely heavily on the *Federal Reserve Bulletin* and the *Economic Report of the President* for data relating to research on financial and economic conditions. Builders and contractors use the information in the *Current Housing Report and Annual Housing Survey* for their research. The *Statistical Abstract of the United States* is an extremely valuable source of information about the social, political, and economic organization of the United States. It abstracts data available in hundreds of other government publications and serves as a convenient reference to more specific statistical data.

The federal government is a leader in making secondary data available on the Internet. Visit FedWorld (http://www.fedworld.gov) for a central access point and links to many of these important documents. STAT-USA/Internet is another authoritative and comprehensive source of U.S. government information that focuses on economic, financial, and trade data. It contains the following types of information:

- More than 18,000 market research reports on individual countries and markets compiled by foreign experts at U.S. embassies
- Economic data series, current and historical, such as gross domestic product, balance of payment, and merchandise trade
- Standard reference works, such as the *Economic Report of the President,* the *Budget of the United States Federal Government,* and the *World Factbook*
- Worldwide listings of businesses interested in buying U.S. products

The STAT-USA/Internet web address is http://www.stat-usa.gov. However, only subscribers who pay a fee have access to this service.

State, county, and local government agencies can also be useful sources of information. Many state governments publish state economic models and forecasts, and many cities have metropolitan planning agencies that provide data about the population, economy, transportation system, and so on. These are similar to federal government data but are more current and are structured to suit local needs.

Many cities and states publish information on the Internet. Many search engines have directory entries that allow easy navigation to a particular state's website. A researcher using Yahoo!, for example, needs only to click Regional Information to find numerous paths to information about states.

Media Sources

Information on a broad range of subjects is available from broadcast and print media. *CNN Financial News* and *Business Week* are valuable sources for information on the economy and many industries. Media frequently commission research studies about various aspects of Americans' lives, such as financial affairs, and make reports of survey findings available to potential advertisers free of charge. Data about the readers of magazines and the audiences for broadcast media typically are profiled in media kits and advertisements.

Information about special-interest topics may also be available. *Hispanic Business* reports that the number of Hispanic-owned companies in the United States is expected to grow at a rate of 55 percent between 2004 and 2010, reaching 3.2 million firms, with revenue growth for the period of 70 percent. According to the magazine, most of these firms are located in twenty states, with over half in California and Florida. For researchers willing to pay a modest $85, *Hispanic Business* offers a more detailed report about Hispanic-owned businesses.[14]

Data such as these are plentiful because the media like to show that their vehicles are viewed or heard by advertisers' target markets. These types of data should be evaluated carefully, however, because often they cover only limited aspects of a topic. Nevertheless, they can be quite valuable for research, and they are generally available free of charge.

Trade Association Sources

Trade associations, such as the Food Marketing Institute or the American Petroleum Institute, serve the information needs of a particular industry. The trade association collects data on a number of topics of specific interest to firms, especially data on market size and market trends. Association members have a source of information that is particularly germane to their industry questions. For example, the Newspaper Advertising Bureau (NAB) has catalogued and listed in its computer the specialized sections that are currently popular in newspapers. The NAB has surveyed all daily, Sunday, and weekend newspapers in the United States and Canada on their editorial content and has stored this information, along with data on rates, circulation, and mechanical requirements, in its computer for advertisers' use.

Commercial Sources

Numerous firms specialize in selling and/or publishing information. For example, the Polk Company publishes information on the automotive field, such as average car values and new-car purchase rates by zip code. Many of these organizations offer information in published formats and as CD-ROM or Internet databases. The following discussion of several of these firms provides a sampling of the diverse data that are available.

Market-Share Data A number of syndicated services supply either wholesale or retail sales volume data based on product movement. Information Resources, Inc., collects market-share data using Universal Product Codes (UPC) and optical scanning at retail store checkouts. INFOSCAN is a syndicated store tracking service that collects scanner data weekly from more than 32,000 supermarket, drug, and mass merchandiser outlets across the United States. Sales in France, Germany, Greece, Italy, the Netherlands, Spain, and the United Kingdom also are tracked by INFOSCAN.

Although it is best known for its television rating operations, ACNielsen also has a scanner-based marketing and sales information service called ScanTrack. This service gathers sales and marketing data from a sample of more than 4,800 stores representing more than 800 retailers in fifty major U.S. markets. As part of Nielsen's Retail Measurement Service, auditors visit the stores at regular intervals to track promotions to customers, retail inventories, displays, brand distribution, out-of-stock conditions, and other retail marketing activity. Scanner data allow researchers to monitor sales data before, during, and after changes in advertising frequency, price changes, distribution of free samples, and similar marketing tactics.

Wal-Mart operates its own in-store scanner system called RetailLink. Key suppliers can have online access to relevant data free of charge.[15] The *Market Share Reporter* is produced each year, made available for sale, and provides market share data for most industries.

Many primary data investigations use scanner data to measure the results of experimental manipulations such as altering advertising copy. For example, scanning systems combined with consumer panels are used to create electronic test-markets. Systems based on UPCs (bar codes) and similar technology have been implemented in factories, warehouses, and transportation companies to research inventory levels, shipments, and the like.

Demographic and Census Updates A number of firms, such as CACI Marketing Systems and Urban Information Systems, offer computerized U.S. census files and updates of these data broken down by small geographic areas, such as zip codes. Many of these research suppliers provide in-depth information on minority customers and other market segments.

Consumer Attitude and Public Opinion Research Many research firms offer specialized syndicated services that report findings from attitude research and opinion polls. For example, Yankelovich provides custom research, tailored for specific projects, and several syndicated services. Yankelovich's public opinion research studies, such as the voter and public attitude surveys that appear in *Time* and other news magazines, are a source of secondary data. One of the firm's services is the *Yankelovich MONITOR,* a syndicated annual census of changing social values and an analysis of how they can affect consumer marketing. The *MONITOR* charts the growth and spread of new social values, characterizes the types of customers who support the new values and those who continue to support traditional values, and outlines the ways in which people's values affect purchasing behavior.

Harris/Interactive is another public opinion research firm that provides syndicated and custom research for business. One of its services is its ABC News/Harris survey. This survey, released three

RESEARCHSNAPSHOT

Fandango and Nielsen Keeping an Eye on Moviegoers

Fandango, which sells movie tickets online, never set out to be a research firm. But in 2002, MGM contacted Fandango to ask for demographic data about customers who bought tickets to war

movies. That was the first sign that the company's data were as valuable as its ticket sales. By looking at purchase data for its 1.7 million registered users, Fandango can tell moviemakers a lot about who is choosing particular movies. It also can use the e-mail addresses (of those who choose to accept e-mail) as a pool of subjects for opinions about movie ideas and ads. Buying histories can help researchers

verify that people who offer an opinion about a particular movie actually spent the money to see it.

ACNielsen set out to offer a similar service when it partnered with Movie Tickets.com, which like Fandango sells tickets online. Supplementing Nielsen's research asking consumers about their awareness of and interest in particular movies, this partnership will investigate actual movie viewing. Nielsen asks customers of MovieTickets.com questions related to their choice of movies and their opinions about movies they saw. In some cases, the surveys will ask the same questions about different movies to provide a standard set of data available for sale. The company also researches particular movies to fulfill requests from inidividual clients.

Sources: Based on Geoff Keighley, "Puppet's Got a Brand-New Bag," Business 2.0, October 2005, downloaded from InfoTrac at http://www.galenet.com; Kate Kelly, "Nielsen Venture to Mine for Data on Moviegoers," The Wall Street Journal, January 17, 2006, http://online.wsj.com.

©STONE+/GETTY IMAGES

times per week, monitors the pulse of the American public on topics such as inflation, unemployment, energy, attitudes toward the president, elections, and so on.

Consumption and Purchase Behavior Data NPD's *National Eating Trends* (NET) is the most detailed database available on consumption patterns and trends for more than 4,000 food and beverage products. This is a syndicated source of data about the types of meals people eat and when and how they eat them. The data, called *diary panel data,* are based on records of meals and diaries kept by a group of households that have agreed to record their consumption behavior over an extended period of time.

National Family Opinion (NFO), Marketing Research Corporation of America (MRCA), and many other syndicated sources sell diary panel data about consumption and purchase behavior. Since the advent of scanner data, diary panels are more commonly used to record purchases of apparel, hardware, home furnishings, jewelry, and other durable goods, rather than purchases of nondurable consumer packaged goods. More recently, services have been tracking consumer behavior online, collecting data about sites visited and purchases made over the Internet.

Advertising Research Advertisers can purchase readership and audience data from a number of firms. W. R. Simmons and Associates measures magazine audiences; Arbitron measures radio audiences; ACNielsen Media Measurement estimates television audience ratings. By specializing in collecting and selling audience information on a continuing basis, these commercial sources provide a valuable service to their subscribers.

Assistance in measuring advertising effectiveness is another syndicated service. For example, Roper Starch Worldwide measures the impact of advertising in magazines. Readership information can be obtained for competitors' ads or the client's own ads. Respondents are classified as noted readers, associated readers, or read-most readers.

Burke Marketing Research provides a service that measures the extent to which respondents recall television commercials aired the night before. It provides product category norms, or average DAR (Day-After Recall) scores, and DAR scores for other products.

An individual advertiser would be unable to monitor every minute of every television program before deciding on the appropriate ones in which to place advertising. However, numerous clients, agencies, television networks, and advertisers can purchase the Nielsen television ratings service.

		EXHIBIT 6.8
CACI Marketing Systems http://www.caci.com	Provides industry-specific marketing services, such as customer profiling and segmentation, custom target analysis, demographic data reports and maps, and site evaluation and selection. CACI offers demographics and data on businesses, lifestyles, consumer spending, purchase potential, shopping centers, traffic volumes, and other statistics.	**Examples of Single-Source Databases**
PRIZM by Claritas Corporation http://www.claritas.com	PRIZM, which stands for Potential Rating Index for Zip Markets, is based on the "birds-of-a-feather" assumption that people live near others who are like themselves. PRIZM combines census data, consumer surveys about shopping and lifestyle, and purchase data to identify market segments. Colorful names such as "Young Suburbia," "Shot Guns," and "Pickups" describe 40 segments that can be identified by zip code. Claritas also has a lifestyle census in the United Kingdom (http://www.claritas.co.uk).	
MRI Cable Report—Mediamark Research Inc. http://www.mediamark.com	Integrates information on cable television viewing with demographic and product usage information.	

Single-Source Data-Integrated Information

ACNielsen Company offers data from both its television meters and scanner operations. The integration of these two types of data helps marketers investigate the impact of television advertising on retail sales. In other ways as well, users of data find that merging two or more diverse types of data into a single database offers many advantages.

PRIZM by Claritas Corporation, CACI, ClusterPlus by SMI, Mediamark Research Inc., and many other syndicated databases report product purchase behavior, media usage, demographic characteristics, lifestyle variables, and business activity by geographic area such as zip code. Although such data are often called *geodemographic,* they cover such a broad range of phenomena that no one name is a good description. These data use small geographic areas as the unit of analysis.

The marketing research industry uses the term **single-source data** for diverse types of data offered by a single company. Exhibit 6.8 identifies three major marketers of single-source data.

Single-source data
Diverse types of data offered by a single company; usually integrated on the basis of a common variable such as geographic area or store.

Sources for Global Research

As business has become more global, so has the secondary data industry. The Japan Management Association Research Institute, Japan's largest provider of secondary research data to government and industry, maintains an office in San Diego. The Institute's goal is to help U.S. firms access its enormous store of data about Japan to develop and plan their business there. The office in San Diego provides translators and acts as an intermediary between Japanese researchers and U.S. clients.

Secondary data compiled outside the United States have the same limitations as domestic secondary data. However, international researchers should watch for certain pitfalls that frequently are associated with foreign data and cross-cultural research. First, data may simply be unavailable in certain countries. Second, the accuracy of some data may be called into question. This is especially likely with official statistics that may be adjusted for the political purposes of foreign governments. Finally, although economic terminology may be standardized, various countries use different definitions and accounting and recording practices for many economic concepts. For example, different countries may measure disposable personal income in radically different ways. International researchers should take extra care to investigate the comparability of data among countries.

The U.S. government and other organizations compile databases that may aid international marketers. For example, *The European Union in the US* (http://www.eurunion.org/) reports on historical and current activity in the European Union, providing a comprehensive reference guide to information about laws and regulations. The *European Union in the US* profiles in detail each European Union member state, investment opportunities, sources of grants and other funding, and other information about business resources.

The U.S. government offers a wealth of data about foreign countries. The CIA's *World Factbook* and the *National Trade Data Bank* are especially useful. Both can be accessed using the Internet. The National Trade Data Bank (NTDB), the U.S. government's most comprehensive source of world trade data, illustrates what is available.

The National Trade Data Bank was established by the Omnibus Trade and Competitiveness Act of 1988.[16] Its purpose was to provide "reasonable public access, including electronic access" to an export promotion data system that was centralized, inexpensive, and easy to use.

EXHIBIT 6.9

Examples of Information Contained in the NTDB

Agricultural commodity production and trade

Basic export information

Calendars of trade fairs and exhibitions

Capital markets and export financing

Country reports on economic and social policies and trade practices

Energy production, supply, and inventories

Exchange rates

Export licensing information

Guides to doing business in foreign countries

International trade terms directory

How-to guides

International trade regulations/agreements

Labor, employment, and productivity

Maritime and shipping information

Market research reports

Overseas contacts

Overseas and domestic industry information

Price indexes

Small business information

State exports

State trade contacts

Trade opportunities

U.S. export regulations

U.S. import and export statistics by country and commodity

U.S. international transactions

World Fact Book

World minerals production

The U.S. Department of Commerce has the responsibility for operating and maintaining the NTDB and works with federal agencies that collect and distribute trade information to keep the NTDB up-to-date. The NTDB has been published monthly on CD-ROM since 1990. Over one thousand public and university libraries offer access to the NTDB through the Federal Depository Library system.

The National Trade Data Bank consists of 133 separate trade- and business-related programs (databases). By using it, small- and medium-sized companies get immediate access to information that until now only Fortune 500 companies could afford.

Topics in the NTDB include export opportunities by industry, country, and product; foreign companies or importers looking for specific products; how-to market guides; demographic, political, and socioeconomic conditions in hundreds of countries; and much more. NTDB offers one-stop shopping for trade information from more than twenty federal sources. You do not need to know which federal agency produces the information: All you need to do is consult NTDB.

Some of the specific information that can be obtained from the NTDB are listed in Exhibit 6.9.

Summary

1. Discuss the advantages and disadvantages of secondary data. Secondary data are data that have been gathered and recorded previously by someone else for purposes other than those of the current researcher. The chief advantage of secondary data is that they are almost always less expensive to obtain than primary data. Generally, they can be obtained rapidly and may provide information not otherwise available to the researcher. The disadvantage of secondary data is that they were not intended specifically to meet the researcher's needs. The researcher must examine secondary data for accuracy, bias, and soundness. One way to do this is to cross-check various available sources.

2. Define objectives and types of secondary data analysis conducted by marketing managers. Secondary research designs address many common marketing problems. There are three general categories of secondary research objectives: fact-finding, model building, and database marketing. A typical fact-finding study might seek to uncover all available information about consumption patterns for a particular product category or to identify business trends that affect an industry.

3. Understand the nature of model building with secondary data. Model building is more complicated than fact-finding; it involves specifying relationships between two or more variables. The practice of database marketing, which involves maintaining customer databases with customers' names, addresses, phone numbers, past purchases, responses to past promotional offers, and other relevant data such as demographic and financial data, is increasingly being supported by marketing research efforts.

4. Describe the concept of data mining. Data mining refers to the use of powerful computers to dig through volumes of data to discover patterns about an organization's customers and products. Data mining is a broad term applying to many different forms of analysis.

5. Identify various internal and proprietary sources of secondary data. Internal sources of secondary data can come from an organization's accounting system, sales records, service records, warranty card returns, and the like. External sources of secondary data come from many sources, such as libraries, the Internet, vendors of databases, producers of books and periodicals, the government, the media, trade associations, and commercial firms.

6. Give examples of various external sources of secondary data. External data are generated or recorded by another entity. The government, newspaper and journal publishers, trade associations, and other organizations create or produce information. Traditionally this information has been distributed in published form, either directly from producer to researcher, or indirectly through intermediaries such as public libraries. Modern computerized data archives, electronic data interchange, and the Internet have changed the distribution of external data, making them almost as accessible as internal data. *Push technology* is a term referring to an Internet information technology that automatically delivers content to the researcher's or manager's desktop. This service helps in environmental scanning.

7. Describe the impact of single-source data and globalization on secondary data research. The marketing of multiple types of related data by single-source suppliers has radically changed the nature of secondary-data research. Businesses can measure promotional efforts and related buyer behavior by detailed customer characteristics. As business has become more global, so has the secondary-data industry. International researchers should watch for pitfalls that can be associated with foreign data and cross-cultural research, such as problems with the availability and reliability of data.

Key Terms and Concepts

Secondary data	Site analysis techniques	Customer discovery
Data conversion	Index of retail saturation	Database marketing
Cross-checks	Data mining	Internal and proprietary data
Market tracking	Neural network	External data
Model building	Market-basket analysis	Single-source data

Questions for Review and Critical Thinking

1. Secondary data have been called the first line of attack for marketing researchers. Discuss this description.
2. Suppose you wish to learn about the size of the soft-drink market, particularly root beer sales, growth patterns, and market shares. Indicate probable sources for these secondary data.
3. What is *push technology?*
4. Identify some typical research objectives for secondary-data studies.
5. How might a marketing researcher doing a job for a company such as Pulte Homes (http://www.pultehomes.com) or David Weekley Homes (http://www.davidweekley.com/) use secondary data and data mining?
6. What would be a source for the following data?
   a. Population, average income, and employment rates for Oregon
   b. Maps of U.S. counties and cities
   c. Trends in automobile ownership
   d. Divorce trends in the United States
   e. Median weekly earnings of full-time, salaried workers for the previous five years
   f. Annual sales of the top ten fast-food companies
   g. Top ten websites ranked by number of unique visitors
   h. Attendance at professional sports events
7. Suppose you are a marketing research consultant and a client comes to your office and says, "I must have the latest information on the supply of and demand for Maine potatoes within the next 24 hours." What would you do?
8. Find the following data in the *Survey of Current Business:*
   a. U.S. gross domestic product for the first quarter of 2004
   b. Exports of goods and services for the fourth quarter of 2004
   c. Imports of goods and services for the fourth quarter of 2004
9. **ETHICS** A newspaper reporter finds data in a study that surveyed children that reports that a high percentage of children can match cartoon characters with the products they represent. For instance, they can match cereal with Captain Crunch and Ronald McDonald with a Big Mac. The reporter used this to write a story about the need to place limits on the use of cartoon characters. However, the study also provided data suggesting that matching the cartoon character and the product did not lead to significantly higher consumption. Would this be a proper use of secondary data?

Research Activities

1. Use secondary data to learn the size of the U.S. golf market and to profile the typical golfer.
2. **'NET** Where could a researcher working for the U.S. Marine Corps (http://www.marines.com) find information that would identify the most productive areas of the United States in which to recruit? What would you recommend?
3. **'NET** POPClocks estimate the U.S. and world populations. Go to the Census Bureau home page (http://www.census.gov), navigate to the population section, and find today's estimate of the U.S. and world populations.
4. **'NET** Try to find the U.S. market share for the following companies within thirty minutes:
   a. Home Depot
   b. Burger King
   c. Marlboro
   d. Was this a difficult task? If so, why do you think it is this difficult?
5. **'NET** Use the Internet to learn what you can about Indonesia.
   a. Check the corruption index for Indonesia at http://www.transparency.org.
   b. What additional kinds of information are available from the following sources?
   - Go to http://freetheworld.com/member.html and view info for Indonesia.
   - Visit the CIA's *World Factbook* at http://www.cia.gov/cia/publications/factbook.
   - Go to Google, Yahoo! Search, or another search engine, and use "Indonesia" as a search word.
6. **'NET** Go to Statistics Norway at http://www.ssb.no. What data, if any, can you obtain in English? What languages can be used to search this website? What databases might be of interest to the business researcher?
7. **'NET** Go to Statistics Canada at http://www.statcan.ca. What languages can be used to search this website? What databases might be of interest to the business researcher?
8. **'NET** Suppose you were working for a company that wanted to start a business selling handmade acoustic guitars that are reproductions of classic vintage guitars. Pricing is a big part of the decision. Secondary information is available via the Internet. Use eBay (http://ebay.com) to identify four key brands of acoustic guitars by studying the vintage acoustic guitars listed for sale. Since the company wishes to charge premium prices, they will model after the most expensive brand. What brand seems to be associated with the highest prices?

Case 6.1 Demand for Gas Guzzlers

In fall 2005, Hurricanes Katrina and Rita churning in the Gulf of Mexico damaged oil rigs and refineries, contributing to a spike in oil prices. Many observers expressed confidence that those events were the long-expected trigger that would kill off demand for SUVs and other gas-guzzling vehicles.[17] They were only partly right.

In the months leading up to the hurricanes, sales of SUVs had already been falling, according to data from *Automotive News*. Automakers had been shifting ad dollars away from these products. CNW Market Research said that in August 2005, consumers had for the first time placed fuel economy ahead of performance when ranking factors for choosing a new vehicle. When gas prices approached three dollars a gallon in September 2005, marketers felt sure that fuel economy would remain a top concern. Advertisers began creating more ads featuring vehicles' gas mileage.

But by the end of the year, attitudes were shifting again. The National Automobile Dealers Association surveyed consumers visiting its website for information about car purchases, and it learned they ranked price as most important, followed by make and model, then performance. Fuel economy ranked last, with 3 percent considering it most important and 11 percent considering it least important. What's a carmaker to do? General Motors gathers data from the shoppers who visit websites such as **www.kbb.com** to look up information, and it is analyzing the data to identify the price of fuel at which car buyers adjust their priorities.

Questions

1. From the standpoint of an automobile company, what sources of information in this article offer secondary data?
2. Suggest two or three other sources of data that might be of interest to auto companies interested in forecasting demand.
3. Online or at your library, look for information about recent trends in SUV purchases. Report what you learned, and forecast whether SUV sales are likely to recover or continue their decline. What role do gas prices play in your forecast?

Video Case 6.2 FedEx Corporation

FedEx's two key descriptors explain its success: relationship-focused and data-intensive.

The company was started by Frederick W. Smith in 1973. Smith had an idea about the coming computerization of society, based on an essay written he was a student at Yale University. (He received a below-average grade on the essay.)* His idea caused him to speculate about a then-existing need in the U.S. economy for a reasonably priced and reliable package air delivery system.

Today, Smith's idea has literally taken off. As the world's largest air and ground express transportation company, FedEx handles 3.2 million packages and deliveries each day to 210 countries worldwide.

The company's marketing efforts are directed at building 100 percent satisfaction-guaranteed relationships with its customers. What it aims to provide for its varied customer base is true reliability and peace of mind in shipping, so customers know that FedEx can be depended on.

Jeff Wyne, manager of marketing, notes that it's important "to understand what your customer wants . . . and needs from you as a supplier." And he adds that it's also important "to anticipate customer needs." One example of how FedEx does this is to offer various shipping channels. Customers, whether large corporations or individuals, have a variety of shipping options from free delivery-service software they can download onto their own computers to shipping centers where non-technically oriented customers can take in their packages for delivery.

FedEx has also been at the forefront in using technology to respond to its customer base. For example, FedEx will install a server directly on-site for companies who have a large number of transactions and require high speed. FedEx has also become known as "the warehouse in the sky" because it can connect production and transportation operations such that companies do not have to stockpile products on their sites. FedEx can communicate with both parties so that parts are manufactured and delivered at appropriate times.

Jeff Wyne says, "I think that what has made [FedEx] so successful is that it's been able to make so many other businesses successful."

Questions

1. How can FedEx use its current customer database to determine or anticipate future customer needs and/or demands?
2. If you were responsible for converting FedEx's technology-resistant consumers into consumers who were comfortable using some of the corporation's automation channels, what market research would you need, and how would you obtain it?

*Interview: Frederick W. Smith, http://www.achievement.org/autodoc/page, accessed April 26, 2005.

CHAPTER 7
SURVEY
RESEARCH:
AN OVERVIEW

After studying this chapter, you should be able to

1. Define surveys, and explain their advantages
2. Describe the type of information that may be gathered in a survey
3. Identify sources of error in survey research
4. Summarize ways researchers gather information through interviews
5. Compare the advantages and disadvantages of conducting door-to-door, mall intercept, telephone, and Internet interviews
6. Discuss the importance of pretesting questionnaires
7. Describe ethical issues that arise in survey research

Chapter Vignette: Intuit Gets Answers to Satisfy Customers

Intuit, maker of Quicken, QuickBooks, and Turbo Tax software for accounting and tax preparation, has enjoyed years of growth and profits, thanks in part to its efforts to learn what customers want.[1] One of its most important marketing research tools is called a "net promoter survey." That survey is extremely simple. Researchers simply ask customers, "On a scale of 0 to 10 [with 10 being most likely], how likely is it that you would recommend our product to your friends or colleagues?" Customers who respond with a 9 or 10 are called "promoters," and customers who respond with 0 through 6 are called "detractors." Subtracting the percentage of respondents who are detractors from the percentage who are promoters yields the net promoter score.

©INDEX STOCK PHOTOGRAPHY/JUPITER IMAGES

Intuit's CEO, Steve Bennett—who says he believes that "anything that can be measured can be improved"—encourages the ongoing collection of net promoter scores as a way to improve products and customer service and thereby build revenues and profits. Of course, making improvements requires that the company not only know *whether* customers are satisfied or dissatisfied but also know *why*. To learn more, the company asks survey respondents who are promoters to go online and provide more detailed opinions. For example, Intuit learned that claiming rebates was an annoying process (the company has simplified it) and that discount stores were offering some products for less than the prices offered online to frequent buyers (the company plans to adjust prices).

For even more in-depth information, Intuit supplements survey research with direct observation of customers. One year the company sent hundreds of employees, including CEO Bennett, to visit customers as they worked at their computers. The observers learned that a significant number of small-business owners were struggling with the accounting know-how they needed to use QuickBooks and were mystified by terms such as *accounts payable* and *accounts receivable*. In response, the company introduced QuickBooks: Simple Start Edition, which replaces the financial jargon with simple terms like *cash in* and *cash out*. In the first year after its launch, Simple Start Edition sold more copies than any other accounting software except the standard QuickBooks.

The purpose of survey research is to collect primary data—data gathered and assembled specifically for the project at hand. This chapter defines the subject. It also discusses typical research objectives that may be accomplished with surveys and various advantages of the survey method. The chapter explains many potential errors that researchers must be careful to avoid. Finally, it classifies surveys according to the media used to deliver the questionnaire.

The Nature of Surveys

Often research entails asking people—called **respondents**—to provide answers to written or spoken questions. These questionnaires or interviews collect data through the mail, on the telephone, online, or face-to-face. Thus, a survey is defined as a method of collecting primary data based on communication with a representative sample of individuals. Surveys provide a snapshot at a given point in time. The more formal term, **sample survey**, emphasizes that the purpose of contacting respondents is to obtain a representative sample of the target population.

Respondents
People who verbally answer an interviewer's questions or provide answers to written questions.

Sample survey
A more formal term for a survey.

Survey Objectives: Type of Information Gathered

The type of information gathered in a survey varies considerably depending on its objectives. Typically, surveys attempt to describe what is happening or to learn the reasons for a particular marketing activity.

Identifying characteristics of target markets, measuring consumer attitudes, and describing consumer purchasing patterns are common survey objectives. Most marketing surveys have multiple objectives; few gather only a single type of factual information. Questions about product use and desirable features help with product development and advertising messages. Demographic information and information on media exposure might also be collected in the survey to help plan a market segmentation strategy. A survey commissioned by eBay learned that almost 60 percent of respondents receive unwanted gifts, and 15 percent of them had sold an unwanted gift online, suggesting a possible source of demand for eBay's auction services.[2] In addition, the survey indicated that selling unwanted gifts online was twice as common among 25- to 34-year-olds. Although consumer surveys are a common form of marketing research, not all survey research is conducted with the ultimate consumer. Frequently, studies focus on wholesalers, retailers, or industrial buyers.

Because most survey research is descriptive research, the term *survey* is most often associated with quantitative findings. Although most surveys are conducted to quantify certain factual information, some aspects of surveys may also be qualitative. In new-product development, a survey often has a qualitative objective of refining product concepts. Stylistic, aesthetic, or functional changes may be made on the basis of respondents' suggestions. Evaluating the qualitative nature of advertising may also be an objective of survey research, as in the following story told to advertiser Michael Arlen about testing a rough commercial for AT&T:

We called it "Fishing Camp." The idea was this: These guys go off to a fishing camp in the north woods, somewhere far away, where they're going to have a terrific time together and do all this great fishing, only what happens is that it rains all the time and the fishing is a bust. Mind you, this was a humorous ad. The emphasis was on the humor. Anyway, the big moment occurs when the fishing guys are talking on the phone to their jealous friends back home—who naturally want to know how great the fishing is—and what you see are the fishing guys, huddled in this cabin, with the rain pouring down outside, and one of the guys is staring at a frying pan full of hamburgers sizzling on the stove while he says into the phone, "Boy, you should see the great trout we've got cooking here."[3]

However, much to the advertisers' astonishment, when they tested the advertisement and gave subjects a questionnaire, respondents recalled that what was cooking was trout. To counteract this misimpression, said the advertiser, "We ended up making it, but what we had to do was, when we came to that segment, we put the camera almost *inside* the frying pan, and in the frying pan we put huge, crude chunks of hamburger that were so raw they were almost red."

Although most marketing surveys are descriptive, they can also be designed to provide insights about causal explanations or to explore ideas.

Advantages of Surveys

Surveys provide a quick, inexpensive, efficient, and accurate means of assessing information about a population. The examples given earlier illustrate that surveys are quite flexible and, when properly conducted, extremely valuable to the manager.

As we discussed in Chapter 1, marketing research has proliferated since the general adoption of the marketing concept. The growth of survey research is related to the simple idea that to find out what consumers think, you need to ask them.[4]

Over the last fifty years, and particularly during the last two decades, survey research techniques and standards have become quite scientific and accurate. When properly conducted, surveys offer managers many advantages. However, they can also be used poorly when researchers do not follow research principles, such as careful survey and sample design. Sometimes even a well-designed and carefully executed survey is not helpful because the results are delivered too late to inform decisions.

The disadvantages of specific forms of survey data collection—personal interview, telephone, mail, Internet, and other self-administered formats—are discussed later in this chapter. However, errors are common to all forms of surveys, so it is appropriate to describe them generally next.

Errors in Survey Research

A manager who is evaluating the quality of a survey must estimate its accuracy. Exhibit 7.1 outlines the various forms of survey error. They have two major sources: random sampling error and systematic error.

Random Sampling Error

Random sampling error
A statistical fluctuation that occurs because of chance variation in the elements selected for a sample.

Most surveys try to portray a representative cross-section of a particular target population. Even with technically proper random probability samples, however, statistical errors will occur because of chance variation in the elements selected for the sample. These statistical problems are unavoidable without very large samples (>400). However, the extent of **random sampling error** can be estimated. Chapters 12 and 13 will discuss these errors and ways they can be estimated in more detail.

Systematic Error

Systematic error
Error resulting from some imperfect aspect of the research design that causes respondent error or from a mistake in the execution of the research.

Sample bias
A persistent tendency for the results of a sample to deviate in one direction from the true value of the population parameter.

The other major source of survey error, **systematic error**, results from some imperfect aspect of the research design or from a mistake in the execution of the research. Because systematic errors include all sources of error other than those introduced by the random sampling procedure, these errors or biases are also called *nonsampling errors*. A **sample bias** exists when the results of a sample show a persistent tendency to deviate in one direction from the true value of the population parameter. The many sources of error that in some way systematically influence answers can be divided into two general categories: respondent error and administrative error.

EXHIBIT 7.1 Categories of Survey Errors

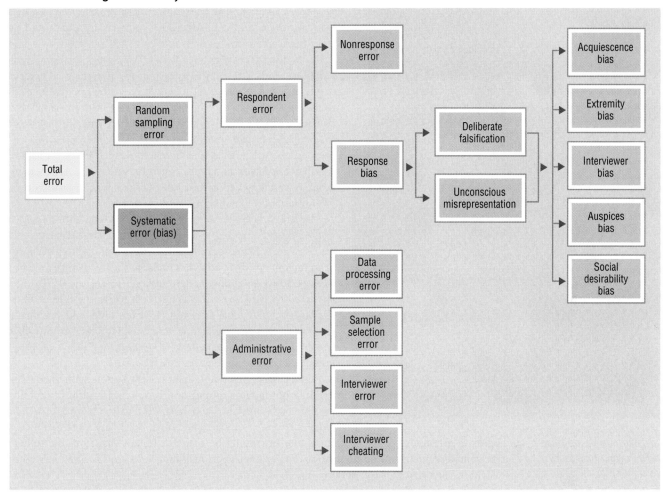

Respondent Error

Surveys ask people for answers. If people cooperate and give truthful answers, a survey will likely accomplish its goal. If these conditions are not met, nonresponse error or response bias, the two major categories of **respondent error**, may cause sample bias.

Nonresponse Error

Few surveys have 100 percent response rates. But a researcher who obtains a 1 percent response to a five-page e-mail questionnaire concerning various brands of spark plugs may face a serious problem. To use the results, the researcher must believe that consumers who responded to the questionnaire are representative of consumers who did not respond. The statistical differences between a survey that includes only those who responded and a survey that also included those who failed to respond are referred to as **nonresponse error**. This problem is especially acute in mail and Internet surveys, but nonresponse also threatens telephone and face-to-face interviews.

People who are not contacted or who refuse to cooperate are called **nonrespondents**. A nonresponse occurs if no one answers the phone at the time of both the initial call and a subsequent callback. The number of **no contacts** in survey research has been increasing because of the proliferation of answering machines and growing use of caller ID to screen telephone calls.[5] A parent who must juggle the telephone and a half-diapered child and refuses to participate in the survey because

Respondent error
A category of sample bias resulting from some respondent action or inaction such as nonresponse or response bias.

Nonresponse error
The statistical differences between a survey that includes only those who responded and a perfect survey that would also include those who failed to respond.

Nonrespondents
People who are not contacted or who refuse to cooperate in the research.

No contacts
People who are not at home or who are otherwise inaccessible on the first and second contact.

Many e-mail addresses are actually inactive. Inactive e-mails contribute to low response rates.

Refusals
People who are unwilling to participate in a research project.

Self-selection bias
A bias that occurs because people who feel strongly about a subject are more likely to respond to survey questions than people who feel indifferent about it.

he or she is too busy also is a nonresponse. **Refusals** occur when people are unwilling to participate in the research. A research team reviewed fifty mail surveys of pediatricians conducted by the American Academy of Pediatrics (AAP) between 1994 and 2002 and found that response rates declined over the period studied. In the early years of the study period, an average 70 percent of pediatricians returned completed surveys; the response rate fell to an average 63 percent in the second half of the period.[6] No contacts and refusals can seriously bias survey data. In the case of the pediatricians, the researchers found little difference in the response rates attributable to differences in such easy-to-measure variables as age, sex, and type of membership in the AAP, leaving them to wonder whether the cause of refusals was some unknown but important difference among these doctors.

Because of this problem, researchers investigate the causes of nonresponse. For example, a study analyzed a large database collected by AT&T and found that the effort required to participate in an ongoing study contributes to the problem.[7] People tend not to respond to questions that are difficult to answer. When they are asked to participate in a long-term panel, the rate of nonresponse to individual items grows over time, and eventually some people stop participating altogether. However, eventually it becomes easier to keep answering the same kinds of panel questions, and nonresponse rates level off.

Comparing the demographics of the sample with the demographics of the target population is one means of inspecting for possible biases in response patterns. If a particular group, such as older citizens, is underrepresented or if any potential biases appear in a response pattern, additional efforts should be made to obtain data from the underrepresented segments of the population. For example, personal interviews may be used instead of telephone interviews for the underrepresented segments.

After receiving a refusal from a potential respondent, an interviewer can do nothing other than be polite. The respondent who is not at home when called or visited should be scheduled to be interviewed at a different time of day or on a different day of the week.

With a mail survey, the researcher never really knows whether a nonrespondent has refused to participate or is just indifferent. Researchers know that those who are most involved in an issue are more likely to respond to a mail survey. **Self-selection bias** is a problem that frequently plagues self-administered questionnaires. In a restaurant, for example, a customer on whom a waiter spilled soup, a person who was treated to a surprise dinner, or others who feel strongly about the service are more likely to complete a self-administered questionnaire left at the table than individuals who are indifferent about the restaurant. Self-selection biases distort surveys because they overrepresent extreme positions while underrepresenting responses from those who are indifferent. Several techniques will be discussed later for encouraging respondents to reply to mail and Internet surveys.

Response Bias

Response bias
A bias that occurs when respondents either consciously or unconsciously tend to answer questions with a certain slant that misrepresents the truth.

A **response bias** occurs when respondents tend to answer questions with a certain slant. People may consciously or unconsciously misrepresent the truth. If a distortion of measurement occurs because respondents' answers are falsified or misrepresented, either intentionally or inadvertently, the resulting sample bias will be a response bias. When researchers identify response bias, they should include a corrective measure.

Response bias falls into four specific categories: acquiescence bias, extremity bias, interviewer bias, and social desirability bias. These categories overlap and are not mutually exclusive. A single biased answer may be distorted for many complex reasons, some distortions being deliberate and some being unconscious misrepresentations.

RESEARCHSNAPSHOT

My Opinion? It Depends on Your Words

It's hard to capture the nuances of a person's opinion with a simple survey question. Word choices seem to shape some respondents' answers. Carl Bialik, a columnist for *The Wall Street Journal,* observed this problem when he looked at responses to public-opinion polls exploring differences of opinion about activities of the National Security Agency. Bialik concluded that opinions varied based on the wording of the questions.

One pollster, Rasmussen Reports, asked, "Should the National Security Agency be allowed to intercept telephone conversations between terrorism suspects in other countries and people living in the United States?" Almost two-thirds of respondents said yes. But in a Gallup survey for *USA Today* and CNN, only 51 percent favored the NSA's wiretapping of "telephone conversations between U.S. citizens living in the United States and suspected terrorists living in other countries without getting a court order allowing it to do so."

One source of the difference might be the language "people" in the first poll and "U.S. citizens" in the second. A *Wall Street Journal*/NBC poll found 53 percent favoring the wiretapping program when it involved "American citizens in the United States," while more (56 percent) favored the program in a *Washington Post*/ABC poll asking about "some people in the United States." Scott Rasmussen, president of Rasmussen Reports, also hypothesizes that results of polls investigating this issue also may be swayed by whether the questions mention the lack of search warrants for the wiretaps. In these examples, the word choices shape which aspects of a complex issue the respondents focus on.

Source: Wall Street Journal. Online [May Be Used] by Carl Bialik. Copyright 2006 by Dow Jones & Co. Inc. Reproduced with permission of Dow Jones & Co. Inc. via Copyright Clearance Center.

Acquiescence Bias

Some respondents are very agreeable. They seem to agree to practically every statement they are asked about. A tendency to agree with all or most questions is known as **acquiescence bias**. This bias is particularly prominent in new-product research. Questions about a new-product idea generally elicit some acquiescence bias because respondents give positive connotations to most new ideas. For example, consumers responded favorably to survey questions about pump baseball gloves (the pump inserts air into the pocket of the glove, providing more cushioning). However, when these expensive gloves hit the market, they sat on the shelves. When conducting new-product research, researchers should recognize the high likelihood of acquiescence bias.

Another form of acquiescence is evident in some people's tendency to disagree with all questions. Thus, acquiescence bias is a response bias due to the respondents' tendency to concur with a particular position.

Acquiescence bias
A tendency for respondents to agree with all or most questions asked of them in a survey.

Extremity Bias

Some individuals tend to use extremes when responding to questions; others consistently avoid extreme positions and tend to respond more neutrally. Response styles vary from person to person, and extreme responses may cause an **extremity bias** in the data.[8]

Extremity bias
A category of response bias that results because some individuals tend to use extremes when responding to questions.

Interviewer Bias

Response bias may arise from the interplay between interviewer and respondent. If the interviewer's presence influences respondents to give untrue or modified answers, the survey will be marred by **interviewer bias**. Many homemakers and retired people welcome an interviewer's visit as a break in routine activities. Other respondents may give answers they believe will please the interviewer rather than the truthful responses. Respondents may wish to appear intelligent and wealthy—of course they read *Scientific American* rather than *Playboy.*

The interviewer's age, sex, style of dress, tone of voice, facial expressions, or other nonverbal characteristics may have some influence on a respondent's answers. If an interviewer smiles and makes a positive statement after a respondent's answers, the respondent will be more likely to give

Interviewer bias
A response bias that occurs because the presence of the interviewer influences respondents' answers.

similar responses. In a research study on sexual harassment against saleswomen, male interviewers might not yield as candid responses from saleswomen as female interviewers would.

Many interviewers, contrary to instructions, shorten or rephrase questions to suit their needs. This potential influence on responses can be avoided to some extent if interviewers receive training and supervision that emphasize the necessity of appearing neutral.

If interviews go on too long, respondents may feel that time is being wasted. They may answer as abruptly as possible with little forethought.

Social Desirability Bias

Social desirability bias
Bias in responses caused by respondents' desire, either conscious or unconscious, to gain prestige or appear in a different social role.

A **social desirability bias** may occur either consciously or unconsciously because the respondent wishes to create a favorable impression or save face in the presence of an interviewer. Incomes may be inflated, education overstated, or perceived respectable answers given to gain prestige. In contrast, answers to questions that seek factual information or responses about matters of public knowledge (zip code, number of children, and so on) usually are quite accurate. An interviewer's presence may increase a respondent's tendency to give inaccurate answers to sensitive questions such as "Did you vote in the last election?," "Do you have termites or roaches in your home?," or "Do you color your hair?"

The social desirability bias is especially significant in the case of research that addresses sensitive or personal topics, including respondents' sexual behavior. A group of researchers recently evaluated responses to questions about homosexual sexual activity, collected by National Opinion Research Center's long-running General Social Survey.[9] The researchers found that over time, as attitudes toward homosexual conduct have softened, the frequency of repeated female-female sexual contacts increased dramatically, suggesting the possibility that reporting levels have been subject to social desirability bias. However, the researchers noted that rates of male-male sexual contact were fairly steady over the period and that the rate of change for female-female sexual contact persisted even when adjusted for measures of greater tolerance. This evidence suggests that the data reflect more phenomena than mere social desirability bias.

Administrative Error

Administrative error
An error caused by the improper administration or execution of the research task.

The result of improper administration or execution of the research task is called an **administrative error**. Administrative errors are caused by carelessness, confusion, neglect, omission, or some other blunder. Four types of administrative error are data-processing error, sample selection error, interviewer error, and interviewer cheating.

Data-Processing Error

Data-processing error
A category of administrative error that occurs because of incorrect data entry, incorrect computer programming, or other procedural errors during data analysis.

Processing data by computer, like any arithmetic or procedural process, is subject to error because data must be edited, coded, and entered into the computer by people. The accuracy of data processed by computer depends on correct data entry and programming. **Data-processing error** can be minimized by establishing careful procedures for verifying each step in the data-processing stage.

Sample Selection Error

Sample selection error
An administrative error caused by improper sample design or sampling procedure execution.

Many kinds of error involve failure to select a representative sample. **Sample selection error** is systematic error that results in an unrepresentative sample because of an error in either the sample design or the execution of the sampling procedure. Executing a sampling plan free of procedural error is difficult. A firm that selects its sample from the phone book will have some systematic error, because unlisted numbers are not included. Stopping respondents during daytime hours in shopping centers excludes working people who shop by mail, Internet, or telephone. In other cases, researchers interview the wrong person. Consider a political pollster who uses random-digit dialing to select a sample, rather than a list of registered voters. Unregistered 17-year-olds may be willing to give their opinions, but they are the wrong people to ask because they cannot vote.

Interviewer Error

Interviewers' abilities vary considerably. **Interviewer error** is introduced when interviewers record answers but check the wrong response or are unable to write fast enough to record answers verbatim. Also, selective perception may cause interviewers to misrecord data that do not support their own attitudes and opinions.

©BANANA STOCK/JUPITER IMAGES

One problem with web-based surveys is that there is no way of knowing who exactly responded to the questionnaire.

Interviewer error
Mistakes made by interviewers failing to record survey responses correctly.

Interviewer cheating
The practice of filling in fake answers or falsifying questionnaires while working as an interviewer.

Interviewer Cheating

Interviewer cheating occurs when an interviewer falsifies entire questionnaires or fills in answers to questions that have been intentionally skipped. Some interviewers cheat to finish an interview as quickly as possible or to avoid questions about sensitive topics.

If interviewers are suspected of faking questionnaires, they should be told that a small percentage of respondents will be called back to confirm whether the initial interview was actually conducted. This practice should discourage interviewers from cheating. The term *curb-stoning* is sometimes used to refer to interviewers filling in responses for respondents that do not really exist.

Rule-of-Thumb Estimates for Systematic Error

The techniques for estimating systematic, or nonsampling, error are less precise than many sample statistics. Researchers have established experience-based, conservative rules of thumb to estimate systematic error. In the case of consumer research, experienced researchers might determine that only a certain percentage of people who say they will definitely buy a new product actually do so. Evidence for a mere-measurement effect suggests asking respondents about their own behavior can be associated with error. For instance, respondents who really like a certain TV show may actually report that they watch the show more often than they actually do. Thus, researchers often present actual survey findings *and* their interpretations of estimated purchase response based on estimates of nonsampling error. For example, one pay-per-view cable TV company surveys geographic areas it plans to enter and estimates the number of people who indicate they will subscribe to its service. The company knocks down the percentage by a "ballpark 10 percent" because experience in other geographic areas has indicated that there is a systematic upward bias of 10 percent on this intentions question.

What Can Be Done to Reduce Survey Error?

Now that we have examined the sources of error in surveys, you may have lost some of your optimism about survey research. Don't be discouraged! The discussion emphasized the bad news because it is important for marketing managers to realize that surveys are not a panacea. There are, however, ways to handle and reduce survey errors. For example, Chapter 11 on questionnaire design discusses the reduction of response bias; Chapters 12 and 13 discuss the reduction of sample selection and random sampling error. Indeed, much of the remainder of this book discusses various techniques for reducing bias in marketing research. The good news lies ahead!

Survey Research by Media

Now that we have discussed some advantages and disadvantages of surveys in general, we will discuss surveys according to the medium of communication.

Survey data are obtained when individuals respond to questions asked by interviewers (interviews) or to questions they have read (questionnaires). Interviews can be categorized based on the medium the researcher uses in communicating with individuals and recording data. For example, interviews may be conducted door-to-door, in shopping malls, through the mail, on the telephone, or, increasingly, through the Internet. Questionnaires may be in paper or electronic format; they may be presented by an interviewer or self-administered, and they may be placed at a variety of points, such as points of purchase or even by fax.

Electronic dating services have become a popular, successful example of electronic interactive media.

©MICHAEL NEWMAN/PHOTOEDIT

Human Interactive Media and Electronic Interactive Media

When two people engage in a conversation, human interaction takes place. Human interactive media are a personal form of communication. One human being directs a message to and interacts with another individual (or a small group). When most people think of interviewing, they envision two people engaged in a face-to-face dialogue or a conversation on the telephone.

Electronic interactive media allow marketers to reach a large audience, personalize individual messages, and interact using digital technology. To a large extent, electronic interactive media are controlled by the users themselves. No other human need be present. Survey respondents today are not passive audience members. They are actively involved in a two-way communication using electronic interactive media.

The Internet is radically altering many organizations' research strategies, providing a prominent example of the new electronic interactive media. Consumers determine what information they will be exposed to by choosing what sites to visit and by blocking or closing annoying pop-up ads. Electronic interactive media also include CD-ROM and DVD materials, touch-tone telephone systems, touch-screen interactive kiosks in stores, and other forms of digital technology.

Noninteractive Media

The traditional questionnaire received by mail and completed by the respondent does not allow a dialogue or an exchange of information providing immediate feedback. So, from our perspective, self-administered questionnaires printed on paper are noninteractive. This fact does not mean that they are without merit, just that this type of survey is less flexible than surveys using interactive communication media.

Each technique for conducting surveys has merits and shortcomings. The purpose of this chapter is to explain when researchers should use different types of surveys. This portion begins with a discussion of surveys that use live interviews. Then we turn to noninteractive, self-administered questionnaires. Finally, we explain how the Internet and digital technology are dramatically changing survey research.

Personal Interviews

To conduct interviews, the researcher may communicate with individuals in person by going door-to-door or intercepting them in shopping malls, or interviews may take place over the telephone. Traditionally, researchers have recorded interview results using paper and pencil, but computers are increasingly supporting survey research. In this section, we examine the general characteristics of face-to-face personal interviews, then compare the characteristics of door-to-door personal interviews and personal interviews conducted in shopping malls. The next section examines telephone interviews.

Researchers have been gathering information through face-to-face contact with individuals for many years. Periodic censuses were used to set tax rates and aid military conscription in the ancient empires of Egypt and Rome.[10] During the Middle Ages, the merchant families of Fugger and Rothschild prospered in part because their far-flung organizations enabled them to get information before their competitors could.[11] Today, survey researchers typically present themselves in shopping centers and street corners throughout the United States and announce, "Good afternoon, my name is _____. I am with _____ Marketing Research Company, and we are conducting a survey on _____."

A **personal interview** is a form of direct communication in which an interviewer asks respondents questions face-to-face. This versatile and flexible method is a two-way conversation between interviewer and respondent.

Personal interview
Face-to-face communication in which an interviewer asks a respondent to answer questions.

Advantages of Personal Interviews

Marketing researchers find that personal interviews offer many unique advantages. One of the most important is the opportunity for feedback.

▇ OPPORTUNITY FOR FEEDBACK

Personal interviews provide the opportunity for feedback and clarification. For example, if a consumer is reluctant to provide sensitive information, the interviewer may offer reassurance that his or her answers will be strictly confidential. Personal interviews offer the lowest chance that respondents will misinterpret questions, because an interviewer who senses confusion can clarify the instruction or questions. Circumstances may dictate that at the conclusion of the interview, the respondent be given additional information concerning the purpose of the study. This clarification is easily accomplished with a personal interview. If the feedback indicates that some question or set of questions is particularly confusing, the researcher can make changes that make the questionnaire easier to understand.

▇ PROBING COMPLEX ANSWERS

Another important characteristic of personal interviews is the opportunity to follow up by probing. If a respondent's answer is too brief or unclear, the researcher may request a more comprehensive or clearer explanation. In probing, the interviewer asks for clarification with standardized questions such as "Can you tell me more about what you had in mind?" Although interviewers are expected to ask questions exactly as they appear on the questionnaire, probing allows them some flexibility. Depending on the research purpose, personal interviews vary in the degree to which questions are structured and in the amount of probing required. The personal interview is especially useful for obtaining unstructured information. Skilled interviewers can handle complex questions that cannot easily be asked in telephone or mail surveys.

LENGTH OF INTERVIEW

If the research objective requires an extremely lengthy questionnaire, personal interviews may be the only option. A general rule of thumb on mail surveys is that they should not exceed six pages, and telephone interviews typically last less than ten minutes. In contrast, a personal interview can be much longer, perhaps an hour and a half. However, the longer the interview, no matter what the form, the more the respondent should be compensated for their time and participation. Researchers should also be clear about how long participation should take in the opening dialog requesting participation. Online surveys should include a completion meter that shows the progress a respondent has made toward completing the task.

COMPLETENESS OF QUESTIONNAIRE

The social interaction between a well-trained interviewer and a respondent in a personal interview increases the likelihood that the respondent will answer all the items on the questionnaire. The respondent who grows bored with a telephone interview may terminate the interview at his or her discretion simply by hanging up the phone. Self-administration of a mail questionnaire requires even more effort by the respondent. Rather than write lengthy responses, the respondent may fail to complete some of the questions. Item nonresponse—failure to provide an answer to a question—is least likely to occur when an experienced interviewer asks questions directly.

Item nonresponse
Failure of a respondent to provide an answer to a survey question.

PROPS AND VISUAL AIDS

Interviewing respondents face-to-face allows the investigator to show them new product samples, sketches of proposed advertising, or other visual aids. When Lego Group wanted to introduce new train model sets for its famous building bricks, the company targeted adults who build complex models with its product. The company invited adults who were swapping ideas at the Lego website to visit the New York office, where they viewed ideas and provided their opinions. The respondents wound up rejecting all the company's ideas, but they suggested something different: the Santa Fe Super Chief set, which sold out within two weeks, after being advertised only by enthusiastic word of mouth.[12] This research could not have been done in a telephone interview or mail survey.

Marketing research that uses visual aids has become increasingly popular with researchers who investigate film concepts, advertising problems, and moviegoers' awareness of performers. Research for movies often begins by showing respondents videotapes of the prospective cast. After the movie has been produced, film clips are shown and interviews conducted to evaluate the movie's appeal, especially which scenes to emphasize in advertisements.

HIGH PARTICIPATION

Although some people are reluctant to participate in a survey, the presence of an interviewer generally increases the percentage of people willing to complete the interview. Respondents typically are required to do no reading or writing—all they have to do is talk. Many people enjoy sharing information and insights with friendly and sympathetic interviewers. People are often more hesitant to tell a person "no" face-to-face than they are over the phone or through some impersonal contact.

Disadvantages of Personal Interviews

Personal interviews also have some disadvantages. Respondents are not anonymous and as a result may be reluctant to provide confidential information to another person. Suppose a survey asked top executives, "Do you see any major internal instabilities or threats (people, money, material, and so on) to the achievement of your marketing objectives?" Many managers may be reluctant to answer this sensitive question honestly in a personal interview in which their identities are known.

INTERVIEWER INFLUENCE

Some evidence suggests that demographic characteristics of the interviewer influence respondents' answers. For example, one research study revealed that male interviewers produced larger amounts of interviewer variance than female interviewers in a survey in which 85 percent of the respondents were female. Older interviewers who interviewed older respondents produced more variance than other age combinations, whereas younger interviewers who interviewed younger respondents produced the least variance.

Differential interviewer techniques may be a source of bias. The rephrasing of a question, the interviewer's tone of voice, and the interviewer's appearance may influence the respondent's answer. Consider the interviewer who has conducted 100 personal interviews. During the next one, he or she may lose concentration and either selectively perceive or anticipate the respondent's answer. The interpretation of the response may differ somewhat from what the respondent intended. Typically, the public thinks of the person who does marketing research as a dedicated scientist. Unfortunately, some interviewers do not fit that ideal. Considerable interviewer variability exists. Cheating is possible; interviewers may cut corners to save time and energy, faking parts of their reports by dummying up part or all of the questionnaire. Control over interviewers is important to ensure that difficult, embarrassing, or time-consuming questions are handled properly.

LACK OF ANONYMITY OF RESPONDENT

Because a respondent in a personal interview is not anonymous and may be reluctant to provide confidential information to another person, researchers often spend considerable time and effort to phrase sensitive questions to avoid social desirability bias. For example, the interviewer may show the respondent a card that lists possible answers and ask the respondent to read a category number rather than be required to verbalize sensitive answers.

COST

Personal interviews are expensive, generally substantially more costly than mail, Internet, or telephone surveys. The geographic proximity of respondents, the length and complexity of the questionnaire, and the number of people who are nonrespondents because they could not be contacted (not-at-homes) will all influence the cost of the personal interview.

Door-to-Door Interviews and Shopping Mall Intercepts

Personal interviews may be conducted at the respondents' homes or offices or in many other places. Increasingly, personal interviews are being conducted in shopping malls. Mall intercept interviews allow many interviews to be conducted quickly. Often, respondents are intercepted in public areas of shopping malls and then asked to come to a permanent research facility to taste new food items or to view advertisements. The locale for the interview generally influences the participation rate, and thus the degree to which the sample represents the general population.

DOOR-TO-DOOR INTERVIEWS

The presence of an interviewer at the door generally increases the likelihood that a person will be willing to complete an interview. Because **door-to-door interviews** increase the participation rate, they provide a more representative sample of the population than mail questionnaires. For example, response rates to mail surveys are substantially lower among Hispanics whether the questionnaire is printed in English or Spanish.[13] People who do not have telephones, who have unlisted telephone numbers, or who are otherwise difficult to contact may be reached using door-to-door interviews. However, door-to-door interviews may underrepresent some groups and overrepresent others based on the geographic areas covered.

Door-to-door interviews may exclude individuals who live in multiple-dwelling units with security systems, such as high-rise apartment dwellers, or executives who are too busy to grant

Door-to-door interviews
Personal interviews conducted at respondents' doorsteps in an effort to increase the participation rate in the survey.

RESEARCHSNAPSHOT

Matters of Taste

Asking an opinion is easy to do over the phone or online, but not if you want people's reactions to a new food, wine, or perfume. For those opinions, you probably want people to sample the new product first. And for best results, they need to try it away from odors that could mask or alter the experience. As a result, researchers arrange for sensory evaluations to take place along with personal interviews, often using the mall intercept format.

By listening to consumers drawn from a mall intercept, marketers can hear the way consumers react to a product.

©FOODPIX/JUPITER IMAGES

Sometimes researchers simply want to know whether consumers like the product; in other situations, they are trying to meet objectives such as maintaining the same taste after substituting a new ingredient. Sartori Foods uses a chart it calls the Italian Cheese Flavor Wheel to ask consumers to describe various cheeses. The chart matches consumer-

friendly terms like *nutty, buttery,* and *creamy* with terms useful in the industry (for example, *aromatic amino acids* and *sulfur compounds*). Other research projects involve a specialized set of subjects who have been trained to discuss wine, cheese, or perfume using technical language.

For sensory research, finding qualified participants is more complicated than for other kinds of interviews. Besides knowing whether individuals buy the category of product, researchers want to eliminate anyone who has a cold, smokes, or has other conditions that could interfere with taste and smell. Sometimes the problem goes beyond screening. A team of researchers who traveled to Venezuela for research discovered that the hosts of the testing room had beautified it with a fresh coat of paint—and the paint odor made the room unusable.

Sources: Based on Claudia D. O'Donnell, "Tips for Sensory Tests," Prepared Foods, January 2005, downloaded from InfoTrac at http://www.galenet.com; Fran LaBell, "International Sensory Tests: When in Rome," Prepared Foods, February 2002, downloaded from Business & Company Resource Center, http://galenet.galegroup.com; and Paula Frank, "Sensory Analysis: An Invaluable Tool," Dairy Field, January 2002, http://galenet.galegroup.com.

personal interviews during business hours. Other people, for security reasons, simply will not open the door when a stranger knocks. Telephoning an individual in one of these subgroups to make an appointment may make the total sample more representative. However, obtaining a representative sample of this security-conscious subgroup based on a listing in the telephone directory may be difficult. For these reasons, door-to-door interviews are becoming a thing of the past.

CALLBACKS

Callbacks
Attempts to recontact individuals selected for a sample who were not available initially.

When a person selected to be in the sample cannot be contacted on the first visit, a systematic procedure is normally initiated to call back at another time. **Callbacks,** or attempts to recontact individuals selected for the sample, are the major means of reducing nonresponse error. Calling back a sampling unit is more expensive than interviewing the person the first time around, because subjects who initially were not at home generally are more widely dispersed geographically than the original sample units. Callbacks in door-to-door interviews are important because not-at-home individuals (for example, working parents) may systematically vary from those who *are* at home (nonworking parents, retired people, and the like).

MALL INTERCEPT INTERVIEWS

Mall intercept interviews
Personal interviews conducted in a shopping mall.

Personal interviews conducted in shopping malls are referred to as **mall intercept interviews,** or *shopping center sampling.* Interviewers typically intercept shoppers at a central point within the mall or at an entrance. The main reason mall intercept interviews are conducted is because their costs are lower. No travel is required to the respondent's home; instead, the respondent comes to the interviewer, and many interviews can be conducted quickly in this way.

A major problem with mall intercept interviews is that individuals usually are in a hurry to shop, so the incidence of refusal is high—typically around 50 percent. Yet the commercial marketing research industry conducts more personal interviews in shopping malls than it conducts door-to-door.

In a mall interview, the researcher must recognize that he or she should not be looking for a representative sample of the total population. Each mall has its own target market's characteristics, and there is likely to be a larger bias than with careful household probability sampling. However, personal interviews in shopping malls are appropriate when the target group is a special market segment such as the parents of children of bike-riding age. If the respondent indicates that he or she has a child of this age, the parent can then be brought into a rented space and shown several bikes. The mall intercept interview allows the researcher to show large, heavy, or immobile visual materials, such as a television commercial. A mall interviewer can give an individual a product to take home to use and obtain a commitment that the respondent will cooperate when recontacted later by telephone. Mall intercept interviews are also valuable when activities such as cooking and tasting of food must be closely coordinated and timed to follow each other. They may also be appropriate when a consumer durable product must be demonstrated. For example, when videocassette recorders and DVD players were innovations in the prototype stage, the effort and space required to set up and properly display these units ruled out in-home testing.

Global Considerations

Willingness to participate in a personal interview varies dramatically around the world. For example, in many Middle Eastern countries women would never consent to be interviewed by a man. And in many countries the idea of discussing grooming behavior and personal-care products with a stranger would be highly offensive. Few people would consent to be interviewed on such topics.

The norms about appropriate business conduct also influence businesspeople's willingness to provide information to interviewers. For example, conducting business-to-business interviews in Japan during business hours is difficult because managers, strongly loyal to their firm, believe that they have an absolute responsibility to oversee their employees while on the job. In some cultures when a businessperson is reluctant to be interviewed, a reputable third party may be asked to intervene so that an interview may take place.

TOTHEPOINT

A man's feet should be planted in his country, but his eyes should survey the world.

—George Santayana

Telephone Interviews

Good evening, I'm with a nationwide marketing research company. Are you watching television tonight?
A: Yes.
Did you see 60 Minutes on CBS?
A: "Click"

For several decades, **telephone interviews** have been the mainstay of commercial survey research. The quality of data obtained by telephone may be comparable to the quality of the data collected in personal interviews. Respondents are more willing to provide detailed and reliable information on a variety of personal topics over the telephone than with personal interviews. Telephone surveys can provide representative samples of the general population in the United States. Conducting telephone interviews may be less possible in developed nations, although the widespread adoption of mobile phones is certain changing the telephone interview landscape. Additionally, the recent no-call laws discussed earlier limit the ability to generate a representative sample.

Telephone interviews
Personal interviews conducted by telephone, the mainstay of commercial survey research.

Characteristics of Telephone Interviews

Telephone interviews have several distinctive characteristics that set them apart from other survey techniques. These characteristics present significant advantages and disadvantages for the researcher.

SPEED

One advantage of telephone interviewing is the speed of data collection. While data collection with mail or personal interviews can take several weeks, hundreds of telephone interviews can be conducted literally overnight. When the interviewer enters the respondents' answers directly into a computerized system, the data processing speeds up even more.

COST

As the cost of personal interviews continues to increase, telephone interviews are becoming relatively inexpensive. The cost of telephone interviews is estimated to be less than 25 percent of the cost of door-to-door personal interviews. Travel time and costs are eliminated. However, the typical Internet survey is less expensive than a telephone survey.

ABSENCE OF FACE-TO-FACE CONTACT

Telephone interviews are more impersonal than face-to-face interviews. Respondents may answer embarrassing or confidential questions more willingly in a telephone interview than in a personal interview. However, mail and Internet surveys, although not perfect, are better media for gathering extremely sensitive information because they seem more anonymous. Some evidence suggests that people provide information on income and other financial matters only reluctantly, even in telephone interviews. Such questions may be personally threatening for a variety of reasons, and high refusal rates for this type of question occur with each form of survey research.

Although telephone calls may be less threatening because the interviewer is not physically present, the absence of face-to-face contact can also be a liability. The respondent cannot see that the interviewer is still writing down the previous comment and may continue to elaborate on an answer. If the respondent pauses to think about an answer, the interviewer may not realize it and may go on to the next question. Hence, there is a greater tendency for interviewers to record no answers and incomplete answers in telephone interviews than in personal interviews.

COOPERATION

One trend is very clear. In the last few decades, telephone response rates have fallen. Analysis of response rates for the long-running Survey of Consumer Attitudes conducted by the University of Michigan found that response rates fell from a high of 72 percent to 67 percent during the period from 1979 to 1996 and then even faster after 1996, dropping to 60 percent.[14] Lenny Murphy of data collection firm Dialtek says he has observed a decline in survey response rates from a typical range of 30 to 40 percent in the past down to below 20 percent.[15] Fewer calls are answered because more households are using caller ID and answering machines to screen their calls, and many individuals do not pick up the phone when the display reads "out of area" or when an unfamiliar survey organization's name and number appear on the display. Also, more phone lines are dedicated to fax machines and computers. However, the University of Michigan study found that the rate of refusal actually grew faster in the more recent period than the rate of not answering researchers' calls.

One way researchers can try to improve response rates is to leave a message on the household's telephone answering machine or voice mail. However, many people will not return a call to help someone conduct a survey. Using a message explicitly stating that the purpose of the call is not sales related may improve responses. Other researchers simply hope to reach respondents when they call back, trying callbacks at different times and on different days.

Further complicating the situation is the use of wireless mobile phone services.[16] Regulations by the Federal Communications Commission make it illegal for researchers to use automated dialing equipment to call mobile phones. Even if researchers dial the calls by hand, they may not contact anyone who would have to pay for the call—that is, most cellphone users. So far, only a small share of U.S. households (less than 4 percent) have given up their landlines, but those numbers are growing, and they include a sizable segment of young adults. Worse for marketers, consumers may keep their phone numbers when they change to a new phone company, so many consumers who have abandoned landlines for cellphones may be keeping a phone number that marketers may no longer dial without penalty.

Other countries may not adopt laws restricting calls to mobile phones. In addition, consumers in other countries are more open to responding to research delivered by voice or by text messaging. Thus, the mobile phone may be a better interview tool outside of the United States than in the United States.

Refusal to cooperate with interviews is directly related to interview length. A major study of survey research found that interviews of 5 minutes or less had a refusal rate of 21 percent; interviews of between 6 and 12 minutes had 41 percent refusal rates; and interviews of 13 minutes or more had 47 percent rates. In unusual cases, a few highly interested respondents will put up with longer interviews. A good rule of thumb is to keep telephone interviews approximately 10 to 15 minutes long. In general, 30 minutes is the maximum amount of time most respondents will spend unless they are highly interested in the survey subject or highly compensated for their time.

Another way to encourage participation is to send households an invitation to participate in a survey. The invitation can describe the purpose and importance of the survey and the likely duration of the survey. The invitation can also encourage subjects to be available and reassure them that the caller will not try to sell anything. In a recent study comparing response rates, the rates were highest among households that received an advance letter, somewhat lower when the notice came on a postcard, and lowest when no notice was sent.[17]

INCENTIVES TO REPOND

Respondents should receive some incentive to respond. Research addresses different types of incentives. For telephone interviews, test-marketing involving different types of survey introduciton suggests that not all introductions are equally effective. A financial incentive or some significant chance to win a desirable prize will produce a higher telephone response rate than a simple assurance that the research is not a sales pitch, a more detailed description of the survey or an assurance of confidentiality.[18]

REPRESENTATIVE SAMPLES

Practical difficulties complicate obtaining representative samples based on listings in the telephone book. About 95 percent of households in the United States have landline telephones. People without phones are more likely to be poor, aged, rural, or living in the South. Unlisted phone numbers and numbers too new to be printed in the directory are a greater problem. People have unlisted phone numbers for two reasons:

- They have recently moved
- They prefer to have unlisted numbers for privacy

Individuals whose phone numbers are unlisted because of a recent move differ slightly from those with published numbers. The unlisted group tends to be younger, more urban, and less likely to own a single-family dwelling. Households that maintain unlisted phone numbers by choice tend to have higher incomes. And, as previously mentioned, a number of low-income households are unlisted by circumstance.

The problem of unlisted phone numbers can be partially resolved through the use of random digit dialing. **Random digit dialing** eliminates the counting of names in a list (for example, calling every fiftieth name in a column) and subjectively determining whether a directory listing is a business, institution, or legitimate household. In the simplest form of random digit dialing, telephone exchanges (prefixes) for the geographic areas in the sample are obtained. Using a table of random numbers, the last four digits of the telephone number are selected. Telephone directories can be ignored entirely or used in combination with the assignment of one or several random digits. Random digit dialing also helps overcome the problem due to new listings and recent changes in numbers. Unfortunately, the refusal rate in commercial random digit dialing studies is higher than the refusal rate for telephone surveys that use only listed telephone numbers.

Random digit dialing
Use of telephone exchanges and a table of random numbers to contact respondents with unlisted phone numbers.

CALLBACKS

An unanswered call, a busy signal, or a respondent who is not at home requires a callback. Telephone callbacks are much easier to make than callbacks in personal interviews. However, as mentioned, the ownership of telephone answering machines is growing, and their effects on callbacks need to be studied.

▓ LIMITED DURATION

Respondents who run out of patience with the interview can merely hang up. To encourage participation, interviews should be relatively short. The length of the telephone interview is definitely limited.

▓ LACK OF VISUAL MEDIUM

Because visual aids cannot be used in telephone interviews, this method is not appropriate for packaging research, copy testing of television and print advertising, and concept tests that require visual materials. Likewise, certain attitude scales and measuring instruments, such as the semantic differential (see Chapter 10), require the respondent to see a graphic scale, so they are difficult to use over the phone.

Central Location Interviewing

Central location interviewing
Telephone interviews conducted from a central location using wats lines at fixed charges.

Research agencies or interviewing services typically conduct all telephone interviews from a central location. Such **central location interviewing** allows firms to hire a staff of professional interviewers and to supervise and control the quality of interviewing more effectively. When telephone interviews are centralized and computerized, an agency or business can benefit from additional cost economies.

Computer-Assisted Telephone Interviewing

Computer-assisted telephone interviewing (CATI)
Technology that allows answers to telephone interviews to be entered directly into a computer for processing.

Advances in computer technology allow responses to telephone interviews to be entered directly into the computer in a process known as **computer-assisted telephone interviewing (CATI)**. Telephone interviewers are seated at computer terminals. Monitors display the questionnaires, one question at a time, along with precoded possible responses to each question. The interviewer reads each question as it appears on the screen. When the respondent answers, the interviewer enters the response directly into the computer, and it is automatically stored in the computer's memory. The computer then displays the next question on the screen. Computer-assisted telephone interviewing requires that answers to the questionnaire be highly structured. If a respondent gives an unacceptable answer (that is, one not precoded and programmed), the computer will reject it.

Computer-assisted telephone interviewing systems include telephone management systems that select phone numbers, dial the numbers automatically, and perform other labor-saving functions. These systems can automatically control sample selection by randomly generating names or fulfilling a sample quota. A computer can generate an automatic callback schedule. A typical call management system might schedule recontact attempts to recall no answers after two hours and busy numbers after ten minutes and allow the interviewer to enter a more favorable time slot (day and hour) when a respondent indicates that he or she is too busy to be interviewed. Software systems also allow researchers to request daily status reports on the number of completed interviews relative to quotas. CATI interviews can also be conducted by a pre-recorded voice with the respondent answering by punching buttons on the phone.

Computerized Voice-Activated Telephone Interview

Technological advances have combined computerized telephone dialing and voice-activated computer messages to allow researchers to conduct telephone interviews without human interviewers. However, researchers have found that computerized voice-activated telephone interviewing works best with very short, simple questionnaires. One system includes a voice-synthesized module controlled by a microprocessor. With it the sponsor is able to register a caller's single response such as "true/false," "yes/no," "like/dislike," or "for/against." This type of system has been used by television and radio stations to register callers' responses to certain issues. One system, Telsol, begins with an announcement that the respondent is listening to a recorded message. Many people are intrigued by the idea of talking to a robot or a computer, so they stay on the line. The computer then asks questions, leaving blank tape in between to record the answers. If respondents do not answer the first two questions, the computer disconnects and goes to the next call. With this process, the entire data collection process can be automated because a recorded voice is used to both ask the questions and record answers.

Global Considerations

Different cultures often have different norms about proper telephone behavior. For example, business-to-business researchers have learned that Latin American businesspeople will not open up to strangers on the telephone. So, researchers in Latin America usually find personal interviews more suitable than telephone surveys. In Japan, respondents consider it ill-mannered if telephone interviews last more than twenty minutes.

Self-Administered Questionnaires

Many surveys do not require an interviewer's presence. Marketing researchers distribute questionnaires to consumers through the mail and in many other ways (see Exhibit 7.2). They insert questionnaires in packages and magazines. They may place questionnaires at points of purchase or in high-traffic locations in stores or malls. They may even fax questionnaires to individuals. Questionnaires can be printed on paper, but they may be posted on the Internet or sent via e-mail. No matter how the **self-administered questionnaires** are distributed, they are different from interviews because the respondent takes responsibility for reading and answering the questions.

Self-administered questionnaires present a challenge to the marketing researcher because they rely on the clarity of the written word rather than on the skills of the interviewer. The nature of self-administered questionnaires is best illustrated by explaining mail questionnaires.

Self-administered questionnaires
Surveys in which the respondent takes the responsibility for reading and answering the questions.

Mail Questionnaires

A **mail survey** is a self-administered questionnaire sent to respondents through the mail. This paper-and-pencil method has several advantages and disadvantages.

Mail survey
A self-administered questionnaire sent to respondents through the mail.

▇ GEOGRAPHIC FLEXIBILITY

Mail questionnaires can reach a geographically dispersed sample simultaneously because interviewers are not required. Respondents (such as farmers) who are located in isolated areas or those (such as executives) who are otherwise difficult to reach can easily be contacted by mail. For example, a pharmaceutical firm may find that doctors are not available for personal or telephone interviews. However, a mail survey can reach both rural and urban doctors who practice in widely dispersed geographic areas.

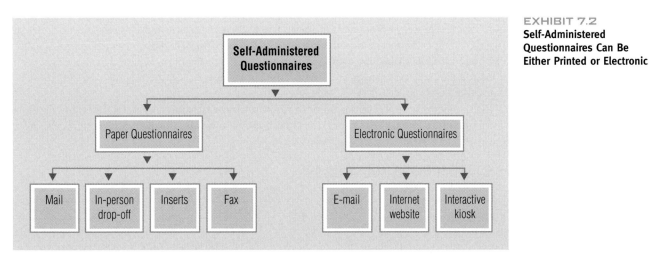

EXHIBIT 7.2
Self-Administered Questionnaires Can Be Either Printed or Electronic

COST

Mail questionnaires are relatively inexpensive compared with personal interviews, though they are not cheap. Most include follow-up mailings, which require additional postage and printing costs. And it usually isn't cost-effective to try to cut costs on printing—questionnaires photocopied on low-grade paper have a greater likelihood of being thrown in the wastebasket than those prepared with more expensive, high-quality printing. The low response rates contribute to the high cost.

RESPONDENT CONVENIENCE

Mail surveys and other self-administered questionnaires can be filled out when the respondents have time, so respondents are more likely to take time to think about their replies. Many hard-to-reach respondents place a high value on convenience and thus are best contacted by mail. In some situations, particularly in business-to-business marketing research, mail questionnaires allow respondents to collect facts, such as sales statistics, that they may not be able to recall without checking. Being able to check information by verifying records or, in household surveys, by consulting with other family members should provide more valid, factual information than either personal or telephone interviews would allow. A catalog retailer may use mail surveys to estimate sales volume for catalog items by sending a mock catalog as part of the questionnaire. Respondents would be asked to indicate how likely they would be to order selected items. Using the mail allows respondents to consult other family members and to make their decisions within a reasonable timespan.

ANONYMITY OF RESPONDENT

In the cover letter that accompanies a mail or self-administered questionnaire, marketing researchers almost always state that the respondents' answers will be confidential. Respondents are more likely to provide sensitive or embarrassing information when they can remain anonymous. For example, personal interviews and a mail survey conducted simultaneously asked the question "Have you borrowed money at a regular bank?" Researchers noted a 17 percent response rate for the personal interviews and a 42 percent response rate for the mail survey. Although random sampling error may have accounted for part of this difference, the results suggest that for research on personal and sensitive financial issues, mail surveys are more confidential than personal interviews.

Anonymity can also reduce social desirability bias. People are more likely to agree with controversial issues, such as extreme political candidates, when completing self-administered questionnaires than when speaking to interviewers on the phone or at their doorsteps.

ABSENCE OF INTERVIEWER

Although the absence of an interviewer can induce respondents to reveal sensitive or socially undesirable information, this lack of personal contact can also be a disadvantage. Once the respondent receives the questionnaire, the questioning process is beyond the researcher's control. Although the printed stimulus is the same, each respondent will attach a different personal meaning to each question. Selective perception operates in research as well as in advertising. The respondent does not have the opportunity to question the interviewer. Problems that might be clarified in a personal or telephone interview can remain misunderstandings in a mail survey. There is no interviewer to probe for additional information or clarification of an answer, and the recorded answers must be assumed to be complete.

Respondents have the opportunity to read the entire questionnaire before they answer individual questions. Often the text of a later question will provide information that affects responses to earlier questions.

STANDARDIZED QUESTIONS

Mail questionnaires typically are highly standardized, and the questions are quite structured. Questions and instructions must be clear-cut and straightforward. Ambiguous questions only create additional error. Interviewing allows for feedback from the interviewer regarding the respondent's comprehension of the questionnaire. An interviewer who notices that the first fifty respondents are having some difficulty understanding a question can report this fact to the research analyst so that revisions can be made. With a mail survey, however, once the questionnaires are mailed, it is difficult to change the format or the questions.

TIME IS MONEY

If time is a factor in management's interest in the research results, or if attitudes are rapidly changing (for example, toward a political event), mail surveys may not be the best communication medium. A minimum of two or three weeks is necessary for receiving the majority of the responses. Follow-up mailings, which usually are sent when the returns begin to trickle in, require an additional two or three weeks. The time between the first mailing and the cut-off date (when questionnaires will no longer be accepted) normally is six to eight weeks. In a regional or local study, personal interviews can be conducted more quickly. However, conducting a national study by mail might be substantially faster than conducting personal interviews across the nation.

LENGTH OF MAIL QUESTIONNAIRE

Mail questionnaires vary considerably in length, ranging from extremely short postcard questionnaires to multipage booklets that require respondents to fill in thousands of answers. A general rule of thumb is that a mail questionnaire should not exceed six pages in length. When a questionnaire requires a respondent to expend a great deal of effort, an incentive is generally required to induce the respondent to return the questionnaire. The following sections discuss several ways to obtain high response rates even when questionnaires are longer than average.

Response Rates

All questionnaires that arrive via bulk mail are likely to get thrown away. Questionnaires that are boring, unclear, or too complex are even more likely to get thrown in the wastebasket. A poorly designed mail questionnaire may be returned by less than 5 percent of those sampled (that is, a 5 percent response rate). The basic calculation for obtaining a **response rate** is to count the number of questionnaires returned or completed, then divide the total by the number of eligible people who were contacted or requested to participate in the survey. Typically, the number in the denominator is adjusted for faulty addresses and similar problems that reduce the number of eligible participants.

Response rate
The number of questionnaires returned or completed divided by the number of eligible people who were asked to participate in the survey.

The major limitations of mail questionnaires relate to response problems. Respondents who complete the questionnaire may not be typical of all people in the sample. Individuals with a special interest in the topic are more likely to respond to a mail survey than those who are indifferent.

A researcher has no assurance that the intended subject is the person who fills out the questionnaire. The wrong person answering the questions may be a problem when surveying corporate executives, physicians, and other professionals, who may pass questionnaires on to subordinates to complete. This probably is not unique to snail mail surveys since electronic surveying suffers similarly.

Evidence suggests that cooperation and response rates rise as home value increases. Also, if the sample has a high proportion of retired and well-off householders, response rates will be lower. Mail survey respondents tend to be better educated than nonrespondents. If they return the questionnaire at all, poorly educated respondents who cannot read and write well may skip open-ended questions to which they are required to write out their answers. Rarely will a mail survey have a 50 percent or greater response rate. However, the use of follow-up mailings and other techniques may increase the response rate to an acceptable percentage. The lower the response rate, the greater the concern that the resulting sample will not adequately represent the population.

Increasing Survey Response Rate

Nonresponse error is always a potential problem. Individuals interested in the general subject of the survey are more likely to respond than those with less interest. Thus, people who hold extreme positions on an issue are more likely to respond than individuals who are largely indifferent to the topic.

To minimize this bias, researchers have developed a number of techniques to increase the response rate to mail surveys. For example, almost all surveys include postage-paid return envelopes. Using a stamped return envelope instead of a business reply envelope increases response rates even more.[19] Designing and formatting attractive questionnaires and wording questions so that they are easy to understand also help ensure a good response rate. However, special efforts may be required even with a sound questionnaire. Several of these methods are discussed in the following subsections.

■ PERSONALIZATION

Cover letter
Letter that accompanies a questionnaire to induce the reader to complete and return the questionnaire.

A personalized **cover letter** or email should accompany a request to participate in a survey. This is an important means of inducing a reader to complete and return the questionnaire. Exhibit 7.3 illustrates a cover letter and some of the points considered by a marketing research professional to be important in gaining respondents' attention and cooperation. The first paragraph of the letter explains why the study is important. The basic appeal alludes to the social usefulness of responding. Two other frequently used appeals are asking for help ("Will you do us a favor?") and the egotistical appeal ("Your opinions are important!"). Most cover letters promise confidentiality, invite

EXHIBIT 7.3
Example of Cover Letter for Household Survey

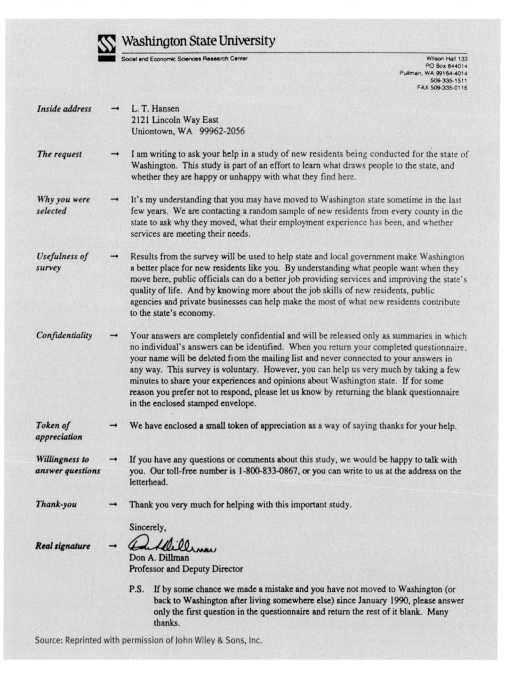

Source: Reprinted with permission of John Wiley & Sons, Inc.

the recipient to use an enclosed postage-paid reply envelope, describe any incentive or reward for participation, explain that answering the questionnaire will not be difficult and will take only a short time, and describe how the person was scientifically selected for participation.

Personalization shows the respondent that he or she is important. Including an individually typed cover letter on letterhead rather than a printed form is an important element in increasing the response rate in mail surveys.[20]

MONEY HELPS

The respondent's motivation for participating in a survey may be increased by offering monetary incentives or premiums. Although pens, lottery tickets, and a variety of premiums have been used, monetary incentives appear to be the most effective and least biasing incentive. Money attracts attention and creates a sense of obligation. Perhaps for this reason, monetary incentives work for all income categories. Often, cover letters try to boost response rates with messages such as "We know that the attached dollar cannot compensate you for your time but please accept it as a token of our appreciation." Response rates increase dramatically when the monetary incentive is to be sent to a charity of the respondent's choice rather than directly to the respondent.

INTERESTING QUESTIONS

The topic of the research—and thus the point of the questions—cannot be manipulated without changing the definition of the marketing problem. However, certain interesting questions can be added to the questionnaire, perhaps at the beginning, to stimulate respondents' interest and to induce cooperation. By including questions that are of little concern to the researchers but that the respondents want to answer, the researchers may give respondents who are indifferent to the major questions a reason for responding.

FOLLOW-UPS

After responses from the first wave of mailings begin to trickle in, most studies use a follow-up letter or postcard reminder, which requests that the questionnaire be returned because a 100 percent return rate is important. A follow-up may include a duplicate questionnaire or may merely be a reminder to return the original questionnaire. Multiple contacts almost always increase response rates. The more attempts made to reach people, the greater the chances of their responding.[21]

ADVANCE NOTIFICATION

Advance notification, by either letter or telephone, that a questionnaire will be arriving has been successful in increasing response rates in some situations. ACNielsen has used this technique to ensure a high cooperation rate in filling out diaries of television watching. Advance notices that go out closer to the questionnaire mailing time produce better results than those sent too far in advance. The optimal lead time for advance notification is three days before a questionnaire is to arrive.

SURVEY SPONSORSHIP

Auspices bias may result from the sponsorship of a survey. One business-to-business marketer wished to conduct a survey of its wholesalers to learn their stocking policies and their attitudes concerning competing manufacturers. A mail questionnaire sent on the corporate letterhead very likely would have received a much lower response rate than the questionnaire actually sent, which used the letterhead of a commercial marketing research firm. Sponsorship by well-known and prestigious organizations such as universities or government agencies may also significantly influence response rates. A survey sent to members of a consumer panel will receive an exceptionally high response rate because panel members have already agreed to cooperate with surveys.

OTHER TECHNIQUES

Numerous other devices have been used for increasing response rates. For example, the type of postage (commemorative versus regular stamp), envelope size, color of the questionnaire paper, and many other factors have been varied in efforts to increase response rates. Each has had at least limited success in certain situations; unfortunately, under other conditions each has failed to increase response rates significantly. The researcher should consider his or her particular situation. For example, the researcher who is investigating consumers faces one situation; the researcher who is surveying corporate executives faces quite another.

▓ KEYING MAIL QUESTIONNAIRES WITH CODES

A marketing researcher planning a follow-up letter, email, or postcard should not disturb respondents who already have returned the questionnaire. One device for eliminating those who have already responded from the follow-up mailing list is to mark the questionnaires so that they may be keyed to identify members of the sampling frame who are nonrespondents. Blind keying of questionnaires on a return envelope (systematically varying the job number or room number of the marketing research department, for example) or a visible code number on the questionnaire has been used for this purpose. Visible keying is indicated with statements such as "The sole purpose of the number on the last page is to avoid sending a second questionnaire to people who complete and return the first one." Ethical researchers key questionnaires only to increase response rates, thereby preserving respondents' anonymity.

Global Considerations

Researchers conducting surveys in more than one country must recognize that postal services and cultural circumstances differ around the world. Some of the issues to consider are the reliability of mail delivery, literacy rates, and trust that researchers can and will provide confidentiality. In some cases, hand delivery of surveys or door-to-door interviewing may be necessary. In other cases, consumers (especially women or children) might be discouraged from talking to an interviewer who is not a family member, so mailed questionnaires would be superior to interviews.

Self-Administered Questionnaires Using Other Forms of Distribution

Many forms of self-administered, printed questionnaires are very similar to mail questionnaires. Airlines frequently pass out questionnaires to passengers during flights. Restaurants, hotels, and other service establishments print short questionnaires on cards so that customers can evaluate the service. *Tennis Magazine, Advertising Age, Wired,* and many other publications have used inserted questionnaires to survey current readers inexpensively, and often the results provide material for a magazine article.

Many manufacturers use their warranty or owner registration cards to collect demographic information and data about where and why products were purchased. Using owner registration cards is an extremely economical technique for tracing trends in consumer habits. Again, problems may arise because people who fill out these self-administered questionnaires differ from those who do not.

Extremely long questionnaires may be dropped off by an interviewer and then picked up later. The **drop-off method** sacrifices some cost savings because it requires traveling to each respondent's location.

Drop-off method
A survey method that requires the interviewer to travel to the respondent's location to drop off questionnaires that will be picked up later.

Fax Surveys

With fax surveys, potential survey respondents receive and/or return questionnaires via fax machines.[22] A questionnaire inserted in a magazine may instruct the respondent to clip out the questionnaire and fax it to a certain phone number. In a mail survey, a prepaid-postage envelope places little burden on the respondent. But faxing a questionnaire to a long-distance number requires that the respondent pay for the transmission of the fax. Thus, a disadvantage of the **fax survey** is that only respondents with fax machines who are willing to exert the extra effort will return questionnaires. Again, people with extreme opinions will be more likely to respond.

Fax survey
A survey that uses fax machines as a way for respondents to receive and return questionnaires.

To address this disadvantage, marketers may use faxing as one of several options for replying to a survey. Recently, the journal *American Family Physician* carried a reader survey that gave respondents the option of either returning the reply by fax or visiting the journal's website to answer the same questions online.[23] For busy physicians who likely have access to office equipment, this approach would improve the response rate.

Fax machines can also be used to distribute questionnaires. These fax surveys reduce the sender's printing and postage costs and can be delivered and returned faster than traditional mail surveys. Questionnaires distributed via fax can deal with timely issues. Although few households have fax machines, when the sample consists of organizations that are likely to have fax machines, the sample coverage may be adequate.

E-Mail Surveys

Questionnaires can be distributed via e-mail, but researchers must remember that some individuals cannot be reached this way. Certain projects do lend themselves to **e-mail surveys**, such as internal surveys of employees or satisfaction surveys of retail buyers who regularly deal with an organization via e-mail. The benefits of incorporating a questionnaire in an e-mail include the speed of distribution, lower distribution and processing costs, faster turnaround time, more flexibility, and less handling of paper questionnaires. The speed of e-mail distribution and the quick response time can be major advantages for surveys dealing with time-sensitive issues.

E-mail surveys
Surveys distributed through electronic mail.

Not much academic research has been conducted on e-mail surveys. Nevertheless, some researchers have argued that many respondents feel they can be more candid in e-mail than in person or on the telephone, for the same reasons they are candid on other self-administered questionnaires. Yet, in many organizations employees know that their e-mails are not secure and "eavesdropping" by a supervisor could possibly occur. Further, maintaining respondents' anonymity is difficult, because a reply to an e-mail message typically includes the sender's address. Researchers designing e-mail surveys should assure respondents that their answers will be confidential.

Not all e-mail systems have the same capacity: Some handle color and graphics well; others are limited to text. The extensive differences in the capabilities of respondents' computers and e-mail software limit the types of questions and the layout of the e-mail questionnaire. For example, the display settings for computer screens vary widely, and wrap-around of lines may put the questions and the answer choices into strange and difficult-to-read patterns.[24] Many novice e-mail users find it difficult to mark answers in brackets on an e-mail questionnaire and/or to send a completed questionnaire using the e-mail Reply function. For this reason, some researchers give respondents the option to print out the questionnaire, complete it in writing, and return it via regular mail. Unless the research is an internal organizational survey, this alternative, of course, requires the respondent to pay postage.

In general, the guidelines for printed mail surveys apply to e-mail surveys. However, some differences exist, because the cover letter and the questionnaire appear in a single e-mail message. A potential respondent who is not immediately motivated to respond, especially one who considers an unsolicited e-mail survey to be spam, can quickly hit the Delete button to remove the e-mail. This response suggests that e-mail cover letters should be brief and the questionnaires relatively short. The cover letter should explain how the company got the recipient's name and should include a valid return e-mail address in the "FROM" box and reveal who is conducting the survey. Also, if the e-mail lists more than one address in the "TO" or "CC" field, all recipients will see the entire list of names. This lack of anonymity has the potential to cause response bias and nonresponse error. When possible, the e-mail should be addressed to a single person. (The blind carbon copy, or BCC, field can be used if the same message must be sent to an entire sample.)

E-mail has another important role in survey research. E-mail letters can be used as cover letters asking respondents to participate in an Internet survey. Such e-mails typically provide a password and a link to a unique website location that requires a password for access.

Internet Surveys

An **Internet survey** is a self-administered questionnaire posted on a website. Respondents provide answers to questions displayed onscreen by highlighting a phrase, clicking an icon, or keying in an answer. Like every other type of survey, Internet surveys have both advantages and disadvantages.

Internet survey
A self-administered questionnaire posted on a website.

SPEED AND COST-EFFECTIVENESS

Internet surveys allow marketers to reach a large audience (possibly a global one), personalize individual messages, and secure confidential answers quickly and cost-effectively. These computer-to-computer self-administered questionnaires eliminate the costs of paper, postage, and data entry, as well as other administrative costs. Once an Internet questionnaire has been developed, the incremental cost of reaching additional respondents is minimal. So, samples can be larger than with interviews or other types of self-administered questionnaires. Even with large samples, surveys that used to take many weeks can be conducted in a week or less.

VISUAL APPEAL AND INTERACTIVITY

Surveys conducted on the Internet can be interactive. The researcher can use more sophisticated lines of questioning based on the respondents' prior answers. Many of these interactive surveys utilize color, sound, and animation, which may help to increase respondents' cooperation and willingness to spend time answering the questionnaires. The Internet is an excellent medium for the presentation of visual materials, such as photographs or drawings of product prototypes, advertisements, and movie trailers. Innovative measuring instruments that take advantage of the ability to adjust backgrounds, fonts, color, and other features have been designed and applied with considerable success.

RESPONDENT PARTICIPATION AND COOPERATION

Participation in some Internet surveys occurs because computer users intentionally navigate to a particular website where questions are displayed. For example, a survey of more than 10,000 visitors to the Ticketmaster website helped Ticketmaster better understand its customer purchase patterns and evaluate visitor satisfaction with the site. In some cases, individuals expect to encounter a survey at a website; in others, it is totally unexpected. In some instances, the visitor cannot venture beyond the survey page without providing information for the organization's "registration" questionnaire. When the computer user does not expect a survey on a website and participation is voluntary, response rates are low. And, as with other questionnaires that rely on voluntary self-selection, participants tend to be more interested in or involved with the subject of the research than the average person.

For many other Internet surveys, respondents are initially contacted via e-mail. Often they are members of consumer panels who have previously indicated their willingness to cooperate. When panel members receive an e-mail invitation to participate, they are given logon instructions and a password. This security feature prevents access by individuals who are not part of the scientifically selected sample. Assigning a unique password code also allows the researchers to track the responses of each respondent, thereby identifying any respondent who makes an effort to answer the questionnaire more than once.

Panel members also need an incentive to respond. A study of German consumers showed that nothing beat financial incentives. In other words, the best way to get responses was to simply pay consumers for participating in surveys.[25]

Welcome screen
The first web page in an Internet survey, which introduces the survey and requests that the respondent enter a password or pin.

Ideally, the **welcome screen** contains the name of the research company and information about how to contact the organization if the respondent has a problem or concern. A typical statement might be "If you have any concerns or questions about this survey or if you experience any technical difficulties, please contact [name of research organization]."

REPRESENTATIVE SAMPLES

The population to be studied, the purpose of the research, and the sampling methods determine the quality of Internet samples, which varies substantially. If the sample consists merely of those who visit a web page and voluntarily fill out a questionnaire, then it is not likely to be representative of the entire U.S. population, because of self-selection error. However, if the purpose of the research is to evaluate how visitors feel about a website, randomly selecting every 100th visitor may accomplish the study's purpose. Scientifically drawn samples from a consumer panel or samples randomly generated in other ways also can be representative.

RESEARCHSNAPSHOT

Personalizing E-mail Invitations

When inviting people to participate in a study, researchers should address them by name. A recent study testing e-mail invitations to a web survey supported this widely held view.

The researcher set up an Internet survey to ask university students a set of questions about marriage and divorce. The objective was not to learn about their attitudes, but to measure their response rates to different kinds of invitations. One set of students received an e-mail invitation addressing them as "Dear student," while the other half received invitations addressing them by first and last name. Both invitations requested that the students visit the website where they could take the survey. A week later, both sets of students received a reminder e-mail, using the same experimental treatment regarding use of their names.

When students were invited by name, they were significantly more likely to visit the website and log in to take the survey.

However, the use of a name was not associated with whether the students finished taking the survey once they had begun.

The researcher also wondered whether students would think the survey was less confidential when the research team contacted them by name. To test this, the survey included questions about the frequency of their sexual activity—a topic that might produce a tendency to bias answers in a socially desirable direction. The research results did not indicate a social desirability bias. Do you think they weren't worried about privacy or didn't care whether their sexual activity met social norms?

Source: Heerwegh, Dirk (2005), "Effects of Personal Salutations in E-mail Invitations to Participate in a Web Survey," Public Opinion Quarterly, 69 (Winter), 588–598.

©PHOTOALTO/GETTY IMAGES

Of course, a disadvantage, albeit ever decreasing, of Internet surveys is that many individuals in the general population cannot access the Internet. Even among people with Internet access, not all of them have the same level of technology. Many people with low-speed Internet connections (low bandwidth) cannot quickly download high-resolution graphic files. Many lack powerful computers or software that is compatible with advanced features programmed into many Internet questionnaires. Some individuals have minimal computer skills. They may not know how to navigate through and provide answers to an Internet questionnaire. For example, the advanced audio- and video-streaming technology of RealPlayer or Windows Media Player software can be used to incorporate a television commercial and questions about its effectiveness into an Internet survey. However, some respondents might find downloading the file too slow or even impossible, others might not have the RealPlayer or Windows Media Player software, and still others might not know how to use the streaming media software to view the commercial.

For the foreseeable future, Internet surveys sampling the general public should be designed with the recognition that problems may arise for the reasons just described. Thus, photographs, animation, or other cutting-edge technological features created on the researcher's/web designer's powerful computer may have to be simplified or eliminated so that all respondents can interact at the same level of technological sophistication.

Because Internet surveys can be accessed anytime (24/7) from anywhere, they can reach certain hard-to-reach respondents, such as doctors. Chapter 12 discusses sampling techniques for Internet surveys.

ACCURATE REAL-TIME DATA CAPTURE

The computer-to-computer nature of Internet surveys means that each respondent's answers are entered directly into the researcher's computer as soon as the questionnaire is submitted. In addition, the questionnaire software may be programmed to reject improper data entry. For example, on a paper questionnaire a respondent might incorrectly check two responses even though the instructions call for a single answer. In an Internet survey, this mistake can be interactively corrected as the survey is taking place. Thus, the data capture is more accurate than when humans are involved.

Real-time data capture allows for real-time data analysis. A researcher can review up-to-the-minute sample size counts and tabulation data from an Internet survey in real time.

CALLBACKS

When the sample for an Internet survey is drawn from a consumer panel, those who have not completed the survey questionnaire can be easily recontacted. Computer software can simply automatically send e-mail reminders to panel members who did not visit the welcome page. Computer software can also identify the passwords of respondents who completed only a portion of the questionnaire and send those people customized messages. Sometimes such e-mails offer additional incentives to those individuals who terminated the questionnaire with only a few additional questions to answer, so that they are motivated to comply with the request to finish the questionnaire.

PERSONALIZED AND FLEXIBLE QUESTIONING

Computer-interactive Internet surveys are programmed in much the same way as computer-assisted telephone interviews. That is, the software that is used allows questioning to branch off into two or more different lines depending on a respondent's answer to a filtered question. The difference is that there is no interviewer. The respondent interacts directly with software on a website. In other words, the computer program asks questions in a sequence determined by the respondent's previous answers. The questions appear on the computer screen, and answers are recorded by simply pressing a key or clicking an icon, thus immediately entering the data into the computer's memory. Of course, these methods avoid labor costs associated with data collection and processing of paper-and-pencil questionnaires.

This ability to sequence questions based on previous responses is a major advantage of computer-assisted surveys. The computer can be programmed to skip from question 6 to question 9 if the answer to question 6 is no. Furthermore, responses to previous questions can lead to questions that can be personalized for individual respondents (for example, "When you cannot buy your favorite brand, Revlon, what brand of lipstick do you prefer?"). Often the respondent's name appears in questions to personalize the questionnaire. Fewer and more relevant questions speed up the response process and increase the respondent's involvement with the survey.

A related advantage of using a web survey is that it can prompt respondents when they skip over a question. In a test comparing telephone and Internet versions of the same survey, the rate of item nonresponse was less for the Internet version, which issued a prompt for each item that was left blank.[26] This was likely not a simple matter of motivation, because the rate of respondents who actually took the web version was less than for the telephone version, even though the researchers offered a larger incentive to those who were asked to go online. (An earlier telephone screening had verified that everyone who was asked to participate had a computer.)

The ability to customize questions and the low cost per recipient also help researchers keep surveys short, an important consideration for boosting responses.[27] Jakob Nielsen, a consultant on Internet usability with the Nielsen Norman Group, emphasizes that "quick and painless" surveys generate the highest response and urges researchers to keep surveys as short as possible. He suggests that if the research objectives call for a long survey, the questions can be divided among several questionnaires, with each version sent to a different group of respondents.

Designers of Internet questionnaires can be creative and flexible in the presentation of questions by using a variety of **dialog boxes**, or windows that prompt the respondent to enter information. Chapter 11 discusses software issues, the design of questions, and questionnaire layouts for Internet surveys.

RESPONDENT CONCERNS

Respondents are more likely to provide sensitive or embarrassing information when they can remain anonymous. The anonymity of the Internet encourages respondents to provide honest answers to sensitive questions.

SECURITY CONCERNS

Many organizations worry that hackers or competitors may access websites to discover new product concepts, new advertising campaigns, and other top-secret ideas. Respondents may worry whether personal information will remain private. So may the organizations sponsoring the research. Recently, McDonald's conducted quality-control research in England and Scotland, automating the transmittal of data with a system in which consultants used handheld devices and sent the numbers to headquarters as e-mail messages. The system saved hours of work, but the company worried that confidential information could be compromised. McDonald's therefore purchased software that encrypted the data and allowed the handhelds to be remotely wiped clean of data if they were lost or stolen.[28]

As in the experience of McDonald's, no system can be 100 percent secure, but risks can be minimized. Many research service suppliers specializing in Internet surveying have developed password-protected systems that are very secure. One important feature of these systems restricts access and prevents individuals from filling out a questionnaire over and over again.

Kiosk Interactive Surveys

A computer with a touch screen may be installed in a kiosk at a trade show, at a professional conference, in an airport, or in any other high-traffic location to administer an interactive survey. Because the respondent chooses to interact with an on-site computer, self-selection often is a problem with this type of survey. Computer-literate individuals are most likely to complete these interactive questionnaires. At temporary locations such as conventions, these surveys often require a fieldworker to be at the location to explain how to use the computer system. This personal assistance is an obvious disadvantage.

Survey Research That Mixes Modes

For many surveys, research objectives dictate the use of some combination of telephone, mail, e-mail, Internet, and personal interview. For example, the researcher may conduct a short telephone screening interview to determine whether respondents are eligible for recontact in a more extensive personal interview. Such a **mixed-mode survey** combines the advantages of the telephone survey (such as fast screening) and those of the personal interview. A mixed-mode survey can employ any combination of two or more survey methods. Conducting a research study in two or more waves, however, creates the possibility that some respondents will no longer cooperate or will be unavailable in the second wave of the survey.

Mixed-mode survey
Study that employs any combination of survey methods.

Several variations of survey research use cable television channels. For example, a telephone interviewer calls a cable subscriber and asks him or her to tune in to a particular channel at a certain time. An appointment is made to interview the respondent shortly after the program or visual material is displayed. NBC uses this type of mixed-mode survey to test the concepts for many proposed new programs.

Selecting the Appropriate Survey Research Design

Earlier discussions of research design and problem definition emphasized that many research tasks may lead to similar decision-making information. There is no best form of survey; each has advantages and disadvantages. A researcher who must ask highly confidential questions may use a mail survey, thus sacrificing speed of data collection to avoid interviewer bias. If a researcher must have considerable control over question phrasing, central location telephone interviewing may be appropriate.

To determine the appropriate technique, the researcher must ask several questions: Is the assistance of an interviewer necessary? Are respondents interested in the issues being investigated? Will cooperation be easily attained? How quickly is the information needed? Will the study require a long and complex questionnaire? How large is the budget? The criteria—cost, speed, anonymity, and so forth—may differ for each project.

Exhibit 7.4 summarizes the major advantages and disadvantages of typical door-to-door, mall intercept, telephone, mail, and Internet surveys. It emphasizes the typical types of surveys. For

EXHIBIT 7.4 **Advantages and Disadvantages of Typical Survey Methods**

	Door-to-Door Personal Interview	**Mall Intercept Personal Interview**	**Telephone Interview**	**Mail Survey**	**Internet Survey**
Speed of data collection	Moderate to fast	Fast	Very fast	Slow; researcher has no control over return of questionnaire	Instantaneous; 24/7
Geographic flexibility	Limited to moderate	Confined, possible urban bias	High	High	High (worldwide)
Respondent cooperation	Excellent	Moderate to low	Good	Moderate; poorly designed questionnaire will have low response rate	Varies depending on website; high from consumer panels
Versatility of questioning	Quite versatile	Extremely versatile	Moderate	Not versatile; requires highly standardized format	Extremely versatile
Questionnaire length	Long	Moderate to long	Moderate	Varies depending on incentive	Moderate; length customized based on answers
Item non-response rate	Low	Medium	Medium	High	Software can assure none
Possibility for respondent misunderstanding	Low	Low	Average	High; no interviewer present for clarification	High
Degree of interviewer influence on answers	High	High	Moderate	None; interviewer absent	None
Supervision of interviewers	Moderate	Moderate to high	High, especially with central-location interviewing	Not applicable	Not applicable
Anonymity of respondent	Low	Low	Moderate	High	Respondent can be either anonymous or known
Ease of callback or follow-up	Difficult	Difficult	Easy	Easy, but takes time	Difficult, unless e-mail address is known
Cost	Highest	Moderate to high	Low to moderate	Lowest	Low
Special features	Visual materials may be shown or demonstrated; extended probing possible	Taste tests, viewing of TV commercials possible	Fieldwork and supervision of data collection are simplified; quite adaptable to computer technology	Respondent may answer questions at own convenience; has time to reflect on answers	Streaming media software allows use of graphics and animation

Note: The emphasis is on *typical* surveys. For example, an elaborate mail survey may be far more expensive than a short personal interview, but this generally is not the case.

example, a creative researcher might be able to design highly versatile and flexible mail questionnaires, but most researchers use standardized questions. An elaborate mail survey may be far more expensive than a short personal interview, but generally this is not the case.

Pretesting

A researcher who is surveying 3,000 consumers does not want to find out after the questionnaires have been completed or returned that most respondents misunderstood a particular question, skipped a series of questions, or misinterpreted the instructions for filling out the questionnaire. To avoid problems such as these, screening procedures, or *pretests,* are often used. **Pretesting** involves a trial run with a group of respondents to iron out fundamental problems in the instructions or design of a questionnaire. The researcher looks for such obstacles as the point at which respondent fatigue sets in and whether there are any particular places in the questionnaire where respondents tend to terminate. Unfortunately, this stage of research is sometimes eliminated because of costs or time pressures.

Broadly speaking, three basic ways to pretest exist. The first two involve screening the questionnaire with other research professionals, and the third—the one most often called pretesting—is a trial run with a group of respondents. When screening the questionnaire with other research professionals, the investigator asks them to look for such problems as difficulties with question wording, leading questions, and bias due to question order. An alternative type of screening might involve a client or the research manager who ordered the research. Often, managers ask researchers to collect information, but when they see the questionnaire, they find that it does not really meet their needs. Only by checking with the individual who has requested the questionnaire does the researcher know for sure that the information needed will be provided. Once the researcher has decided on the final questionnaire, data should be collected with a small number of respondents (perhaps 100) to determine whether the questionnaire needs refinement.

Pretesting
Screening procedure that involves a trial run with a group of respondents to iron out fundamental problems in the survey design.

TOTHEPOINT

Practice is the best of all instructors.

—Publius Syrus,
Circa 42 BC

Ethical Issues in Survey Research

Chapter 4 mentioned that the American Marketing Association's code of ethics expresses researchers' obligation to protect the public from misrepresentation and exploitation under the guise of marketing research. Many ethical issues apply to survey research, such as respondents' right to privacy, the use of deception, respondents' right to be informed about the purpose of the research, the need for confidentiality, the need for honesty in collecting data, and the need for objectivity in reporting data. You may wish to reexamine Chapter 4's coverage of these issues now that various survey research techniques have been discussed.[29]

Summary

1. Define surveys, and explain their advantages. The survey is a common tool for asking respondents questions. Surveys can provide quick, inexpensive, and accurate information for a variety of objectives. The term *sample survey* is often used because a survey is expected to obtain a representative sample of the target population.

2. Describe the type of information that may be gathered in a survey. The typical survey is a descriptive research study with the objective of measuring awareness, product knowledge, brand usage behavior, opinions, attitudes, and so on.

3. Identify sources of error in survey research. Two major forms of error are common in survey research. The first, random sampling error, is caused by chance variation and results in a sample that is not absolutely representative of the target population. Such errors are inevitable, but they can be predicted using the statistical methods discussed in later chapters on sampling. The second major category of error, systematic error, takes several forms. Nonresponse error is caused by subjects' failing to respond to a survey. This type of error can be reduced by comparing the demographics of the sample population with those of the target population and making a special effort to contact underrepresented groups. There are four specific categories of response bias: acquiescence bias, extremity bias, interviewer bias, and social desirability bias. An additional source of survey error comes from administrative problems such as inconsistencies in interviewers' abilities, cheating, coding mistakes, and so forth.

4. Summarize ways researchers gather information through interviews. Interviews can be categorized based on the medium used to communicate with respondents. Interviews can be conducted door-to-door, in shopping malls, or on the telephone. Traditionally, interviews have been recorded using paper and pencil, but survey researchers are increasingly using computers. Personal interviews are a flexible method that allows researchers to use visual aids and various kinds of props. However, the presence of an interviewer may influence subjects' responses.

5. Compare the advantages and disadvantages of conducting door-to-door, mall intercept, telephone, and Internet interviews. Door-to-door personal interviews can get high response rates, but they are more costly to administer than other types of surveys. When a sample need not represent the entire country, mall intercept interviews may reduce costs. Telephone interviewing has the advantage of providing data fast and at a lower cost per interview. However, not all households have telephones, and not all telephone numbers are listed in directories. This causes problems in obtaining a representative sample, so researchers often use random digit dialing. Absence of face-to-face contact and inability to use visual materials also limit telephone interviewing. Computer-assisted telephone interviewing from central locations can improve the efficiency of certain kinds of telephone surveys.

6. Discuss the importance of pretesting questionnaires. Pretesting a questionnaire on a small sample of respondents is a useful way to discover problems while they can still be corrected. Pretests may involve screening the questionnaire with other research professionals or conducting a trial run with a set of respondents.

7. Describe ethical issues that arise in survey research. Researchers must protect the public from misrepresentation and exploitation. This obligation includes honesty about the purpose of a research project and protection of subjects' right to refuse to participate or to answer particular questions. Researchers also should protect the confidentiality of participants and record responses honestly.

Key Terms and Concepts

Respondents
Sample survey
Random sampling error
Systematic error
Sample bias
Respondent error
Nonresponse error
Nonrespondents
No contacts
Refusals
Self-selection bias
Response bias
Acquiescence bias
Extremity bias
Interviewer bias

Social desirability bias
Administrative error
Data-processing error
Sample selection error
Interviewer error
Interviewer cheating
Personal interview
Item nonresponse
Door-to-door interviews
Callbacks
Mall intercept interviews
Telephone interviews
Random digit dialing
Central location interviewing

Computer-assisted telephone
    interviewing (CATI)
Self-administered questionnaires
Mail survey
Response rate
Cover letter
Drop-off method
Fax survey
E-mail surveys
Internet survey
Welcome screen
Dialog boxes
Mixed-mode survey
Pretesting

Questions for Review and Critical Thinking

1. Name several nonbusiness applications of survey research.
2. Do surveys tend to gather qualitative or quantitative data? What types of information are commonly measured with surveys?
3. Give an example of each type of error listed in Exhibit 7.1.
4. In a survey, chief executive officers (CEOs) indicated that they would prefer to relocate their businesses to Atlanta

(first choice), San Diego, Tampa, Los Angeles, or Boston. The CEOs who said they were going to build the required office space in the following year were asked where they were going to build. They indicated they were going to build in New York, Los Angeles, San Francisco, or Chicago. Explain the difference.

5. What potential sources of error might be associated with the following situations?
   a. In a survey of frequent fliers age fifty and older, researchers concluded that price does not play a significant role in airline travel because only 25 percent of the respondents check off price as the most important consideration in determining where and how they travel, while 35 percent rate price as being unimportant.
   b. A survey of voters finds that most respondents do not like negative political ads—that is, advertising by one political candidate that criticizes or exposes secrets about the opponent's "dirty laundry."
   c. Researchers who must conduct a 45-minute personal interview decide to offer $10 to each respondent because they believe that people who will sell their opinions are more typical than someone who will talk to a stranger for 45 minutes.
   d. A survey comes with a Water Hardness Packet to test the hardness of the water in a respondent's home. The packet includes a color chart and a plastic strip to dip into hot water. The respondent is given instructions in six steps on how to compare the color of the plastic strip with the color chart that indicates water hardness.

6. A sample of 14-year-old school children is asked if they have ever smoked a cigarette. The students are asked to respond orally in the presence of other students. What types of error might enter into this process?

7. A survey conducted by the National Endowment for the Arts asked, "Have you read a book within the last year?" What response bias might arise from this question?

8. What type of communication medium would you use to conduct the following surveys? Why?
   a. Survey of the buying motives of industrial engineers
   b. Survey of the satisfaction levels of rental car users
   c. Survey of television commercial advertising awareness
   d. Survey of top corporate executives

9. A publisher offers college professors one of four best-selling mass-market books as an incentive for filling out a ten-page mail questionnaire about a new textbook. What advantages and disadvantages does this incentive have?

10. Do most surveys use a single communication mode (for example, the telephone), as most textbooks suggest?

11. Evaluate the following survey designs:
    a. A researcher suggests mailing a small safe (a metal file box with a built-in lock) without the lock combination to respondents, with a note explaining that respondents will be called in a few days for a telephone interview. During the telephone interview, the respondent is given the combination and the safe may be opened.
    b. A shopping mall that wishes to evaluate its image places packets including a questionnaire, cover letter, and stamped return envelope in the mall where customers can pick them up if they wish.
    c. An e-mail message is sent to individuals who own computers, asking them to complete a questionnaire on a website. Respondents answer the questions and then have the opportunity to play a slot-machine game on the website. Each respondent is guaranteed a monetary incentive

    but has the option to increase it by playing the slot-machine game.
    d. A mall intercept interviewing service is located in a regional shopping center. The facility contains a small room for television and movie presentations. Shoppers are used as sampling units. However, mall intercept interviewers recruit additional subjects for television commercial experiments by offering them several complimentary tickets for special sneak previews. Individuals contacted at the mall are allowed to bring up to five guests. In some cases the complimentary tickets are offered through ads in a local newspaper.
    e. *Time* magazine opts to conduct a mail survey rather than a telephone survey for a study to determine the demographic characteristics and purchasing behavior of its subscribers.

12. What type of research studies lend themselves to the use of e-mail for survey research? What are the advantages and disadvantages of using e-mail?

13. **ETHICS** Comment on the ethics of the following situations:
    a. A researcher plans to use invisible ink to code questionnaires to identify respondents in a distributor survey.
    b. A political action committee conducts a survey about its cause. At the end of the questionnaire, it includes a request for a donation.
    c. A telephone interviewer calls at 1 p.m. on Sunday and asks the person who answers the phone to take part in an interview.
    d. An industrial marketer wishes to survey its own distributors. It invents the name "Mountain States Marketing Research" and sends out a mail questionnaire under this name.
    e. A questionnaire is printed on the back of a warranty card included inside the package of a food processor. The questionnaire includes a number of questions about shopping behavior, demographics, and customer lifestyles. At the bottom of the warranty card is a short note in small print that says "Thank you for completing this questionnaire. Your answers will be used for marketing studies and to help us serve you better in the future. You will also benefit by receiving important mailings and special offers from a number of organizations whose products and services relate directly to the activities, interests, and hobbies in which you enjoy participating on a regular basis. Please indicate if there is some reason you would prefer not to receive this information."

14. **ETHICS** How might the marketing research industry take action to ensure that the public believes that telephone surveys and door-to-door interviews are legitimate activities and that firms that misrepresent and deceive the public using marketing research as a sales ploy are not true marketing researchers?

15. Why is the mobile phone likely to be an ineffective way of reaching potential respondents in America?

16. **'NET** Go to the Pew Internet and American Life page at http://www.pewinternet.org. Several reports based on survey research will be listed. Select one of the reports. What were the research objectives? What were the first three questions on the survey?

17. **'NET** Go to the NPD Group website (http://www.npd.com) and click on the Store link. What types of custom and syndicated survey research services does the company offer?

Research Activities

1. **'NET** Visit this web site: http://www.zoomerang.com. What unique service does this company offer? Then visit this site: http://www.websurveyor.com. How does this service differ from zoomerang? Create a short survey and email it to ten of your friends without any advanced notice. At the end of the survey, ask them if they would have responded had they not noticed the survey came from you. What is the response rate? What would it have been if the respondent did not know you?

Case 7.1 National Do Not Call Registry

Citizens' annoyance with phone calls from salespeople prompted Congress to pass a law setting up a National Do Not Call Registry. The registry was soon flooded with requests to have phone numbers removed from telemarketers' lists. By law, salespeople may not call numbers listed on this registry. The law makes exceptions for charities and researchers. However, a recent poll suggests that even though phone calls from researchers may be legal, they are not always well received.[30]

In late 2005, Harris Interactive conducted an Internet survey in which almost 2,000 adults answered questions about the National Do Not Call Registry. About three-quarters of the respondents said they had signed up for the registry, and a majority (61 percent) said they had since received "far less" contact from telemarketers. In addition, 70 percent said that since registering, they had been contacted by someone "who was doing a poll or survey" and wanted them to participate. But apparently respondents weren't sure whether this practice was acceptable. Only one-fourth (24 percent) of respondents said they knew that researchers "are allowed to call," and over half (63 percent) weren't sure about researchers' rights under the law.

Questions

1. Was an online survey the best medium for a poll on this subject? What were some pros and cons of conducting this poll online?
2. How might the results have differed if this poll had been conducted by telephone?
3. As a researcher, how would you address people's doubts about whether pollsters may contact households listed on the Do Not Call Registry?

Case 7.2 Royal Bee Electric Fishing Reel

Royal Barton started thinking about an electric fishing reel when his father had a stroke and lost the use of an arm. To see that happen to his dad, who had taught him the joys of fishing and hunting, made Barton realize what a chunk a physical handicap could take out of a sports enthusiast's life. Being able to cast and retrieve a lure and experience the thrill of a big bass trying to take your rig away from you were among the joys of life that would be denied Barton's father forever.

Barton was determined to do something about it, if not for his father, then at least for others who had suffered a similar fate. So, after tremendous personal expense and years of research and development, Barton perfected what is sure to be the standard bearer for all future freshwater electric reels. Forget those saltwater jobs, which Barton refers to as "winches." He has developed something that is small, compact, and has incredible applications.

He calls it the Royal Bee. The first word is obviously his first name. The second word refers to the low buzzing sound the reel makes when in use.

The Royal Bee system looks simple enough and probably is if you understand the mechanical workings of a reel. A system of gears ties into the gears of the spool, and a motor in the back drives the gears attached to the triggering system.

All gearing of the electrical system can be disengaged so that you can cast normally. But pushing the button for "Retrieve" engages two gears. After the gears are engaged, the trigger travels far enough to touch the switch that tightens the drive belt, and there is no slipping. You cannot hit the switch until the gears are properly engaged. This means that you cast manually, just as you would normally fish, then you reengage the reel for the levelwind to work. And you can do all that with one hand!

The system works on a 6-volt battery that you can attach to your belt or hang around your neck if you are wading. If you have a boat with a 6-volt battery, the reel can actually work off of the battery. There is a small connector that plugs into the reel, so you could easily use more than one reel with the battery. For instance, if you have two or three outfits equipped with different lures, you just switch the connector from reel to reel as you use it. A reel with the Royal Bee system can be used in a conventional manner. You do not have to use it as an electric reel unless you choose to do so.

Barton believes the Royal Bee may not be just for handicapped fishermen. Ken Cook, one of the leading professional anglers in the country, is sold on the Royal Bee. After he suffered a broken arm, he had to withdraw from some tournaments because fishing with one hand was difficult. By the time his arm healed, he was hooked on the Royal Bee because it increased bassing efficiency. As Cook explains, "The electric reel has increased my efficiency in two ways. One is in flipping, where I use it all the time. The other is for fishing topwater, when I have to make a long cast. When I'm flipping, the electric reel gives me instant control over slack line. I can keep both hands on the rod. I never have to remove them to take up slack. I flip, engage the reel, and then all I have to do is push the lever with my thumb to take up slack instantly."

Cook's reel (a Ryobi 4000) is one of several that can be converted to the electric retrieve. For flipping, Cook loads his reel with

20-pound test line. He uses a similar reel with lighter line when fishing a surface lure. "What you can do with the electric reel is eliminate unproductive reeling time," Cook says.

A few extra seconds may not mean much if you are out on a neighborhood pond just fishing on the weekend. But it can mean a lot if you are in tournament competition, where one extra cast might keep you from going home with $50,000 tucked in your pocket. "Look at it this way," Cook explains. "Let's suppose we're in clear water and it's necessary to make a long cast to the cover we want to fish with a topwater lure. There's a whole lot of unproductive water between us and the cover. With the electric reel, I make my long cast and fish the cover. Then, when I'm ready to reel in, I just press the retrieve lever so the battery engages the necessary gears, and I've got my lure back ready to make another cast while you're still cranking."

When Royal Barton retired from his veterinary supply business, he began enjoying his favorite pastimes: hunting, fishing, and developing the Royal Bee system. He realized he needed help in marketing his product, so he sought professional assistance to learn how to reach the broadest possible market for the Royal Bee system.

Questions

1. What marketing problem does Royal Barton face? What are his information needs? Outline some survey research objectives for a research project on the Royal Bee system.
2. What type of survey—personal interview, telephone interview, or mail survey—should be selected?
3. What sources of survey error are most likely to occur in a study of this type?
4. What means should be used to obtain a high response rate?

CHAPTER 8
OBSERVATION

LEARNING OUTCOMES

After studying this chapter, you should be able to

1. Discuss the role of observation as a marketing research method
2. Describe the use of direct observation and contrived observation
3. Identify ethical issues in observation studies
4. Explain the observation of physical objects and message content
5. Describe major types of mechanical observation
6. Summarize techniques for measuring physiological reactions

Chapter Vignette: Neuroco Peers into the Consumer's Brain

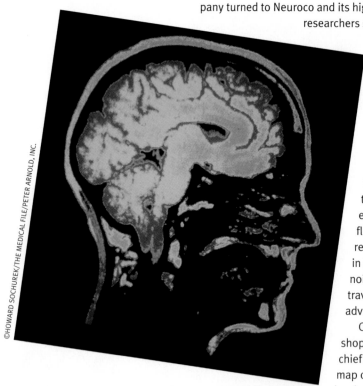

©HOWARD SOCHUREK/THE MEDICAL FILE/PETER ARNOLD, INC.

When Hewlett-Packard was developing advertisements for its digital photography products, the firm wanted to ensure its ad images would evoke the desired response. For guidance, the company turned to Neuroco and its high-tech research method, known as neuromarketing.[1] Neuroco researchers showed subjects a pair of photos of the same woman, and about half of them preferred each picture. Then Neuroco measured the electrical activity in the brains of subjects looking at the same images, and the analysis showed a definite preference for one of the pictures in which the woman's smile was a little warmer.

Neuroco's approach uses a technology called *quantified electroencephalography (QEEG)*. Subjects wear light and portable EEG equipment that records brain activity; software presents the data in computer maps that display activity levels in areas of the brain. Researchers can then evaluate whether the person is attentive and whether brain activity signifies emotional involvement or analytical thinking. QEEG is more flexible than the better-known use of functional magnetic resonance imaging (fMRI), which has provided many advances in brain research but requires all subjects to lie still in a large, noisy machine. With QEEG, the measuring equipment can travel with subjects as they walk around a store or watch advertisements.

Consider a young woman demonstrating a Neuroco study by shopping with electrodes discreetly attached to her head. Neuroco chief scientist David Lewis observes a computer screen showing a map of her brain waves in red and green, with the colors signaling levels of alpha-wave activity. The zigzag pattern tells Lewis that this shopper is alert but not engaged in making purchase decisions. As the woman walks into a store's shoe department, however, the pattern changes when she picks up a pair of stiletto heels. An explosion of brain activity occurs, then the woman heads for the cash register, decision made.

As this example illustrates, observation can provide significant insights to marketers, and advances in observation technology are literally providing a view of what is happening in customers' brains. This chapter introduces the observation method of data gathering in marketing research.

Observation in Marketing Research

In marketing research, **observation** is a systematic process of recording behavioral patterns of people, objects, and occurrences as they happen. No questioning or communicating with people is needed. Researchers who use observation method data collection either witness and record information while watching events take place or take advantage of some tracking system such as checkout scanners or Internet activity records. These tracking systems can observe and provide data such as whether or not a specific consumer purchased more products on discount or at regular price or how much time a consumer spent viewing a particular web page before either exiting or clicking through to the next page.

Observation becomes a tool for scientific inquiry when it meets several conditions:

- The observation serves a formulated research purpose.
- The observation is planned systematically.
- The observation is recorded systematically and related to general propositions rather than simply reflecting a set of interesting curiosities.
- The obseravtion is subjected to checks or controls on validity and reliability.[2]

What Can Be Observed?

Observational studies gather a wide variety of information about behavior. Exhibit 8.1 lists seven kinds of observable phenomena: physical actions, such as shopping patterns (in-store or via a web interface) or television viewing; verbal behavior, such as sales conversations; expressive behavior, such as tone of voice or facial expressions; spatial relations and locations, such as traffic patterns; temporal patterns, such as amount of time spent shopping or driving; physical objects, such as the amount of newspapers recycled; and verbal and pictorial records, such as the content of advertisements. (Investigation of secondary data also uses observation, but that subject was described in Chapter 6 and is not extensively discussed in this chapter.)

The observation method may be used to describe a wide variety of behavior, but cognitive phenomena such as attitudes, motivations, and preferences cannot be observed. As a result, observation research cannot provide an explanation of why a behavior occurred or what actions were intended. Another limitation is that the observation period generally is short. Observing behavior patterns that occur over a period of several days or weeks generally is too costly or even impossible.

Observation
The systematic process of recording the behavioral patterns of people, objects, and occurrences as they are witnessed.

TOTHEPOINT

Where observation is concerned, chance favors only the prepared mind.

—Louis Pasteur

EXHIBIT 8.1
What Can Be Observed

Phenomenon	Example
Physical action	A shopper's movement pattern in a store
Verbal behavior	Statements made by airline travelers while waiting in line
Expressive behavior	Facial expressions, tones of voices, and other forms of body language
Spatial relations and locations	How close visitors at an art museum stand to paintings
Temporal patterns	How long fast-food customers wait for their orders to be served
Physical objects	What brand-name items are stored in consumers' pantries
Verbal and pictorial records	Bar codes on product packages

The Nature of Observation Studies

Marketing researchers can observe people, objects, events, or other phenomena using either human observers or machines designed for specific observation tasks. Human observation best suits a situation or behavior that is not easily predictable in advance of the research. Mechanical observation, as performed by supermarket scanners or traffic counters, can very accurately record situations or types of behavior that are routine, repetitive, or programmatic.

Human or mechanical observation is generally *unobtrusive,* meaning no communication with a respondent takes place. For example, rather than asking customers how much time they spend shopping in the store, a supermarket manager might observe and record the intervals between when shoppers enter and leave the store. The unobtrusive or nonreactive nature of the observation method often generates data without a subject's knowledge. A situation in which an observer's presence is known to the subject involves **visible observation**. A situation in which a subject is unaware that observation is taking place is **hidden observation**. Hidden, unobtrusive observation minimizes respondent error. Asking subjects to participate in the research is not required when they are unaware that they are being observed.

The major advantage of observation studies over surveys, which obtain self-reported data from respondents, is that the data are free from distortions, inaccuracies, or other response biases due to memory error, social desirability bias, and so on. The data are recorded when the actual behavior takes place.

Visible observation
Observation in which the observer's presence is known to the subject.

Hidden observation
Observation in which the subject is unaware that observation is taking place.

Observation of Human Behavior

Whereas surveys emphasize verbal responses, observation studies emphasize and allow for the systematic recording of nonverbal behavior. Toy manufacturers such as Fisher Price use the observation technique because children often cannot express their reactions to products. By observing children at play with a proposed toy, doll, or game, marketing researchers may be able to identify the elements of a potentially successful product. Toy marketing researchers might observe play to answer the following questions:

- How long does the child's attention stay with the product?
- Does the child put the toy down after two minutes or twenty minutes?
- Are the child's peers equally interested in the toy?

Behavioral scientists have recognized that nonverbal behavior can be a communication process by which meanings are exchanged among individuals. Head nods, smiles, raised eyebrows, and other facial expressions or body movements have been recognized as communication symbols. Observation of nonverbal communication may hold considerable promise for the marketing researcher. For example, a hypothesis about customer-salesperson interactions is that the salesperson would signal status based on the importance of each transaction. In low-importance transactions, in which potential customers are plentiful and easily replaced (say, a shoe store), the salesperson may show definite nonverbal signs of higher status than the customer. When customers are scarce, as in big-ticket purchase situations (real estate sales), the opposite should be true, with the salesperson showing many nonverbal indicators of deference. One way to test this hypothesis would be with an observation study using the nonverbal communication measures shown in Exhibit 8.2.

Of course, researchers would not ignore verbal behavior. In fact, in certain observation studies, verbal expression is very important.

Complementary Evidence

The results of observation studies may amplify the results of other forms of research by providing *complementary evidence* concerning individuals' "true" feelings. Focus group interviews often are conducted behind one-way mirrors from which marketing executives observe as well as listen to

EXHIBIT 8.2 **Nonverbal Communication: Status and Power Gestures**

Behavior	Between People of Equal Status		Between People of Unequal Status		Between Men and Women	
	Intimate	Nonintimate	Used by Superior	Used by Subordinate	Used by Men	Used by Women
Posture	Relaxed	Tense (less relaxed)	Relaxed	Tense	Relaxed	Tense
Personal space	Closeness	Distance	Closeness (optional)	Distance	Closeness	Distance
Touching	Touch	Don't touch	Touch (optional)	Don't touch	Touch	Don't touch
Eye gaze	Establish	Avoid	Stare, ignore	Avert eyes, watch	Stare, ignore	Avert eyes
Demeanor	Informal	Circumspect	Informal	Circumspect	Informal	Circumspect
Emotional expression	Show	Hide	Hide	Show	Hide	Show
Facial expression	Smile	Don't smile	Don't smile	Smile	Don't smile	Smile

Source: Reprinted with permission of Simon & Schuster Adult Publishing Group, from *Body Politics* by Nancy C. Henley. Copyright © 1977 by Prentice-Hall, Inc.

what is occurring. This additional source allows for interpretation of nonverbal behavior such as facial expressions or head nods to supplement information from interviews.

For example, in one focus group session concerning women's use of hand lotion, researchers observed that all the women's hands were above the table while they were casually waiting for the session to begin. Seconds after the women were told that the topic was to be hand lotion, all their hands were placed out of sight. This observation, along with the group discussion, revealed the women's anger, guilt, and shame about the condition of their hands. Although they felt they were expected to have soft, pretty hands, their housework required them to wash dishes, clean floors, and do other chores that were hard on their hands.

When focus group behavior is videotaped, observation of the nonverbal communication symbols can add even more to marketers' knowledge of the situation.

Direct Observation

Direct observation can produce detailed records of what people actually do during an event. The observer plays a passive role, making no attempt to control or manipulate a situation, instead merely recording what occurs. Many types of data can be obtained more accurately through direct observation than by questioning. For example, recording traffic counts or observing the direction of traffic flows within a supermarket can help managers design store layouts that maximize the exposure of departments that sell impulse goods. A manufacturer can determine the number of facings, shelf locations, display maintenance, and other characteristics that improve store conditions. If directly questioned in a survey, most shoppers would be unable to accurately portray the time they spent in each department. The observation method, in contrast, could determine this without difficulty.

With the direct observation method, the data consist of records of events made as they occur. An observation form often helps keep researchers' observations consistent and ensures that they record all relevant information. A respondent is not required to recall—perhaps inaccurately—an event after it has occurred; instead, the observation is instantaneous.

Direct observation
A straightforward attempt to observe and record what naturally occurs; the investigator does not create an artificial situation.

In many cases, direct observation is the most straightforward form of data collection—or the only form possible. A produce manager for Auchan (a France-based hypermart firm) may periodically gather competitive price information from Carrefour (also a France-based hypermart firm) stores within competing areas. Both Carrefour and Auchan can monitor each other's promotions by observing promotions posted on the competitor's website (see http://www.Auchan.fr and http://www.carrefour.fr, for example). In other situations, observation is the most economical technique. In a common type of observation study, a shopping center manager may observe the license plate (tag) numbers on cars in its parking lot. These data, along with automobile registration information, provide an inexpensive means of determining where customers live.

Certain data may be obtained more quickly or easily using direct observation than by other methods—gender, race, and other respondent characteristics can simply be observed. Researchers investigating a diet product may use observation when selecting respondents in a shopping mall. Overweight people may be prescreened by observing pedestrians, thus eliminating a number of screening interviews.

In a quality-of-life survey, researchers asked respondents a series of questions that were compiled into an index of well-being. But interviewers also used direct observation because the researchers wanted to investigate the effect of weather conditions on people's answers. The researchers quickly and easily observed and recorded outside weather conditions on the day of the interviews, as well as the temperature and humidity in the building in which the interviews were conducted.[3]

Recording the decision time necessary to make a choice between two alternatives is a relatively simple, unobtrusive task easily accomplished through direct observation. The choice time recorded as a measure of the strength of the preference between alternatives is called **response latency**. This measure is based on the hypothesis that the longer a decision maker takes to choose between two alternatives, the closer the two alternatives are in terms of preference. In contrast, making a quick decision presumably indicates a considerable psychological distance between alternatives—that is, the choice is obvious. A computer can record decision times, so the response latency measure is gaining popularity now that computer-assisted data collection methods are becoming more common.

Response latency
The amount of time it takes to make a choice between two alternatives; used as a measure of the strength of preference.

ERRORS ASSOCIATED WITH DIRECT OBSERVATION

Although direct observation involves no interaction with the subject, the method is not error-free; the observer may record events subjectively. The same visual cues that may influence the interplay between interviewer and respondent (e.g., the subject's age or sex) may come into play in some direct observation settings, such as when the observer subjectively attributes a particular economic status or educational background to a subject. A distortion of measurement resulting from the cognitive behavior or actions of the witnessing observer is called **observer bias**. For example, in a research project using observers to evaluate whether sales clerks are rude or courteous, fieldworkers may be required to rely on their own interpretations of people or situations during the observation process.

Also, accuracy may suffer if the observer does not record every detail that describes the persons, objects, and events in a given situation. Generally, the observer should record as much detail as possible. However, the pace of events, the observer's memory, the observer's writing speed, and other factors will limit the amount of detail that can be recorded.

Interpretation of observation data is another potential source of error. Facial expressions and other nonverbal communication may have several meanings. Does a smile always mean happiness? Does the fact that someone is standing or seated next to the president of a company necessarily indicate the person's status?

Observer bias
A distortion of measurement resulting from the cognitive behavior or actions of a witnessing observer.

TOTHEPOINT

What we see depends mainly on what we look for.

—Sir John Lubbock

SCIENTIFICALLY CONTRIVED OBSERVATION

Most observation takes place in a natural setting, but sometimes the investigator intervenes to create an artificial environment in order to test a hypothesis. This approach is called **contrived observation**. Contrived observation can increase the frequency of occurrence of certain behavior patterns, such as employee responses to complaints. An airline passenger complaining about a meal or service from the flight attendant may actually be a researcher recording that person's reactions. If situations were not contrived, the research time spent waiting and observing would expand

Contrived observation
Observation in which the investigator creates an artificial environment in order to test a hypothesis.

RESEARCHSNAPSHOT

Hand Washing Overreported, Says Observational Research

People know that hand washing is a fundamental way to stay healthy, not to mention simple good manners. So, when you ask them, most people say they faithfully wash their hands. But according to observational research, what people say about this behavior is not what they necessarily do.

The American Society for Microbiology and the Soap and Detergent Association together arranged for a nationwide study of hand washing by U.S. adults. In an online survey by Harris Interactive, 91 percent of adults said they always wash their hands after using a public restroom. Men were somewhat less likely to make this claim—88 percent, versus 94 percent of women. The researchers followed up on the survey results by observing adults in public restrooms in Atlanta, Chicago, New York City, and San Francisco. A tally of the percentage who washed their hands found that only 83 percent did so. Keep in mind that some of the people observed to wash their hands might be people who would claim to do it only some of the time; so, the difference between the proportion of people who say they wash their hands and those who are observed doing it is probably more than the 8 percentage points observed. The difference between reporting of hand washing and actual hand washing was greater for the men (about a 16 percent difference) than for the women (12 percent).

This research showing a divide between what individuals believe they should be doing and what they actually do could help the American Society for Microbiology and government agencies to craft messages aimed at improving citizens' health. In addition, soap marketers may want to learn more about what keeps individuals from washing their hands (Is it inconvenient? Are public sinks a turnoff?), even while being prepared for some response bias.

Source: Based on Harris Interactive, "Many Adults Report Not Washing Their Hands When They Should, and More People Claim to Wash Their Hands Than Who Actually Do," news release, December 14, 2005, http://www.harrisinteractive.com; Soap and Detergent Association (SDA), "Women Better at Hand Hygiene Habits, Hands Down," news release, September 21, 2005, www.cleaning101.com; SDA, "Hand Washing Survey Fact Sheet," 2005, http://www.cleaning101.com, accessed February 24, 2006; and Harris Interactive, "A Survey of Hand Washing Behavior (2005 Findings)," September 2005, accessed at "2005 ASM/SDA Hand Hygiene Survey Results," http://www.cleaning101.com (SDA website), February 24, 2006.

©M. THOMSEN/ZEFA/CORBIS

considerably. A number of retailers use observers called *mystery shoppers* to visit a store and pretend to be interested in a particular product or service. After leaving the store, the "shopper" evaluates the salesperson's performance.

Combining Direct Observation and Interviewing

Some research studies combine visible observation with personal interviews. During or after in-depth observations, individuals are asked to explain their actions.[4] For example, direct observation of women applying hand and body lotion identified two kinds of users. Some women slapped on the lotion, rubbing it briskly into their skin. Others caressed their skin as they applied the lotion. When the women were questioned about their behavior, the researchers discovered that women who slapped the lotion on were using the lotion as a remedy for dry skin. Those who caressed their skin were more interested in making their skin smell nice and feel soft.

Ethical Issues in the Observation of Humans

Observation methods introduce a number of ethical issues. Hidden observation raises the issue of the respondent's right to privacy. Suppose a research firm is approached by a company interested in acquiring information about how women put on their bras by observing behavior in a spa dressing area. The researcher considers approaching spas in several key cities about placing small cameras inconspicuously to observe women getting dressed. Obviously, such a situation raises an ethical question. While to some extent the dressing room is an area where women often do dress where others can observe them, women do not expect to have their dressing behavior recorded. Therefore, unless a way can be found to have some women consent to such observation, this observational approach is unethical.

Some people might see contrived observation as entrapment. To *entrap* means to deceive or trick into difficulty, which clearly is an abusive action. The problem is one of balancing values. If the researcher obtains permission to observe someone, the subject may not act naturally. So, at times there is a stront temptation to observe without obtaining consent. At other times, such as monitoring mall traffic, obtaining consent just to observe people walking through the mall would be difficult.

So, when should researchers feel comfortable collecting observational data? While exceptions exist to every rule, here are three questions that can help address this question:

1. Is the behavior being observed commonly performed in public where it is expected that others can observe the behavior?
2. Is the behavior performed in a setting in which the anonymity of the person being observed is assured (meaning there is no way to identify individuals)?
3. Has the person agreed to be observed?

If the answer to the first two questions is yes, then there is not likely a violation of privacy in collecting observational research data. If the answer to the third question is yes, then gathering the data also is likely to be ethical.

Observation of Physical Objects

Picking through the garbage on the side of the road can reveal behaviors of fast-food customers.

©ROBERT BRENNER/PHOTOEDIT

Physical phenomena may be the subject of observation study. Physical-trace evidence is a visible mark of some past event or occurrence. For example, the wear on library books indirectly indicates which books are actually read (handled most) when checked out. A classic example of physical-trace evidence in a nonprofit setting was erosion on the floor tiles around the hatching-chick exhibit at Chicago's Museum of Science and Industry. These tiles had to be replaced every six weeks; tiles in other parts of the museum did not need to be replaced for years. The selective erosion of tiles, indexed by the replacement rate, was a measure of the relative popularity of exhibits.

Clearly, a creative marketing researcher has many options for determining the solution to a problem. The story about Charles Coolidge Parlin, generally recognized as one of the founders of commercial marketing research, counting garbage cans at the turn of the twentieth century illustrates another study of physical traces.

Parlin designed an observation study to persuade Campbell's Soup Company to advertise in the *Saturday Evening Post*. Campbell's was reluctant to advertise because it believed that the *Post* was read primarily by working people who would prefer to make soup from scratch, peeling the potatoes and scraping the carrots, rather than paying ten cents for a can of soup. To demonstrate that rich people weren't the target market, Parlin selected a sample of Philadelphia garbage routes. Garbage from each specific area of the city that was selected was dumped on the floor of a local National Guard Armory. Parlin had the number of Campbell's soup cans in each pile counted. The results indicated that the garbage from the rich people's homes didn't contain many cans of Campbell's soup. Although they may not have made soup from scratch themselves, their housekeepers may have. The garbage piles from the blue-collar area showed a larger number of Campbell's soup cans. This observation study was enough evidence for Campbell's. They advertised in the *Saturday Evening Post.*[5]

The method used in this study has since been used in a scientific project at the University of Arizona in which aspiring archaeologists have sifted through garbage for over thirty years. They examine soggy cigarette butts, empty milk cartons, and half-eaten Big Macs in an effort to understand modern life.

What is most interesting about the garbage project is that observations can be compared with the results of surveys about food consumption—and garbage does not lie. This type of observation can correct for overreporting consumption of healthful items and underreporting of, say, cigarette or alcohol consumption.

Another application of observing physical objects is to count and record physical inventories through retail or wholesale audits. This method allows researchers to investigate brand sales on regional and national levels, market shares, seasonal purchasing patterns, and so on. Marketing research suppliers offer audit data at both the retail and the wholesale levels.

An observer can record physical-trace data to discover information a respondent could not recall accurately. For example, measuring the number of ounces of a liquid bleach used during a test provides precise physical-trace evidence without relying on the respondent's memory. The accuracy of respondents' memories is not a problem for the firm that conducts a pantry audit. The pantry audit requires an inventory of the brands, quantities, and package sizes in a consumer's home rather than responses from individuals. The problem of untruthfulness or some other form of response bias is avoided. For example, the pantry audit prevents the possible problem of respondents erroneously claiming to have purchased prestige brands. However, gaining permission to physically check consumers' pantries is not easy, and the fieldwork is expensive. In addition, the brand in the pantry may not reflect the brand purchased most often if consumers substituted it because they had a coupon, the usual brand was out of stock, or another reason.

Content Analysis

Besides observing people and physical objects, researchers may use **content analysis**, which obtains data by observing and analyzing the contents or messages of advertisements, newspaper articles, television programs, letters, and the like. This method involves systematic analysis as well as observation to identify the specific information content and other characteristics of the messages. Content analysis studies the message itself and involves the design of a systematic observation and recording procedure for quantitative description of the manifest content of communication. This technique measures the extent of emphasis or omission of a given analytical category. For example, content analysis of advertisements might evaluate their use of words, themes, characters, or space and time relationships. Another topic of content analysis is the frequency with which women, African-Americans, or ethnic minorities appear in mass media.

Content analysis might be used to investigate questions such as whether some advertisers use certain themes, appeals, claims, or deceptive practices more than others or whether recent consumer-oriented actions by the Federal Trade Commission have influenced the content of advertising. A cable television programmer might do a content analysis of network programming to evaluate its competition. Every year researchers analyze the Super Bowl telecast to see how much of the visual material is live-action play and how much is replay, or how many shots focus on the cheerleaders and how many on spectators. Content analysis also can explore the information content of television commercials directed at children, the company images portrayed in ads, and numerous other aspects of advertising.

Study of the content of communications is more sophisticated than simply counting the items; it requires a system of analysis to secure relevant data. After one employee role-playing session involving leaders and subordinates, researchers analyzed videotapes to identify categories of verbal behaviors (e.g., positive reward statements, positive comparison statements, and self-evaluation requests). Trained coders, using a set of specific instructions, then recorded and coded the leaders' behavior into specific verbal categories.

Mechanical Observation

In many situations, the primary—and sometimes the only—means of observation is mechanical rather than human. Video cameras, traffic counters, and other machines help observe and record behavior. Some unusual observation studies have used motion-picture cameras and time-lapse

TOTHEPOINT

What would you rather believe? What I say, or what you saw with your own eyes?

—Groucho Marx

Content analysis
The systematic observation and quantitative description of the manifest content of communication.

photography. An early application of this observation technique photographed train passengers and determined their levels of comfort by observing how they sat and moved in their seats. Another time-lapse study filmed traffic flows in an urban square and resulted in a redesign of the streets. Similar techniques may help managers design store layouts and resolve problems in moving people or objects through spaces over time.

Television Monitoring

Television monitoring
Computerized mechanical observation used to obtain television ratings.

Perhaps the best-known marketing research project involving mechanical observation and computerized data collection is ACNielsen's **television monitoring** system for estimating national television audiences. Nielsen Media Research uses a consumer panel and a monitoring device called a People Meter to obtain ratings for television programs nationwide.[6] The Nielsen People Meter gathers data on what each television in a household is playing and who is watching it at the time. Researchers attach electronic boxes to television sets and remote controls to capture information on program choices and the length of viewing time. Nielsen matches the signals captured through these devices with its database of network broadcast and cable program schedules so that it can identify the specific programs being viewed.

When a television in the panel household is turned on, a red light on the People Meter periodically flashes to remind viewers to indicate who is watching. The viewer then uses a remote control to record who is watching. One button on the control is assigned to each member of the household and a separate visitor button is used for potential guests. The household member presses his or her button to indicate the sex and age of the person who is watching. Knowing who in the family is watching allows executives to match television programs with demographic profiles.

Each night, Nielsen's computers automatically retrieve the data stored in the People Meter's recording box. In this way, Nielsen gathers daily estimates of when televisions are in use, which channels are used, and who is viewing each program. The panel includes more than five thousand households, selected to be representative of the U.S. population. For local programming, Nielsen uses additional panels equipped with recording devices but not People Meters to record viewer demographics. (Nielsen uses surveys to record demographic data for local programming.)

Critics of the People Meter argue that subjects in Nielsen's panel grow bored over time and do not always record when they begin or stop watching television. Arbitron, best known for measuring radio audiences, has attempted to answer this objection with its own measuring system, which it calls the Portable People Meter.[7] The Portable People Meter, which occupies about 4 cubic inches and weighs less than 3 ounces, reads inaudible codes embedded in audio signals to identify their source. Study participants wear or carry the meter throughout the day, and it automatically picks up codes embedded in whatever radio and television signals they encounter. At the end of the day, the participant inserts the meter into a "base station," which extracts the data collected, sends it to a household hub, and recharges the battery. The household hub then sends the data to Arbitron's computer over phone lines. To encourage cooperation, the meter has a motion sensor connected to a green light signaling that the meter senses it is being carried. Each participant is awarded points for the amount of time the meter is on. Total points are displayed in the base station and used to determine the size of the incentive paid to each participant. Arbitron's meter simplifies the participants' role and collects data on exposure to radio and television programming outside the home. However, the device records only signals that the radio or television system embeds using Arbitron's equipment.

Other devices gather data about the viewing of advertisements. The TiVo digital television recorder, so far used by only a small percentage of the population, collects detailed viewing data, such as what commercials people skip by using fast-forward. The PreTesting Company sets up contrived observational studies in which viewers equipped with a remote control are invited to watch any of three prerecorded channels playing different programs and advertisements, including the client's ads to be tested.[8] The system records the precise points at which the viewer changes the channel. By combining the results from many participants, the company arrives at a Cumulative Zapping Score, that is, the percentage of viewers who had exited the client's advertisement by each point in the ad. So that viewing behavior will be more natural, subjects are told they are evaluating the programming, not the ads.

RESEARCHSNAPSHOT

Klipmart Watches Ad Viewership Online

As bandwidth widens, more and more computer users are going online to download audio and video content. Providers of that content are earning revenues through a combination of user fees and advertising. This situation is creating demand for information about how many people are seeing Internet ads and whether they are paying attention. Klipmart not only provides video content online but also is finding ways to measure the behavior of computer users—in particular, their viewership of ads using video.

Klipmart sets up tests in which computer users are presented with 30-second video ads as they perform other tasks. The company's equipment then measures how long the users spend watching each advertisement. The assumption is that a 30-second ad is too long for a computer user, so the company can get an upper limit of viewers' interest in the ads by seeing how many seconds out of the 30 the viewers keep watching. Early results suggest that the length of time spent viewing an online video ad averages 21 seconds but varies according to what the

user is trying to accomplish. Users stayed with an ad the longest—an average of 22.5 seconds—when they were waiting for the download of a home video. They were least patient, clicking away from the ad after 19 seconds, if they were downloading a finance video. The results surprised some people, who expected that computer users would exit advertisements within a few seconds.

Klipmart also can measure the user's interaction with an advertisement. Data from Klipmart indicate that users interact more with ads that contain more interactive elements.

Source: Based on Zachary Rodgers, "What's the Optimal Length for Video Ads?" ClickZ Internet Advertising News, October 4, 2005, http://www.clickz.com; Klipmart, "About Us" and "Research," http://www.klipmart.com, accessed February 6, 2006.

Monitoring Website Traffic

Computer technology makes gathering detailed data about online behavior easy and inexpensive. The greater challenges are to identify which measures are meaningful and to interpret the data correctly. For instance, most organizations record the level of activity at their websites. They may count the number of *hits*—mouse clicks on a single page of a website. If the visitor clicks on many links, that page receives multiple hits. Similarly, they can track *page views,* or single, discrete clicks to load individual pages of a website. Page views more conservatively indicate how many users visit each individual page on the website and may also be used to track the path or sequence of pages that each visitor follows.

▇ CLICK-THROUGH RATES

A **click-through rate** (CTR) is the percentage of people who are exposed to an advertisement who actually click on the corresponding hyperlink which takes them to the company's web site. Counting hits or page views can suggest the amount of interest or attention a website is receiving, but these measures are flawed. First, hits do not differentiate between a lot of activity by a few visitors and a little activity by many visitors. In addition, the researcher lacks information about the meaning behind the numbers. If a user clicks on a site many times, is the person finding a lot of useful or enjoyable material, or is the user trying unsuccessfully to find something by looking in several places? Additionally, some hits are likely made by mistake. The consumers may have had no intention of clicking through the ad or may not have known what they were doing when they clicked on the ad.

Google has benefited from CTR research indicating that the highest click-through rates tend to occur on pages displaying search results. (Not surprisingly, someone who searches for the term *kayaks* is more likely to be interested in an advertisement offering a good deal on kayaks.) The company showed Vanguard, for example, that its banner ads cost the financial firm less than fifty cents per click and generated a 14 percent click-through rate. That CTR is far above typical response rates for direct-mail advertising, but it does not indicate whether online clicks are as valuable in terms of sales.[9]

Click-through rate
Proportion of people who are exposed to an Internet ad who actually click on its hyperlink to enter the website; click-through rates are generally very low.

Scanner-Based Research

Lasers performing optical character recognition and barcode technology like the universal product code (UPC) have accelerated the use of mechanical observation in marketing research. Chapter 6 noted that a number of syndicated services offer secondary data about product category movement generated from retail stores using scanner technology.

This technology allows researchers to investigate questions that are demographically or promotionally specific. Scanner research has investigated the different ways consumers respond to price promotions and the effects of those differences on a promotion's profitability. One of the primary means of implementing this type of research is through the establishment of a **scanner-based consumer panel** to replace consumer purchase diaries. In a typical scanner panel, each household is assigned a barcoded card, like a frequent-shopper card, which members present to the clerk at the register. The household's code number is coupled with the purchase information recorded by the scanner. In addition, as with other consumer panels, background information about the household obtained through answers to a battery of demographic and psychographic survey questions can also be coupled with the household code number.

> **Scanner-based consumer panel**
> A type of consumer panel in which participants' purchasing habits are recorded with a laser scanner rather than a purchase diary.

Aggregate data, such as actual store sales as measured by scanners, are available to clients and industry groups. Data may also be aggregated by product category. To interpret the aggregated data, researchers can combine them with secondary research and panel demographics. For instance, data from Information Resources Inc. (IRI) have indicated a downward trend in sales of hair-coloring products. Demographic data suggest that an important reason is the aging of the population; many consumers who dye their hair reach an age at which they no longer wish to cover their gray hair. A smaller segment of the population is at an age where consumers typically begin using hair coloring.[10]

Data from scanner research parallel data provided by a standard mail diary panel, with some important improvements:

1. The data measure observed (actual) purchase behavior rather than reported behavior (recorded later in a diary).
2. Substituting mechanical for human record-keeping improves accuracy.
3. Measures are unobtrusive, eliminating interviewing and the possibility of social desirability or other bias on the part of respondents.
4. More extensive purchase data can be collected, because all UPC categories are measured. In a mail diary, respondents could not possibly reliably record all items they purchased. Because all UPC-coded items are measured in the panel, users can investigate many product categories to determine loyalty, switching rates, and so on for their own brands as well as for other companies' products and locate product categories for possible market entry.
5. The data collected from computerized checkout scanners can be combined with data about advertising, price changes, displays, and special sales promotions. Researchers can scrutinize them with powerful analytical software provided by the scanner data providers.

Scanner data can show a marketer week by week how a product is doing, even in a single store, and track sales in response to local ads or promotions. Also, several organizations have developed scanner panels, such as Information Resources Inc. Behavior Scan System, and expanded them into electronic test-market systems. These issues are discussed in greater detail in Chapter 9.

Advances in bar-code technology have led to **at-home scanning systems** that use handheld wands to read UPC symbols. Consumer panelists perform their own scanning *after* they have taken home the products. This advance makes it possible to investigate purchases made at stores that lack in-store scanning equipment.

> **At-home scanning systems**
> Systems that allow consumer panelists to perform their own scanning after taking home products, using handheld wands that read UPC symbols.

Measuring Physiological Reactions

Marketing researchers have used a number of other mechanical devices to evaluate consumers' physical and physiological reactions to advertising copy, packaging, and other stimuli. Researchers use such means when they believe consumers are unaware of their own reactions to stimuli such as advertising or that consumers will not provide honest responses. Four major categories of mechanical devices are used to measure physiological reactions: (1) eye-tracking monitors, (2) pupilometers, (3) psychogalvanometers, and (4) voice-pitch analyzers.

A magazine or newspaper advertiser may wish to grab readers' attention with a visual scene and then direct it to a package or coupon. Or a television advertiser may wish to identify which selling points to emphasize. Eye-tracking equipment records how the subject reads a print ad or views a television commercial and how much time is spent looking at various parts of the stimulus. In physiological terms, the gaze movement of a viewer's eye is measured with an **eye-tracking monitor**, which measures unconscious eye movements. Originally developed to measure astronauts' eye fatigue, modern eye-tracking systems need not keep a viewer's head in a stationary position. The devices track eye movements with invisible infrared light beams that lock onto a subject's eyes. The light reflects off the eye, and eye-movement data are recorded while another tiny video camera monitors which magazine page is being perused. The data are analyzed by computer to determine which components in an ad (or other stimuli) were seen and which were overlooked. Eye-tracking monitors have recently been used to measure the way subjects view e-mail and web marketing messages. OgilvyOne has used this technology to learn that people often skip over more than half of the words in e-mail advertising, especially words on the right side of the message. Interestingly, consumers generally ignore the word *free*.[11]

Other physiological observation techniques are based on a common principle: that adrenaline is released when the body is aroused. This hormone causes the heart to enlarge and to beat harder and faster. These changes increase the flow of blood to the fingers and toes. The blood vessels dilate, and perspiration increases, affecting the skin's electrical conductivity. Other physical changes following the release of adrenaline include dilation of the pupils, more frequent brain wave activity, higher skin temperature, and faster breathing. Methods that measure these and other changes associated with arousal can apply to a variety of marketing questions, such as subjects' reactions to advertising messages or product concepts.

A **pupilometer** observes and records changes in the diameter of a subject's pupils. A subject is instructed to look at a screen on which an advertisement or other stimulus is projected. When the brightness and distance of the stimulus from the subject's eyes are held constant, changes in pupil size may be interpreted as changes in cognitive activity that result from the stimulus, rather than from eye dilation and constriction in response to light intensity, distance from the object, or other physiological reactions to the conditions of observation. This method of research is based on the assumption that increased pupil size reflects positive attitudes toward and interest in advertisements.

A **psychogalvanometer** measures galvanic skin response (GSR), a measure of involuntary changes in the electrical resistance of the skin. This device is based on the assumption that physiological changes, such as increased perspiration, accompany emotional reactions to advertisements, packages, and slogans. Excitement increases the body's perspiration rate, which increases the electrical resistance of the skin. The test is an indicator of emotional arousal or tension.

Voice-pitch analysis is a relatively new physiological measurement technique that gauges emotional reactions as reflected in physiological changes in a person's voice. Abnormal frequencies in the voice caused by changes in the autonomic nervous system are measured with sophisticated, audio-adapted computer equipment. Computerized analysis compares the respondent's voice

Eye-tracking monitor
A mechanical device used to observe eye movements; some eye monitors use infrared light beams to measure unconscious eye movements.

Pupilometer
A mechanical device used to observe and record changes in the diameter of a subject's pupils.

Psychogalvanometer
A device that measures galvanic skin response, a measure of involuntary changes in the electrical resistance of the skin.

Voice-pitch analysis
A physiological measurement technique that records abnormal frequencies in the voice that are supposed to reflect emotional reactions to various stimuli.

Physiological responses to advertising can be recorded with a device like this one.

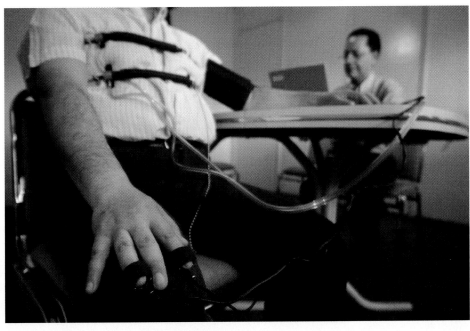

©ASSOCIATED PRESS/AP

pitch during warm-up conversations (normal range) with verbal responses to questions about his or her evaluative reaction to television commercials or other stimuli. This technique, unlike other physiological devices, does not require the researcher to surround subjects with mazes of wires or equipment.

All of these devices assume that physiological reactions are associated with persuasiveness or predict some cognitive response. This assumption has not yet been clearly demonstrated. No strong theoretical evidence supports the argument that such a physiological change is a valid measure of future sales, attitude change, or emotional response. Another major problem with physiological research is the *calibration,* or sensitivity, of measuring devices. Identifying arousal is one thing, but precisely measuring *levels* of arousal is another. In addition, most of these devices are expensive. However, as a prominent researcher points out, physiological measurement is coincidental: "Physiological measurement isn't an exit interview. It's not dependent on what was remembered later on. It's a live blood, sweat, and tears, moment-by-moment response, synchronous with the stimulus."[12]

Each of these mechanical devices has another limitation: The subjects are usually placed in artificial settings, such as watching television in a laboratory rather than at home, and they know they are being observed.

Summary

1. Discuss the role of observation as a marketing research method. Observation is a powerful tool for the marketing researcher. Scientific observation is the systematic process of recording the behavioral patterns of people, objects, and occurrences as they are witnessed. Questioning or otherwise communicating with subjects does not occur. A wide variety of information about the behavior of people and objects can be observed. Seven kinds of phenomena are observable: physical actions, verbal behavior, expressive behavior, spatial relations and locations, temporal patterns, physical objects, and verbal and pictorial records. Thus, both verbal and nonverbal behavior may be observed. Observation may not, however, be used for cognitive phenomena. Attitudes, motivations, expectations, intentions, and preferences are not observable; only overt behavior of short duration can be observed.

2. Describe the use of direct observation and contrived observation. Human observation, whether direct or contrived, is commonly used when the situation or behavior to be recorded is not easily predictable in advance of the research. Observation may be unobtrusive, and many types of data can be obtained more accurately through direct observation than by questioning respondents. Direct observation involves watching and recording what naturally occurs, without creating an artificial situation. For some data, observation is the most direct or the only method of collection. For example, researchers can measure response latency, the time it takes individuals to choose between alternatives. Observer bias may be a problem in correctly perceiving the behaviors being observed. Observation can also be contrived by creating the situations to be observed. This can reduce the time and expense of obtaining reactions to certain circumstances.

3. Identify ethical issues in observation studies. Contrived observation, hidden observation, and other observation research designs have the potential to involve deception. For this reason, these methods often raise ethical concerns about subjects' right to privacy and right to be informed.

4. Explain the observation of physical objects and message content. Physical-trace evidence serves as a visible record of past events. Researchers may examine whatever evidence provides such a record, including inventory levels, the contents of garbage cans, or the items in a consumer's pantry. Content analysis obtains data by observing and analyzing the contents of the messages in written or spoken communications.

5. Describe major types of mechanical observation. Mechanical observation uses a variety of devices to record behavior directly. Mechanically observing behavior may be an efficient and accurate choice when the situation being recorded is routine, repetitive, or programmatic. National television audience ratings are based on mechanical observation (for example, People Meters) and computerized data collection. Website traffic may be measured electronically. Scanner-based research provides product category sales data recorded by laser scanners in retail stores. Many syndicated services offer secondary data collected through scanner systems.

6. Summarize techniques for measuring physiological reactions. Physiological reactions, such as arousal or eye movement patterns, may be observed using a number of mechanical devices. Eye-tracking monitors identify the direction of a person's gaze, and a pupilometer observes and records changes in the diameter of the pupils of subjects' eyes, based on the assumption that a larger pupil signifies a positive attitude. A psychogalvanometer measures galvanic skin response as a signal of a person's emotional reactions. Voice-pitch analysis measures changes in a person's voice and associates the changes with emotional response.

Key Terms and Concepts

Observation	Contrived observation	Eye-tracking monitor
Visible observation	Content analysis	Pupilometer
Hidden observation	Television monitoring	Psychogalvanometer
Direct observation	Click-through rate	Voice-pitch analysis
Response latency	Scanner-based consumer panel	
Observer bias	At-home scanning systems	

Questions for Review and Critical Thinking

1. Yogi Berra, former New York Yankee catcher, said, "You can observe a lot just by watching." How does this fit in with the definition of scientific observation?

2. What are the advantages and disadvantages of observation studies relative to surveys?

3. Under what conditions are observation studies most appropriate?

4. **ETHICS** Consider the increasingly common use of surveillance cameras to monitor driving bahavior. Do you think the use of these cameras to issue speeding tickets is ethical? What types of behavior might cameras like these capture that would help automobile designers produce products that better match our needs as drivers?

5. A multinational fast-food corporation plans to locate a restaurant in La Paz, Bolivia. Secondary data for this city are sketchy and outdated. How might you determine the best location using observation?

6. Discuss how an observation study might be combined with a personal interview.

7. **'NET** Click-through rates for advertisements placed in websites are usually very, very low (less than 1 percent). What types of error might exist in using click-through rate data as a measure of an ad's success?

8. Outline a research design using observation for each of the following situations:
   a. A bank wishes to collect data on the number of customer services and the frequency of customer use of these services.
   b. A state government wishes to determine the driving public's use of seat belts.
   c. A researcher wishes to know how many women have been featured on *Time* covers over the years.
   d. A fast-food franchise wishes to determine how long a customer entering a store has to wait for his or her order.
   e. A magazine publisher wishes to determine exactly what people look at and what they pass over while reading one of its magazines.
   f. A food manufacturer wishes to determine how people use snack foods in their homes.

   g. An overnight package delivery service wishes to observe delivery workers beginning at the moment when they stop the truck, continuing through the delivery of the package, and ending when they return to the truck.

9. What is a scanner-based consumer panel?

10. What are the major types of mechanical observation?

11. **ETHICS** Comment on the ethics of the following situations:
   a. During the course of telephone calls to investors, a stockbroker records respondents' voices when they are answering sensitive investment questions and then conducts a voice pitch analysis. The respondents do not know that their voices are being recorded.
   b. A researcher plans to invite consumers to be test users in a simulated kitchen located in a shopping mall and then to videotape their reactions to a new microwave dinner from behind a two-way mirror (one that an observer behind the mirror can see through but the person looking into the mirror sees only the reflection).
   c. A marketing researcher arranges to purchase the trash from the headquarters of a major competitor. The purpose is to sift through discarded documents to determine the company's strategic plans.

12. What is a psychogalvanometer?

13. **'NET** William Rathje, a researcher at the University of Arizona, Department of Anthropology, has become well-known for the "Garbage Project." The project involves observational research. Use http://www.ask.com to find information about the garbage project at the University of Arizona. What is the name of the book that describes some of the key findings of the Garbage Project? How do you think it involves observational research?

14. **'NET** The Internet is filled with webcams. For example, Pebble Beach Golf Club has several webcams (http://www.pebblebeach.com). How could a researcher use webcams like these to collect behavioral data?

Case 8.1 Mazda and Syzygy

When Mazda Motor Europe set out to improve its website, the company wanted details about how consumers were using the site and whether finding information was easy. Mazda hired a research firm called Syzygy to answer those questions with observational research.[13] Syzygy's methods include the use of an eye-tracking device that uses infrared light rays to record what areas of a computer screen a user is viewing. For instance, the device measured the process computer users followed in order to look for a local dealer or arranging a test drive. Whenever a process seemed confusing or difficult, the company looked for ways to make the website easier to navigate.

To conduct this observational study, Syzygy arranged for sixteen subjects in Germany and the United Kingdom to be observed as they used the website. The subjects in Germany were observed with the eye-tracking equipment. As the equipment measured each subject's gaze, software recorded the location on the screen and graphed the data. Syzygy's results included three-dimensional contour maps highlighting the "peak" areas where most of the computer users' attention was directed.

Questions

1. What could Mazda learn from eye-tracking software that would be difficult to learn from other observational methods?
2. What are the shortcomings of this method?
3. Along with the eye-tracking research, what other research methods could help Mazda assess the usability of its website? Summarize your advice for how Mazda could use complementary methods to obtain a complete understanding of its website usability.

Case 8.2 Texas Instruments and E-Lab

E-Lab, LLC is a business research and design firm in Chicago that specializes in observing people, identifying patterns in behavior, and developing an understanding of why these patterns exist.[14] The company then uses the knowledge that it gains as a framework in the product development process. Texas Instruments (TI) used E-Lab to investigate the mobility, connectivity, and communications needs of law enforcement officers, which led to ideas for a set of computing and communications products. As part of its product development research, TI's Advanced Integrated Systems Department and E-Lab researchers spent 320 hours shadowing police officers in three Texas police departments. Shadowing involves asking questions while observing. Researchers walked foot patrols, rode in patrol cars, and pedaled with bike patrols. They spent time with crowd control, narcotics, homicide, dispatch, and juvenile teams. They recorded their observations and interviews on paper, digital camera, and video.

A number of interesting findings emerged from all this research. First, police officers are very social, so it was important that any product TI developed should enhance socialization rather than detract from it. For example, an in-car computing and communications device should be able to access a database that lists names and numbers of experts on the force so officers can call or e-mail the experts directly. Second, police officers are not driven by procedure. That told TI that the procedures for an investigation should reside in the device and that the device should prompt the officer at each step in the process. And third, officers rely on informal information about people and activities on their beats. This information may be kept on scraps of paper, on a spreadsheet back in the office, or in the police officer's head. Business researchers concluded that any device that TI develops should have a place to compile and share informal information.

Questions

1. Identify the research design used by E-Lab.
2. Compare this research design with a survey research design. What advantages, if any, did this research design have over a survey?

CHAPTER 9
EXPERIMENTAL RESEARCH:
AN OVERVIEW

After studying this chapter, you should be able to

1. Create an experimental, independent variable through a valid experimental manipulation of its value
2. Understand and minimize the systematic experimental error
3. Know ways of minimizing experimental demand characteristics
4. Avoid unethical experimental practices
5. Weigh the trade-off between internal and external validity
6. Recognize the appropriate uses of test-marketing

Chapter Vignette: The Color of Fish

Marketing managers often like to show off by proving that their brand is superior to a competitor's offering. When Brand "X" managers claim that customers prefer its product over Brand "Y's" product, they had best be prepared to defend that claim in court. As a result, lawyers often need marketing research. This vignette describes just such a situation.

Sea Snapper brand gourmet frozen fish products claimed in advertising that their fish sticks are preferred more than two to one over the most popular brand, Captain John's.[1] The advertisements all include a definitive statement indicating that research existed which substantiated this claim.

Captain John's reaction was *war;* or at least legal war. They decided to sue Sea Snapper claiming that the advertisements include false claims based on faulty research. In court, the research was described in great detail. Sea Snapper conducted taste tests involving four hundred consumers who indicated that they regularly ate frozen food products. Two hundred tasted Sea Snapper premium fish sticks and the other two hundred tasted Captain John's premium fish sticks. Consumer preference was measured with a 100-point rating scale. The results showed the average preference score for Sea Snapper was 78.2 compared to 39.0 for Captain John's. Case closed?

Captain John's attorney hired a marketing research firm to assist in the lawsuit. They claimed that the research was faulty because the procedures were improperly conducted. First, it turned out that Sea Snapper fish sticks were always presented to consumers on a blue plate while Captain John's were always presented to consumers on an orange plate. Second, the Sea Snapper products used in the experiment were taken directly from the Sea Snapper kitchens to the testing facility, while the Captain John's products were purchased at a local warehouse store. Therefore, because the research was invalid, the claims were invalid and Sea Snapper should stop making the claims and pay for any damages to Captain John's in the form of lost sales and damaged image. Who will win this lawsuit?

The Nature of Experiments

Most students are familiar with scientific experiments from studying physical sciences like physics and chemistry. The term *experiment* typically conjures up an image of a chemist surrounded by bubbling test tubes and Bunsen burners. Behavioral and physical scientists have used experimentation far longer than have marketing researchers. Nevertheless, both social scientists and physical scientists use experiments for much the same purpose.

As described in Chapter 3, experiments are widely used in causal research designs. Experimental research allows a researcher to control the research situation so that *causal* relationships among variables may be evaluated. The marketing experimenter manipulates one or more independent variables and holds constant all other possible independent variables while observing effects on dependent variables. Events may be controlled in an experiment to a degree not possible in a survey.

Independent variables are expected to determine the outcomes of interest. In an experiment, they are controlled by the researcher through manipulations. Dependent variables are the outcomes of interest to the researcher and the decision makers. A simple example would be thinking about how changes in price would influence sales. Price would be an independent variable and sales would be a dependent variable. In our opening vignette, the brand (Sea Snapper or Captain John's) would be an experimental independent variable and the 100-point ratings scale indicating liking would be the important dependent variable.

The researcher's goal in conducting an experiment is to determine whether changing an experimental independent variable causes changes in an important dependent variable. Sea Snapper's preference claim is based on the brand causing preference. In other words, when a consumer is presented with Sea Snapper brand instead of Captain John's, it causes him or her to rate the product higher. If everything else is the same each time a consumer tried the product in the experiment, then a causal inference is supported.

A famous marketing experiment investigated the influence of brand name on consumers' taste perceptions. An experimenter manipulated whether consumers preferred the taste of beer in labeled or unlabeled bottles. One week respondents were given a six-pack containing bottles labeled only with letters (A, B, C). The following week, respondents received another six-pack with brand labels (like Budweiser, Coors, Miller, and so forth). The experimenter measured reactions to the beers after each tasting. In every case, the beer itself was the same. So, every person involved in the experiment drank the very same beer. Therefore, the differences observed in taste, the key dependent variable, could only be attributable to the difference in labeling. When the consumers participating in the experiment expressed a preference for the branded beer, the conclusion is that brand name does influence consumers' taste perceptions.

Basic Issues in Experimental Design

Experimental design is a major research topic. In fact, there are courses and books devoted only to that topic.[2] Here, an introduction into experimental design is provided. A student should be able to design and implement basic experimental designs with this introduction. Fortunately, most experimental designs in marketing are relatively simple.

Experimental designs involve no less than four important design elements. These issues include (1) manipulation of the independent variable, (2) selection and measurement of the dependent variable, (3) selection and assignment of experimental subjects, and (4) control over extraneous variables.[3] Each is discussed below.

Manipulation of the Independent Variable

Independent variable
In an experimental design, a variable that can be manipulated, or altered, independently of any other variable.

Recall from Chapter 3, the thing that makes **independent variables** special in experimentation is that the researcher actually creates his or her values. This is how the researcher manipulates, and therefore controls, independent variables. Experimental independent variables are hypothesized to be causal influences. Therefore, experiments are very appropriate in causal designs.

An **experimental treatment** is the term referring to the way an experimental variable is manipulated. For example, the opening vignette manipulated the brand with an experimental treatment assigning consumers to taste either Sea Snapper or Captain John's fish sticks. Thus, there were two levels (or values) of the brand variable. A medical researcher may manipulate an experimental variable by treating some subjects with one drug and the other subjects with a separate drug. Experimental variables often involve treatments with more than two levels. For instance, prices of $1.29, $1.69, and $1.99 might represent treatments in a pricing experiment examining how price affects sales.

A lot of marketing research involves experiments that manipulate different elements of physical environments.

Experimental variables like these can not only be described as independent variables, but they also can be described as a *categorical variable* because they take on a value to represent some classifiable or qualitative aspect. Color, for example, is either orange or blue. Advertising copy style is another example of a categorical or classificatory variable that might be manipulated in an experiment. In other situations an independent variable may truly be a *continuous variable*. When this is the case, the researcher must select appropriate levels of that variable as experimental treatments. For example, lighting can actually be varied over any level from no brightness onward. Before conducting the experiment, the researcher decides on levels that would be relevant to study. The levels should be noticeably different and realistic.

Experimental treatment
The term referring to the way an experimental variable is manipulated.

EXPERIMENTAL AND CONTROL GROUPS

In perhaps the simplest experiment, an independent variable is manipulated over two treatment levels resulting in two groups, an experimental group and a control group. An **experimental group** is one in which an experimental treatment is administered. A **control group** is one in which no experimental treatment is administered. For example, consider an experiment studying how advertising affects sales. In the experimental group, the advertising budget may be set at $200,000. In the control condition, advertising may remain at zero or may not change from its current level. By holding conditions constant in the control group, the researcher controls for potential sources of error in the experiment. Sales (the dependent variable) in the two treatment groups are compared at the end of the experiment to determine whether the level of advertising (the independent variable) had any effect. Note that this simple experiment can only produce a main effect.

Experimental group
A group of subjects to whom an experimental treatment is administered.

Control group
A group of subjects to whom no experimental treatment is administered.

SEVERAL EXPERIMENTAL TREATMENT LEVELS

The advertising/sales experiment with one experimental and one control group may not tell the advertiser everything he or she wishes to know. If the advertiser wished to understand the functional nature of the relationship between sales and advertising at several treatment levels, additional experimental groups with advertising expenditures of $250,000, $500,000, and $1 million might be studied. This experiment may still involve a control variable. By analyzing more groups, each with a different treatment level, a more precise result may be obtained than in the simple experimental group–control group experiment described above. This design also can produce only a main effect.

TOTHEPOINT

You never know what is enough unless you know what is more than enough.

—William Blake

We are never deceived; we deceive ourselves.

—Johann Wolfgang von Goethe

RESEARCHSNAPSHOT

Does Promotion Cause Intoxication?

One of the most pressing issues on college campuses is over-indulgence in alcohol. What are all of the factors that lead to the abuse of alcohol among undergraduate college students? Cultural influences such as the rite of passage can be identified in qualitative research. However, when it comes to setting policies that govern the sale of alcohol on and near universities, decision makers need to know what controllable practices cause drunkenness among college students and what behaviors are caused by drunkenness.

If heavy price promotion leads to drunkenness, which leads to detrimental behaviors, bars may reconsider their use and policy makers may consider restricting the types of promotions allowable if they wish to maintain their license to sell alcoholic beverages. These decision questions have led to numerous market experiments. For instance, the type of price promotion used by bars can be manipulated either in the field or in a lab experiment by exposing some subjects to an ad with one type of promotion and exposing others to a different type of promotion. This may allow a test of the causal influence of promotion on alcohol consumption. These studies show results like those shown in the chart titled "Mean Number of Drinks":

Mean Number of Drinks

[Bar chart with y-axis from 0 to 9, showing three conditions on the x-axis: "Free food", "1/2 price drinks", "50 cent drinks". Male and Female bars. Free food: Male ~7, Female ~4; 1/2 price drinks: Male ~7.3, Female ~4; 50 cent drinks: Male ~8, Female ~5. Legend: Male, Female]

This experiment involves an experimental manipulation varying the promotion over three levels. One-third of the student-subjects were exposed to each condition. The results show that reduced price drinks do lead to an increase in the number of drinks that a student estimates he or she would drink. This effect looks to be slightly larger among men than among women, although

©JEFF GREENBERG/PHOTOEDIT

women simply estimate they will drink less than men no matter what the experimental condition.

An experiment can also be used to show potentially negative results of too much drinking among college students. Researchers have designed simple experiments to examine how likely over-drinking is to lead a woman to experience an unwanted sexual encounter. An experimental variable can be created that manipulates the amount of alcohol a student-subject actually consumes. This experiment can be performed in a lab environment, and one experimental condition could involve non-alcoholic drinking and another could involve heavy drinking and then asking subjects how likely they would be to consent to or actively resist unwanted sexual advances. A similar experiment showed results like those depicted in the chart below:

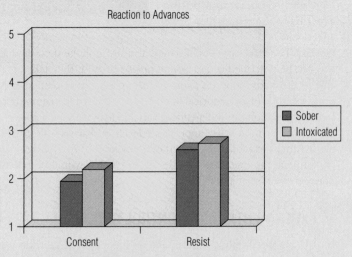

Reaction to Advances

[Bar chart with y-axis from 1 to 5, showing two conditions: "Consent" and "Resist". Sober and Intoxicated bars. Consent: Sober ~1.9, Intoxicated ~2.1; Resist: Sober ~2.5, Intoxicated ~2.6. Legend: Sober, Intoxicated]

These results show that although self-reported consent is low in both cases (on a 1 – 5 scale with 5 indicating probable consent), it is slightly higher in the intoxicated case. There appears to be very little difference in self-reported aggressive resistance. Thus, the manipulation did not seem to affect the means on aggressive resistance. Other experiments looked at different interactions that have further implications for policy makers.

Thus, experimental manipulations like these are very helpful in implementing causal designs studying drinking related behaviors.

Sources: Christie, J., D. Fisher, J. Kozup, S. Smith, S. Burton, and E. Creyer (2001), "The Effects of Bar-Sponsored Alcohol Beverage Promotions Across Binge and Non-binge Drinkers," Journal of Public Policy and Marketing, 20 (Fall), 240–253; Davis, K.C., W. H. George, and J. Norris (2004), "Women's Responses to Unwanted Sexual Advances: The Role of Alcohol and Inhibition Conflict," Psychology of Women Quarterly, 28 (December), 333–343.

◼ MORE THAN ONE INDEPENDENT VARIABLE

It is possible to assess the effects of more than one independent variable. In basic experimental designs, a single independent variable is manipulated to observe its effect on another single dependent variable. However, complex marketing-depenent variables such as sales, product usage, and brand preference are influenced by several factors such as sales, product usage, and brand preferences. The simultaneous changes in independent variables such as price and advertising may have a greater influence on sales than a change in either variable alone. *Factorial experimental designs* are more sophisticated than basic experimental designs; they allow for an investigation of the interaction of two or more independent variables. Whether the experiment is basic or factorial, the purpose of marketing research experimentation is to measure and compare the effects of experimental treatments on the dependent variable.

Selection and Measurement of the Dependent Variable

The **dependent variable** is so named because its value is expected to be dependent on the experimenter's manipulation of the independent variable; it is the criterion or standard by which the results are judge. Changes in the dependent variable are presumed to be a consequence of changes in the independent variable.

Dependent variable
The criterion by which the results of an experiment are judged; a variable expected to be dependent on the experimenter's manipulation of the independent variable.

Selecting dependent variables is crucial in experimental design. Unless the dependent variables are relevant and truly represent an outcome of interest, the experiment will not be useful. Sometimes, the logical dependent variable is fairly obvious. If researchers introduce a new cinnamon, pink grapefruit tea mix in a test-market, sales volume is most likely to be a key dependent variable. However, if researchers are experimenting with different forms of advertising copy appeals, defining the dependent variable may be more difficult. For example, measures of advertising awareness, recall, changes in brand preference, or sales might be possible dependent variables.

Choosing the right dependent variable is part of the problem definition process. Like the problem definition process in general, it sometimes is considered less carefully than it should be. The experimenter's choice of a dependent variable determines what type of answer is given to assist managers in decision making.

Consider how difficult it can be to select the right dependent variable in a test-market. While sales are almost certainly important, when should sales be measured? The amount of time needed for effects to become evident should be considered in choosing the dependent variable. Sales may be measured several months after the experiment to determine if there were any carryover effects. Changes that are relatively permanent or longer lasting than changes generated only during the period of the experiment should be considered. Repeat purchase behavior may be important too since some consumers may try a product once but then never choose that product again. Consumers often try a "loser" once, but they do not buy a "loser" again and again.

The introduction of the original Crystal Pepsi illustrates the need to think beyond consumers' initial reactions. When Crystal Pepsi, a clear cola, was introduced, the initial trial rate was high, but only a small percentage of customers made repeat purchases. The brand never achieved high repeat sales within a sufficiently large market segment. Brand awareness, trial purchase, and repeat purchase are all possible dependent variables in an experiment. The dependent variable therefore should be considered carefully. Thorough problem definition will help the researcher select the most important dependent variable(s).

Selection and Assignment of Test Units

Test units are the subjects or entities whose responses to the experimental treatment are measured or observed. Individual consumers, employees, organizational units, sales territories, market segments, brands, stores, or other entities may be the test units. People are the most common test units in most marketing and consumer behavior experiments.

Test units
The subjects or entities whose responses to the experimental treatment are measured or observed.

©DIGITAL VISION/GETTY IMAGES

Although experiments are often administered in groups, if all groups are not the same, then systematic error is introduced.

SAMPLE SELECTION AND RANDOM SAMPLING ERRORS

As in other forms of marketing research, random sampling errors and sample selection errors may occur in experimentation. For example, experiments sometimes go awry even when a geographic area is specially chosen for a particular investigation. A case in point was the experimental testing of a new lubricant for outboard motors by Dow Chemical Company. The lubricant was tested in Florida. Florida was chosen because researchers thought the hot, muggy climate would provide the most demanding test. In Florida the lubricant was a success. However, the story was quite different when the product was sold in Michigan. Although the lubricant sold well and worked well during the sum-

mer, the following spring Dow discovered the oil had congealed, allowing the outboard motors, idle all winter, to rust. The rusting problem never came to light in Florida, where the motors were in year-round use. Thus, sample selection error occurs because of flaws in procedures used to assign experimental test units. Florida conditions made the experiment irrelevant in Michigan.

Systematic or nonsampling error
Occurs if the sampling units in an experimental cell are somehow different than the units in another cell, and this difference affects the dependent variable.

Systematic or nonsampling error may occur if the sampling units in an experimental cell are somehow different than the units in another cell, and this difference affects the dependent variable. For example, suppose some professors are interested in testing the effect of providing snacks during exams on students' scores. The experimental variable is snacks, manipulated over three levels: (1) fruit, (2) cookies, and (3) chocolate. The test units in this case are individual students. When the professors conduct the experiment, for convenience, they decide to give all of the 8 a.m. classes chocolate for a snack, all of the 1 p.m. classes get fruit, and all of the 7 p.m. classes get cookies. While this type of procedure is often followed, if our tastes and digestive systems react differently to different foods at different times of the day, systematic error is introduced into the experiment. Furthermore, because the night classes contain students who are older on average, the professors may reach the conclusion that students perform better when they eat cookies, when it may really be due to the fact that students who are older perform better no matter what they are fed.

RANDOMIZATION

Randomization
The random assignment of subject and treatments to groups; it is one device for equally distributing the effects of extraneous variables to all conditions.

Randomization—the random assignment of subjects and treatments to groups—is one device for equally distributing the effects of extraneous variables to all conditions. The presence of nuisance variables will not be eliminated, but they will be controlled because they are likely to exist to the same degree in every experimental cell. Thus, all cells would be expected to yield similar average scores on the dependent variables if it were not for the experimental treatments administered in a particular cell. In other words, the researcher would like to set up a situation where everything in every cell is the same except for the experimental treatment. Random assignment of subjects allows the researcher to make this assumption.

MATCHING

Random assignment of subjects to the various experimental groups is the most common technique used to prevent test units from differing from each other on key variables; it assumes that all characteristics of the subjects have been likewise randomized. **Matching** the respondents on the basis of pertinent background information is another technique for controlling systematic error by assigning subjects in a way that their characteristics are the same in each group. This is best thought of in terms of demographic characteristics. If a subject's sex is expected to influence dependent variable responses, as in a taste test, then the researcher may make sure that there are equal numbers of men and women in each experimental cell. In general, if a researcher believes that certain extraneous variables may affect the dependent variable, he or she can make sure that the subjects in each group are the same on these characteristics.

For example, in a taste test experiment for a dog food, it might be important to match the dogs in various experimental groups on the basis of age or breed. That way, the same number of Basset Hounds and Dobermans will test formula A, formula B, and formula C. While matching can be a useful approach, the researcher can never be sure that sampling units are matched on all characteristics. Here, for example, even though breeds can be matched, it is difficult to know if all dogs live in the same type of environment (indoors, outdoors, spacious, cramped, with table scraps or without, and so on).

REPEATED MEASURES

Experiments in which an individual subject is exposed to more than one level of an experimental treatment are referred to as **repeated measures** designs. Although this approach has advantages, including being more economical since the same subject provides more data than otherwise, it has several drawbacks that can limit its usefulness. We will discuss these in more detail later.

CONTROL OVER EXTRANEOUS VARIABLES

The fourth decision about the basic elements of an experiment concerns control over extraneous variables. This is related to the various types of experimental error. In Chapter 7 we classified total survey error into two basic categories: random sampling error and systematic error. The same dichotomy applies to all research designs, but the terms *random (sampling) error* and *systematic error* are more frequently used when discussing experiments.

EXPERIMENTAL CONFOUNDS

We have already discussed how systematic error can occur when the extraneous variables or the conditions of administering the experiment are allowed to influence the dependent variables. When this occurs, the results will be confounded because the extraneous variables have not been controlled or eliminated. The results can be confounded by an extraneous cause. A **confound** in an experiment means that there is an alternative explanation beyond the experimental variables for any observed differences in the dependent variable. Once a potential confound is identified, the validity of the experiment is severely questioned.

Recall from the opening vignette that the experimental procedures involved a taste test. Sea Snapper fish sticks were always presented on a blue plate and Captain John's fish sticks were always presented on an orange plate. Since the color of the plates coincides with the assignment of the brand, there is no way of knowing from these results whether any observed differences in liking are due to the brand or the color of the plate. The plate's color is confounding the explanation that the difference in brands is responsible for the difference in liking.

In a simple experimental group–control group experiment, if subjects in the experimental group are always administered treatment in the morning and subjects in the control group always receive the treatment in the afternoon, a systematic error occurs. In such a situation, time of day represents a confound. In a training experiment the sources of constant error might be the persons who do the training (line or external specialists) or whether the training is conducted on the employees' own time or on company time. These and other characteristics of the training may have an impact on the dependent variable and will have to be taken into account:

The effect of a constant error is to distort the results in a particular direction, so that an erroneous difference masks the true state of affairs. The effect of a random error is not to distort the results in any particular direction,

Matching
A procedure for the assignment of subjects to groups that ensures that each group of respondents is matched on the basis of pertinent characteristics.

Repeated measures
Experiments in which an individual subject is exposed to more than one level of an experimental treatment.

Confound
Means that there is an alternative explanation beyond the experimental variables for any observed differences in the dependent variable.

but to obscure them. Constant error is like a distorting mirror in a fun house; it produces a picture that is clear but incorrect. Random error is like a mirror that has become cloudy with age; it produces a picture that is essentially correct but unclear.[4]

EXTRANEOUS VARIABLES

Most students of marketing realize that the marketing mix variables—price, product, promotion, and distribution—interact with uncontrollable forces in the market, such as competitors' activities and consumer trends. Thus, marketing experiments are subject to the effect of extraneous variables. Since extraneous variables can produce confounded results, they must be identified before the experiment if at all possible.

Cigarette smoking has been a topic of much debate and research. Does cigarette advertising cause young people to smoke? Although this is an often asked question, it is far from settled. One of the primary reasons for the inconclusiveness of this debate is the failure for most of the research to control for extraneous variables.[5] For instance, consider a study in which two groups of U.S. high school students are studied over the course of a year. One is exposed to a greater percentage of foreign television media in which American cigarettes are more often shown in a flattering and glamorous light. In fact, the programming includes cigarette commercials. The other group is a control group in which their exposure to media is not controlled. At the end of the year, the experimental group reports a greater frequency and incidence of cigarette smoking. Did the increased media exposure involving cigarettes cause smoking behavior?

While the result seems plausible at first, the careful researcher may ask the following questions:

- Was the demographic makeup of the two groups the same? While it is clear that the ages of the two groups are likely the same, it is well known that different ethnic groups have different smoking rates. Approximately 28 percent of all high school students report smoking, but the rate is higher among Hispanic teens, for example.[6] Therefore, if one group contained more Hispanics or Asians, we might expect it to report different smoking rates than otherwise. Similarly, smoking varies with social class.
- How did the control group fill the time consumed by the experimental group in being exposed to the experimental treatment? Could it be that it somehow dissuaded them from smoking? Perhaps they were exposed to media with more anti-smoking messages?
- Were the two groups of the same general achievement profiles? Those who are high in the need for achievement may be less prone to smoke than are other students.
- Although it is a difficult task to list all possible extraneous factors, some that even sound unusual can sometimes have an effect. For example, did the students have equally dispersed birthdays? Researchers have even shown that smoking rates correspond to one's birthday, meaning that different astrological groups have different smoking rates.[7]

Because an experimenter does not want extraneous variables to affect the results, he or she must control or eliminate such variables. It is always better to spend time thinking about how to control for possible extraneous variables before the experiment since often there is nothing that can be done to salvage results after a confounding effect is identified.

Demand Characteristics

What are Demand Characteristics?

Demand characteristic
Experimental design element or procedure that unintentionally provides subjects with hints about the research hypothesis.

Demand effect
Occurs when demand characteristics actually affect the dependent variable.

The term **demand characteristic** refers to an experimental design element that unintentionally provides subjects with hints about the research hypothesis. Researchers cannot reveal the research hypothesis to subjects before the experiment or else they can create a confounding effect. In addition, once subjects know the hypothesis, there is little hope that they will respond naturally.

So, knowledge of the experimental hypothesis creates a confound. This particular type of confound is known as a **demand effect**. Demand characteristics make demand effects very likely.

EXHIBIT 9.1
**By Smiling or Looking
Solemn, Experimenters Can
Modify Subjects' Behavior**

Experimenter Bias and Demand Effects

Demand characteristics are aspects of an experiment that *demand* (encourage) that the subjects respond in a particular way. Hence, they are a source of systematic error (see Exhibit 9.1). If participants recognize the experimenter's expectation or demand, they are likely to act in a manner consistent with the experimental treatment. Even slight nonverbal cues may influence their reactions.

Prominent demand characteristics are often presented by the person administering experimental procedures. If an experimenter's presence, actions, or comments influence the subjects' behavior or sway the subjects to slant their answers to cooperate with the experimenter, the experiment has introduced *experimenter bias*. When subjects slant their answers to cooperate with the experimenter, they are exhibiting behaviors that might not represent their behavior in the marketplace. For example, if subjects in an advertising experiment understand that the experimenter is interested in whether they changed their attitudes in accord with a given advertisement, they may answer in the desired direction. Acting in this manner reflects a demand effect rather than a true experimental treatment effect.

Reducing Demand Characteristics

Although it is practically impossible to eliminate demand characteristics from experiments, there are steps that can be taken to reduce them. Many of these steps make it difficult for subjects to know what the researcher is trying to find out. Some or all of these may be appropriate in a given experiment.

1. Use an experimental disguise.
2. Isolate experimental subjects.
3. Use a "blind" experimental administrator.
4. Administer only one experimental treatment level to each subject.

▨ USE AN EXPERIMENTAL DISGUISE

Subjects taking part in the experiment can be told that the purpose of the experiment is somewhat different than the actual purpose. Most often, they are simply told less than the complete "truth" about what is going to happen. Psychologists studying how much pain one person may be willing to inflict on another might use a ruse telling the subject that they are actually interested in the effect of pain on human performance. The researcher tells the actual subject to administer a series of questions to another person (who is actually a research assistant) and to provide them with an increasingly strong electric shock each time an incorrect answer is given. In reality, the real dependent variable has something to do with how long the actual subject will continue to administer shocks before stopping.

ISOLATE EXPERIMENTAL SUBJECTS

Researchers should minimize the extent to which subjects are able to talk about the experimental procedures with each other. Although it may be unintentional, discussion among subjects may lead them to guess the experimental hypothesis. For instance, it could be that different subjects received different treatments. The experimental integrity will be higher when each only knows enough to participate in the experiment.

USE A "BLIND" EXPERIMENTAL ADMINISTRATOR

When possible, the people actually administering the experiment may not be told the experimental hypothesis. The advantage is that if they do not know what exactly is being studied, then they are less likely to give off clues that result in demand effects. Like the subjects, when there is some reason to expect that their knowledge may constitute a demand characteristic, administrators best know only enough to do their job.

ADMINISTER ONLY ONE EXPERIMENTAL CONDITION PER SUBJECT

When subjects know more than one experimental treatment condition, they are much more likely to guess the experimental hypothesis. So, even though there are cost advantages to administering multiple treatment levels to the same subject, it should be avoided when possible. For example, in the retail atmospherics example, if subjects responded first to a blue retail store concept, and then saw the same store that was exactly the same except the walls had become orange, then he or she is very likely to know that the researcher is interested in color.

Establishing Control

The major difference between experimental research and descriptive research is an experimenter's ability to control variables by either holding conditions constant or manipulating the experimental variable. If the color of beer causes preference, a brewery experimenting with a new clear beer must determine the possible extraneous variables other than color that may affect an experiment's results and attempt to eliminate or control those variables. Marketing theory tells us that brand image and packaging design are important factors in beer drinkers' reactions. Therefore, the researcher may wish to control the influence of these variables. He or she may eliminate these two extraneous variables by packaging the test beers in plain brown packages without any brand identification.

Constancy of conditions
Means that subjects in all experimental groups are exposed to identical conditions except for the differing experimental treatments.

When extraneous variables cannot be eliminated, experimenters may strive for **constancy of conditions**. This means that subjects in all experimental groups are exposed to identical conditions except for the differing experimental treatments. The principle of matching discussed earlier helps make sure that constancy is achieved.

A supermarket experiment involving four test products shows the care that must be taken to hold all factors constant. The experiment required that all factors other than shelf space be kept constant throughout the testing period. In all stores the shelf level that had existed before the tests began was to be maintained throughout the test period. Only the *amount* of shelf space (the treatment) was changed. One problem involved store personnel accidentally changing shelf level when stocking the test products. This deviation from the constancy of conditions was minimized by auditing each store four times a week. In this way, any change could be detected in a minimum amount of time. The experimenter personally stocked as many of the products as possible, and the cooperation of stock clerks also helped reduce treatment deviations.

If an experimental method requires that the same subjects be exposed to two or more experimental treatments, an error may occur due to the *order of presentation*. For instance, if subjects are examining the effects of different levels of graphical interface on video game enjoyment, and they are asked to view each of four different levels, the order in which they are presented may influence enjoyment. Subjects might perform one level simply because it follows a very poor level. **Counterbalancing** attempts to eliminate the confounding effects of order of presentation by requiring that one fourth of the subjects be exposed to treatment A first, one fourth to treatment B first, one fourth to treatment C first, and finally one fourth to treatment D first. Likewise, the other levels are counterbalanced so that the order of presentation is rotated among subjects.

Counterbalancing
Attempts to eliminate the confounding effects of order of presentation by requiring that one fourth of the subjects be exposed to treatment A first, one fourth to treatment B first, one fourth to treatment C first, and finally one fourth to treatment D first.

Problems Controlling Extraneous Variables

In marketing experiments it is not always possible to control every possible extraneous variable. For example, competitors may bring out a product during the course of a test-market. This form of competitive interference occurred in a Boston test-market for Anheuser-Busch's import beer, Wurzburger Hofbrau. During the test, Miller Brewing Company introduced its own brand, Munich Oktoberfest, and sent eight salespeople out to blitz the Boston market. A competitor who learns of a test-market experiment may knowingly change its prices or increase advertising to confound the test results. This brings us to ethical issues in experimentation.

Ethical Issues in Experimentation

Ethical issues with experimentation were discussed in Chapter 4. There, the question of deception was raised. Although deception is necessary in most experiments, when subjects can be returned to their prior condition through **debriefing**, then the experiment is probably consistent with high moral standards. When subjects have been injured significantly or truly psychologically harmed, debriefing will not return them to their formal condition and the experiment should not proceed. Therefore, some additional commentary on debriefing is presented.

Debriefing
The process of providing subjects with all pertinent facts about the nature and purpose of an experiment after its completion.

Debriefing experimental subjects by communicating the purpose of the experiment and the researcher's hypotheses about the nature of consumer behavior is expected to counteract negative effects of deception, relieve stress, and provide an educational experience for the subject.

Proper debriefing allows the subject to save face by uncovering the truth for himself. The experimenter should begin by asking the subject if he has any questions or if he found any part of the experiment odd, confusing, or disturbing. This question provides a check on the subject's suspiciousness and effectiveness of manipulations. The experimenter continues to provide the subject cues to the deception until the subject states that he believes there was more to the experiment than met the eye. At this time the purpose and procedure of the experiment [are] revealed.[8]

Additionally, there is the issue of test-markets and efforts extended toward interfering with a competitor's test-market. The research snapshot dealing with Hidden Valley Ranch salad dressings described just such a situation. When a company puts a product out for public consumption, they should be aware that competitors may also now freely consume the product. When attempts to interfere with a test-market are aimed solely at invalidating test results or they are aimed at infringing on some copyright protection, those acts are ethically questionable.

Fundamental Questions in Experimentation

Basic versus Factorial Experimental Designs

In *basic experimental designs* a single independent variable is manipulated to observe its effect on a single dependent variable. However, we know that complex marketing dependent variables such as sales, product usage, and preference are influenced by several factors. The simultaneous change in independent variables such as price and advertising may have a greater influence on sales than if either variable is changed alone. *Factorial experimental designs* are more sophisticated than basic experimental designs and allow for an investigation of the interaction of two or more independent variables.

Laboratory Experiments

A marketing experiment can be conducted in a natural setting (a field experiment) or in an artificial or laboratory setting. In social sciences, the actual laboratory may be a behavioral lab, which is somewhat like a focus group facility. However, it may simply be a room or classroom dedicated to collecting data, or it can even take place in one's home.

In a **laboratory experiment** the researcher has more complete control over the research setting and extraneous variables. For example, subjects are recruited and brought to an advertising agency's office, a research agency's office, or perhaps a mobile unit designed for research purposes. They are exposed to a television commercial within the context of a program that includes competitors' ads among the commercials shown. They are then allowed to purchase either the advertised product or one of several competing products in a simulated store environment. Trial purchase measures are thus obtained. A few weeks later, subjects are contacted again to measure their satisfaction and determine repeat purchasing intention. This laboratory experiment gives the consumer an opportunity to "buy" and "invest." In a short timespan, the marketer is able to collect information on decision making. Our retail atmospheric experiment also illustrates a laboratory experiment.

Other laboratory experiments may be more controlled or artificial. For example, a **tachistoscope** allows a researcher to experiment with the visual impact of advertising, packaging, and so on by controlling the amount of time a subject is exposed to a visual image. Each stimulus (for example, package design) is projected from a slide to the tachistoscope at varying exposure lengths (1/10 of a second, 2/10, 3/10, and so on). The tachistoscope simulates the split-second duration of a customer's attention to a package in a mass display.

Laboratory experiment
The researcher has more complete control over the research setting and extraneous variables.

Tachistoscope
Device that controls the amount of time a subject is exposed to a visual image.

Field experiments
Research projects involving experimental manipulations that are implemented in a natural environment.

Field Experiments

Field experiments are research projects involving experimental manipulations that are implemented in a natural environment. They can be useful in fine-tuning marketing strategies and determining sales forecasts for different marketing mix designs. Test-markets are field experiments. Betty Crocker's Squeezit (a 10 percent fruit juice drink in a squeeze bottle) was so successful in a test-market that production could not keep up with demand. As a result, the product's national introduction was postponed until production capacity could be increased.

The naturally occurring noise that exists in the field can interfere with experimental manipulations.

©MIKE MCQUEEN/CORBIS

McDonald's conducted a field experiment testing the Triple Ripple, a three-flavor ice cream product. The product was dropped because the experiment revealed distribution problems reduced product quality and limited customer acceptance. In the distribution system the product would freeze, defrost, and refreeze. Solving the problem would have required each McDonald's city to have a local ice cream plant with special equipment to roll the three flavors into one. A naturalistic setting for the experiment helped McDonald's executives realize the product was impractical.

Experiments vary in their degree of artificiality and control.

RESEARCHSNAPSHOT

The Hidden in Hidden Valley Ranch

A few years ago, Hidden Valley Ranch (HVR) conducted a field market experiment to examine how effective three new flavors of salad dressings would be in the marketplace. Thus, there were three levels of the experimental variable, each representing a different flavor. Tests like this can be expensive. HVR had to produce small batches of each flavor, get them bottled, and ship them to their sales representatives, who then had to stock the dressings in the participating retail stores. All of this is very expensive.

So, the first day of the test was consumed with sales reps placing the products in the salad dressing sections of retail stores. The second day, each rep went back to each store to record the number of sales for each flavor. By the third day, all of the bottles of all flavors had sold! Amazing! Was every flavor a huge success? Actually, one of HVR's competitors had sent its sales reps around beginning on the second day of the test to buy every bottle of the new HVR dressings in every store it had been placed in. Thus, HVR was unable to produce any valid sales data (the dependent variable) and the competitor was able to break down the dressing in its labs and determine the recipe.

This illustrates one risk that comes along with field tests. Once a product is available for sale, there are no secrets. Also, you risk espionage of this type that can render the experiment invalid.

©SUSAN VAN ETTEN

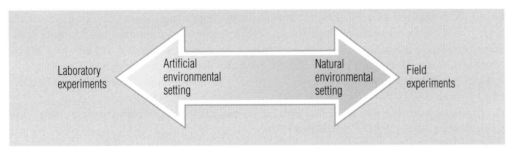

EXHIBIT 9.2
The Artificiality of Laboratory versus Field Experiments

Exhibit 9.2 shows that as experiments increase in naturalism, they begin to approach a pure field experiment. As they become more artificial, they approach a pure laboratory experiment.

In field experiments, a researcher manipulates experimental variables but cannot possibly control all the extraneous variables. An example is NBC's research on new television programs. Viewers who subscribe to a cable television service are asked to watch a cable preview on their home television sets at a certain time on a certain cable channel. While the program is being aired, telephone calls from the viewers' friends cannot be controlled. In contrast, an advertising professor may test some advertising effect by showing subjects advertising in a classroom setting. Here, there are no phone calls and little to distract the subject. Which produces a better experiment?

Issues of Experimental Validity

An experiment's quality is judged by two types of validity. These are known as internal and external validity.

Internal Validity

Internal validity exists to the extent that an experimental variable is truly responsible for any variance in the dependent variable. In other words, does the experimental manipulation truly cause changes in the specific outcome of interest? If the observed results were influenced or confounded by extraneous factors, the researcher will have problems making valid conclusions about the relationship between the experimental treatment and the dependent variable.

Internal validity
Exists to the extent that an experimental variable is truly responsible for any variance in the dependent variable.

Thus, a lab experiment enhances internal validity because it maximizes control of outside forces. If we wish to know whether a certain odor causes increased productivity among service workers, we may set up a task in a room with a tightly controlled airflow so we can be sure that the specific odor exists in the air in the amount and intensity desired. We can also control temperature, lighting, density, sounds, and many other factors that would be difficult or impossible to control outside of a lab environment. If the only thing that varies from subject to subject is the odor, then we can safely say that any differences in performance must be attributable to human reactions to the scent.

▨ MANIPULATION CHECKS

Internal validity depends in large part on successful manipulations. Manipulations should be carried out in a way that varies the experimental variable over meaningfully different levels. If the levels are too close together, the experiment may lack the power necessary to observe differences in the dependent variable. In a pricing experiment, it may be that manipulating the price of an automobile over two levels, $24,800 and $24,600, would not be successful in creating truly different price categories.

Manipulation check
A validity test of an experimental manipulation to make sure that the manipulation does produce differences in the independent variable.

The validity of manipulations can often be checked with a manipulation check. If a drug is administered in different dosages that should affect blood sugar levels, the researcher could actually measure blood sugar level after administering the drug to make sure that the dosages were different enough to produce a change in blood sugar. In marketing, the manipulation check is often conducted by asking a survey question or two. In the pricing example above, subjects may be asked a question about how low they believe the price of the car to be. A valid manipulation would produce substantially different average responses to that question in a "high" and "low" price group. Manipulation checks should always be administered after dependent variables in self-response format experiments. This keeps the manipulation check item from becoming a troublesome demand characteristic.

Extraneous variables can jeopardize internal validity. The six major ones are *history, maturation, testing, instrumentation, selection,* and *mortality.*

▨ HISTORY

History effect
Occurs when some change other than the experimental treatment occurs during the course of an experiment that affects the dependent variable.

A history effect occurs when some change other than the experimental treatment occurs during the course of an experiment that affects the dependent variable. A common history effect occurs when competitors change their marketing strategies during a test marketing experiment. History effects are particularly prevalent in repeated measures experiments that take place over an extended time. If we wanted to assess how much a change in recipe improves individual subjects' consumption of a food product, we would first measure their consumption and then compare it with consumption after the change. Since several weeks may pass between the first and second measurement, there are many things that could occur that would also influence subjects' diets.

Although it may sound extreme, examining the effect of some dietary supplement on various health-related outcomes may require that a subject be confined during the experiment's course. This may take several weeks. Without confining the subject in something like a hospital setting, there would be little way of controlling food and drink consumption, exercise activities, and other factors that may also affect the dependent variables.

Cohort effect
Refers to a change in the dependent variable that occurs because members of one experimental group experienced different historical situations than members of other experimental groups.

A special case of the history effect is the cohort effect, which refers to a change in the dependent variable that occurs because members of one experimental group experienced different historical situations than members of other experimental groups. For example, two groups of managers used as subjects may be in different cohorts because one group encountered different experiences over the course of an experiment. If the experimental manipulation involves different levels of financial incentives and performance is the dependent variable, one group may be affected by an informative article appearing in a trade magazine during the experiment. Since the other group participated prior to this group, members of that group could not benefit from the article. Therefore, the possibility exists that the article rather than the change in incentive is truly causing differences in performance.

MATURATION

Maturation effects are effects that are a function of time and the naturally occurring events that coincide with growth and experience. Experiments taking place over longer timespans may see lower internal validity as subjects simply grow older or more experienced. Suppose an experiment were designed to test the impact of a new compensation program on sales productivity. If this program were tested over a year's time, some of the salespeople probably would mature as a result of more selling experience or perhaps gain increased knowledge. Their sales productivity might improve because of their knowledge and experience rather than the compensation program.

Maturation effects
Effects that are a function of time and the naturally occurring events that coincide with growth and experience.

TESTING

Testing effects are also called *pretesting effects* because the initial measurement or test alerts or primes subjects in a way that affects their response to the experimental treatments. Testing effects only occur in a before-and-after study. A before-and-after study is one requiring an initial baseline measure be taken before an experimental treatment is administered. So, before-and-after experiments are a special case of a repeated measures design. For example, students taking standardized achievement and intelligence tests for the second time usually do better than those taking the tests for the first time. The effect of testing may increase awareness of socially approved answers, increase attention to experimental conditions (that is, the subject may watch more closely), or make the subject more conscious than usual of the dimensions of a problem.

Testing effects
A nuisance effect occurring when the initial measurement or test alerts or primes subjects in a way that affects their response to the experimental treatments.

INSTRUMENTATION

A change in the wording of questions, a change in interviewers, or a change in other procedures used to measure the dependent variable causes an **instrumentation effect**, which may jeopardize internal validity. If the same interviewers are used to ask questions for both before and after measurement, some problems may arise. With practice, interviewers may acquire increased skill in interviewing, or they may become bored and decide to reword the questionnaire in their own terms. To avoid this problem, new interviewers are hired, but different individuals are also a source of extraneous variation due to instrumentation variation. There are numerous other sources of instrument decay or variation. Again, instrumentation effects are problematic with any type of repeated measures design.

Instrumentation effect
A nuisance that occurs when a change in the wording of questions, a change in interviewers, or a change in other procedures causes a change in the dependent variable.

SELECTION

The selection effect is a sample bias that results from differential selection of respondents for the comparison groups, or sample selection error, discussed earlier.

MORTALITY

If an experiment is conducted over a period of a few weeks or more, some sample bias may occur due to the **mortality effect (sample attrition)**. Sample attrition occurs when some subjects withdraw from the experiment before it is completed. Mortality effects may occur if subjects drop from one experimental treatment group disproportionately from other groups. Consider a sales training experiment investigating the effects of close supervision of salespeople (high pressure) versus low supervision (low pressure). The high-pressure condition may misleadingly appear superior if those subjects who completed the experiment did very well. If, however, the high-pressure condition caused more subjects to drop out than the other conditions, this apparent superiority may be due to the fact that only very determined and/or talented salespeople stuck with the program.

Mortality effect (sample attrition)
Occurs when some subjects withdraw from the experiment before it is completed.

External Validity

External validity is the accuracy with which experimental results can be generalized beyond the experimental subjects. External validity is increased when the subjects comprising the sample truly

External validity
Is the accuracy with which experimental results can be generalized beyond the experimental subjects.

represent some population and when the results extend to market segments or other groups of people. The higher the external validity, the more researchers and managers can count on the fact that any results observed in an experiment will also be seen in the "real world" (marketplace, workplace, sales floor, and so on).

For instance, to what extent would results from a retail atmosphere experiment, which represents a simulated shopping experiment, transfer to a real-world retail store in a shopping mall, downtown mall, or lifestyle center? Can one extrapolate the results from a tachistoscope to an in-store shopping situation? Lab experiments are associated with low external validity because the limited set of experimental conditions, holding all else constant, do not adequately represent all the influences existing in the real world. In other words, the experimental situation may be too artificial. When a study lacks external validity, the researcher will have difficulty repeating the experiment with any change in subjects, settings, or time.

Trade-Offs Between Internal and External Validity

Naturalistic field experiments tend to have greater external validity than artificial laboratory experiments. Marketing researchers often must trade internal validity for external validity. A researcher who wishes to test advertising effectiveness by manipulating treatments via a split-cable experiment has the assurance that the advertisement will be viewed in an externally valid situation, the subjects' homes. However, the researcher has no assurance that some interruption (for example, a telephone call) will not have some influence that will reduce the internal validity of the experiment. Laboratory experiments with many controlled factors usually are high in internal validity, while field experiments generally have less internal validity, but greater external validity. Ideally, results from lab experiments would be followed up with some type of field test.

Classification of Experimental Designs

An experimental design may be compared to an architect's plans for a building. The basic requirements for the structure are given to the architect by the prospective owner. Several different plans may be drawn up as options for meeting the basic requirements. Some may be more costly than others. One may offer potential advantages that another does not.

There are various types of experimental designs. If only one variable is manipulated, the experiment has a **basic experimental design**. If the experimenter wishes to investigate several levels of the independent variable (for example, four price levels) or to investigate the interaction effects of two or more independent variables, the experiment requires a *complex,* or *statistical,* experimental design.

Basic experimental design
An experimental design in which only one variable is manipulated.

Symbolism for Diagramming Experimental Designs

The work of Campbell and Stanley has helped many students master the subject of basic experimental designs.[9] The following symbols will be used in describing the various experimental designs:

X = *exposure of a group to an experimental treatment*

O = *observation or measurement of the dependent variable; if more than one observation or measurement is taken, subscripts (that is, O_1, O_2, etc.) indicate temporal order*

$\boxed{R}$ = *random assignment of test units; $\boxed{R}$ symbolizes that individuals selected as subjects for the experiment are randomly assigned to the experimental groups*

The diagrams of experimental designs that follow assume a time flow from left to right. Our first example will make this clearer.

Three Examples of Quasi-Experimental Designs

Quasi-experimental designs do not involve random allocation of subjects to treatment combinations. In this sense, they do not qualify as true experimental designs because they do not adequately control for the problems associated with loss of internal validity. However, they are used particularly when it is the only way to implement a study.

ONE-SHOT DESIGN

The **one-shot design**, or *after-only design,* is diagrammed as follows:

$$X \qquad O_1$$

Suppose that during a very cold winter an automobile dealer finds herself with a large inventory of cars. She decides to experiment for the month of January with a promotional scheme. She offers a free trip to Miami with every car sold. She experiments with the promotion ($X =$ experimental treatment) and measures sales ($O_1 =$ measurement of sales after the treatment is administered).

This one-shot design is a case study of a research project fraught with problems. Subjects or test units participate because of voluntary self-selection or arbitrary assignment, not because of random assignment. The study lacks any kind of comparison or any means of controlling extraneous influences. There should be a measure of what will happen when the test units have not been exposed to X to compare with the measures of when subjects have been exposed to X. Nevertheless, under certain circumstances, even though this design lacks internal validity, it is the only viable choice.

ONE-GROUP PRETEST–POSTTEST DESIGN

Suppose a real estate franchiser wishes to provide a training program for franchisees. If the franchiser measures subjects' knowledge of real estate selling before (O_1) they are exposed to the experimental treatment (X) and then measures real estate selling knowledge after (O_2) they are exposed to the treatment, the design will be as follows:

$$O_1 \qquad X \qquad O_2$$

In this example the trainer is likely to conclude that the difference between O_2 and O_1 ($O_2 - O_1$) is the measure of the influence of the experimental treatment. This **one-group pretest-posttest design** offers a comparison of the same individuals before and after training. Although this is an improvement over the one-shot design, this research still has several weaknesses that may jeopardize internal validity. For example, if the time lapse between O_1 and O_2 was a period of several months, the trainees may have matured as a result of experience on the job (maturation effect). History effects may also influence this design. Perhaps some subjects dropped out of the training program (mortality effect). The effect of testing may also have confounded the experiment.

Although this design has a number of weaknesses, it is used in marketing research. Remember, the cost of the research is a consideration in most business situations. While there will be some problems of internal validity, the researcher must always take into account questions of time and cost.

STATIC GROUP DESIGN

In a **static group design** each subject is identified as a member of either an experimental group or a control group (for example, exposed or not exposed to a commercial). The experimental group is measured after being exposed to an experimental treatment, and the control group is measured without having been exposed to this experimental treatment:

Experimental group: $\quad X \qquad O_1$
Control group: $\qquad\qquad\quad\ O_2$

The results of the static group design are computed by subtracting the observed results in the control group from those in the experimental group ($O_1 - O_2$). A major weakness of this design is its lack of assurance that the groups were equal on variables of interest before the experimental group received the treatment. If the groups were selected arbitrarily by the investigator, or if entry into either group was voluntary, systematic differences between the groups could invalidate the conclusions about the effect of the treatment. Random assignment of subjects may eliminate problems with group differences. If groups are established by the experimenter rather than existing as a function of some other causation, the static group design is referred to as an *after-only design with control group*.

On many occasions, an after-only design is the only possible option. This is particularly true when conducting use tests for new products or brands. Cautious interpretation and recognition of the design's shortcomings may make this design valuable.

Three Alternative Experimental Designs

In a formal scientific sense, the three designs just discussed are not pure experimental designs. Subjects for the experiments were not selected from a common pool of subjects and randomly assigned to one group or another. In the following discussion of three basic experimental designs, the symbol $\boxed{R}$ to the left of the diagram indicates that the first step in a true experimental design is the randomization of subject assignment.

◼ PRETEST-POSTTEST CONTROL GROUP DESIGN (BEFORE–AFTER WITH CONTROL)

Pretest-posttest control group design
A true experimental design in which the experimental group is tested before and after exposure to the treatment and the control group is tested at the same two times without being exposed to the experimental treatment.

A **pretest-posttest control group design**, or *before–after with control group design*, is the classic experimental design:

Experimental group: $\boxed{R}$ O_1 X O_2
Control group: $\boxed{R}$ O_3 O_4

As the diagram indicates, the subjects in the experimental group are tested before and after being exposed to the treatment. The control group is tested at the same two times as the experimental group, but subjects are not exposed to the experimental treatment. This design has the advantages of the before–after design with the additional advantages gained by its having a control group. The effect of the experimental treatment equals

$$(O_2 - O_1) - (O_4 - O_3)$$

If there is brand awareness among 20 percent of the subjects ($O_1 = 20$ percent, $O_3 = 20$ percent) before an advertising treatment and then 35 percent awareness in the experimental group ($O_2 = 35$ percent) and 22 percent awareness in the control group ($O_4 = 22$ percent) after exposure to the treatment, the treatment effect equals 13 percent:

$$(0.35 - 0.20) - (0.22 - 0.20) = (0.15) - (0.02) = 0.13 \text{ } or \text{ } 13\%$$

The effect of all extraneous variables is assumed to be the same on both the experimental and the control groups. For instance, since both groups receive the pretest, no difference between them is expected for the pretest effect. This assumption is also made for effects of other events between the before and after measurements (history), changes within the subjects that occur with the passage of time (maturation), testing effects, and instrumentation effects. In reality there will be some differences in the sources of extraneous variation. Nevertheless, in most cases assuming that the effect is approximately equal for both groups is reasonable.

However, a testing effect is possible when subjects are sensitized to the subject of the research. This is analogous to what occurs when people learn a new vocabulary word. Soon they discover that they notice it much more frequently in their reading. In an experiment the combination of being interviewed on a subject and receiving the experimental treatment might be a potential source of error. For example, a subject exposed to a certain advertising message in a split-cable experiment might say, "Ah, there is an ad about the product I was interviewed about yesterday!" The subject may pay more attention than normal to the advertisement and be more prone to change his or her attitude than in a situation with no interactive testing effects. This weakness in the before–after with control group design can be corrected (see the next two designs).

EXHIBIT 9.3 **Product Preference Measure in an Experiment**

We are going to give away a series of prizes. If you are selected as one of the winners, which brand from each of the groups listed below would you truly want to win?

Special arrangements will be made for any product for which bulk, or one-time, delivery is not appropriate.

Indicate your answers by filling in the box like this: ■

Do not "X," check, or circle the boxes please.

Cookies			**Allergy Relief Products**		
(A 3-month supply, pick ONE.)			(A year's supply, pick ONE.)		
NABISCO OREO	☐	(1)	ALLEREST	☐	(1)
NABISCO OREO DOUBLE STUFF	☐	(2)	BENADRYL	☐	(2)
NABISCO NUTTER BUTTER	☐	(3)	CONTAC	☐	(3)
NABISCO VANILLA CREMES	☐	(4)	TAVIST–D	☐	(4)
HYDROX CHOCOLATE	☐	(5)	DRISTAN	☐	(5)
HYDROX DOUBLES	☐	(6)	SUDAFED	☐	(6)
NABISCO COOKIE BREAK	☐	(7)	CHLOR–TRIMETON	☐	(7)
NABISCO CHIPS AHOY	☐	(8)			
KEEBLER E.L. FUDGE	☐	(9)			
KEEBLER FUDGE CREMES	☐	(10)			
KEEBLER FRENCH VANILLA CREMES	☐	(11)			

Testing the effectiveness of television commercials in movie theaters provides an example of the before–after with control group design. Subjects are selected for the experiments by being told that they are going to preview several new television shows. When they enter the theater, they learn that a drawing for several types of products will be held, and they are asked to complete a product preference questionnaire (see Exhibit 9.3). Then a first drawing is held. Next, the television pilots and commercials are shown. Then the emcee announces additional prizes and a second drawing. Finally, subjects fill out the same questionnaire about prizes. The information from the first questionnaire is the before measurement, and that from the second questionnaire is the after measurement. The control group receives similar treatment except that on the day they view the pilot television shows, different (or no) television commercials are substituted for the experimental commercials.

POSTTEST-ONLY CONTROL GROUP DESIGN (AFTER-ONLY WITH CONTROL)

In some situations pretest measurements are impossible. In other situations selection error is not anticipated to be a problem because the groups are known to be equal. The **posttest-only control group design**, or *after-only with control group design,* is diagrammed as follows:

Experimental group: $\boxed{R}$ $\quad$ X $\quad$ O_1
Control group: $\quad$ $\boxed{R}$ $\quad\quad\quad$ O_2

The effect of the experimental treatment is equal to $O_2 - O_1$.

Suppose the manufacturer of an athlete's-foot remedy wishes to demonstrate by experimentation that its product is better than a competing brand. No pretest measure about the effectiveness of the remedy is possible. The design is to randomly select subjects, perhaps students, who have contracted athlete's foot and randomly assign them to the experimental or the control group. With only the posttest measurement, the effects of testing and instrument variation are eliminated. Furthermore, researchers make the same assumptions about extraneous variables described above—that is, that they operate equally on both groups, as in the before–after with control group design.

COMPROMISE DESIGNS

True experimentation is often simply not possible. The researcher may compromise by approximating an experimental design. A compromise design is one that falls short of assigning subjects or treatments randomly to experimental groups.

Posttest-only control group design
An after-only design in which the experimental group is tested after exposure to the treatment and the control group is tested at the same time without having been exposed to the treatment; no premeasure is taken. Random assignment of subjects and treatment occurs.

Consider a situation in which a researcher would ideally implement a pretest–posttest control group design to study the effect of training on employee performance. In this case, subjects may not be able to be assigned randomly to the experimental and control group because the researcher cannot take workers away from their work groups. Thus, one entire work group is used as the experimental group and a separate work group is used as a control group. The researcher has no assurance that the groups are equivalent. The situation has forced a compromise to experimental integrity.

The alternative to the compromise design when random assignment of subjects is not possible is to conduct the experiment *without* a control group. Generally this is considered a greater weakness than using groups that have already been established. When the experiment involves a longitudinal study, circumstances usually dictate a compromise with true experimentation.

Using Test-Markets

Test-marketing involves scientific testing and controlled field experimentation. As such, test-marketing goes well beyond merely "trying something out in the marketplace." Just because a product is introduced in a small marketing area before deciding whether to do a national launch does not mean a test-market has been conducted. Those who underestimate the need for a rigorous approach to test-marketing often "succeed" in their test-market but fail in their product launch. Test-marketing is the most prominent type of field experiment.

Chapter 3 briefly introduced test-marketing. Recall that a *test-market* is a market experiment conducted in an actual product market, meaning under real-world conditions. While we most often think of test-markets in conjunction with a decision about the viability of some newly developed product, they are equally useful in examining other elements of marketing strategy. Even though test-markets are not "small scale" research projects, they do test-marketing questions under a smaller scale than the entire market. So, before implementing a marketing strategy throughout the United States or Europe, test cities such as Tampa, Florida, and Frankfurt, Germany, may be used to represent the way consumers in other cities might react.

Effective Uses of Test-marketing

Test-marketing has three broad primary uses in marketing research. Each use can be broken down more specifically to look at some issue in close detail. The three broad uses are

1. Forecasting the success of a newly developed product.
2. Testing hypotheses about different options for marketing mix elements.
3. Identifying weaknesses in product designs or marketing strategies.

■ FORECASTING NEW PRODUCT SUCCESS

Test-markets have long been used as a pilot test for a new product introduction. While test-markets can be complicated to implement, the basic idea is simple. A product can be marketed on a small scale under actual market conditions and the results used to forecast the success or failure once the product is introduced on a large scale.

Companies using test-markets should realize that a new product concept also involves issues like advertising, pricing, supply chains, and retail placement. These issues may also be manipulated within a test-market. Estimates can then be made about the optimal advertising level, the need for product sampling, retail channel fit, or perhaps even advertising and retail channel selection interaction. Test-marketing permits evaluation of the entire new product concept, not just the physical good itself.

A marketing manager for Life Savers candies vividly portrays this function of experimentation in the marketplace:

A market test may be likened to an orchestra rehearsal. The violinists have adjusted their strings, the trumpeters have tested their keys, and the drummer has tightened his drums. Everything is ready to go. But all these instruments have not worked in unison. So a test-market is like an orchestra rehearsal where you can practice with everything together before the big public performance.[10]

RESEARCHSNAPSHOT

Test-marketing Channels

Traditionally, most construction material companies have focused their advertising on B2B efforts by targeting their sales and promotional efforts at construction material wholesalers, retailers, and contractors. The emphasis as a result was often centered around price in one way or another.

Construction products today are changing the way these products are sold and promoted. They are going right to the end-consumers in a classic pull strategy. The hope is that by advertising and selling directly to consumers, they will demand that contractors use a certain material and that home centers stock these products. Both Hardi Plank siding products and Georgia-Pacific drywall products have seen success in communicating emotionally about the importance of building and repairing one's home "right."

GP has test-marketing advertising campaigns aimed squarely at end-consumers in Atlanta, Minneapolis, Tampa, Charlotte, and Raleigh-Durham, North Carolina. The campaigns include commercials that address consumers' fears about mold in their homes. They tout drywall products that can "stop feeding the mold." Similarly, Hardi Plank ads show how their products can help homeowners relax without fear of rotting or constant repainting. Both companies are excited about the results of marketing directly to consumers. However, the building industry is slow to change and most building product companies continue to target business markets.

Sources: Lovel, J. (2005), "New GP Ads Take Drywall to the Masses," Adweek, 46 (8/8), 11; Rodriguez, Dennis. (2004), "Shea Homes," Professional Builder, 69 (Mid-December), 34.

▇ TESTING THE MARKETING MIX

Test-markets are not confined to studying new products or product modifications. They also are equally useful as a field experiment manipulating different marketing plans for existing products. Any element of the marketing mix can be examined with a test-market.

As we all know, retailers rely heavily on weekly flyers distributed through newspapers or through direct mail. This is particularly true in France, where retail advertising is restricted by law in many ways, including the ability to advertise on television. In France, the average French household receives over 12 kg (26.4 lbs) of retail flyers annually![11] Yet many have little idea about the effectiveness of different approaches. Should the flyers simply promote low price, or should they emphasize products related to a specific theme? In fact, different flyer styles can significantly affect not only sales, but retailer image too.[12] Test-marketing can provide an effective way of estimating the effect of a different flyer approach.

▇ IDENTIFYING PRODUCT WEAKNESSES

Test-market experimentation also allows identification of previously undetected product or marketing plan weaknesses. The weaknesses can then be dealt with before the company commits to the actual sales launch. Although often this use of test-markets is accidental, in the sense that it isn't the reason for conducting the test-markets, huge sums of resources can be saved by spotting problems before the full-scale marketing effort begins. Often, this use of test-marketing occurs when a product underperforms in at least one location. Researchers can then follow up with other research approaches to try and reveal the reason for the lack of performance. Once identified, product modifications can be made that address these reasons specifically.

McDonald's test-marketed pizza periodically for years. The first test-market provided lower than expected sales results. The reasons for the underperformance included a failure to consider learned competitors' reactions and problems associated with the small, single portion pizza, which was the only way McPizza was sold. Additionally, McPizza didn't seem to bring any new customers to McDonald's. In the next round of test-marketing, the marketing strategy repositioned the pizza, shifting to a 14-inch pizza that was only sold from about 4 p.m. until closing. With still underwhelming results, McDonalds test-marketed "Pizza Shoppes" within the test McDonald's where employees could be seen assembling ingredients on ready-made pizza dough. Although the concept is still alive, McDonald's has shied away from pizza for the U.S. adult market. A McPizza Happy Meal remains as a sole pizza concept with promise for American stores. Pizza-like products, however, exist and succeed at many McDonald's locations in other nations.

Factors to Consider in Test-market Selection

Obtaining a representative test-market requires considering many factors that may not be obvious to the inexperienced researcher. Consider the observation of a vice president of ITT Continental Banking:

When I started in the business, I thought people picked cities like Columbus, Ohio, because their populations were typical. But I found the main reasons were that they were isolated media markets and the distribution patterns were such that they didn't have to worry about the chain warehouse shipping outside of Columbus. It's difficult to translate information from a city which represents 0.1 percent of the United States and multiply that to get 99.9 percent. I think it is much more important to get control of the distribution and the advertising message.[13]

As with all decisions, the objectives of the decision makers will influence the choice of alternative. The following factors should be considered in the selection of a test-market.

■ POPULATION SIZE

No one size represents the best population for a test-market city. Practically all metropolitan areas in the United States are large enough. The population simply should be large enough to provide meaningful results with respect to the larger population, yet small enough to ensure that costs are not prohibitive. New York City is far too large to be a popular test-market, as is Chicago and Los Angeles in the United States. Likewise, Tokyo and Mexico City are considered too large for practical test-markets.

■ DEMOGRAPHIC COMPOSITION AND LIFESTYLE CONSIDERATIONS

Ethnic backgrounds, incomes, age distributions, lifestyles, and so on within the market should be representative of the market segment to which an offering is targeted. If a product is intended to be equally targeted toward the entire U.S. market, the product should then be test-marketed in cities that most closely match the entire U.S. population, like Wichita Falls, Texas. Test-marketing on the West Coast may not be representative because people residing in metropolitan areas along the Pacific tend to be unique in some ways. For instance, West Coast consumers are quick to accept innovations that might not ever be adopted on a large scale elsewhere. Additionally, most of these cities have large percentages of either Hispanic and/or Asian populations, making them less appropriate for representing the entire country.

■ COMPETITIVE SITUATION

Competitive market shares, competitive advertising, and distribution patterns should be typical so that test-markets will represent other geographic regions. If they are not representative, it will be difficult to project the test-market results to other markets.

Consider a firm that test-markets a new product in a specific geographical area in which the company has a dominant market share. Here, the sales force may have a much easier time getting shelf space than in an area where market share is low. The result is a higher acceptance level among retailers, lower cost of sell-in (obtaining initial distribution), and a greater upside potential for test-market results. Hence, projecting the results of this particular test-market into those where the same level of past success is not enjoyed proves difficult.

■ MEDIA COVERAGE AND EFFICIENCY

Local media (television spots, newspapers) will never exactly replicate national media. However, duplicating the national media plan or using one similar to it is important. Sunday newspaper supplements are sometimes used as a substitute for national magazine advertising. This does not duplicate a national plan, but may provide a rough estimate of the plan's impact. Ideally, a market should be represented by the major television networks, typical cable television programming, and newspaper coverage. Some magazines have regional editions or advertising inserts.

MEDIA ISOLATION

Advertising in communities outside of the test-market may contaminate the test-market. Furthermore, advertising money is wasted when it reaches consumers who cannot buy the advertised product because they live outside the test area. Markets such as Tulsa, Oklahoma, and Green Bay, Wisconsin, are highly desirable because advertising does not spill over into other areas.

SELF-CONTAINED TRADING AREA

Distributors should sell primarily or exclusively in the test-market area. Shipments in and out of markets from chain warehouses can produce confusing shipping figures. Frito-Lay test-marketed Olean-based versions of Ruffles, Lay's, Doritos, and Tostitos under the Max name in Cedar Rapids, Iowa. However, large amounts of the chips were purchased by droves of consumers in markets far from the test site.[14] Publicity about the no-fat chips had retailers fielding telephone orders from as far away as California, Texas, and New Jersey. Had the company relied solely on shipment information, the plants it built for what became WOW! Chips would have been much larger than needed.

OVERUSED TEST-MARKETS

If consumers or retailers become aware of the tests, they will react in a manner different from their norm. Thus, it is not a good idea to establish one great test-market and use it time and time again. Tucson, Arizona, is one area now used less frequently than in the past because Tuscsonian consumers now display atypical reactions to new-product introductions. Perhaps they are so accustomed to in-store promotion and advertising of new products that the reaction to innovative marketing is now below average.

Summary

1. Create an experimental, independent variable through a valid experimental manipulation of its value. Independent variables are created through manipulation in experiments rather than through measurement. The researcher creates unique experimental conditions that represent unique levels of an independent variable. The levels should be different enough to represent meaningful categorie of the dependent variable.

2. Understand and minimize the systematic experimental error. Systematic experimental error occurs because sampling units (research subjects) in one experimental cell are different from those in another cell in a way that affects the dependent variable. In an experiment involving how people respond to color, the researcher would not want to have all males in one color group and all females in another. Randomization is an important way of minimizing systematic experimental error. If research subjects are randomly assigned to different treatment combinations, then the differences among people that exist naturally within a population should also exist within each experimental cell.

3. Know ways of minimizing experimental demand characteristics. Demand characteristics are experimental procedures that somehow inform the subject about the actual research purpose. Demand effects can result from demand characteristics. When this happens, the results are confounded. Demand characteristics can be minimized by following these simple rules: using an experimental disguise, isolating experimental subjects, using a "blind" experimental administrator, and administering only one experimental treatment combination to each subject.

4. Avoid unethical experimental practices. Experiments involve deception. Additionally, research subjects are sometimes exposed to stressful or possibly dangerous manipulations. Every precaution should be made to ensure that subjects are not harmed. Debriefing subjects about the true purpose of the experiment following its conclusion is important for the ethical treatment of subjects. If debriefing can restore subjects to their pre-experimental condition, the experimental procedures are likely consistent with ethical practice. If subjects are affected in some way that makes it difficult to return them to their prior condition, then the experimental procedures probably go beyond what is considered ethical.

5. Weigh the trade-off between internal and external validity. Lab experiments offer higher internal validity because they maximize control of extraneous variables. High internal validity is a good thing because we can be more certain that the experimental variable is truly the cause of any variance in the dependent variable. Field experiments maximize external validity because they are conducted in a more natural setting, meaning that the results are more likely to generalize to the actual business situation. The increased external validity comes at the expense of internal validity.

6. Recognize the appropriate uses of test-marketing. Major uses of test-marketing include forecasting the success of a newly developed product, testing hypotheses about different options for marketing mix elements, and identifying weaknesses in product designs or marketing strategies. Whereas the first two reasons are usually intentional results in that they are the reason a test-market is implemented in the first place, the last reason often occurs when results from a test-market are less favorable than expected.

Key Terms and Concepts

Independent variable
Experimental treatment
Experimental group
Control group
Dependent variable
Test units
Systematic or nonsampling error
Randomization
Matching
Repeated measures
Confound
Demand characteristic

Demand effect
Constancy of conditions
Counterbalancing
Debriefing
Laboratory experiment
Tachistoscope
Field experiments
Internal validity
Manipulation check
History effect
Cohort effect
Maturation effects

Testing effects
Instrumentation effect
Mortality effect (sample attrition)
External validity
Basic experimental design
Quasi-experimental designs
One-shot design
One-group pretest–posttest design
Static group design
Pretest–posttest control group design
Posttest–only control group design

Questions for Review and Critical Thinking

1. Name some independent and dependent variables frequently studied in marketing.
2. A tissue manufacturer that has the fourth-largest market share plans to experiment with a 50-cents-off coupon during November. It plans to measure sales volume for November using store scanners to determine the effectiveness of the coupon. What is the independent variable? The dependent variable? Do you see any problems with the dependent variable?
3. What purpose does the random assignment of subjects serve?
4. In a test of a new coffee, three Styrofoam cups labeled A, B, and C are placed before subjects. The subjects are instructed to taste the coffee from each cup. What problems might arise in this situation?
5. What are demand characteristics? Give some examples.
6. Do you think the guinea pig effect is a common occurrence in experiments? Why or why not?
8. Provide an example for each of the six major factors that influence internal validity.
9. Consider a research project conducted by a company to investigate a self-contained heating and lighting source designed to be used during power failures. The product was given to the experimental subjects, who were asked to wait until dark, then turn off their heat and lights and test the product. A few days later, they were telephoned and interviewed about their opinions of the product. Discuss the external and internal validity of this experiment.
10. A nighttime cough relief formula contains alcohol. An alternative formulation contains no alcohol. During an experiment, subjects are asked to try the product in their homes. Alternative

formulations are randomly assigned to subjects. No mention of alcohol is given in the instructions to subjects. Is this ethical?
11. What purpose does the random assignment of subjects serve?
12. Why is an experimental confound so damaging to the conclusions drawn from an experiment?
13. 'NET Suppose you wanted to test the effect of three different e-mail requests inviting people to participate in a survey posted on the Internet. One simply contained a hyperlink with no explanation, the other said if someone participated $10 would be donated to charity, and the other said if someone participated he or she would have a chance to win $1,000. How would this experiment be conducted differently based on whether it was a between-subjects or within-subjects design? What are the advantages of a between-subjects design?
14. **ETHICS** What role does debriefing play in ensuring that experimental procedures are consistent with good ethical practice?
15. List three typical uses of test-markets.
16. When is test-marketing likely to be conducted? When is it unlikely?
17. Which of the following products or marketing strategies are likely to be test-marketed? Why or why not?
    a. A computerized robot lawn mower
    b. A line of 8-ounce servings of vegetarian dishes for senior citizens
    c. A forklift truck
    d. A new brand of eye drops especially for brown-eyed people
    e. A new, heavy-duty KitchenAid mixer
    f. An advertising campaign to get people to drink a cola drink in the morning

Research Activities

1. Consider the situation of a researcher approached by Captain John's in the opening vignette.
   a. Provide a critique of the procedures used to support the claim that Sea Snapper's product is superior. Prepare it in a way that it could be presented as evidence in court.
   b. Design an experiment that would provide a more valid test of the research question, "Do consumers prefer Sea Snapper fish sticks compared to Captain John's fish sticks?"
2. Conduct a taste test involving some soft drinks with a group of friends. Pour them several ounces of three popular soft drinks and simply label the cups A, B, and C. Make sure they are blind to the actual brands. Then, let them drink as much as they want and record how much of each they drink. You may also ask them some questions about the drinks. Then, allow other subjects to participate in the same test, but this time, let them know what the three brands are. Record the same data and draw conclusions. Does brand knowledge affect behavior and attitudes about soft drinks?

Case 9.1 Examining Product Failure at No-Charge Electronics

No-Charge Electronics owner Buzz Auphf needs to know how much product failure affects customer loyalty. Buzz contacts David Handy, a local market researcher, and they ultimately decide on examining a research question asking, "How do current customers react to different levels of product failure?" David designs the following experiment to examine the causal effect of product failure on customer purchase intentions, satisfaction, and loyalty.

The experiment is implemented via e-mail using a sample of current and prospective customers. Three free mp3 movies are provided as an incentive to participate. Subjects are asked to click through to an Internet site to download a product that will enhance their computer's graphics capability. In the low-failure condition, after the subjects click to the site, there is no change in the graphics of their computers. In the high-failure condition, once they click through to the site, the subjects' computers go into an infinite loop of obscene graphical images until a message arrives indicating that a severe virus has infected their computer and some files may be permanently damaged. This goes on for forty-five minutes with no remedy. At that time, a debriefing message pops up telling subjects that it was all part of an experiment and that their computer should now function properly. Prepare a position statement either agreeing or disagreeing that the experiment is consistent with good ethical practice.

Case 9.2 Tooheys

Sixty-six willing Australian drinkers helped a Federal Court judge decide that Tooheys didn't engage in misleading or deceptive advertising for its 2.2 beer. The beer contains 2.2 percent alcohol, compared to 6 percent for other beers, leading to a claim that could be interpreted as implying it was non-alcoholic.

Volunteers were invited to a marathon drinking session after the Aboriginal Legal Service claimed Tooheys' advertising implied beer drinkers could imbibe as much 2.2 as desired without becoming legally intoxicated. Drunken driving laws prohibit anyone with a blood-alcohol level above 0.05 from getting behind the wheel in Australia.

So, an experiment was conducted to see what happens when a lot of 2.2 is consumed. But the task wasn't easy or that much fun. Some subjects couldn't manage to drink the required 10 "middies," an Aussie term for a beer glass of 10 fluid ounces, over the course of an hour.

Thirty-six participants could manage only nine glasses. Four threw up and were excluded. Two more couldn't manage the "minimum" nine glasses and had to be replaced.

Justice J. Beaumont observed that consuming enough 2.2 in an hour to reach the 0.05 level was "uncomfortable and therefore an unlikely process." Because none of the ads mentioned such extreme quantities, he ruled they couldn't be found misleading or deceptive.[15]

Questions

1. Would a lab experiment or a field experiment be more "valid" in determining whether Tooheys could cause a normal beer consumer to become intoxicated? Explain.
2. Describe an alternate research design that would have higher validity.
3. Is the experiment described in this story consistent with good ethical practice? Likewise, comment on how the design described in part 2 would be made consistent with good ethical practices.
4. Is validity or ethics more important?

Part 3
Measurement

©BRAND X PICTURES/JUPITER IMAGES

CHAPTER 10
Measurement and Attitude Scaling

CHAPTER 11
Questionnaire Design

CHAPTER 10
MEASUREMENT AND ATTITUDE SCALING

After studying this chapter, you should be able to

1. Explain what needs to be measured to address a research question or hypothesis
2. Define operationalization
3. Distinguish levels of scale measurement
4. Explain the need for index or composite measures
5. List the three criteria for good measurement
6. Explain the significance of scale reliability and validity
7. Describe how marketing researchers think of attitudes
8. Identify basic approaches to measuring attitudes
9. Discuss the use of rating scales for measuring attitudes
10. Represent a latent construct by constructing a summated scale
11. Summarize ways to measure attitudes with ranking and sorting techniques

Chapter Vignette—Money Matters?

Griff Mitchell is the Vice President of Customer Relationship Management (CRM) for one of the world's largest suppliers of industrial heavy equipment. In this role, he oversees all sales and service operations. This year, for the first time, the company has decided to perform a CRM employee evaluation process that will allow an overall ranking of all CRM employees. Griff knows this will be a difficult task for many reasons, not the least of which is that he oversees over a thousand employees worldwide.

The ranking will be used to single out the best performers. These employees will be recognized at the company's annual CRM conference. The rankings will also be used to identify the lowest 20 percent of performers. These employees will be put on a probationary list with specific targeted improvement goals that will have to be met within twelve months or they will be fired. Griff becomes really stressed out trying to define the performance ranking process.

Griff's key question is, What is performance? Although these employees are now often referred to as CRM employees, they have traditionally performed the sales function. Griff calls a meeting of senior CRM managers to discuss how ranking decisions should be made.

One manager simply argues that sales volume should be the sole criterion. She believes that "sales figures provide an objective performance measure that will make the task easy and difficult to refute." Another counters that for the past twenty-two years, he has simply used his opinion of each employee's performance to place each of them into one of three groups: top performers, good performers, and underperformers. "I think about who is easy to work with and doesn't cause much trouble. It has worked for twenty-two years, why won't it work now?" Another responds curtly, "It's margin! It's margin! I don't care about sales volume; I want my guys selling things that improve my division's profit!" One of the newer managers sits silently through most of the meeting and finally summons up the courage to speak. "Aren't we CRM? That means performance should not be tied to sales, profits, or convenience, it should be based on how well a salesperson builds and maintains relationships with customers. So, we should see how satisfied the customers assigned to the employee are and use this in the evaluation process!" After this, the meeting disintegrates into a shouting match, with each manager believing the others' ideas are flawed.

Griff feels like he is back to square one. "How do I make sure I have a valid performance measure so that all of our people are treated fairly?" He decides to seek out an opinion from a long-time friend in the research business, Robin Donald. Robin suggests that a research project may be needed to define a reliable and valid measure. She also brings up the fact that because employees from all over the world will be considered, the measure will have to maintain its reliability and validity anywhere it is used! Griff agrees to the project. He also feels good about letting someone outside the company develop the measure.

What Do I Measure?

The chapter vignette describes a situation in which Griff must develop a recipe for distinguishing employees based on job performance. Before the measurement process can be defined, he will have to decide exactly what it is that needs to be produced. In this case, the outcome should be a valid job performance measure.

The decision statement, corresponding research questions, and research hypotheses can be used to decide what concepts need to be measured in a given project. **Measurement** is the process of describing some property of a phenomenon of interest, usually by assigning numbers in a reliable and valid way. The numbers convey information about the property being measured. When numbers are used, the researcher must have a rule for assigning a number to an observation in a way that provides an accurate description.

Measurement can be illustrated by thinking about the way instructors assign students' grades. A grade represents a student's performance in a class. Students with higher performance should receive a different grade than do students with lower performance. Even the apparently simple concept of student performance is measured in many different ways. Consider the following options:

1. A student can be assigned a letter corresponding to his/her performance.
   a. A — Represents excellent performance
   b. B — Represents good performance
   c. C — Represents average performance
   d. D — Represents poor performance
   e. F — Represents failing performance
2. A student can be assigned a number from 1 to 20.
   a. 20 — Represents outstanding performance
   b. 11–20 — Represent differing degrees of passing performance
   c. Below 11 — Failing performance
3. A student can be assigned a number corresponding to a percentage performance scale.
   a. 100 percent — Represents a perfect score. All assignments are performed correctly.
   b. 60–99 percent — Represents differing degrees of passing performance, each number representing the proportion of correct work.
   c. 0–59 percent — Represents failing performance but still captures proportion of correct work.
4. A student can be assigned one of two letters corresponding to performance.
   a. P — Represents a passing mark
   b. F — Represents a failing mark

Measurement
The process of describing some property of a phenomenon of interest, usually by assigning numbers in a reliable and valid way.

EXHIBIT 10.1
**Are There Any Validity Issues
with This Measurement?**

Student	Percentage Grade	Difference from Next Highest Student	Letter Grade
1	79.4%	0.5%	C
2	70.0%	9.4%	C
3	69.0%	1.0%	D
4	79.9%	NA	B

Actually, this is not terribly different than a manager who must assign performance scores to employees. In each case, students with different marks are distinguished in some way. However, some scales may better distinguish students. Each scale also has the potential of producing error or some lack of validity. Exhibit 10.1 illustrates a common measurement application.

Often, instructors may use a percentage scale all semester long and then be required to assign a letter grade for a student's overall performance. Does this produce any measurement problems? Consider two students who have percentage scores of 79.4 and 70.0, respectively. The most likely outcome when these scores are translated into "letter grades" is that each receives a C (the common ten-point spread would yield a 70–80 percent range for a C). Consider a third student who finishes with a 69.0 percent average and a fourth student who finishes with a 79.9 percent average.

Which students are happiest with this arrangement? The first two students receive the same grade, even though their scores are 9.4 percent apart. The third student gets a grade lower (D) than the second student, even though their percentage scores are only 1.0 percentage point different. The fourth student, who has a score only 0.5 percent higher than the first student, would receive a B. Thus, the measuring system (final grade) suggests that the fourth student outperformed the first (assuming that 79.9 is rounded up to 80) student (B versus C), but the first student did not outperform the second (each gets a C), even though the first and second students have the greatest difference in percentage scores.

A strong case can be made that error exists in this measurement system. All measurement, particularly in the social sciences, contains error. Researchers, if we are to represent concepts truthfully, must make sure that the measures used, if not perfect, are accurate enough to yield correct conclusions. Ultimately, research and measurement are tied closely together.

Concepts

A researcher has to know what to measure before knowing how to measure something. The problem definition process should suggest the concepts that must be measured. A **concept** can be thought of as a generalized idea that represents something of meaning. Concepts such as *age, sex,*

Concept
A generalized idea that represents something of meaning.

education, and *number of children* are relatively concrete properties. They present few problems in either definition or measurement. Other concepts are more abstract. Concepts such as *loyalty, personality, channel power, trust, corporate culture, customer satisfaction, value,* and so on are more difficult to both define and measure. For example, *loyalty* has been measured as a combination of customer share, the relative proportion of a person's purchases going to one competing brand/store and commitment, or the degree to which a customer will sacrifice to do business with a brand/store.[1] The first component is a behavioral measure and the second is attitudinal.

Operational Definitions

Operationalization
The process of identifying scales that correspond to variance in a concept to be involved in a research process.

Scales
A device providing a range of values that correspond to different values in a concept being measured.

Correspondence rules
Indicate the way that a certain value on a scale corresponds to some true value of a concept.

Researchers measure concepts through a process known as **operationalization**. This process involves identifying scales that correspond to variance in the concept. **Scales**, just as a scale you may use to check your weight, provide a range of values that correspond to different values in the concept being measured. In other words, scales provide **correspondence rules** that indicate that a certain value on a scale corresponds to some true value of a concept. Hopefully, they do this in a truthful way.

Here is an example of a correspondence rule: "Assign the numerals 1 through 7 to individuals according to how much trust that person has in a sales representative. If the sales representative is completely trustworthy, assign a 7. If the sales rep is perceived as completely untrustworthy, assign the numeral 1."

VARIABLES

Researchers use variance in concepts to make diagnoses. Therefore, when we defined variables in an earlier chapter, we really were suggesting that variables capture different concept values. Scales capture variance in concepts and, as such, the scales provide the researcher's variables. Thus, for practical purposes, once a research project is underway, there is little difference between a concept and a variable. Consider the following hypothesis:

H1: Experience *is positively related to* job performance.

The hypothesis implies a relationship between two variables, experience and job performance. The variables capture variance in the experience and performance concepts. One employee may have fifteen years of experience and be a top performer. A second may have ten years experience and be a good performer. The scale used to measure experience is quite simple in this case and would involve simply providing the number of years an employee has been with the company. Job performance is captured by a scale in which a supervisor places the employee into a category as described in the vignette.

CONSTRUCTS

Sometimes, a single variable cannot capture a concept alone. Using multiple variables to measure one concept can often provide a more complete account of some concept than could any single variable. Even in the physical sciences, multiple measurements are often used to make sure an accurate representation is obtained. In social science, many concepts are measured with multiple measurements.

Construct
A term used to refer to concepts measured with multiple variables.

A **construct** is a term used for concepts that are measured with multiple variables. For instance, when a marketing researcher wishes to measure the customer orientation of a salesperson, several variables like these may be used, each captured on a 1–5 scale:

1. I offer the product that is best suited to a customer's problem.
2. A good employee has to have the customer's best interests in mind.
3. I try to find out what kind of products will be most helpful to a customer.[2]

Constructs can be very helpful in operationalizing a concept.

An operational definition is like a manual of instructions or a recipe: Even the truth of a statement like "Gaston Gourmet likes key lime pie" depends on the recipe. Different instructions lead to different results.[3]

EXHIBIT 10.2 Media Skepticism: An Operational Definition

Concept	Conceptual Definition	Operational Definition
Media skepticism	*Media skepticism* is the degree to which individuals are skeptical of the reality presented in the mass media. Media skepticism varies across individuals, from those who are mildly skeptical and accept most of what they see and hear in the media to those who completely discount and disbelieve the facts, values, and portrayal of reality in the media.	Please tell me how true each statement is about the media. Is it very true, not very true, or not at all true? 1. The program was *not* very accurate in its portrayal of the problem. 2. Most of the story was staged for entertainment purposes. 3. The presentation was slanted and unfair. 4. I think the story was fair and unbiased. 5. I think important facts were purposely left out of the story. Individual items were scored on a 4-point scale with values from 1 to 4; higher scores represented greater skepticism. Media skepticism is defined as the sum of these five scores.

Source: Michael D. Cozzens and Noshir S. Contractor, "The Effects of Conflicting Information on Media Skepticism," Communications Research, August 1987, pp. 437–451.

An operational definition tells the investigator, "Do such-and-such in so-and-so manner."[4] Exhibit 10.2 presents a concept definition and an operational definition from a study on a construct called *media skepticism*.

Levels of Scale Measurement

Marketing researchers use many scales or number systems. Not all scales capture the same richness in a measure. Not all concepts require a rich measure. Traditionally, the level of scale measurement is seen as important because it determines the mathematical comparisons that are allowable. The four levels or types of scale measurement are *nominal, ordinal, interval,* and *ratio level scales.* Each type offers the researcher progressively more power in analyzing and testing the validity of a scale.

Nominal Scale

Nominal scales represent the most elementary level of measurement. A nominal scale assigns a value to an object for identification or classification purposes. The value can be, but does not have to be, a number because no quantities are being represented. In this sense, a nominal scale is truly a qualitative scale. Nominal scales are extremely useful even though they can be considered elementary.

Marketing researchers use nominal scales quite often. For instance, suppose Barq's Root Beer was experimenting with three different types of sweeteners (cane sugar, corn syrup, or fruit extract). The researchers would like the experiment to be blind, so when subjects are asked to taste one of the three root beers, the drinks are labeled A, B, or C, not cane sugar, corn syrup, or fruit extract.

Nominal scaling is arbitrary in the sense that each label can be assigned to any of the categories without introducing error; for instance, in the root beer example above, the researcher can assign the letter C to any of the three options without damaging scale validity. The researcher could just as easily use numbers instead of letters. If so, cane sugar, corn syrup, and fruit extract might be identified with the numbers 1, 2, and 3, respectively, or even 543, 26, and 2010, respectively. Either set of numbers is equally valid since the numbers are not representing different quantities. They are simply identifying the type of sweetener.

Nominal scales
Represent the most elementary level of measurement, in which values are assigned to an object for identification or classification purposes only.

EXHIBIT 10.3
Nominal, Ordinal, Interval, and Ratio Scales Provide Different Information

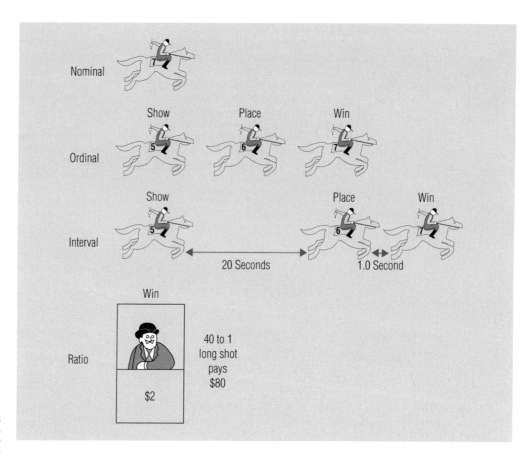

Ordinal scales
Ranking scales allowing things to be arranged based on how much of some concept they possess.

Without nominal scales, how would you know which terminal to go to at this airport?

The first drawing in Exhibit 10.3 depicts the number 7 on a horse's colors. This is merely a label to allow bettors and racing enthusiasts to identify the horse. The assignment of a 7 to this horse does not mean that it is the seventh fastest horse or that it is the seventh biggest, or anything else meaningful. But the 7 does let you know when you have won or lost your bet!

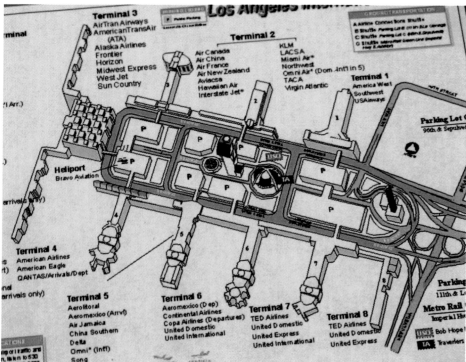

Exhibit 10.4 lists some nominal scales commonly used by marketing researchers. Nominal scale properties mean the numbering system simply identifies things.

Ordinal Scale

Ordinal scales have nominal properties, but they also allow things to be arranged based on how much of some concept they possess. In other words, an ordinal scale is a ranking scale. When a professor assigns an A, B, C, D, or F to a student at the end of the semester, he or she is using an ordinal scale.

Research participants often are asked to *rank order* things based on preference. So preference is the concept, and the ordinal scale lists the options from most to least preferred, or vice versa. In this

EXHIBIT 10.4 **Facts About the Four Levels of Scales**

Level	Examples	Numerical Operations	Descriptive Statistics
Nominal	Yes – No Female – Male Buy – Did Not Buy Postal Code: ____	Counting	• Frequencies • Mode
Ordinal	Rankings Choose from the Following: • Dissatisfied • Satisfied • Very Satisfied • Delighted Indicate Your Level of Education: • HS Diploma • Some College • Bachelor's Degree • Graduate Degree	Counting and Ordering	• Frequencies • Mode • Median • Range
Interval	100-Point Job Performance Ratings Assigned by Supervisors: 0% = Worst Performers 100% = Best Performers Temperature-Type Attitude Scales: Low Temperature = Bad Attitude High Temperature = Good Attitude	Common Arithmetic Operations	• Mean • Median • Variance • Standard Deviation
Ratio	Amount Purchased Salesperson Sales Volume Likelihood of performing some act: • 0%=No Likelihood to • 100%=Certainty Number of stores visited Time spent viewing a particular web page Number of web pages viewed	All Arithmetic Operations	• Mean • Median • Variance • Standard Deviation

sense, ordinal scales are somewhat arbitrary, but not nearly as arbitrary as a nominal scale. Five objects can be ranked from 1–5 (least preferred to most preferred) or 1–5 (most preferred to least preferred) with no loss of meaning.

Interval Scale

Interval scales have both nominal and ordinal properties, but they also capture information about differences in quantities of a concept. So, not only would a sales manager know that a particular salesperson outperformed a colleague, but the manager would know by how much. If a professor assigns grades to term papers using a numbering system ranging from 1.0–20.0, not only does the scale represent the fact that a student with a 16.0 outperformed a student with 12.0, but the scale would show by how much (4.0).

The third drawing in Exhibit 10.3 depicts a horse race in which the win horse is one second ahead of the place horse, which is 20 seconds ahead of the show horse. Not only are the horses identified by the order of finish, but the difference between each horse's performance is known. So, horse number 7 and horse number 6 performed similarly, but horse number 5 performed not nearly as well.

The classic example of an interval scale is the Fahrenheit temperature scale. Consider the following weather:

- June 6 was 80° F
- December 7 was 40° F

Interval scales
Scales that have both nominal and ordinal properties, but that also capture information about differences in quantities of a concept from one observation to the next.

The interval Fahrenheit scale lets us know that December 7 was 40° F colder than June 6. But we cannot conclude that December 7 was twice as cold as June 6. Although the actual numeral 80 is indeed twice as great as 40, remember that this is a scaling system. In this case, the scale is not iconic, meaning that it does not exactly represent some phenomenon. These temperatures can be converted to the more common Celsius scale. Then, the following would result:

- June 6 was 26.7° C
- December 7 was 4.4° C

Obviously, now we can see that December 7 was not twice as cold as June 6. December 7 was 40° F or 22.3° C cooler, depending upon your thermometer. Interval scales are very useful because they capture relative quantities in the form of distances between observations. No matter what thermometer is used, December 7 was colder than June 6.

Ratio Scale

Ratio scales
Represent the highest form of measurement in that they have all the properties of interval scales with the additional attribute of representing absolute quantities; characterized by a meaningful absolute zero.

Ratio scales represent the highest form of measurement in that they have all the properties of interval scales with the additional attribute of representing absolute quantities. Interval scales represent only relative meaning, whereas ratio scales represent absolute meaning. In other words, ratio scales provide iconic measurement. Zero, therefore, has meaning in that it represents an absence of some concept.

An absolute zero is a defining characteristic in determining between ratio and interval scales. For example, money is a way to measure economic value. Consider the following items offered for sale in an online auction:

- Antique railroad pocket watch circa 1910—sold for $50
- Authentic Black Forest cuckoo clock—sold for $75
- Antique gold-filled Elgin wristwatch circa 1950—sold for $100
- "Antique" 1970s digital watch—did not sell and there were no takers for free

We can make the ordinal conclusions that the cuckoo clock was worth more than the pocket watch and that the wristwatch was worth more than the cuckoo, all of which were worth more than the 1970s digital watch. We can make interval conclusions such as that the cuckoo was worth $25 more than the pocket watch. We can also conclude that the wristwatch was worth twice as much as the pocket watch and that the 1970s watch was worthless (selling price = $0.00). The latter two conclusions are possible because money price represents a ratio scale.

Temperature can also be captured by a ratio scale. The Kelvin scale begins at 0 K, corresponding to −273.2° on the Celsius scale (an interval scale). This temperature is known as absolute zero. Zero K is the point at which the kinetic energy of atoms in a water molecule approaches 0, meaning that they are moving as slowly as possible. This is as cold as water can get since there is no way of slowing the molecules further (they never completely stop). Thus, 0 K indeed has absolute meaning.

When a manager assigns a performance commission based directly on the amount of sales produced, the bonus is based on a ratio scale. Zero has an absolute meaning, particularly if you are the one without a bonus! Griff could decide to use a ratio sales measure to rank performance for the CRM division. This would be valid only if performance was truly equal to sales.

TOTHEPOINT

When you can measure what you are talking about and express it in numbers, you know something about it.

—William Thompson,
Lord Kelvin

Mathematical and Statistical Analysis of Scales

While it is true that mathematical operations can be performed with numbers from nominal scales, the result may not have a great deal of meaning. For instance, a school district may perform mathematical operations on the nominal school bus numbers. With this, they may find that the average school bus number is 77.7 with a standard deviation of 20.5. Will this help them use the buses more efficiently or better assign bus routes? Probably not. Thus, although you can put numbers into formulas and perform calculations with almost any numbers, the researcher has to know the meaning behind the numbers before useful conclusions can be drawn.[5]

RESEARCHSNAPSHOT

Football Follies

The subject of whether or not certain mathematical properties can be conducted with certain types of scales has been debated in the social science literature for decades. One famous statistician used a funny parable about a football folly to make a point about this very well. The story goes something like this:

A football coach purchased a vending machine that would assign numbers (0 to 99) to the school's football players randomly. Over the years, then, all numbers should be equally used. By randomly assigning the numbers in this way, no players were treated unequally because no one could choose one of their favorite numbers. Everybody simply got the number the machine spit out.

Professor Aaron Urd, naturally curious about anything having to do with numbers, became suspicious that the football players had secretly been breaking into the machine to select more preferred numbers. Professor Urd believed that football had no place in college and would have loved to show how unscrupulous the football players really are—stealing numbers no less! However, Professor Urd had a problem. Football numbers are nominal numbers; all they do is identify! Therefore, as all good statisticians knew, you cannot compute averages with nominal numbers. In fact, all you can do is count nominal numbers. This problem tormented Professor Urd for years. He desperately wanted to test his hypothesis about the football number theft. Many times he entered the football numbers into a spreadsheet but could not bring himself to add, multiply, or divide them. It just wouldn't be right!

One fall, Aleck Smart, a star defensive tackle on the football team, wrote a term paper for Professor Aaron Urd entitled "A Statistical Treatment of the Football Team Numbering System." Aleck, not being the brightest student, missed the day when Professor Urd taught students that you could not do arithmetic with nominal numbers. So, Aleck Smart computed all manner of statistics with data consisting of the last ten years of football numbers worn by the team. Among these, he showed that the average football number over those years was 40.1. Professor Aaron Urd was conflicted with this result. How can this be? If the numbers were assigned randomly, then shouldn't the average be 50? This must confirm his suspicion about the football number theft. But even to think this troubled him because it meant his brain was unintentionally computing the average of nominal numbers!

A few days later, Aleck dropped by Professor Aaron Urd's office to pick up his paper (after office hours of course). Professor Urd lit into Aleck: "I have given you a failing grade, Mr. Smart. Numbers from football jerseys are nominal numbers! Don't you know that you cannot take the average of nominal numbers?"

Aleck thought about that a while and answered, "Professor Urd, the numbers don't know where they came from."

Professor Urd decided to change Aleck's grade to a B−. He then used Aleck's calculations to try and show the faculty senate that the football team was indeed breaking into the machine.

Sources: Lord, F. M. (1953), "On the Statistical Treatment of Football Numbers," American Psychologist, 8, 750–751; Cohen, Jacob (1990), "Things I Have Learned (So Far)," American Psychologist, 45 (December), 1304–1312.

©DAVE KAUP/CORBIS

Index Measures

Earlier, we distinguished constructs as concepts that require multiple variables to measure them adequately. Looking back to the chapter vignette, could it be that multiple items will be required to adequately represent job performance? Likewise, a consumer's attitude toward some product is usually a function of multiple attributes. An **attribute** is a single characteristic or fundamental feature of an object, person, situation, or issue.

Attribute
A single characteristic or fundamental feature of an object, person, situation, or issue.

Indexes and Composites

Multi-item instruments for measuring a construct are called *index measures,* or *composite measures.* An **index measure** assigns a value based on how much of the concept being measured is associated with an observation. Indexes often are formed by putting several variables together. For example, a social class index is based on three weighted variables: income, occupation, and education. Usually, occupation is seen as the single best indicator and would be weighted highest. With an index, the different attributes may not be strongly correlated with each other. A person's income does not always relate strongly to their education. The American Consumer Satisfaction Index shows how satisfied American consumers are based on an index of satisfaction scores. Readers are likely not surprised to know that Americans appear more satisfied with soft drinks than they are with cable TV companies based on this index.[6]

Index measure
An index assigns a value based on how much of the concept being measured is associated with an observation. Indexes often are formed by putting several variables together.

Composite measures
Assign a value to an observation based on a mathematical derivation of multiple variables.

Composite measures also assign a value based on a mathematical derivation of multiple variables. For example, salesperson satisfaction may be measured by combining questions such as "How satisfied are you with your job? How satisfied are you with your territory? How satisfied are you with the opportunity your job offers?" For most practical applications, composite measures and indexes are computed in the same way.[7]

Three Criteria for Good Measurement

The three major criteria for evaluating measurements are reliability, validity, and sensitivity.

Reliability

Reliability
An indicator of a measure's internal consistency.

Reliability is an indicator of a measure's internal consistency. Consistency is the key to understanding reliability. A measure is reliable when different attempts at measuring something converge on the same result. If a professor's marketing research tests are reliable, a student should tend toward consistent scores on all tests. In other words, a student who makes an 80 on the first test should make scores close to 80 on all subsequent tests. Another way to look at this is that the student who makes the best score on one test will exhibit scores close to the best score in the class on the other tests. If it is difficult to predict what students would make on a test by examining their previous test scores, the tests probably lack reliability. When a measuring process provides reproducible results, the measuring instrument is reliable.

Coefficient alpha (α)
The most commonly applied estimate of a multiple item scale's reliability. It represents the average of all possible split-half reliabilities for a construct.

Coefficient alpha (α) is a commonly applied estimate of a multiple item scale's reliability.[8] Coefficient α represents internal consistency by computing the average of all possible split-half reliabilities for a multiple-item scale. The coefficient demonstrates whether or not the different items converge. Although coefficient α does not address validity, many researchers use α as the sole indicator of a scale's quality. Coefficient alpha ranges in value from 0, meaning no consistency, to 1, meaning complete consistency (all items yield matching values). Generally speaking, scales with a coefficient α between 0.80 and 0.95 are considered to have very good reliability. Scales with a coefficient α between 0.70 and 0.80 are considered to have good reliability, and an α value between 0.60 and 0.70 indicates fair reliability. When the coefficient α is below 0.6, the scale has poor reliability.[9] Most statistical software such as SPSS will easily compute coefficient α.

Validity

Good measures should be both precise and accurate. Reliability represents how precise a measure is in that the different attempts at measuring the same thing converge on the same point. Accuracy deals more with how a measure assesses the intended concept. **Validity** is the accuracy of a measure or the extent to which a score truthfully represents a concept.

Validity
The accuracy of a measure or the extent to which a score truthfully represents a concept.

Achieving validity is not a simple matter. The opening vignette describes this point. The job performance measure should truly reflect job performance. If a supervisor's friendship affects the performance measure, then the scale's validity is diminished. Likewise, if the performance scale is defined as effort, the result may well be a reliable scale but not one that maximizes validity. Effort may well lead to performance but effort probably does not equal performance.

Another example of a validity question might involve a media researcher who wonders what it means when respondents indicate they have been *exposed* to a magazine. The researcher wants to know if the measure is valid. The question of validity expresses the researcher's concern with accurate measurement. Validity addresses the problem of whether a measure (for example, an attitude measure used in marketing) indeed measures what it is supposed to measure. When a measure lacks validity, any conclusions based on that measure are also likely to be faulty.

Students should be able to empathize with the following validity problem. Consider the controversy about highway patrol officers using radar guns to clock speeders. A driver is clocked at 75 mph in a 55 mph zone, but the same radar gun aimed at a house registers 28 mph. The error occurred because the radar gun had picked up impulses from the electrical system of the squad car's idling engine. The house wasn't speeding—and the test was not completely valid.

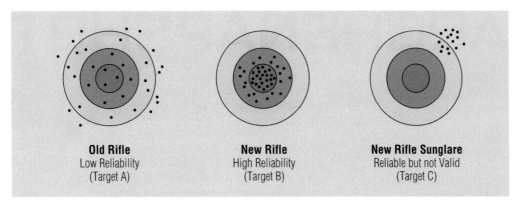

EXHIBIT 10.5
**Reliability and Validity
on Target**

Old Rifle
Low Reliability
(Target A)

New Rifle
High Reliability
(Target B)

New Rifle Sunglare
Reliable but not Valid
(Target C)

Construct validity exists when a measure reliably measures and truthfully represents a unique concept. Construct validity consists of several components, including

- Face or Content validity
- Convergent validity
- Criterion or validity
- Discriminant validity

Convergent validity is another way of expressing internal consistency. Highly reliable scales contain convergent validity. Criterion validity and face validity were discussed above.

Reliability versus Validity

The differences between reliability and validity can be illustrated by the rifle targets in Exhibit 10.5. Suppose an expert sharpshooter fires an equal number of rounds with a century-old rifle and a modern rifle.[10] The shots from the older gun are considerably scattered, but those from the newer gun are closely clustered. The variability of the old rifle compared with that of the new one indicates it is less reliable. The target on the right illustrates the concept of a systematic bias influencing validity. The new rifle is reliable (because it has little variance), but the sharpshooter's vision is hampered by glare. Although shots are consistent, the sharpshooter is unable to hit the bull's-eye.

Sensitivity

The sensitivity of a scale is an important measurement concept, particularly when *changes* in attitudes or other hypothetical constructs are under investigation. **Sensitivity** refers to an instrument's ability to accurately measure variability in a concept. A dichotomous response category, such as "agree or disagree," does not allow the recording of subtle attitude changes. A more sensitive measure with numerous categories on the scale may be needed. For example, adding "strongly agree," "mildly agree," "neither agree nor disagree," "mildly disagree," and "strongly disagree" will increase the scale's sensitivity.

The sensitivity of a scale based on a single question or single item can also be increased by adding questions or items. In other words, because composite measures allow for a greater range of possible scores, they are more sensitive than single-item scales. Thus, sensitivity is generally increased by adding more response points or adding scale items.

Attitudes in Marketing Research

For social scientists, an **attitude** is an enduring disposition to respond consistently in a given manner to various aspects of the world, including persons, events, and objects. One way to understand attitudes is to think of their components. Consider this brief statement: "Sally loves shopping at Sam's. She believes the store is clean and conveniently located and that it has the lowest prices. She

Construct validity
Exists when a measure reliably measures and truthfully represents a unique concept; consists of several components including face validity, convergent validity, criterion validity, and discriminant validity.

Convergent validity
Another way of expressing internal consistency; highly reliable scales contain convergent validity.

Sensitivity
A measurement instrument's ability to accurately measure variability in stimuli or responses.

Attitude
An enduring disposition to consistently respond in a given manner to various aspects of the world, composed of affective, cognitive, and behavioral components.

RESEARCHSNAPSHOT

This Hypothetical Construct Is a Four-Letter Word

©ROYALTY-FREE/CORBIS

Love is a four-letter word. And a hypothetical construct—that is, a term that psychologists use to describe or explain consistent patterns of human behavior. Love, hate, thirst, learning, intelligence—all of these are hypothetical constructs. They are hypothetical in that they do not exist as physical entities; therefore, they cannot be seen, heard, felt, or measured directly. There is no love center in the brain that, if removed, would leave a person incapable of responding positively and affectionately toward other people and things. Love and hate are constructs in that we invent these terms to explain why, for instance, a young man spends all his time with one young woman while completely avoiding another. From a scientific point of view, we might be better off if we said that this young man's behavior suggested that he had a relatively enduring, positive-approach attitude toward the first woman and a negative-avoidance attitude toward the second.

Source: *Psychology Today: An Introduction* (Del Mar, CA: CRM Books, 1970), p. 613.

©DON MASON/CORBIS

Generally, consumers act in a way consistent with their attitudes. Therefore, attitudes are a popular marketing research topic.

Hypothetical constructs
Variables that are not directly observable but are measurable through indirect indicators, such as verbal expression or overt behavior.

intends to shop there every Thursday." As in this example, an attitude has three components: affective, cognitive, and behavioral. The affective component refers to an individual's general feelings or emotions toward an object. Statements such as "I love my Chevrolet Corvette," "I enjoyed reading *A Corporate Bestiary,*" and "I hate cranberry juice" reflect the emotional character of attitudes. The way a person feels about a product, an advertisement, or an object is usually tied to his or her *beliefs* or *cognitions.* This cognitive component represents an individual's awareness of and knowledge about an object. One person might feel happy about the purchase of an automobile because she believes the car "gets great gas mileage" or knows that the dealer is "the best in New Jersey." The behavioral component of an attitude reflects a predisposition to action by reflecting a consumer's buying or purchase intentions.

Attitudes as Hypothetical Constructs

Many variables that marketing researchers wish to investigate are psychological variables that cannot be observed directly. For example, someone may have an attitude toward a particular brand of shaving cream, but we cannot observe this attitude. To measure an attitude, we make an inference based on the way a person responds to multiple individual scale items. Unobserved or latent variables are known as **hypothetical constructs** or just constructs. Common constructs include consumer commitment, values, feelings, organizational commitment, salesperson orientation, role stress, and many more.

Techniques for Measuring Attitudes

A remarkable variety of techniques has been devised to measure attitudes. This variety stems in part from lack of consensus about the exact definition of the concept. In addition, the affective, cognitive, and behavioral components of an attitude may be measured by different means. For example, sympathetic nervous system responses may be recorded using physiological measures to quantify affect, but they are not good measures of behavioral intentions. Direct verbal statements concerning affect, belief, or behavior are used to measure behavioral intent. However, attitudes may also be interpreted using qualitative techniques like those discussed in Chapter 5.

Research may assess the affective (emotional) components of attitudes through physiological measures such as galvanic skin response (GSR), blood pressure, and pupil dilation (see Chapter 8). These measures provide a means of assessing attitudes without verbally questioning the respondent. In general, they can provide a gross measure of likes or dislikes, but they are not extremely sensitive to the different gradients of an attitude.

Obtaining verbal statements from respondents generally requires that the respondents perform a task such as ranking, rating, sorting, or making choices. A **ranking** task requires the respondent to rank order a small number of stores, brands, feelings, or objects on the basis of overall preference or some characteristic of the stimulus. **Rating** asks the respondent to estimate the magnitude or the extent to which some characteristic exists. A quantitative score results. The rating task involves marking a response indicating one's position using one or more attitudinal or cognitive scales. A **sorting** task might present the respondent with several product concepts printed on cards and require the respondent to classify the concepts by placing the cards into groups (stacks of cards). Another type of attitude measurement is **choice** between two or more alternatives. If a respondent chooses one object over another, the researcher assumes that the respondent prefers the chosen object, at least in this setting. The following sections describe the most popular techniques for measuring attitudes.

Ranking
A measurement task that requires respondents to rank order a small number of stores, brands, or objects on the basis of overall preference or some characteristic of the stimulus.

Rating
A measurement task that requires respondents to estimate the magnitude of a characteristic or quality that a brand, store, or object possesses.

Attitude Rating Scales

Perhaps the most common practice in marketing research is using rating scales to measure attitudes. This section discusses many rating scales designed to enable respondents to report the intensity of their attitudes.

Sorting
A measurement task that presents a respondent with several objects or product concepts and requires the respondent to arrange the objects into piles or classify the product concepts.

Simple Attitude Scales

In its most basic form, attitude scaling requires that an individual agree or disagree with a statement or respond to a single question. For example, respondents in a political poll may be asked whether they agree or disagree with the statement "The president should run for re-election." Or, an individual might indicate whether he or she likes or dislikes jalapeño bean dip. This type of self-rating scale merely classifies respondents into one of two categories, thus having only the properties of a nominal scale, and the types of mathematical analysis that may be used with this basic scale are limited.

Choice
A measurement task that identifies preferences by requiring respondents to choose between two or more alternatives.

Despite the disadvantages, simple attitude scaling may be used when questionnaires are extremely long, when respondents have little education, or for other specific reasons. A number of simplified scales are merely checklists: A respondent indicates past experience, preference, and the like merely by checking an item. In many cases the items are adjectives that describe a particular object. In a survey of small-business owners and managers, respondents indicated whether they found working in a small firm more rewarding than working in a large firm, as well as whether they agreed with a series of attitude statements about small businesses. For example, 77 percent said small and mid-sized businesses "have less bureaucracy," and 76 percent said smaller companies "have more flexibility" than large ones.[11]

Most attitude theorists believe that attitudes vary along continua. Early attitude researchers pioneered the view that the task of attitude scaling is to measure the distance from "good" to "bad," "low" to "high," "like" to "dislike," and so on. Thus, the purpose of an attitude scale is to find an individual's position on the continuum. However, simple scales do not allow for fine distinctions between attitudes. Several other scales have been developed for making more precise measurements.

Category Scales

The simplest rating scale contains only two response categories: agree/disagree. Expanding the response categories provides the respondent with more flexibility in the rating task. Even more information is provided if the categories are ordered according to a particular descriptive or evaluative dimension. Consider the following question:

How often do you disagree with your spouse about how much to spend on vacation?

☐ *Never*   ☐ *Rarely*   ☐ *Sometimes*   ☐ *Often*   ☐ *Very often*

EXHIBIT 10.6 **Selected Category Scales**

Quality				
Excellent	Good	Fair	Poor	
Very good	Fairly good	Neither good nor bad	Not very good	Not good at all
Well above average	Above average	Average	Below average	Well below average
Importance				
Very important	Fairly important	Neutral	Not so important	Not at all important
Interest				
Very interested		Somewhat interested		Not very interested
Satisfaction				
Completely satisfied	Somewhat satisfied	Neither satisfied nor dissatisfied	Somewhat dissatisfied	Completely dissatisfied
Very satisfied	Quite satisfied	Somewhat satisfied	Not at all satisfied	
Frequency				
All of the time	Very often	Often	Sometimes	Hardly ever
Very often	Often	Sometimes	Rarely	Never
All of the time	Most of the time	Some of the time	Just now and then	
Truth				
Very true	Somewhat true	Not very true	Not at all true	
Definitely yes	Probably yes	Probably no	Definitely no	
Uniqueness				
Very different	Somewhat different	Slightly different	Not at all different	
Extremely unique	Very unique	Somewhat unique	Slightly unique	Not at all unique

Category scale
A rating scale that consists of several response categories, often providing respondents with alternatives to indicate positions on a continuum.

This **category scale** is a more sensitive measure than a scale that has only two response categories. By having more choices for a respondent, the potential exists to provide more information. However, if the researcher tries to represent something that is truly bipolar (yes/no, female/male, member/non-member, and so on) with more than two categories, error may be introduced.

Question wording is an extremely important factor in the usefulness of these scales. Exhibit 10.6 shows some common wordings used in category scales. The issue of question wording is discussed in Chapter 11.

Method of Summated Ratings: The Likert Scale

Likert scale
A measure of attitudes designed to allow respondents to rate how strongly they agree or disagree with carefully constructed statements, ranging from very positive to very negative attitudes toward some object.

A method that is simple to administer and therefore extremely popular is marketing researchers' adaptation of the method of summated ratings, developed by Rensis Likert.[12] With the **Likert scale**, respondents indicate their attitudes by checking how strongly they agree or disagree with carefully constructed statements, ranging from very positive to very negative attitudes toward some object. Individuals generally choose from approximately five response alternatives—strongly agree, agree, uncertain, disagree, and strongly disagree—although the number of alternatives may range from three to nine. In the following example, from a study of food-shopping behavior, there are five alternatives:

In buying food for my family, price is no object.

Strongly Disagree	*Disagree*	*Uncertain*	*Agree*	*Strongly Agree*
☐	☐	☐	☐	☐
(1)	*(2)*	*(3)*	*(4)*	*(5)*

Researchers assign scores, or weights, to each possible response. In this example, numerical scores of 1, 2, 3, 4, and 5 are assigned to each level of agreement, respectively. The numerical scores, shown in parentheses, may not be printed on the questionnaire or computer screen. Strong agreement indicates the most favorable attitude on the statement, and a numerical score of 5 is assigned to this response.

REVERSE RECODING

The statement given in this example is positively framed. If a statement is framed negatively (such as "I carefully budget my food expenditures"), the numerical scores would need to be reversed. This is done by **reverse recoding** (sometimes referred to more simply as reverse coding) the negative item so that a strong agreement really indicates an unfavorable response rather than a favorable attitude. In the case of a five-point scale, the recoding is done as follows:

Old Value	New Value
1	5
2	4
3	3
4	2
5	1

Reverse recoding
A method of making sure all the items forming a composite scale are scored in the same direction. Negative items can be recoded into the equivalent responses for a non-reverse coded item.

Recoding in this fashion turns agreement with a negatively worded item into a mirror image, meaning the result is the same as disagreement with a positively worded item. SPSS has a recode function that allows simple recoding to be done by entering "old" and "new" scale values. Alternatively, a simple mathematical formula can be entered. In this case, the formula

$$X_{new\ value} = 6 - X_{old\ value}$$

would result in the same recoding.

COMPOSITE SCALES

A Likert scale may include several scale items to form a **composite scale**. Each statement is assumed to represent an aspect of a common attitudinal domain. For example, Exhibit 10.7 shows the items in a Likert scale for measuring attitudes toward patients' interaction with a physician's service staff. The total score is the summation of the numerical scores assigned to an individual's responses. Here the maximum possible score for the composite would be 20 if a 5 were assigned to "strongly agree"

Composite scale
A way of representing a latent construct by summing or averaging respondents' reactions to multiple items, each assumed to indicate the latent construct.

EXHIBIT 10.7
Likert Scale Items for Measuring Attitudes toward Patients' Interaction with a Physician's Service Staff

1. My doctor's office staff takes a warm and personal interest in me.
2. My doctor's office staff is friendly and courteous.
3. My doctor's office staff is more interested in serving the doctor's needs than in serving my needs.
4. My doctor's office staff always acts in a professional manner.

Source: Brown, Stephen W. and Teresa A. Swartz (1989), "A Gap Analysis of Professional Service Quality," *Journal of Marketing*, 53 (April), 92–98. Copyright 1989 by Am. Marketing Assn (AMA (Chic). Reproduced with permission of Am. Marketing Assn (AMA (Chic) in the format Textbook via Copyright Clearance Center.

responses for each of the positively worded statements and a 5 to "strongly disagree" responses for the negative statement. Item 3 is negatively worded and therefore it is reverse coded.

In Likert's original procedure, a large number of statements are generated, and an *item analysis* is performed. The purpose of the item analysis is to ensure that final items evoke a wide response and discriminate among those with positive and negative attitudes. Items that are poor because they lack clarity or elicit mixed response patterns are eliminated from the final statement list. Scales that use multiple items can be analyzed for reliability and validity. Only a set of items that shows good reliablity and validity should be summed or averaged to form a composite scale representing a hypothetical construct. Unfortuantely, not all researchers are willing or able to thoroughly assess reliability and validity. Without this test, the use of Likert scales can be disadvantageous because there is no way of knowing exactly what the items represent or how well they represent anything of interest.

Semantic Differential

Semantic differential
A measure of attitudes that consists of a series of seven-point rating scales that use bipolar adjectives to anchor the beginning and end of each scale.

The **semantic differential** is actually a series of attitude scales. This popular attitude measurement technique consists of getting respondents to react to some concept using a series of seven-point bipolar rating scales. Bipolar adjectives—such as "good" and "bad," "modern" and "old-fashioned," or "clean" and "dirty"—anchor the beginning and the end (or poles) of the scale. The subject makes repeated judgments about the concept under investigation on each of the scales. Exhibit 10.8 shows seven of eighteen scales used in a research project that measured attitudes toward supermarkets.

The scoring of the semantic differential can be illustrated using the scale bounded by the anchors "modern" and "old-fashioned." Respondents are instructed to check the place that indicates the nearest appropriate adjective. From left to right, the scale intervals are interpreted as "extremely modern," "very modern," "slightly modern," "both modern and old-fashioned," "slightly old-fashioned," "very old-fashioned," and "extremely old-fashioned":

Modern __ __ __ __ __ __ __ *Old-fashioned*

The semantic differential technique originally was developed as a method for measuring the meanings of objects or the "semantic space" of interpersonal experience.[13] Marketing researchers have found the semantic differential versatile and useful in business applications. The validity of the semantic differential depends on finding scale anchors that are semantic opposites. This can sometimes prove difficult. However, in attitude or image studies simple anchors such as very unfavorable and very favorable work well.

For scoring purposes, a numerical score is assigned to each position on the rating scale. Traditionally, scores are 1, 2, 3, 4, 5, 6, 7 or $-3, -2, -1, 0, +1, +2, +3$. Many marketing researchers find it desirable to assume that the semantic differential provides interval data. This assumption, although widely accepted, has its critics, who argue that the data have only ordinal properties because the numerical scores are arbitrary. Practically, marketing researchers treat semantic differential scales as

EXHIBIT 10.8
Semantic Differential Scales for Measuring Attitudes toward Supermarkets

Inconvenient location __ __ __ __ __ __ __ Convenient location

Low prices __ __ __ __ __ __ __ High prices

Pleasant atmosphere __ __ __ __ __ __ __ Unpleasant atmosphere

Modern __ __ __ __ __ __ __ Old-fashioned

Cluttered __ __ __ __ __ __ __ Spacious

Fast checkout __ __ __ __ __ __ __ Slow checkout

Dull __ __ __ __ __ __ __ Exciting

Source: Julie H. Yu, Gerald Albaum, and Michael Swenson, "Is a Central Tendency Error Inherent in the Use of Semantic Differential Scales in Different Cultures?" International Journal of Market Research, Summer 2003, downloaded from Business & Company Resource Center, http://galenet.galegroup.com.

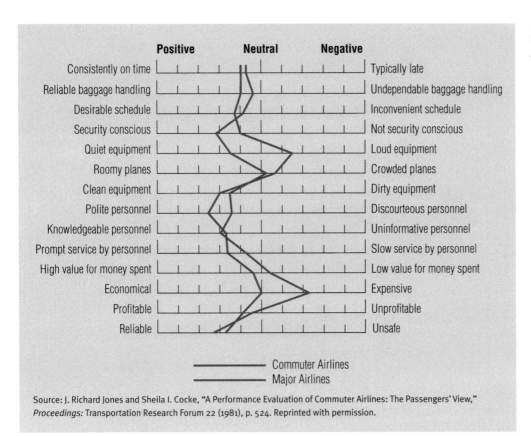

EXHIBIT 10.9
Image Profile of Commuter Airlines versus Major Airlines

Source: J. Richard Jones and Sheila I. Cocke, "A Performance Evaluation of Commuter Airlines: The Passengers' View," *Proceedings:* Transportation Research Forum 22 (1981), p. 524. Reprinted with permission.

metric (at least interval). This is because the amount of error introduced by assuming the intervals between choices are equal (even though this is uncertain) is fairly small.

Exhibit 10.9 illustrates a typical **image profile** based on semantic differential data. Because the data are assumed to be interval, either the arithmetic mean or the median will be used to compare the profile of one product, brand, or store with that of a competing product, brand, or store.

Image profile
A graphic representation of semantic differential data for competing brands, products, or stores to highlight comparisons.

Numerical Scales

In a **numerical scale**, numbers, rather than semantic space or verbal descriptions, serve as the response options to identify categories (response positions). For example, if scale items have five response positions, the scale is called a five-point numerical scale. A six-point scale has six positions and a seven-point scale seven positions, and so on. Consider the following numerical scale:

Numerical scale
An attitude rating scale similar to a semantic differential except that it uses numbers, instead of verbal descriptions, as response options to identify response positions.

> *Now that you've had your automobile for about one year, please tell us how satisfied you are with your Ford Taurus.*

> *Extremely Dissatisfied   1   2   3   4   5   6   7   Extremely Satisfied*

This numerical scale uses bipolar adjectives in the same manner as the semantic differential.

In practice, researchers have found that a scale with numerical labels for intermediate points on the scale is as effective a measure as the true semantic differential.

Stapel Scale

The **Stapel scale** was originally developed in the 1950s to measure simultaneously the direction and intensity of an attitude. Modern versions of the scale, with a single adjective, are used as a substitute for the semantic differential when it is difficult to create pairs of bipolar adjectives. The modified Stapel scale places a single adjective in the center of an even number of numerical values

Stapel scale
A measure of attitudes that consists of a single adjective in the center of an even number of numerical values.

A Stapel Scale for Measuring a Store's Image

Bloomingdale's

+3

+2

+1

Wide Selection

−1

−2

−3

Select a *plus* number for words that you think describe the store accurately. The more accurately you think the word describes the store, the larger the plus number you should choose. Select a *minus* number for words you think do not describe the store accurately. The less accurately you think the word describes the store, the larger the minus number you should choose. Therefore, you can select any number from +3 for words that you think are very accurate all the way to −3 for words that you think are very inaccurate.

Source: Dennis Menezes and Norbert F. Elbert, "Alternative Semantic Scaling Formats for Measuring Store Image: An Evaluation," Journal of Marketing Research, February 1979, pp. 80–87. Reprinted by permission of the American Marketing Association.

(ranging, perhaps, from +3 to −3). The scale measures how close to or distant from the adjective a given stimulus is perceived to be. Exhibit 10.10 illustrates a Stapel scale item used in measurement of a retailer's store image.

The advantages and disadvantages of the Stapel scale are very similar to those of the semantic differential. However, the Stapel scale is markedly easier to administer, especially over the telephone. Because the Stapel scale does not require bipolar adjectives, it is easier to construct than the semantic differential. Research comparing the semantic differential with the Stapel scale indicates that results from the two techniques are largely the same.[14]

Constant-Sum Scale

Constant-sum scale
A measure of attitudes in which respondents are asked to divide a constant sum to indicate the relative importance of attributes; respondents often sort cards, but the task may also be a rating task.

With a **constant-sum scale**, respondents are asked to divide a fixed number of points among several attributes to indicate their relative importance. Suppose United Parcel Service (UPS) wishes to determine the importance of the attributes of accurate invoicing, delivery as promised, and price to organizations that use its service in business-to-business marketing. Respondents might be asked to divide a constant sum of 100 points to indicate the relative importance of those attributes:

Divide 100 points among the following characteristics of a delivery service according to how important each characteristic is to you when selecting a delivery company.
Accurate invoicing _____
Delivery as promised _____
Lower price _____

The constant-sum scale works best with respondents who have high educational levels. If respondents follow the instructions correctly, the results will approximate interval measures. As the number of stimuli increases, this technique becomes increasingly complex.

This technique may be used for measuring brand preference. The approach, which is similar to the paired-comparison method, is as follows:

Divide 100 points among the following brands according to your preference for each brand:
Brand A _____
Brand B _____
Brand C _____

RESEARCHSNAPSHOT

A Measuring Stick for Website Usability

Two technology experts looking for a standard way to measure websites' usability developed metrics emphasizing attitudes. Rather than, say, measuring how long it took users to accomplish a particular task, they asked users to rate their experiences using each site. Each rater evaluated the site's content (information and transactions), ease of use, promotion (advertising on the site), "made for the medium" (features that make the site fit the user's particular needs), and emotions (sense of accomplishment, interest in the site's content, credibility, and control over the flow of content).

Of course, what is very important on one site may be minor on another. A prospective investor looking for information about an airline would likely seek a different online experience than a consumer visiting the same site to plan a vacation, and they both would have still different expectations for an online bookstore. As a result, the usability assessment begins by asking respondents to rate each category being evaluated in terms of how important it is for a particular kind of company, assuming the

rater is either a consumer or an investor. For example, a user might rate an airline website's content, ease of use, and so on for a consumer. These ratings use a 100-point constant-sum scale. Each rater divides 100 points among the five categories. The rater then evaluates, on a scale of 1 to 10, how well the site performs in each category. The importance ratings weight those scores. So, if a rater assigns 5 points to the emotion category and thinks the site performs at a 6 on the 1-to-10 scale, the weighted score is 30. By combining all the ratings for a website, a site can earn between 0 and 1,000 points. In the researchers' test of this rating system, it delivered helpful insights.

Source: Based on Ritu Agarwal and Viswanath Venkatesh, "Assessing a Firm's Web Presence: A Heuristic Evaluation Procedure for the Measurement of Usability," *Information Systems Research*, June 2002, downloaded from Business & Company Resource Center at http://galenet.galegroup .com; and G.A. Buchholz, "Losability vs. Usability," *Digital Web*, http://www .digital-web.com, July 11, 2005,

©PHOTODISC/GETTY IMAGES

In this case, the constant-sum scale is a rating technique. However, with minor modifications, it can be classified as a sorting technique. Although the constant sum scale is widely used, strictly speaking, the scale is flawed because the last response is completely determined by the way the respondent has scored the other choices. Although this is probably somewhat complex to understand, the fact is that practical reasons often outweigh this concern.

Graphic Rating Scales

A **graphic rating scale** presents respondents with a graphic continuum. The respondents are allowed to choose any point on the continuum to indicate their attitude. Exhibit 10.11 shows a traditional graphic scale, ranging from one extreme position to the opposite position. Typically a respondent's score is determined by measuring the length (in millimeters) from one end of the graphic continuum to the point marked by the respondent. Many researchers believe that scoring in this manner strengthens the assumption that graphic rating scales of this type are interval scales. Alternatively, the researcher may divide the line into predetermined scoring categories (lengths) and record respondents' marks accordingly. In other words, the graphic rating scale has the advantage of allowing the researcher to choose any interval desired for scoring purposes. The disadvantage of the graphic rating scale is that there are no standard answers.

Graphic rating scale
A measure of attitude that allows respondents to rate an object by choosing any point along a graphic continuum.

EXHIBIT 10.11
Graphic Rating Scale

Please evaluate each attribute in terms of how important it is to you by placing an X at the position on the horizontal line that most reflects your feelings.

Seating comfort	Not important _____ Very important	
In-flight meals	Not important _____ Very important	
Airfare	Not important _____ Very important	

EXHIBIT 10.12
A Ladder Scale

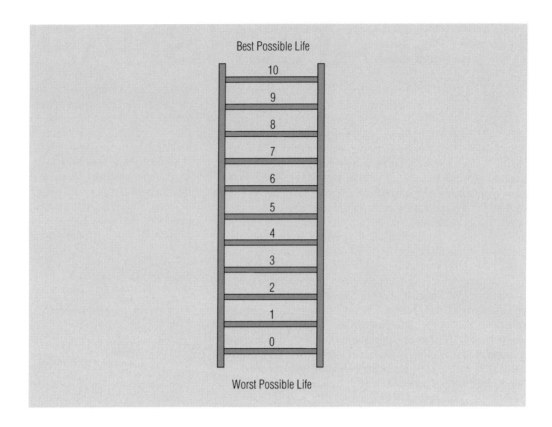

Graphic rating scales are not limited to straight lines as sources of visual communication. Picture response options or another type of graphic continuum may be used to enhance communication with respondents. A variation of the graphic ratings scale is the ladder scale. This scale also includes numerical options:

Here is a ladder scale [response scale is shown Exhibit 10.12]. It represents the "ladder of life." As you see, it is a ladder with eleven rungs numbered 0 to 10. Let's suppose the top of the ladder represents the best possible life for you as you describe it, and the bottom rung represents the worst possible life for you as you describe it.

On which rung of the ladder do you feel your life is today?

0   1   2   3   4   5   6   7   8   9   10

Research to investigate children's attitudes has used happy-face scales (see Exhibit 10.13). The children are asked to indicate which face shows how they feel about candy, a toy, or some other concept. Research with the happy-face scale indicates that children tend to choose the faces at the ends of the scale. Although this may be because children's attitudes fluctuate more widely than

EXHIBIT 10.13
Graphic Rating Scale with Picture Response Categories Stressing Visual Communication

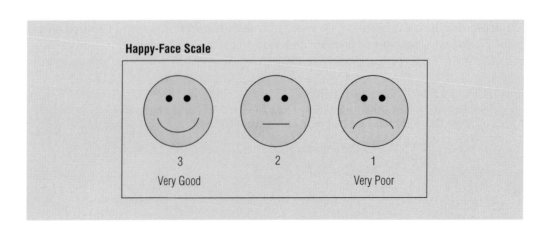

EXHIBIT 10.14 **Summary of Advantages and Disadvantages of Rating Scales**

Rating Measure	Subject Must	Advantages	Disadvantages
Category scale	Indicate a response category	Flexible, easy to respond to	Items may be ambiguous; with few categories, only gross distinctions can be made
Likert scale	Evaluate statements on a scale of agreement	Easiest scale to construct	Hard to judge what a single score means
Semantic differential and numerical scales	Choose points between bipolar adjectives on relevant dimensions	Easy to construct; norms exist for comparison, such as profile analysis	Bipolar adjectives must be found; data may be ordinal, not interval
Stapel scale	Choose points on a scale with a single adjective in the center	Easier to construct than semantic differential, easy to administer	Endpoints are numerical, not verbal, labels
Constant-sum scale	Divide a constant sum among response alternatives	Approximates an interval measure	Difficult for respondents with low education levels
Graphic scale	Choose a point on a continuum	Visual impact, unlimited scale points	No standard answers
Graphic scale with picture response categories	Choose a visual picture	Visual impact, easy for poor readers	Hard to attach a verbal explanation to a response

adults' or because they have stronger feelings both positively and negatively, the tendency to select the extremes is a disadvantage of the scale.

Exhibit 10.14 summarizes the attitude–rating techniques discussed in this section.

Measuring Behavioral Intention

The behavioral component of an attitude involves the behavioral expectations of an individual toward an attitudinal object. Typically, the component of interest to marketers is a buying intention, a tendency to seek additional information, or plans to visit a showroom. Category scales for measuring the behavioral component of an attitude ask about a respondent's likelihood of purchase or intention to perform some future action, using questions such as the following:

How likely is it that you will purchase an mp3 player?

- *I definitely will buy*
- *I probably will buy*
- *I might buy*
- *I probably will not buy*
- *I definitely will not buy*

I would write a letter to my representative in Congress or other government official in support of this company if it were in a dispute with government.

- *Extremely Likely*
- *Very Likely*
- *Somewhat Likely*
- *Likely, about a 50–50 chance*
- *Somewhat Unlikely*
- *Very Unlikely*
- *Absolutely Unlikely*

The wording of statements used in these scales often includes phrases such as "I would recommend," "I would write," or "I would buy" to indicate action tendencies.

Expectations also may be measured using a scale of subjective probabilities, ranging from 100 for "absolutely certain" to 0 for "absolutely no chance." Researchers have used the following subjective probability scale to estimate the chance that a job candidate will accept a sales position:

_____	100%	(Absolutely certain) I will accept
_____	90%	(Almost sure) I will accept
_____	80%	(Very big chance) I will accept
_____	70%	(Big chance) I will accept
_____	60%	(Not so big a chance) I will accept
_____	50%	(About even) I will accept
_____	40%	(Smaller chance) I will accept
_____	30%	(Small chance) I will accept
_____	20%	(Very small chance) I will accept
_____	10%	(Almost certainly not) I will accept
_____	0%	(Certainly not) I will accept

Behavioral Differential

Behavioral differential
A rating scale instrument similar to a semantic differential, developed to measure the behavioral intentions of subjects toward future actions.

A general instrument, the **behavioral differential**, is used to measure the behavioral intentions of subjects toward an object or category of objects. As in the semantic differential, a description of the object to be judged is followed by a series of scales on which subjects indicate their behavioral intentions toward this object. For example, one item might be something like this:

A 25-year-old female sales representative

Would __ __ __ __ __ __ __ __ __ Would not

Ask this person for advice.

Ranking

Consumers often *rank order* their preferences. An ordinal scale may be developed by asking respondents to rank order (from most preferred to least preferred) a set of objects or attributes. Respondents easily understand the task of rank ordering the importance of product attributes or arranging a set of brand names according to preference. Like the constant sum scale, technically the ranking scale also suffers from inflexibility in that if we know how some ranked five out of six alternatives, we know the answer to the sixth.

TOTHEPOINT

My tastes are very simple. I only want the best.

—Oscar Wilde

Paired comparison
A measurement technique that involves presenting the respondent with two objects and asking the respondent to pick the preferred object; more than two objects may be presented, but comparisons are made in pairs.

Paired Comparisons

Consider a situation in which a chainsaw manufacturer learned that a competitor had introduced a new lightweight (6-pound) chain saw. The manufacturer's lightest chain saw weighed 9 pounds. Executives wondered if they needed to introduce a 6-pound chain saw into the product line. The research design chosen was a **paired comparison**. A 6-pound chain saw was designed and a prototype built. To control for color preferences, the competitor's chain saw was painted the same color as the 9- and 6-pound chain saws. Respondents were presented with two chain saws at a time and asked to pick the one they preferred. Three pairs of comparisons were required to determine the most preferred chain saw.

The following question illustrates the typical format for asking about paired comparisons.

I would like to know your overall opinion of two brands of adhesive bandages. They are Curad and Band-Aid. Overall, which of these two brands—Curad or Band-Aid—do you think is the better one? Or are both the same?

Curad is better _____
Band-Aid is better _____
They are the same _____

If researchers wish to compare four brands of pens on the basis of attractiveness or writing quality, six comparisons $[(n)(n - 1)/2]$ will be necessary.

When comparing only a few items, such as products or advertisements, ranking objects with respect to one attribute is not difficult. As the number of items increases, the number of comparisons increases geometrically. If the number of comparisons is too large, respondents may become fatigued and no longer carefully discriminate among them.

Sorting

Sorting tasks require that respondents indicate their attitudes or beliefs by arranging items on the basis of perceived similarity or some other attribute. One advertising agency has had consumers sort photographs of people to measure their perceptions of a brand's typical user. Another agency used a sorting technique in which consumers used a deck of fifty-two cards illustrating elements from advertising for the brand name being studied. The study participants created a stack of cards showing elements they recalled seeing or hearing, and the interviewer then asked the respondent to identify the item on each of those cards. National City Corporation, a banking company, has used sorting as part of its research into the design of its website. Consumers participating in the research were given a set of cards describing various parts of processes that they might engage in when they are banking online. The participants were asked to arrange the cards to show their idea of a logical way to complete these processes. This research method showed the website designers how consumers go about doing something—sometimes very differently from the way the bankers expected.[15]

A variant of the constant-sum technique uses physical counters (for example, poker chips or coins), to be divided among the items being tested. In an airline study of customer preferences, the following sorting technique could be used:

Here is a sheet that lists several airlines. Next to the name of each airline is a pocket. Here are ten cards. I would like you to put these cards in the pockets next to the airlines you would prefer to fly on your next trip. Assume that all of the airlines fly to wherever you would choose to travel. You can put as many cards as you want next to an airline, or you can put no cards next to an airline.

Cards

American Airlines	_____
Delta Airlines	_____
United Airlines	_____
Southwest Airlines	_____
Northwest Airlines	_____

Summary

1. Explain what needs to be measured to address a research question or hypothesis. Researchers can determine what concepts must be measured by examining research questions and hypotheses. A hypothesis often states that one concept is related to another. Therefore, the concepts listed in the hypotheses must have operational measures if the research is to be performed.

2. Define operationalization. This is the process of identifying scales that correspond to variance in a concept to be involved in a research process.

3. Distinguish levels of scale measurement. Four levels of scale measurement can be identified. Each level is associated with increasingly complex properties. Nominal scales assign numbers or letters to objects for identification or classification. Ordinal scales arrange objects based on relative magnitude of a concept. Thus, ordinal scales represent rankings. Interval scales also represent an ordering based on relative amounts of a concept, but they also capture the differences between scale values. Thus, interval scales allow stimuli to be compared to each other based on the difference in their scale scores. Ratio scales are absolute scales, starting with absolute zeros, at which there is a total absence of the attribute. Nominal and ordinal scales are discrete. The mode is the best way to represent central tendency for discrete measures. Ratio measures are continuous and interval scales are generally treated as continuous. For continuous measures, the mean represents a valid representation of central tendency.

4. Explain the need for index or composite measures. Indexes and composite measures are formed by combining scores from multiple items. For instance, a composite score can be formed by adding the scores to multiple items, each intended to represent the same concept.

5. List the three criteria for good measurement. Good measurement exists when a measure is reliable, valid, and sensitive. Thus, reliability, validity, and sensitivity are characteristics of good measurement. Reliability represents the consistency and repeatability of a measure. Validity refers to the degree to which the instrument measures the concept the researcher wants to measure. Sensitivity is the instrument's ability to accurately measure variability in stimuli or responses.

6. Explain the significance of scale reliability and validity. Reliability is an indicator of a measure's internal consistency. A measure that is reliable when different attempts at measuring something converge on the same result. Validity is the accuracy or a measure or the extent to which a score truthfully represents a concept.

7. Describe how marketing researchers think of attitudes. Attitudes are enduring dispositions to consistently respond in a given manner to various aspects of the world, including persons, events, and objects. Attitudes consist of three components: the affective, or the emotions or feelings involved; the cognitive, or awareness or knowledge; and the behavioral, or the predisposition to action. Attitudes are latent constructs and because of this, they are not directly observable.

8. Identify basic approaches to measuring attitudes. Many methods for measuring attitudes have been developed for attitude measurement. Most fall into the categories of ranking, rating, sorting, and choice techniques.

9. Discuss the use of rating scales for measuring attitudes. One class of rating scales, category scales, provides several response categories to allow respondents to indicate the intensity of their attitudes. The Likert scale uses a series of statements with which subjects indicate agreement or disagreement. The levels of agreement with some statement are assigned numerical scores. A semantic differential uses a series of attitude scales anchored by bipolar adjectives. The respondent indicates where his or her attitude falls between the polar attitudes. Variations on this method, such as numerical scales and the Stapel scale, are also used. The Stapel scale puts a single adjective in the center of a range of numerical values from $+3$ to -3. Constant-sum scales require the respondent to divide a constant sum into parts, indicating the weights to be given to various attributes of the item being studied.

10. Represent a latent construct by constructing a summated scale. Researchers use composite scales to represent latent constructs. An easy way to create a composite scale is to add the responses to multiple items together to form a total. Thus, a respondent's scores to four items can simply be added together to form a summated scale. The researcher must check to make sure that each scale item is worded positively, or at least all in the same direction. For example, if multiple items are used to form a satisfaction construct, a higher score for each item should lead to higher satisfaction. If one of the items represents dissatisfaction, such that a higher score represents lower satisfaction, this item must be reverse recoded prior to creating the composite scale.

11. Summarize ways to measure attitudes with ranking and sorting techniques. People often rank order their preferences. Thus, ordinal scales that ask respondents to rank order a set of objects or attributes may be developed. In the paired-comparison technique, two alternatives are paired and respondents are asked to pick the preferred one. Sorting requires respondents to indicate their attitudes by arranging items into piles or categories.

Key Terms and Concepts

Measurement	Reliability	Category scale
Concept	Coefficient alpha (α)	Likert scale
Operationalization	Validity	Reverse recoding
Scales	Construct validity	Composite scale
Correspondence rules	Convergent validity	Semantic differential
Construct	Sensitivity	Image profile
Nominal scales	Attitude	Numerical scale
Ordinal scales	Hypothetical constructs	Stapel scale
Interval scales	Ranking	Constant-sum scale
Ratio scales	Rating	Graphic rating scale
Attribute	Sorting	Behavioral differential
Index measure	Choice	Paired comparison
Composite measures		

Questions for Review and Critical Thinking

1. Define *measurement*. How is your performance in a marketing research class being measured?
2. What is the difference between a *concept* and a *construct*?
3. Describe the four different levels of scale measurement.
4. Look at the responses to the following survey items that describe how stressful consumers believed a Christmas shopping trip was using a ten-point scale ranging from 1 (= no stress at all) to 10 (= extremely stressful):
   a. How stressful was finding a place to park? _7_
   b. How stressful was the checkout procedure? _5_
   c. How stressful was trying to find exactly the right product? _8_
   d. How stressful was finding a store employee? _6_
      i. What would be the stress score for this respondent based on a summated scale score?
      ii. What would be the stress score for this respondent based on an average composite scale score?
      iii. Do any items need to be reverse-coded? Why or why not?
5. Why might a researcher wish to use more than one question to measure satisfaction with a particular aspect of retail shopping?
6. Comment on the validity and reliability of the following:
   a. A respondent's report of an intention to subscribe to *Consumer Reports* is highly reliable. A researcher believes this constitutes a valid measurement of dissatisfaction with the economic system and alienation from big business.
   b. A general-interest magazine claimed that it was a better advertising medium than television programs with similar content. Research had indicated that for a soft drink and other test products, recall scores were higher for the magazine ads than for thirty-second commercials.
   c. A respondent's report of frequency of magazine reading consistently indicates that she regularly reads *Good Housekeeping* and *Gourmet* and never reads *Cosmopolitan*.
7. Indicate whether the following measures use a nominal, ordinal, interval, or ratio scale:
   a. Prices on the stock market
   b. Marital status, classified as "married" or "never married"
   c. Whether a respondent has ever been unemployed
   d. Professorial rank: assistant professor, associate professor, or professor
   e. Grades: A, B, C, D, or F
8. What is an *attitude*? Is there a consensus concerning its definition?
9. Distinguish between *rating* and *ranking*. Which is a better attitude measurement technique? Why?
10. Assume the researcher wanted to create a summated scale indicating a respondent's attitude toward the trucking industry. What would the result be for the respondent whose response is as indicated below?

	Strongly Disagree	Disagree	Somewhat Disagree	Somewhat Agree	Agree	Strongly Agree
6. I feel the trucking industry in Canada is very important to our economy.	☐	☐	☐	☒	☐	☐
7. Truck drivers go out of their way to help make the roads safer.	☐	☐	☐	☐	☒	☐
8. The trucking industry is harmful to Canadians in more ways than one.	☐	☒	☐	☐	☐	☐
9. Without the trucking industry, our communities would be much better off.	☐	☐	☒	☐	☐	☐
10. Truck drivers are among the most courteous drivers.	☐	☐	☐	☐	☐	☒

11. What advantages do numerical scales have over semantic differential scales?
12. Identify the issues a researcher should consider when choosing a measurement scale.
13. Name some situations in which a semantic differential might be useful.
14. In each of the following, identify the type of scale and evaluate it:
   a. A U.S. representative's questionnaire sent to constituents:

   Do you favor or oppose the Fair Tax Proposal?

In Favor	Opposed	No Opinion
☐	☐	☐

   b. How favorable are you toward the Fair Tax Proposal?

   Very Unfavorable ☐ ☐ ☐ ☐ ☐ ☐ *Very Favorable*

   c. A psychographic statement asking the respondent to circle the appropriate response:

   I shop a lot for specials.

Strongly Disagree	Disagree	Neutral	Agree	Strongly Agree
1	2	3	4	5

15. If a semantic differential has ten scale items, should all the positive adjectives be on the right and all the negative adjectives on the left?

16. **ETHICS** A researcher thinks many respondents will answer "don't know" or "can't say" if these options are printed on an attitude scale along with categories indicating level of agreement. The researcher does not print either "don't know" or "can't say"

on the questionnaire because the resulting data would be more complicated to analyze and report. Is this proper?

17. **'NET** SRI International investigates U.S. consumers by asking questions about their attitudes and values. It has a website so people can VALS-type themselves. To find out your VALS type, go to http://www.sric-bi.com/VALS/presurvey.shtml.

Research Activities

1. Go to the library and find out how *Sales and Marketing Management* magazine constructs its buying-power index.

2. Define each of the following concepts, and then operationally define each one by providing correspondence rules between the definition and the scale:
    a. A good bowler
    b. The television audience for *The Tonight Show*
    c. Purchasing intention for a palm-sized computer
    d. Consumer involvement with cars
    e. A workaholic
    f. Fast-food restaurant
    g. The American Dream

3. **'NET** Use the ACSI scores found at http://www.theacsi.org to respond to this question. Using the most recent two years of data, test the following two hypotheses:

a. American consumers are more satisfied with breweries than they are with wireless telephone services.

b. **'NET** American consumers are more satisfied with discount and department stores than they are with automobile companies.

4. Refer back to the opening vignette. Use the *Business Resource Center* to search for stories dealing with job performance. In particular, pay attention to stories that may be related to CRM. Make a recommendation to Griff concerning a way that job performance should be measured. Would your scale be nominal, ordinal, interval, or ratio?

5. **'NET** Go to http://www.queendom.com/tests. Click on the lists of personality tests. Take the hostility test. Do you think this is a reliable and valid measure of how prone someone is to generally act in a hostile manner?

Case 10.1 FlyAway Airways

Wesley Shocker, research analyst for FlyAway Airways, was asked by the director of research to make recommendations regarding the best approach for monitoring the quality of service provided by the airline.[16] FlyAway Airways is a national air carrier that has a comprehensive route structure consisting of long-haul, coast-to-coast routes and direct, nonstop routes between short-haul metropolitan areas. Current competitors include Midway and Alaska Airlines. FlyAway Airlines is poised to surpass the billion-dollar revenue level required to be designated as a major airline. This change in status brings a new set of competitors. To prepare for this move up in competitive status, Shocker was asked to review the options available for monitoring the quality of FlyAway Airways service and the service of its competitors. Such monitoring would involve better understanding the nature of service quality and the ways in which quality can be tracked for airlines.

After some investigation, Shocker discovered two basic approaches to measuring quality of airline service that can produce similar ranking results. His report must outline the important aspects to consider in measuring quality as well as the critical points of difference and similarity between the two approaches to measuring quality.

Some Background on Quality

In today's competitive airline industry, it's crucial that an airline do all it can do to attract and retain customers. One of the best ways to do this is by offering quality service to consumers. Perceptions of service quality vary from person to person, but an enduring element of service quality is the consistent achievement of customer satisfaction.

For customers to perceive an airline as offering quality service, they must be satisfied, and that usually means receiving a service outcome that is equal to or greater than what they expected.

An airline consumer usually is concerned most with issues of schedule, destination, and price when choosing an airline. Given that most airlines have competition in each of these areas, other factors that relate to quality become important to the customer when making a choice between airlines. Both subjective aspects of quality (that is, food, pleasant employees, and so forth) and objective aspects (that is, on-time performance, safety, lost baggage, and so forth) have real meaning to consumers. These secondary factors may not be as critical as schedule, destination, and price, but they do affect quality judgments of the customer.

There are many possible combinations of subjective and objective aspects that could influence a customer's perception of quality at different times. Fortunately, since 1988, consumers of airline services have had access to objective information from the Department of Transportation regarding service performance in some basic categories. Unfortunately, the average consumer is most likely unaware of or uninterested in these data on performance; instead, consumers rely on personal experience and subjective opinion to judge quality of service. Periodic surveys of subjective consumer opinion regarding airline service experience are available through several sources. These efforts rely on contact with a sample of consumers who may or may not have informed opinions regarding the quality of airline service for all airlines being compared.

A Consumer Survey Approach

In his research, Shocker discovered a recent study conducted to identify favorite airlines of frequent fliers. This study is typical of the

Ranking of Major Airlines: Consumer Survey Approach

1. American	11. Lufthansa
2. United	12. USAir
3. Delta	13. KLM
4. TWA	14. America West
5. SwissAir	15. JAL
6. Singapore	16. Alaska
7. British Airways	17. Qantas
8. Continental	18. Midway
9. Air France	19. Southwest
10. Pan Am	20. SAS

survey-based, infrequent (usually only annually), subjective efforts conducted to assess airline quality. A New York firm, Research & Forecasts, Inc., published results of a consumer survey of frequent fliers that used several criteria to rate domestic and international airlines. Criteria included comfort, service, reliability, food quality, cost, delays, routes served, safety, and frequent-flier plans. The questionnaire was sent to 25,000 frequent fliers.

The 4,462 people who responded were characterized as predominantly male (59 percent) professional managers (66 percent) whose average age was 45 and who traveled an average of at least 43 nights a year for both business and pleasure. This group indicated that the most important factors in choosing an airline were 1) route structure (46 percent), 2) price (42 percent), 3) reliability (41 percent), 4) service (33 percent), 5) safety (33 percent), 6) frequent-flier plans (33 percent), and 7) food (12 percent). When asked to rate twenty different airlines, respondents provided the rankings in Case Exhibit 10.1–1.

A Weighted Average Approach

Shocker also discovered a newer, more objective approach to measuring airline quality in a study recently published by the National Institute for Aviation Research at the Wichita State University in Wichita, Kansas. The Airline Quality Rating (AQR) is a weighted average of nineteen factors that have relevance when judging the quality of airline services (see Case Exhibit 10.1–2). The AQR is based on data that are readily obtainable (most of the data are updated monthly) from published sources for each major airline operating in the United States. Regularly published data on such factors as consumer complaints, on-time performance, accidents, number of aircraft, and financial performance are available from the Department of Transportation, the National Transportation Safety Board, Moody's Bond Record, industry trade publications, and annual reports of individual airlines.

To establish the nineteen weighted factors, an opinion survey was conducted with a group of sixty-five experts in the aviation field. These experts included representatives of most major airlines, air travel experts, Federal Aviation Administration (FAA) representatives, academic researchers, airline manufacturing and support firms, and individual consumers. Each expert was asked to rate the importance that each individual factor might have to a consumer of airline services using a scale of 0 (no importance) to 10 (great importance). The average importance ratings for each of the nineteen factors were then used as the weights for those factors in the AQR. Case Exhibit 10.1–2 shows the factors included in the Airline Quality Rating, the weight associated with each factor, and whether

Factors Included in the Airline Quality Rating (AQR)[a]

Factor	Weight
1. Average age of fleet	−5.85
2. Number of aircraft	+4.54
3. On-time performance	+8.63
4. Load factor	−6.98
5. Pilot deviations	−8.03
6. Number of accidents	−8.38
7. Frequent-flier awards	−7.35
8. Flight problems[b]	−8.05
9. Denied boardings[b]	−8.03
10. Mishandled baggage[b]	−7.92
11. Fares[b]	−7.60
12. Customer service[b]	−7.20
13. Refunds	−7.32
14. Ticketing/boarding[b]	−7.08
15. Advertising[b]	−6.82
16. Credit[b]	−5.94
17. Other[b]	−7.34
18. Financial stability	−6.52
19. Average seat-mile cost	−4.49

$$AQR = \frac{w_1F_1 - w_2F_2 + w_3F_3 + \cdots - w_{19}F_{19}}{w_1 + w_2 + w_3 + \cdots + w_{19}}$$

a. The 19-item rating has a reliability coefficient (Cronbach's Alpha) of 0.87.
b. Data for these factors come from consumer complaints registered with the Department of Transportation.

Airline Rankings

Rank	Airline	AQR Score
1	American	+0.328
2	Southwest	+0.254
3	Delta	+0.209
4	United	+0.119
5	USAir	+0.054
6	Pan Am	+0.003
7	Northwest	−0.063
8	Continental	−0.346
9	America West	−0.377
10	TWA	−0.439

the factor has a positive or negative impact on quality from the consumer's perspective.

Using the Airline Quality Rating formula and recent data, produce AQR scores and rankings for the 10 major U.S. airlines shown in Case Exhibit 10.1–3.

What Course to Chart?

Shocker has discovered what appear to be two different approaches to measuring quality of airlines. One relies on direct consumer opinion and is mostly subjective in its approach to quality and the elements considered. The other relies on performance data that are available through public sources and appear to be more objective.

Both approaches incorporate pertinent elements that could be used by consumers to judge the quality of an airline. Shocker's recommendation must consider the comprehensiveness and usefulness of these approaches for FlyAway Airways as it moves into a more competitive environment. What course of action should he recommend?

Questions

1. How comparable are the two different methods? In what ways are they similar? In what ways are they different?

2. What are the positive and negative aspects of each approach that Shocker should consider before recommending a course of action for FlyAway Airways?

3. What aspects of service quality does each approach address well and not so well?

4. Considering the two methods outlined, what types of validity would you consider to be demonstrated by the two approaches to measuring quality? Defend your position.

5. Which of the methods should Shocker recommend? Why?

Case 10.2 Ha-Pah-Shu-Tse

 Raymond RedCorn is an Osage Indian. The Ha-Pah-Shu-Tse (Osage for "red corn") restaurant in Pawhuska, Oklahoma, is the only authentic Native American restaurant in the state and one of few in the country.

The Ha-Pah-Shu-Tse restaurant opened in 1972 with a seating capacity of eight; today, after expansion, crowds of up to ninety keep RedCorn and his wife busy. They are currently marketing an Indian fry bread mix, and they are planning on increased sales for their only packaged good. Indian fry bread mix has long been a staple of the Native American diet. The bread is sweet and contains basic ingredients such as flour, shortening, and sugar.

The Restaurant

Waltina RedCorn married into the Osage tribe forty-seven years ago and learned how to cook from two women named Grandma Baconrind and Grandma Lookout. They must have taught her well, because customers of the Ha-Pah-Shu-Tse are not content just to eat there—they often have the RedCorns mail them fry bread mix. Raymond RedCorn finds that people who eat the unusual native dish usually request the recipe. He says, "I have not found anyone who does not like the bread." Customers aren't limited to local fans of Indian food. Because the fry bread is sold or served in restaurants and stores in Oklahoma as well as at a museum, people from as far away as Europe have tried it.

According to RedCorn, "About once a week, someone from England comes in." He serves these British customers fry bread or the restaurant's "best-sellers," Indian Meat Pie or Navaho Taco, and tells them the story of fry bread and how it got him an invitation to Buckingham Palace. When he was eighteen years old, he was in London for a Boy Scout Jamboree. One evening he was frying the Indian bread when the British Boy Scout organizer approached with two young men. It was only after everyone had tasted RedCorn's culinary effort that the Prince of Wales was introduced. "The Indian delegation from Oklahoma was invited to set up their tents on the ground at the palace and spend the weekend being entertained by the young royalty," RedCorn says.

The Product

The product as it is today took several years to perfect. The Red-Corns wanted a mix that would need only the addition of water. Each batch was sent to relatives and friends for judgment on the taste until everyone was convinced it was the best it could be.

The mix, consisting of Indian flour, is already distributed in Tulsa, Bartlesville, and surrounding towns under the Ha-Pah-Shu-Tse brand name. It is packaged in 2- and 5-pound silver bags with Raymond RedCorn in Osage tribal costume pictured on the front. Directions for making the fry bread are listed on the back of the package.

The Research Problem

When planning the marketing for the Indian fry bread mix, student consultants working with the Small Business Administration suggested some attitude research. They felt that successfully marketing the Ha-Pah-Shu-Tse product depended on knowing what consumer reactions to Indian foods would be. They believed that if the image of Indian foods and consumers' awareness of them were measured, RedCorn would have a better chance of marketing his product. In addition, the student consultants felt that the name Ha-Pah-Shu-Tse violated many of the requirements for a good brand name—it was not short, simple, or easy to recall, and was difficult to pronounce and spell.

Questions

1. What marketing questions must be answered as Ha-Pah-Shu-Tse plans for expansion? How can marketing research help answer those questions?

2. What type of attitude scale would you recommend? How would you generate a set of items (attributes) to be measured?

CHAPTER 11
QUESTIONNAIRE DESIGN

After studying this chapter, you should be able to

1. Explain the significance of decisions about questionnaire design and wording
2. Define alternatives for wording open-ended and fixed-alternative questions
3. Summarize guidelines for questions that avoid mistakes in questionnaire design
4. Describe how the proper sequence of questions may improve a questionnaire
5. Discuss how to design a questionnaire layout
6. Describe criteria for pretesting and revising a questionnaire and for adapting it to global markets

Chapter Vignette: J.D. Power Asks Consumers to Get Real

Are you driving your dream car? Most of us can't, because we bump up against the practical reality that we can't pay for every great new feature. As car makers consider adding new features, they have to evaluate not only which ones appeal to consumers but also which ones will actually sell, considering their likely cost. J.D. Power and Associates recently addressed this issue in a survey of about seventeen thousand consumers.[1]

©ROYALTY FREE/CORBIS

In the J.D. Power survey, consumers were asked whether they were familiar with twenty-two different emerging technologies. Then they were asked about their interest in each technology, rating their interest using a scale ("definitely interested," "probably interested," and so on). Next, the study indicated the likely price of each technology, and consumers were asked their interest, given the price. The results ranked the features according to interest level, based on the percentage who indicated they were either definitely or probably interested in the feature.

Learning price information often changed consumers' interest levels. Night vision systems appealed to 72 percent of consumers, placing it in second place in the rankings. But when consumers learned the systems would likely add $1,500 to the price of a car, this technology dropped to a rank of 17, near the bottom. In contrast, HD radio ranked in sixteenth place until consumers saw a price tag of just $150. That price pushed the feature up to third place. Still, two features remained in the top five even with pricing information: run-flat tires and stability control. And three of the bottom-five features—a reconfigurable cabin, lane departure warning system, and smart sensing power-swing front doors—stayed in the bottom rankings. Automakers can use findings such as these to determine which features are price-sensitive and which might be appealing even at a higher price.

In the J.D. Power survey, answers changed when respondents were given more information. This chapter outlines a procedure for questionnaire design, which addresses concerns such as the wording and order of questions and the layout of the questionnaire.

Questionnaire Quality and Design: Basic Considerations

Each stage in the interdependent marketing research process is important. Yet a marketing research survey is only as good as the questions asked. The importance of question wording is easily overlooked, but questionnaire design is one of the most critical stages in the survey research process.

Businesspeople who are inexperienced at marketing research frequently believe that constructing a questionnaire is a simple task. Amateur researchers think a short questionnaire can be written in minutes. Unfortunately, newcomers who naively believe that good grammar is all a person needs to construct a questionnaire generally end up with useless results. Ask a bad question, get bad results.

Good questionnaire design requires far more than correct grammar. People don't understand questions just because they are grammatically correct. Respondents simply may not know what is being asked. They may be unaware of the product or topic of interest. They may confuse the subject with something else. The question may not mean the same thing to everyone interviewed. Finally, people may refuse to answer personal questions. Most of these problems can be minimized, however, if a skilled researcher composes the questionnaire.

For a questionnaire to fulfill a researcher's purposes, the questions must meet the basic criteria of *relevance* and *accuracy*. To achieve these ends, a researcher who is systematically planning a questionnaire's design will be required to make several decisions—typically, but not necessarily, in the following order:

1. What should be asked?
2. How should questions be phrased?
3. In what sequence should the questions be arranged?
4. What questionnaire layout will best serve the research objectives?
5. How should the questionnaire be pretested? Does the questionnaire need to be revised?

This chapter provides guidelines for answering each question.

TOTHEPOINT

How often misused words generate misleading thoughts.

—Herbert Spencer

What Should Be Asked?

Certain decisions made during the early stages of the research process will influence the questionnaire design. The preceding chapters stressed good problem definition and clear research questions. This leads to specific research hypotheses that, in turn, clearly indicate what must be measured. Different types of questions may be better at measuring certain things than are others. In addition, the communication medium used for data collection—that is, telephone interview, personal interview, or self-administered questionnaire—must be determined. This decision is another forward linkage that influences the structure and content of the questionnaire. The specific questions to be asked will be a function of the previous decisions.

The latter stages of the research process will have an important impact on questionnaire wording. When designing the questionnaire, for instance the researcher should consider the types of statistical analysis that will be conducted.

Questionnaire Relevancy

A questionnaire is *relevant* to the extent that all information collected addresses a research question that will help the decision maker address the current marketing problem. Asking a wrong question or an irrelevant question is a common pitfall. If the marketing task is to pinpoint store image problems, questions asking for political opinions may be irrelevant. The researcher should be specific about data needs and have a rationale for each item requesting information. Irrelevant questions are more than a nuisance because they make the survey needlessly long. In a study where two samples of the same group of businesses received either a one-page or a three-page questionnaire, the response rate was nearly twice as high for the one-page survey.[2]

Conversely, many researchers, after conducting surveys, find that they omitted some important questions. Therefore, when planning the questionnaire design, researchers must think about possible omissions. Is information on the relevant demographic and psychographic variables being collected? Would certain questions help clarify the answers to other questions? Will the results of the study provide the answer to the marketing manager's problem?

Questionnaire Accuracy

Once a researcher decides what should be asked, the criterion of accuracy becomes the primary concern. *Accuracy* means that the information is reliable and valid. While experienced researchers generally believe that questionnaires should use simple, understandable, unbiased, unambiguous, and nonirritating words, no step-by-step procedure for ensuring accuracy in question writing can be generalized across projects. Obtaining accurate answers from respondents depends strongly on the researcher's ability to design a questionnaire that will facilitate recall and motivate respondents to cooperate. Respondents tend to be more cooperative when the subject of the research interests them. When questions are not lengthy, difficult to answer, or ego threatening, there is a higher probability of obtaining unbiased answers.

Question wording and sequence also substantially influence accuracy, which can be particularly challenging when designing a survey for technical audiences. The Department of the Treasury commissioned a survey of insurance companies to evaluate their offering of terrorism insurance as required by the government's terrorism reinsurance program. But industry members complained that the survey misused terms such as "contract" and "high risk," which have precise meanings for insurers, and asked for policy information "to date," without specifying which date. These questions caused confusion and left room for interpretation, calling the survey results into question.[3]

How Should Questions Be Phrased?

There are many ways to phrase questions, and many standard question formats have been developed in previous research studies. This section presents a classification of question types and provides some helpful guidelines for writing questions.

Open-Ended Response versus Fixed-Alternative Questions

Two basic types of questions can be identified based on the amount of freedom respondents have in answering. Thus, they call for responses that are either open-ended or closed (from a fixed set of choices).

Open-ended response questions pose some problem or topic and ask respondents to answer in their own words. If the question is asked in a personal interview, the interviewer may probe for more information, as in the following examples:

What names of local banks can you think of offhand?
What comes to mind when you look at this advertisement?
In what way, if any, could this product be changed or improved? I'd like you to tell me anything you can think of, no matter how minor it seems.
What things do you like most about Federal Express's service?
Why do you buy more of your clothing in Nordstrom than in other stores?
How can our stores better serve your needs?
Please tell me anything at all that you remember about the BMW commercial you saw last night.

Open-ended response questions
Questions that pose some problem and ask respondents to answer in their own words.

**Fixed-alternative
questions**
Questions in which respondents
are given specific, limited-
alternative responses and
asked to choose the one closest
to their own viewpoint.

Open-ended response questions are free-answer questions. They may be contrasted with **fixed-alternative questions**—sometimes called *closed questions*—which give respondents specific limited-alternative responses and ask them to choose the one closest to their own viewpoints. For example

Did you use any commercial feed or supplement for livestock or poultry in 2006?

- *Yes*
- *No*

As compared with ten years ago, would you say that the quality of most products made in Japan is higher, about the same, or not as good?

- *Higher*
- *About the same*
- *Not as good*

Do you think the Renewable Energy Partnership Program has affected your business?

- *Yes, for the better*
- *Yes, for the worse*
- *Not especially*

In which type of bookstore is it easier for you to shop—a regular bookstore or a bookstore on the Internet?

- *Regular bookstore*
- *Internet bookstore*

How much of your shopping for clothes and household items do you do in wholesale club stores?

- *All of it*
- *Most of it*
- *About one-half of it*
- *About one-quarter of it*
- *Less than one-quarter of it*

USING OPEN-ENDED RESPONSE QUESTIONS

Open-ended response questions are most beneficial when the researcher is conducting exploratory research, especially when the range of responses is not known. Such questions can be used to learn which words and phrases people spontaneously give to the free-response question. Respondents are free to answer with whatever is uppermost in their minds. By obtaining free and uninhibited responses, the researcher may find some unanticipated reaction toward the product. Such responses will reflect the flavor of the language that people use in talking about goods or services and thus may provide a source of new ideas for advertising copywriting. Also, open-ended response questions are valuable at the beginning of an interview. They are good first questions because they allow respondents to warm up to the questioning process.

The cost of administering open-ended response questions is substantially higher than that of administering fixed-alternative questions because the job of editing, coding, and analyzing the data is quite extensive. As each respondent's answer is somewhat unique, there is some difficulty in categorizing and summarizing the answers. The process requires that an editor go over a sample of questions to develop a classification scheme. This scheme is then used to code all answers according to the classification scheme.

Another potential disadvantage of the open-ended response question is the possibility that interviewer bias will influence the answer. While most interviewer instructions state that answers are to be recorded verbatim, rarely does even the best interviewer get every word spoken by the respondent. Interviewers have a tendency to take shortcuts. When this occurs, the interviewer may well introduce error because the final answer may reflect a combination of the respondent's and interviewer's ideas.

Also, articulate individuals tend to give longer answers to open-ended response questions. Such respondents often are better educated and from higher income groups and therefore may not be representative of the entire population, and yet they may give a large share of the responses.

USING FIXED-ALTERNATIVE QUESTIONS

In contrast, fixed-alternative questions require less interviewer skill, take less time, and are easier for the respondent to answer. This is because answers to closed questions are classified into standardized groupings prior to data collection. Standardizing alternative responses to a question provides comparability of answers, which facilitates coding, tabulating, and ultimately interpreting the data.

However, when a researcher is unaware of the potential responses to a question, fixed-alternative questions obviously cannot be used. If the researcher assumes what the responses will be but is in fact wrong, he or she will have no way of knowing the extent to which the assumption was incorrect. Sometimes this type of error comes to light after the questionnaire has been used. Researchers found cross-cultural misunderstandings in a survey of mothers called the Preschooler Feeding Questionnaire. By talking to a group of African-American mothers, a researcher at the University of Chicago determined that they had experience with encouraging children to eat more and using food to calm children, but they used different language for these situations than the questionnaire used, so they misinterpreted some questions.[4]

Unanticipated alternatives emerge when respondents believe that closed answers do not adequately reflect their feelings. They may make comments to the interviewer or write additional answers on the questionnaire indicating that the exploratory research did not yield a complete array of responses. After the fact, little can be done to correct a closed question that does not provide enough alternatives. Therefore, a researcher may find exploratory research with open-ended responses valuable before writing a descriptive questionnaire. The researcher should strive to ensure that there are sufficient response choices to include almost all possible answers.

Respondents may check off obvious alternatives, such as price or durability, if they do not see the choice they would prefer. Also, a fixed-alternative question may tempt respondents to check an answer that is more prestigious or socially acceptable than the true answer. Rather than stating that they do not know why they chose a given product, they may select an alternative among those presented, or as a matter of convenience, they may select a given alternative rather than think of the most correct response.

Most questionnaires mix open-ended and closed questions. As we have discussed, each form has unique benefits. In addition, a change of pace can eliminate respondent boredom and fatigue.

Types of Fixed-Alternative Questions

Earlier in the chapter a variety of fixed-alternative questions were presented. We will now identify and categorize the various types.

The **simple-dichotomy (dichotomous-alternative) question** requires the respondent to choose one of two alternatives. The answer can be a simple "yes" or "no" or a choice between "this" and "that." For example:

Did you make any long-distance calls last week?

☐ *Yes*   ☐ *No*

Several types of questions provide the respondent with *multiple-choice alternatives*. The **determinant-choice question** requires the respondent to choose one—and only one—response from among several possible alternatives. For example:

Please give us some information about your flight. In which section of the aircraft did you sit?

• *First class*
• *Business class*
• *Coach class*

Simple-dichotomy (dichotomous-alternative) question
A fixed-alternative question that requires the respondent to choose one of two alternatives.

Determinant-choice question
A fixed-alternative question that requires the respondent to choose one response from among multiple alternatives.

Frequency-determination question
A fixed-alternative question that asks for an answer about general frequency of occurrence.

The **frequency-determination question** is a determinant-choice question that asks for an answer about the general frequency of occurrence. For example:

How frequently do you watch the MTV television channel?

- *Every day*
- *5–6 times a week*
- *2–4 times a week*
- *Once a week*
- *Less than once a week*
- *Never*

Attitude rating scales, such as the Likert scale, semantic differential, Stapel scale, and so on, are also fixed-alternative questions. These scales were discussed in Chapter 10.

Checklist question
A fixed-alternative question that allows the respondent to provide multiple answers to a single question by checking off items.

The **checklist question** allows the respondent to provide multiple answers to a single question. The respondent indicates past experience, preference, and the like merely by checking off items. In many cases the choices are adjectives that describe a particular object. A typical checklist question might ask the following:

Please check which of the following sources of information about investments you regularly use, if any.

- *Personal advice of your broker(s)*
- *Brokerage newsletters*
- *Brokerage research reports*
- *Investment advisory service(s)*
- *Conversations with other investors*
- *Web page(s)*
- *None of these*
- *Other (please specify) _____*

A major problem in developing dichotomous or multiple-choice alternatives is the framing of the response alternatives. There should be no overlap among categories. Alternatives should be *mutually exclusive,* meaning only one dimension of an issue should be related to each alternative. The following listing of income groups illustrates a common error:

- *Under $15,000*
- *$15,000–$30,000*
- *$30,000–$55,000*
- *$55,000–$70,000*
- *Over $70,000*

How many people with incomes of $30,000 will be in the second group, and how many will be in the third group? Researchers have no way to determine the answer. Grouping alternatives without forethought about analysis is likely to diminish accuracy.

Also, few people relish being in the lowest category. To negate the potential bias caused by respondents' tendency to avoid an extreme category, researchers often include a category lower than the lowest expected answers.

Phrasing Questions for Self-Administered, Telephone, and Personal Interview Surveys

The means of data collection—telephone interview, personal interview, self-administered questionnaire—will influence the question format and question phrasing. In general, questions for mail, Internet, and telephone surveys must be less complex than those used in personal interviews. Questionnaires for telephone and personal interviews should be written in a conversational style. Exhibit 11.1 illustrates how a question may be revised for a different medium.

In a telephone survey about attitudes toward police services, the questionnaire not only asked about general attitudes, such as how much respondents trust their local police officers and whether the police are "approachable," "dedicated," and so on, but also provided basic scenarios to help

EXHIBIT 11.1
**Reducing Question
Complexity by Providing
Fewer Responses**

Mail Form:

How satisfied are you with your community?

1 Very satisfied
2 Quite satisfied
3 Somewhat satisfied
4 Slightly satisfied
5 Neither satisfied nor dissatisfied
6 Slightly dissatisfied
7 Somewhat dissatisfied
8 Quite dissatisfied
9 Very dissatisfied

Revised for Telephone:

How satisfied are you with your community? Would you say you are very satisfied, somewhat satisfied, neither satisfied nor dissatisfied, somewhat dissatisfied, or very dissatisfied?

Very satisfied	1
Somewhat satisfied	2
Neither satisfied nor dissatisfied	3
Somewhat dissatisfied	4
Very dissatisfied	5

Source: Don A. Dillman, *Mail and Telephone Surveys: The Total Design Method* (New York: John Wiley & Sons, 1978), p. 209. Reprinted with permission.

respondents put their expectations into words. For example, the interviewer asked respondents to imagine that someone had broken into their home and stolen items, and that the respondent called the police to report the crime. The interviewer asked how quickly or slowly the respondent expected the police to arrive.[5]

When a question is read aloud, remembering the alternative choices can be difficult. Consider the following question from a personal interview:

There has been a lot of discussion about the potential health risks to nonsmokers from tobacco smoke in public buildings, restaurants, and business offices. How serious a health threat to you personally is the inhaling of this secondhand smoke, often called passive smoking: *Is it a very serious health threat, somewhat serious, not too serious, or not serious at all?*

1. *Very serious*
2. *Somewhat serious*
3. *Not too serious*
4. *Not serious at all*
5. *(Don't know)*

The last portion of the question was a listing of the four alternatives that serve as answers. This listing at the end is often used in interviews to remind the respondent of the alternatives, since they are not presented visually. The fifth alternative, "Don't know," is in parentheses because, although the interviewer knows it is an acceptable answer, it is not read. The researcher only uses this response when the respondent truly cannot provide an answer.

The data collection technique also influences the layout of the questionnaire. Layout will be discussed later in the chapter.

The Art of Asking Questions

No hard-and-fast rules determine how to develop a questionnaire. Fortunately, research experience has yielded some guidelines that help prevent the most common mistakes.

TOTHEPOINT

I don't know the rules of grammar. . . . If you're trying to persuade people to do something, or buy something, it seems to me you should use their language, the language they use every day, the language in which they think. We try to write in the vernacular.

—David Ogilvy

Avoid Complexity: Use Simple, Conversational Language

Words used in questionnaires should be readily understandable to all respondents. The researcher usually has the difficult task of adopting the conversational language of people at the lower education levels without talking down to better-educated respondents. Remember, not all people have the vocabulary of a college graduate. Many consumers, for instance, have never gone beyond a high school education.

Respondents can probably tell an interviewer whether they are married, single, divorced, separated, or widowed, but providing their *marital status* may present a problem. The technical jargon of top corporate executives should be avoided when surveying retailers or industrial users. "Brand image," "positioning," "marginal analysis," and other corporate language may not have the same meaning for or even be understood by a store owner-operator in a retail survey. The vocabulary used in the following question from an attitude survey on social problems probably would confuse many respondents:

When effluents from a paper mill can be drunk and exhaust from factory smokestacks can be breathed, then humankind will have done a good job in saving the environment. . . . Don't you agree that what we want is zero toxicity: no effluents?

Besides being too long and confusing, this question is leading.

Avoid Leading and Loaded Questions

Leading question
A question that suggests or implies certain answers.

Leading and loaded questions are a major source of bias in question wording. A **leading question** suggests or implies certain answers. A study of the dry cleaning industry asked this question:

Many people are using dry cleaning less because of improved wash-and-wear clothes. How do you feel wash-and-wear clothes have affected your use of dry cleaning facilities in the past 4 years?

☐ *Use less*   ☐ *No change*   ☐ *Use more*

The potential "bandwagon effect" implied in this question threatens the study's validity. *Partial mention of alternatives* is a variation of this phenomenon:

Do small imported cars, such as Volkswagens, get better gas mileage than small U.S. cars?
How do you generally spend your free time, watching television or what?

Loaded question
A question that suggests a socially desirable answer or is emotionally charged.

A **loaded question** suggests a socially desirable answer or is emotionally charged. Consider the following question from a survey about media influence on cooking and home-decorating behavior:[6]

What most influences you to buy food equipment?

- *My own need for equipment at the time*
- *Salesperson at store*
- *Food magazines*
- *Food shows on TV*
- *Internet food sites*
- *Family or friends*
- *Food/dining section of newspaper*
- *Other*
- *I rarely/never buy food preparation equipment*

Over half the respondents chose the first alternative. Although this question is not emotionally loaded, many people could be reluctant to say they are swayed by the media rather than making purchases out of their own, independently experienced need.

A television station produced the following 10-second spot asking for viewer feedback:

We are happy when you like programs on Channel 7. We are sad when you dislike programs on Channel 7. Write us and let us know what you think of our programming.

Few people wish to make others sad. This question is likely to elicit only positive comments.

RESEARCHSNAPSHOT

What to Do with the Clubhouse?

Mathematician Jennifer Lewis Priestley helps the managers of golf and country clubs collect and interpret data. One club showed her a member survey containing the following question:

We need to make some decisions about our clubhouse. The clubhouse itself is too small and requires substantial physical improvement, and it's been a long time since we undertook a major redecorating project. Do you favor

a. *remodeling the current clubhouse?*
b. *building a new clubhouse?*
c. *doing nothing?*

The wording of the question and the answer choices are biased in favor of action. The question criticizes the current clubhouse and places the question in the context of "a long time since we

undertook a major redecorating project." To select choice *c*, the respondent would have to disregard the premise of the question.

To eliminate the bias and include neutral wording so that the responses could more accurately represent the members' opinions, Priestley recommended some changes:

Considering the current clubhouse, which of the following statements most closely reflects your views?

a. *The current clubhouse should remain the same.*
b. *The current clubhouse should be remodeled (size will remain the same).*
c. *The current clubhouse should be remodeled and expanded.*
d. *The club needs a new clubhouse (current clubhouse torn down).*

Source: Based on Jennifer Lewis Priestley, "Determining What Your Marketing Members Want," Club Management, October 2004, downloaded from Info-Trac at http://infotrac.galegroup.com.

©JEFF GREENBERG/PHOTOEDIT

Certain answers to questions are more socially desirable than others. For example, a truthful answer to the following classification question might be painful:

Where did you rank academically in your high school graduating class?

- *Top quarter*
- *2nd quarter*
- *3rd quarter*
- *4th quarter*

When taking personality or psychographic tests, respondents frequently can interpret which answers are most socially acceptable even if those answers do not portray their true feelings. For example, which are the socially desirable answers to the following questions on a self-confidence scale?

I feel capable of handling myself in most social situations.

☐ *Agree*   ☐ *Disagree*

I seldom fear my actions will cause others to have low opinions of me.

☐ *Agree*   ☐ *Disagree*

Invoking the status quo is a form of loading that results in bias because most people tend to resist change.[7] An experiment conducted in the early days of polling illustrates the unpopularity of change.[8] Comparable samples of respondents were simultaneously asked two questions about the presidential succession. One sample was asked, **"Would you favor or oppose adding a law to the Constitution preventing a president from succeeding himself more than once?"** The other sample was asked, **"Would you favor or oppose changing the Constitution in order to prevent a president from succeeding himself more than once?"** Fifty percent of respondents answered negatively to the first question. For the second question, 65 percent of respondents answered negatively. Thus, the public would rather add to than change the Constitution.

Asking respondents "how often" they use a product or visit a store leads them to generalize about their habits, because there usually is some variance in their behavior. In generalizing, a person is likely to portray an *ideal* behavior rather than an *average* behavior. For instance, brushing your teeth after each meal may be ideal, but busy people may skip a brushing or two. An introductory **counterbiasing statement** or preamble to a question that reassures respondents that their "embarrassing" behavior is not abnormal may yield truthful responses:

Some people have the time to brush three times daily but others do not. How often did you brush your teeth yesterday?

If a question embarrasses the respondent, it may elicit no answer or a biased response. This is particularly true with respect to personal or classification data such as income or education. The problem may be mitigated by introducing the section of the questionnaire with a statement such as this:

To help classify your answers, we'd like to ask you a few questions. Again, your answers will be kept in strict confidence.

A question statement may be leading because it is phrased to reflect either the negative or the positive aspects of an issue. To control for this bias, the wording of attitudinal questions may be reversed for 50 percent of the sample. This **split-ballot technique** is used with the expectation that two alternative phrasings of the same question will yield a more accurate total response than will a single phrasing. For example, in a study on small-car buying behavior, one-half of a sample of imported-car purchasers received a questionnaire in which they were asked to agree or disagree with the statement **"Small U.S. cars are cheaper to maintain than small imported cars."** The other half of the import-car owners received a questionnaire in which the statement read **"Small imported cars are cheaper to maintain than small U.S. cars."**

Avoid Ambiguity: Be as Specific as Possible

Items on questionnaires often are ambiguous because they are too general. Consider such indefinite words as *often, occasionally, regularly, frequently, many, good,* and *poor.* Each of these words has many different meanings. For one consumer *frequent* reading of *Fortune* magazine may be reading six or seven issues a year. Another consumer may think reading two issues a year is frequent.

Questions such as the following one, used in a study measuring the reactions of consumers to a television boycott, should be interpreted with care:

Please indicate the statement that best describes your family's television viewing during the boycott of Channel 7.

- *We did* not *watch any television programs on Channel 7.*
- *We watched* hardly any *television programs on Channel 7.*
- *We occasionally watched television programs on Channel 7.*
- *We frequently watched television programs on Channel 7.*

Some marketing scholars have suggested that the rate of diffusion of an innovation is related to the perception of product attributes such as *divisibility,* which refers to the extent to which the innovation may be tried or tested on a limited scale.[9] An empirical attempt to test this theory using semantic differentials was a disaster. Pretesting found that the bipolar adjectives *divisible–not divisible* were impossible for consumers to understand because they did not have the theory in mind as a frame of reference. A revision of the scale used these bipolar adjectives:

Testable ____ ____ ____ ____ ____ ____ *Not testable*
(sample use possible)   *(sample use not possible)*

However, the question remained ambiguous because the meaning was still unclear.

A brewing industry study on point-of-purchase advertising (store displays) asked:

What degree of durability do you prefer in your point-of-purchase advertising?

- *Permanent (lasting more than 6 months)*
- *Semipermanent (lasting from 1 to 6 months)*
- *Temporary (lasting less than 1 month)*

Counterbiasing statement
An introductory statement or preamble to a potentially embarrassing question that reduces a respondent's reluctance to answer by suggesting that certain behavior is not unusual.

Split-ballot technique
Using two alternative phrasings of the same question for respective halves of a sample to elicit a more accurate total response than would a single phrasing.

Here the researchers clarified the terms *permanent, semipermanent,* and *temporary* by defining them for the respondent. However, the question remained somewhat ambiguous. Beer marketers often use a variety of point-of-purchase devices to serve different purposes—in this case, what is the purpose? In addition, analysis was difficult because respondents were merely asked to indicate a preference rather than a *degree* of preference. Thus, the meaning of a question may not be clear because the frame of reference is inadequate for interpreting the context of the question.

A student research group asked this question:

What media do you rely on most?

- *Television*
- *Radio*
- *Internet*
- *Newspapers*

This question is ambiguous because it does not ask about the content of the media. "Rely on most" for what—news, sports, entertainment?

Avoid Double-Barreled Items

A question covering several issues at once is referred to as a **double-barreled question** and should always be avoided. Making the mistake of asking two questions rather than one is easy—for example, **"Please indicate your degree of agreement with the following statement: 'Wholesalers and retailers are responsible for the high price of meat.'"** Which intermediaries are responsible, the wholesalers or the retailers? When multiple questions are asked in one question, the results may be exceedingly difficult to interpret. Consider the following question from a magazine's survey entitled "How Do You Feel about Being a Woman?":

Double-barreled question
A question that may induce bias because it covers two issues at once.

Between you and your husband, who does the housework (cleaning, cooking, dishwashing, laundry) over and above that done by any hired help?

- *I do all of it.*
- *I do almost all of it.*
- *I do over half of it.*
- *We split the work fifty-fifty.*
- *My husband does over half of it.*

The answers to this question do not tell us if the wife cooks and the husband washes the dishes.

A survey by a consumer-oriented library asked,

Are you satisfied with the present system of handling "closed-reserve" and "open-reserve" readings? (Are enough copies available? Are the required materials ordered promptly? Are the borrowing regulations adequate for students' use of materials?)

☐ *Yes*   ☐ *No*

A respondent may feel torn between a "yes" to one part of the question and a "no" to another part. The answer to this question does not tell the researcher which problem or combination of problems concerns the library user.

The following comment offers good advice regarding double-barreled questions:

Generally speaking, it is hard enough to get answers to one idea at a time without complicating the problem by asking what amounts to two questions at once. If two ideas are to be explored, they deserve at least two questions. Since question marks are not rationed, there is little excuse for the needless confusion that results [from] the double-barreled question.[10]

Avoid Making Assumptions

Consider the following question:

Should Macy's continue its excellent gift-wrapping program?

☐ *Yes*   ☐ *No*

RESEARCHSNAPSHOT

Who's *Really* Doing the Housework?

Married women have been a large part of the workforce for decades, but wives continue to complain that when both spouses hold jobs, women bear the heavier responsibility for housework. Researchers have recently considered whether the problem is one of fairness or misperception.

Some evidence suggests that the difference in estimates depends partly on data gathering. First, it matters whom the researchers question and when they ask. If the study asks men and women to recall how they used their time at home, both groups tend to overestimate the time they devote to housework.

Also, defining time spent on housework turns out to be more complex than you might guess. Why? People often combine activities. For example, someone might grab an armload of dirty clothes to shove into the washing machine on the way to the den to use the computer. Is that housework?

Detailed data from the long-term Sloan 500 Family Study provide some insights. This study used the Experi-ence Sampling Method (ESM) to overcome problems associated with asking people to remember how they used their time. With ESM, participants wear programmed wristwatches that beep at randomly chosen times. Whenever the watch beeps, participants are supposed to answer a short questionnaire indicating what their primary and secondary activities are and what they are thinking about at that time. With regard to housework, researchers found that if they count time spent on housework as either a primary or secondary activity, the overreporting of housework time shrinks. If the definition of housework is further expanded to include time spent thinking about it—not necessarily procrastinating, but maybe planning or managing household tasks—the overreporting shrinks again. The way housework is defined also affects the size of the gap between husbands' and wives' contributions.

Source: Based on Yun-Suk Lee and Linda J. Waite, "Husbands' and Wives' Time Spent on Housework: A Comparison of Measures," Journal of Marriage and Family 67(2) (2005): 328–36, abstract downloaded from OCLC FirstSearch, http://firstsearch.oclc.org; Barbara Schneider and Linda Waite, "Timely and Timeless: Working Parents and Their Children," Conference on Work, Family, Health and Well-Being, Washington, DC, June 16–18, 2003, downloaded from Maryland Population Research Center Web site, http://www.popcenter.umd.edu; Alfred P. Sloan Center on Parents, Children and Work, "Overview of Center Research," http://www.sloanworkingfamilies.org, accessed March 8, 2006.

This question has a built-in assumption: that people believe the gift-wrapping program is excellent. By answering "yes," the respondent implies that the program is, in fact, excellent and that things are fine just as they are. When a respondent answers "no," he or she implies that the store should discontinue the gift wrapping. The researchers should not place the respondent in that sort of bind by including an implicit assumption in the question.

Another frequent mistake is assuming that the respondent had previously thought about an issue. For example, the following question appeared in a survey concerning Jack-in-the-Box: **"Do you think Jack-in-the-Box restaurants should consider changing their name?"** Respondents have not likely thought about this question beforehand. Most respondents answered the question even though they had no prior opinion concerning the name change. Research that induces people to express attitudes on subjects they do not ordinarily think about is meaningless.

Avoid Burdensome Questions That May Tax the Respondent's Memory

A simple fact of human life is that people forget. Researchers writing questions about past behavior or events should recognize that certain questions may make serious demands on the respondent's memory. Writing questions about prior events requires a conscientious attempt to minimize the problems associated with forgetting.

In many situations, respondents cannot recall the answer to a question. For example, a telephone survey conducted during the 24-hour period following the airing of the Super Bowl might establish whether the respondent watched the Super Bowl and then ask, "Do you recall any commercials on that program?" If the answer is positive, the interviewer might ask, "What brands were advertised?" These two questions measure *unaided recall,* because they give the respondent no clue as to the brand of interest.

If the researcher suspects that the respondent may have forgotten the answer to a question, he or she may rewrite the question in an *aided-recall* format—that is, in a format that provides a clue to help jog the respondent's memory. For instance, the question about an advertised beer in an aided-recall format might be "Do you recall whether there was a brand of beer advertised on that program?" or "I am going to read you a list of beer brand names. Can you pick out the name of the beer that was advertised on the program?" While aided recall is not as strong a test of attention or memory as unaided recall, it is less taxing to the respondent's memory.

Telescoping and squishing are two additional consequences of respondents' forgetting the exact details of their behavior. *Telescoping* occurs when respondents believe that past events happened more recently than they actually did. The opposite effect, *squishing,* occurs when respondents think that recent events took place longer ago than they really did. A solution to this problem may be to refer to a specific event that is memorable—for example, "How often have you gone to a sporting event since the World Series?" Because forgetting tends to increase over time, the question may concern a recent period: "How often did you watch HBO on cable television last week?" (During the editing stage, the results can be transposed to the appropriate time period.)

In situations in which "I don't know" or "I can't recall" is a meaningful answer, simply including a "don't know" response category may solve the question writer's problem.

What Is the Best Question Sequence?

The order of questions, or the question sequence, may serve several functions for the researcher. If the opening questions are interesting, simple to comprehend, and easy to answer, respondents' cooperation and involvement can be maintained throughout the questionnaire. Asking easy-to-answer questions teaches respondents their role and builds their confidence.

A mail survey among department store buyers drew an extremely poor return rate. A substantial improvement in response rate occurred, however, when researchers added some introductory questions seeking opinions on pending legislation of great importance to these buyers. Respondents completed all the questions, not only those in the opening section.

In their attempt to "warm up" respondents toward the questionnaire, student researchers frequently ask demographic or classificatory questions at the beginning. This generally is not advisable, because asking for personal information such as income level or education may embarrass or threaten respondents. Asking potentially embarrassing questions at the middle or end of the questionnaire usually is better, after rapport has been established between respondent and interviewer.

Order bias can result from a particular answer's position in a set of answers or from the sequencing of questions. In political elections in which candidates lack high visibility, such as elections for county commissioners and judges, the first name listed on the ballot often receives the highest percentage of votes. For this reason, many election boards print several ballots so that each candidate's name appears in every possible position on the ballot.

Order bias
Bias caused by the influence of earlier questions in a questionnaire or by an answer's position in a set of answers.

Order bias can also distort survey results. For example, suppose a questionnaire's purpose is to measure levels of awareness of several charitable organizations. If Big Brothers and Big Sisters is always mentioned first, the American Red Cross second, and the American Cancer Society third, Big Brothers and Big Sisters may receive an artificially high awareness rating because respondents are prone to yea-saying (by indicating awareness of the first item in the list).

Asking specific questions before asking about broader issues is a common cause of order bias. For example, bias may arise if questions about a specific clothing store are asked prior to those

RESEARCHSNAPSHOT

What Citizens (Don't) Know about Climate Change

Climate change as a result of global warming has frequently been featured in the news, especially in stories related to science and technology. Scientists at the Massachusetts Institute of Technology's Laboratory for Energy and the Environment (LFEE) have dedicated themselves to researching a variety of approaches to slow down climate change. The scientists recognize, however, that these innovations have a cost, so their use will depend partly on public interest in the problem and demand for solutions. As a result, LFEE conducted an online survey, which it sent to a national panel.

One challenge for the study was that before researchers could gauge citizens' willingness to pay for new technologies, they needed to know whether most people were even aware of the energy alternatives. They asked, "Have you heard of or read about any of the following in the past year? Check all that apply," followed by a list of ten technologies for mitigating climate change. Only three technologies—more efficient cars, solar energy, and nuclear energy—were checked by a majority of respondents. Seventeen percent admitted to not hearing

about any of the technologies, a number that the researchers acknowledge may be too low, because some people might want to appear better informed than they are.

Perhaps lack of interest is a factor as well. Another question gave respondents a list of twenty-two issues and asked them to choose the most important. The environment was ranked thirteenth. In a question asking respondents to rank the importance of specific environmental problems, "global warming" was in sixth place, trailing water pollution, destruction of ecosystems, and toxic waste.

All of these questions presented respondents with a list of alternatives to check. What precautions should the survey have taken to minimize the chance that the order of alternatives influenced respondents' opinions that some items were familiar or important?

Source: Based on "U.S. Public in the Dark on Climate Change Issues," Bulletin of the American Meteorological Society 86(6) (June 2005), downloaded from FirstSearch at http://firstsearch.oclc.org; and Howard J. Herzog, Thomas E. Curry, David M. Reiner, and Stephen Ansolabehere, "Climate Change Poorly Understood, Not a High Priority, Shows MIT Public Survey," *Energy and Environment* (Massachusetts Institute of Technology Laboratory for Energy and the Environment), December 2004, pp. 7–8, accessed at http://lfee.mit.edu.

©LESTER LEFKOWITZ/CORBIS

---

concerning the general criteria for selecting a clothing store. Suppose a respondent indicates in the first portion of a questionnaire that she shops at a store where parking needs to be improved. Later in the questionnaire, to avoid appearing inconsistent, she may state that parking is less important than she really believes it is. Specific questions may thus influence the more general ones. As a result, it is advisable to ask general questions before specific questions to obtain the freest of open-ended responses. This procedure, known as the **funnel technique**, allows the researcher to understand the respondent's frame of reference before asking more specific questions about the level of the respondent's information and the intensity of his or her opinions.

Funnel technique
Asking general questions before specific questions in order to obtain unbiased responses.

Consider how later answers might be biased by previous questions in this questionnaire on environmental pollution:

Circle the number on the following table that best expresses your feelings about the severity of each environmental problem:

Problem	Not a Problem				Very Severe Problem
Air pollution from automobile exhausts	1	2	3	4	5
Air pollution from open burning	1	2	3	4	5
Air pollution from industrial smoke	1	2	3	4	5
Air pollution from foul odors	1	2	3	4	5
Noise pollution from airplanes	1	2	3	4	5
Noise pollution from cars, trucks, motorcycles	1	2	3	4	5
Noise pollution from industry	1	2	3	4	5

Not surprisingly, researchers found that the responses to the air pollution questions were highly correlated—in fact, almost identical.

With attitude scales, there also may be an *anchoring effect*. The first concept measured tends to become a comparison point from which subsequent evaluations are made. Randomization of items on a questionnaire susceptible to the anchoring effect helps minimize order bias.

A related problem is bias caused by the order of alternatives on closed questions. To avoid this problem, the order of these choices should be rotated if producing alternative forms of the questionnaire is possible. However, marketing researchers rarely print alternative questionnaires to eliminate problems resulting from order bias. A more common practice is to pencil in Xs or check marks on printed questionnaires to indicate where the interviewer should start a series of repetitive questions. For example, the capitalized phrases in the following question provide instructions to the interviewer to "rotate" brands, starting with the one checked:

I would like to determine how likely you would be to buy certain brands of candy in the future. Let's start with (X'ED BRAND). (RECORD BELOW UNDER APPROPRIATE BRAND. REPEAT QUESTIONS FOR ALL REMAINING BRANDS.)

Start Here:	*( ) Mounds*	*(X) Almond Joy*	*( ) Snickers*
Definitely would buy	−1	−1	−1
Probably would buy	−2	−2	−2
Might or might not buy	−3	−3	−3
Probably would not buy	−4	−4	−4
Definitely would not buy	−5	−5	−5

One advantage of Internet surveys is the ability to reduce order bias by having the computer randomly order questions and/or response alternatives. With complete randomization, question order is random and respondents see response alternatives in different random positions.

Asking a question that does not apply to the respondent or that the respondent is not qualified to answer may be irritating or cause a biased response because the respondent wishes to please the interviewer or to avoid embarrassment. Including a **filter question** minimizes the chance of asking questions that are inapplicable. Asking **"Where do you generally have check-cashing problems in Springfield?"** may elicit a response even though the respondent has had no check-cashing problems. He or she may wish to please the interviewer with an answer. A filter question such as **"Do you ever have a problem cashing a check in Springfield? — Yes — No"** would screen out the people who are not qualified to answer.

Filter question
A question that screens out respondents who are not qualified to answer a second question.

Another form of filter question, the **pivot question**, can be used to obtain income information and other data that respondents may be reluctant to provide. For example,

Pivot question
A filter question used to determine which version of a second question will be asked.

"Is your total family income over or under $50,000?" IF UNDER, ASK, "Is it over or under $25,000?" IF OVER, ASK, "Is it over or under $75,000?"

Under $25,000	*$50,001–$75,000*
$25,001–$50,000	*Over $75,000*

Exhibit 11.2 gives an example of a flowchart plan for a questionnaire. Structuring the order of the questions so that they are logical will help to ensure the respondent's cooperation and eliminate confusion or indecision. The researcher maintains legitimacy by making sure that the respondent can comprehend the relationship between a given question (or section of the questionnaire) and the overall purpose of the study. Furthermore, a logical order may aid the individual's memory. Transitional comments explaining the logic of the questionnaire may ensure that the respondent continues. Here are two examples:

We have been talking so far about general shopping habits in this city. Now I'd like you to compare two types of grocery stores—regular supermarkets and grocery departments in wholesale club stores.

So that I can combine your answers with those of other farmers who are similar to you, I need some personal information about you. Your answers to these questions—as to all of the others you've answered—are confidential, and you will never be identified to anyone without your permission. Thanks for your help so far. If you'll answer the remaining questions, it will help me analyze all your answers.

EXHIBIT 11.2 **Flow of Questions to Determine the Level of Prompting Required to Stimulate Recall**

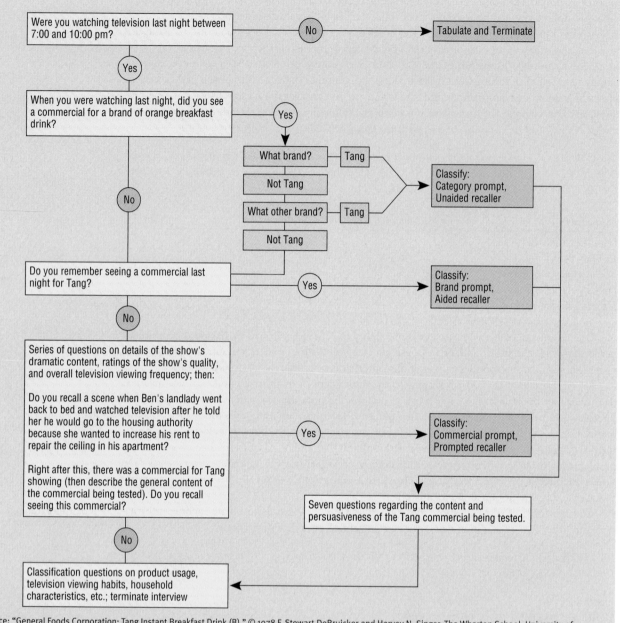

Source: "General Foods Corporation: Tang Instant Breakfast Drink (B)," © 1978 F. Stewart DeBruicker and Harvey N. Singer, The Wharton School, University of Pennsylvania. Reprinted with permission.

What Is the Best Layout?

Good layout and physical attractiveness are crucial in mail, Internet, and other self-administered questionnaires. For different reasons, a good layout in questionnaires designed for personal and telephone interviews is also important.

Traditional Questionnaires

Exhibit 11.3 shows a page from a telephone questionnaire. The layout is neat and attractive, and the instructions for the interviewer (all boldface capital letters) are easy to follow. The responses "It

EXHIBIT 11.3 **Layout of a Page from a Telephone Questionnaire**

5. Now I'm going to read you some types of professions. For each one, please tell me whether you think the work that profession does, on balance, has a very positive impact on society, a somewhat positive impact, a somewhat negative impact, a very negative impact, or not much impact either way on society. First . . . **(START AT X'D ITEM. CONTINUE DOWN AND UP THE LIST UNTIL ALL ITEMS HAVE BEEN READ AND RATED.)**

(DO NOT READ)

START HERE:	Very Positive Impact	Some-what Positive Impact	Some-what Negative Impact	Very Negative Impact	Not Much Impact	It Depends	Refused	Don't Know
[ ] Members of Congress	1	2	3	4	5	0	X	Y (24)
[ ] Business executives	1	2	3	4	5	0	X	Y (25)
[ ] Physicians	1	2	3	4	5	0	X	Y (26)
[ ] Political pollsters—that is, people who conduct surveys for public officials or political political candidates	1	2	3	4	5	0	X	Y (27)
[ ] Researchers in the media—that is, people in media such as television, newspapers, magazines, and radio, who conduct surveys about issues later reported in the media	1	2	3	4	5	0	X	Y (28)
[ ] Telemarketers—that is, people who sell products or services over the phone	1	2	3	4	5	0	X	Y (29)
[ ] Used car salesmen	1	2	3	4	5	0	X	Y (30)
[ ] Market researchers—that is, people who work for commercial research firms who conduct surveys to see what the public thinks about certain kinds of consumer products or services	1	2	3	4	5	0	X	Y (31)
[ ] Biomedical researchers	1	2	3	4	5	0	X	Y (32)
[ ] Public-opinion researchers—that is, people who work for commercial research firms who conduct surveys to see what the public thinks about important social issues	1	2	3	4	5	0	X	Y (33)
[ ] College and university professors	1	2	3	4	5	0	X	Y (34)
[ ] Attorneys	1	2	3	4	5	0	X	Y (35)
[ ] Members of the clergy	1	2	3	4	5	0	X	Y (36)
[ ] Journalists	1	2	3	4	5	0	X	Y (37)

depends," "Refused," and "Don't Know" are enclosed in a box to indicate that these answers are acceptable but responses from the five-point scale are preferred.

Often rate of return can be increased by using money that might have been spent on an incentive to improve the attractiveness and quality of the questionnaire. Mail questionnaires should never be overcrowded. Margins should be of decent size, white space should be used to separate blocks of print, and the unavoidable columns of multiple boxes should be kept to a minimum. A question should not begin on one page and end on another page. Splitting questions may cause a respondent to read only part of a question, to pay less attention to answers on one of the pages, or to become confused.

Questionnaires should be designed to appear as short as possible. Sometimes it is advisable to use a booklet form of questionnaire rather than stapling a large number of pages together. In situations in which it is necessary to conserve space on the questionnaire or to facilitate data entry or tabulation of the data, a multiple-grid layout may be used. The **multiple-grid question** presents several similar questions and corresponding response alternatives arranged in a grid format. For example,

Multiple-grid question
Several similar questions arranged in a grid format.

Airlines often offer special fare promotions. On a vacation trip would you take a connecting flight instead of a nonstop flight if the connecting flight were longer?

	Yes	No	Not sure
One hour longer?	☐	☐	☐
Two hours longer?	☐	☐	☐
Three hours longer?	☐	☐	☐

Experienced researchers have found that the title of a questionnaire should be phrased carefully. In self-administered and mail questionnaires, a carefully constructed title may capture the respondent's interest, underline the importance of the research ("Nationwide Study of Blood Donors"), emphasize the interesting nature of the study ("Study of Internet Usage"), appeal to the respondent's ego ("Survey among Top Executives"), or emphasize the confidential nature of the study ("A Confidential Survey among . . . "). The researcher should take steps to ensure that the wording of the title will not bias the respondent in the same way that a leading question might.

By using several forms, special instructions, and other tricks of the trade, the researcher can design the questionnaire to facilitate the interviewer's job of following interconnected questions. Exhibits 11.4 and 11.5 illustrate portions of telephone and personal interview questionnaires. Note how the layout and easy-to-follow instructions for interviewers in Questions 1, 2, and 3 of Exhibit 11.4 help the interviewer follow the question sequence.

Instructions are often capitalized or printed in bold to alert the interviewer that it may be necessary to proceed in a certain way. For example, if a particular answer is given, the interviewer or respondent may be instructed to skip certain questions or go to a special sequence of questions. To facilitate coding, question responses should be precoded when possible, as in Exhibit 11.4.

Exhibit 11.5 illustrates some other useful techniques that are possible with personal interviews. Questions 3 and 6 instruct the interviewer to hand the respondent a card bearing a list of alternatives. Cards may help respondents grasp the intended meaning of the question and remember all the brand names or other items they are being asked about. Also, Questions 2, 3, and 6 instruct the interviewer that rating of the banks will start with the bank that has been checked in red pencil on the printed questionnaire. The name of the red-checked bank is not the same on every questionnaire. By rotating the order of the check marks, the researchers attempted to reduce order bias caused by respondents' tendency to react more favorably to the first set of questions.

Exhibit 11.6 illustrates a series of questions that includes a *skip question*. Either skip instructions or an arrow drawn pointing to the next question informs the respondent which question comes next.

Layout is extremely important when questionnaires are long or require the respondent to fill in a large amount of information. In many circumstances, using headings or subtitles to indicate groups of questions will help the respondent grasp the scope or nature of the questions to be asked. Thus, at a glance, the respondent can follow the logic of the questionnaire.

EXHIBIT 11.4 **Telephone Questionnaire with Skip Questions**

1. Did you take the car you had checked to the Standard Auto Repair Center for repairs?

    –1 Yes **(SKIP TO Q. 3)**   –2 No

2. **(IF NO, ASK:)** Did you have the repair work done?

    –1 Yes   –2 No

    ⬇   ⬇

1. Where was the repair work done? _____   1. Why didn't you have the car repaired?
   _____   _____

2. Why didn't you have the repair work done   _____
   at the Standard Auto Repair Center? _____   _____
   _____
   _____
   _____

3. **(IF YES TO Q. 1, ASK:)** How satisfied were you with the repair work? Were you . . .

    –1 Very satisfied

    –2 Somewhat satisfied

    –3 Somewhat dissatisfied

    –4 Very dissatisfied

    (IF SOMEWHAT OR VERY DISSATISFIED:) In what way were you dissatisfied?
    _____
    _____
    _____

4. **(ASK EVERYONE:)** Do you ever buy gas at the 95th Street Standard Center?

    –1 Yes   –2 No **(SKIP TO Q. 6)**

5. **(IF YES, ASK:)** How often do you buy gas there?

    –1 Always

    –2 Almost always

    –3 Most of the time

    –4 Part of the time

    –5 Hardly ever

6. Have you ever had your car washed there?

    –1 Yes   –2 No

7. Have you ever had an oil change or lubrication done there?

    –1 Yes   –2 No

Internet Questionnaires

Layout is also an important issue for questionnaires appearing on the Internet. A questionnaire on a website should be easy to use, flow logically, and have a graphic look and overall feel that motivate the respondent to cooperate from start to finish. Many of the guidelines for layout of paper questionnaires apply to Internet questionnaires. There are, however, some important differences.

EXHIBIT 11.5 **Personal Interview Questionnaire**

"Hello, my name is _____. I'm a Public Opinion Interviewer with Research Services, Inc. We're making an opinion survey about banks and banking, and I'd like to ask you . . ."

1. What are the names of local banks you can think of offhand? (INTERVIEWER: List names in order mentioned.)

a. _____

b. _____

c. _____

d. _____

e. _____

f. _____

g. _____

2. Thinking now about the experiences you have had with the different banks here in Boulder, have you ever talked to or done business with . . . (INTERVIEWER: Insert name of bank checked in red below.)

a. Are you personally acquainted with any of the employees or officers at _____?

b. (If YES) Who is that? _____

c. How long has it been since you have been inside _____?

(INTERVIEWER: Now go back and repeat 2–2c for all other banks listed.)

	(2) Talked		(2a and 2b) Know Employee Or Officer		(2c) Been in Bank in:				
	Yes	No	No	Name	Last Year	1–5	5-Plus	No	DK
Arapahoe National Bank	1	2	1	_____	1	2	3	4	5
First National Bank	1	2	1	_____	1	2	3	4	5
Boulder National Bank	1	2	1	_____	1	2	3	4	5
Security Bank	1	2	1	_____	1	2	3	4	5
United Bank of Boulder	1	2	1	_____	1	2	3	4	5
National State Bank	1	2	1	_____	1	2	3	4	5

3. (HAND BANK RATING CARD) On this card there are a number of contrasting phrases or statements—for example, "Large" and "Small." We'd like to know how you rate (NAME OF BANK CHECKED IN RED BELOW) in terms of these statements or phrases. Just for example, let's use the terms "fast service" and "slow service." If you were to rate a bank #1 on this scale, it would mean you find their service "very fast." On the other hand, a 7 rating would indicate you feel their service is "very slow," whereas a 4 rating means you don't think of them as being either "very fast" or "very slow." Are you ready to go ahead? Good! Tell me then how you would rate (NAME OF BANK CHECKED IN RED) in terms of each of the phrases or statements on that card. How about (READ NEXT BANK NAME)? . . . (INTERVIEWER: Continue on until respondent has evaluated all six banks.)

	Arapahoe National	First National	Boulder National	Security Bank	United Bank	National State
a. Service	_____	_____	_____	_____	_____	_____
b. Size	_____	_____	_____	_____	_____	_____
c. Business vs. Family	_____	_____	_____	_____	_____	_____
d. Friendliness	_____	_____	_____	_____	_____	_____
e. Big/Small Business	_____	_____	_____	_____	_____	_____
f. Rate of Growth	_____	_____	_____	_____	_____	_____
g. Modernness	_____	_____	_____	_____	_____	_____
h. Leadership	_____	_____	_____	_____	_____	_____
i. Loan Ease	_____	_____	_____	_____	_____	_____
j. Location	_____	_____	_____	_____	_____	_____
k. Hours	_____	_____	_____	_____	_____	_____
l. Ownership	_____	_____	_____	_____	_____	_____
m. Community Involvement	_____	_____	_____	_____	_____	_____

(continued)

EXHIBIT 11.5 **Personal Interview Questionnaire** (*continued*)

4. Suppose a friend of yours who has just moved to Boulder asked you to recommend a bank. Which local bank would you recommend? Why would you recommend that particular bank?

Arapahoe National	1
First National	2
Boulder National	3
Security Bank	4
United Bank of Boulder	5
National State Bank	6
Other (Specify) _____	
DK/Wouldn't	9

5. Which of the local banks do you think of as: (INTERVIEWER: Read red-checked item first, then read each of the other five.)

the newcomer's bank? _____

the student's bank? _____

the Personal Banker bank? _____

the bank where most C.U. faculty and staff bank? _____

the bank most interested in this community? _____

the most progressive bank? _____

6. Which of these financial institutions, if any, (HAND CARD 2) are you or any member of your immediate family who lives here in this home doing business with now?

Bank	1
Credit Union	2
Finance Company	3
Savings and Loan	4
Industrial Bank	5
None of these	6
DK/Not sure	7

(IF NONE, Skip to 19.)

7. If a friend asked you to recommend a place where he or she could get a loan with which to buy a home, which financial institution would you probably recommend? (INTERVIEWER: Probe for specific name.) Why would you recommend (INSTITUTION NAMED)?

Would Recommend: _____

_____

Wouldn't	0
DK/Not Sure	9

Source: Reprinted with permission from the Council of American Survey Research, http://www.casro.org.

With *graphical user interface (GUI) software,* the researcher can exercise control over the background, colors, fonts, and other visual features displayed on the computer screen so as to create an attractive and easy-to-use interface between the computer user and the Internet survey. GUI software allows the researcher to design questionnaires in which respondents click on the appropriate answer rather than having to type answers or codes.

EXHIBIT 11.6
Example of a Skip Question

1. If you had to buy a computer tomorrow, which of the following three types of computers do you think you would buy?

    1 Desktop—Go to Q. 3
    2 Laptop—Go to Q. 3
    3 Palm-sized (PDA)

2. (If "Palm-sized" on Q. 1, ask): What brand of computer do you think you would buy?

3. What is your age?

Researchers often use web publishing software, such as WebSurveyor, FrontPage, or Netscape Composer, to format a questionnaire so that they will know how it should appear online. Questionnaire publishing also is available through survey host sites such as www.zoomerang.com. However, several features of a respondent's computer may influence the appearance of an Internet questionnaire. For example, discrepancies between the designer's and the respondent's computer settings for screen configuration (e.g., 640×480 pixels versus 800×600 pixels) may result in questions not being fully visible on the respondent's screen, misaligned text, or other visual problems. The possibility that the questionnaire the researcher/designer constructs on his or her computer may look different from the questionnaire that appears on the respondent's computer should always be considered when designing Internet surveys. One sophisticated remedy is to use the first few questions on an Internet survey to ask about operating system, browser software, and other computer configuration issues so that the questionnaire that is delivered is as compatible as possible with the respondent's computer. A simpler solution is to limit the horizontal width of the questions to seventy characters or less, to decrease the likelihood of wrap-around text.

▣ LAYOUT ISSUES

Even if the questionnaire designer's computer and the respondents' computers are compatible, a web questionnaire designer should consider several layout issues. The first decision is whether the questionnaire will appear page by page, with individual questions on separate screens (web pages), or on a scrolling basis, with the entire questionnaire appearing on a single web page that the respondent scrolls from top to bottom. The *paging layout* (going from screen to screen) greatly facilitates skip patterns. Based on a respondent's answers to filter questions, the computer can automatically insert relevant questions on subsequent pages. If the entire questionnaire appears on one page (the *scrolling layout*), the display should advance smoothly, as if it were a piece of paper being moved up or down. The scrolling layout gives the respondent the ability to read any portion of the questionnaire at any time, but the absence of page boundaries can cause problems. For example, suppose a Likert scale consists of fifteen statements in a grid-format layout, with the response categories **Strongly Agree, Agree, Disagree,** and **Strongly Disagree** at the beginning of the questionnaire. Once the respondent has scrolled down beyond the first few statements, he or she may not be able to see both the statements at the end of the list and the response categories at the top of the grid simultaneously. Thus, avoiding the problems associated with splitting questions and response categories may be difficult with scrolling questionnaires.

When a scrolling questionnaire is long, category or section headings are helpful to respondents. It is also a good idea to provide links to the top and bottom parts of each section, so that users can navigate through the questionnaire without having to scroll through the entire document.[11]

Push button
In a dialog box on an Internet questionnaire, a small outlined area, such as a rectangle or an arrow, that the respondent clicks on to select an option or perform a function, such as submit.

Whether a web survey is page-by-page or scrolling format, a **push button** with a label should clearly describe the actions to be taken. For example, if the respondent is to go to the next page, a large arrow labeled "NEXT" might appear in color at the bottom of the screen.

Decisions must be made about the use of color, graphics, animation, sound, and other special features that the Internet makes possible. One point to remember is that, although sophisticated graphics are not a problem for people with very powerful computers, many respondents' computers are not powerful enough to deliver complex graphics at a satisfactory speed, if at all. A textured background, colored headings, and small graphics can make a questionnaire more interesting and appealing, but they may present problems for respondents with older computers and/or low-bandwidth Internet connections.

Status bar
In an Internet questionnaire, a visual indicator that tells the respondent what portion of the survey he or she has completed.

With a paper questionnaire, the respondent knows how many questions he or she must answer. Because many Internet surveys offer no visual clues about the number of questions to be asked, it is important to provide a **status bar** or some other visual indicator of questionnaire length. For example, including a partially filled rectangular box as a visual symbol and a statement such as "The status bar at top right indicates approximately what portion of the survey you have completed" increases the likelihood that the respondent will finish the entire sequence of questions. Exhibit 11.7 shows a question from an online survey that uses a simple and motivating design. The survey presents one question at a time for simplicity. So that respondents can see their progress toward the end of the questionnaire, a gauge in the upper right corner fills from left to right as the respondent proceeds from Start to Finish.

EXHIBIT 11.7

Question in an Online Screening Survey for Joining a Consumer Panel

Though your plans may change, approximately when do you plan to purchase or lease your next automobile? Please indicate both the year and month.

Start ▮ Finish

Select Year ⌄ Select Month ⌄

Next page

©2006 J.D. Power and Associates, The McGraw-Hill Companies, Inc. All Rights Reserved.

Source: J.D. Power and Associates, "JDPowerPanel," https://ia.jdpa.com/20/survey/onsurvey.phtml, accessed March 9, 2006.

An Internet questionnaire uses windows known as dialog boxes to display questions and record answers. Exhibit 11.8 portrays four common ways of displaying questions on a computer screen. Many Internet questionnaires require the respondent to activate his or her answer by clicking on the **radio button** for a response. Radio buttons work like push buttons on automobile radios: Clicking on an alternative response deactivates the first choice and replaces it with the new response. A **drop-down box**, such as the one shown in Exhibit 11.8, is a space-saving device that allows the researcher to provide a list of responses that are hidden from view until they are needed. A general statement, such as "Please select" or "Click here," is shown initially. Clicking on the downward-facing arrow makes the full range of choices appear. If the first choice in a list, such as "Strongly Agree," is shown while the other responses are kept hidden, the chance that response bias will occur is increased. Drop-down boxes may present a problem for individuals with minimal computer skills, as they may not know how to reveal hidden responses behind a drop-down menu or how to move from one option to another in a moving-bar menu.

Checklist questions may be followed by **check boxes**, several, none, or all of which may be checked by the respondent. **Open-ended boxes** are boxes in which respondents type their answers to open-ended questions. Open-ended boxes may be designed as *one-line text boxes* or *scrolling text boxes,* depending on the breadth of the expected answer. Of course, open-ended questions require that respondents have both the skill and the willingness to keyboard lengthy answers on the computer. Some open-ended boxes are designed so that respondents can enter numbers for frequency response, ranking, or rating questions. For example,

Below you will see a series of statements that might or might not describe how you feel about your career. Please rate each statement using a scale from 1 to 4, where 4 means "Totally Agree," 3 means "Somewhat Agree," 2 means "Somewhat Disagree," and 1 means "Totally Disagree." Please enter your numeric answer in the box provided next to each statement. Would you say that . . .

 A lack of business knowledge relevant to my field/career could hurt my career advancement.
 My career life is an important part of how I define myself.

Pop-up boxes are message boxes that can be used to highlight important information. For example, pop-up boxes may be use to provide a privacy statement, such as the following:

IBM would like your help in making our website easier to use and more effective. Choose to complete the survey now or not at all.

Clicking on Privacy Statement opens the following pop-up box:

Survey Privacy Statement
 This overall Privacy Statement verifies that IBM is a member of the TRUSTe program and is in compliance with TRUSTe principles. This survey is strictly for market research purposes. The information you provide will be used only to improve the overall content, navigation, and usability of ibm.com.

In some cases, respondents can learn more about how to use a particular scale or get a definition of a term by clicking on a link, which generates a pop-up box. One of the most common reasons for using pop-up boxes is *error trapping,* a topic discussed in the next section.

Radio button
In an Internet questionnaire, a circular icon, resembling a button, that activates one response choice and deactivates others when a respondent clicks on it.

Drop-down box
In an Internet questionnaire, a space-saving device that reveals responses when they are needed but otherwise hides them from view.

Check boxes
In an Internet questionnaire, small graphic boxes, next to answers, that a respondent clicks on to choose an answer; typically, a check mark or an **X** appears in the box when the respondent clicks on it.

Open-ended boxes
In an Internet questionnaire, boxes where respondents can type in their own answers to open-ended questions.

Pop-up boxes
In an Internet questionnaire, boxes that appear at selected points and contain information or instructions for respondents.

EXHIBIT 11.8
**Alternative Ways of
Displaying Internet Questions**

Radio button

Last month, did you purchase products or services over the Internet?

○ Yes

○ No

How familiar are you with Microsoft's Xbox video game player?

Know Extremely Well	Know Fairly Well	Know a Little	Know Just Name	Never Heard of
○	○	○	○	○

Drop-down box, closed position

In which country or region do you currently reside?

Click Here ▼

Drop-down box, open position

In which country or region do you currently reside?

Click Here ▼

Click Here
United States
Asia/Pacific (excluding Hawaii)
Africa
Australia or New Zealand
Canada
Europe
Latin America, South America, or Mexico
Middle East
Other

Check box

From which location(s) do you access the Internet? Select all that apply.
☐ Home
☐ Work
☐ Other Location

**Please indicate which of the following Web sites you have
ever visited or used. (CHOOSE ALL THAT APPLY.)**
☐ E*Trade's Web site
☐ Waterhouse's Web site
☐ Merrill Lynch's Web site
☐ Fidelity's Web site
☐ Schwab's Web site
☐ Powerstreet
☐ Yahoo! Finance
☐ Quicken.com
☐ Lycos Investing
☐ AOL's Personal Finance
☐ None of the above

Open-ended, one-line box

What company do you think is the most visible sponsor of sports?

Open-ended, scrolling text box

What can we do to improve our textbook?

▲

▼

Chapter 10 described graphic rating scales, which present respondents with a graphic continuum. On the Internet, researchers can take advantage of scroll bars or other GUI software features to make these scales easy to use. For example, the graphic continuum may be drawn as a measuring rod with a plus sign on one end and a minus sign on the other. The respondent then moves a small rectangle back and forth between the two ends of the scale to scroll to any point on the continuum. Scoring, as discussed in Chapter 10, is in terms of some measure of the length (millimeters) from one end of the graphic continuum to the point marked by the respondent.

Finally, researchers often include a customized thank-you page at the end of an Internet questionnaire, so that a brief thank-you note pops onto respondents' screens when they click on the Submit push button.[12]

SOFTWARE THAT MAKES QUESTIONNAIRES INTERACTIVE

Computer code can be written to make Internet questionnaires interactive and less prone to errors. The writing of software programs is beyond the scope of this discussion. However, several of the interactive functions that software makes possible should be mentioned here.

As discussed in Chapter 7, Internet software allows the branching off of questioning into two or more different lines, depending on a particular respondent's answer, and the skipping or filtering of questions. Questionnaire-writing software with Boolean skip and branching logic is readily available. Most of these programs have *hidden skip logic* so that respondents never see any evidence of skips. It is best if the questions the respondent sees flow in numerical sequence. However, some programs number all potential questions sequentially, and the respondent sees only the numbers on the questions he or she answers. Thus, a respondent may answer questions 1 through 11 and then next see a question numbered 15 because of the skip logic.

Software can systematically or randomly manipulate the questions a respondent sees. **Variable piping software** allows variables, such as answers from previous questions, to be inserted into unfolding questions. Other software can randomly rotate the order of questions, blocks of questions, and response alternatives from respondent to respondent.

Researchers can use software to control the flow of a questionnaire. Respondents can be blocked from backing up, or they can be allowed to stop in mid-questionnaire and come back later to finish. A questionnaire can be designed so that if the respondent fails to answer a question or answers it with an incorrect type of response, an immediate error message appears. This is called **error trapping**. With **forced answering software**, respondents cannot skip over questions as they do in mail surveys. The program will not let them continue if they fail to answer a question. The software may insert a boldfaced error message on the question screen or insert a pop-up box instructing the respondent how to continue. For example, if a respondent does not answer a question and tries to proceed to another screen, a pop-up box might present the following message:

You cannot leave a question blank. On questions without a "Not sure" or "Decline to answer" option, please choose the response that best represents your opinions or experiences.

The respondent must close the pop-up box and answer the question in order to proceed to the next screen.

Some designers include an **interactive help desk** in their web questionnaire so that respondents can solve problems they encounter in completing a questionnaire. A respondent might e-mail questions to the survey help desk or get live, interactive, real-time support via an online help desk.

Some respondents will leave the questionnaire website, prematurely terminating the survey. In many cases sending an e-mail message to these respondents at a later date, encouraging them to revisit the website, will persuade them to complete the questionnaire. Through the use of software and cookies, researchers can make sure that the respondent who revisits the website will be able to pick up at the point where he or she left off.

Once an Internet questionnaire has been designed, it is important to pretest it to ensure that it works with Internet Explorer, Netscape, AOL, WebTV, and other browsers. Some general-purpose programming languages, such as Java, do not always work with all browsers. Because different browsers have different peculiarities, a survey that works perfectly well with one may not function at all with another.[13]

Variable piping software
Software that allows variables to be inserted into an Internet questionnaire as a respondent is completing it.

Error trapping
Using software to control the flow of an Internet questionnaire—for example, to prevent respondents from backing up or failing to answer a question.

Forced answering software
Software that prevents respondents from continuing with an Internet questionnaire if they fail to answer a question.

Interactive help desk
In an Internet questionnaire, a live, real-time support feature that solves problems or answers questions respondents may encounter in completing the questionnaire.

How Much Pretesting and Revising Are Necessary?

Many novelists write, rewrite, revise, and rewrite again certain chapters, paragraphs, or even sentences. The researcher works in a similar world. Rarely does he or she write only a first draft of a questionnaire. Usually the questionnaire is tried out on a group, selected on a convenience basis, that is similar in makeup to the one that ultimately will be sampled. Although the researcher should not select a group too divergent from the target market—for example, selecting business students as surrogates for businesspeople—pretesting does not require a statistical sample. The **pretesting** process allows the researcher to determine whether respondents have any difficulty understanding the questionnaire and whether there are any ambiguous or biased questions. This process is exceedingly beneficial. Making a mistake with twenty-five or fifty subjects can avoid the potential disaster of administering an invalid questionnaire to several hundred individuals. For a questionnaire investigating teaching students' experience with web-based instruction, the researcher had the questionnaire reviewed first by university faculty members to ensure the questions were valid, then asked twenty teaching students to try answering the questions and indicate any ambiguities they noticed. Their feedback prompted changes in the format and wording. Pretesting was especially helpful because the English-language questionnaire was used in a school in the United Arab Emirates, where English is spoken but is not the primary language.[14]

Tabulating the results of a pretest helps determine whether the questionnaire will meet the objectives of the research. A **preliminary tabulation** often illustrates that, although respondents can easily comprehend and answer a given question, that question is inappropriate because it does not provide relevant information to help solve the marketing problem. Consider the following example from a survey among distributors of powder-actuated tools such as stud drivers concerning the percentage of sales to given industries:

Please estimate what percentage of your fastener and load sales go to the following industries:

- *% heating, plumbing, and air conditioning*
- *% carpentry*
- *% electrical*
- *% maintenance*
- *% other (please specify)*

The researchers were fortunate to learn that asking the question in this manner made it virtually impossible to obtain the information actually desired. Most respondents' answers did not total 100 percent, and the question had to be revised. In general, getting respondents to add everything correctly is a problem. Pretesting difficult questions such as these is essential.

What administrative procedures should be implemented to maximize the value of a pretest? Administering a questionnaire exactly as planned in the actual study often is not possible. For example, mailing out a questionnaire might require several weeks that simply cannot be spared. Pretesting a questionnaire in this manner would provide important information on response rate but may not point out why questions were skipped or what questions are ambiguous or confusing. Personal interviewers can record requests for additional explanation or comments that indicate respondents' difficulty with question sequence or other factors. This is the primary reason why interviewers are often used for pretest work. Self-administered questionnaires are not reworded to be personal interviews, but interviewers are instructed to observe respondents and ask for their comments after they complete the questionnaire. When pretesting personal or telephone interviews, interviewers may test alternative wordings and question sequences to determine which format best suits the intended respondents.

No matter how the pretest is conducted, the researcher should remember that its purpose is to uncover any problems that the questionnaire may cause. Thus, pretests typically are conducted to answer questions about the questionnaire such as the following:

- Can the questionnaire format be followed by the interviewer?
- Does the questionnaire flow naturally and conversationally?

Pretesting
Administering a questionnaire to a small group of respondents to detect ambiguity or bias in the questions or to iron out fundamental problems in the instructions or administrative procedures.

Preliminary tabulation
A tabulation of the results of a pretest to help determine whether the questionnaire will meet the objectives of the research.

- Are the questions clear and easy to understand?
- Can respondents answer the questions easily?
- Which alternative forms of questions work best?

Pretests also provide means for testing the sampling procedure—to determine, for example, whether interviewers are following the sampling instructions properly and whether the procedure is efficient. Pretests also provide estimates of the response rates for mail surveys and the completion rates for telephone surveys.

Usually a questionnaire goes through several revisions. The exact number of revisions depends on the researcher's and client's judgment. The revision process usually ends when both agree that the desired information is being collected in an unbiased manner.

Designing Questionnaires for Global Markets

Now that marketing research is conducted around the globe, researchers must take cultural factors into account when designing questionnaires. The most common problem involves translating a questionnaire into other languages. A questionnaire developed in one country may be difficult to translate because equivalent language concepts do not exist or because of differences in idiom and vernacular. Although Spanish is spoken in both Mexico and Venezuela, one researcher found out that the Spanish translation of the English term *retail outlet* works in Mexico but not in Venezuela. Venezuelans interpreted the translation to refer to an electrical outlet, an outlet of a river into an ocean, or the passageway onto a patio.

Counting on an international audience to speak a common language such as English does not necessarily bridge these gaps, even when the respondents actually do speak more than one language. Cultural differences incorporate many shades of meaning that may not be captured by a survey delivered in a language used primarily for, say, business transactions. In a test of this idea, undergraduate students in twenty-four countries completed questionnaires about attitudes toward school and career. Half received the questionnaire in English, and half in their native language. The results varied, with country-to-country differences being smaller when students completed the questionnaire in English.[15]

International marketing researchers often have questionnaires back translated. **Back translation** is the process of taking a questionnaire that has previously been translated from one language to another and having it translated back again by a second, independent translator. The back translator is often a person whose native tongue is the language that will be used for the questionnaire. This process can reveal inconsistencies between the English version and the translation. For example, when a soft-drink company translated its slogan "Baby, it's cold inside" into Cantonese for research in Hong Kong, the result read "Small Mosquito, on the inside, it is very cold." In Hong Kong, *small mosquito* is a colloquial expression for a small child. Obviously the intended meaning of the advertising message had been lost in the translated questionnaire.[16]

As indicated in Chapter 7, literacy influences the designs of self-administered questionnaires and interviews. Knowledge of the literacy rates in foreign countries, especially those that are just developing modern economies, is vital.

Back translation
Taking a questionnaire that has previously been translated into another language and having a second, independent translator translate it back to the original language.

Summary

1. Explain the significance of decisions about questionnaire design and wording. Good questionnaire design is a key to obtaining accurate survey results. The specific questions to be asked will be a function of the type of information needed to answer the manager's questions and the communication medium of data collection. Relevance and accuracy are the basic criteria for judging questionnaire results. A questionnaire is *relevant* if no unnecessary information is collected and the information needed for solving the marketing problem is obtained. *Accuracy* means that the information is reliable and valid.

2. Define alternatives for wording open-ended and fixed-alternative questions. Knowing how each question should be phrased requires some knowledge of the different types of questions possible. Open-ended response questions pose some problem or question and ask the respondent to answer in his or her own words. Fixed-alternative questions require less interviewer skill, take less time, and are easier to answer. In fixed-alternative questions the respondent is given specific limited alternative responses and asked to choose the one closest to his or her own viewpoint. Standardized responses are easier to code, tabulate, and interpret. Care must be taken to formulate the responses so that they do not overlap. Respondents whose answers do not fit any of the fixed alternatives may be forced to select alternatives that do not communicate what they really mean. Open-ended response questions are especially useful in exploratory research or at the beginning of a questionnaire. They make a questionnaire more expensive to analyze because of the uniqueness of the answers. Also, interviewer bias can influence the responses to such questions.

3. Summarize guidelines for questions that avoid mistakes in questionnaire design. Some guidelines for questionnaire construction have emerged from research experience. The language should be simple to allow for variations in educational level. Researchers should avoid leading or loaded questions, which suggest answers to the respondents, as well as questions that induce them to give socially desirable answers. Respondents have a bias against questions that suggest changes in the status quo. Their reluctance to answer personal questions can be reduced by explaining the need for the questions and by assuring respondents of the confidentiality of their replies. The researcher should carefully avoid ambiguity in questions. Another common problem is the double-barreled question, which asks two questions at once.

4. Describe how the proper sequence of questions may improve a questionnaire. Question sequence can be very important to the success of a survey. The opening questions should be designed to capture respondents' interest and keep them involved. Personal questions should be postponed to the middle or end of the questionnaire. General questions should precede specific ones. In a series of attitude scales the first response may be used as an anchor for comparison with the other responses. The order of alternatives on closed questions can affect the results. Filter questions are useful for avoiding unnecessary questions that do not apply to a particular respondent. Such questions may be put into a flowchart for personal or telephone interviewing.

5. Discuss how to design a questionnaire layout. The layout of a mail or other self-administered questionnaire can affect its response rate. An attractive questionnaire encourages a response, as does a carefully phrased title. Internet questionnaires present unique design issues. Decisions must be made about the use of color, graphics, animation, sound, and other special layout effects that the Internet makes possible.

6. Describe criteria for pretesting and revising a questionnaire and for adapting it to global markets. Pretesting helps reveal errors while they can still be corrected easily. A preliminary tabulation may show that, even if respondents understand questions, the responses are not relevant to the marketing problem. Often, the most efficient way to conduct a pretest is with interviewers to generate quick feedback. International marketing researchers must take cultural factors into account when designing questionnaires. The most widespread problem involves translation into another language. International questionnaires are often back translated.

Key Terms and Concepts

Open-ended response questions
Fixed-alternative questions
Simple-dichotomy
    (dichotomous-alternative) question
Determinant-choice question
Frequency-determination question
Checklist question
Leading question
Loaded question
Counterbiasing statement
Split-ballot technique

Double-barreled question
Order bias
Funnel technique
Filter question
Pivot question
Multiple-grid question
Push button
Status bar
Radio button
Drop-down box
Check boxes

Open-ended boxes
Pop-up boxes
Variable piping software
Error trapping
Forced answering software
Interactive help desk
Pretesting
Preliminary tabulation
Back translation

Questions for Review and Critical Thinking

1. Evaluate and comment on the following questions, taken from several questionnaires:

   a. A university computer center survey on SPSS usage:

   How often do you use SPSS statistical software? Please check one.

   - *Infrequently (once a semester)*
   - *Occasionally (once a month)*
   - *Frequently (once a week)*
   - *All the time (daily)*

   b. A survey of advertising agencies:

   Do you understand and like the Federal Trade Commission's new corrective advertising policy?

   _____ *Yes*   _____ *No*

   c. A survey on a new, small electric car:

   Assuming 90 percent of your driving is in town, would you buy this type of car?

   _____ *Yes*   _____ *No*

   If this type of electric car had the same initial cost as a current "Big 3" full-size, fully equipped car, but operated at one-half the cost over a five-year period, would you buy one?

   _____ *Yes*   _____ *No*

   d. A student survey:

   Since the beginning of this semester, approximately what percentage of the time do you get to campus using each of the forms of transportation available to you per week?

   Walk _____ Bicycle _____
   Public transportation _____ Motor vehicle _____

   e. A survey of motorcycle dealers:

   Should the company continue its generous cooperative advertising program?

   f. A survey of media use by farmers:

   Thinking about yesterday, *put an X in the box below for* each *quarter-hour time period during which, so far as you can recall, you* personally *listened to* radio. *Do the same for* television.

   6:00 to 10:00 A.M. by quarter-hours

   If you did not watch TV any time yesterday, X here ☐
   If you did not listen to radio any time yesterday, X here ☐

   g. A government survey of gasoline retailers:

   Suppose the full-service pump selling price for regular gasoline is 232.8 cents per gallon on the first day of the month. Suppose on the 10th of the month the price is raised to 234.9 cents per gallon, and on the 25th of the month it is reduced to 230.9 cents per gallon. In order to provide the required data you should list the accumulator reading on the full-service regular gasoline pump when the station opens on the 1st day, the 10th day, and the 25th day of the month and when the station closes on the last day of the month.

   h. An anti-gun-control group's survey:

   Do you believe that private citizens have the right to own firearms to defend themselves, their families, and their property from violent criminal attack?

   _____ *Yes*   _____ *No*

   i. A survey of the general public:

   In the next year, after accounting for inflation, do you think your real personal income will go up or down?

   1. *Up*
   2. *(Stay the same)*
   3. *Down*
   4. *(Don't know)*

   j. **ETHICS** A survey of the general public:

   Some people say that companies should be required by law to label all chemicals and substances that the government states are potentially harmful. The label would tell what the chemical or substance is, what dangers it might pose, and what safety procedures should be used in handling the substance. Other people say that such laws would be too strict. They say the law should require labels on only those chemicals and substances that the companies themselves decide are potentially harmful. Such a law, they say, would be less costly for the companies and would permit them to exclude those chemicals and substances they consider to be trade secrets. Which of these views is closest to your own?

   1. *Require labels on all chemicals and substances that the government states are potentially harmful.*
   2. *(Don't know)*
   3. *Require labels on only those chemicals and substances that companies decide are potentially harmful.*

   k. A survey of voters:

   Since agriculture is vital to our state's economy, how do you feel about the administration's farm policies?

   Strongly favor
   Somewhat favor
   Somewhat oppose
   Strongly oppose
   Unsure

2. The following question was asked of a sample of television viewers:

   We are going to ask you to classify the type of fan you consider yourself to be for different sports and sports programs.

   - **Diehard Fan: Watch games, follow up on scores and sports news multiple times a day**
   - **Avid Fan: Watch games, follow up on scores and sports news once a day**

- **Casual Fan: Watch games, follow up on scores and sports news occasionally**
- **Championship Fan: Watch games, follow up on scores and sports news only during championships or playoffs**
- **Non-Fan: Never watch games or follow up on scores**
- **Anti-Fan: Dislike, oppose, or object to a certain sport**

Does this question do a good job of avoiding ambiguity?

3. How might the wording of a question about income influence respondents' answers?

4. What is the difference between a *leading question* and a *loaded question?*

5. Design one or more open-ended response questions to measure reactions to a magazine ad for a Xerox photocopier.

6. Design one or more questions to measure how a person who has just been shown a television commercial might describe the commercial.

7. Evaluate the layout of the filter question that follows:

> **Are you employed either full time or part time?**
>
> | *Mark (x) one.* | ☐ Yes | ☐ No |
> | --- | --- | --- |
>
> If yes: How many hours per week are you usually employed? *Mark (x) one.*
>
> ☐ Less than 35   ☐ 35 or more
>
> What is the zip code at your usual place of work?
>
> _____

8. It has been said that surveys show that consumers hate advertising, but like specific ads. Comment.

9. Design a complete questionnaire to evaluate a new fast-food fried chicken restaurant.

10. Design a short but complete questionnaire to measure consumer satisfaction with an airline.

11. Develop a checklist of things to consider in questionnaire construction.

12. Design a complete personal interview questionnaire for a zoo that wishes to determine who visits the zoo and how they evaluate it.

13. Design a complete self-administered questionnaire for a bank to give to customers immediately after they open new accounts.

14. Design a questionnaire for your local Big Brothers and Big Sisters organization to investigate awareness of and willingness to volunteer time to this organization.

15. Design a questionnaire for a bank located in a college town to investigate the potential for attracting college students as checking account customers.

16. The Apple Assistance Center is a hotline to solve problems for users of Macintosh computers and other Apple products. Design a short (postcard-size) consumer satisfaction/service quality questionnaire for the Apple Assistance Center.

17. **'NET** Visit the following website: http://www.history.org. What type of questions might be asked in a survey to evaluate the effectiveness of this website in terms of being informative and in terms of being an effective sales medium?

18. A client tells a researcher that she wants a questionnaire that evaluates the importance of thirty product characteristics and rates her brand and ten competing brands on these characteristics. The researcher believes that this questionnaire will induce respondent fatigue because it will be far too long. Should the researcher do exactly what the client says or risk losing the business by suggesting a different approach?

19. **ETHICS** A lobbying organization designs a short questionnaire about its political position. It also includes a membership solicitation with the questionnaire. Is this approach ethical?

20. **'NET** Visit Mister Poll at http://www.misterpoll.com, where you will find thousands of user-contributed polls on every imaginable topic from the controversial to the downright zany. What you find will depend on when you visit the site. However, you might find something such as a Movie Poll, where you pick your favorite film of the season. Evaluate the questions in the poll.

21. **'NET** Try to find two friends that know the same foreign language. Write ten Likert questions that measure how exciting a retail store environment is to shop in. Have one of your friends interpret the question into the foreign language. Have the other take the translation and state each question in English. How similar is the translated English to the original English? Comment.

Research Activity

1. Design eight questions that assess how effective an undergraduate college business course has been.

Case 11.1 Agency for Healthcare Research and Quality

At the U.S. Department of Health and Human Services, the Agency for Healthcare Research and Quality (AHRQ) developed a survey to measure hospital employees' attitudes about patient safety in their facilities.[17] The survey is designed to help hospitals ensure safety by creating an environment in which employees share information, improve safety when problems are identified, and if necessary, change the way employees

deliver care. The AHRQ suggests that hospitals use the survey to identify areas needing improvement and repeat its use to track changes over time.

The survey is shown in Case Exhibit 11.1–1.

Questions

1. Evaluate the questionnaire. Can you suggest any improvements?

2. Will this survey meet its objectives? Explain.

CASE EXHIBIT 11.1-1 AHRQ Hospital Questionnaire

 # HOSPITAL SURVEY ON PATIENT SAFETY CULTURE

INSTRUCTIONS

This survey asks for your opinions about patient safety issues, medical error, and event reporting in your hospital and will take about 10 to 15 minutes to complete.

- An "_event_" is defined as any type of error, mistake, incident, accident, or deviation, regardless of whether or not it results in patient harm.

- "_Patient safety_" is defined as the avoidance and prevention of patient injuries or adverse events resulting from the processes of health care delivery.

SECTION A: Your Work Area/Unit

In this survey, think of your "unit" as the work area, department, or clinical area of the hospital where you spend _most_ of your work time or provide _most_ of your clinical services.

What is your primary work area or unit in this hospital? Mark ONE answer by filling in the circle.

○ a. Many different hospital units/No specific unit

○ b. Medicine (non-surgical)	○ g. Intensive care unit (any type)	○ l. Radiology
○ c. Surgery	○ h. Psychiatry/mental health	○ m. Anesthesiology
○ d. Obstetrics	○ i. Rehabilitation	○ n. Other, please specify:
○ e. Pediatrics	○ j. Pharmacy	
○ f. Emergency department	○ k. Laboratory	

Please indicate your agreement or disagreement with the following statements about your work area/unit. Mark your answer by filling in the circle.

Think about your hospital work area/unit...	Strongly Disagree ▼	Disagree ▼	Neither ▼	Agree ▼	Strongly Agree ▼
1. People support one another in this unit	①	②	③	④	⑤
2. We have enough staff to handle the workload	①	②	③	④	⑤
3. When a lot of work needs to be done quickly, we work together as a team to get the work done	①	②	③	④	⑤
4. In this unit, people treat each other with respect	①	②	③	④	⑤
5. Staff in this unit work longer hours than is best for patient care	①	②	③	④	⑤
6. We are actively doing things to improve patient safety	①	②	③	④	⑤
7. We use more agency/temporary staff than is best for patient care	①	②	③	④	⑤
8. Staff feel like their mistakes are held against them	①	②	③	④	⑤
9. Mistakes have led to positive changes here	①	②	③	④	⑤
10. It is just by chance that more serious mistakes don't happen around here	①	②	③	④	⑤
11. When one area in this unit gets really busy, others help out	①	②	③	④	⑤
12. When an event is reported, it feels like the person is being written up, not the problem	①	②	③	④	⑤

(continued)

CASE EXHIBIT 11.1–1 **AHRQ Hospital Questionnaire** (*continued*)

SECTION A: Your Work Area/Unit (continued)

Think about your hospital work area/unit...	Strongly Disagree ▼	Disagree ▼	Neither ▼	Agree ▼	Strongly Agree ▼
13. After we make changes to improve patient safety, we evaluate their effectiveness	①	②	③	④	⑤
14. We work in "crisis mode" trying to do too much, too quickly.........	①	②	③	④	⑤
15. Patient safety is never sacrificed to get more work done	①	②	③	④	⑤
16. Staff worry that mistakes they make are kept in their personnel file.........	①	②	③	④	⑤
17. We have patient safety problems in this unit	①	②	③	④	⑤
18. Our procedures and systems are good at preventing errors from happening	①	②	③	④	⑤

SECTION B: Your Supervisor/Manager

Please indicate your agreement or disagreement with the following statements about your immediate supervisor/manager or person to whom you directly report. Mark your answer by filling in the circle.

	Strongly Disagree ▼	Disagree ▼	Neither ▼	Agree ▼	Strongly Agree ▼
1. My supervisor/manager says a good word when he/she sees a job done according to established patient safety procedures.......	①	②	③	④	⑤
2. My supervisor/manager seriously considers staff suggestions for improving patient safety...........	①	②	③	④	⑤
3. Whenever pressure builds up, my supervisor/manager wants us to work faster, even if it means taking shortcuts...........	①	②	③	④	⑤
4. My supervisor/manager overlooks patient safety problems that happen over and over	①	②	③	④	⑤

SECTION C: Communications

How often do the following things happen in your work area/unit? Mark your answer by filling in the circle.

Think about your hospital work area/unit...	Never ▼	Rarely ▼	Some- times ▼	Most of the time ▼	Always ▼
1. We are given feedback about changes put into place based on event reports	①	②	③	④	⑤
2. Staff will freely speak up if they see something that may negatively affect patient care	①	②	③	④	⑤
3. We are informed about errors that happen in this unit.............	①	②	③	④	⑤
4. Staff feel free to question the decisions or actions of those with more authority.............	①	②	③	④	⑤
5. In this unit, we discuss ways to prevent errors from happening again.........	①	②	③	④	⑤
6. Staff are afraid to ask questions when something does not seem right.........	①	②	③	④	⑤

(*continued*)

CASE EXHIBIT 11.1-1 **AHRQ Hospital Questionnaire** (*continued*)

SECTION D: Frequency of Events Reported
In your hospital work area/unit, when the following mistakes happen, *how often are they reported?*
Mark your answer by filling in the circle.

	Never ▼	Rarely ▼	Some-times ▼	Most of the time ▼	Always ▼
1. When a mistake is made, but is *caught and corrected before affecting the patient*, how often is this reported?..........	①	②	③	④	⑤
2. When a mistake is made, but has *no potential to harm the patient*, how often is this reported?.............................	①	②	③	④	⑤
3. When a mistake is made that *could harm the patient*, but does not, how often is this reported?.......................	①	②	③	④	⑤

SECTION E: Patient Safety Grade
Please give your work area/unit in this hospital an overall grade on patient safety. Mark ONE answer.

O	O	O	O	O
A	**B**	**C**	**D**	**E**
Excellent	Very Good	Acceptable	Poor	Failing

SECTION F: Your Hospital
Please indicate your agreement or disagreement with the following statements about your hospital.
Mark your answer by filling in the circle.

Think about your hospital…	Strongly Disagree ▼	Disagree ▼	Neither ▼	Agree ▼	Strongly Agree ▼
1. Hospital management provides a work climate that promotes patient safety..............................	①	②	③	④	⑤
2. Hospital units do not coordinate well with each other..................	①	②	③	④	⑤
3. Things "fall between the cracks" when transferring patients from one unit to another...............	①	②	③	④	⑤
4. There is good cooperation among hospital units that need to work together	①	②	③	④	⑤
5. Important patient care information is often lost during shift changes.................	①	②	③	④	⑤
6. It is often unpleasant to work with staff from other hospital units .	①	②	③	④	⑤
7. Problems often occur in the exchange of information across hospital units	①	②	③	④	⑤
8. The actions of hospital management show that patient safety is a top priority................ .	①	②	③	④	⑤
9. Hospital management seems interested in patient safety only after an adverse event happens	①	②	③	④	⑤
10. Hospital units work well together to provide the best care for patients.................	①	②	③	④	⑤
11. Shift changes are problematic for patients in this hospital............	①	②	③	④	⑤

SECTION G: Number of Events Reported
In the past 12 months, how many event reports have you filled out and submitted? Mark ONE answer.

O a. No event reports   O d. 6 to 10 event reports
O b. 1 to 2 event reports   O e. 11 to 20 event reports
O c. 3 to 5 event reports   O f. 21 event reports or more

(*continued*)

CASE EXHIBIT II.1-1 **AHRQ Hospital Questionnaire** (*continued*)

SECTION H: Background Information
This information will help in the analysis of the survey results. Mark ONE answer by filling in the circle.

1. How long have you worked in this <u>hospital</u>?
    - ○ a. Less than 1 year
    - ○ b. 1 to 5 years
    - ○ c. 6 to 10 years
    - ○ d. 11 to 15 years
    - ○ e. 16 to 20 years
    - ○ f. 21 years or more

2. How long have you worked in your current hospital <u>work area/unit</u>?
    - ○ a. Less than 1 year
    - ○ b. 1 to 5 years
    - ○ c. 6 to 10 years
    - ○ d. 11 to 15 years
    - ○ e. 16 to 20 years
    - ○ f. 21 years or more

3. Typically, how many <u>hours per week</u> do you work in this hospital?
    - ○ a. Less than 20 hours per week
    - ○ b. 20 to 39 hours per week
    - ○ c. 40 to 59 hours per week
    - ○ d. 60 to 79 hours per week
    - ○ e. 80 to 99 hours per week
    - ○ f. 100 hours per week or more

4. What is your staff position in this hospital? Mark ONE answer that best describes your staff position.
    - ○ a. Registered Nurse
    - ○ b. Physician Assistant/Nurse Practitioner
    - ○ c. LVN/LPN
    - ○ d. Patient Care Assistant/Hospital Aide/Care Partner
    - ○ e. Attending/Staff Physician
    - ○ f. Resident Physician/Physician in Training
    - ○ g. Pharmacist
    - ○ h. Dietician
    - ○ i. Unit Assistant/Clerk/Secretary
    - ○ j. Respiratory Therapist
    - ○ k. Physical, Occupational, or Speech Therapist
    - ○ l. Technician (e.g., EKG, Lab, Radiology)
    - ○ m. Administration/Management
    - ○ n. Other, please specify:

5. In your staff position, do you typically have direct interaction or contact with patients?
    - ○ a. YES, I typically have direct interaction or contact with patients.
    - ○ b. NO, I typically do NOT have direct interaction or contact with patients.

6. How long have you worked in your current specialty or profession?
    - ○ a. Less than 1 year
    - ○ b. 1 to 5 years
    - ○ c. 6 to 10 years
    - ○ d. 11 to 15 years
    - ○ e. 16 to 20 years
    - ○ f. 21 years or more

SECTION I: Your Comments
Please feel free to write any comments about patient safety, error, or event reporting in your hospital.

THANK YOU FOR COMPLETING THIS SURVEY.

Source: Agency for Healthcare Research and Quality, "Hospital Survey on Patient Safety Culture," http://www.ahrq.gov/qual/hospculture/.

Case 11.2 McDonald's Spanish Language Questionnaire

The questions in Case Exhibit 11.2–1, about a visit to McDonald's, originally appeared in Spanish.

Questions

1. What is the typical process for developing questionnaires for markets where consumers speak a language other than English?

2. Find someone who speaks Spanish and have him or her back translate the questions that appear in Case Exhibit 11.2–1. Are these Spanish-language questions adequate?

CASE EXHIBIT 11.2–1 **McDonald's Questionnaire**

			NADA SATISFECHO/A				MUY SATISFECHO/A
AQUI → SE EMPIEZA	**1. En general, ¿qué tan satisfecho/a quedó con su visita a este McDonald's hoy?**		☹	①	②	③ ④	⑤ ☺
	2. Su visita fue....... Adentro (**A**) o en el Drive-thru (**DT**)	Ⓐ Adentro		Ⓓ⫶ Drive-thru			
	3. Su visita fue....... Durante el Desayuno (**D**), Almuerzo (**A**), Cena (**C**)		Ⓓ Desayuno	Ⓐ Almuerzo		Ⓐ Cena	
	4. Su visita fue....... Entre semana (**E**) o Fin de semana (**F**)		Ⓔ Entre semana	Ⓕ Fin de semana			
COMIDA	**5. ¿Quedó satisfecho/a con la comida que recibio hoy?** Si NO, ¿cuál fue el problema? Favor de rellenar el(los) círculo(s) apropiado(s).	Ⓢ Si	Sandwich / platillo frío	Ⓝ No ⬚			
			Apariencia desagradable	⬚			
			Mal sabor de la comida	⬚			
			Pocas papas en la bolsa / caja	⬚			
			Papas / tortitas de papa frías	⬚			
			Papas no bien saladas	⬚			
			Bebida aguada / de mal sabor	⬚			

Part 4
Sampling and
Statistical Theory

©MATTHIAS CLAMER/STONE+/GETTY IMAGES

CHAPTER 12
SAMPLING DESIGNS AND SAMPLING PROCEDURES

After studying this chapter, you should be able to

1. Define *sample, population, population element,* and *census*
2. Explain reasons for taking a sample rather than a complete census
3. Describe the process of identifying a target population and selecting a sampling frame
4. Compare random sampling and systematic (nonsampling) errors
5. Identify the types of nonprobability sampling, including their advantages and disadvantages
6. Summarize the advantages and disadvantages of the various types of probability samples
7. Discuss how to choose an appropriate sample design, as well as challenges for Internet sampling

Chapter Vignette: At Cadbury, Gum Chewing Takes Expertise

After Cadbury Schweppes acquired Pfizer's candy brands, including Bubbaloo, Dentyne, and Trident, new technology and marketing research pointed the company to a new product idea.[1] From a consumer survey, Cadbury knew that most Americans chew gum, and more than two-thirds of those gum chewers said one reason was to avoid snacking. Looking for a product that would serve as a junk-food alternative, company researchers identified gum pellets with liquid centers as a possible new product. Pfizer's sale to Cadbury had included a man-ufacturing technology that used different flavors for the candy coating and liquid filling. By delivering two flavors and three textures (crunchy, chewy, and liquid), Cadbury hoped the new gum would satisfy customers' crav-ings for more substantial snacks. And the small pellets of gum seemed more adult-friendly than other liquid-center gums, which were sold under the Freshen Up and Bubbaloo brands.

The developers' next step was to come up with appealing flavor combinations. Peppermint was one obvious choice since most gum has a mint flavor, which tends to maintain a good taste in the chewer's mouth. Another idea came from consumer testing showing that the most popular fruit flavor is strawberry. Cadbury worked with food scien-tists to select a strawberry flavoring that was less like the jam-sweet flavor popular with children and more like the taste of a fresh strawberry. Then company marketers selected vanilla centers for the mint gum and lime centers for the strawberry gum.

Finally, the new products were ready for consumer testing. Here, Cadbury faced a problem typically associated with testing foods: Most consumers don't pay enough attention to tastes and smells to give helpful feedback. Their comments are vague, so a truly random sample of the consumer population would not give the company the information it needed. Instead, Cadbury recruited a sample from a sensory panel. Panel members passed tests rating their sense of smell and even the rate at which they salivate. Cadbury trained the panelists for the gum-chewing job, teaching them to chew steadily along with the beats of a metronome.

Testers chewed samples of the gum for precisely three minutes, timing themselves with electronic clocks. At the end of each chewing period, a panel leader asked for comments. Panelists cleared their palates with crackers and water before trying the next sample. Eventually, the panelists provided enough feedback for the company to pinpoint winning flavor combinations and move on to engineering the production process.

Just as Cadbury needed a sample of gum chewers to make judgments about its products, sampling is a familiar part of daily life. A customer in a bookstore picks up a book, looks at the cover, and skims a few pages to get a sense of the writing style and content before deciding whether to buy. A high school student visits a college classroom to listen to a professor's lecture. Selecting a university on the basis of one classroom visit may not be scientific sampling, but in a personal situation, it may be a practical sampling experience. When measuring every item in a population is impossible, inconvenient, or too expensive, we intuitively take a sample.

Although sampling is commonplace in daily activities, these familiar samples are seldom scientific. For researchers, the process of sampling can be quite complex. Sampling is a central aspect of marketing research, requiring in-depth examination. This chapter explains the nature of sampling and ways to determine the appropriate sample design.

Sampling Terminology

Sample
A subset, or some part, of a larger population.

Population (universe)
Any complete group of entities that share some common set of characteristics.

Population element
An individual member of a population.

Census
An investigation of all the individual elements that make up a population.

The process of sampling involves using a a portion of a population to make conclusions about the whole population. A **sample** is a subset, or some part, of a larger population. The purpose of sampling is to estimate an unknown characteristic of a population.

Sampling is defined in terms of the population being studied. A **population (universe)** is any complete group—for example, of people, sales territories, stores, or college students—that shares some common set of characteristics. The term **population element** refers to an individual member of the population.

Researchers could study every element of a population to draw some conclusion. A **census** is an investigation of all the individual elements that make up the population—a total enumeration rather than a sample. Thus, if we wished to know whether more adult Texans drive pickup trucks than sedans, we could contact every adult Texan and find out whether or not they drive a pickup truck or a sedan. We would then know the answer to this question definitively.

Why Sample?

At a wine-tasting party, guests sample wine by having a small taste from each of a number of bottles of wine. From this, the consumer decides if he or she likes a particular wine. If an entire bottle were consumed to decide, the guest may end up too inebriated to care about the next bottle. However, in a scientific study in which the objective is to determine an unknown population value, why should a sample rather than a complete census be taken?

Pragmatic Reasons

Applied marketing research projects usually have budget and time constraints. If Ford Motor Corporation wished to take a census of past purchasers' reactions to the company's recalls of defective models, the researchers would have to contact millions of automobile buyers. Some of them would be inaccessible (for example, out of the country), and it would be impossible to contact all these people within a short time period.

A researcher who wants to investigate a population with an extremely small number of population elements may elect to conduct a census rather than a sample because the cost, labor, and time drawbacks would be relatively insignificant. For a company that wants to assess salespersons' satisfaction with its computer networking system, circulating a questionnaire to all twenty-five of its employees is practical. In most situations, however, many practical reasons favor sampling. Sampling cuts costs, reduces labor requirements, and gathers vital information quickly. These advantages may be sufficient in themselves for using a sample rather than a census, but there are other reasons.

Accurate and Reliable Results

Another major reason for sampling is that most properly selected samples give results that are reasonably accurate. If the elements of a population are quite similar, only a small sample is necessary to accurately portray the characteristic of interest. Thus, a population consisting of 10,000 eleventh grade students in all-boys Catholic high schools will require a smaller sample than a broader population consisting of 10,000 high school students from coeducational secondary schools.

A sample may on occasion be more accurate than a census. Interviewer mistakes, tabulation errors, and other nonsampling errors may increase during a census because of the increased volume of work. In a sample, increased accuracy may sometimes be possible because the fieldwork and tabulation of data can be more closely supervised. In a field survey, a small, well-trained, closely supervised group may do a more careful and accurate job of collecting information than a large group of nonprofessional interviewers who try to contact everyone. An interesting case in point is the use of samples by the Bureau of the Census to check the accuracy of the U.S. Census. If the sample indicates a possible source of error, the census is redone.

Destruction of Test Units

Many research projects, especially those in quality-control testing, require the destruction of the items being tested. If a manufacturer of firecrackers wished to find out whether each unit met a specific production standard, no product would be left after the testing. This is the exact situation in many marketing strategy experiments. For example, if an experimental sales presentation were presented to every potential customer, no prospects would remain to be contacted after the experiment. In other words, if there is a finite population and everyone in the population participates in the research and cannot be replaced, no population elements remain to be selected as sampling units. The test units have been destroyed or ruined for the purpose of the research project.

Practical Sampling Concepts

Before taking a sample, researchers must make several decisions. Exhibit 12.1 presents these decisions as a series of sequential stages, but the order of the decisions does not always follow this sequence. These decisions are highly interrelated. The issues associated with each of these stages are discussed in this chapter and Chapter 13.

Defining the Target Population

Once the decision to sample has been made, the first question concerns identifying the target population. What is the relevant population? In many cases this question is easy to answer. Registered voters may be clearly identifiable. Likewise, if a company's 106-person sales force is the population of concern, there are few definitional problems. In other cases the decision may be difficult. One survey concerning organizational buyer behavior incorrectly defined the population as purchasing agents whom sales representatives regularly contacted. After the survey, investigators discovered that industrial engineers within the customer companies rarely talked with the salespeople but substantially affected buying decisions. For consumer research, the appropriate population element frequently is the household rather than an individual member of the household. This presents some problems if household lists are not available.

EXHIBIT 12.1
**Stages in the Selection
of a Sample**

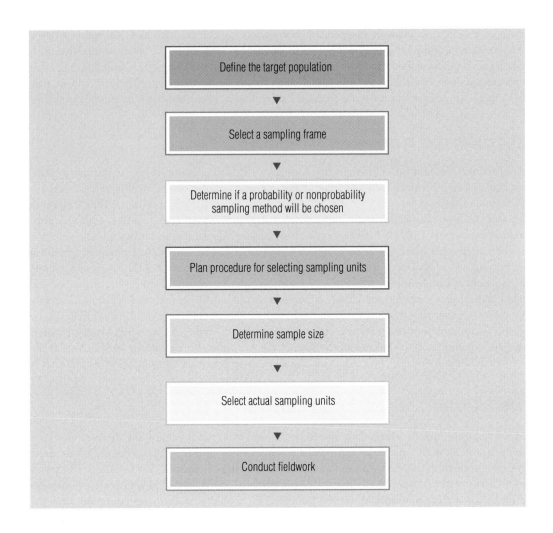

At the outset of the sampling process, the target population must be carefully defined so that the proper sources from which the data are to be collected can be identified. The usual technique for defining the target population is to answer questions about the crucial characteristics of the population. Does the term *comic book reader* include children under six years of age who do not actually read the words? Does *all persons west of the Mississippi* include people in east bank towns that border the river, such as East St. Louis, Illinois? The question to answer is, "Whom do we want to talk to?" The answer may be users, nonusers, recent adopters, or brand switchers.

To implement the sample in the field, tangible characteristics should be used to define the population. A baby food manufacturer might define the population as all women still capable of bearing children. However, a more specific *operational definition* would be women between the ages of twelve and fifty. While this definition by age may exclude a few women who are capable of childbearing and include some who are not, it is still more explicit and provides a manageable basis for the sample design.

The Sampling Frame

In practice, the sample will be drawn from a list of population elements that often differs somewhat from the defined target population. A list of elements from which the sample may be drawn is called a **sampling frame**. The sampling frame is also called the *working population* because these units will eventually provide units involved in analysis. A simple example of a sampling frame would be a list of all members of the American Medical Association.

In practice, almost every list excludes some members of the population. For example, would a university e-mail directory provide an accurate sampling frame for a given university's student population? Perhaps the sampling frame excludes students who registered late and includes students

Sampling frame
A list of elements from which a sample may be drawn; also called working population.

RESEARCHSNAPSHOT

George Gallup's Nation of Numbers

George H. Gallup . . . born in 1901 . . . left [his] hometown, Jefferson, [Iowa,] as soon as he could find his way in a bigger world. The first step was Iowa City and the State University of Iowa. Then in 1922, between his junior and senior years, George answered an advertisement for summer employment in St. Louis. The Post-Dispatch *hired fifty students to survey the city, questioning readers about what they liked and didn't like in the newspaper.*

Each and every reader was to be surveyed. The students were hired to go to every door in St. Louis—there were 55,000 homes in the city then—and ask the same questions. Gallup, one hot day, knocked on one door too many, got the same answers one time too many, and decided, there's got to be a better way.

"A New Technique for Objective Methods for Measuring Reader Interest in Newspapers" was the way, and the title of Gallup's doctoral thesis at Iowa. Working with the Des Moines *Register* and *Tribune* and the 200-year-old statistical theory probabilities of the Swiss mathematician Jakob Bernoulli, Gallup developed "sampling" techniques. You didn't have to talk to everybody, he said, as long as you randomly selected interviews according to a sampling plan that took into account whatever diversity was relevant in the universe of potential respondents— geographic, ethnic, economic, and so on.

Well, it seemed to work for newspapers, and George Gallup, instructor, was in great demand around the country. He became head of the journalism department at Drake University and then switched to a professorship at Northwestern University—all the while doing readership surveys for papers in Chicago, Cleveland, Buffalo, and points east and west. He was hot, and in that summer of 1932, a new advertising agency, Young & Rubicam, invited him to New York to create a research department and procedures for evaluating the effectiveness of advertising. He did that, too. One of his first Y&R surveys, based on newspaper experience, indicated that the number of readers of advertisements was proportional to the length of the paragraphs in a piece of copy.

©BETTMANN/CORBIS

Source: Excerpted from "George Gallup's Nation of Numbers," Esquire, December 1983, pp. 91–92.

---

who have resigned from the university. The e-mail directory also will likely list only the student's official university e-mail address. However, many students may not ever use this address, opting to use a private e-mail account instead. Thus, the university e-mail directory could not be expected to perfectly represent the student population. However, a perfect representation isn't always possible or needed.

Some firms, called *sampling services* or *list brokers,* specialize in providing lists or databases that include the names, addresses, phone numbers, and e-mail addresses of specific populations. Exhibit 12.2 on the next page shows a page from a mailing list company's offerings. Lists offered by companies such as this are compiled from subscriptions to professional journals, credit card applications, warranty card registrations, and a variety of other sources. One sampling service obtained its listing of households with children from an ice cream retailer who gave away free ice cream cones on children's birthdays. The children filled out cards with their names, addresses, and birthdays, which the retailer then sold to the mailing list company.

A valuable source of names is Equifax's series of city directories. Equifax City Directory provides complete, comprehensive, and accurate business and residential information. The city directory records the name of each resident over eighteen years of age and lists pertinent information about each household. The reverse directory pages offer a unique benefit. A **reverse directory** provides, in a different format, the same information contained in a telephone directory. Listings may be by city and street address or by phone number, rather than alphabetical by last name. Such a directory is particularly useful when a retailer wishes to survey only a certain geographical area of a city or when census tracts are to be selected on the basis of income or another demographic criterion.

A **sampling frame error** occurs when certain sample elements are excluded or when the entire population is not accurately represented in the sampling frame. Election polling that used a telephone directory as a sampling frame would be contacting households with listed phone numbers, not households whose members are likely to vote. A better sampling frame might be voter registration records. Another potential sampling frame error involving phone records is the possibility that a phone survey could underrepresent people with disabilities. Some disabilities, such as hearing and speech impairments, might make telephone use impossible. However, when researchers in

Reverse directory
A directory similar to a telephone directory except that listings are by city and street address or by phone number rather than alphabetical by last name.

Sampling frame error
An error that occurs when certain sample elements are not listed or are not accurately represented in a sampling frame.

EXHIBIT 12.2 **Mailing List Directory Page**

Lists Available - Alphabetical

S.I.C. Code	List Title	United States Total Count	United States State Count Page	Canadian Count	S.I.C. Code	List Title	United States Total Count	United States State Count Page	Canadian Count
	A				7313-03	Advertising-Radio	2866	59	247
5122-02	Abdominal Supports	201	‡	28	7311-07	Advertising-Shoppers' Guides	392	‡	4
8399-03	Abortion Alternatives Organizations`	946	‡	•	5199-17	Advertising-Specialties	12827	52	1648
8093-04	Abortion Information & Services	551	‡	•	7389-12	Advertising-Telephone	120	‡	•
5085-23	Abrasives	1811	‡	277	7313-05	Advertising-Television	1746	‡	102
5169-04	Absorbents	145	‡	•	7319-02	Advertising-Transit & Transportation	179	‡	38
6541-03	Abstracters	4057	58	•	0721-03	Aerial Applicators (Service)	1479	‡	61
6411-06	Accident & Health Insurance	2113	‡	9	3999-01	Aerosols	158	‡	•
8748-52	Accident Reconstruction Service	125	‡	•	3812-01	Aerospace Industries	426	‡	•
8721-01	Accountants	127392	64	6933		Affluent Americans		73	
8721-02	Accounting & Bookkeeping General Svc	27996	64	2072	5191-04	Agricultural Chemicals	549	‡	210
5044-08	Accounting & Bookkeeping Machines/Supls	889	‡	50	8748-20	Agricultural Consultants	1047	‡	474
5044-01	Accounting & Bookkeeping Systems	624	‡	1230	9999-32	Air Balancing	353	‡	•
8711-02	Acoustical Consultants	381	‡	91	5084-64	Air Brushes	219	‡	•
1742-02	Acoustical Contractors	3063	47	433	4512-02	Air Cargo Service	6005	48	•
1742-01	Acoustical Materials	878	‡	210	5075-01	Air Cleaning & Purifying Equipment	2055	‡	342
8999-10	Actuaries	1185	‡	•	5084-02	Air Compressors	4358	50	717
8049-13	Acupuncture (Acupuncturists)	2921	62	493		(See Compressors Air & Gas)			
5044-02	Adding & Calculating Machines/Supplies	5524	49	648	1711-17	Air Conditioning Contractors & Systems	50951	47	2667
5044-09	Addressing Machines & Supplies	345	‡	29		***Available By Brands Sold***			
5169-12	Adhesives & Glues	1187	‡	4		Airtemp (A)	187		
3579-02	Adhesives & Gluing Equipment	170	‡	204		Amana (B)	1450		
6411-02	Adjusters	6164	57	8357		Arco Aire (2)	673		
6411-01	Adjusters-Public	161	‡	•		Armstrong/Magic Chef (C)	395		
8322-07	Adoption Agencies	1621	‡	32		Arvin (4)	106		
8059-03	Adult Care Facilities	596	‡	•		Bryant (D)	2223		
8361-08	Adult Congregate Living Facilities	170	‡	•		Carrier (E)	5927		
7319-03	Advertising-Aerial	337	‡	26		Coleman (5)	1176		
7311-01	Advertising-Agencies & Counselors	27753	59	2552		Comfortmaker/Singer (O)	989		
7336-05	Advertising-Art Layout & Production Svc	457	‡	101		Day & Night (Z)	749		
7331-05	Advertising-Direct Mail	6347	59	540		Fedders (H)	318		
7311-03	Advertising-Directory & Guide	2465	‡	124		Heli/Quaker (3)	1977		
7319-01	Advertising-Displays	3441	59	571		Janitrol (7)	587		
7319-11	Advertising-Indoor	209	‡	63		Kero-Sun (W)	2		
7311-05	Advertising-Motion Picture	143	‡	11		Lennox (K)	4390		
7311-06	Advertising-Newspaper	4274	59	404		Luxaire (L)	510		
7312-01	Advertising-Outdoor	3052	59	297		Payne (M)	553		
7311-08	Advertising-Periodical	817	‡	78					

Washington State tested for this possible sampling frame error by comparing Census Bureau data on the prevalence of disability with the responses to a telephone survey, they found the opposite effect. The reported prevalence of a disability was actually higher in the phone survey.[2] These findings could be relevant for research into a community's health status or the level of demand for services for disabled persons.

As in this example, population elements can be either under- or overrepresented in a sampling frame. A savings and loan defined its population as all individuals who had savings accounts. However, when it drew a sample from the list of accounts rather than from the list of names of individuals, individuals who had multiple accounts were overrepresented in the sample.

SAMPLING FRAMES FOR INTERNATIONAL MARKETING RESEARCH

The availability of sampling frames around the globe varies dramatically. Not every country's government conducts a census of population. In some countries telephone directories are incomplete, no voter registration lists exist, and accurate maps of urban areas are unobtainable. However, in Taiwan, Japan, and other Asian countries, a researcher can build a sampling frame relatively easily because those governments release some census information. If a family changes households, updated census information must be reported to a centralized government agency before communal services (water, gas, electricity, education, and so on) are made available.[3] This information is then easily accessible in the local *Inhabitants' Register.*

Sampling Units

During the actual sampling process, the elements of the population must be selected according to a certain procedure. The **sampling unit** is a single element or group of elements subject to selection in the sample. For example, if an airline wishes to sample passengers, it may take every twenty-fifth name on a complete list of passengers. In this case the sampling unit would be the same as the element. Alternatively, the airline could first select certain flights as the sampling unit and then select certain passengers on each flight. In this case the sampling unit would contain many elements.

If the target population has first been divided into units, such as airline flights, additional terminology must be used. A unit selected in the first stage of sampling is called a **primary sampling unit (PSU)**. A unit selected in a successive stages of sampling is called a **secondary sampling unit** or (if three stages are necessary) **tertiary sampling unit**. When there is no list of population elements, the sampling unit generally is something other than the population element. In a random-digit dialing study, the sampling unit will be telephone numbers.

Sampling unit
A single element or group of elements subject to selection in the sample.

Primary sampling unit (PSU)
A term used to designate a unit selected in the first stage of sampling.

Secondary sampling unit
A term used to designate a unit selected in the second stage of sampling.

Tertiary sampling unit
A term used to designate a unit selected in the third stage of sampling.

Random Sampling and Nonsampling Errors

An advertising agency sampled a small number of shoppers in grocery stores that used Shopper's Video, an in-store advertising network. The agency hoped to measure brand awareness and purchase intentions. Investigators expected this sample to be representative of the grocery-shopping population. However, if a difference exists between the value of a sample statistic of interest (for example, the sample group's average willingness to buy the advertised brand) and the value of the corresponding population parameter (the population's average willingness to buy), a *statistical error* has occurred. Chapter 7 classified two basic causes of differences between statistics and parameters:

1. random sampling errors
2. systematic (nonsampling) error

An estimation made from a sample is not the same as a census count. **Random sampling error** is the difference between the sample result and the result of a census conducted using identical procedures. Of course, the result of a census is unknown unless one is taken, which is rarely done. Other sources of error also can be present. Random sampling error occurs because of chance variation in the scientific selection of sampling units. The sampling units, even if properly selected according to sampling theory, may not perfectly represent the population, but generally they are reliable estimates. Our discussion on the process of randomization (a procedure designed to give everyone in the population an equal chance of being selected as a sample member) will show that, because random sampling errors follow chance variations, they tend to cancel one another out when averaged. This means that properly selected samples generally are good approximations of the population. Still, the true population value almost always differs slightly from the sample value, causing a small random sampling error. Every once in a while, an unusual sample is selected because too many atypical people were included in the sample and a large random sampling error occurred.

Random sampling error
The difference between the sample result and the result of a census conducted using identical procedures.

Random Sampling Error

The theories behind the concept of sample reliability and other basic statistical concepts are reviewed in detail in Chapter 13, which discusses sample size. At this point, simply recognize that *random sampling error* is a technical term that refers *only* to statistical fluctuations that occur because of chance variations in the elements selected for the sample.

Random sampling error is a function of sample size. As sample size increases, random sampling error decreases. Of course, the resources available will influence how large a sample may be taken. Random sampling error associated with different sample sizes can be estimated. Suppose a survey of approximately 1,000 people has been taken in Fresno to determine the feasibility of a new soccer franchise. Assume that 30 percent of the respondents favor the idea of a new professional sport in town. The researcher will know, based on the laws of probability, that 95 percent of the time a survey of slightly fewer than 900 people will produce results with an error of approximately plus or minus 3 percent. If the survey were conducted with only 325 people, the margin of error would increase to approximately plus or minus 5 percentage points. This example illustrates random sampling errors.

Systematic Sampling Error

Systematic (nonsampling) error
Error resulting from factors not due to chance fluctuations, such as the nature of a study's design and imperfections in executions.

Systematic (nonsampling) errors result from nonsampling factors, primarily the nature of a study's design and the correctness of execution. These errors are *not* due to chance fluctuations. For example, highly educated respondents are more likely to cooperate with mail surveys than poorly educated ones, for whom filling out forms is more difficult and intimidating. Sample biases such as these account for a large portion of errors in marketing research. The term *sample bias* is somewhat unfortunate, because many forms of bias are not related to the selection of the sample.

We discussed nonsampling errors in Chapter 7. Errors due to sample selection problems, such as sampling frame errors, are systematic (nonsampling) errors and should not be classified as random sampling errors.

Less Than Perfectly Representative Samples

Random sampling errors and systematic errors associated with the sampling process may combine to yield a sample that is less than perfectly representative of the population. Exhibit 12.3 illustrates two nonsampling errors (sampling frame error and nonresponse error) related to sample design.

EXHIBIT 12.3 **Errors Associated with Sampling**

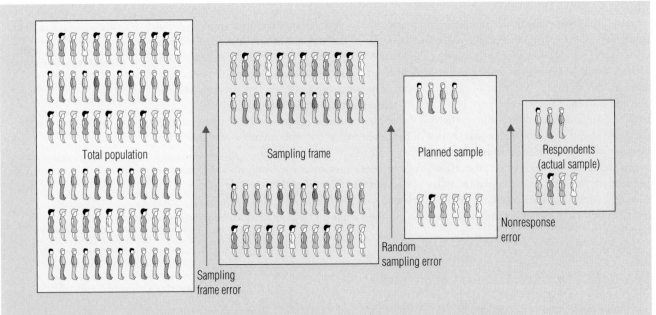

Source: Adapted from Keith K. Cox and Ben M. Enis, *The Marketing Research Process* (Pacific Palisades, CA: Goodyear, 1972); and Danny N. Bellenger and Barnet A. Greenberg, *Marketing Research: A Management Information Approach* (Homewood, IL: Richard D. Irwin, 1978), pp. 154–155.

The total population is represented by the area of the largest square. Sampling frame errors eliminate some potential respondents. Random sampling error (due exclusively to random, chance fluctuation) may cause an imbalance in the representativeness of the group. Additional errors will occur if individuals refuse to be interviewed or cannot be contacted. Such nonresponse error may also cause the sample to be less than perfectly representative. Thus, the actual sample is drawn from a population different from (or smaller than) the ideal.

Probability versus Nonprobability Sampling

Several alternative ways to take a sample are available. The main alternative sampling plans may be grouped into two categories: probability techniques and nonprobability techniques.

In **probability sampling**, every element in the population has a *known, nonzero probability* of selection. The simple random sample, in which each member of the population has an equal probability of being selected, is the best-known probability sample.

In **nonprobability sampling**, the probability of any particular member of the population being chosen is unknown. The selection of sampling units in nonprobability sampling is quite arbitrary, as researchers rely heavily on personal judgment. Technically, no appropriate statistical techniques exist for measuring random sampling error from a nonprobability sample. Therefore, projecting the data beyond the sample is, technically speaking, statistically inappropriate. Nevertheless, researchers sometimes find nonprobability samples best suited for a specific researcher purpose. As a result, nonprobability samples are pragmatic and are used in market research.

Probability sampling
A sampling technique in which every member of the population has a known, nonzero probability of selection.

Nonprobability sampling
A sampling technique in which units of the sample are selected on the basis of personal judgment or convenience; the probability of any particular member of the population being chosen is unknown.

Nonprobability Sampling

Although probability sampling is preferred, we will discuss nonprobability sampling first to illustrate some potential sources of error and other weaknesses in sampling.

Convenience Sampling

As the name suggests, **convenience sampling** refers to sampling by obtaining people or units that are conveniently available. A research team may determine that the most convenient and economical method is to set up an interviewing booth from which to intercept consumers at a shopping center. Just before elections, television stations often present person-on-the-street interviews that are presumed to reflect public opinion. (Of course, the television station generally warns that the survey was "unscientific and random" [*sic*].) The college professor who uses his or her students has a captive sample—convenient, but perhaps not always so representative.

Researchers generally use convenience samples to obtain a large number of completed questionnaires quickly and economically, or when obtaining a sample through other means is impractical. For example, many Internet surveys are conducted with volunteer respondents who, either intentionally or by happenstance, visit an organization's website. Although this method produces a large number of responses quickly and at a low cost, selecting all visitors to a website is clearly convenience sampling. Respondents may not be representative because of the haphazard manner by which many of them arrived at the website or because of self-selection bias.

Similarly, research looking for cross-cultural differences in organizational or consumer behavior typically uses convenience samples. Rather than selecting cultures with characteristics relevant to the hypothesis being tested, the researchers conducting these studies often choose cultures to which they have access (for example, because they speak the language or have contacts in that culture's organizations). Further adding to the convenience, cross-cultural research often defines "culture" in terms of nations, which are easier to identify and obtain statistics for, even though many nations include several cultures and some people in a given nation may be more involved

Convenience sampling
The sampling procedure of obtaining those people or units that are most conveniently available.

TOTHEPOINT

A straw vote only shows which way the hot air blows.

—O. Henry

with the international business or academic community than with a particular ethnic culture.[4] Here again, the use of convenience sampling limits how well the research represents the intended population.

The user of research based on a convenience sample should remember that projecting the results beyond the specific sample is inappropriate. Convenience samples are best used for exploratory research when additional research will subsequently be conducted with a probability sample.

Judgment Sampling

Judgment (purposive) sampling
A nonprobability sampling technique in which an experienced individual selects the sample based on personal judgment about some appropriate characteristic of the sample member.

Judgment (purposive) sampling is a nonprobability sampling technique in which an experienced individual selects the sample based on his or her judgment about some appropriate characteristics required of the sample member. Researchers select samples that satisfy their specific purposes, even if they are not fully representative. The consumer price index (CPI) is based on a judgment sample of market-basket items, housing costs, and other selected goods and services expected to reflect a representative sample of items consumed by most Americans. Test-market cities often are selected because they are viewed as typical cities whose demographic profiles closely match the national profile. A fashion manufacturer regularly selects a sample of key accounts believed to be capable of providing information needed to predict what may sell in the fall. Thus, the sample is selected to achieve this specific objective.

Judgment sampling often is used in attempts to forecast election results. People frequently wonder how a television network can predict the results of an election with only 2 percent of the votes reported. Political and sampling experts judge which small voting districts approximate overall state returns from previous election years; then these *bellwether precincts* are selected as the sampling units. Of course, the assumption is that the past voting records of these districts are still representative of the political behavior of the state's population.

Quota Sampling

Suppose a firm wishes to investigate consumers who currently subscribe to an HDTV (high definition television) service. The researchers may wish to ensure that each brand of HDTV televisions is included proportionately in the sample. Strict probability sampling procedures would likely underrepresent certain brands and overrepresent other brands. If the selection process were left strictly to chance, some variation would be expected.

Quota sampling
A nonprobability sampling procedure that ensures that various subgroups of a population will be represented on pertinent characteristics to the exact extent that the investigator desires.

The purpose of **quota sampling** is to ensure that the various subgroups in a population are represented on pertinent sample characteristics to the exact extent that the investigators desire. Stratified sampling, a probability sampling procedure described in the next section, also has this objective, but it should not be confused with quota sampling. In quota sampling, the interviewer has a quota to achieve. For example, an interviewer in a particular city may be assigned 100 interviews, 35 with owners of Sony TVs, 30 with owners of Samsung TVs, 18 with owners of Panasonic TVs, and the rest with owners of other brands. The interviewer is responsible for finding enough people to meet the quota. Aggregating the various interview quotas yields a sample that represents the desired proportion of each subgroup.

■ POSSIBLE SOURCES OF BIAS

The logic of classifying the population by pertinent subgroups is essentially sound. However, because respondents are selected according to a convenience sampling procedure rather than on a probability basis (as in stratified sampling), the haphazard selection of subjects may introduce bias. For example, a college professor hired some of his students to conduct a quota sample based on age. When analyzing the data, the professor discovered that almost all the people in the "under twenty-five years" category were college-educated. Interviewers, being human, tend to prefer to interview people who are similar to themselves.

Quota samples tend to include people who are easily found, willing to be interviewed, and middle class. Fieldworkers are given considerable leeway to exercise their judgment concerning selection of actual respondents. Interviewers often concentrate their interviewing in areas with heavy pedestrian traffic such as downtowns, shopping malls, and college campuses. Those who interview door-to-door learn quickly that quota requirements are difficult to meet by interviewing whoever happens to appear at the door. People who are more likely to stay at home generally share a less active lifestyle and are less likely to be meaningfully employed. One interviewer related a story of working in an upper-middle-class neighborhood. After a few blocks, he arrived in a neighborhood of mansions. Feeling that most of the would-be respondents were above his station, the interviewer skipped these houses because he felt uncomfortable knocking on doors that would be answered by these people or their hired help.

ADVANTAGES OF QUOTA SAMPLING

The major advantages of quota sampling over probability sampling are speed of data collection, lower costs, and convenience. Although quota sampling has many problems, carefully supervised data collection may provide a representative sample of the various subgroups within a population. Quota sampling may be appropriate when the researcher knows that a certain demographic group is more likely to refuse to cooperate with a survey. For instance, if older men are more likely to refuse, a higher quota can be set for this group so that the proportion of each demographic category will be similar to the proportions in the population. A number of laboratory experiments also rely on quota sampling because it is difficult to find a sample of the general population willing to visit a laboratory to participate in an experiment.

Snowball Sampling

A variety of procedures known as **snowball sampling** involve using probability methods for an initial selection of respondents and then obtaining additional respondents through information provided by the initial respondents. This technique is used to locate members of rare populations by referrals. Suppose a manufacturer of sports equipment is considering marketing a mahogany croquet set for serious adult players. This market is certainly small. An extremely large sample would be necessary to find 100 serious adult croquet players. It would be much more economical to survey, say, 300 people, find 15 croquet players, and ask them for the names of other players.

Reduced sample sizes and costs are clearcut advantages of snowball sampling. However, bias is likely to enter into the study because a person suggested by someone also in the sample has a higher probability of being similar to the first person. If there are major differences between those who are widely known by others and those who are not, this technique may present some serious problems. However, snowball sampling may be used to locate and recruit heavy users, such as consumers who buy more than fifty compact disks per year, for focus groups. As the focus group is not expected to be a generalized sample, snowball sampling may be appropriate.

Snowball sampling
A sampling procedure in which initial respondents are selected by probability methods and additional respondents are obtained from information provided by the initial respondents.

Probability Sampling

All probability sampling techniques are based on chance selection procedures. Because the probability sampling process is random, the bias inherent in nonprobability sampling procedures is eliminated. Note that the term *random* refers to the procedure for selecting the sample; it does not describe the data in the sample. *Randomness* characterizes a procedure whose outcome cannot be predicted because it depends on chance. Randomness should not be thought of as unplanned or unscientific—it is the basis of all probability sampling techniques. This section will examine the various probability sampling methods.

Simple Random Sampling

The sampling procedure that ensures each element in the population will have an equal chance of being included in the sample is called **simple random sampling**. Examples include drawing names from a hat and selecting the winning raffle ticket from a large drum. If the names or raffle

Simple random sampling
A sampling procedure that assures each element in the population of an equal chance of being included in the sample.

tickets are thoroughly stirred, each person or ticket should have an equal chance of being selected. In contrast to other, more complex types of probability sampling, this process is simple because it requires only one stage of sample selection.

Although drawing names or numbers out of a fishbowl, using a spinner, rolling dice, or turning a roulette wheel may be an appropriate way to draw a sample from a small population, when populations consist of large numbers of elements, sample selection is based on tables of random numbers (see Table A.1 in the Appendix) or computer-generated random numbers.

Suppose a researcher is interested in selecting a simple random sample of all the Honda dealers in California, New Mexico, Arizona, and Nevada. Each dealer's name is assigned a number from 1 to 105. The numbers can be written on paper slips, and all the slips can be placed in a bowl. After the slips of paper have been thoroughly mixed, one is selected for each sampling unit. Thus, if the sample size is 35, the selection procedure must be repeated 34 times after the first slip has been selected. Mixing the slips after each selection will ensure that those at the bottom of the bowl will continue to have an equal chance of being selected in the sample.

To use a table of random numbers, a serial number is first assigned to each element of the population. Assuming the population is 99,999 or fewer, five-digit numbers may be selected from the table of random numbers merely by reading the numbers in any column or row, moving up, down, left, or right. A random starting point should be selected at the outset. For convenience, we will assume that we have randomly selected as our starting point the first five digits in columns 1 through 5, row 1, of Table A.1 in the Appendix. The first number in our sample would be 37751; moving down, the next numbers would be 50915, 99142, and so on.

The random-digit dialing technique of sample selection requires that the researcher identify the exchange or exchanges of interest (the first three numbers) and then use a table of numbers to select the next four numbers. In practice, the exchanges are not always selected randomly. Researchers who wanted to find out whether Americans of African descent prefer being called "black" or "African-American" narrowed their sampling frame by selecting exchanges associated with geographic areas where the proportion of the population (African-Americans/blacks) was at least 30 percent. The reasoning was that this made the survey procedure far more efficient, considering that the researchers were trying to contact a group representing less than 15 percent of U.S. households. This initial judgment sampling raises the same issues we discussed regarding non-probability sampling. In this study, the researchers found that respondents were most likely to prefer the term *black* if they had attended schools that were about half black and half white.[5] If such experiences influence the answers to the question of interest to the researchers, the fact that blacks who live in predominantly white communities are underrepresented may introduce bias into the results.

Systematic Sampling

Systematic sampling
A sampling procedure in which a starting point is selected by a random process and then every n^{th} number on the list is selected.

Suppose a researcher wants to take a sample of 1,000 from a list of 200,000 names. With **systematic sampling**, every 200th name from the list would be drawn. The procedure is extremely simple. A starting point is selected by a random process; then every n^{th} number on the list is selected. To take a sample of consumers from a rural telephone directory that does not separate business from residential listings, every 23rd name might be selected as the *sampling interval*. In the process, Mike's Restaurant might be selected. This unit is inappropriate because it is a business listing rather than a consumer listing, so the next eligible name would be selected as the sampling unit, and the systematic process would continue.

Periodicity
A problem that occurs in systematic sampling when the original list has a systematic pattern.

While systematic sampling is not actually a random selection procedure, it does yield random results if the arrangement of the items in the list is random in character. The problem of **periodicity** occurs if a list has a systematic pattern—that is, if it is not random in character. Collecting retail sales information every seventh day would result in a distorted sample because there would be a systematic pattern of selecting sampling units—sales for only one day of the week (perhaps Monday) would be sampled. If the first 50 names on a list of contributors to a charity were extremely large donors, periodicity bias might occur in sampling every 200th name. Periodicity is rarely a problem for most sampling in marketing research, but researchers should be aware of the possibility.

Stratified Sampling

The usefulness of dividing the population into subgroups, or *strata,* whose members are more or less equal with respect to some characteristic was illustrated in our discussion of quota sampling. The first step is the same for both stratified and quota sampling: choosing strata on the basis of existing information—for example, classifying retail outlets based on annual sales volume. However, the process of selecting sampling units within the strata differs substantially. In **stratified sampling**, a subsample is drawn using simple random sampling within each stratum. This is not true of quota sampling.

The reason for taking a stratified sample is to obtain a more efficient sample than would be possible with simple random sampling. Suppose, for example, that urban and rural groups have widely different attitudes toward energy conservation, but members within each group hold very similar attitudes. Random sampling error will be reduced with the use of stratified sampling, because each group is internally homogeneous but there are comparative differences between groups. More technically, a smaller standard error may result from this stratified sampling because the groups will be adequately represented when strata are combined.

Another reason for selecting a stratified sample is to ensure that the sample will accurately reflect the population on the basis of the criterion or criteria used for stratification. This is a concern because occasionally simple random sampling yields a disproportionate number of one group or another and the sample ends up being less representative than it could be.

A researcher can select a stratified sample as follows. First, a variable (sometimes several variables) is identified as an efficient basis for stratification. A stratification variable must be a characteristic of the population elements known to be related to the dependent variable or other variables of interest. The variable chosen should increase homogeneity within each stratum and increase heterogeneity between strata. The stratification variable usually is a categorical variable or one easily converted into categories (that is, subgroups). For example, a pharmaceutical company interested in measuring how often physicians prescribe a certain drug might choose physicians' training as a basis for stratification. In this example the mutually exclusive strata are MDs (medical doctors) and ODs (osteopathic doctors).

Next, for each separate subgroup or stratum, a list of population elements must be obtained. (If such lists are not available, they can be costly to prepare, and if a complete listing is not available, a true stratified probability sample cannot be selected.) Using a table of random numbers or some other device, a *separate* simple random sample is then taken within each stratum. Of course, the researcher must determine how large a sample to draw for each stratum. This issue is discussed in the following section.

Stratified sampling
A probability sampling procedure in which simple random subsamples that are more or less equal on some characteristic are drawn from within each stratum of the population.

Cluster Sampling

The purpose of **cluster sampling** is to sample economically while retaining the characteristics of a probability sample. Consider a researcher who must conduct five hundred personal interviews with consumers scattered throughout the United States. Travel costs are likely to be enormous because the amount of time spent traveling will be substantially greater than the time spent in the interviewing process. If an aspirin marketer can assume the product will be equally successful in Phoenix and Baltimore, or if a frozen pizza manufacturer assumes its product will suit the tastes of Texans equally as well as Oregonians, cluster sampling may be used to represent the United States.

In a cluster sample, the primary sampling unit is no longer the individual element in the population (for example, grocery stores) but a larger cluster of elements located in proximity to one another (for example, cities). The *area sample* is the most popular type of cluster sample. A grocery store researcher, for example, may randomly choose several geographic areas as primary sampling units and then interview all or a sample of grocery stores within the geographic clusters. Interviews are confined to these clusters only. No interviews occur in other clusters. Cluster sampling is classified as a probability sampling technique because of either the random selection of clusters or the random selection of elements within each cluster. Some examples of clusters appear in Exhibit 12.4 on the next page.

Cluster sampling
An economically efficient sampling technique in which the primary sampling unit is not the individual element in the population but a large cluster of elements; clusters are selected randomly.

EXHIBIT 12.4
Examples of Clusters

Population Element	Possible Clusters in the United States
U.S. adult population	States Counties Metropolitan Statistical Areas Census Tracts Blocks Households
College seniors	Colleges
Manufacturing firms	Counties Metropolitan Statistical Areas Localities Plants
Airline travelers	Airports Planes
Sports fans	Football Stadiums Basketball Arenas Baseball Parks

Cluster samples frequently are used when lists of the sample population are not available. For example, when researchers investigating employees and self-employed workers for a downtown revitalization project found that a comprehensive list of these people was not available, they decided to take a cluster sample, selecting organizations (business and government) as the clusters. A sample of firms within the central business district was developed, using stratified probability sampling to identify clusters. Next, individual workers within the firms (clusters) were randomly selected and interviewed concerning the central business district.

Ideally, a cluster should be as heterogeneous as the population itself—a mirror image of the population. A problem may arise with cluster sampling if the characteristics and attitudes of the elements within the cluster are too similar. For example, geographic neighborhoods tend to have residents of the same socioeconomic status. Students at a university tend to share similar beliefs. This problem may be mitigated by constructing clusters composed of diverse elements and by selecting a large number of sampled clusters.

Multistage Area Sampling

Multistage area sampling
Sampling that involves using a combination of two or more probability sampling techniques.

So far we have described two-stage cluster sampling. **Multistage area sampling** involves two or more steps that combine some of the probability techniques already described. Typically, geographic areas are randomly selected in progressively smaller (lower-population) units. For example, a political pollster investigating an election in Arizona might first choose counties within the state to ensure that the different areas are represented in the sample. In the second step, precincts within the selected counties may be chosen. As a final step, the pollster may select blocks (or households) within the precincts, then interview all the blocks (or households) within the geographic area. Researchers may take as many steps as necessary to achieve a representative sample. Exhibit 12.5 graphically portrays a multistage area sampling process frequently used by a major academic research center. Progressively smaller geographic areas are chosen until a single housing unit is selected for interviewing.

The Bureau of the Census provides maps, population information, demographic characteristics for population statistics, and so on, by several small geographical areas; these may be useful in sampling. Census classifications of small geographic areas vary, depending on the extent of urbanization within Metropolitan Statistical Areas (MSAs) or counties.

EXHIBIT 12.5 **Illustration of Multistage Area Sampling**

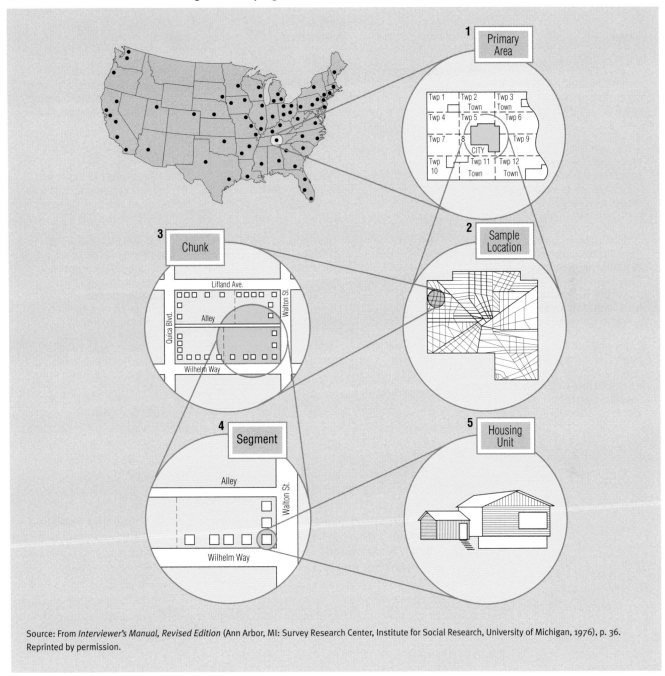

Source: From *Interviewer's Manual, Revised Edition* (Ann Arbor, MI: Survey Research Center, Institute for Social Research, University of Michigan, 1976), p. 36. Reprinted by permission.

What Is the Appropriate Sample Design?

A researcher who must decide on the most appropriate sample design for a specific project will identify a number of sampling criteria and evaluate the relative importance of each criterion before selecting a sampling design. This section outlines and briefly discusses the most common criteria. Exhibit 12.6 on the next page summarizes the advantages and disadvantages of each nonprobability sampling technique, and Exhibit 12.7 does the same for the probability sampling techniques.

EXHIBIT 12.6 **Comparison of Sampling Techniques: Nonprobability Samples**

Description	Nonprobability Samples Cost and Degree of Use	Advantages	Disadvantages
1. *Convenience:* The researcher uses the most convenient sample or economical sample units.	Very low cost, extensively used	No need for list of population	Unrepresentative samples likely; random sampling error estimates cannot be made; projecting data beyond sample is relatively risky
2. *Judgment:* An expert or experienced researcher selects the sample to fulfill a purpose, such as ensuring that all members have a certain characteristic.	Moderate cost, average use	Useful for certain types of forecasting; sample guaranteed to meet a specific objective	Bias due to expert's beliefs may make sample unrepresentative; projecting data beyond sample is risky
3. *Quota:* The researcher classifies the population by pertinent properties, determines the desired proportion to sample from each class, and fixes quotas for each interviewer.	Moderate cost, very extensively used	Introduces some stratification of population; requires no list of population	Introduces bias in researcher's classification of subjects; nonrandom selection within classes means error from population cannot be estimated; projecting data beyond sample is risky
4. *Snowball:* Initial respondents are selected by probability samples; additional respondents are obtained by referral from initial respondents.	Low cost, used in special situations	Useful in locating members of rare populations	High bias because sample units are not independent; projecting data beyond sample is risky

Degree of Accuracy

Selecting a representative sample is important to all researchers. However, the degree of accuracy required or the researcher's tolerance for sampling and nonsampling error may vary from project to project, especially when cost savings or another benefit may be a trade-off for a reduction in accuracy.

For example, when the sample is being selected for an exploratory research project, a high priority may not be placed on accuracy because a highly representative sample may not be necessary. For other, more conclusive projects, the sample result must precisely represent a population's characteristics, and the researcher must be willing to spend the time and money needed to achieve accuracy.

Resources

The cost associated with the different sampling techniques varies tremendously. If the researcher's financial and human resources are restricted, certain options will have to be eliminated. For a graduate student working on a master's thesis, conducting a national survey is almost always out of the question because of limited resources. Managers concerned with the cost of the research versus the value of the information often will opt to save money by using a nonprobability sampling design rather than make the decision to conduct no research at all.

Time

A researcher who needs to meet a deadline or complete a project quickly will be more likely to select a simple, less time-consuming sample design. A telephone survey that uses a sample based on random-digit dialing takes considerably less time than a survey that uses an elaborate disproportional stratified sample.

EXHIBIT 12.7 **Comparison of Sampling Techniques: Probability Samples**

Description	**Probability Samples** Cost and Degree of Use	Advantages	Disadvantages
1. *Simple random:* The researcher assigns each member of the sampling frame a number, then selects sample units by random method.	High cost, moderately used in practice (most common in random digit dialing and with computerized sampling frames)	Only minimal advance knowledge of population needed; easy to analyze data and compute error	Requires sampling frame to work from; does not use knowledge of population that researcher may have; larger errors for same sampling size than in stratified sampling; respondents may be widely dispersed, hence cost may be higher
2. *Systematic:* The researcher uses natural ordering or the order of the sampling frame, selects an arbitrary starting point, then selects items at a preselected interval.	Moderate cost, moderately used	Simple to draw sample; easy to check	If sampling interval is related to periodic ordering of the population, may introduce increased variability
3. *Stratified:* The researcher divides the population into groups and randomly selects subsamples from each group. Variations include proportional, disproportional, and optimal allocation of subsample sizes.	High cost, moderately used	Ensures representation of all groups in sample; characteristics of each stratum can be estimated and comparisons made; reduces variability for same sample size	Requires accurate information on proportion in each stratum; if stratified lists are not already available, they can be costly to prepare
4. *Cluster:* The researcher selects sampling units at random, then does a complete observation of all units or draws a probability sample in the group.	Low cost, frequently used	If clusters geographically defined, yields lowest field cost; requires listing of all clusters, but of individuals only within clusters; can estimate characteristics of clusters as well as of population	Larger error for comparable size than with other probability samples; researcher must be able to assign population members to unique cluster or else duplication or omission of individuals will result
5. *Multistage:* Progressively smaller areas are selected in each stage by some combination of the first four techniques.	High cost, frequently used, especially in nationwide surveys	Depends on techniques combined	Depends on techniques combined

Advance Knowledge of the Population

Advance knowledge of population characteristics, such as the availability of lists of population members, is an important criterion. In many cases, however, no list of population elements will be available to the researcher. This is especially true when the population element is defined by ownership of a particular product or brand, by experience in performing a specific job task, or on a qualitative dimension. A lack of adequate lists may automatically rule out systematic sampling, stratified sampling, or other sampling designs, or it may dictate that a preliminary study, such as a short telephone survey using random digit dialing, be conducted to generate information to build a sampling frame for the primary study. In many developing countries, things like reverse directories are rare. Thus, researchers planning sample designs have to work around this limitation.

National versus Local Project

Geographic proximity of population elements will influence sample design. When population elements are unequally distributed geographically, a cluster sample may become much more attractive.

RESEARCHSNAPSHOT

Reactions to Handbills in Hong Kong

On busy city sidewalks, pedestrians often encounter a form of advertising called *handbills,* leaflets handed to passersby, informing them of a new store, a theater event, or some other nearby product or service. In highly populated urban centers, handbills are a common and successful method of direct marketing promotion—reaching tens of thousands of potential customers. Two marketing researchers in Hong Kong recently decided that this form of advertising had received little research attention, so they conducted exploratory research into consumer attitudes about handbills.

The selection of a sample design started with advance knowledge of the researchers' population. They decided to interview people in Hong Kong because the city has an extremely dense population—6 million people within 419 square miles. As a result, pedestrian traffic is heavy, and handbill distribution is a common sight on Hong Kong streets. A sample drawn from the Hong Kong population would be likely to include many people who have experiences with and attitudes toward handbills. The Hong Kong population provided another advantage. The researchers wished to use a telephone questionnaire, and the majority of households in Hong Kong have a telephone line with a registered number. Finally, language was unlikely to be a problem; the survey was conducted in Chinese, spoken by all but a small percentage of Hong Kong's population.

In a sense, this survey involved a convenience sample, drawn from a population where the researchers live and work, rather than other parts of the world, where perhaps opinions would have been more diverse. Nevertheless, for an exploratory study into a formerly unexplored topic, the greater resources required for a more complex sampling method might not have been justified. The researchers were able to find response patterns for further investigation: People who accepted handbills were more likely to be female, relatively young, and have the equivalent of a high school education. Most of them took the handbills to help the distributor finish his or her work, and most read the handbills.

Source: Gerard Prendergast and Yuen Sze Man, "Perceptions of Handbills as a Promotional Medium: An Exploratory Study," Journal of Advertising Research, 45 (March 2005), 124–131; "Direct Delivery," Direct Marketing of Asia, Limited, http://www.dm-asia.com, accessed March 20, 2006.

Internet Sampling Is Unique

Internet surveys allow researchers to reach a large sample rapidly—both an advantage and a disadvantage. Sample size requirements can be met overnight or in some cases almost instantaneously. A researcher can, for instance, release a survey during the morning in the Eastern Standard Time zone and have all sample size requirements met before anyone on the West Coast wakes up. If rapid response rates are expected, the sample for an Internet survey should be metered out across all time zones. In addition, people in some populations are more likely to go online during the weekend than on a weekday. If the researcher can anticipate a day-of-the-week effect, the survey should be kept open long enough so that all sample units have the opportunity to participate in the research project.

The ease and low cost of an Internet survey also has contributed to a flood of online questionnaires, some more formal than others. As a result, frequent Internet users may be more selective about which surveys they bother answering. Researchers investigating college students' attitudes toward environmental issues found that those who responded to an e-mail request that had been sent to all students tended to be more concerned about the environment than students who were contacted individually through systematic sampling. The researchers concluded that students who cared about the issues were more likely to respond to the online survey.[6]

Another disadvantage of Internet surveys is the lack of computer ownership and Internet access among certain segments of the population. A sample of Internet users is representative only of Internet users, who tend to be younger, better educated, and more affluent than the general population. This is not to say that all Internet samples are unrepresentative of all target populations. Nevertheless, when using Internet surveys, researchers should be keenly aware of potential sampling problems that can arise due to systematic characteristics of heavy computer users.

Website Visitors

As noted earlier, many Internet surveys are conducted with volunteer respondents who visit an organization's website intentionally or by happenstance. These *unrestricted samples* are clearly convenience samples. They may not be representative because of the haphazard manner by which many respondents arrived at a particular website or because of self-selection bias.

A better technique for sampling website visitors is to randomly select sampling units. SurveySite, a company that specializes in conducting Internet surveys, collects data by using its "pop-up survey" software. The software selects web visitors at random and "pops up" a small javascript window asking the person if he or she wants to participate in an evaluation survey. If the person clicks "Yes," a new window containing the online survey opens up. The person can then browse the site at his or her own pace and switch to the survey at any time to express an opinion.[7]

Randomly selecting website visitors can cause a problem. It is possible to overrepresent frequent visitors to the site and thus represent site visits rather than visitors. Several programming techniques and technologies (using cookies, registration data, or prescreening) are available to help accomplish more representative sampling based on site traffic.[8] Details of these techniques are beyond the scope of this discussion.

This type of random sampling is most valuable if the target population is defined as visitors to a particular website. Evaluation and analysis of visitors' perceptions and experiences of the website would be a typical survey objective with this type of sample. Researchers who have broader interests may obtain Internet samples in a variety of other ways.

Panel Samples

Drawing a probability sample from an established consumer panel or other prerecruited membership panel is a popular, scientific, and effective method for creating a sample of Internet users. Typically, sampling from a panel yields a high response rate because panel members have already agreed to cooperate with the research organization's e-mail or Internet surveys. Often panel members are compensated for their time with a sweepstakes, a small cash incentive, or redeemable points. Further, because the panel has already supplied demographic characteristics and other information from previous questionnaires, researchers are able to select panelists based on product ownership, lifestyle, or other characteristics. A variety of sampling methods and data transformation techniques can be applied to assure that sample results are representative of the general public or a targeted population.

Consider Harris Interactive Inc., an Internet survey research organization that maintains a panel of more than 6.5 million individuals in the United States. In the early twenty-first century, Harris plans to expand this panel to between 10 million and 15 million and to include an additional 10 million people internationally.[9] A database this large allows the company to draw simple random samples, stratified samples, and quota samples from its panel members.

Harris Interactive finds that two demographic groups are not fully accessible via Internet sampling: people ages 65 and older—a group that is rapidly growing—and those with annual incomes of less than $15,000. In contrast, 18- to 25-year-olds—a group that historically has been very hard to reach by traditional research methods—are now extremely easy to reach over the Internet.[10]

To ensure that survey results are representative, Harris Interactive uses a *propensity-weighting* scheme. The research company does parallel studies—by phone as well as over the Internet—to test the accuracy of its Internet data-gathering capabilities. Researchers look at the results of the telephone surveys and match those against the Internet-only survey results. Next, they use propensity weighting to adjust the results, taking into account the motivational and behavioral differences between the online and offline populations. (How propensity weighting adjusts for the difference between the Internet population and the general population is beyond the scope of this discussion.)

Recruited Ad Hoc Samples

Another means of obtaining an Internet sample is to obtain or create a sampling frame of e-mail addresses on an *ad hoc* basis. Researchers may create the sampling frame offline or online. Databases containing e-mail addresses can be compiled from many sources, including customer/client lists, advertising banners on pop-up windows that recruit survey participants, online sweepstakes, and registration forms that must be filled out in order to gain access to a particular website. Researchers may contact respondents by "snail mail" or by telephone to ask for their e-mail addresses and obtain permission for an Internet survey. Using offline techniques, such as random-digit dialing and short telephone screening interviews, to recruit respondents can be a very practical way to get a representative sample for an Internet survey. Companies anticipating future Internet research can develop a valuable database for sample recruitment by including e-mail addresses in their customer relationship databases (by inviting customers to provide that information on product registration cards, in telephone interactions, through on-site registration, etc.).[11]

Opt-in Lists

Opt in
To give permission to receive selected e-mail, such as questionnaires, from a company with an Internet presence.

Survey Sampling International specializes in providing sampling frames and scientifically drawn samples. The company offers more than 3,500 lists of high-quality, targeted e-mail addresses of individuals who have given permission to receive e-mail messages related to a particular topic of interest. Survey Sampling International's database contains millions of Internet users who **opt in** for limited participation. An important feature of Survey Sampling International's database is that the company has each individual confirm and reconfirm interest in communicating about a topic before the person's e-mail address is added to the company's database.[12]

By whatever technique the sampling frame is compiled, it is important *not* to send unauthorized e-mail to respondents. If individuals do not *opt in* to receive e-mail from a particular organization, they may consider unsolicited survey requests to be spam. A researcher cannot expect high response rates from individuals who have not agreed to be surveyed. Spamming is not tolerated by experienced Internet users and can easily backfire, creating a host of problems—the most extreme being complaints to the Internet service provider (ISP), which may shut down the survey site.

Summary

1. Define *sample, population, population element,* and *census.* A sample is a subset, or some part, of a larger population. The purpose of sampling is to estimate an unknown characteristic of a population. A population (universe) is any complete group; the term population element refers to an individual member of the population. A census is an investigation of all the individual elements that make up the population—a total enumeration rather than a sample.

2. Explain reasons for taking a sample rather than a complete census. Sampling is a procedure that uses a small number of units of a given population as a basis for drawing conclusions about the whole population. Sampling often is necessary because it would be practically impossible to conduct a census to measure characteristics of all units of a population. Samples also are needed in cases where measurement involves destruction of the measured unit.

3. Describe the process of identifying a target population and selecting a sampling frame. The first problem in sampling is to define the target population. Incorrect or vague definition of this population is likely to produce misleading results. A sampling frame is a list of elements, or individual members, of the overall population from which the sample is drawn. A sampling unit is a single element or group of elements subject to selection in the sample.

4. Compare random sampling and systematic (nonsampling) errors. There are two sources of discrepancy between the sample results and the population parameters. One, random sampling error, arises from chance variations of the sample from the population. Random sampling error is a function of sample size and may be estimated using the central-limit theorem, discussed in Chapter 13. Systematic, or nonsampling, error comes from sources such as sampling frame error, mistakes in recording responses, or nonresponses from persons who are not contacted or who refuse to participate.

5. Identify the types of nonprobability sampling, including their advantages and disadvantages. The two major classes of sampling methods are probability and nonprobability techniques. Nonprobability techniques include convenience sampling, judgment sampling, quota sampling, and snowball sampling. They are convenient to use, but there are no statistical techniques with which to measure their random sampling error.

6. **Summarize the advantages and disadvantages of the various types of probability samples.** Probability samples are based on chance selection procedures. These include simple random sampling, systematic sampling, stratified sampling, and cluster sampling. With these techniques, random sampling error can be accurately predicted.

7. **Discuss how to choose an appropriate sample design, as well as challenges for Internet sampling.** A researcher who must determine the most appropriate sampling design for a specific project will identify a number of sampling criteria and evaluate the relative importance of each criterion before selecting a design. The most common criteria concern accuracy requirements, available resources, time constraints, knowledge availability, and analytical requirements. Internet sampling presents some unique issues. Researchers must be aware that samples may be unrepresentative because not everyone has a computer or access to the Internet. Convenience samples drawn from website visitors can create problems. Drawing a probability sample from an established consumer panel or an ad hoc sampling frame whose members opt in can be effective.

Key Terms and Concepts

Sample
Population (universe)
Population element
Census
Sampling frame
Reverse directory
Sampling frame error
Sampling unit
Primary sampling unit (PSU)

Secondary sampling unit
Tertiary sampling unit
Random sampling error
Systematic (nonsampling) error
Probability sampling
Nonprobability sampling
Convenience sampling
Judgment (purposive) sampling
Quota sampling

Snowball sampling
Simple random sampling
Systematic sampling
Periodicity
Stratified sampling
Cluster sampling
Multistage area sampling
Opt in

Questions for Review and Critical Thinking

1. If you decide whether you want to see a new movie or television program on the basis of the "coming attractions" or television commercial previews, are you using a sampling technique? A scientific sampling technique?
2. Name some possible sampling frames for the following:
   a. Electrical contractors
   b. Tennis players
   c. Dog owners
   d. Foreign-car owners
   e. Wig and hair goods retailers
   f. Minority-owned businesses
   g. Men over six feet tall
3. Describe the difference between a probability sample and a nonprobability sample.
4. In what types of situations is conducting a census more appropriate than sampling? When is sampling more appropriate than taking a census?
5. Comment on the following sampling designs:
   a. A citizen's group interested in generating public and financial support for a new university basketball arena prints a questionnaire in area newspapers. Readers return the questionnaires by mail.
   b. A department store that wishes to examine whether it is losing or gaining customers draws a sample from its list of credit card holders by selecting every tenth name.
   c. A motorcycle manufacturer decides to research consumer characteristics by sending one hundred questionnaires to each of its dealers. The dealers will then use their sales records to

track down buyers of this brand of motorcycle and distribute the questionnaires.
   d. An advertising executive suggests that advertising effectiveness be tested in the real world. A one-page ad is placed in a magazine. One-half of the space is used for the ad itself. On the other half, a short questionnaire requests that readers comment on the ad. An incentive will be given for the first thousand responses.
   e. A research company obtains a sample for a focus group through organized groups such as church groups, clubs, and schools. The organizations are paid for securing respondents; no individual is directly compensated.
   f. A researcher suggests replacing a consumer diary panel with a sample of customers who regularly shop at a supermarket that uses optical scanning equipment. The burden of recording purchases by humans will be replaced by computerized longitudinal data.
   g. A banner ad on a business-oriented website reads, "Are you a large company Sr. Executive? Qualified execs receive $50 for under 10 minutes of time. Take the survey now!" Is this an appropriate way to select a sample of business executives?
6. When would a researcher use a judgment, or purposive, sample?
7. A telephone interviewer asks, "I would like to ask you about race. Are you Native American, Hispanic, African-American, Asian, or white?" After the respondent replies, the interviewer says, "We have conducted a large number of surveys with people of your background, and we do not need to question you further. Thank you for your cooperation." What type of sampling is likely being used?

8. If researchers know that consumers in various geographic regions respond quite differently to a product category, such as tomato sauce, is area sampling appropriate? Why or why not?

9. What are the benefits of stratified sampling?

10. What geographic units within a metropolitan area are useful for sampling?

11. Selection for jury duty is supposed to be a totally random process. Comment on the following computer selection procedures, and determine if they are indeed random:

   a. A program instructs the computer to scan the list of names and pick names that were next to those from the last scan.

   b. Three-digit numbers are randomly generated to select jurors from a list of licensed drivers. If the weight information listed on the license matches the random number, the person is selected.

   c. The juror source list is obtained by merging a list of registered voters with a list of licensed drivers.

12. **ETHICS** To ensure a good session, a company selects focus group members from a list of articulate participants instead of conducting random sampling. The client did not inquire about sample selection when it accepted the proposal. Is this ethical?

13. **'NET** Go to http://www.reversephonedirectory.com and put in your phone number. How accurate is this database?

Case 12.1 Who's Fishing?

Washington Times columnist Gene Mueller writes about fishing and other outdoor sporting activities.[13] Mueller commented recently that although interest groups express concerns about the impact of saltwater fishers on the fish population, no one really knows how many people fish for recreation or how many fish they catch. This situation would challenge marketers interested in the population of anglers.

How could a marketer get an accurate sample? One idea would be to contact residents of coastal counties using random-digit dialing. This sampling frame would include many, if not all, of the people who fish in the ocean, but it would also include many people who do not fish—or who fish for business rather than recreation. A regional agency seeking to gather statistics on anglers, the Atlantic Coastal Cooperative Statistics Program, prefers to develop a sampling frame more related to people who fish.

Another idea would be to use state fishing license records. Privacy would be a drawback, however. Some people might not want their records shared, and they might withhold phone numbers. Further complicating this issue for Atlantic fishing is that most states in the Northeast do not require a license for saltwater fishing. Also exempt in some states are people who fish from the shore and from piers.

A political action group called the Recreational Fishing Alliance suggests that charter fishing businesses collect data.

Questions

1. Imagine that an agency or business has asked for help in gathering data about the number of sports anglers who fish off the coast of Georgia. What advice would you give about sampling? What method or combination of methods would generate the best results?

2. What other criteria besides accuracy would you expect to consider? What sampling methods could help you meet those criteria?

Case 12.2 Scientific Telephone Samples

Scientific Telephone Samples (STS), located in Santa Ana, California, specializes in selling sampling frames for marketing research.[14] The STS sampling frame is based on a database of all working residential telephone exchanges in the United States. Thus, STS can draw from any part of the country—no matter how large or how small. The information is updated several times per year and cross-checked against area code and assigned exchange lists furnished by telephone companies. Exchange and/or working blocks designated for business or governmental telephones, mobile phones, and other commercial services are screened out.

STS can furnish almost any type of random digit sample desired, including

- National samples (continental United States only, or with Alaska and Hawaii)
- Stratified national samples (by census region or division)
- Census region or division samples
- State samples
- Samples by MSA

- County samples
- Samples by zip code
- City samples by zip code
- Exchange samples generated from lists of three-digit exchanges
- Targeted random–digit dialing samples (including over forty variables and special databases for high-income areas, Hispanics, African-Americans, and Asians)

STS offers two different methods for pulling working blocks. Either method can be used regardless of the geographic sampling unit (for example, state, county, zip). The two versions are Type A (unweighted) and Type B (weighted/efficient).

Type A samples are pulled using a strict definition of randomness. They are called "unweighted" samples because each working block has an equal chance of being selected to generate a random digit number. Completed interviews from a Type A sample that has been dialed to exhaustion should be highly representative of the population under study.

Type B, or "efficient," samples are preweighted, so random digit dialing numbers are created from telephone working blocks in proportion to the number of estimated household listings in each working block. Working blocks that are more filled with numbers will be more prevalent in a sample. For example, a working block that had fifty known numbers in existence would have twice the probability of being included as one that had just twenty-five numbers.

Type B samples are most useful when a researcher is willing to overlook a strict definition of randomness in favor of slightly more calling efficiency because of fewer "disconnects." In theory, completed interviews from Type B samples may tend to overrepresent certain types of working blocks, but many researchers feel there is not much difference in representativeness.

Questions

1. Evaluate the geographic options offered by STS. Do they seem to cover all the bases?
2. Evaluate the STS method of random-digit dialing.

CHAPTER 13
DETERMINATION OF SAMPLE SIZE: A REVIEW OF STATISTICAL THEORY

LEARNING OUTCOMES

After studying this chapter, you should be able to

1. Explain the difference between descriptive and inferential statistics
2. Know the difference between population parameters and sample statistics
3. Interpret frequency distributions, proportions, and measures of central tendency
4. Identify and calculate the various measures of dispersion
5. Distinguish among population, sample, and sampling distributions and to identify the mean and standard deviation of each distribution
6. Summarize the use of confidence interval estimates
7. Discuss the major issues in specifying sample size

Chapter Vignette: Federal Reserve Finds Cards Are Replacing Cash

Payment options have gone high-tech. Businesses that sell to consumers—and even charities that seek donations from individuals—need to plan for a wide range of choices beyond traditional cash or checks. Today's spenders are more likely to pay with a debit or credit card or through a variety of methods for electronic transfer of funds. To measure this trend in more detail, researchers at the Federal Reserve conducted surveys of depository institutions (banks, savings and loan institutions, and credit unions), asking them to report the number of each type of payment the institutions processed.[1]

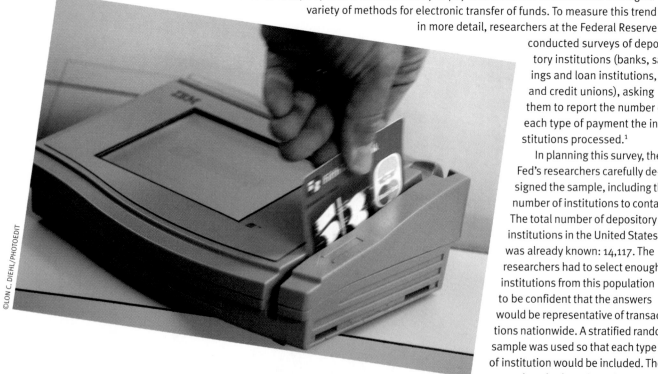

©LON C. DIEHL/PHOTOEDIT

In planning this survey, the Fed's researchers carefully designed the sample, including the number of institutions to contact. The total number of depository institutions in the United States was already known: 14,117. The researchers had to select enough institutions from this population to be confident that the answers would be representative of transactions nationwide. A stratified random sample was used so that each type of institution would be included. The researchers had conducted a similar survey three years earlier and obtained a 54 percent response rate, so they assumed the rate would be similar. Using techniques such as those described in this chapter, the researchers determined that, given the total number of institutions and the response rate, they would need to sample 2,700 depository institutions to obtain results that they could say, with 95 percent confidence, were accurate to within ±5 percent of the responses.

With a response rate just above that of the prior survey, 1,500 institutions responded, giving data on the number of transactions processed in each payment category. Their responses confirmed earlier analysis showing that the number of checks paid in the United States is declining while the number of electronic payments is increasing. Because this survey measured institutional transactions, it could not count the number of purchases made with cash.

Formally identifying the proper sample size requires applied statistical theory. Statistics often inspires dread among students. However, when a would-be researcher learns a few tricks of the trade, using statistics can become second nature. Many of these "tricks" involve learning the specialized language of statisticians. Simply put, if you do not understand the basics of the language, you will have problems in conversation. Statistics is the language of the researcher. This chapter reviews some of the basic terminology of statistical analysis and applies statistical principles to the process of determining a sample size.

Review of Basic Terminology

The first part of this chapter summarizes key statistical concepts necessary for understanding the theory that underlies the derivation of sample size. These sections are intended for students who need to review basic aspects of statistics theory. Even students who received good grades in their elementary statistics classes probably will benefit from a quick review of the basic statistical concepts. Some students will prefer to just skim this material and proceed to page 307, where actual determination of sample size is discussed. Others need to study these sections carefully.

Descriptive and Inferential Statistics

The *Statistical Abstract of the United States* presents table after table of figures associated with numbers of births, number of employees in each county of the United States, and other data that the average person calls "statistics." They are descriptive statistics. Another type of statistics, inferential statistics, is used to make inferences about a whole population from a sample. For example, a firm test-markets a new product in Sacramento and Birmingham, to make an inference from these sample markets about what would happen if the product were sold all over the United States. So, two applications of statistics exist: (1) to describe characteristics of the population or sample and (2) to generalize from a sample to a population.

Sample Statistics and Population Parameters

The primary purpose of inferential statistics is to make a judgment about a population, or the total collection of all elements about which a researcher seeks information. A sample is a subset or relatively small portion of the total number of elements in a given population. Data from a sample are always uncertain but when data come from all elements of a population, certainty is possible.

Sample statistics are measures computed from sample data. **Population parameters** are measured characteristics of a specific population. Sample statistics are used to make inferences (guesses) about population parameters.[2] In our notation, we will generally represent population parameters with Greek lowercase letters—for example, μ or σ—and sample statistics with English letters, such as X or S.

Sample statistics
Variables in a sample or measures computed from sample data.

Population parameters
Variables in a population or measured characteristics of the population.

Making Data Usable

Suppose a telephone survey has been conducted for a savings and loan association. The data have been recorded on a large number of questionnaires. To make the data usable, this information must be organized and summarized. Methods for doing this include frequency distributions, proportions, and measures of central tendency and dispersion.

EXHIBIT 13.1
Frequency Distribution of Deposits

Amount	Frequency (Number of People Who Hold Deposits in Each Range)
Under $3,000	499
$3,000–$4,999	530
$5,000–$9,999	562
$10,000–$14,999	718
$15,000 or more	811
	3,120

Frequency Distributions

Frequency distribution
A set of data organized by summarizing the number of times a particular value of a variable occurs.

One of the most common ways to summarize a set of data is to construct a *frequency table,* or *frequency distribution.* The process begins with recording the number of times a particular value of a variable occurs. This is the frequency of that value. Continuing the example of a telephone survey for a savings and loan association, Exhibit 13.1 represents a frequency distribution of respondents' answers to a question that asked how much money customers had deposited in the institution.

Percentage distribution
A frequency distribution organized into a table (or graph) that summarizes percentage values associated with particular values of a variable.

A similar method that is also simple is to construct a distribution of relative frequency, or a *percentage distribution.* To develop a frequency distribution of percentages, divide the frequency of each value by the total number of observations, and multiply the result by 100. Based on the data in Exhibit 13.1, Exhibit 13.2 shows the percentage distribution of deposits; that is, the percentage of people holding deposits within each range of values.

Probability
The long-run relative frequency with which an event will occur.

Probability is the long-run relative frequency with which an event will occur. Inferential statistics uses the concept of a probability distribution, which is conceptually the same as a percentage distribution except that the data are converted into probabilities. Exhibit 13.3 shows the probability distribution of the savings and loan deposits.

Proportions

Proportion
The percentage of elements that meet some criterion.

When a frequency distribution portrays only a single characteristic in terms of a percentage of the total, it defines the *proportion* of occurrence. A proportion, such as the proportion of tenured professors at a university, indicates the percentage of population elements that successfully meet some standard concerning the particular characteristic. A proportion may be expressed as a percentage, a fraction, or a decimal value.

EXHIBIT 13.2
Percentage Distribution of Deposits

Amount	Percent (Percentage of People Who Hold Deposits in Each Range)
Under $3,000	16
$3,000–$4,999	17
$5,000–$9,999	18
$10,000–$14,999	23
$15,000 or more	26
	100

Amount	Probability
Under $3,000	.16
$3,000–$4,999	.17
$5,000–$9,999	.18
$10,000–$14,999	.23
$15,000 or more	.26
	1.00

EXHIBIT 13.3
Probability Distribution of Deposits

Measures of Central Tendency

On a typical day, a sales manager counts the number of sales calls each sales representative makes. He or she wishes to inspect the data to find the center, or middle area, of the frequency distribution. Central tendency can be measured in three ways—the mean, median, or mode—each of which has a different meaning.

THE MEAN

We all have been exposed to the measure known as the **mean**. The mean is simply the arithmetic average and is a common measure of central tendency. To express this mathematically, we use the summation symbol, the capital Greek letter *sigma* (Σ). A typical use might look like this:

$$\sum_{i=1}^{n} X_i$$

which is a shorthand way to write the sum

$$X_1 + X_2 + X_3 + X_4 + X_5 + \cdots + X_n$$

Below the Σ is the initial value of an index, usually $i, j,$ or k, and above it is the final value, in this case n, the number of observations. The shorthand expression says to replace i in the formula with the values from 1 to 8 and total the observations obtained. Without changing the basic formula, the initial and final index values may be replaced by other values to indicate different starting and stopping points.

Suppose a sales manager supervises the eight salespeople listed in Exhibit 13.4. To express the sum of the salespeople's calls in Σ notation, we just number the salespeople (this number becomes the index number) and associate subscripted variables with their numbers of calls:

Mean
A measure of central tendency; the arithmetic average.

Index		Salesperson	Variable		Number of Calls
1	=	Mike	X_1	=	4
2	=	Patty	X_2	=	3
3	=	Billie	X_3	=	2
4	=	Bob	X_4	=	5
5	=	John	X_5	=	3
6	=	Frank	X_6	=	3
7	=	Chuck	X_7	=	1
8	=	Samantha	X_8	=	5

EXHIBIT 13.4
**Number of Sales Calls
per Day by Salesperson**

Salesperson	Number of Sales Calls
Mike	4
Patty	3
Billie	2
Bob	5
John	3
Frank	3
Chuck	1
Samantha	5
Total	26

We then write an appropriate Σ formula and evaluate it:

$$\sum_{i=1}^{8} X_i = X_1 + X_2 + X_3 + X_4 + X_5 + X_6 + X_7 + X_8$$
$$= 4 + 3 + 2 + 5 + 3 + 3 + 1 + 5$$
$$= 26$$

This notation is the numerator in the formula for the arithmetic mean:

$$\text{Mean} = \frac{\sum_{i=1}^{n} X}{n} = \frac{26}{8} = 3.25$$

The sum $\sum_{i=1}^{n} X$ tells us to add all the Xs whose subscripts are between 1 and n inclusive, where n equals the number of observations. The formula shows that the mean number of sales calls in this example is 3.25.

Researchers generally wish to know the population mean, μ (lowercase Greek letter mu), which is calculated as follows:

$$\mu = \frac{\sum_{i=1}^{N} X}{N}$$

where

N = number of all observations in the population

Often we will not have enough data to calculate the population mean, μ, so we will calculate a sample mean, $\overline{X}$ (read "X bar"), with the following formula:

$$\overline{X} = \frac{\sum_{i=1}^{n} X}{n}$$

where

n = number of observations made in the sample

More likely than not, you already know how to calculate a mean. However, knowing how to distinguish among the symbols Σ, μ, and X is helpful to understand statistics.

In this introductory discussion of the summation sign (Σ), we have used very detailed notation that includes the subscript for the initial index value (i) and the final index value (n). However,

RESEARCHSNAPSHOT

Are Incomes Growing? It Depends What You Measure

When marketers investigate demand, they often are interested in income levels. And if the income of a population is growing, marketers hope that trend signals potential growth in demand. So, marketers may have been pleased to hear the former U.S. Treasury Secretary, John Snow, comment on the strength of the national economy. Snow mentioned data showing that income had grown 8.2 percent between January 2001 and January 2006.

In evaluating these numbers, it's important to consider what is being measured. The growth Snow reported was in per capita after-tax income. Because he measured income after taxes, he was looking at taxation as well as pay rates, which certainly would affect the amount of funds available to consumers. By using *per capita* income, he referred to the total earnings divided by the population—in other words, the statistical mean.

When measuring income, statisticians generally look at the median. Data available for changes in median income paint a less rosy picture. Between 2000 and 2005, the median hourly wage rose by only 2.9 percent. Growth among salaried employees was even stronger. Similarly, marketers are interested in buying power. During the last few years, income and energy prices have increased. However, buying power has increased faster than energy prices leading to an increase in buying power and good news for American retailers. Thus, if one focused on only energy prices or only income, the picture of the economy could be fuzzy.

Sources: Based on Greg Ip, "Snow Defends President's Handling of Economy," The Wall Street Journal, March 20, 2006, http://online.wsj.com; Chain Store Age (2006), "$468 Billion: Disposable Incrome Growth," 82 (January), 141.

©JOE TREE/ALAMY

from this point on, references to Σ will sometimes omit the subscript for the initial index value (i) and the final index value (n).

THE MEDIAN

The next measure of central tendency, the **median**, is the midpoint of the distribution, or the 50th percentile. In other words, the median is the value below which half the values in the sample fall. In the sales manager example, 3 is the median because half the observations are greater than 3 and half are less than 3.

Median
A measure of central tendency that is the midpoint; the value below which half the values in a distribution fall.

THE MODE

In apparel *mode* refers to the most popular fashion. In statistics the **mode** is the measure of central tendency that identifies the value that occurs most often. In our example of sales calls, Patty, John, and Frank each made three sales calls. The value 3 occurs most often, so 3 is the mode. The mode is determined by listing each possible value and noting the number of times each value occurs.

Mode
A measure of central tendency; the value that occurs most often.

Measures of Dispersion

The mean, median, and mode summarize the central tendency of frequency distributions. Accurate analysis of data also requires knowing the tendency of observations to depart from the central tendency. Thus, another way to summarize the data is to calculate the dispersion of the data, or how the observations vary from the mean. Consider, for instance, the twelve-month sales patterns of the two products shown in Exhibit 13.5 on the next page. Both have a mean monthly sales volume of 200 units, but the dispersion of observations for product B is much greater than that for product A. There are several measures of dispersion.

THE RANGE

The simplest measure of dispersion is the range. It is the distance between the smallest and the largest values of a frequency distribution. In Exhibit 13.5, the range for product A is between 196

EXHIBIT 13.5
**Sales Levels for Two
Products with Identical
Average Sales**

	Units Product A	Units Product B
January	196	150
February	198	160
March	199	176
April	200	181
May	200	192
June	200	200
July	200	201
August	201	202
September	201	213
October	201	224
November	202	240
December	202	261
Average	**200**	**200**

units and 202 units (6 units), whereas for product B the range is between 150 units and 261 units (111 units). The range does not take into account all the observations; it merely tells us about the extreme values of the distribution.

Just as people may be fat or skinny, distributions may be fat or skinny. While we do not expect all observations to be exactly like the mean, in a skinny distribution they will lie a short distance from the mean. Product A is an example; the observations are close together and reasonably close to the mean. In a fat distribution, such as the one for Product B, they will be spread out. Exhibit 13.6 illustrates this concept graphically with two frequency distributions that have identical modes, medians, and means but different degrees of dispersion.

The interquartile range is the range that encompasses the middle 50 percent of the observations—in other words, the range between the bottom quartile (lowest 25 percent) and the top quartile (highest 25 percent).

DEVIATION SCORES

A method of calculating how far any observation is from the mean is to calculate individual deviation scores. To calculate a deviation from the mean, use the following formula:

$$d_{i_i} = X_i - \overline{X}$$

EXHIBIT 13.6
**Low Dispersion versus
High Dispersion**

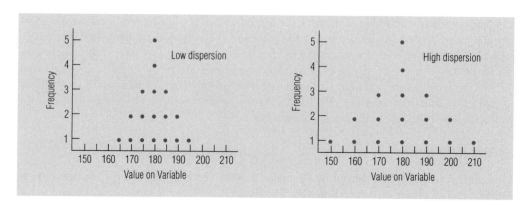

For the value of 150 units for product B for the month of January, the deviation score is -50; that is, $150 - 200 = -50$. If the deviation scores are large, we will have a fat distribution because the distribution exhibits a broad spread.

■ WHY USE THE STANDARD DEVIATION?

Statisticians have derived several quantitative indexes to reflect a distribution's spread, or variability. The *standard deviation* is perhaps the most valuable index of spread, or dispersion. Students often have difficulty understanding it. Learning about the standard deviation will be easier if we first look at several other measures of dispersion that may be used. Each of these has certain limitations that the standard deviation does not.

First is the average deviation. We compute the average deviation by calculating the deviation score of each observation value (that is, its difference from the mean), summing these scores, and then dividing by the sample size (n):

$$\text{Average deviation} = \frac{\sum \left(X_i - \overline{X} \right)}{n}$$

While this measure of spread seems interesting, it is never used. Positive deviation scores are canceled out by negative scores with this formula, leaving an average deviation value of zero no matter how wide the spread may be. Hence, the average deviation is a useless spread measure.

One might correct for the disadvantage of the average deviation by computing the absolute values of the deviations. In other words, we ignore all the positive and negative signs and use only the absolute value of each deviation. The formula for the mean absolute deviation is

$$\text{Mean absolute deviation} = \frac{\sum \left| X_i - \overline{X} \right|}{n}$$

While this procedure eliminates the problem of always having a zero score for the deviation measure, some technical mathematical problems make it less valuable than some other measures.

Variance

Another means of eliminating the sign problem caused by the negative deviations canceling out the positive deviations is to square the deviation scores. The following formula gives the mean squared deviation:

$$\text{Mean squared deviation} = \frac{\sum \left(X_i - \overline{X} \right)^2}{n}$$

This measure is useful for describing the sample variability. However, we typically wish to make an inference about a population from a sample, and so the divisor $n - 1$ is used rather than n in most pragmatic marketing research problems.[3] This new measure of spread, called **variance**, has the following formula:

$$\text{Variance} = S^2 = \frac{\sum \left(X_i - \overline{X} \right)^2}{n - 1}$$

Variance
A measure of variability or dispersion. Its square root is the standard deviation.

Variance is a very good index of dispersion. The variance, S^2, will equal zero if and only if each and every observation in the distribution is the same as the mean. The variance will grow larger as the observations tend to differ increasingly from one another and from the mean.

Standard Deviation

While the variance is frequently used in statistics, it has one major drawback. The variance reflects a unit of measurement that has been squared. For instance, if measures of sales in a territory are made in dollars, the mean number will be reflected in dollars, but the variance will be in squared dollars. Because of this, statisticians often take the square root of the variance. Using the square root of the variance for a distribution, called the **standard deviation**, eliminates the drawback of

Standard deviation
A quantitative index of a distribution's spread, or variability; the square root of the variance for a distribution.

EXHIBIT 13.7
Calculating a Standard Deviation: Number of Sales Calls per Day for Eight Salespeople

X	$(X - \bar{X})$	$(X - \bar{X})^2$
4	$(4 - 3.25) =$ .75	.5625
3	$(3 - 3.25) =$ $-.25$	.0625
2	$(2 - 3.25) = -1.25$	1.5625
5	$(5 - 3.25) =$ 1.75	3.0625
3	$(3 - 3.25) =$ $-.25$	.0625
3	$(3 - 3.25) =$ $-.25$	.0625
1	$(1 - 3.25) = -2.25$	5.0625
5	$(5 - 3.25) =$ 1.75	3.0625
Σ[a]	[a]	13.5000

$$n = 8 \quad \bar{X} = 3.25$$

$$S = \sqrt{\frac{\sum(X - \bar{X})^2}{n - 1}} = \sqrt{\frac{13.5}{8 - 1}} = \sqrt{\frac{13.5}{7}} = \sqrt{1.9286} = 1.3887$$

[a]The summation of this column is not used in the calculation of the standard deviation.

having the measure of dispersion in squared units rather than in the original measurement units. The formula for the standard deviation is

$$S = \sqrt{S^2} = \sqrt{\frac{\sum \left(X_i - \bar{X} \right)^2}{n - 1}}$$

Exhibit 13.7 illustrates that the calculation of a standard deviation requires the researcher to first calculate the sample mean. In the example with eight salespeople's sales calls (Exhibit 13.4), we calculated the sample mean as 3.25. Exhibit 13.7 illustrates how to calculate the standard deviation for these data.

At this point we can return to thinking about the original purpose for measures of dispersion. We want to summarize the data from survey research and other forms of marketing research. Indexes of central tendency, such as the mean, help us interpret the data. In addition, we wish to calculate a measure of variability that will give us a quantitative index of the dispersion of the distribution. We have looked at several measures of dispersion to arrive at two very adequate means of measuring dispersion: the variance and the standard deviation. The formula given is for the sample standard deviation, S.

The formula for the population standard deviation, σ, which is conceptually very similar, has not been given. Nevertheless, you should understand that σ measures the dispersion in the population and S measures the dispersion in the sample. These concepts are crucial to understanding statistics. Remember, the student must learn the language of statistics to use it in a research project. If you do not understand the language at this point, review this material now.

The Normal Distribution

Normal distribution
A symmetrical, bell-shaped distribution that describes the expected probability distribution of many chance occurrences.

One of the most common probability distributions in statistics is the **normal distribution**, commonly represented by the *normal curve.* This mathematical and theoretical distribution describes the expected distribution of sample means and many other chance occurrences. The normal curve is bell shaped, and almost all (99 percent) of its values are within ± 3 standard deviations from its mean. An example of a normal curve, the distribution of IQ scores, appears in Exhibit 13.8. In this

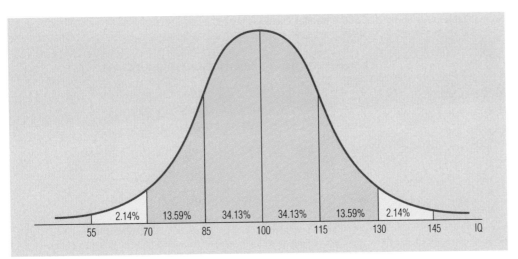

example, 1 standard deviation for IQ equals 15. We can identify the proportion of the curve by measuring a score's distance (in this case, standard deviation) from the mean (100).

The **standardized normal distribution** is a specific normal curve that has several characteristics:

1. It is symmetrical about its mean.
2. The mean identifies the normal curve's highest point (the mode) and the vertical line about which this normal curve is symmetrical.
3. The normal curve has an infinite number of cases (it is a continuous distribution), and the area under the curve has a probability density equal to 1.0.
4. The standardized normal distribution has a mean of 0 and a standard deviation of 1.

Exhibit 13.9 illustrates these properties. Exhibit 13.10 is a summary version of the typical standardized normal table found at the end of most statistics textbooks. A more complex table of areas under the standardized normal distribution appears in Table A.2 in the appendix.

The standardized normal distribution is a purely theoretical probability distribution. Statisticians have spent a great deal of time and effort making it convenient for researchers to find the probability of any portion of the area under the standardized normal distribution. All we have to do is transform, or convert, the data from other observed normal distributions to the standardized normal curve. In other words, the standardized normal distribution is extremely valuable because

Standardized normal distribution
A purely theoretical probability distribution that reflects a specific normal curve for the standardized value, z.

TOTHEPOINT

Order is heaven's law.

—Alexander Pope

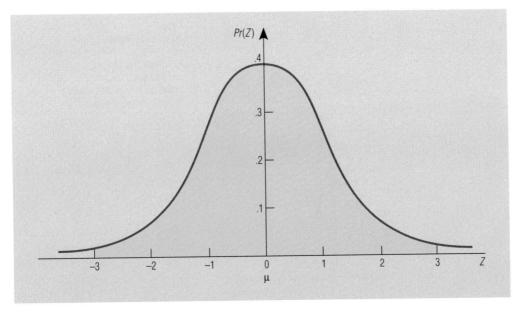

EXHIBIT 13.9
**Standardized Normal
Distribution**

EXHIBIT 13.10 **Standardized Normal Table: Area under Half of the Normal Curve**[a]

Z Standard Deviations from the Mean (Units)	Z Standard Deviations from the Mean (Tenths of Units)									
	.0	.1	.2	.3	.4	.5	.6	.7	.8	.9
0.0	.000	.040	.080	.118	.155	.192	.226	.258	.288	.315
1.0	.341	.364	.385	.403	.419	.433	.445	.455	.464	.471
2.0	.477	.482	.486	.489	.492	.494	.495	.496	.497	.498
3.0	.499	.499	.499	.499	.499	.499	.499	.499	.499	.499

[a]Area under the segment of the normal curve extending (in one direction) from the mean to the point indicated by each row-column combination. For example, about 68 percent of normally distributed events can be expected to fall within 1.0 standard deviation on either side of the mean (0.341 × 2). An interval of almost 2.0 standard deviations around the mean will include 95 percent of all cases.

we can translate, or transform, any normal variable, X, into the standardized value, Z. Exhibit 13.11 illustrates how either a skinny distribution or a fat distribution can be converted into the standardized normal distribution. This ability to transform normal variables has many pragmatic implications for the marketing researcher. The standardized normal table in the back of most statistics and marketing research books allows us to evaluate the probability of the occurrence of many events without any difficulty.

Computing the standardized value, Z, of any measurement expressed in original units is simple: Subtract the mean from the value to be transformed, and divide by the standard deviation (all

EXHIBIT 13.11

Standardized Values Can be Computed from Flat or Peaked Distributions Resulting in a Standardized Normal Curve

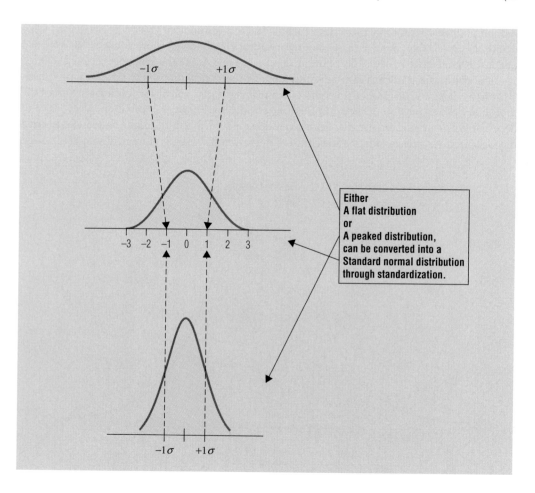

expressed in original units). The formula for this procedure and its verbal statement follow. In the formula, note that σ, the population standard deviation, is used for calculation.[4]

$$\text{Standardized value} = \frac{\text{Value to be transformed} - \text{Mean}}{\text{Standard deviation}}$$

$$Z = \frac{X - \mu}{\sigma}$$

where

$\mu =$ hypothesized or expected value of the mean

Suppose that in the past a toy manufacturer has experienced mean sales, μ, of 9,000 units and a standard deviation, σ, of 500 units during September. The production manager wishes to know whether wholesalers will demand between 7,500 and 9,625 units during September of the upcoming year. Because no tables are available showing the distribution for a mean of 9,000 and a standard deviation of 500, we must transform our distribution of toy sales, X, into the standardized form using our simple formula. The following computation shows that the probability (Pr) of obtaining sales in this range is equal to .893:

$$Z = \frac{X - \mu}{\sigma} = \frac{7,500 - 9,000}{500} = -3.00$$

$$Z = \frac{X - \mu}{\sigma} = \frac{9,625 - 9,000}{500} = 1.25$$

Using Exhibit 13.10 (or Table A.2 in the appendix), we find that

When $Z = -3.00$, the area under the curve (probability) equals 0.499.

When $Z = 1.25$, the area under the curve (probability) equals 0.394.

Thus, the total area under the curve is .499 + .394 = .893. (The area under the curve corresponding to this computation is the shaded area in Exhibit 13.12.) The sales manager, therefore, knows there is a .893 probability that sales will be between 7,500 and 9,625.

At this point, it is appropriate to repeat that understanding statistics requires an understanding of the language that statisticians use. Each concept discussed so far is relatively simple, but a clear-cut command of this terminology is essential for understanding what we will discuss later on.

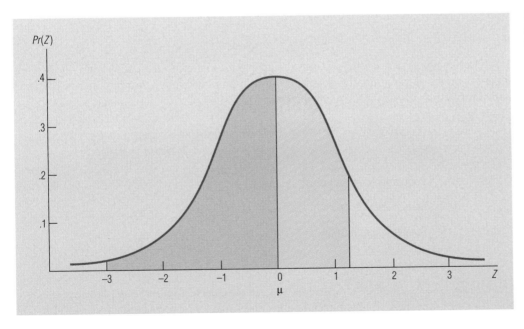

EXHIBIT 13.12
Standardized Distribution Curve

Population Distribution, Sample Distribution, and Sampling Distribution

Before we outline the technique of statistical inference, three additional types of distributions must be defined: population distribution, sample distribution, and sampling distribution. When conducting a research project or survey, the researcher's purpose is not to describe the sample of respondents, but to make an inference about the population. As defined previously, a population, or universe, is the total set, or collection, of potential units for observation. The sample is a smaller subset of this population.

Population distribution
A frequency distribution of the elements of a population.

Sample distribution
A frequency distribution of a sample.

A frequency distribution of the population elements is called a **population distribution**. The mean and standard deviation of the population distribution are represented by the Greek letters μ and σ. A frequency distribution of a sample is called a **sample distribution**. The sample mean is designated $\overline{X}$, and the sample standard deviation is designated S.

The concepts of population distribution and sample distribution are relatively simple. However, we must now introduce another distribution, which is the crux of understanding statistics: the *sampling distribution of the sample mean*. The sampling distribution is a theoretical probability distribution that in actual practice would never be calculated. Hence, practical, business-oriented students have difficulty understanding why the notion of the sampling distribution is important. Statisticians, with their mathematical curiosity, have asked themselves, "What would happen if we were to draw a large number of samples (say, 50,000), each having *n* elements, from a specified population?" Assuming that the samples were randomly selected, the sample means, $\overline{X}$s, could be arranged in a frequency distribution. Because different people or sample units would be selected in the different samples, the sample means would not be exactly equal. The shape of the sampling distribution is of considerable importance to statisticians. If the sample size is sufficiently large and if the samples are randomly drawn, we know from the central-limit theorem that the sampling distribution of the mean will be approximately normally distributed.

A formal definition of the sampling distribution is as follows:

Sampling distribution
A theoretical probability distribution of sample means for all possible samples of a certain size drawn from a particular population.

A **sampling distribution** *is a theoretical probability distribution that shows the functional relation between the possible values of some summary characteristic of n cases drawn at random and the probability (density) associated with each value over all possible samples of size n from a particular population.*[5]

Standard error of the mean
The standard deviation of the sampling distribution.

The sampling distribution's mean is called the *expected value* of the statistic. The expected value of the mean of the sampling distribution is equal to μ. The standard deviation of a sampling distribution of $\overline{X}$ is called **standard error of the mean** ($S_{\overline{X}}$) and is approximately equal to

$$S_{\overline{X}} = \frac{\sigma}{\sqrt{n}}$$

To review, for us to make an inference about a population from a sample, we must know about three important distributions: the population distribution, the sample distribution, and the sampling distribution. They have the following characteristics:

	Mean	**Standard Deviation**
Population distribution	μ	σ
Sample distribution	$\overline{X}$	S
Sampling distribution	$\mu_{\overline{X}} = \mu$	$S_{\overline{X}}$

We now have much of the information we need to understand the concept of statistical inference. To clarify why the sampling distribution has the characteristic just described, we will elaborate

EXHIBIT 13.13
**Fundamental Types of
Distributions**

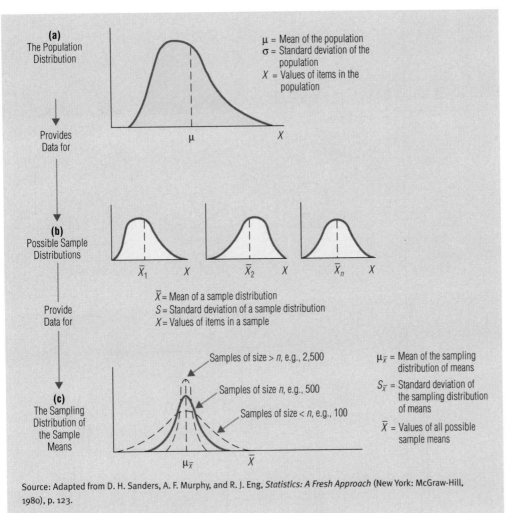

(a)
The Population
Distribution

μ = Mean of the population
σ = Standard deviation of the population
X = Values of items in the population

Provides
Data for

(b)
Possible Sample
Distributions

$\bar{X}_1$ X $\bar{X}_2$ X $\bar{X}_n$ X

$\bar{X}$ = Mean of a sample distribution
S = Standard deviation of a sample distribution
X = Values of items in a sample

Provide
Data for

Samples of size > n, e.g., 2,500

Samples of size n, e.g., 500

Samples of size < n, e.g., 100

$\mu_{\bar{X}}$ = Mean of the sampling distribution of means
$S_{\bar{X}}$ = Standard deviation of the sampling distribution of means
$\bar{X}$ = Values of all possible sample means

(c)
The Sampling
Distribution of
the Sample
Means

$\mu_{\bar{X}}$ $\bar{X}$

Source: Adapted from D. H. Sanders, A. F. Murphy, and R. J. Eng, *Statistics: A Fresh Approach* (New York: McGraw-Hill, 1980), p. 123.

on two concepts: the standard error of the mean and the central-limit theorem. You may be wondering why the standard error of the mean, $S_{\bar{X}}$, is defined as $S_{\bar{X}} = \sigma/\sqrt{n}$. The reason is based on the notion that the variance or dispersion within the sampling distribution of the mean will be less if we have a larger sample size for independent samples. We can see intuitively that a larger sample size allows the researcher to be more confident that the sample mean is closer to the population mean. In actual practice, the standard error of the mean is estimated using the sample's standard deviation. Thus, $S_{\bar{X}}$ is estimated using $S/\sqrt{n}$.

Exhibit 13.13 shows the relationship among a population distribution, the sample distribution, and three sampling distributions for varying sample sizes. In part (a) the population distribution is not a normal distribution. In part (b) the sample distribution resembles the distribution of the population; however, there may be some differences. In part (c) each sampling distribution is normally distributed and has the same mean. Note that as sample size increases, the spread of the sample means around μ decreases. Thus, with a larger sample size we will have a skinnier sampling distribution.

Central-limit theorem
The theory that, as sample size increases, the distribution of sample means of size n, randomly selected, approaches a normal distribution.

Central-Limit Theorem

Finding that the means of random samples of a sufficiently large size will be approximately normal in form and that the mean of the sampling distribution will approach the population mean is very useful. Mathematically, this is the assertion of the **central-limit theorem**, which states, as the

EXHIBIT 13.14
Distribution of Sample Means for Samples of Various Sizes and Population Distributions

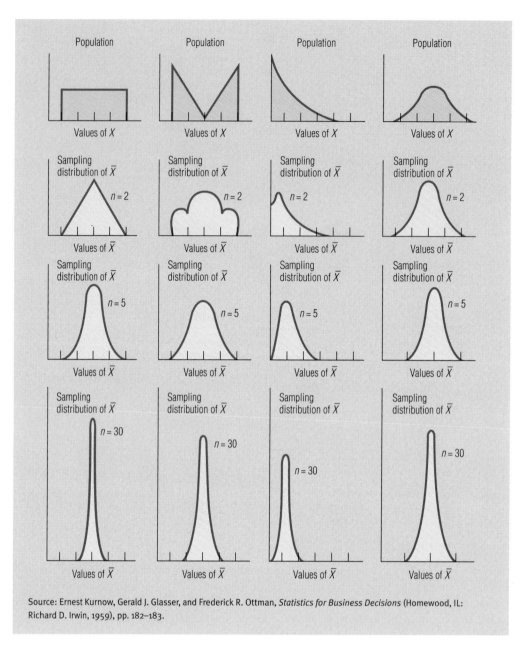

Source: Ernest Kurnow, Gerald J. Glasser, and Frederick R. Ottman, *Statistics for Business Decisions* (Homewood, IL: Richard D. Irwin, 1959), pp. 182–183.

sample size, n, increases, the distribution of the mean, $\overline{X}$, of a random sample taken from practically any population approaches a normal distribution (with a mean μ and a standard deviation $\sigma/\sqrt{n}$).[6] The central-limit theorem works regardless of the shape of the original population distribution (see Exhibit 13.14).

A simple example will demonstrate the central-limit theorem. Assume that a consumer researcher is interested in the number of dollars children spend on toys each month. Assume further that the population the consumer researcher is investigating consists of eight-year-old children in a certain school. In this example, the population consists of only six individuals. (This is a simple and perhaps somewhat unrealistic example; nevertheless, assume that the population size is only six elements.) Exhibit 13.15 shows the population distribution of toy expenditures. Alice, a relatively deprived child, has only $1 per month, whereas Freddy, the rich kid, has $6 to spend. The average expenditure on toys each month is $3.50, so the population mean, μ, equals 3.5 (see Exhibit 13.16).

EXHIBIT 13.15
Population Distribution: Hypothetical Toy Expenditures

Child	Toy Expenditures
Alice	$1.00
Becky	2.00
Noah	3.00
Tobin	4.00
George	5.00
Freddy	6.00

Now assume that we do not know everything about the population, and we wish to take a sample size of two, to be drawn randomly from the population of the six individuals. How many possible samples are there? The answer is 15, as follows:

```
1, 2
1, 3    2, 3
1, 4    2, 4    3, 4
1, 5    2, 5    3, 5    4, 5
1, 6    2, 6    3, 6    4, 6    5, 6
```

Exhibit 13.17 lists the sample mean for each of the possible fifteen samples and the frequency distribution of these sample means with their appropriate probabilities. These sample means comprise a sampling distribution of the mean, and the distribution is *approximately* normal. If we increased the sample size to three, four, or more, the distribution of sample means would more closely approximate a normal distribution. While this simple example is not a proof of the central-limit theorem, it should give you a better understanding of the nature of the sampling distribution of the mean.

This theoretical knowledge about distributions can be used to solve two practical marketing research problems: estimating parameters and determining sample size.

EXHIBIT 13.16
Calculation of Population Mean

X
$1.00
2.00
3.00
4.00
5.00
6.00
$\sum$ $21.00

$$\text{Calculations: } \mu = \frac{\sum X}{N} = \frac{21}{6} = 3.5 = \mu_{\bar{X}}$$

Arithmetic Means of Samples and Frequency Distribution of Sample Means

	Sample Means		
Sample	**ΣX**	**$\overline{X}$**	**Probability**
$1, $2	$3.00	$1.50	1/15
1, 3	4.00	2.00	1/15
1, 4	5.00	2.50	1/15
1, 5	6.00	3.00	1/15
1, 6	7.00	3.50	1/15
2, 3	5.00	2.50	1/15
2, 4	6.00	3.00	1/15
2, 5	7.00	3.50	1/15
2, 6	8.00	4.00	1/15
3, 4	7.00	3.50	1/15
3, 5	8.00	4.00	1/15
3, 6	9.00	4.50	1/15
4, 5	9.00	4.50	1/15
4, 6	10.00	5.00	1/15
5, 6	11.00	5.50	1/15

	Frequency Distribution	
Sample Mean	**Frequency**	**Probability**
$1.50	1	1/15
2.00	1	1/15
2.50	2	2/15
3.00	2	2/15
3.50	3	3/15
4.00	2	2/15
4.50	2	2/15
5.00	1	1/15
5.50	1	1/15

Estimation of Parameters

A catalog retailer, such as Horchow, may rely on sampling and statistical estimation to prepare for Christmas orders. The company can expect that twenty-eight days after mailing a catalog, it will have received X percent of the orders it will get. With this information, the company can tell within 5 percent how many ties it will sell by Christmas. Making a proper inference about population parameters is highly practical for a marketer that must have the inventory appropriate for a short selling season.

Suppose you are a product manager for Beatrice Foods and you recently conducted a taste test to measure intention to buy a reformulated Swiss Miss Lite Cocoa Mix. The results of the research indicate that when the product was placed in eight hundred homes and a callback was made two weeks later, 80 percent of the respondents said they would buy it: 76 percent of those who had not previously used low-calorie cocoa and 84 percent of those who had. How can you be sure there were no statistical errors in this estimate? How confident can you be of these figures?

Students often wonder whether statistics are really used in the business world. The two situations just described provide contemporary examples of the need for statistical estimation of parameters and the value of statistical techniques as managerial tools.

Point Estimates

Our goal in using statistics is to make an estimate about population parameters. A population mean, μ, and standard deviation, σ, are constants, but in most instances of marketing research, they are unknown. To estimate population values, we are required to sample. As we have discussed, $\overline{X}$ and S are random variables that will vary from sample to sample with a certain probability (sampling) distribution.

Our previous example of statistical inference was somewhat unrealistic because the population had only six individuals. Consider the more realistic example of a prospective racquetball entrepreneur who wishes to estimate the average number of days players participate in this sport each week. When statistical inference is needed, the population mean, μ, is a constant but unknown parameter. To estimate the average number of playing days, we could take a sample of three hundred racquetball players throughout the area where our entrepreneur is thinking of building club facilities. If the sample mean, $\overline{X}$, equals 2.6 days per week, we might use this figure as a **point estimate**. This single value, 2.6, would be the best estimate of the population mean. However, we would be extremely lucky if the sample estimate were exactly the same as the population value. A less risky alternative would be to calculate a confidence interval.

Point estimate
An estimate of the population mean in the form of a single value, usually the sample mean.

Confidence Intervals

If we specify a range of numbers, or interval, within which a population mean should lie, we can be more confident that our inference is correct. A **confidence interval estimate** is based on the knowledge that $\mu = \overline{X} \pm$ a small sampling error. After calculating an interval estimate, we can determine how probable it is that the population mean will fall within this range of statistical values. In the racquetball project, the researcher, after setting up a confidence interval, would be able to make a statement such as "With 95 percent confidence, I think that the average number of days played per week is between 2.3 and 2.9." This information can be used to estimate market demand because the researcher has a certain confidence that the interval contains the value of the true population mean.

Confidence interval estimate
A specified range of numbers within which a population mean is expected to lie; an estimate of the population mean based on the knowledge that it will be equal to the sample mean plus or minus a small sampling error.

The crux of the problem for a researcher is to determine how much random sampling error to tolerate. In other words, what should the confidence interval be? How much of a gamble should be taken that μ will be included in the range? Do we need to be 80 percent, 90 percent, or 99 percent sure? A **confidence level** is a percentage or decimal indicating the long-run probability that the results will be correct. Traditionally, researchers have used the 95 percent confidence level. While there is nothing magical about the 95 percent confidence level, it is useful to select this confidence level in our examples.

As mentioned, the point estimate gives no information about the possible magnitude of random sampling error. A confidence interval gives the estimated value of the population parameter, plus or minus an estimate of the error. We can express the idea of the confidence interval as follows:

Confidence level
A percentage or decimal value that tells how confident a researcher can be about being correct; it states the long-run percentage of confidence intervals that will include the true population mean.

$$\mu = \overline{X} \pm \text{ a small sampling error}$$

More formally, assuming that the researchers select a large sample (more than thirty observations), the small sampling error is given by

$$\text{Small sampling error} = Z_{c.l.} S_{\overline{X}}$$

where

$Z_{c.l.}$ = value of Z, or standardized normal variable, at a specified confidence level (*c.l.*)

$S_{\overline{X}}$ = standard error of the mean

The precision of our estimate is indicated by the value of $Z_{c.l.} S_{\overline{X}}$. It is useful to define the range of possible error, E, as follows:

$$E = Z_{c.l.} S_{\overline{X}}$$

Thus,

$$\mu = \overline{X} \pm E$$

where

$\overline{X}$ = sample mean

E = range of sampling error

or

$$\mu = \overline{X} \pm Z_{c.l.} S_{\overline{X}}$$

The confidence interval $\pm E$ is always stated as one-half of the total confidence interval.

The following step-by-step procedure can be used to calculate confidence intervals:

1. Calculate $\overline{X}$ from the sample.
2. Assuming σ is unknown, estimate the population standard deviation by finding S, the sample standard deviation.
3. Estimate the standard error of the mean, using the following formula:

$$S_{\overline{X}} = \frac{S}{\sqrt{n}}$$

4. Determine the Z-value associated with the desired confidence level. The confidence level should be divided by 2 to determine what percentage of the area under the curve to include on each side of the mean.
5. Calculate the confidence interval.

The following example shows how calculation of a confidence interval can be used in preparing a demographic profile, a useful tool for market segmentation. Suppose you plan to open a sporting goods store to cater to working women who golf. In a survey of 100 women in your market area, you find that the mean age ($\overline{X}$) is 37.5 years, with a standard deviation (S) of 12.0 years. Even though 37.5 years is the "expected value" and the best guess for the true mean age in the population (μ), the likelihood is that the mean is not exactly 37.5. Thus, a confidence interval around the sample mean computed using the steps just given will be useful:

1. $\overline{X}$ = 37.5 years
2. S = 12.0 years
3. $S_{\overline{X}} = \dfrac{12.0}{\sqrt{100}} = 1.2$
4. Suppose you wish to be 95 percent confident—that is, assured that 95 times out of 100, the estimates from your sample will include the population parameter. Including 95 percent of the area requires that 47.5 percent (one-half of 95 percent) of the distribution on each side be included. From the Z-table (Table A.2 in the appendix), you find that 0.475 corresponds to the Z-value 1.96.
5. Substitute the values for $Z_{c.l.}$ and $S_{\overline{X}}$ into the confidence interval formula:

$$\mu = 37.5 \pm (1.96)(1.2)$$
$$= 37.5 \pm 2.352$$

You can thus expect that μ is contained in the range from 35.148 to 39.852 years. Intervals constructed in this manner will contain the true value of μ 95 percent of the time.

Step 3 can be eliminated by entering S and n directly in the confidence interval formula:

$$\mu = \overline{X} \pm Z_{c.l.} \frac{S}{\sqrt{n}}$$

Remember that $S/\sqrt{n}$ represents the standard error of the mean, $S_{\overline{X}}$. Its use is based on the central-limit theorem.

If you wanted to increase the probability that the population mean will lie within the confidence interval, you could use the 99 percent confidence level, with a Z-value of 2.57. You may want to calculate the 99 percent confidence interval for the preceding example; you can expect that μ will be in the range between 34.416 and 40.584 years.

We have now examined the basic concepts of inferential statistics. You should understand that sample statistics such as the sample means, $\overline{X}$s, can provide good estimates of population parameters such as μ. You should also realize that there is a certain probability of being in error when you estimate a population parameter from sample statistics. In other words, there will be a random sampling error, which is the difference between the survey results and the results of surveying the entire population. If you have a firm understanding of these basic terms and ideas, which are the essence of statistics, the remaining statistics concepts will be relatively simple for you. Several ramifications of the simple ideas presented so far will permit you to make better decisions about populations based on surveys or experiments.

Sample Size

Random Error and Sample Size

When asked to evaluate a marketing research project, most people, even those with little marketing research training, begin by asking, "How big was the sample?" Intuitively we know that the larger the sample, the more accurate the research. This is in fact a statistical truth; random sampling error varies with samples of different sizes. In statistical terms, increasing the sample size decreases the width of the confidence interval at a given confidence level. When the standard deviation of the population is unknown, a confidence interval is calculated using the following formula:

$$\text{Confidence interval} = \overline{X} \pm Z \frac{S}{\sqrt{n}}$$

Observe that the equation for the plus or minus error factor in the confidence interval includes n, the sample size:

$$E = Z \frac{S}{\sqrt{n}}$$

If n increases, E is reduced. Exhibit 13.18 illustrates that the confidence interval (or magnitude of error) decreases as the sample size, n, increases.

We already noted that it is not necessary to take a census of all elements of the population to conduct an accurate study. The laws of probability give investigators sufficient confidence regarding the accuracy of data collected from a sample. Knowledge of the characteristics of the sampling distribution helps researchers make reasonably precise estimates.

Students familiar with the law of diminishing returns in economics will easily grasp the concept that increases in sample size reduce sampling error at a *decreasing rate*. For example, doubling a sample of 1,000 will reduce random sampling error by 1 percentage point, but doubling the sample from 2,000 to 4,000 will reduce random sampling error by only another half percentage point. More technically, random sampling error is inversely proportional to the square root of n. (Exhibit 13.18 gives an approximation of the relationship between sample size and error.) Thus, the main issue becomes one of determining the optimal sample size.

RESEARCHSNAPSHOT

Target and Wal-Mart Shoppers Really Are Different

Scarborough Research conducts ongoing consumer research that combines a telephone interview on media behavior with a mail survey about shopping habits and lifestyle and a television diary for detailed data about television viewing. Scarborough recognizes the importance of sample size for minimizing errors. Its sample includes over 200,000 adults so that it can make estimates of the U.S. population.

An example is a recent comparison of consumers who shop exclusively at either Target or Wal-Mart. When respondents were asked to identify the stores at which they had shopped during the preceding three months, the largest share (40 percent) named both Target and Wal-Mart. However, 31 percent shopped at Wal-Mart but not Target, and 12 percent shopped at Target but not Wal-Mart. Scarborough compared

the consumer behavior of the latter two groups.

Target shoppers who shunned Wal-Mart were more likely to shop at more upscale stores, including Macy's and Nordstrom. They also were more likely than the average shopper to visit many different stores. Wal-Mart shoppers who stayed away from Target were more likely to shop at discounters such as Dollar General and Kmart, and they were more likely to be at least fifty years old. Target-only shoppers tended to be younger and were more likely to have a high household income.

Given a U.S. adult population of approximately 220 million, do you think the sample size was adequate to make these comparisons?

Source: Based on Scarborough Research, "In the Battle for Discount Shoppers, Target and Wal-Mart Find Brand Loyalty in Different Customer Groups," news release, September 19, 2005, http://www.scarborough.com; Scarborough Research, "About Scarborough: Methodology," http://www.scarborough.com, accessed March 16, 2006; U.S. Census Bureau, *Statistical Abstract of the United States*, 2006, table 11, p. 13.

Factors in Determining Sample Size for Questions Involving Means

Three factors are required to specify sample size: (1) the variance, or heterogeneity, of the population; (2) the magnitude of acceptable error; and (3) the confidence level. Suppose a researcher wishes to find out whether nine-year-old boys are taller than four-year-old boys. Intuitively we know that even with a very small sample size, the correct information probably will be obtained. This is based on the fact that the determination of sample size depends on the research question and the variability within the sample.

The *variance,* or *heterogeneity,* of the population is the first necessary bit of information. In statistical terms, this refers to the *standard deviation* of the population. Only a small sample is required

EXHIBIT 13.18
Relationship between Sample Size and Error

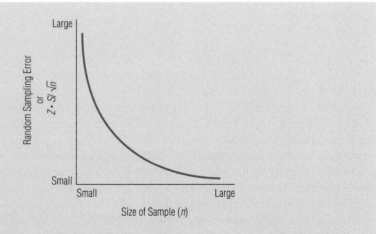

Source: From Foundations of Behavioral Research 3rd edition by Kerlinger. © 1986. Reprinted with permission of Wadsworth, a division of Thomson Learning: http://www.thomsonrights.com. Fax 800-730-2215.

EXHIBIT 13.19 **Statistical Information Needed to Determine Sample Size for Questions Involving Means**

Variable	Symbol	Typical Source of Information
Standard deviation	S	Pilot study or rule of thumb
Magnitude of error	E	Managerial judgment or calculation ($Z\,S_{\bar{x}}$)
Confidence level	$Z_{c.l.}$	Managerial judgment

if the population is homogeneous. For example, predicting the average age of college students requires a smaller sample than predicting the average age of people who visit the zoo on a given Sunday afternoon. As *heterogeneity* increases, so must sample size. Thus, to test the effectiveness of an acne medicine, the sample must be large enough to cover the range of skin types.

The *magnitude of error*, or the confidence interval, is the second necessary bit of information. Defined in statistical terms as E, the magnitude of error indicates how precise the estimate must be. It indicates a certain precision level. From a managerial perspective, the importance of the decision in terms of profitability will influence the researcher's specifications of the range of error. If, for example, favorable results from a test-market sample will result in the construction of a new plant and unfavorable results will dictate not marketing the product, the acceptable range of error probably will be small; the cost of an error would be too great to allow much room for random sampling errors. In other cases, the estimate need not be extremely precise. Allowing an error of $\pm\$1,000$ in total family income instead of $E = \pm 50$ may be acceptable in most market segmentation studies.

The third factor of concern is the *confidence level*. In our examples, we will typically use the 95 percent confidence level. This, however, is an arbitrary decision based on convention; there is nothing sacred about the 0.05 chance level (that is, the probability of 0.05 of the true population parameter being incorrectly estimated). Exhibit 13.19 summarizes the information required to determine sample size.

Estimating Sample Size for Questions Involving Means

Once the preceding concepts are understood, determining the actual size for a simple random sample is quite easy. The researcher must follow three steps:

1. Estimate the standard deviation of the population.
2. Make a judgment about the allowable magnitude of error.
3. Determine a confidence level.

The only problem is estimating the standard deviation of the population. Ideally, similar studies conducted in the past will give a basis for judging the standard deviation. In practice, researchers who lack prior information conduct a pilot study to estimate the population parameters so that another, larger sample of the appropriate sample size may be drawn. This procedure is called *sequential sampling* because researchers take an initial look at the pilot study results before deciding on a larger sample to provide more precise information.

A rule of thumb for estimating the value of the standard deviation is to expect it to be one-sixth of the range. If researchers conducting a study on television purchases expected the price paid to range from $100 to $700, a rule-of-thumb estimate for the standard deviation would be $100.

For the moment, assume that the standard deviation has been estimated in some preliminary work. If our concern is to estimate the mean of a particular population, the formula for sample size is

$$n = \left(\frac{ZS}{E}\right)^2$$

where

> Z = standardized value that corresponds to the confidence level
>
> S = sample standard deviation or estimate of the population standard deviation
>
> E = acceptable magnitude of error, plus or minus error factor (range is one-half of the total confidence interval)[7]

Suppose a survey researcher studying annual expenditures on lipstick wishes to have a 95 percent confidence level ($Z = 1.96$) and a range of error (E) of less than \$2. If the estimate of the standard deviation is \$29, the sample size can be calculated as follows:

$$n = \left(\frac{ZS}{E}\right)^2 = \left(\frac{(1.96)(29)}{2}\right)^2 = \left(\frac{56.84}{2}\right)^2 = 28.42^2 = 808$$

If a range of error (E) of \$4 is acceptable, sample size can be reduced:

$$n = \left(\frac{ZS}{E}\right)^2 = \left(\frac{(1.96)(29)}{4}\right)^2 = \left(\frac{56.84}{4}\right)^2 = 14.21^2 = 202$$

Thus, doubling the range of acceptable error reduces sample size to approximately one-quarter of its original size. Stated conversely in a general sense, doubling sample size will reduce error by only approximately one-quarter.

The Influence of Population Size on Sample Size

The ACNielsen Company estimates television ratings. Throughout the years, it has been plagued with questions about how it is possible to rate 98 million or more television homes with such a small sample (approximately 5,000 households). The answer to that question is that in most cases the size of the population does not have a major effect on the sample size. As we have indicated, the variance of the population has the largest effect on sample size. However, a finite correction factor may be needed to adjust a sample size that is more than 5 percent of a finite population. If the sample is large relative to the population, the foregoing procedures may overestimate sample size, and the researcher may need to adjust sample size. The finite correction factor is $\sqrt{(N-n)(N-1)}$, where N = population size and n = sample size.

Factors in Determining Sample Size for Proportions

Researchers frequently are concerned with determining sample size for problems that involve estimating population proportions or percentages. When the question involves the estimation of a proportion, the researcher requires some knowledge of the logic for determining a confidence interval around a sample proportion estimation (p) of the population proportion (π). For a confidence interval to be constructed around the sample proportion (p), an estimate of the standard error of the proportion (S_p) must be calculated and a confidence level specified.

The precision of the estimate is indicated by the value $Z_{c.l.}S_p$. Thus, the plus-or-minus estimate of the population proportion is

$$\text{Confidence interval} = p \pm Z_{c.l.}S_p$$

If the researcher selects a 95 percent probability for the confidence interval, $Z_{c.l.}$ will equal 1.96 (see Table A.2 in the appendix). The formula for S_p is

$$S_p = \sqrt{\frac{pq}{n}} \text{ or } S_p = \sqrt{\frac{p(1-n)}{n}}$$

where

S_p = estimate of the standard error of the proportion

p = proportion of successes

$q = 1 - p$, or proportion of failures

Suppose that 20 percent of a sample of 1,200 television viewers recall seeing an advertisement. The proportion of successes (p) equals 0.2, and the proportion of failures (q) equals 0.8. We estimate the 95 percent confidence interval as follows:

$$\text{Confidence interval} = p \pm Z_{c.l.} S_p$$

$$= 0.2 \pm 1.96 S_p$$

$$= 0.2 \pm 1.96 \sqrt{\frac{p(1 - n)}{n}}$$

$$= 0.2 \pm 1.96 \sqrt{\frac{(0.2)(0.8)}{1,200}}$$

$$= 0.2 \pm 1.96(0.0115)$$

$$= 0.2 \pm 0.022$$

Thus, the population proportion who see an advertisement is estimated to be included in the interval between 0.178 and 0.222, or roughly between 18 and 22 percent, with a 95 percent confidence coefficient.

To determine *sample size* for a proportion, the researcher must make a judgment about confidence level and the maximum allowance for random sampling error. Furthermore, the size of the proportion influences random sampling error, so an estimate of the expected proportion of successes must be made, based on intuition or prior information. The formula is

$$n = \frac{Z_{c.l.}^2 pq}{E^2}$$

where

n = number of items in sample

$Z_{c.l.}^2$ = square of the confidence level in standard error units

p = estimated proportion of successes

$q = 1 - p$, or estimated proportion of failures

E^2 = square of the maximum allowance for error between the true proportion and the sample proportion, or $Z_{c.l.} S_p$ squared

Suppose a researcher believes that a simple random sample will show that 60 percent of the population (p) recognizes the name of an automobile dealership. The researcher wishes to estimate with 95 percent confidence ($Z_{c.l.} = 1.96$) that the allowance for sampling error is not greater than 3.5 percentage points (E). Substituting these values into the formula gives

$$n = \frac{(1.96)^2 (0.6)(0.4)}{0.035^2}$$

$$= \frac{(3.8416)(0.24)}{0.001225}$$

$$= \frac{0.922}{0.001225}$$

$$= 753$$

EXHIBIT 13.20 **Selected Tables for Determining Sample Size when the Characteristic of Interest Is a Proportion**

**Sample Size for a 95 Percent Confidence Level when Parameter in Population
Is Assumed to Be over 70 Percent or under 30 Percent**

Size of Population	Reliability			
	±1% Point	±2% Points	±3% Points	±5% Points
1,000	a	a	473	244
2,000	a	a	619	278
3,000	a	1,206	690	291
4,000	a	1,341	732	299
5,000	a	1,437	760	303
10,000	4,465	1,678	823	313
20,000	5,749	1,832	858	318
50,000	6,946	1,939	881	321
100,000	7,465	1,977	888	321
500,000 to ∞	7,939	2,009	895	322

**Sample Size for a 95 Percent Confidence Level when Parameter in Population
Is Assumed to Be over 85 Percent or under 15 Percent**

Size of Population	Reliability			
	±1% Point	±2% Points	±3% Points	±5% Points
1,000	a	a	353	235
2,000	a	760	428	266
3,000	a	890	461	278
4,000	a	938	479	284
5,000	a	984	491	289
10,000	3,288	1,091	516	297
20,000	3,935	1,154	530	302
50,000	4,461	1,195	538	304
100,000	4,669	1,210	541	305
500,000 to ∞	4,850	1,222	544	306

[a]In these cases, more than 50 percent of the population is required in the sample. Since the normal approximation of the hypergeometric distribution is a poor approximation in such instances, no sample value is given.

Source: Nan Lin, *Foundations of Social Research* (New York: McGraw-Hill, 1976), p. 447. Copyright © 1976 by Nan Lin. Used with permission.

Calculating Sample Size for Sample Proportions

In practice, a number of tables have been constructed for determining sample size. Exhibit 13.20 illustrates a sample size table for problems that involve sample proportions (p).

EXHIBIT 13.21 **Allowance for Random Sampling Error (Plus and Minus Percentage Points) at 95 Percent Confidence Level**

Response	Sample Size						
	2,500	1,500	1,000	500	250	100	50
10 (90)	1.2	1.5	2.0	3.0	4.0	6.0	8.0
20 (80)	1.6	2.0	2.5	4.0	5.0	8.0	11.0
30 (70)	1.8	2.5	3.0	4.0	6.0	9.0	13.0
40 (60)	2.0	2.5	3.0	4.0	6.0	10.0	14.0
50 (50)	2.0	2.5	3.0	4.0	6.0	10.0	14.0

Source: Nan Lin, *Foundations of Social Research* (New York: McGraw-Hill, 1976).

The theoretical principles underlying calculation of sample sizes of proportions are similar to the concepts discussed in this chapter. Suppose we wish to take samples in two large cities, New Orleans and Miami. We wish no more than 2 percentage points of error, and we will be satisfied with a 95 percent confidence level (see Exhibit 13.20). If we assume all other things are equal, then in the New Orleans market, where 15 percent of the consumers favor our product and 85 percent prefer competitors' brands, we need a sample of 1,222 to get results with only 2 percentage points of error. In the Miami market, however, where 30 percent of the consumers favor our brand and 70 percent prefer other brands (a less heterogeneous market), we need a sample size of 2,009 to get the same sample reliability.

Exhibit 13.21 shows a sampling error table typical of those that accompany research proposals or reports. Most studies will estimate more than one parameter. Thus, in a survey of 100 people in which 50 percent agree with one statement and 10 percent with another, the sampling error is expected to be 10 and 6 percentage points of error, respectively.

Determining Sample Size on the Basis of Judgment

Just as sample units may be selected to suit the convenience or judgment of the researcher, sample size may also be determined on the basis of managerial judgments. Using a sample size similar to those used in previous studies provides the inexperienced researcher with a comparison with other researchers' judgments.

Another judgmental factor that affects the determination of sample size is the selection of the appropriate item, question, or characteristic to be used for the sample size calculations. Several different characteristics affect most studies, and the desired degree of precision may vary for these items. The researcher must exercise some judgment to determine which item will be used. Often the item that will produce the largest sample size will be used to determine the ultimate sample size. However, the cost of data collection becomes a major consideration, and judgment must be exercised regarding the importance of such information.

Another consideration stems from most researchers' need to analyze various subgroups within the sample. For example, suppose an analyst wishes to look at differences in retailers' attitudes by geographic region. The analyst will want to make sure to sample an adequate number of retailers in the New England, Mid-Atlantic, and South Atlantic regions to ensure that subgroup comparisons are reliable. There is a judgmental rule of thumb for selecting minimum subgroup sample size: Each subgroup to be separately analyzed should have a minimum of 100 units in each category of the major breakdowns. With this procedure, the total sample size is computed by totaling the sample sizes necessary for these subgroups.

Determining Sample Size for Stratified and Other Probability Samples

Stratified sampling involves drawing separate probability samples within the subgroups to make the sample more efficient. With a stratified sample, the sample variances are expected to differ by strata. This makes the determination of sample size more complex. Increased complexity may also characterize the determination of sample size for cluster sampling and other probability sampling methods. The formulas are beyond the scope of this book. Students interested in these advanced sampling techniques should investigate advanced sampling textbooks.

A Reminder about Statistics

Learning the terms and symbols defined in this chapter will provide you with the basics of the language of statisticians and researchers. As you learn more about the pragmatic use of statistics in marketing research, do not forget these concepts. Rules are important in learning a foreign language and when the rules are forgotten, being understood becomes very difficult. The same is true for the student who forgets the basics of the "foreign language" of statistics.

Summary

1. Explain the difference between descriptive and inferential statistics. Determination of sample size requires a knowledge of statistics. Statistics is the language of the researcher, and this chapter introduced its vocabulary. Descriptive statistics describe characteristics of a population or sample. Thus, calculating a mean and a standard deviation to "describe" or profile a sample is a commonly applied descriptive statistical approach. Inferential statistics investigate samples to draw conclusions about entire populations. If a mean is computed and then compared to some preconceived standard, then inferential statistics are being implemented.

2. Know the difference between population parameters and sample statistics. Inferential statistics investigate samples to draw conclusions about entire populations. Sample statistics are measures computed from sample data. Population parameters are measured characteristics of a specific population.

3. Interpret frequency distributions, proportions, and measures of central tendency. A frequency distribution shows how frequently each response or classification occurs. A simple tally count illustrates a frequency distribution. A proportion indicates the percentage of group members that have a particular characteristic. Three measures of central tendency are commonly used: the mean, or arithmetic average; the median, or halfway value; and the mode, or most frequently observed value. These three values may differ, and care must be taken to understand distortions that may arise from using the wrong measure of central tendency.

4. Identify and calculate the various measures of dispersion. Measures of dispersion further describe a distribution. The range is the difference between the largest and smallest values observed. The most useful measures of dispersion are the variance (the summation of each observation's deviation from the mean, divided by one less than the number of observations) and standard deviation, which is the square root of the variance.

5. Distinguish among population, sample, and sampling distributions and to identify the mean and standard deviation of each distribution. The techniques of statistical inference are based on the relationship among the population distribution, the sample distribution, and the sampling distribution. The population distribution is a frequency distribution of the elements of a population. The sample distribution is a frequency distribution of a sample. A sampling distribution is a theoretical probability distribution of sample means for all possible samples of a certain size drawn from a particular population. The sampling distribution's mean is the expected value of the mean, which equals the population's mean. The standard deviation of the sampling distribution is the standard error of the mean, approximately equal to the standard deviation of the population, divided by the square root of the sample size.

6. Summarize the use of confidence interval estimates. Estimating a population mean with a single value gives a point estimate. The confidence interval estimate is a range of numbers within which the researcher is confident that the population mean will lie. The confidence level is a percentage that indicates the long-run probability that the confidence interval estimate will be correct. Many research problems involve the estimation of proportions. Statistical techniques may be used to determine a confidence interval around a sample proportion.

7. Discuss the major issues in specifying sample size. The statistical determination of sample size requires knowledge of (1) the variance of the population, (2) the magnitude of acceptable error, and (3) the confidence level. Several computational formulas are available for determining sample size. Furthermore, a number of easy-to-use tables have been compiled to help researchers calculate sample size. The main reason a large sample size is desirable is that sample size is related to random sampling error. A smaller sample makes a larger error in estimates more likely. Calculation of sample size for a sample proportion is not difficult. However, most researchers use tables that indicate predetermined sample sizes.

Key Terms and Concepts

Sample statistics	Median	Sample distribution
Population parameters	Mode	Sampling distribution
Frequency distribution	Variance	Standard error of the mean
Percentage distribution	Standard deviation	Central-limit theorem
Probability	Normal distribution	Point estimate
Proportion	Standardized normal distribution	Confidence interval estimate
Mean	Population distribution	Confidence level

Questions for Review and Critical Thinking

1. What is the difference between descriptive and inferential statistics?

2. Suppose the speed limits in thirteen countries in miles per hour are as follows:

Country	Highway Miles per Hour
Italy	87
France	81
Hungary	75
Belgium	75
Portugal	75
Great Britain	70
Spain	62
Denmark	62
Netherlands	62
Greece	62
Japan	62
Norway	56
Turkey	56

What are the mean, median, and mode for these data? Feel free to use your computer (statistical software or spreadsheet) to get the answer.

3. Prepare a frequency distribution for the data in question 2.

4. Why is the standard deviation rather than the average deviation typically used?

5. Calculate the standard deviation for the data in question 2.

6. Draw three distributions that have the same mean value but different standard deviation values. Draw three distributions that have the same standard deviation value but different mean values.

7. A manufacturer of MP3 players surveyed one hundred retail stores in each of the firm's sales regions. An analyst noticed that in the South Atlantic region the average retail price was $165 (mean) and the standard deviation was $30. However, in the Mid-Atlantic region the mean price was $170, with a standard deviation of $15. What do these statistics tell us about these two sales regions?

8. What is the sampling distribution? How does it differ from the sample distribution?

9. What would happen to the sampling distribution of the mean if we increased sample size from 5 to 25?

10. Suppose a fast-food restaurant wishes to estimate average sales volume for a new menu item. The restaurant has analyzed the sales of the item at a similar outlet and observed the following results:

$$\overline{X} = 500 \text{ (mean daily sales)}$$
$$S = 100 \text{ (standard deviation of sample)}$$
$$n = 25 \text{ (sample size)}$$

The restaurant manager wants to know into what range the mean daily sales should fall 95 percent of the time. Perform this calculation.

11. In the example on page 310 of research on lipstick, where $E = \$2$ and $S = \$29$, what sample size would we require if we desired a 99 percent confidence level?

12. Suppose you are planning to sample cat owners to determine the average number of cans of cat food they purchase monthly. The following standards have been set: a confidence level of 99 percent and an error of less than five units. Past research has indicated that the standard deviation should be 6 units. What is the required sample size?

13. In a survey of 500 people, 60 percent responded positively to an attitude question. Calculate a confidence interval at 95 percent to get an interval estimate for a proportion.

14. What is a standardized normal curve?

15. A researcher expects the population proportion of Cubs fans in Chicago to be 80 percent. The researcher wishes to have an error of less than 5 percent and to be 95 percent confident of an estimate to be made from a mail survey. What sample size is required?

16. **ETHICS** Using the formula in this chapter, a researcher determines that at the 95 percent confidence level, a sample of 2,500 is required to satisfy a client's requirements. The researcher actually uses a sample of 1,200, however, because the client has specified a budget cap for the survey. What are the ethical considerations in this situation?

17. **'NET** Go to http://www.dartmouth.edu/~chance/ to visit the Chance course. The Chance course is an innovative program to creatively teach introductory materials about probability and statistics. The Chance course is designed to enhance quantitative literacy. Numerous videos can be played online.

18. **'NET** Go to http://www.researchinfo.com. Click on "Marketing Research Calculators." Which of the calculators can be used to help find the sample size required? How big of a sample is needed to make an inference about the U.S. population $+/- 5$ percent? How large a sample is needed to make an inference about the population of Norway $+/- 5$ percent? Remember, population statistics can be found in the *CIA World Factbook* online. Comment.

Research Activities

1. **'NET** Go to http://www.surveypro.com. Click on pricing. Write a brief report that describes how prices are charged to someone wishing to use this service to host a survey. What happens as the desired sample size increases? Why is this?

2. **'NET** Use an online library service to find basic business research studies that report a "response rate" or number of respondents compared to number of contacts. You may wish to consult journals such as the *Journal of Business Research,* the *Journal of Marketing,* or the *Journal of Personal Selling and Sales Management.* Find at least 25 such studies. What is the average response rate across all of these studies? Do there appear to be any trends or factors that are associated with lower response rates? Write a brief report on your findings.

Case 13.1 Pointsec Mobile Technologies

When salespeople, construction supervisors, managers, and other employees are away from the workplace, many of them carry mobile devices such as laptop computers and PDAs, often containing valuable, private data related to their jobs. Pointsec provides security systems to protect such data. To bring home the vulnerability of mobile devices, Pointsec decided to share information about the number of such devices left behind in taxis.[8]

The research involved conducting a survey of taxi drivers. Staff members at Pointsec's public relations firm called major taxi companies in nine cities in Australia, Denmark, Finland, France, Germany, Norway, Sweden, Great Britain, and the United States. Each of the cooperating companies put these interviewers in touch with about one hundred drivers. Drivers were asked how many devices of each type—cell phones, PDAs, computers, and so on—had been left in their cab over the preceding six months. From these numbers, they came up with the rate of items left behind. Multiplying by the size of taxi fleets in each city, the researchers came up with city-by-city numbers: 3.42 cell phones per cab yielded 85,619 cell phones left behind in Chicago, for example. In London, the researchers concluded 63,135 cell phones were left in cabs, a startling increase of 71 percent compared to four years earlier.

Questions

1. Discuss why the sampling method and sample size make these results questionable, even though the numbers were reported as if they were precise.

2. The simple survey method described in the case may have been sufficient as a way to draw attention to the issue of data security. However, if the company were using data on lost mobile devices to predict demand for a product, accuracy might be more significant. Imagine that you have been asked to collect data on mobile devices left in cabs, and you wish to be able to report results with a 95 percent confidence level. How can you improve the sample design and select an appropriate sample size?

Case 13.2 Coastal Star Sales Corporation (A)

Download the data sets for this case from www. thomsonedu.com/marketing/zikmund or request them from your instructor.

Coastal Star Sales Corporation is a West Coast wholesaler that markets leisure products from several manufacturers. Coastal Star has an eighty-person sales force that sells to wholesalers in a six-state area, which is divided into two sales regions. Case Exhibit 13.2–1 shows the names of a sample of eleven salespeople, some descriptive information about each person, and sales performance for each of the last two years.

Questions

1. Calculate a mean and a standard deviation for each variable.

2. Set a 95 percent confidence interval around the mean for each variable.

3. Calculate the median, mode, and range for each variable.

4. Organize the data for current sales into a frequency distribution with three classes: (a) under $500,000, (b) $500,001 to $999,999, and (c) $1,000,000 and over.

5. Organize the data for years of selling experience into a frequency distribution with two classes: (a) less than five years and (b) five or more years.

6. Convert the frequency distributions from question 5 to percentage distributions.

CASE EXHIBIT 13.2–1 **Salesperson Data: Coastal Star Sales Corporation**

Region	Salesperson	Age	Years of Experience	Sales Previous Year	Sales Current Year
Northern	Jackson	40	7	$ 412,744	$ 411,007
Northern	Gentry	60	12	1,491,024	1,726,630
Northern	La Forge	26	2	301,421	700,112
Northern	Miller	39	1	401,241	471,001
Northern	Mowen	64	5	448,160	449,261
Southern	Young	51	2	518,897	519,412
Southern	Fisk	34	1	846,222	713,333
Southern	Kincaid	62	10	1,527,124	2,009,041
Southern	Krieger	42	3	921,174	1,030,000
Southern	Manzer	64	5	463,399	422,798
Southern	Weiner	27	2	548,011	422,001

Part 5
Analysis and Reporting

©NONSTOCK/JUPITER IMAGES

After studying this chapter, you should be able to

1. Know that analysis consists of summarizing, rearranging, ordering, or manipulating data
2. Create and interpret simple tabulation and cross-tabulation tables
3. Understand how cross-tabulations can reveal relationships
4. Perform basic data transformations
5. Define *hypothesis* and *significance level*
6. Discuss the steps in the hypothesis-testing procedure
7. Describe the factors that influence the choice of statistical methods to use for analysis

Chapter Vignette: Choose Your "Poison"

Most Americans enjoy an adult beverage occasionally. But not all Americans like the same drink. Many decision makers are interested in what Americans like to drink. Retailers need to have the correct product mix for their particular customers if profits are to be increased and customers made more satisfied. Restaurants need to know what their customers like to have with the types of food they serve. Policy makers need to know what types of restrictions should be placed on what types of products to prevent underage drinking and alcohol abuse. Researchers could apply sophisticated statistics to address questions related to Americans' drinking preferences, but a lot can be learned from just counting what people are buying.

©STEPHEN OLIVER/DORLING KINDERSLEY/GETTY IMAGES

A grocery store built in 1975 in Chicago allocates 15 percent of their floor space to adult beverage products. Out of this 15 percent, 60 percent is allocated to beer, 25 percent to spirits, and 15 percent to wine. Since the products are not merchandised the same way (different types of shelving, aisles, and racking are needed), adjusting the floor space to change these percentages is not an easy task. Over the three-decade history of the store, the customer base has changed. Originally, stay-at-home moms buying groceries for the family best characterized the customer base. During the 1990s, empty-nesters, including retirees with high disposable incomes, characterized the customer base. More recently, younger singles just starting careers have moved into the nearby neighborhoods. Should the store reconsider its adult beverage merchandising?

In 1992, American consumers showed a heavy preference toward beer. Among American adults who drank adult beverages,[1]

- 47 percent drank beer
- 21 percent drank spirits
- 27 percent drank wine

By 2005, Americans had changed their drinking preferences. Now,

- 36 percent drink beer
- 21 percent drink spirits
- 39 percent drink wine

A couple of other facts have become clear. A count of the preferred beverages among American adult consumers twenty-nine and younger shows the following preferences:[2]

- 48 percent drink beer
- 32 percent drink spirits
- 17 percent drink wine

Across America, grocers account for 35 percent of all beer sales, but convenience stores, where younger consumers tend to shop, account for 45 percent.[3] If the grocery store is converting more to a convenience store, maybe a continued emphasis on beer is wise. However, wine consumers are more *attractive* from several perspectives. Wine now ranks among the top ten food categories in America, based on grocery store dollar sales volume. Forty-five percent of all wine is sold in grocery stores. What we find is that the consumer who buys wine is also more likely to buy products like prime or choice beef and imported cheeses, instead of lower quality and lower priced meat and cheese products. As a result, the average $13.44 spent on wine in a grocery store (as opposed to $11.94 on beer) is only part of the story in explaining why wine customers may be *grape* customers![4]

What should the grocer emphasize in marketing adult beverages? Perhaps the research based on counting can address this decision.

The Nature of Descriptive Analysis

Descriptive analysis
The elementary transformation of raw data in a way that describes the basic characteristics such as central tendency, distribution, and variability.

Perhaps the most basic statistical analysis is descriptive analysis. **Descriptive analysis** is the elementary transformation of data in a way that describes the basic characteristics such as central tendency, distribution, and variability. A researcher takes responses from 1,000 American consumers and tabulates their favorite soft drink brand and the price they expect to pay for a six-pack of that product. The mode for favorite soft drink and the average price across all 1,000 consumers would be descriptive statistics that describe central tendency in two different ways. Averages, medians, modes, variance, range, and standard deviation typify widely applied descriptive statistics.

Descriptive statistics can summarize responses from large numbers of respondents in a few simple statistics. When a sample is used, the sample descriptive statistics are used to make inferences about characteristics of the entire population of interest. Descriptive statistics are simple but powerful. The researcher enters the area of univariate statistical analysis when this is the case. Chapter 15 will focus on this extension of basic descriptive statistics. Because they are so simple, descriptive statistics are used very widely.

Chapter 10 indicated that the level of scale measurement helps the researcher choose the most appropriate form of statistical analysis. Exhibit 14.1 shows how the level of scale measurement influences the choice of descriptive statistics. Remember that all statistics appropriate for lower-order scales (nominal is the lowest) are suitable for higher-order scales (ratio is the highest).

Consider the following data. Sample consumers were asked where they most often purchased beer. The result is a nominal variable which can be described with a frequency distribution (see the bar chart in Exhibit 14.1). Ten percent indicated they most often purchased beer in a drug store, 45 percent indicated a convenience store, 35 percent indicated a grocery store, and 7 percent indicated a specialty store. Three percent listed "other" (not shown in the bar chart). The mode is convenience store since more respondents chose this than any other category. A similar distribution may have been obtained if the chart plotted the number of respondents ranking each store as their favorite type of place to purchase beer.

The bottom part of Exhibit 14.1 displays example descriptive statistics for interval and ratio variables. In this case, the chart displays results of a question asking respondents how much they typically spend on a bottle of wine purchased in a store. The mean and standard deviation are displayed beside the chart as 11.7 and 4.5, respectively. Additionally, a frequency distribution is shown with a histogram. A **histogram** is graphical way of showing a frequency distribution in which the height of a bar corresponds to the frequency of a category. Histograms are useful for any type of data, but with continuous variables (interval or ratio) the histogram is useful for providing a quick assessment of the distribution of the data. A normal distribution line is superimposed over the histogram providing an easy comparison to see if the data are skewed or multi-modal.

Histogram
A graphical way of showing a frequency distribution in which the height of a bar corresponds to the observed frequency of the category.

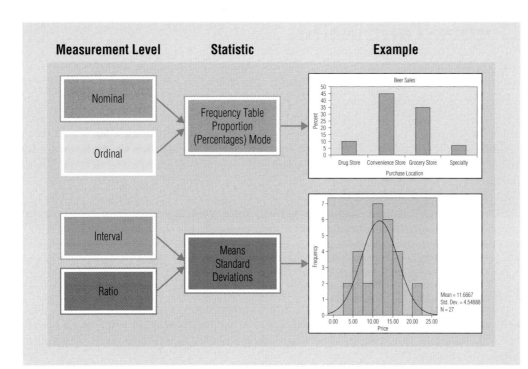

Tabulation

Tabulation refers to the orderly arrangement of data in a table or other summary format. When this tabulation process is done by hand the term *tallying* is used. Counting the different ways respondents answered a question and arranging them in a simple tabular form yields a **frequency table**. The actual number of responses to each category is a variable's frequency distribution. A simple tabulation of this type is sometimes called a *marginal tabulation*.

Simple tabulation tells the researcher how frequently each response occurs. This starting point for analysis requires the researcher to count responses or observations for each category or code assigned to a variable. A frequency table showing where consumers generally purchase beer can be computed easily. The tabular results that correspond to the chart would appear as follows:

Response	Frequency	Percent	Cumulative Percentage
Drug Store	50	10	10
Convenience Store	225	45	55
Grocery Store	175	35	90
Specialty	35	7	97
Other	15	3	100

Tabulation
The orderly arrangement of data in a table or other summary format showing the number of responses to each response category; tallying.

Frequency table
A table showing the different ways respondents answered a question.

The frequency column shows the tally result or the number of respondents listing each store, respectively. The percent column shows the total percentage in each category. The cumulative percentage shows the percentage indicating either a particular category or any preceding category as their preferred place to purchase beer. From this chart, the mode indicates that the typical consumer buys beer at the convenience store since more people indicated this as their top response.

Similarly, a recent tabulation of Americans' responses to the simple question of "Who is your favorite TV personality?" revealed the response varied by age. For respondents aged 18–24, Conan O'Brien was listed first. For respondents aged 30–39, Bill O'Reilly was the preferred TV personality, and among consumers 65 and older, Oprah Winfrey was the modal response.[5] The idea that age may influence choice of favorite celebrity brings us to cross-tabulation.

Cross-Tabulation

Cross-tabulation

The appropriate technique for addressing research questions involving relationships among multiple less-than interval variables; results in a combined frequency table displaying one variable in rows and another in columns.

A frequency distribution or tabulation can address many research questions. As long as a question deals with only one categorical variable, tabulation is probably the best approach. Although frequency counts, percentage distributions, and averages summarize considerable information, simple tabulation may not yield the full value of the research. **Cross-tabulation** is the appropriate technique for addressing research questions involving relationships among multiple less-than interval variables. A cross-tabulation is a combined frequency table. Cross-tabulation allows the inspection and comparison of differences among groups based on nominal or ordinal categories. One key to interpreting a cross-tabulation table is comparing the observed table values with hypothetical values that would result from pure chance.

Exhibit 14.2 summarizes several cross-tabulations from consumers' responses to a questionnaire on ethical behavior in the United States.[6] Panel A suggests how two questionable behaviors (variables—taking home supplies, calling in sick) may vary with basic demographic variables. A researcher interested in the relative ethical perspectives of business executives and the general public can inspect panel B and compare the two groups. If business executives and the general public have the same ethical attitudes, the observed percentages should be equal for each question. This does not appear to be the case. The data lead to the conclusion that business executives participate in these behaviors more than the general public. However, before reaching the conclusion that business executives are less ethical than the general public, one must carefully scrutinize this finding for possible extraneous variables.

Contingency table

A data matrix that displays the frequency of some combination of possible responses to multiple variables; cross-tabulation results.

Contingency Tables

Exhibit 14.3 shows example cross-tabulation results using contingency tables. A **contingency table** is a data matrix that displays the frequency of some combination of possible responses to multiple

EXHIBIT 14.2 **Cross-Tabulation Tables from a Survey on Ethics in America**

(A) Reported Behavior (Percentage of General Public Who Have Ever Done Each Activity)

Activity	Age		Gender		Education	
	Under 50 Years Old	**Over 50 Years Old**	**Men**	**Women**	**College Graduate**	**High School Graduate**
Taken home work supplies	50	26	47	33	58	21
Called in sick to work when not ill	40	18	Not reported		36	21

(B) Reported Behavior (Percentage Who Have Ever Done Each Activity)

Activity	Business Executives	General Public
Taken home work supplies	74	40
Called in sick to work when not ill	14	31
Used company telephone for personal long-distance calls	78	15
Overstated deductions somewhat on tax forms	35	13
Driven while drunk	80	33
Saw a fellow employee steal something at work and did not report it	7	26

From Roger Ricklefs, "Ethics in America," The Wall Street Journal, October 31, 1983, p. 33, 42; November 1, 1983, p. 33; November 2, 1983, p. 33; and November 3, 1983, pp. 33, 37.

EXHIBIT 14.3

Possible Cross-Tabulations of One Question

(A) Cross-Tabulation of Question "Do you shop at Target?" by Sex of Respondent

	Yes	No	Total
Men	150	75	225
Women	180	45	225
Total	330	120	450

(B) Percentage Cross-Tabulation of Question "Do you shop at Target?" by Sex of Respondent, Row Percentage

	Yes	No	Total (Base)
Men	66.7%	33.3%	100% (225)
Women	80.0%	20.0%	100% (225)

(C) Percentage Cross-Tabulation of Question "Do you shop at Target?" by Sex of Respondent, Column Percentage

	Yes	No
Men	45.5%	62.5%
Women	54.5%	37.5%
Total	100%	100%
(Base)	(330)	(120)

variables. Two-way contingency tables, meaning they involve two less-than interval variables, are used most often. A three-way contingency table involves three less-than interval variables. Beyond three variables, contingency tables become difficult to analyze and thus, they are seldom used.

Two variables are depicted in the contingency table shown in panel A:

- Row Variable: Biological Sex _____M _____F
- Column Variable: "Do you shop at Target? YES or NO"

Several conclusions can be drawn initially by examining the row and column totals:

1. 225 men and 225 women responded as can be seen in the row totals column.
2. Out of 450 total consumers responding, 330 consumers indicated that "yes," they do shop at Target and 120 indicated "no," they do not shop at Target. This can be observed in the column totals at the bottom of the table. These row and column totals often are called **marginals** because they appear in the table's margins.

Researchers usually are more interested in the inner cells of a contingency table. The inner cells display conditional frequencies (combinations). Using these values, we can draw some more specific conclusions:

3. Out of 330 consumers who shop at Target, 150 are male and 180 are female.
4. Alternatively, out of the 120 respondents not shopping at Target, 75 are male and 45 are female.

This finding helps us know whether the two variables are related. If men and women equally patronized Target, we would expect that hypothetically 165 of the 330 shoppers would be female and 165 would be female. Because we have equal numbers of men and women, the 330 would be equally male and female. The hypothetical expectations (165m/165f) are not observed. What is the implication? Target shoppers are more likely to be female than male. Notice that the same meaning could be drawn by analyzing non-Target shoppers.

Marginals
Row and column totals in a contingency table, which are shown in its margins.

RESEARCHSNAPSHOT

Contingent Personalities

Who is the world's favorite celebrity? This is an important question because the answer helps to determine how much a celebrity endorsement is worth. Sports stars like Tiger Woods are effective in shaping consumers' product preferences worldwide. Pop stars like the Spice Girls have been effectively used to increase soft drink sales in the United Kingdom. In other parts of the world, perhaps Sharon Cumeta could do the same. Perhaps some celebrities are effective nearly everywhere, but others may only be effective in a given country. Their effectiveness is contingent upon region.

Television personalities also influence the public's opinion by giving their own. But all opinions may not be equal. Polling agencies like the Harris interactive poll (http://www.harrisinteractive.com) monitor the popularity of celebrities. Who is America's favorite television personality? Oprah Winfrey has achieved the top rating by Americans for several years. But is Oprah's likeability contingent upon other factors? Cross-tabulations can help answer this question. Consider the following 2-by-2 contingency table showing results of 1,000 respondents asked to choose whether they prefer Oprah Winfrey or David Letterman:

	Oprah Winfrey	David Letterman	Totals
Men	150	350	500
Women	380	120	500
	530	470	1,000

Or, consider the 3-by-3 contingency table:

	Oprah Winfrey	Bill O'Reilly	Jon Stewart	Totals
Conservatives	60	260	20	340
Liberals	100	20	200	320
Moderates	210	70	60	340
	370	350	280	1000

In either case, opinions about the preferred celebrity seem to be contingent, or to depend on some characteristic. Results like these would suggest that although Oprah is preferred overall, men prefer David Letterman over Oprah. Also, one's favorite celebrity depends on political orientation. Thus, marketing managers should consider the contingencies when trying to identify preferred celebrities.

Sources: Erdogan, B., Zater, Michael J. Baker, and Stephen Tagg (2001), "Selecting Celebrity Endorsers: The Practitioner's Perspective," Journal of Advertising Research, 41 (May/June), 39–48; Goetzl, David and Wayne Friedman (2002), "What We're Talking About," Advertising Age, 73 (12/2), 51–57; The Wall Street Journal Online (2006), "Harris Poll: Oprah Again Tops America's List of Favorite TV Personalities," (February 3), http://online.wsj.com/article/SB113889692780763347-search.html?KEYWORDS=Oprah&COLLECTION=wsjie/6month.

D. VAN/UPI/LANDOV

A two-way contingency table like the one shown in part A is referred to as a *2 × 2 table* because it has two rows and two columns. Each variable has two levels. A two-way contingency table displaying two variables one (the row variable) with three levels and the other with four levels would be referred to as a *3 × 4 table*. Any cross-tabulation table may be classified according to the number of rows by the number of columns (*R* by *C*).

Percentage Cross-Tabulations

When data from a survey are cross-tabulated, percentages help the researcher understand the nature of the relationship by making relative comparisons simpler. The total number of respondents or observations may be used as a **statistical base** for computing the percentage in each cell. When the objective of the research is to identify a relationship between answers to two questions (or two variables), one of the questions is commonly chosen to be the source of the base for determining percentages. For example, look at the data in parts A, B, and C of Exhibit 14.3. Compare part B with part C. Selecting either the row percentages or the column percentages will emphasize a particular comparison or distribution. The nature of the problem the researcher wishes to answer will determine which marginal total will serve as a base for computing percentages.

Fortunately, a conventional rule determines the direction of percentages. The rule depends on which variable is identified as an independent variable and which is a dependent variable. Simply put, independent variables should form the rows in a contingency table. The marginal total of the

Statistical base
The number of respondents or observations (in a row or column) used as a basis for computing percentages.

independent variable should be used as the base for computing the percentages. Although survey research does not establish cause-and-effect evidence, one might argue that it would be logical to assume that a variable such as biological sex might predict beverage preference. This makes more sense than thinking that beverage preference would determine biological sex.

Elaboration and Refinement

The *Oxford Universal Dictionary* defines *analysis* as "the resolution of anything complex into its simplest elements." Once a researcher has examined the basic relationship between two variables, he or she may wish to investigate this relationship under a variety of different conditions. Typically, a third variable is introduced into the analysis to elaborate and refine the researcher's understanding by specifying the conditions under which the relationship between the first two variables is strongest and weakest. In other words, a more elaborate analysis asks, "Will interpretation of the relationship be modified if other variables are simultaneously considered?"

Elaboration analysis involves the basic cross-tabulation within various subgroups of the sample. The researcher breaks down the analysis for each level of another variable. If the researcher has cross-tabulated shopping preference by sex (see Exhibit 14.3) and wishes to investigate another variable (say, marital status), a more elaborate analysis may be conducted. Exhibit 14.4 breaks down the responses to the question "Do you shop at Target?" by sex and marital status. The data show women display the same preference whether married or single. However, married men are much more likely to shop at Target than are single men. The analysis suggests that the original conclusion about the relationship between sex and shopping behavior for women be retained. However, a relationship that was not discernible in the two-variable case is evident. Married men more frequently shop at Target than do single men.

The finding is consistent with an interaction effect. The combination of the two variables, sex and marital status, is associated with differences in the dependent variable. Interactions between variables examine moderating variables. A moderator variable is a third variable that changes the nature of a relationship between the original independent and dependent variables. Marital status is a moderator variable in this case. The interaction effect suggests that marriage changes the relationship between sex and shopping preference.

In other situations the addition of a third variable to the analysis may lead us to reject the original conclusion about the relationship. When this occurs, the elaboration analysis suggests the relationship between the original variables is spurious (see Chapter 3).

The chapter vignette described data suggesting a relationship between the type of store in which a consumer shops and beverage preference. Convenience store shoppers seem to choose beer over wine while grocery store shoppers choose wine over beer. Does store type drive drinking preference? Perhaps age determines both the type of store consumers choose to buy in and their preference for adult beverages. Younger consumers both disproportionately shop in convenience stores and drink beer.

How Many Cross-Tabulations?

Surveys may ask dozens of questions and hundreds of categorical variables can be stored in a data warehouse. Computer-assisted marketing researchers can "fish" for relationships by cross-tabulating every categorical variable with every other categorical variable. Thus, every possible response

TOTHEPOINT

The more we study, the more we discover our ignorance.

—Percy Bysshe Shelley

Elaboration analysis
An analysis of the basic cross-tabulation for each level of a variable not previously considered, such as subgroups of the sample.

Moderator variable
A third variable that changes the nature of a relationship between the original independent and dependent variables.

EXHIBIT 14.4
Cross-Tabulation of Marital Status, Sex, and Responses to the Question "Do You Shop at Target?"

	Single		Married	
	Men	Women	Men	Women
"Do you shop at Target?"				
Yes	55%	80%	86%	80%
No	45%	20%	14%	20%

becomes a possible explanatory variable. A researcher addressing an exploratory research question may find some benefit in such a fishing expedition. Software exists that can automatically search through volumes of cross-tabulations. These may even provide some insight into the market segment structure for some product. Alternatively, the program may flag the cross-tabulations suggesting the strongest relationship. CHAID (chi-square automatic interaction detection) software exemplifies software that makes searches through large numbers of variables possible.[7] Data-mining can be conducted in a similar fashion and may suggest relationships that are worth considering further.

Outside of exploratory research, researchers should conduct cross-tabulations that address specific research questions or hypotheses. When hypotheses involve relationships among two categorical variables, cross-tabulations are the right tool for the job.

Data Transformation

Simple Transformations

Data transformation
Process of changing the data from their original form to a format suitable for performing a data analysis addressing research objectives.

TOTHEPOINT

All that we do is done with an eye to something else.

—Aristotle

Data transformation (also called *data conversion*) is the process of changing the data from their original form to a format suitable for performing a data analysis that will achieve research objectives. Researchers often modify the values of scalar data or create new variables. For example, many researchers believe that less response bias will result if interviewers ask respondents for their year of birth rather than their age. This presents no problem for the research analyst, because a simple data transformation is possible. The raw data coded as birth year can easily be transformed to age by subtracting the birth year from the current year.

In earlier chapters, we discussed recoding and creating summated scales. These also are common data transformations.

Collapsing or combining adjacent categories of a variable is a common form of data transformation used to reduce the number of categories. A Likert scale may sometimes be collapsed into a smaller number of categories. For instance, consider the following Likert item administered to a sample of state university seniors:

	Strongly Disagree	Disagree	Neutral	Agree	Strongly Agree
I am satisfied with my college experience at this university	☐	☐	☐	☐	☐

The following frequency table describes results for this survey item:

Strongly Disagree	Disagree	Neutral	Agree	Strongly Agree
110	30	15	35	210

The distribution of responses suggests the responses are bimodal. That is, two peaks exist in the distribution, one at either end of the scale. Since the vast majority of respondents (80 percent = (110 + 210)/400) indicated either strongly disagree or strongly agree, the variable closely resembles a categorical variable. Customers either strongly disagreed or strongly agreed with the statement. So, the research may wish to collapse the responses into two categories. While multiple ways exist to accomplish this, the researcher may assign the value of one to all respondents who either strongly disagreed or disagreed and the value two to all respondents who either agreed or strongly agreed. Respondents marking neutral would be deleted from the analysis.

RESEARCHSNAPSHOT

Wine Index Can Help Retailers

Indexes can be very useful, and researchers are sometimes asked to create index values from secondary data. The chapter vignette described a situation where a retailer was making decisions about merchandising based on the consumption habits of store customers. If a U.S. grocer is considering wine merchandising in another country, he/she may be interested to know wine indexes of other countries.

Using 1968 U.S. wine consumption as a base, the current wine consumption index for the United Kingdom is 4.1, South Africa's index value is 2.2 (almost the same as the United States), Israel's index is 0.4, and Luxembourg's wine index is 14.1 (59.2 liters/person/year)! This information would be helpful in making decisions about the amount of space and attention given to wine in different countries. Similarly, the retailer could compute wine or beer indices by state. Policy agencies could also chart indices on alcohol consumption that may be helpful in regulating underage consumption.

Sources: http://www.wineinstitute.com.

©SUSAN VAN ETTEN

Calculating Rank Order

Survey respondents are often asked to rank order brand or store preferences. Employee respondents may provide rankings of several different employee benefit plans. Ranking data can be summarized by performing a data transformation. The transformation involves multiplying the frequency by the ranking score for each choice to result in a new scale.

For example, suppose a manager of a frequent-flier program had ten executives rank their preferences for locations in which to hold the company's annual conference. Exhibit 14.5 shows how executives ranked each of four locations: Hawaii, Paris, Greece, and Hong Kong. Exhibit 14.6 on the next page tabulates frequencies for these rankings. A ranking summary can be computed by assigning the destination with the highest preference the lowest number (1) and the least preferred destination the highest consecutive number (4). The summarized rank orderings were obtained with the following calculations:

Hawaii:	$(3 \times 1) + (5 \times 2) + (1 \times 3) + (1 \times 4) = 20$
Paris:	$(3 \times 1) + (1 \times 2) + (3 \times 3) + (3 \times 4) = 26$
Greece:	$(2 \times 1) + (2 \times 2) + (4 \times 3) + (2 \times 4) = 26$
Hong Kong:	$(2 \times 1) + (2 \times 2) + (2 \times 3) + (4 \times 4) = 28$

Three executives chose Hawaii as the best destination (ranked "1"), five executives selected Hawaii as the second best destination, and so forth. The lowest total score indicates the first (highest) preference ranking. The results show the following rank ordering: (1) Hawaii, (2) Paris, (3) Greece, and (4) Hong Kong. Company employees may be glad to hear their conference will be in Hawaii.

EXHIBIT 14.5

Executive Rankings of Potential Conference Destinations

Executive	Hawaii	Paris	Greece	Hong Kong
1	1	2	4	3
2	1	3	4	2
3	2	1	3	4
4	2	4	3	1
5	2	1	3	4
6	3	4	1	2
7	2	3	1	4
8	1	4	2	3
9	4	3	2	1
10	2	1	3	4

Destination	Preference Rankings			
	1st	**2nd**	**3rd**	**4th**
Hawaii	3	5	1	1
Paris	3	1	3	3
Greece	2	2	4	2
Hong Kong	2	2	2	4

Tabular and Graphic Methods of Displaying Data

Tables, graphs, and charts may simplify and clarify data. Graphical representations of data may take a number of forms, ranging from a computer printout to an elaborate pictograph. Tables, graphs, and charts, however, all facilitate summarization and communication.

Today's researcher has many convenient tools to quickly produce charts, graphs, or tables. Even basic word processing programs like Word include chart functions that can construct the chart within the text document. Bar charts (histograms), pie charts, curve/line diagrams, and scatter plots are among the most widely used tools. Some choices match well with certain types of data and analyses.

Tables

Tables are most useful for presenting numerical information, especially when several pieces of information have been gathered about each item discussed. The purpose of each table, however, is to facilitate the summarization and communication of the data's meaning. For example, Exhibit 14.7 illustrates the relationships among education, income, and regional airline usage expenditures for

EXHIBIT 14.7 **Table of Regional Airline Usage for Vacation/Pleasure by Income and Education Class**

	Total	Under $20,000	$20,000–$39,000	$40,000–$59,000	$60,000 and Over
All consumers					
Expenditures (%)	100	10	7	16	67
Consumer units (%)	100	42	19	16	23
Index	100	26	36	100	291
Non–high school graduate					
Expenditures (%)	8	1	2	1	4
Consumer units (%)	35	21	6	4	4
Index	21	5	33	25	100
High school graduate					
Expenditures (%)	29	4	2	8	15
Consumer units (%)	30	11	6	6	7
Index	96	36	33	133	214
Attended/graduated college					
Expenditures (%)	63	5	3	7	48
Consumer units (%)	35	10	6	6	13
Index	180	50	50	116	369
				Percentage population = 32	Percentage expenditures = 78

EXHIBIT 14.8 **A Stubhead Format Table Allowing Several Cross-Tabulations to Be Included in a Single Table**

Confidence in Church/Organized Religion

Question: I am going to read you a list of institutions in American society. Would you tell me how much confidence you, yourself, have in each one—a great deal, quite a lot, some, or very little?

The Church or Organized Religion

	Great Deal	Quite a Lot	Some	Very Little	None	No Opinion	Number of Interviews
National	42%	24%	21%	11%	1%	1%	1,528
Sex							
Men	36	27	22	13	1	1	755
Women	48	21	20	9	1	1	773
Age							
Total under 30	39	26	24	10	1	*	320
18–24 years	38	28	24	9	1	*	138
25–29 years	40	23	23	13	1	*	182
30–49 years	38	25	23	12	1	1	593
Total 50 & older	50	21	18	10	*	1	608
50–64 years	48	23	18	10	*	1	302
65 and older	52	18	18	10	1	1	306
Region							
East	33	24	28	13	1	1	388
Midwest	44	26	20	9	*	1	398
South	51	24	14	9	1	1	444
West	39	20	25	15	1	*	298
Race							
Whites	42	23	22	11	1	1	1,334
Nonwhites	45	27	18	8	1	1	184
Blacks	47	26	18	7	*	2	151
Hispanics	42	25	21	10	1	1	104

*Less than 1 percent.
From "Confidence in Church/Organized Religion," *The Gallup Report 238,* July 1985, p. 4.

vacation/pleasure trips. The shaded area emphasizes a key conclusion about market share. (To summarize the information in the shaded box: 32 percent of the population makes 78 percent of the expenditures.) This form of presentation simplifies interpretation.

Suppose an airline asks a question about customers' satisfaction with its baggage-handling service. In addition to showing the simple frequency for each category, most research analysts would cross-tabulate answers to the baggage-handling questions with several demographic variables such as gender, income, education, and age. Presenting multiple cross-tabulations individually in a separate table requires considerable space. Thus, many research reports use a space-saving format with either *stubheads* for rows or *bannerheads* for columns, to allow the reader to view several cross-tabulations at the same time. Exhibit 14.8 presents several cross-tabulations in a single table with stubheads.

Charts and Graphs

Charts translate numerical information into visual form so that relationships may be easily grasped. Although a number of standardized forms exist for presenting data in charts or graphs, the researcher may use his or her creativity to increase the effectiveness of a particular presentation. Bar charts, pie charts, line charts, and other graphic forms of presentation create strong visual impressions. Exhibit 14.9 on the next page shows simple versions of a pie chart, horizontal bar graph, vertical bar graph, and line graph.

PIE CHARTS

One of the most useful kinds of charts is the *pie chart,* which shows the composition of some total quantity at a particular time. Each angle, or "slice," is proportional to its percentage of the whole and

EXHIBIT 14.9
The Basic Forms of Graphic Presentation

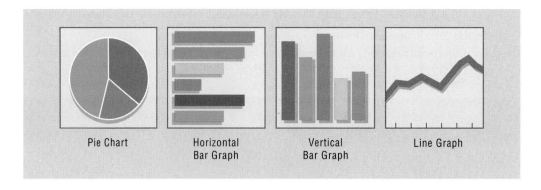

| Pie Chart | Horizontal Bar Graph | Vertical Bar Graph | Line Graph |

should be labeled with its description and percentage. The writer should not try to include too many small slices; about six slices is a typical maximum. Companies commonly use pie charts to show how revenues were used or the composition of their sales.

LINE GRAPHS

Line graphs are useful for showing the relationship of one variable to another. The dependent variable generally is shown on the vertical axis and the independent variable on the horizontal axis. The most common independent variable for such charts is time, but it is by no means the only one. Exhibit 14.10 depicts a multiple line graph. It shows how line graphs can display comparisons among groups over time. The line for each dependent variable should be in a different color or pattern and should be clearly labeled. The researcher should not try to squeeze in too many variables; this can quickly lead to confusion rather than clarification.

BAR CHARTS

Bar charts show changes in the value of a dependent variable (plotted on the vertical axis) at discrete intervals of the independent variable (on the horizontal axis). A simple bar chart often presents the frequency of response to various questions. A multiple bar chart shows how multiple variables are related to the primary variable. In every case, each bar needs to be clearly identified with a different color or pattern. The researcher should not use too many divisions or dependent variables. Too much detail obscures the essential advantage of charts, which is to make relationships easy to grasp.

EXHIBIT 14.10
Line Graphs Highlighting Comparisons over Time

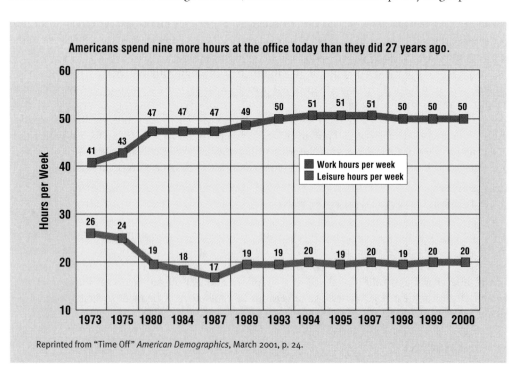

Reprinted from "Time Off" *American Demographics*, March 2001, p. 24.

Computer Programs for Analysis

Statistical Packages

In the 1980s and early 1990s, when the PC was still a relatively novel innovation, specialized statistical software formerly used on mainframe computers made their way into the personal computing market. Today, most spreadsheet packages can perform a wide variety of basic statistical options. Excel's basic data analysis tool will allow descriptive statistics including frequencies and measures of central tendency to be easily computed.[8] Most of the basic statistical features are now menu driven, reducing the need to memorize function labels. Spreadsheet packages like Excel continue to evolve and become more viable for performing many basic statistical analyses (see Exhibit 14.11).

Despite the advances in spreadsheet applications, commercialized statistical software packages remain extremely popular among researchers. They continue to become easier to use and more compatible with other data interface tools, including spreadsheets and word processors. Like any specialized tool, statistical packages are more tailored to the types of analyses performed by statistical analysts, including marketing researchers. Thus, any serious business or social science researcher should still become familiar with at least one general computer software package.

Two of the most popular general statistical packages are SAS (http://www.sas.com) and SPSS (http://www.spss.com). SAS revenues exceed $1.4 billion and its software can be found on computers worldwide. SAS was founded in 1976, and its statistical software historically has been widely used in engineering and other technical fields. SPSS sales exceed $224 million and the company was founded in 1968. SPSS stands for *Statistical Package for the Social Sciences.* SPSS is commonly used by university business and social science students. Marketing researchers have traditionally used SPSS more than any other statistical software tool. SPSS has been viewed as more user-friendly in the past. However, today's versions of both SPSS and SAS are very user-friendly and give the user the option of using drop-down menus to conduct analysis rather than writing computer code.

Excel, SAS, and SPSS account for most of the statistical analysis conducted in marketing research. University students are sometimes exposed to MINITAB. MINITAB's revenues are

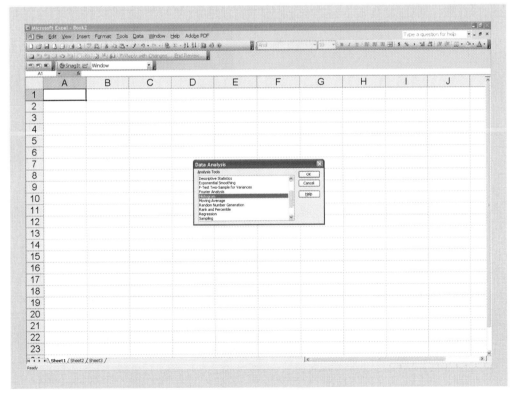

EXHIBIT 14.11

The Basic Data Analysis Window

EXHIBIT 14.12 **SAS Computer Output of Descriptive Statistics**

State = NY Variable	N	Mean	Standard Deviation	Minimum Value	Maximum Value	Std Error of Mean	Sum	Variance	C.V.
EMP	10	142.930	232.665	12.800	788.800	73.575	1429.300	54133.0	162.782
SALES	10	5807.800	11905.127	307.000	39401.000	3764.732	58078.000	141732049.1	204.985

Key: EMP = number of employees (000)   SALES = Sales (000)

approximately $10 million per year. Economists sometimes favor MINITAB; however, it has traditionally been viewed as being less user-friendly than other choices.

In the past, data entry was an issue as specific software required different types of data input. Today, however, all the major software packages including SAS and SPSS can work from data entered into a spreadsheet. The spreadsheets can be imported into the data windows or simply read by the program. Most conventional online survey tools will return data to the user in the form of either an SPSS data file, an Excel spreadsheet, or a plain text document.

Exhibit 14.12 shows a printout of descriptive statistics generated by SAS for two variables: EMP (number of employees working in an MSA, or Metropolitan Statistical Area) and SALES (sales volume in dollars in an MSA) for ten MSAs. The number of data elements (N), mean, standard deviation, and other descriptive statistics are displayed. SAS output is generally simple and easy to read. A histogram is similar to a bar chart. Exhibit 14.13 shows an SPSS histogram plot of purchase price data from a survey. Each bar indicates the number of purchases.

Exhibit 14.14 shows an SPSS cross-tabulation of two variables, class status and smoking behavior. The data come from a sample intercepted on an urban university campus. It addresses the research question, "Does smoking on campus vary across groups?" More non-smokers than smokers are found. However, the results show that graduate students, and to a lesser extent instructors,

EXHIBIT 14.13
SPSS Histogram Output

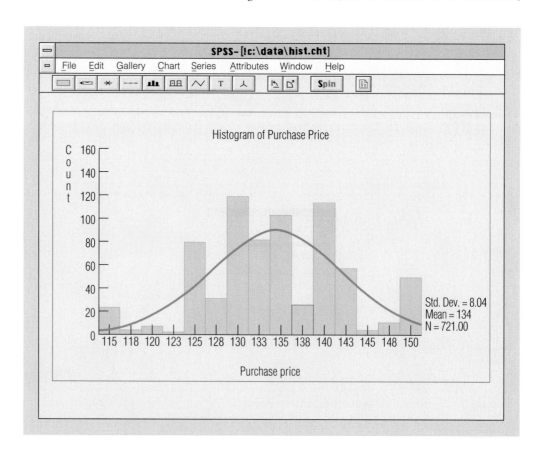

CLASS * SMOKING Cross-Tabulation				
Count		**Smoking**		
		Smoker	**Non-smoker**	**Total**
Class	high school	7	9	16
	undergraduate	9	22	31
	graduate	15	10	25
	career	6	6	12
Total		37	47	84

From *Real Stats Real Easy: SPSS for Windows*. Copyright © 1992, SPSS, Inc.

EXHIBIT 14.14

Examples of SPSS Output for Cross-Tabulation

smoke more than the norm. The SPSS user can ask for any number of statistics and percentages to be included with this output by clicking on the corresponding options.

Univariate Statistics: Stating a Hypothesis

In marketing theory, a **hypothesis** is an unproven proposition or supposition offering an explanation of certain facts or phenomena. In other words, a hypothesis is a guess. A sales manager may hypothesize that salespeople who are highest in product knowledge will be the most productive. An advertising manager may hypothesize that if consumers' attitudes toward a product change in a positive direction, there will be an increase in consumption of the product. Statistical techniques allow us to decide whether or not our theoretical hypothesis is confirmed by the empirical evidence.

Because scientists should be bold in conjecturing but extremely cautious in testing, statistical hypotheses generally are stated in null form. A **null hypothesis** is a statement about a status quo. The true purpose of the null hypothesis is to provide an opportunity for nullifying it. For example, suppose academic researchers expect that highly dogmatic (that is, closed-minded) consumers will be less likely to try a new product than will less dogmatic consumers. The researchers would generally formulate a conservative null hypothesis. A null hypothesis in this case would be that there is *no difference* between high dogmatics and low dogmatics in their willingness to try an innovation. The **alternative hypothesis** would be that there *is* a difference between high dogmatics and low dogmatics. It states the opposite of the null hypothesis.

Hypothesis
An unproven proposition or supposition that tentatively explains certain facts or phenomena; a proposition that is empirically testable.

Null hypothesis
A statement about a status quo asserting that any change from what has been thought to be true will be due entirely to random sampling error.

Alternative hypothesis
A statement indicating the opposite of the null hypothesis.

Hypothesis Testing

Generally, we assign the symbol H_0 to the null hypothesis and the symbol H_1 to the alternative hypothesis. The purpose of hypothesis testing is to determine which of the two hypotheses is correct. The process of hypothesis testing is slightly more complicated than that of estimating parameters because the decision maker must choose between the two hypotheses. However, the student need not worry because the mathematical calculations are no more difficult than those we have already made.

The Hypothesis-Testing Procedure

The process of hypothesis testing goes as follows. First, we translate the substantive hypothesis into a statistical hypothesis. One result of this is determining the measurement level(s) involved. We then imagine what the sampling distribution of the mean would be if this hypothesis were a true statement of the nature of the population. Next, we take an actual sample and calculate the sample mean (or appropriate statistic, if we are not concerned about the mean). We know from our previous discussions of the sampling distribution of the mean that obtaining a sample value that is exactly the same as the population parameter is highly unlikely; we expect some small difference (although it may be large) between the sample mean and the population mean. We then must determine if the deviation between the obtained value of the sample mean and its expected value (based on the statistical hypothesis) would have occurred by chance alone—say, 5 times out of 100—if in fact the statistical hypothesis had been true. In other words, we ask this question: "Has the sample mean deviated substantially from the mean of the hypothesized sampling distribution by a value large enough for us to conclude that this large a deviation would be somewhat rare if the statistical hypothesis were true?" Suppose we observe that the sample value differs from the expected value. Before we can conclude that these results are improbable (or even probable), we must have some standard, or decision rule, for determining if in fact we should reject the null hypothesis and accept the alternative hypothesis. Statisticians define this decision criterion as the *significance level*.

Significance level
The critical probability in choosing between the null and alternative hypotheses; the probability level that is too low to warrant support of the null hypothesis.

The **significance level** is the critical probability in choosing between the null hypothesis and the alternative hypothesis. The level of significance determines the probability level—say, .05 or .01—that is to be considered too low to warrant support of the null hypothesis. Assuming the null hypothesis being tested is true, if the probability of occurrence of the observed data is smaller than the significance level, then the data suggest that the null hypothesis should be rejected. In other words, there has been evidence to support contradiction of the null hypothesis, which is equivalent to supporting the alternative hypothesis.

In discussing confidence intervals (the set of acceptable hypotheses), statisticians use the term *confidence level,* or *confidence coefficient,* to refer to the level of probability associated with an interval estimate. However, when discussing hypothesis testing, statisticians change their terminology and call this the *significance level,* α (the Greek letter *alpha*).

An Example of Hypothesis Testing

An example should help to clarify the nature of hypothesis testing. Suppose the Red Lion restaurant is concerned about its store image, one aspect of which is the friendliness of the service. In a personal interview customers are asked to indicate their perceptions of service on a 5-point scale, where 1 indicates "very unfriendly" service and 5 indicates "very friendly" service. The scale is assumed to be an interval scale, and experience has shown that the previous distribution of this attitudinal measurement assessing the service dimension was approximately normal.

Now, suppose the researcher entertains the hypothesis that customers feel the restaurant has neither friendly nor unfriendly service. The researcher formulates the null hypothesis that the mean is equal to 3.0:

$$H_0: \mu = 3.0$$

The alternative hypothesis is that the mean does not equal 3.0:

$$H_1: \mu \neq 3.0$$

Next, the researcher must decide on a region of rejection. Exhibit 14.15 shows a sampling distribution of the mean assuming the null hypothesis (that is, assuming $\mu = 3.0$). The darkly shaded area shows the region of rejection when $\alpha = .025$ in each tail of the curve. In other words, the *region of rejection* shows those values that are very unlikely to occur if the null hypothesis is true, but relatively probable if the alternative hypothesis is true. The values within the lighter area are called *acceptable at the 95 percent confidence level* (or 5 percent significance level, or .05 alpha level), and if we find that our sample mean lies within this region of acceptance, we conclude that the null hypothesis is true. More precisely, we fail to reject the null hypothesis. In other words, the range of acceptance (1) identifies those acceptable values that reflect a difference from the hypothesized mean in the null hypothesis and (2) shows the range within which any difference is so minuscule that we would conclude that this difference was due to random sampling error rather than to a false null hypothesis.

In our example, the Red Lion restaurant hired research consultants who collected a sample of 225 interviews. The mean score on the 5-point scale equaled 3.78. (If σ is known, it is used in the analysis; however, this is rarely true and was not true in this case.[9]) The sample standard deviation was $S = 1.5$. Now we have enough information to test the hypothesis.

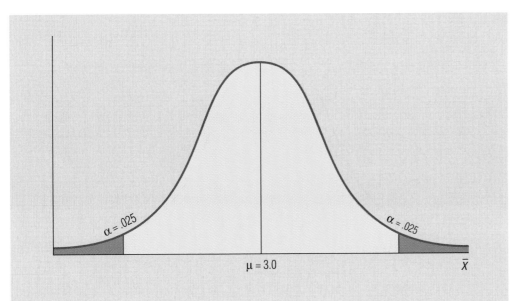

EXHIBIT 14.15
A Sampling Distribution of
the Mean Assuming $\mu = 3.0$

The researcher has decided that the decision rule will be to set the significance level at the .05 level. This means that in the long run the probability of making an erroneous decision when H_0 is true will be fewer than 5 times in 100 (.05). From the table of the standardized normal distribution, the researcher finds that the Z score of 1.96 represents a probability of .025 that a sample mean will lie above 1.96 standard errors from μ. Likewise, the table shows that about .025 of all sample means will fall below -1.96 standard errors from μ.

The values that lie exactly on the boundary of the region of rejection are called the **critical values** of μ. Theoretically, the critical values are $Z = -1.96$ and $+1.96$. Now we must transform these critical Z-values to the sampling distribution of the mean for this image study. The critical values are:

Critical values
The values that lie exactly on the boundary of the region of rejection.

$$\text{Critical value—lower limit} = \mu - ZS_{\bar{X}} \text{ or } \mu - Z\frac{S}{\sqrt{n}}$$

$$= 3.0 - 1.96\left(\frac{1.5}{\sqrt{225}}\right)$$

$$= 3.0 - 1.96(.1)$$

$$= 3.2 - .196$$

$$= 2.804$$

$$\text{Critical value—upper limit} = \mu + ZS_{\bar{X}} \text{ or } \mu + Z\frac{S}{\sqrt{n}}$$

$$= 3.0 + 1.96\left(\frac{1.5}{\sqrt{225}}\right)$$

$$= 3.0 + 1.96(.1)$$

$$= 3.0 + .196$$

$$= 3.196$$

Based on the survey, $\bar{X} = 3.78$. In this case, the sample mean is contained in the region of rejection (see Exhibit 14.16 on the next page). Since the sample mean is greater than the critical value, 3.196, the researcher says that the sample result is statistically significant beyond the .05 level. In other words, fewer than 5 of each 100 samples will show results that deviate this much from the hypothesized null hypothesis when in fact H_0 is actually true.

EXHIBIT 14.16

A Hypothesis Test Using the Sampling Distribution of $\bar{X}$ under the Hypothesis $\mu = 3.0$

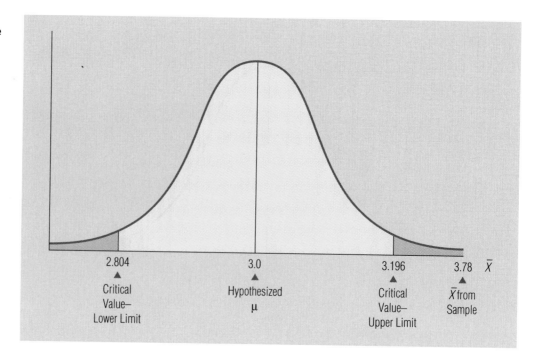

2.804	3.0	3.196	3.78 $\bar{X}$
▲	▲	▲	▲
Critical Value– Lower Limit	Hypothesized μ	Critical Value– Upper Limit	$\bar{X}$ from Sample

What does this mean to the management of the Red Lion? The results indicate that customers believe the service is friendly. It is unlikely (probability of less than 5 in 100) that this result would occur because of random sampling error. This means that the restaurant should worry about factors other than the friendliness of the service personnel.

An alternative way to test the hypothesis is to formulate the decision rule in terms of the Z-statistic. Using the following formula, we can calculate the observed value of the Z-statistic given a certain sample mean, $\bar{X}$:

$$Z_{obs} = \frac{\bar{X} - \mu}{S_{\bar{X}}}$$

$$= \frac{3.78 - \mu}{S_{\bar{X}}}$$

$$= \frac{3.78 - 3.0}{.1}$$

$$= \frac{.78}{.1}$$

$$= 7.8$$

In this case, the Z-value is 7.8 and we find that we have met the criterion of statistical significance at the .05 level. This result is statistically significant at the .000001 level.

The Chi-Square Test for Goodness of Fit

Exhibit 14.17 shows the responses to a survey to investigate awareness of a particular brand of automobile tire. This frequency distribution, a one-dimensional table from a sample of 100, suggests that the majority of the population (60 percent) is aware of the brand.

The **chi-square (χ^2) test** allows us to test for significance in the analysis of frequency distributions. Thus, categorical data on variables such as sex, education, or dichotomous answers may be statistically analyzed. Suppose, for example, that we wish to test the null hypothesis that the

Chi-square (χ^2) test
A hypothesis test that allows for investigation of statistical significance in the analysis of a frequency distribution.

Awareness of Tire Manufacturer's Brand	Frequency
Aware	60
Unaware	$\frac{40}{100}$

EXHIBIT 14.17
One-Way Frequency Table
for Brand Awareness

number of consumers aware of a certain tire brand equals the number unaware of the brand. The logic inherent in the χ^2 test allows us to compare the observed frequencies (O_i) with the expected frequencies (E_i) based on our theoretical ideas about the population distribution or our presupposed proportions. In other words, the technique tests whether the data come from a certain probability distribution. It tests the "goodness of fit" of the observed distribution with the expected distribution.

Calculation of the chi-square statistic allows us to determine whether the difference between the observed frequency distribution and the expected frequency distribution can be attributed to sampling variation. The steps in this process are as follows:

1. Formulate the null hypothesis and determine the expected frequency of each answer.
2. Determine the appropriate significance level.
3. Calculate the χ^2 value, using the observed frequencies from the sample and the expected frequencies.
4. Make the statistical decision by comparing the calculated χ^2 value with the critical χ^2 value.

To analyze the brand awareness data in Exhibit 14.17, start with a null hypothesis that suggests that the number of respondents aware of the brand will equal the number of respondents unaware of it. Thus, the expected probability of each answer (aware or unaware) is .5. In a sample of 100, 50 people would be expected to respond yes, or aware, and 50 would be expected to respond no, or unaware. After the researcher has determined that the chi-square test is appropriate at the .05 level of significance (or some other probability level), the chi-square statistic may be calculated. To calculate the chi-square statistic, use the following formula:

$$\chi^2 = \sum \frac{(O_i - E_i)^2}{E_i}$$

where

$X^2 = $ chi-square statistic

$O_i = $ observed frequency in the ith cell

$E_i = $ expected frequency in the ith cell

Sum the squared differences:

$$\chi^2 = \frac{(O_1 - E_1)^2}{E_1} + \frac{(O_2 - E_2)^2}{E_2}$$

Thus, we determine that the chi-square value equals 4:

$$\chi^2 = \frac{(60 - 50)^2}{50} + \frac{(40 - 50)^2}{50}$$

$$= 4$$

Exhibit 14.18 on the next page shows the detailed calculation for this problem.

Like many other probability distributions, the χ^2 distribution is not a single probability curve, but a family of curves. These curves, although similar, vary according to the number of degrees of freedom ($k - 1$). Thus, we must calculate the number of degrees of freedom. (*Degrees of freedom*

EXHIBIT 14.18 **Table Calculating the Chi-Square Statistic**

Brand Awareness	Observed Frequency (O_i)	Expected Probability	Expected Frequency (E_i)	$(O_i - E_i)$	$\dfrac{(O_i - E_i)^2}{E_i}$
Aware	60	.5	50	10	$\dfrac{100}{50} = 2.0$
Unaware	40	.5	50	−10	$\dfrac{100}{50} = 2.0$
Total	100	1.0	100	0	$\chi^2 = 4.0$

refers to the number of observations that can be varied without changing the constraints or assumptions associated with a numerical system.) We do this as follows:

$$d.f. = k - 1$$

where

k = number of cells associated with column or row data[10]

In the brand awareness problem there are only two categorical responses. Thus, the degrees of freedom equal 1 ($d.f. = 2 - 1 = 1$).

Now the computed chi-square value needs to be compared with the critical chi-square values associated with the .05 probability level with 1 degree of freedom. In Table 4 of the Appendix the critical chi-square value is 3.84. Since the calculated chi-square is larger than the tabular chi-square, the null hypothesis—that the observed values are comparable to the expected values—is rejected.[11]

Choosing the Appropriate Technique

Now that we have looked at two statistical techniques for hypothesis testing, note that a number of descriptive and statistical techniques are available to assist the researcher in interpreting data. The choice of the method of analysis depends on (1) the number of variables, (2) the scale of measurement, and (3) the type of question to be answered.

Number of Variables

The number of variables to be simultaneously investigated is a primary consideration in the choice of statistical technique. A researcher who is interested only in the average number of times a prospective home buyer visits financial institutions to shop for interest rates concentrates on investigating only one variable at a time. The researcher conducts *univariate statistical analysis* when attempting to generalize from a sample about one variable at a time. Statistically describing the relationship between two variables at one time, such as the relationship between advertising expenditures and sales volume, requires *bivariate statistical analysis*. Tests of group differences and measuring the relationship (association) among variables are the subjects of Chapter 15.

Scale of Measurement

The scale of measurement on which the data are based or the type of measurement reflected in the data determines the permissible statistical techniques and appropriate empirical operations to perform. As we discussed earlier, testing a hypothesis about a mean requires interval-scaled or ratio-scaled data. We have also seen that the chi-square test can be used when the researcher employs a nominal scale to measure consumer awareness versus unawareness.

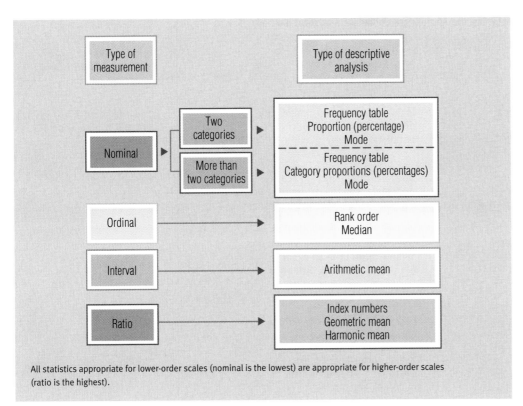

Descriptive Statistics Permissible with Different Types of Measurement

Exhibit 14.19 shows the appropriate descriptive statistics for each type of scale. It is important to remember that all statistics appropriate for lower-order scales (nominal is the lowest) are suitable for higher-order scales (ratio is the highest).

The most sophisticated form of statistical analysis for nominal-scale data is counting. Because numbers are merely labels for classification purposes, they have no quantitative meaning. The researcher tallies the frequency in each category and identifies which category contains the highest number of observations (individuals, objects, etc.). An ordinal scale provides data that may be rank ordered from lowest to highest. For example, the ranking of brand preferences generally employs an ordinal scale. Observations may be associated with percentile ranks. With ordinal data, the median may be used as the average. Because all statistical analyses appropriate for lower-order scales are suitable for higher-order scales, an interval scale may be used as a nominal scale to uniquely classify or as an ordinal scale to preserve order. In addition, an interval scale's property of equal intervals allows researchers to compare differences among scale values and to perform arithmetic operations such as addition and subtraction. Numbers may be changed, but the numerical operations must preserve order and relative magnitudes of differences. The mean and standard deviation may be calculated from true interval-scale data. A ratio scale has all the properties of nominal, ordinal, and interval scales. In addition, it allows researchers to compare absolute magnitudes, because the scale has an absolute zero point. Using the actual quantities for arithmetic operations is permissible. Thus, the ratios of scale values are meaningful.

Type of Question to Be Answered

The type of question the researcher is attempting to answer is a consideration in the choice of statistical technique. For example, we already illustrated a hypothesis test for a researcher who wants to determine whether the calculated mean value of a variable differs from the expected value. Marketing researchers frequently question whether a mean, a proportion, or a distribution differs from what was expected.

Two other frequently asked questions are (1) Are there differences between two (or more) groups and (2) is there a relationship between two or more variables? These topics are discussed in the following chapter.

EXHIBIT 14.20 **Examples of Selecting the Appropriate Univariate Statistical Method**

Sample Marketing Problem	Statistical Question to Be Asked	Possible Test of Statistical Significance
Interval or Ratio Scales Compare actual vs. hypothetical values of average salary	Is the sample mean significantly different from the hypothesized population mean?	Z-test (if sample is large) t-test (if sample is small)
Ordinal Scales Compare actual evaluations and expected evaluations	Does the distribution of scores on a scale with the categories excellent, good, fair, and poor differ from the expected distribution?	chi-square test
Determine ordered preferences for all brands in a product class	Does a set of rank orderings in a sample differ from an expected or hypothetical rank ordering?	Kolmogorov-Smirnov test
Nominal Scales Identify sex of key executives	Is the number of female executives equal to the number of male executives?	chi-square test
Indicate percentage of key executives who are male	Is the proportion of male executives the same as the hypothesized proportion?	t-test of a proportion

Exhibit 14.20 provides guidelines for selecting the appropriate statistical method. Although you may be unfamiliar with most of them, the exhibit illustrates that a variety of statistical techniques exist and the proper one may be selected based on the research situation. A complete discussion of all the relevant techniques is beyond the scope of our discussion thus far. The important point is that the researcher should anticipate the method of statistical analysis before selecting the research design and before determining the type of data to collect. Once the data are collected, the research design will reflect the initial approach to analysis of the problem.

Summary

1. Know that analysis consists of summarizing, rearranging, ordering, or manipulating data. Descriptive analysis refers to the transformation of raw data into an understandable form. Descriptive information is obtained by summarizing, categorizing, rearranging, and other forms of analysis.

2. Create and interpret simple tabulation and cross-tabulation tables. Statistical tabulation is another way of saying that we count the number of observations in each possible response category. In other words, tabulation is the same as tallying. Tabulation is an appropriate descriptive analysis for less–than interval variables. Frequency tables and histograms are used to display tabulation results.

3. Understand how cross-tabulations can reveal relationships. Cross-tabulation is the appropriate technique for assessing relationships among multiple less–than interval variables. The key to interpreting a cross-tabulation result is to compare actual observed values with hypothetical values that would result from pure chance. When observed results vary from these values, a relationship is indicated.

4. Perform basic data transformations. Data transformations are often needed to assist in data analysis and involve changing the mathematical form of data in some systematic way. Basic data transformations include reverse coding, summating scales, creating index numbers, and collapsing a variable based on a median split.

5. Define *hypothesis* and *significance level*. A hypothesis is a statement of assumption about the nature of the world. Significance level is the critical probability in choosing between the null hypothesis and the alternative hypothesis.

6. Discuss the steps in the hypothesis-testing procedure. Hypothesis-testing can be thought of as a three step process. First, the researcher translates the hypothesis into a statistical form based on the measurement level of the variables involved. Second, the researcher computes a test value using the appropriate statistic. Third, the researcher determines whether the resulting value is "significant" using the concept of significance level or a confidence interval.

7. Describe the factors that influence the choice of statistical methods to use for analysis. A number of appropriate statistical techniques are available to assist the researcher in interpreting data. The choice of statistical analysis method depends on (1) the number of variables, (2) the scale of measurement, and (3) the type of question to be answered.

Key Terms and Concepts

Descriptive analysis	Marginals	Null hypothesis
Histogram	Statistical base	Alternative hypothesis
Tabulation	Elaboration analysis	Significance level
Frequency table	Moderator variable	Critical values
Cross-tabulation	Data transformation	Chi-square (χ^2) test
Contingency table	Hypothesis	

Questions for Review and Critical Thinking

1. What are five descriptive statistics used to describe the basic properties of variables?
2. What is a *histogram?* What is the advantage of overlaying a normal distribution over a histogram?
3. A survey asks respondents to respond to the statement "My work is interesting." Interpret the frequency distribution shown here (taken from an SPSS output):
   a. My work in interesting:

Category Label	Code	Abs. Freq.	Rel. Freq. (Pct.)	Adj. Freq. (Pct.)	Cum. Freq. (Pct.)
Very true	1	650	23.9	62.4	62.4
Somewhat true	2	303	11.2	29.1	91.5
Not very true	3	61	2.2	5.9	97.3
Not at all true	4	28	1.0	2.7	100.0
	•	1,673	61.6	Missing	
	Total	2,715	100.0	100.0	
Valid cases	1,042		Missing cases	1,673	

4. Use the data in the following table to
   a. prepare a frequency distribution of the respondents' ages
   b. cross-tabulate the respondents' genders with cola preference

Individual	Gender	Age	Cola Preference	Weekly Unit Purchases
John	M	19	Coke	2
Al	M	17	Pepsi	5
Bill	M	20	Pepsi	7
Mary	F	20	Coke	2
Jim	M	18	Coke	4
Karen	F	16	Coke	4
Tom	M	17	Pepsi	12
Sassi	F	22	Pepsi	6
Amie	F	20	Pepsi	2
Dawn	F	19	Pepsi	3

5. The following computer output shows a cross-tabulation of frequencies and provides frequency number (N) and row (R) percentages.
   a. Interpret this output, including a conclusion about whether or not the row and column variables are related.
   b. Critique the way the analysis is presented.
   c. Draw a pie chart indicating percentages for having read a book in the past three months for those with and those without high school diplomas.

Have You Read a Book in Past 3 Months?	Have High School Diploma?		Total
	Yes	No	
Yes	489 73.8	174 : 26.2 :	663
No	473 55.6	378 : 44.4 :	851
	. . . . . .	. . . . . .	. . . . . .
TOTAL	962	552 :	1514

6. What types of scalar data (that is, nominal, ordinal, interval, or ratio) typically are used in cross-tabulation analysis?
7. List and describe at least three basic data transformations.
8. **ETHICS** A data processing analyst for a research supplier finds that preliminary computer runs of survey results show that consumers love a client's new product. The employee buys a large block of the client's stock. Is this ethical?
9. What is the purpose of a statistical hypothesis?
10. What is significance level? How does a researcher choose a significance level?
11. List the steps in the hypothesis-testing procedure.
12. After a bumper crop, a mushroom grower hypothesizes that mushrooms will remain at the wholesale average price of $1 per pound. State the null hypothesis and the alternative hypothesis.
13. Assume you have the following data: $H_0: \mu = 200$, $S = 30$, $n = 64$, and $\bar{X} = 218$. Conduct a two-tailed hypothesis test at the .05 significance level.
14. Assume you have the following data: $H_0: \mu = 2,450$, $S = 400$, $n = 100$, and $\bar{X} = 2,300$. Conduct a hypothesis test at the .01 significance level.
15. The answers to a researcher's question will be nominally scaled. What statistical test is appropriate to compare the sample data with the hypothesized population data?
16. What factors determine the choice of the appropriate statistical technique?
17. A researcher plans to ask employees whether they favor, oppose, or are indifferent to a change in the company retirement program. Formulate a null hypothesis for a chi-square test, and determine the expected frequencies for each answer.
18. A researcher finds that in a survey of 100 people, 15 respondents answer "don't know" to a question that has "yes" and "no" as alternatives. The researcher uses 85 as a base for calculating the percentage of respondents who answer "yes" or "no." Is this the correct choice?

Research Activities

1. **'NET** Go the website for the Chicago Cubs baseball team (http://chicago.cubs.mlb.com). Use either the schedule listing or the stats information to find their record in the most recent season. Create a data file with a variable indicating whether each game was won or lost and a variable indicating whether the game was played at home in Wrigley Field or away from home. Using computerized software like SPSS or SAS,
   a. Compute a frequency table and histogram for each variable.
   b. Use cross-tabulations to examine whether a relationship exists between where the game is played (home or away) and winning.
   c. Extra Analysis: Repeat the analyses for the Houston Astros baseball team (http://www.astros.com). What does this suggest for the relationship between playing at home and winning?
2. **'NET** Go to http://www.spss.com and click on Industries and Market Research. What services does the company provide?

Case 14.1 Body on Tap

A few years ago Vidal Sassoon, Inc., took legal action against Bristol-Myers over a series of TV commercials and print ads for a shampoo that had been named Body on Tap because of its beer content.[12] The prototype commercial featured a well-known high fashion model saying, "In shampoo tests with over 900 women like me, Body on Tap got higher ratings than Prell for body. Higher than Flex for conditioning. Higher than Sassoon for strong, healthy-looking hair."

The evidence showed that several groups of approximately 200 women each tested just one shampoo. They rated it on a six-step qualitative scale, from "outstanding" to "poor," for twenty-seven separate attributes, such as body and conditioning. It became clear that 900 women did not, after trying both shampoos, make product-to-product comparisons between Body on Tap and Sassoon or between Body on Tap and any of the other brands mentioned. In fact, no woman in the tests tried more than one shampoo.

The claim that the women preferred Body on Tap to Sassoon for "strong, healthy-looking hair" was based on combining the data for the "outstanding" and "excellent" ratings and discarding the lower four ratings on the scale. The figures then were 36 percent for Body

on Tap and 24 percent (of a separate group of women) for Sassoon. When the "very good" and "good" ratings were combined with the "outstanding" and "excellent" ratings, however, there was only a difference of 1 percent between the two products in the category of "strong, healthy-looking hair."

The research was conducted for Bristol-Myers by Marketing Information Systems, Inc. (MISI), using a technique known as blind monadic testing. The president of MISI testified that this method typically is employed when what is wanted is an absolute response to a product "without reference to another specific product." Although he testified that blind monadic testing was used in connection with comparative advertising, that was not the purpose for which Bristol-Myers retained MISI. Rather, Bristol-Myers wished to determine consumer reaction to the introduction of Body on Tap. And Sassoon's in-house research expert stated flatly that blind monadic testing cannot support comparative advertising claims.

Question

Comment on the professionalism of the procedures used to make the advertising claim. Why do you believe the researchers performed the data transformations described?

Case 14.2 Downy-Q Quilt

The research for Downy-Q is an example of a commercial test that was conducted when an advertising campaign for an established brand had run its course.[13] The revised campaign, "Fighting the Cold," emphasized that Downy-Q was an "extra-warm quilt"; previous research had demonstrated that extra warmth was an important and deliverable product quality. The commercial test was requested to measure the campaign's ability to generate purchase interest.

The marketing department had recommended this revised advertising campaign and was now anxious to know how effectively this commercial would perform. The test concluded that "Fighting the Cold" was a persuasive commercial. It also demonstrated that the new campaign would have greater appeal to specific market segments.

Method

Brand choices for the same individuals were obtained before and after viewing the commercial. The commercial was tested in thirty-second, color-moving, storyboard form in a theater test. Invited viewers were shown programming with commercial inserts. Qualified respondents were women who had bought quilts in outlets that carried Downy-Q. The results are shown in Case Exhibits 14.2–1 through 14.2–4.

Question

Interpret the data in these tables. What recommendations and conclusions would you offer to Downy-Q management?

CASE EXHIBIT 14.2–1 **Shifts in Brand Choice Before and After Showing of Downy-Q Quilt Commercial**

Question: We are going to give away a series of prizes. If you are selected as one of the winners, which of the following would you truly want to win?

Brand Choice after Commercial	Brand Choice before Commercial (%)	
	Downy-Q (n = 23)	Other Brand (n = 237)
Downy-Q	78	19
Other brand	22	81

CASE EXHIBIT 14.2-2 Pre/Post Increment in Choice of Downy-Q

Question: We are going to give away a series of prizes. If you are selected as one of the winners, which of the following would you truly want to win? (Check list.)

Demographic Group	"Fighting the Cold"		Norm: All Quilt Commercials	
	Base	Score	Average	Range
Total audience	(260)	+15	+10	6–19
By marital status				
Married	(130)	+17		
Not married	(130)	+12		
By age				
Under 35	(130)	+14		
35 and over	(130)	+15		
By employment status				
Not employed	(90)	+13		
Employed	(170)	+18		

CASE EXHIBIT 14.2-3 Adjective Checklist for Downy-Q Quilt Commercial

Question: Which of these words do you feel come closest to describing the commercial you've just seen? (Check all the apply.) (Check list.)

Adjective	"Fighting the Cold" (%)	Norm: All Quilt Commercials (%)
Positive		
Appealing	18	24
Clever	11	40
Convincing	20	14
Effective	19	23
Entertaining	5	24
Fast moving	12	21
Genuine	7	4
Imaginative	7	21
Informative	24	18
Interesting	13	17
Original	7	20
Realistic	8	3
Unusual	3	8
Negative		
Amateurish	9	11
Bad Taste	4	4
Dull	33	20
Repetitious	17	16
Silly	8	19
Slow	8	7
Unbelievable	3	5
Unclear	3	2
Unimportant	14	14
Uninteresting	32	19

CASE EXHIBIT 14.2-4 Product Attribute Checklist for Downy-Q

Question: Which of the following statements do you feel apply to Downy-Q? (Mark as many or as few as you feel apply.)

Attributes	"Fighting the Cold" (%)
Extra warm	56
Lightweight	48
Pretty designs	45
Durable fabrics	28
Nice fabrics	27
Good construction	27

LEARNING OUTCOMES

After studying this chapter, you should be able to

1. Understand what multivariate statistical analysis involves and know the two types of multivariate analysis
2. Interpret results from multiple regression analysis
3. Interpret results from multivariate analysis of variance (MANOVA)
4. Interpret basic exploratory factor analysis results

CHAPTER 15
DIFFERENCES BETWEEN GROUPS AND RELATIONSHIPS AMONG VARIABLES

Chapter Vignette: Is the Price Right?

The objective in most of the pricing games on *The Price is Right* is knowing the right price. When consumers know the right price, they save money and saving money can be very exciting. Perhaps *The Price is Right* is ready for a new pricing game called "Bricks or Clicks." Bricks and Clicks would involve examining several products and then letting Bob know whether or not a specific product is priced lower on the Internet (clicks) or in a traditional retailer (bricks).

Are prices lower on the Internet? This has been a subject of much debate over the last decade. In the early days of Internet retailing, so-called experts made many grand predictions about how e-tailing would evolve. A few predictions may have been correct, but most have provided wrong. For instance, many predicted that e-tailing would make many traditional retailers obsolete. Almost all predictions involving price forecast that the wide availability of price information that would exist via the Internet would force prices to their lowest level. Smart software systems called bots would quickly search the Internet and inform the consumer where any item could be purchased at the lowest price. However, consumers that think the Internet is always the avenue to the lowest price may not be right.[1]

Are prices offered by e-tailers really lower? The question isn't that easy and the answer depends on what a consumer is trying to buy. A 2001 study of the prices of DVDs showed the following average prices:[2]

Retail Type	Average Price	Percentage-Price
E-tailers	$19.92	72.0%
Multi-Channel Retailers	$23.19	83.9%

A comparison of the prices suggests that "dot-com" retailers offer better prices.

Case closed? Not so fast! If consumers need a DVD player instead of a DVD, they may have better luck with a more traditional retailer, or at least one that offers both real and virtual retail shopping opportunities. Among consumer electronics, the following results are seen:

Retail Type	DVD Player Average Price	Percentage-Price
E-tailers	$371.95	75.6%
Multi-Channel Retailers	$360.30	74.8%

A comparison of these prices suggests that the multi-channel retailers offer better prices. Even though they may never appear on a television game show, consumers and businesses alike find many occasions to compare prices.

Introduction

Making comparisons such as the preceding ones involves bivariate analysis, the topic of this chapter. The purpose of descriptive analysis is to summarize data. After summarizing the data, the researcher may wish to measure the association between variables or test the differences between groups of objects. This chapter goes beyond univariate statistics, in which the analysis focuses on one variable at a time, and into the realm of bivariate statistics, in which the researcher is concerned with scores on two variables. The chapter also briefly discusses multiple regression, a form of multivariate analysis.

What Is the Appropriate Test of Difference?

Researchers commonly test hypotheses stating that two groups differ. In marketing research, differences in behavior, characteristics, beliefs, opinions, emotions, or attitudes are commonly examined. A researcher tests differences between subjects assigned to an experimental group and subjects assigned to a control group. A survey researcher may be interested in whether male and female consumers purchase a product in the same amount. Business researchers may also test whether or not business units in Europe are as profitable as business units in the U.S.A. Such tests are bivariate tests of differences because only two variables are involved. Although researchers do not always make the distinction, the test allows a variable to act like a dependent variable while the other variable acts like an independent variable.

Exhibit 15.1 illustrates that both the type of measurement and the number of groups to be compared influence the statistical choice. Often researchers are interested in testing differences in mean scores between groups or in comparing how two groups' scores are distributed across possible response categories. We will focus our attention on these issues.

Construction of contingency tables for chi-square analysis gives a procedure for comparing the distribution of one group with that of another group. This is a good starting point from which to discuss testing of differences.

Cross-Tabulation Tables: The χ^2 Test for Goodness of Fit

Cross-tabulation is among the most widely used statistical techniques among marketing researchers. Cross-tabs are intuitive and easily understood. They also lend themselves well to graphical analysis using tools like bar charts.

EXHIBIT 15.1 **Choosing the Right Statistic**

	Dolly	Lori	Measurement Levels Involved	Statistic Comment
Driver Distance	203.1 meters	185.0 meters	Distance = Ratio Golfer = Nominal, creating 2 groups	An independent samples *t*-test could be used to compare the average distance (ratio variable) by golfer (nominal variable) assuming we had observed 28 drives for each.
3-Wood Distance	185 meters	179.5 meters	Distance = Ratio Club = Nominal, creating 2 groups	As above, we could compare distance between the two with an independent samples *t*-test, but suppose we wished to know whether or not Lori's distance with the 3-wood is different than her distance with her driver. When we compare one ratio variable observed on one person grouped by a nominal variable (club type—driver/3-wood), a paired-samples *t*-test would be used.
Nationality	Brazil	New Zealand	Nationality = Nominal Rank = Ordinal	If we wished to know whether nationality affected a golfer's ranking in some competition, we could use a cross-tab with χ^2.
Favorite Brand	Mizuno	Callaway	Brand = Nominal Nationality = Nominal	If we observed 50 women golfers, and wished to know whether nationality affected whether they were more likely to prefer Mizuno to Callaway, again the appropriate analysis would be a cross-tab with χ^2.
	Driver Distance = 220 meters		Dependent Variable is Distance = Ratio Independent Variable is Nominal (Golfer) and results in 3 groups (distance for Dolly, Lori, and now Mel)	If we add a 3rd golfer (Mel), and we wished to test for differences in driver distance, we would move to one way ANOVA.

Cross-tabulation (contingency table)
A joint frequency distribution of observations on two or more sets of variables.

TOTHEPOINT

You got to be careful if you don't know where you're going, because you might not get there.

—Yogi Berra

A **cross-tabulation**, or **contingency table**, is a joint frequency distribution of observations on two more variables. Researchers generally rely on two-variable cross-tabs the most since the results can be easily communicated. Cross-tabs are much like tallying. When two variables exist, each with two categories, four cells result. The χ^2 distribution provides a means for testing the statistical significance of contingency table. Put in other words, the bivariate χ^2 test examines statistical significance of relationships among two less–than interval variables.

What Is a χ^2 Test?

The χ^2 test for a contingency table involves comparing the observed frequencies (O_i) with the expected frequencies (E_i) in each cell of the table. The goodness of fit of the observed distribution with the expected distribution is captured by this statistic. Remember that the convention is that the row variable is considered the independent variable and the column variable is considered the dependent variable.

Let's first begin with a very simple application of a χ^2 test to a one-way frequency table. Suppose a Papa John's manager wished to know whether more of their customers were male or female. A CSU student is hired to examine this research question. She does so by observing 100 customers exiting a Papa John's location. Her results are shown in the one-dimensional (one-way) table below:

Customer Sex	One-Way Frequency Table
Male	60 customers
Female	40 customers
Total	100 customers

As can be seen above, the sample includes 10 more male customers than female customers. Is this difference enough to reach a conclusion that more men patronize Papa John's than women? A χ^2 test can answer this question.

Steps in Computing a χ^2 Test Value

Is there any effect of gender on Papa John's patronage? The example above is comparable to testing a hypothesis suggesting more Papa John's customers are men.

Ha: Papa John's customers are more likely to be male than female.

The researcher can compute a χ^2 test result to test this hypothesis. Here are the steps to follow in conducting such a test:

1. Gather data and tally the observed frequencies for a categorical variable.

    • In this case, the frequencies indicate 40 women and 60 men.

2. Compute the expected values for each cell of a contingency table. These are the values that would be seen if the units are randomly distributed (with no pattern) to category values.

    • This is another way of asking the central tendency for each cell. In this case, there is only a one-way frequency table with two possible values, male and female. So, the expected values are easily seen to be 50 in each cell (100/2). This is another way of saying that the expected probability of a Papa John's customer being male is 50 percent.

3. Calculate the χ^2 test value using the following formula:

$$\chi^2 = \sum_{i=1}^{k} \frac{(O_i - E_i)^2}{E_i}$$

where

O_i = observed frequency in ith cell

E_i = expected frequency in ith cell

K = number of cells (categories)

We can sum the squared differences as follows:

$$\chi^2 = \frac{(O_1 - E_1)^2}{E_1} + \frac{(O_2 + E_2)^2}{E_2}$$

Thus, in the present example we determine that the χ^2 test value equals 4:

$$\chi^2 = \frac{(60 - 50)^2}{50} + \frac{(40 - 50)^2}{50} = 4.0$$

4. Find degrees of freedom for the test:

  • For a one-way table, the $d.f.$ are simply the number of cells containing tabulations (number of groups) $- 1$.

    • In this case, there are two cells so the $d.f. = 2 - 1 = 1$.

  • For a two-way table, the $d.f.$ are equal to the number of rows in a contingency table less one $(R - 1)$ times the number of columns less one $(C - 1)$. This will be illustrated shortly below.

5. Make the statistical decision by comparing the p-value associated with the test against a predetermined significance level (acceptable type I error).

  • The computed χ^2 test value is compared with a critical value associated with the desired significance level. Assuming the significance level is .05, we find the critical χ^2 value, with 1 $d.f.$, to be 3.84. A table of critical values is included in the end of book appendix. Numerous critical value calculators exist on the Internet as well. So, since the calculated test value (4) is greater than the theoretical critical value (3.84), the conclusion is that the hypothesis is supported. More men patronize Papa John's than women.

χ^2 Tests for Two-Way Contingency Tables: Cross-Tabs

In practice, researchers are generally interested in more than one variable. Papa John's may benefit from knowing whether or not more customers are male or female. However, what if female customers make more purchases? Tests involving one variable are called **univariate analysis**. **Bivariate analysis** refers to statistical tests involving two variables.

Thus, extending the example above, the student is asked whether male and female employees are equally profitable. Papa John's has determined that customers who buy only pizza are not very profitable. Customers who buy pizza and any other menu item are profitable. Theoretically, women may be buying pizza for the family rather than just themselves. Therefore, the student sought to test the following hypothesis:

  • Female employees are more profitable than male employees.

Thus, an additional variable, profitability, is introduced into this equation. In a sense, the hypothesis implies that one variable, gender, is determining another, profitability. Cross-tabulation using a χ^2 test is appropriate for testing this hypothesis when:

  → The independent variable (gender) is less than interval.

  → The dependent variable (profitable/not profitable) also is less than interval.

In other words, cross-tabulation is another term for the analysis of contingency tables.

Originally, the student was interested in only one variable—customer gender. However, she also recorded whether the customer left with only pizza or whether they had additional purchases.

Univariate analysis
Tests of hypotheses involving only one variable.

Bivariate analysis
Tests of hypotheses involving two variables.

Since Papa John's determines additional purchases are the key to profitability, those who made additional purchases were recorded as profitable while those who purchased only pizza were recorded as not profitable. The Papa John's data can be recorded in the following 2 × 2 contingency table:

Gender	Profitable	Not Profitable	Total
Men	50	10	60
Women	15	25	40
Totals	65	35	100

Several conclusions appear evident. One, it seems that more customers are profitable than not profitable (65 versus 35, respectively). Secondly, more of the profitable customers seem to be men (50/65). However, is the difference strong enough to be statistically significant? Is the observed difference between customer profitability the result of chance variation or is it due to the independent variable—gender? Is the discrepancy more than sampling variation?

The χ^2 test allows us to conduct tests for significance in the analysis of the $R \times C$ contingency table (where R = row and C = column). The formula for the χ^2 statistic is the same as that used for a one-way frequency table above:

$$\chi^2 = \sum_{i=1}^{k} \frac{(O_i - E_i)^2}{E_i}$$

where

χ^2 = chi-square statistic

O_i = observed frequency in the ith cell

E_i = expected frequency in the ith cell

Again, as in the univariate χ^2 test, a frequency count of data that nominally identify or categorically rank groups is sufficient for statistical analysis.

If the researcher's hypothesis is true, the frequencies shown in the contingency table should not resemble a random distribution. If a random distribution truly existed, then profitable and nonprofitable customers would be spread evenly across the two gender categories. This is really the logic of the test in that a χ^2 test compares the observed frequencies with the theoretical expected values for each cell.

After obtaining the observations for each cell, the expected values for each cell must be obtained. The expected values for each cell can be computed easily using this formula:

$$E_{ij} = \frac{R_i C_j}{n}$$

where

R_i = total observed frequency in the ith row

C_j = total observed frequency in the jth column

n = sample size

Only the total column and total row values are needed for this calculation. So, the calculation could be performed before the data displayed in the individual cells are even collected. The following values represent the expected values for each cell:

Gender	Profitable	Not Profitable	Total
Men	(60 × 65)/100 = 39	(60 × 35)/100 = 21	60
Women	(65 × 40)/100 = 26	(40 × 35)/100 = 14	40
Totals	65	35	100

Notice that the row and column totals are the same for both the observed and expected contingency matrices. These values also become useful in providing the substantive interpretation of the relationship. Variance from the expected value indicates a relationship.

The actual bivariate χ^2 test value can be calculated in the same manner as for the univariate test. The one difference is that the degrees of freedom are now obtained by multiplying the number of rows minus one $(R - 1)$ times the number of columns minus one $(C - 1)$: The observed and expected values can be plugged into the formula as shown here:

$$\chi^2 = \frac{(50 - 39)^2}{39} + \frac{(10 - 21)^2}{21} + \frac{(15 - 26)^2}{26} + \frac{(25 - 14)^2}{14}$$
$$= 3.102 + 5.762 + 4.654 + 8.643$$
$$= 22.161$$

The number of degrees of freedom equals 1:

$$(R - 1)(C - 1) = (2 - 1)(2 - 1) = 1$$

From Table 4 in the appendix, we see that the critical value at the .05 probability level with 1 $d.f.$ is 3.84. Thus, we are very confident that the observed values do not equal the expected values. Before the hypothesis can be supported, however, the researcher must check and see that the deviations from the expected values are in the hypothesized direction. Since the difference between the males' observed profitability and the expected values for that cell are positive, the hypothesis is actually not supported. Although the result is significant, the result is the opposite of the hypothesized condition. Based on this sample, men appear more profitable rather than women. A contingency table analysis involves more than a χ^2 test. Testing a hypothesis using cross-tabs involves two key steps:

1. Examine the statistical significance of the observed contingency table.
2. Examine to see if the differences between the observed and expected values are consistent with the hypothesized prediction.

Proper use of the chi-square test requires that each expected cell frequency (E_{ij}) have a value of at least 5. If this sample size requirement is not met, the researcher should take a larger sample or combine (collapse) response categories.

The *t*-Test for Comparing Means

Independent Samples *t*-Test

When a researcher needs to compare means for a variable grouped into two categories based on some less-than interval variable, a **t-test** is appropriate. One way to think about this is as testing the way a dichotomous (two-level) independent variable is associated with changes in a continuous dependent variable. Several variations of the *t*-test exist.

Most typically, the researcher will apply the **independent samples t-test**, which tests the differences between means taken from two independent samples or groups So, for example, if we measure the price for some designer jeans at thirty different retail stores, of which fifteen are Internet-only stores (pure clicks) and fifteen are traditional stores, we can test whether or not the prices are different based on store type with an independent samples *t*-test. The *t*-test for difference of means assumes the two samples (one Internet and one traditional store) are drawn from normal distributions and that the variances of the two populations are approximately equal (homoscedasticity).

▨ INDEPENDENT SAMPLES *t*-TEST CALCULATION

The *t*-test actually tests whether or not the differences between two means is 0. Not surprisingly, this idea can be expressed as the difference between two population means:

$$\mu_1 = \mu_2,$$

which is equivalent to

$$\mu_1 - \mu_2 = 0$$

However, since this is inferential statistics, we test the idea by comparing two sample means $(\overline{X}_1 - \overline{X}_2)$.

The t-value is a ratio with information about the difference between means (provided by the sample) in the numerator and the standard error of that difference in the denominator. The question is whether the observed differences have occurred by chance alone. To calculate t, we use the following formula:

$$t = \frac{\overline{X}_1 - \overline{X}_2}{S_{\overline{X}_1 - \overline{X}_2}}$$

where

$\overline{X}_1$ = sample mean for group 1

$\overline{X}_2$ = sample mean for group 2

$S_{\overline{X}_1 - \overline{X}_2}$ = pooled standard error of difference between means

A pooled estimate of the standard error is more appropriate than one based on the variance from either sample. The pooled standard error of the difference between means of independent samples can be calculated using the following formula:

$$S_{\overline{X}_1 - \overline{X}_2} = \sqrt{\left(\frac{(n_1 - 1)S_1^2 + (n_2 - 1)S_2^2}{n_1 + n_2 - 2}\right)\left(\frac{1}{n_1} + \frac{1}{n_2}\right)}$$

where

S_1^2 = variance of group 1

S_2^2 = variance of group 2

n_1 = sample size of group 1

n_2 = sample size of group 2

Are business majors or sociology majors more positive about a career in business? A t-test can be used to test the difference between sociology majors and business majors on scores on a scale measuring attitudes toward business. We will assume that the attitude scale is an interval scale. Major is a nominal measure. An independent samples t-test is appropriate when an independent variable is nominal (with two groups) and the dependent variable is interval or ratio. The result of the simple random sample of these two groups of college students is shown below:

Business Students	Sociology Students
$\overline{X}_1 = 16.5$	$\overline{X}_2 = 12.2$
$S_1 = 2.1$	$S_2 = 2.6$
$n_1 = 21$	$n_2 = 14$

A high score indicates a favorable attitude toward business. This particular t-test tests whether the difference in attitudes between sociology and business students is significant. A higher t-value is associated with a lower p-value. As t gets higher and the p-value gets lower, the researcher has more confidence that the means are truly different. The relevant data computation is

$$S_{\overline{X}_1 - \overline{X}_2} = \sqrt{\left(\frac{(n_1 - 1)S_1^2 + (n_2 - 1)S_2^2}{n_1 + n_2 - 2}\right)\left(\frac{1}{n_1} + \frac{1}{n_2}\right)}$$

$$= \sqrt{\left(\frac{(20)(2.1)^2 + (13)(2.6)^2}{33}\right)\left(\frac{1}{21} + \frac{1}{14}\right)}$$

$$= 0.797$$

RESEARCHSNAPSHOT

Expert "T-eeze"

When is an independent samples *t*-test appropriate? Once again, we can find out by answering some simple questions:

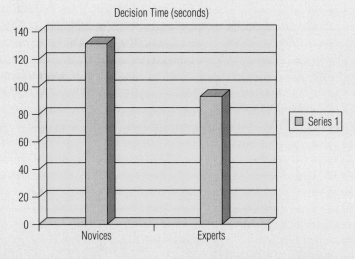

- Is the dependent variable interval or ratio?
- Can the dependent variable scores be grouped based upon some categorical variable?
- Does the grouping result in scores drawn from independent samples?
- Are two groups involved in the research question?

When the answer to all questions is yes, an independent samples *t*-test is appropriate. Often, business researchers may wish to examine how some process varies between novices and experts. Consider the following example.

Researchers looked at the difference in decision speed for expert and novice salespeople faced with the same situation. Decision speed is a ratio dependent variable and the scores are grouped based on whether or not the salesperson is an expert or a novice. Thus, this categorical variable produces two groups. The results across forty respondents, twenty experts and twenty novices, are shown at the top right.

The average difference in decision time is 38 seconds. Is this significantly different from 0? The calculated *t*-test is 2.76 with 38 *d.f.* The one-tailed p-value is 0.0045; thus, the conclusion is reached that experts do take less time to make a decision than do novices.

Source: Shepherd, D.G., S.F. Gardial, M.G. Johnson, and J.O. Rentz (2006), "Cognitive Insights into the Highly Skilled or Expert Salesperson," *Psychology and Marketing*, 23 (February), 115–138. Reprinted with permission of John Wiley & Sons, Inc.

The calculation of the observed *t*-value is:

$$t = \frac{\bar{X}_1 - \bar{X}_2}{S_{\bar{X}_1 - \bar{X}_2}} = \frac{16.5 - 12.2}{0.797}$$

$$= \frac{4.3}{0.797} = 5.395$$

In a test of two means, degrees of freedom are calculated as follows:

$$d.f. = n - k$$

where

$n = n_1 + n_2$

$k = $ number of groups

In our example, *d.f.* equals 33. If the 0.01 level of significance is selected, reference to Table 3 in the end of book appendix yields the critical *t*-value. The *t*-value of 2.75 must be surpassed by the observed *t*-value if the hypothesis test is to be statistically significant at the 0.01 level. The calculated value of *t*, 5.39, far exceeds the critical value of *t* for statistical significance, so it is significant at $\alpha = 0.01$. The p-value is less than 0.01. In other words, this research shows that business students have significantly more positive attitudes toward business than do sociology students.

PRACTICALLY SPEAKING

In practice, computer software is used to compute the *t*-test results. Exhibit 15.2 on the next page displays a typical *t*-test printout. These particular results examine the following research question:

RQ: Does religion relate to price sensitivity?

EXHIBIT 15.2 Independent Samples *t*-Test Results

Group Statistics

	rel	N	Mean	Std. Deviation	Std. Error Mean
price	Catholic	57	61.00	43.381	5.746
	Protestant	43	50.27	64.047	9.767

1. Shows mean, standard deviation, and standard error for each group (Catholic and Protestant)

Independent Samples Test

NOTE: Top row shows results assuming equal variances. Bottom row assumes variance is different in each.

		Levene's Test for Equality of Variances		*t*-Test for Equality of Means						95% Confidence Interval of the Difference	
		F	Sig.	t	d.f.	Sig. (2-tailed)	Mean Difference	Std. Error Difference		Lower	Upper
price	Equal variances assumed	.769	.383	.998	98	.321	10.734	10.752		−10.603	32.070
	Equal variances not assumed			.947	69.829	.347	10.734	11.332		−11.868	33.336

2. Computed *t*-test value shown in this column (*t* = 0.998).

3. P-value for *t*-value and associated degrees of freedom (*t* = 0.998, 98 *d.f.*)

4. Confidence intervals for α = 0.05 (100% − 95%). In this case, it includes 0.

The sample included 57 Catholics and 43 Protestants. Because no direction of the relationship is stated (no hypotheses is offered), a two–tailed test is appropriate. While instructors still find some value in having students learn to perform the *t*-test calculations, employing a statistical software package is the procedure by which *t*-test results are most often generated and interpreted today.

The interpretation of the *t*-test is made simple by focusing on either the p-value or the confidence interval and the group means. Here are the basic steps:

1. Examine the difference in means to find the "direction" of any difference. In this case, Catholics are willing to pay nearly $9 more than Protestants.
2. Compute or locate the computed *t*-test value. In this case, *t* = 0.998.
3. Find the p-value associated with this *t* and the corresponding degrees of freedom. Here, the p-value (two-tailed significance level) is 0.321 (shown in printout). This suggests a 32 percent chance that the means are actually equal given the observed sample means. Assuming a 0.05 acceptable type I error rate (α), the appropriate conclusion is that the means are not significantly different.
4. The difference can also be examined using the 95 percent confidence interval ($-10.603 < \bar{X}_1 - \bar{X}_2 < 32.070$). Since the confidence interval includes 0, we lack sufficient confidence that the true difference between the population means is 0.

A few points are worth noting about this particular result. First, strictly speaking, the *t*-test assumes that the two population variances are equal. A slightly more complicated formula exists which will compute the *t*-statistic assuming the variances are not equal.[3] SPSS and SAS provide both results when an independent samples *t*-test is performed. The sample variances appear considerably different in this case (43.4, 64.0). Nonetheless, the conclusions are the same using either assumption. In marketing research, we often deal with values that have variances close enough to assume equal variance. This isn't always the case in the physical sciences, where variables may take on values of drastically different magnitude. Thus, the rule of thumb in marketing research is to use the equal variance assumption. In the vast majority of cases, the same conclusion will be drawn using either assumption.

Second, notice that even though the means appear to be not so close to each other, the statistical conclusion is that they are the same. The substantive conclusion is that Catholics and Protestants would not be expected to pay different prices. Why is it that means do not appear to be similar yet that is the conclusion? The answer lies in the variance. Respondents provided a very wide range of acceptable prices. Notice how large the standard deviations are compared to the mean for each group. Since the *t*-statistic is a function of the standard error, which is a function of the standard deviation, a lot of variance means a smaller *t*-value for any given observed difference. When this occurs, the researcher may wish to double check for outliers. A small number of wild price estimates could be inflating the variance for one or both groups.

Third, a *t*-test is used even though the sample size is greater than 30. Strictly speaking, a *Z*-test could be used to test this difference. Researchers often employ a *t*-test even with large samples. As samples get larger, the *t*-test and *Z*-test will tend to yield the same result. Although a *t*-test can be used with large samples, a *Z*-test should not be used with small samples. Also, a *Z*-test can be used in instances where the population variance is known ahead of time.

Analysis of Variance (ANOVA)

What Is ANOVA?

When the means of more than two groups or populations are to be compared, one-way **analysis of variance (ANOVA)** is the appropriate statistical tool. ANOVA involving only one grouping variable is often referred to as *one-way* ANOVA because only one independent variable is involved. Another way to define ANOVA is as the appropriate statistical technique to examine the effect of a less-than interval independent variable on an at least interval-dependent variable. Thus, a categorical independent variable and a continuous dependent variable are involved. An independent samples *t*-test can be thought of as a special case of ANOVA in which the independent variable has only two levels. When more levels exist, the *t*-test alone cannot handle the problem.

The statistical null hypothesis for ANOVA is stated as follows:

$$\mu_1 = \mu_2 = \mu_3 = \cdots = \mu_k$$

The symbol k is the number of groups or categories for an independent variable. In other words, all group means are equal. The substantive hypothesis tested in ANOVA is[4]

At least one group mean is not equal to another group mean.

As the term *analysis of variance* suggests, the problem requires comparing variances to make inferences about the means.

The chapter vignette discussed how a sample of prices taken from the Internet could be explained by the source of the price. Specifically, the independent variable could be thought of as "source," meaning either Internet or multi-channel retailer. The dependent variable is price. Since only two groups exist for the independent variable, either an independent samples *t*-test or one-way ANOVA could be used. The results would be identical.

However, assume that source involved three group levels. Prices would now be compared based on whether the retailer was a bricks-and-clicks retailer (multi-channel, meaning real and virtual stores), a bricks-only store (only physical stores), or a clicks-only retailer (virtual or Internet stores only). One-way ANOVA would be the choice for this analysis.

Analysis of variance (ANOVA)
Analysis involving the investigation of the effects of one treatment variable on an interval-scaled dependent variable; a hypothesis-testing technique to determine whether statistically significant differences on means occur among three or more groups.

Simple Illustration of ANOVA

ANOVA's logic is fairly simple. Look at the data table below that describe how much coffee respondents report drinking each day based on which shift they work (GY stands for Graveyard shift).

Day	1
Day	3
Day	4
Day	0
Day	2
GY	7
GY	2
GY	1
GY	6
Night	6
Night	8
Night	3
Night	7
Night	6

The following table displays the means for each group and the overall mean:

Shift	Mean	Std. Deviation	N
Day	2.00	1.58	5
GY	4.00	2.94	4
Night	6.00	1.87	5
Total	4.00	2.63	14

Exhibit 15.3 plots each observation with a bar. The long blue vertical line illustrates the total range of observations. The lowest is 0 cups and the highest is 8 cups of coffee for a range of 8. The overall mean is 4 cups. Each group mean is shown with a different colored line that matches the bars corresponding to the group. The day shift averages 2 cups of coffee a day, the graveyard shift 4 cups, and the night shift 6 cups of coffee per day.

Here is the basic idea of ANOVA. Look at the dark double-headed arrow in Exhibit 15.3. This line represents the range of the differences between group means. In this case, the lowest mean is 2 cups and the highest mean is 6 cups. Thus, the blue vertical line corresponds to the total variation (range) in the data and the thick double headed black line corresponds to the variance accounted for by the group differences. As the thick black line accounts for more of the total variance, then the ANOVA model suggests that the group means are not all the same, and in particular,

EXHIBIT 15.3 Illustration of ANOVA Logic

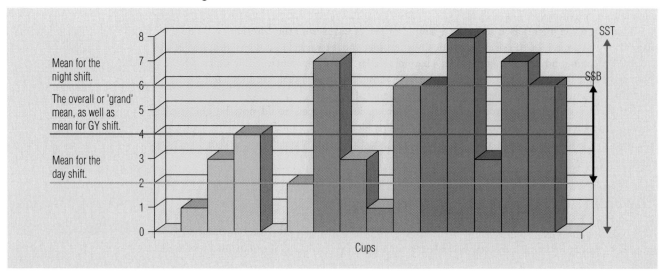

not all the same as the overall mean. This also means that the independent variable, in this case work shift, explains the dependent variable. Here, the results suggest that knowing when someone works explains how much coffee they drink. Night-shirt workers drink the most coffee.

Partitioning Variance in ANOVA

TOTAL VARIABILITY

An implicit question with the use of ANOVA is, How can the dependent variable best be predicted? Absent any additional information, the error in predicting an observation is minimized by choosing the central tendency, or mean for an interval variable. For the coffee example, if no information was available about the work shift of each respondent, the best guess for coffee drinking consumption would be four cups. The total error (or variability) that would result from using the **grand mean**, meaning the mean over all observations, can be thought of as

$$SST = \text{Total of (Observed value} - \text{Grand mean)}^2$$

Grand mean
The mean over all observations.

Although the term error is used, this really represents how much total variation exists among the measures.

Using the first observation, the error of observation would be:

$$(1 \text{ cup} - 4 \text{ cups})^2 = 9$$

The same error could be computed for each observation and these squared errors totaled to give SST.

BETWEEN-GROUPS VARIANCE

ANOVA tests whether "grouping" observations explains variance in the dependent variable. In Exhibit 15.3, the three colors reflect three levels of the independent variable, work shift. Given this additional information about which shift a respondent works, the prediction changes. Now, instead of guessing the grand mean, the group mean would be used. So, once we know that someone works the day shift, the prediction would be that he or she consumes 2 cups of coffee per day. Similarly, the graveyard and night-shift predictions would be 4 and 6 cups, respectively. Thus, the **between-groups variance** can be found by taking the total sum of the weighted difference between group means and the overall mean as shown:

$$SSB = \text{Total of } n_{\text{group}}(\text{Group mean} - \text{Grand mean})^2$$

Between-groups variance
The sum of differences between the group mean and the grand mean summed overall groups for a given set of observations.

The weighting factor (n_{group}) is the specific group sample size. Let's consider the first observation once again. Since this observation is in the day shift, we predict 2 cups of coffee will be consumed. Looking at the day shift group observations in Exhibit 15.3, the new error in prediction would be:

$$(2 \text{ cups} - 4 \text{ cups})^2 = (2)^2 = 4$$

The error in prediction has been reduced from 3 using the grand mean to 2 using the group mean. This squared difference would be weighted by the group sample size of 5, to yield a contribution to SSB of 20.

Next, the same process could be followed for the other groups yielding two more contributions to SSB. Because the graveyard shift group mean is the same as the grand mean, that group's contribution to SSB is 0. Notice that the night shift group mean is also 2 different than the grand mean, like the day shift, so this group's contribution to SSB is likewise 20. The total SSB then represents the variation explained by the experimental or independent variable. In this case, total SSB is 40. The reader may look at the statistical results shown in Exhibit 15.4 to find this value in the sums of squares column.

WITHIN-GROUP ERROR

Finally, error within each group would remain. While the group means explain the variation between the total mean and the group mean, the distance from the group mean and each individual

Within-group error or variance
The sum of the differences between observed values and the group mean for a given set of observations; also known as total error variance.

observation remains unexplained. This distance is called **within-group error or variance**. The values for each observation can be found by

$$SSE = \text{Total of (Observed mean} - \text{Group mean)}^2$$

Again, looking at the first observation, the SSE component would be

$$SSE = (1 \text{ cup} - 2 \text{ cups})^2 = 1 \text{ cup}$$

This process could be computed for all observations and then totaled. The result would be the total error variance—a name sometimes used to refer to SSE since it is variability not accounted for by the group means. These three components are used in determining how well an ANOVA model explains a dependent variable.

The *F*-Test

F-test
A procedure to determine whether there is more variability in the scores of one sample than in the scores of another sample.

The **F-test** is the key statistical test for an ANOVA model. The *F*-test determines whether there is more variability in the scores of one sample than in the scores of another sample. The key question is whether the two sample variances are different from each other or whether they are from the same population. Thus, the test breaks down the variance in a total sample and illustrates why ANOVA is *analysis of variance*.

The *F*-statistic (or *F*-ratio) can be obtained by taking the larger sample variance and dividing by the smaller sample variance. Using Table 5 or 6 in the end-of-book appendix is much like using the tables of the *Z*- and *t*-distributions that we have previously examined. These tables portray the *F*-distribution, which is a probability distribution of the ratios of sample variances. These tables indicate that the distribution of *F* is actually a family of distributions that change quite drastically with changes in sample sizes. Thus, degrees of freedom must be specified. Inspection of an *F*-table allows the researcher to determine the probability of finding an *F* as large as a calculated *F*.

USING VARIANCE COMPONENTS TO COMPUTE *F*-RATIOS

Within-group variation
The sum of the differences between observed values and the group mean for a given set of observations; also known as total error variance

Between-group variance
The sum of differences between the group mean and the grand mean summed over all groups for a given set of observations

In ANOVA, the basic consideration for the *F*-test is identifying the relative size of variance components. The three forms of variation described briefly above are:

1. SSE—variation of scores due to random error or **within-group variation** due to individual differences from the group mean. This is the error of prediction.
2. SSB—systematic variation of scores between groups due to manipulation of an experimental variable or group classifications of a measured independent variable or **between-group variance**.
3. SST—the total observed variation across all groups and individual observations.

Total variability (SST)
The sum of within-group variance and between-group variance. The sum of the differences between a set of observed values and the grand mean of all observations.

Thus, we can partition **total variability (SST)** into *within-group variance* and *between-group variance*. The *F*-distribution is a function of the ratio of these two sources of variances:

$$F = f\left(\frac{SSB}{SSE}\right)$$

A larger ratio of variance between groups to variance within groups implies a greater value of *F*. If the *F*-value is large, the results are likely to be statistically significant.

A DIFFERENT BUT EQUIVALENT REPRESENTATION

F also can be thought of as a function of the between group variance and total variance.

$$F = f\left(\frac{SSB}{SST - SSB}\right)$$

In this sense, the ratio of the thick black line to the blue line representing the total range of data presents the basic idea of the *F*-value.

RESEARCHSNAPSHOT

More Than One-Way

An independent samples *t*-test is a special case of one-way ANOVA. When the independent variable in ANOVA has only two groups, the results for an independent samples *t*-test and ANOVA will be the same. The two sets of statistical results below demonstrate this fact. Both outputs are taken from the same data. The test considers whether men or women are more excited about a new Italian restaurant in their town. Sex2 is dummy coded so that 0 = men and 1 = women. Excitement was measured on a scale ranging from 0 to 6.

Independent Samples *t*-test Results:

Group Statistics

	Sex2	N	Mean	Std. Deviation	Std. Error Mean
excitement	0.00	69	2.64	2.262	0.272
	1.00	73	2.32	2.140	0.250

Independent Samples Test

		Levene's Test for Equality of Variances		*t*-Test for Equality of Means					95% Confidence Interval of the Difference	
		F	Sig.	t	d.f.	Sig. (two-tailed)	Mean Difference	Std. Error Difference	Lower	Upper
excitement	Equal variances assumed	1.768	.186	.873	140	.384	.323	.369	−.408	1.053
	Equal variances not assumed			.872	138.265	.385	.323	.370	−.409	1.054

In this case, we would conclude that men and women are equally excited—or unexcited, as the case may be. The *t* of 0.873 with 140 *d.f.* is not significant (p = 0.384).

ANOVA Results:

Descriptives

		N	Mean	Std. Deviation	Std. Error	95% Confidence Interval for Mean		Minimum	Maximum
						Lower Bound	Upper Bound		
excitement	0.00	69	2.64	2.262	0.272	2.09	3.18	0	7
	1.00	73	2.32	2.140	0.250	1.82	2.81	0	7
	Total	142	2.47	2.198	0.184	2.11	2.84	0	7

ANOVA

		Sum of Squares	d.f.	Mean Square	F	Sig.
excitement	Between Groups	3.692	1	3.692	0.763	0.384
	Within Groups	677.695	140	4.841		
	Total	681.387	141			

Notice that the *F*-ratio shown in the ANOVA table is associated with the same p-value as is the *t*-value above. This is no accident, since the *F* and *t* are mathematical functions of one another. So, when two groups are involved, the researcher can skin the cat either way!

©ARIEL SKELLEY/CORBIS

EXHIBIT 15.4 **Interpreting ANOVA**

Tests of Between-Subjects Effects (Dependent Variable: Coffee)

Source	Type III Sum of Squares	d.f.	Mean Square	F	Sig.
Corrected Model	40.000[a]	2	20.000	4.400	.039
Intercept	221.538	1	221.538	48.738	.000
Shift	40.000	2	20.000	4.400	.039
Error	50.000	11	4.545		
Total	314.000	14			

1. This row shows overall F-value testing whether all group means are equal. The sums of squares column calculates the SST, SSE, and SSB (shift row).

[a]R Squared = .444 (Adjusted R Squared = .343)

Shift	Mean	Std. Error	95% Confidence Interval	
			Lower Bound	Upper Bound
Day	2.000	.953	−.099	4.099
GY	4.000	1.066	1.654	6.346
Night	6.000	.953	3.901	8.099

2. This column shows the group means for each level of the independent variable.

Practically Speaking

Exhibit 15.4 displays the ANOVA result for the coffee-drinking example. Again, one advantage of living in modern times is that even a simple problem like this one need not be hand computed. Even though this example presents a small problem, one-way ANOVA models with more observations or levels would be interpreted similarly.

The first thing to check is whether or not the overall model F is significant. In this case, the computed $F = 4.40$ with 2 and 11 degrees of freedom. The p-value associated with this value is 0.039. Thus, we have high confidence in concluding that the group means are not all the same. Second, the researcher must remember to examine the actual means for each group to properly interpret the result. Doing so, the conclusion reached is that the night shift people drink the most coffee, followed by the graveyard-shift workers, and then lastly, the day-shift workers.

As there are three groups, we may wish to know whether or not group 1 is significantly different than group 3 or group 2, and so on. In this particular example, the answer is fairly obvious.

Correlation Analysis

Correlation coefficient
A statistical measure of the covariation, or association, between two variables.

The most popular technique for indicating the relationship of one variable to another is simple correlation analysis. The **correlation coefficient** is a statistical measure of the covariation, or association, between two variables. The correlation coefficient, r, ranges from $+1.0$ to -1.0. If the value of r equals $+1.0$, there is a perfect positive linear (straight-line) relationship. If the value of r equals -1.0, there is a perfect negative linear relationship, or a perfect inverse relationship. No correlation is indicated if r equals 0. A correlation coefficient indicates both the magnitude of the linear relationship and the direction of that relationship. For example, if we find that $r = -.92$, we know we have a relatively strong inverse relationship—that is, the greater the value measured by variable X, the lower the value measured by variable Y.

The formula for calculating the correlation coefficient for two variables X and Y is as follows:

$$r_{xy} = r_{yx} = \frac{\sum (X_i - \overline{X})(Y_i - \overline{Y})}{\sqrt{\sum (X_i - \overline{X})(Y_i - \overline{Y})}}$$

where the symbols $\overline{X}$ and $\overline{Y}$ represent the sample averages of X and Y, respectively.

An alternative way to express the correlation formula is

$$r_{xy} = r_{yx} = \frac{\sigma_{xy}}{\sqrt{\sigma_x^2 \sigma_y^2}}$$

where

$\sigma_x^2 = $ variance of X

$\sigma_y^2 = $ variance of Y

$\sigma_{xy} = $ covariance of X and Y

with

$$\sigma_{xy} = \frac{\sum (X_i - \overline{X})(Y_i - \overline{Y})}{N}$$

If associated values of X_i and Y_i differ from their means in the same direction, their covariance will be positive. If the values of X_i and Y_i tend to deviate in opposite directions, their covariance will be negative.

The simple correlation coefficient actually is a standardized measure of covariance. In the formula the numerator represents covariance and the denominator is the square root of the product of the sample variances. Researchers find the correlation coefficient useful because they can compare two correlations without regard for the amount of variance exhibited by each variable separately.

Correlation and Causation

Correlation does not mean causation. No matter how highly correlated the rooster's crow is to the rising of the sun, the rooster does not cause the sun to rise. A high correlation exists between teachers' salaries and the consumption of liquor over a period of years. The approximate correlation coefficient is $r = .9$. This high correlation does not indicate how much teachers drink, nor does it indicate that the sale of liquor increases teachers' salaries. The more likely case is that teachers' salaries and liquor sales covary because they are both influenced by a third variable, such as long-run growth in national income and/or population.

Coefficient of Determination

If we wish to know the proportion of *variance* in Y that is explained by X (or vice versa), we can calculate the **coefficient of determination (r^2)** by squaring the correlation coefficient:

$$r^2 = \frac{\text{Explained variance}}{\text{Total variance}}$$

The coefficient of determination, r^2, measures that part of the total variance of Y that is accounted for by knowing the value of X. In the example about unemployment and hours worked, $r = -.635$; therefore, $r^2 = .403$. About 40 percent of the variance in unemployment can be explained by the variance in hours worked, and vice versa.

The Regression Equation

The discussion here concerns **simple linear regression**. Simple regression investigates a *straight-line relationship* of the type:

$$Y = \alpha + \beta X,$$

TOTHEPOINT

Statistics are like a bikini. What they reveal is suggestive, but what they conceal is vital.

—Aaron Levenstein

Coefficient of determination (r^2)
A measure obtained by squaring the correlation coefficient; that proportion of the total variance of a variable that is accounted for by knowing the value of another variable.

Simple linear regression
A measure of linear association that investigates a straight-line relationship of the type $Y = a + \beta X$, where X is the independent variable and a and β are two constants to be estimated.

where Y is a continuous dependent variable, X is an independent variable that is usually continuous, although dichotomous nominal or ordinal variables can be included in the form of a dummy variable. Alpha (α) and beta (β) are two parameters that must be estimated so that the equation best represents a given set of data. These two parameters determine the height of the regression line and the angle of the line relative to horizontal. When these parameters change, the line changes. Regression techniques have the job of estimating values for these parameters that make the line *fit* the observations the best.

The result is simply a linear equation, or the equation for a line, just as in basic algebra! α represents the Y intercept (where the line cross the y-axis) and β is the slope coefficient. The slope is the change in Y associated with a change of one unit in X. Slope may also be thought of as rise over run. That is, how much does Y rise (or fall if negative) for every one unit change in the X-axis.

Parameter Estimate Choices

The estimates for α and β are the key to regression analysis. In most business research, the estimate of β is most important. The explanatory power of regression rests with β because this is where the direction and strength of the relationship between the independent and dependent variable is explained.

A Y-intercept term is sometimes referred to as a constant because α represents a fixed point. An estimated slope coefficient is sometimes referred to as a regression weight, regression coefficient, parameter estimate or sometimes even as a *path* estimate. The term path estimate is a descriptive term adapted because of the way hypothesized causal relationships are often represented in diagrams:

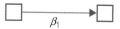

For all practical purposes, these terms are used interchangeably.

Parameter estimates can be presented in either raw or standardized form. One potential problem with raw parameter estimates is due to the fact that they reflect the measurement scale range. So, if a simple regression involved distance measured with miles, very small parameter estimates may indicate a strong relationship. In contrast, if the very same distance is measured with centimeters, a very large parameter estimate would be needed to indicate a strong relationship.

Exhibit 15.5 provides an illustration. Suppose a researcher was interested in how much space was allocated to a specific snack food on a shelf and how it related to sales. Fifteen observations are taken from 15 different stores. The blue line represents a typical distance showing shelf-space measured in cm. The green line is the same distance shown in miles. The top frame shows hypothetical regression results if the independent variable is measured in centimeters. The bottom frame shows the very same regression results if the independent variable is measured in miles. Even though these two regression lines are the same, the parameter coefficients do not seem comparable.

Thus, researchers often explain regression results by referring to a **standardized regression coefficient** (β). A standardized regression coefficient provides a common metric allowing regression results to be compared to one another no matter what the original scale range may have been.

Standardized regression coefficient (β)
The estimated coefficient indicating the strength of relationship between an independent variable and dependent variable expressed on a standardized scale where higher absolute values indicate stronger relationships (range is from -1 to 1).

EXHIBIT 15.5
The Advantage of Standardized Regression Weights

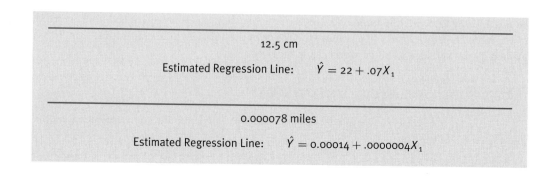

12.5 cm

Estimated Regression Line: $\hat{Y} = 22 + .07X_1$

0.000078 miles

Estimated Regression Line: $\hat{Y} = 0.00014 + .0000004X_1$

Due to the mathematics involved in standardization, the standardized y-intercept term is always 0.[5] The regression equation for the shelf space example would then become:

$$\hat{Y} = 0 + .16X_1$$

Even if the distance measures for the 15 observations were converted to some other metric (feet, meters, . . .), the standardized regression weight would still be .16.

Researchers use short-hand to label regression coefficients as either "raw" or "standardized." The most common short-hand is as follows:

→ $\mathbf{B_0}$ or $\mathbf{b_0}$ = raw (unstandardized) y-intercept term. What was referred to as α above.

→ $\mathbf{B_1}$ or $\mathbf{b_1}$ = raw regression coefficient or estimate.

→ $\boldsymbol{\beta_1}$ = standardized regression coefficients.

RAW REGRESSION ESTIMATES (b_1)

Raw regression weights have the advantage of retaining the scale metric—which is also their key disadvantage. Where should the researcher focus then? Should the standardized or unstandardized coefficients be interpreted? The answer to this question is fairly simple.

→ If the purpose of the regression analysis is forecasting, then raw parameter estimates must be used. This is another way of saying when the researcher is interested only in prediction.

Thus, when the researcher above wants to predict how much will be consumed based on the amount of shelf space, raw regression coefficients must be used. For instance, the forecast for 14 cm of shelf space can be found as follows:

$$\hat{Y} = 22 + .07(14) = 23.0$$

The same result can be found by using the equation representing the distance in miles.

STANDARDIZED REGRESSION ESTIMATES (β_1)

Standardized regression estimates have the advantage of a constant scale. No matter what range of values the independent variables take on, β will not be affected. When should standardized regression estimates be used?

→ Standardized regression estimates should be used when the researcher is testing explanatory hypotheses. In other words, when the purpose of the research is more explanation than prediction.

Multiple Regression Analysis

Multiple regression analysis is an extension of simple regression analysis allowing a metric dependent variable to be predicted by multiple independent variables. For instance, we often are interested in predicting sales using things like shelf space. Thus, one dependent variable is explained by one independent variable. Yet reality is more complicated and several additional factors probably affect sales. The other plausible independent variables include prices, economic factors, advertising intensity, and consumers' incomes in the area. The simple regression equation can be expanded to represent multiple regression analysis:

$$Y_i = \mathbf{b_0} + \mathbf{b_1}X_1 + \mathbf{b_2}X_2 + \mathbf{b_3}X_3 + \cdots + \mathbf{b_n}X_n + e_i$$

Multiple regression analysis
An analysis of association in which the effects of two or more independent variables on a single, interval-scaled dependent variable are investigated simultaneously.

Thus, as a form of the GLM, dependent variable predictions ($\hat{Y}$) are made by adjusting the constant ($\mathbf{b_0}$—which would be equal to the mean if all slope coefficients are zero) based on the slope coefficients associated with each independent variable.[6]

Less than interval (non-metric) independent variables can be used in multiple regression. This can be done by implementing dummy variable coding. A dummy variable is a variable that uses a 1 and a 0 to code the different levels of dichotomous variable. Multiple dummy variables can be included in a regression model. Dummy coding is appropriate when data from two countries are being compared. Suppose the average labor rate for automobile production is included in a sample taken from respondents in Mexico and in South Korea. A response from Mexico could be assigned a 0 and responses from South Korea could be assigned 1 to create a country variable appropriate for use with multiple regression.

A SIMPLE EXAMPLE

Assume that a toy manufacturer wishes to explain store sales (dependent variable) using a sample of stores from Canada and Europe. Several hypotheses are offered:

→ H1: *Competitor's sales* are related negatively to sales.

→ H2: Sales are higher in communities with a *sales office* than when no sales office is present.

→ H3: *Grammar school enrollment* in a community is related positively to sales.

Competitor's sales is how much the primary competitor sold in the same stores over the same time period. Both the dependent variable and the competitor's sales are ratio variables measured in Euros (Canadian sales were converted to Euros). The presence of a sales office is a categorical variable that can be represented with dummy coding (0 = no office in this particular region, 1 = office in this region). Grammar school enrollment is also a ratio variable simply represented by the number of students enrolled in elementary schools in each community (in thousands).[7] A sample of 24 communities is gathered and the data are entered into a regression program to produce the following results:

$$\text{Regression equation: } \hat{Y} = 102.18 + .387 X_1 + 115.2 X_2 + 6.73 X_3$$

$$\text{Coefficient of multiple determination } (R^2) = .845$$

$$F\text{-value} = 14.6; p < .05$$

The regression equation indicates that sales are positively related to X_1, X_2, and X_3. The coefficients show the effect on the dependent variable of a 1-unit increase in any of the independent variables. The value $b_2 = 115.2$ indicates that an increase of \$115,200 (000 included) in toy sales is expected with each additional unit of X_2. Thus, it appears that having a company sales office in a community is associated with a very positive effect on sales. Grammar school enrollments also may help predict sales. An increase of 1 unit of enrollment (1,000 students) indicates a sales increase of \$6,730. A 1-unit increase in competitors' sales volume (X_1) in the territory adds little to the toy manufacturer's sales (\$387).

Because the effect associated with X_1 is positive, H1 is not supported because the sign of the regression coefficient is opposite the prediction. Instead of losing sales to the competition, as competitors sales go up, so do the sales of this toy company. The effects associated with H2 and H3 are in the hypothesized direction. Thus, if the coefficients are statistically significant, each will be supported.

REGRESSION COEFFICIENTS IN MULTIPLE REGRESSION

Recall that in simple regression, the coefficient $\mathbf{b}_1$ represents the slope of X on Y. Multiple regression involves multiple slope estimates, or regression weights. One challenge in regression models is to understand how one independent variable affects the dependent variable considering the effect of other independent variables. As long as the independent variables are related to each other, the regression weight associated with one independent variable is affected by the regression weight of another. Regression coefficients are unaffected by each other only when independent variables are independent.

Conventional regression methods provide standardized parameter estimates, β_1, β_2, and so on, that can be thought of as *partial* regression coefficients. The correlation between Y and X_1, controlling for the correlation that X_2 has with the Y, is called partial correlation. Consider a standardized regression model with only two independent variables:[8]

$$Y = \beta_1 X_1 + \beta_2 X_2 + e_i$$

The coefficients β_1 and β_2 are partial regression coefficients which express the relationship between the independent variable and dependent variable taking into consideration that the other

RESEARCHSNAPSHOT

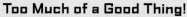

Too Much of a Good Thing!

Researchers often test hypotheses by examining regression coefficients. Thus, we are often looking for correlations, sometimes in all the wrong places. Financial data can be problematic to analyze. Consider the case of a financial manager trying to analyze gross margin (dependent variable = margin per employee) using the following independent variables:

- Average sales per square foot per quarter
- Average labor costs per week
- Years of experience for the manager
- Job performance rating for the previous year (100-point scale)

Regression results can be obtained in SPSS by clicking on ANALYZE, REGRESSION, and then LINEAR. The VIF column must be requested by clicking on STATISTICS and then checking COLINEARITY DIAGNOSTICS. After doing so, the following results are obtained. For the overall model,

ANOVA(b)

Model		Sum of Squares	d.f.	Mean Square	F	Sig.
1	Regression	142566.5332	4	35641.6333	13.56899	.0000008
	Residual	91934.43848	35	2626.698242		
	Total	234500.9717	39			

A	Predictors: (constant), performance, experience, labor, sales
B	Dependent Variable: margin

The *F* of 13.57 is highly significant (<.001), so the variables explain a large portion of the variance in the dependent variable. The model R^2 is .61 also supporting this conclusion. The results for the independent variable tests show the following:

Coefficients(a)

Model		Unstandardized Coefficients B	Std. Error	Standardized Coefficients Beta	t	Sig.	VIF
1	(Constant)	171.242614	235.9374392		0.725797	0.47279	
	Sales	0.090784631	0.030835442	2.339759409	2.944165	0.00572	56.3836
	Labor	−0.070267446	0.035014493	−1.587938574	−2.00681	0.05254	55.8971
	Experience	−0.488078747	0.955764142	−0.054331204	−0.51067	0.61279	1.0105
	Performance	−1.856084354	3.034080822	−0.068978263	−0.61175	0.54466	1.1351

a	Dependent Variable: margin

Even though the model results appear strong, only one independent variable is significant at a Type I error rate of 0.050 – sales. However, the β coefficients do not make sense. The β coefficients for both sales and labor are beyond the range that β should theoretically take (−1.0 to 1.0). Nothing can be correlated with something more than perfectly (which would be a correlation of 1.0 or −1.0). Notice also that the two VIF factors for sales and labor are in the 50s. Generally, when multiple VIF factors approach 5 or greater, problems with multicollinearity can be expected. The high correlation between sales and labor are a problem.

As often occurs with financial data, they can be difficult to use as independent variables. In this case, the researcher may wish to rerun the model after dropping one of the offending variables.

©PHOTODISC/GETTY IMAGES

variable also is related to the dependent variable. As long as the correlation between independent variables is modest, partial regression coefficients adequately represent the relationships. When the correlation between two independent variables becomes high, the regression coefficients may not be reliable. We return to this issue later in the chapter.

When researchers want to know which independent variable is most predictive of the dependent variable, the standardized regression coefficient (β) is used. One huge advantage of β is that it provides a constant scale. Therefore, the greater the absolute value of the standardized regression coefficient, the more that particular independent variable is responsible for explaining the dependent variable. For example, suppose in the toy example above, the following standardized regression coefficients were found:

→ $\beta_1 = .10$

→ $\beta_2 = .30$

→ $\beta_3 = .10$

The resulting standardized regression equation would be:

$$Y = .10X_1 + .30X_2 + .10X_3$$

Using these standardized coefficients, the researcher could conclude that the relationships between competitors' sales and grammar school enrollment and sales with are the same. Perhaps more importantly, though, the conclusion can also be reached that the relationship between having a sales office in the area is three times as strong as the other two relationships. Thus, management may wish to place more emphasis on locating sales offices in major markets.

R^2 IN MULTIPLE REGRESSION

The coefficient of multiple determination in multiple regression indicates the percentage of variation in Y explained by *all* independent variables. A value of $R^2 = .845$ means that 84.5 percent of the variance in the dependent variable is explained by the independent variables. If two independent variables are truly independent (uncorrelated with each other), the R^2 for a multiple regression model is equal to the separate R^2 values that would result from two separate simple regression models. More typically, the independent variables are related to one another, meaning that the model R^2 from a multiple regression model will be less than the separate R^2 values resulting from individual simple regression models. This reduction in R^2 is proportionate to the extent to which the independent variables are interrelated or *collinear*.

STATISTICAL SIGNIFICANCE IN MULTIPLE REGRESSION

Following from simple regression, an F-test is used to test statistical significance by comparing the variation explained by the regression equation to the residual error variation. The F-test allows for testing of the relative magnitudes of the sum of squares due to the regression (SSR) and the error sum of squares (SSE).

$$F = \frac{(\text{SSR})/k}{(\text{SSE})/(n - k - 1)} = \frac{\text{MSR}}{\text{MSE}}$$

where

k = number of independent variables

n = number of observations

MSR = Mean Squares Regression

MSE = Mean Squares Error

Degrees of freedom for the F-test (*d.f.*) are:

d.f. for the numerator = k

d.f. for the denominator = $n - k - 1$

For the example above,

$$d.f. \text{ (numerator)} = 3$$

$$d.f. \text{ (denominator)} = 12 - 3 - 1 = 8$$

A table of critical F-values shows that for 3 and 8 $d.f.$ and a .05 type I error rate, a value of 4.07 or more is necessary for the regression model to be considered significant, meaning that it explains a significant portion of the total variation in the dependent variable. In practice, statistical programs will report the p-value associated with the F-test directly. Similarly, the programs report the statistical test for each individual independent variable. Independent variables with p-values below the acceptable type I error rate are considered significant predictors of the dependent variable.

STEPS IN INTERPRETING A MULTIPLE REGRESSION MODEL

Multiple regression models often are used to test some proposed theoretical model. For instance, a researcher may be asked to develop and test a model explaining business unit performance. Why do some business units outperform others? Multiple regression models can be interpreted using these steps:

1. Examine the model F-test. If the test result is not significant, the model should be dismissed and there is no need to proceed to further steps.
2. Examine the individual statistical tests for each parameter estimate. Independent variables with significant results can be considered a significant explanatory variable.
3. Examine the model R^2. No cut-off values exist that can distinguish an acceptable amount of explained variation across all regression models. However, the absolute value of R^2 is more important when the researcher is more interested in prediction than explanation. In other words, the regression is run for pure forecasting purposes. When the model is more oriented toward explaining which variables are most important in explaining the dependent variable, cut-off values for the model R^2 are inappropriate.
4. Examine collinearity diagnostics. Multicollinearity in regression analysis refers to how strongly interrelated the independent variables in a model are. When multicollinearity is too high, the individual parameter estimates become difficult to interpret. Most regression programs can compute variance inflation factors (VIF) for each variable. As a rule of thumb, VIF above 5.0 suggests problems with multicollinearity.[9]

Exhibit 15.6 on the next page illustrates these steps. The regression model explains business unit profitability for a sample of 28 business units for a Fortune 500 company. The independent variables are hours (average hours spent in training for the workforce), budget (the percentage of the promotional budget used) and state (a dummy variable indicating whether the business unit is in Arizona— coded 0—or Ohio—coded 1). In this case, the researcher is using a maximum acceptable type I error rate of .05. The conclusion reached from this analysis is that hours spent in training seem to pay off in increased business unit profitability as evidenced by the significant, positive regression coefficient ($\beta = .55, \text{p} < .05$).

Other Multivariate Techniques

Multivariate data analysis is a general term referring to statistical techniques involving the simultaneous analysis of three or more variables. Multiple regression analysis is a multivariate data analysis procedure. Many other multivariate techniques exist, including tools such as exploratory factor analysis, confirmatory factor analysis, multivariate analysis of variance (MANOVA), multiple discriminant analysis, and cluster analysis. These tools can be very useful in market segmentation, scale measurement, marketing experiments, and product design, among many other applications. Entire books are devoted to multivariate data analysis and further discussion of these techniques is beyond the scope of this book. The reader should be aware that more intricate data analysis tools are available.

Multivariate data analysis
A group of statistical techniques allowing for the simultaneous analysis of three or more variables.

EXHIBIT 15.6 Interpreting Multiple Regression Results

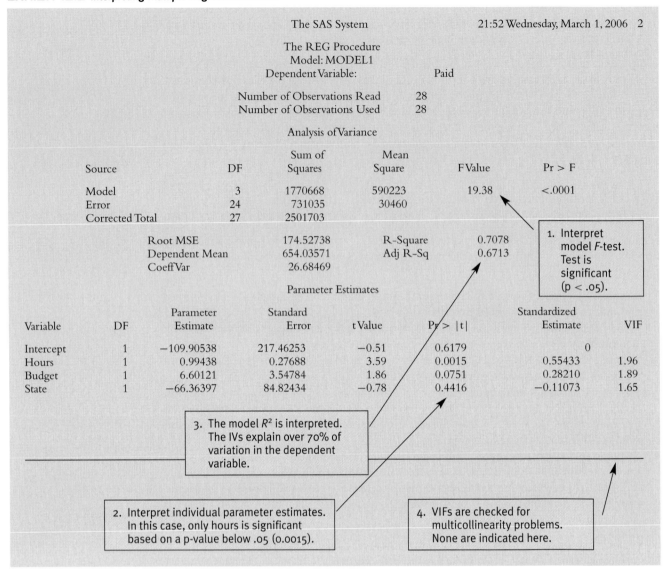

The SAS System   21:52 Wednesday, March 1, 2006   2

The REG Procedure
Model: MODEL1
Dependent Variable: Paid

Number of Observations Read   28
Number of Observations Used   28

Analysis of Variance

Source	DF	Sum of Squares	Mean Square	F Value	Pr > F
Model	3	1770668	590223	19.38	<.0001
Error	24	731035	30460		
Corrected Total	27	2501703			

Root MSE	174.52738	R-Square	0.7078
Dependent Mean	654.03571	Adj R-Sq	0.6713
Coeff Var	26.68469		

1. Interpret model *F*-test. Test is significant (p < .05).

Parameter Estimates

Variable	DF	Parameter Estimate	Standard Error	t Value	Pr > |t|	Standardized Estimate	VIF
Intercept	1	−109.90538	217.46253	−0.51	0.6179	0	
Hours	1	0.99438	0.27688	3.59	0.0015	0.55433	1.96
Budget	1	6.60121	3.54784	1.86	0.0751	0.28210	1.89
State	1	−66.36397	84.82434	−0.78	0.4416	−0.11073	1.65

3. The model R^2 is interpreted. The IVs explain over 70% of variation in the dependent variable.

2. Interpret individual parameter estimates. In this case, only hours is significant based on a p-value below .05 (0.0015).

4. VIFs are checked for multicollinearity problems. None are indicated here.

Summary

1. Understand what multivariate statistical analysis involves and know the two types of multivariate analysis. Multivariate statistical methods analyze multiple variables or even multiple sets of variables simultaneously. They are particularly useful for identifying latent constructs using multiple individual measures. Multivariate techniques represent data through the use of variates. Variates are mathematical combinations of variables. The two major types of multivariate procedures are interdependence and dependence techniques. Interdependence techniques do not distinguish dependent and interdependent variables, whereas dependence techniques do make this distinction.

2. Interpret results from multiple regression analysis. Multiple regression analysis predicts a continuous dependent variable with multiple independent variables. The independent variables can be either continuous or categorical. Categorical variables must be coded as dummy variables. Multiple regression results are analyzed by examining the significance of the overall model using the *F*-test results, the individual parameter estimates, the overall model R^2, and the model collinearity diagnostics. Standardized regression coefficients have the advantage of a common scale making them comparable from model to model and variable to variable.

3. **Interpret results from multivariate analysis of variance (MANOVA).** MANOVA is an extension of ANOVA involving multiple related dependent variables. Thus, MANOVA represents a form of the GLM predicting that multiple categorical independent variables affect multiple, related dependent variables. Interpretation of a MANOVA model is similar to interpretation of a regression model. However, the multivariate F-test results associated with Wilke's Lambda (Λ) are interpreted first, followed by interpretation of the individual ANOVA results.

4. **Interpret basic exploratory factor analysis results.** EFA is a data reduction technique in which the variance in multiple variables is represented by a smaller number of factors. The factors generally represent latent factors or indexes. Factor loading resulting from rotated factor solutions are important in properly interpreting factor analysis results. The pattern of loadings that results suggests both the number of latent factors that may exist and helps validate scales that may be used in other statistical analysis.

Key Terms and Concepts

Cross-tabulation (contingency table)	Within-group error or variance	Coefficient of determination (r^2)
Univariate analysis	F-test	Simple linear regression
Bivariate analysis	Within-group variation	Standardized regression coefficient (β)
Analysis of variance (ANOVA)	Between-group variance	Multiple regression analysis
Grand mean	Total variability (SST)	Multivariate data analysis
Between-groups variance	Correlation coefficient	

Questions for Review and Critical Thinking

1. What tests of difference are appropriate in the following situations?
   a. Average campaign contributions of Democrats, Republicans, and independents are to be compared.
   b. Advertising managers and brand managers have responded "yes," "no," or "not sure" to an attitude question. Their answers are to be compared.
   c. One-half of a sample received an incentive in a mail survey; the other half did not. A comparison of response rates is desired.
   d. A researcher believes that married men will push the grocery cart when grocery shopping with their wives.

2. What type of analysis should be used to analyze the following data on responses to the statement "Regulation is the best way to ensure safe products"?

	Managers	Blue-Collar Workers
Agree	58	66
Disagree	34	24
No opinion	8	10
Totals	100	100

3. A store manager's computer-generated list of all retail sales employees indicates that 70 percent are full-time employees, 20 percent are part-time employees, and 10 percent are furloughed or laid-off employees. A sample of 50 employees from the list indicates that 40 are full-time employees, 6 are part-time employees, and 4 are furloughed/laid-off employees. What statistical test should be used to determine whether the sample is representative of the population?

4. A sales force ($n = 67$) received some management-by-objectives training. The mean scores for salespeople's job performance are shown below. What type of data analysis is appropriate?

Skill	Before	After
Planning ability	4.84	5.43
Territory coverage	5.24	5.51
Activity reporting	5.37	5.42

5. Perform a χ^2 test on the following data:
   a. Regulation is the best way to ensure safe products.

	Agree	Disagree	No Opinion
Managers	58	66	8
Line employees	34	24	10
Totals	92	90	18

   b. Ownership of residence

	Yes	No
Male	25	20
Female	16	14

6. The incomes of owners of trash compactors were compared with those of nonowners. The average income in a sample of 200 was as follows:

	Owners	Nonowners
$\bar{X}$	4.6	3.5

Higher values represent higher levels of income. (Actual scaled average: less than \$7,500 = 1; \$7,501–\$15,000 = 2; \$15,001–\$25,000 = 3; \$25,001–\$40,000 = 4; \$40,001–\$60,000 = 5; over \$60,000 = 6.) Is a *t*-test appropriate?

7. The discussion in this chapter is limited to linear relationships. Try to diagram some nonlinear relationships that show *r* values of zero using the test methods shown in the text.

8. Comment on the following:
   a. Suppose Abraham Lincoln answered a survey questionnaire and indicated he had not received a grade-school diploma. The researcher found that Lincoln's educational score did not correlate highly with the expected variables. What was wrong?
   b. An international marketer has said, "When political instability increases, the price of quality increases." Is this a testable hypothesis?
   c. In 8 out of 11 years, when a racehorse won the Triple Crown (Kentucky Derby, Preakness, and Belmont Stakes), the stock market dropped.

9. A manufacturer of disposable washcloths/wipes told a retailer that sales for this product category closely correlated with sales of disposable diapers. The retailer thought he would check this out for his own sales-forecasting purposes. The researcher tells him, "Disposable washcloth/wipes sales can be predicted with knowledge of disposable diaper sales." Is this the right thing to say?

10. The territories in a company's eastern and western regions were rated for sales potential based on the company's evaluation system. A sales manager wishes to conduct a *t*-test of means to determine whether there is a difference between the two regions. Conduct this test preferably using a statistical software package:

Region	Territory	Rating	Region	Territory	Rating
West	1	74	East	8	81
West	2	88	East	9	63
West	3	78	East	10	56
West	4	85	East	11	68
West	5	100	East	12	80
West	6	114	East	13	79
West	7	98	East	14	69

11. Interpret the following data:
   a. $\hat{Y} = 5.0 + .30X_1$
      i. Where the dependent variable equals turnover intentions for line managers and the independent variable equals number of employees supervised.
   b. $\hat{Y} = 250 - 4.0X_1$
      i. **'NET** Where the dependent variable is the number of hits on a new banner ad and the independent variable is the number of weeks the ad has run.

12. The following table gives a football team's season-ticket sales, percentage of games won, and number of active alumni for the years 1996–2005.

Year	Season-Ticket Sales	Percentage of Games Won	Number of Active Alumni
1996	4,995	40	NA
1997	8,599	54	3,450
1998	8,479	55	3,801
1999	8,419	58	4,000
2000	10,253	63	4,098
2001	12,457	75	6,315
2002	13,285	36	6,860
2003	14,177	27	8,423
2004	15,730	63	9,000
2005	15,805	70	9,500

   a. Compute a correlation matrix for the variables. A software statistical package is recommended. Interpret the correlation between each pair of variables.
   b. Estimate a regression model for sales = Percentage of games won.
   c. Estimate a regression model for sales = Number of active alumni.
   d. If *sales* is the dependent variable, which of the two independent variables do you think explains sales better? Explain.

Exploring the Internet

1. Go to the Chance Web site at http:// www.dartmouth.edu/~chance/ChanceLecture/AudioVideo.html and view the very interesting streaming video "Streaks in Sports."
2. The Federal Reserve Bank of St. Louis maintains a database called FRED (Federal Reserve Economic Data). Navigate to the FRED database at http://www.stls.frb.org/fred/index.html.

Randomly select a five-year period between 1970 and 1995 and then find the correlation between average U.S. employment in retail trade and U.S. employment in wholesale trade. What statistical test is appropriate?

Case 15.1 Springfield Electric Company

Download the data sets for this case from http://www.thomsonedu.com/marketing/zikmund or request them from your instructor.
Springfield Electric Company is a manufacturer of electric pencil sharpeners. The company had always operated in New York and New Jersey and decided to expand beyond that region. The company president thought a new plant needed to be constructed. Seeing no need for contiguous expansion, the president favored a West Coast plant.

The marketing manager believed that sales were correlated with the number of workers employed in the geographic area; in fact, she felt that electric pencil sharpener sales were correlated with the number of white-collar workers in an area. However, all she could get were statistics for total employees. Case Exhibit 15.1–1 shows

Springfield's sales of electric pencil sharpeners and the total number of employees in 17 Metropolitan Statistical Areas (MSAs) in New York and New Jersey. Case Exhibit 15.1–2 shows the number of employees in the MSAs in Washington, Oregon, and California. The marketing manager thought she could forecast sales for the western expansion with these data.

Questions

1. Calculate and interpret the correlation coefficient data in Case Exhibit 15.1–1.
2. Estimate the regression equation coefficient for the data (using sales as the independent variable).
3. Forecast sales in the states of California, Washington, and Oregon based on the data in Case Exhibit 15.1–2.

CASE EXHIBIT 15.1-1 **Data on Total Employees and Springfield Sales in New York and New Jersey MSAs**

Metropolitan Statistical Area	Number of Employees (thousands)	Sales
New York		
Albany–Schenectady–Troy	58.3	3,749
Binghamton	37.0	2,695
Buffalo	135.6	4,926
Elmira	12.8	2,808
Nassau–Suffolk	149.0	7,423
New York	788.8	43,401
Poughkeepsie	24.3	3,254
Rochester	139.1	8,924
Syracuse	53.6	13,119
Utica–Rome	30.8	3,151
New Jersey		
Pennsylvania	110.7	6,123
Atlantic City	8.7	2,666
Jersey City	74.2	3,210
Long Branch–Asbury Park	22.8	2,078
New Brunswick–Perth		
Amboy–Sayreville	78.9	2,894
Newark	252.1	14,989
Paterson–Clifton–Passaic	60.1	3,806

CASE EXHIBIT 15.1-2 **Number of Employees in Selected MSAs**

Metropolitan Statistical Area	Number of Employees (thousands)
Washington	
Richland–Kennewick	7.8
Seattle–Everett	123.6
Spokane	11.1
Tacoma	18.7
Yakima	8.8
Oregon	
Eugene–Springfield	18.2
Portland	90.5
Salem	12.5
California	
Anaheim–Santa Ana–Garden Grove	149.0
Bakersfield	7.1
Fresno	20.5
Los Angeles–Long Beach	750.3
Modesto	18.7
Oxnard–Simi Valley–Ventura	14.9
Riverside–San Bernardino–Ontario	51.8
Sacramento	20.5
Salinas–Seaside–Monterey	8.0
San Diego	71.4
San Francisco–Oakland	172.7
San Jose	151.1
Santa Barbara–Santa Maria–Lompoc	14.0
Santa Cruz	5.7
Santa Rosa	8.6
Stockton	20.0
Vallejo–Fairfield–Napa	7.4

Case 15.2 Center for American Enterprise: A Study of Psychological and Demographic Contributors to Consumerism

 A few years ago the Center for American Enterprise commissioned a study to determine the causes of consumerism.[10] This was done in an effort to stem the tide of growing disenchantment with American business and its practices among a wide number of consumers.

The center, located in Dallas, Texas, was a private foundation funded by a large number of corporations to spread the ideal of the free enterprise system. It conducted a number of projects to better understand what Americans knew about business and published numerous brochures that were sent to high schools and elementary schools throughout the United States. The center believed consumerism—that is, consumer discontent—was a major problem facing business and wished to pursue it as an area of study.

Since the center did not have the expertise to properly formulate the research problem and its accompanying theory, it decided to seek outside assistance for this project. Commissioned to do the study were three professors at Southern Methodist University, Thomas, Rogers, and Michaels, who had done considerable research on the topic. The report they generated follows.

Report on Psychological and Demographic Correlates of Consumer Discontent

The study of consumerism and the allied psychological state of consumer discontent has been theoretically and empirically examined within the confines of the economic system. Although these market interfaces provide discrete areas for analyzing consumerism or consumer discontent, they may be only symptomatic of broader psychological states currently existing in society. With the exception of one study relating consumer alienation to marketing activities, little research has actively explored potential relationships between psychological states and discontent with the market system. Identification of those psychological states and demographic characteristics associated with consumer discontent would provide valuable insight into the dynamics of this phenomenon and assist in the development of constructive approaches for dealing with it from a public policy perspective.

Study Purpose

The purpose of this study is to examine the relationships among selected psychological states, demographic variables, and consumer discontent. Specific objectives of this study are threefold:

1. To determine if consumer discontent with the marketplace is rooted in more basic conceptions of an individual's life-space.

2. To determine the appropriateness of psychological constructs as potential contributors and explanatory states for investigating consumer discontent.

3. To identify demographic correlates of consumer discontent.

Method

A two-stage area sampling procedure was used to select 228 individuals from the Dallas, Texas, metropolitan area. A subsequent analysis of demographic data indicated that the sample represented a cross section of the area. Individuals were personally contacted in their homes by trained interviewers.

Respondents were given a self-administered questionnaire containing a list of 145 statements designed to measure life satisfaction, powerlessness, anomie, alienation, normlessness, social isolation, aggression, and consumer discontent. All statements were scored on a five-point Likert-type scale except for the six-point Likert-type scale of consumer discontent. Demographic data on the respondents were also collected.

Results

Results of the study are shown in Case Exhibits 15.2–1 and 15.2–2. Case Exhibit 15.2–1 presents the correlation matrix between the measures of psychological states and the consumer discontent scale. The correlations indicate that consumer discontent is indeed related to basic psychological states.

Case Exhibit 15.2–2 presents the correlation matrix between demographic variables and the consumer discontent scale. Examination of demographic variables also reveals that discontent is related to certain characteristics of the populace.

Together, the psychological and demographic correlates of consumer discontent provide a profile of the discontented consumer. Consumer discontent may be an outgrowth of more basic psychological states that reflect disassociation with society in general and specifically with the marketplace. One may speculate that dislocation in society will produce consumer discontent. Given the growing complexity of business and society, it appears that this may become an even more pervasive problem in the future and thus warrants further research at this time.

Questions

1. Interpret the results of the correlation matrix.

2. Develop a profile of the discontented consumer and the contented consumer.

3. What policy implications would you suggest based on these results?

CASE EXHIBIT 15.2-1 **Correlation Matrix of Scale Responses**

(N = 228)	CD	LS	AN	AL	PO	NO	SI	AG
Consumer discontent (CD)	1.00	−.11[b]	.37[a]	.42[a]	.37[a]	.28[a]	.34[a]	.21[a]
Life satisfaction (LS)		1.00	−.44[a]	−.44[a]	−.33[a]	−.25[a]	−.44[a]	−.27[a]
Anomie (AN)			1.00	.66[a]	.56[a]	.47[a]	.54[a]	.25[a]
Alienation (AL)				1.00	.80[a]	.77[a]	.79[a]	.31[a]
Powerlessness (PO)					1.00	.46[a]	.42[a]	.15[b]
Normlessness (NO)						1.00	.42[a]	.32[a]
Social isolation (SI)							1.00	.28[a]
Aggression (AG)								1.00

[a] $p < .01$.
[b] $p < .05$; Pearson product-moment correlation coefficients.

CASE EXHIBIT 15.2-2 **Correlation of Scale Responses with Demographic Characteristics**

(N = 228)	CD	LS	AN	AL	PO	NO	SI	AG
Age	.13[b]	.14[b]	.10	.31[a]	.07	.29[a]	.37[a]	.13[b]
Sex[1]	−.13[b]	−.05	.02	−.15[b]	−.11	−.06	−.18[b]	.11
Race[2]	−.06	.08	.04	−.15[b]	−.13[b]	−.21[a]	−.03	−.06
Family Size	.02	−.16[a]	.21[a]	.24[a]	.11[b]	.17[b]	.27[a]	.09
Income	.31[a]	−.29[a]	.22[a]	.37[a]	.30[a]	.31[a]	.30[a]	.17[b]
Occupation[3]	−.26[a]	.08	−.20[a]	−.26[a]	−.23[a]	−.15[b]	−.23[a]	.01
Education	.15[b]	−.03	−.11	.20[a]	.27[a]	.16[b]	.06	.11

[a] $p < .01$.
[b] $p < .05$.
[1] Scored: male = 1, female = 2.
[2] Scored: Caucasian = 1, Black = 2, Mexican American = 3, other = 4.
[3] Scored: professional = 1, skilled worker = 2, unskilled worker = 3, unemployed = 4, retired = 5.

CHAPTER 16
COMMUNICATING RESEARCH RESULTS:
RESEARCH REPORT, ORAL PRESENTATION, AND RESEARCH FOLLOW-UP

After studying this chapter, you should be able to

1. Discuss the research report from the perspective of the communications process
2. Define the parts of a research report following a standard format
3. Describe how to give an effective oral presentation
4. Discuss the importance of Internet reporting and research follow-up

Chapter Vignette: What the World Needs Now Is . . . Mathematicians Who Can Write

As computing power has placed analytical tools into the hands of every manager, the need for people who understand what these tools can do and what the results mean is greater than ever.[1] Think about the power of search engines such as Google, which operate based on mathematical formulas. These programs can track the sites consumers visit, the links they click on, and even what they buy. Using such data for several large companies that agreed to participate in a study, the Interactive Advertising Bureau used mathematics-based analysis to measure the effectiveness of each company's advertising. For example, the bureau told Ford Motor Company that it could have earned $625 million more from the sale of trucks if its advertising budget had been 6 percent rather than 2.5 percent of its total ad spending.

The ability to provide such practical information makes employees with quantitative skills extremely valuable. Harrah's Entertainment, for example, has analyzed data to develop detailed customer profiles, segmenting customers by age, gender, zip code, the amount of time spent gambling, and the value of their winnings or losses. Using mathematical modeling, Harrah's can select groups and match them with special offers—not just to draw in more customers but to maximize the company's profits.

To apply the power of mathematics, organizations need managers who can understand the data—but also numbers experts who can effectively communicate what they have learned. If understanding math adds value to an organization, being able to share that knowledge multiplies the value. Effectively communicating quantitative information is all the more valuable because the skill is, unfortunately, rare. A survey of major corporations found that in seven out of ten companies, at least two-thirds of their employees have writing responsibility, and more than half said their employees frequently produced technical reports. Over three-fourths of the companies said their employees also prepare oral reports incorporating presentation software such as PowerPoint. But more than four out of ten companies said they had to provide training for employees with deficient writing skills.

Why should a careful researcher have to be a good writer, too? After the researcher has spent days, weeks, or even months working on a project, preparation of the report may feel like an anticlimactic formality. All the "real" work has been done; it just has to be put on paper. This attitude can be disastrous, however. Even if the project was well designed, the data carefully obtained and analyzed by sophisticated statistical methods, and important conclusions reached, unless the reporting is effective, all of the earlier efforts will have been wasted. Often the research report is the only part of the project that others ever see. If people who need to use the research results have to wade through a disorganized presentation, are confused by technical jargon, or find sloppiness of language or thought, they will probably discount the report and make decisions without it, just as if the project had never been done. So, the research report is a crucial means for communicating the whole project. This chapter explains the communication of research results with written reports, oral presentations, and follow-up conversations.[2]

Insights from the Communications Model

Some insights from the theory of communications help to clarify the importance of the research report. Several elements influence a successful **communication process**:

- The *communicator*—the source or sender of the message (the writer of the report)
- The *message*—the set of meanings being sent to or received by the audience (the *findings* of the research project)
- The *medium*—the way in which the message is delivered to the audience (the oral or written report itself)
- The *audience*—the receiver or destination of the message (the manager who will make a decision based—we hope—on the report findings)
- *Feedback*—a communication, also involving a message and channel, that flows in the reverse direction (from the audience to the original communicator) and that may be used to modify subsequent communications (the manager's response to the report)

This model may make communication seem simple. Perhaps communication is simple when the message flows smoothly from writer to reader, and then in return, from reader to writer to provide feedback. Actually, communication is more complex. The communicator and the audience each have individual fields of experience. These overlap to some extent; otherwise no communication would be possible. Still, a great deal of experience is not common to both parties. As communicators send a message, they encode it in terms that make sense to them based on their fields of experience. As the individuals in the audience receive the message, they decode it based on their own fields of experience. The message is successfully communicated only if the parties share enough common experience for it to be encoded, transmitted, and decoded with roughly the same meaning.

In the research setting, the communicator (the researcher) has spent a great deal of time studying a problem. He or she has looked at secondary sources, gathered primary data, used statistical techniques to analyze the data, and reached conclusions. When the report on the project is written, all this "baggage" will affect its contents. On the assumption that the reader has a lot of background information on the project, the researcher may produce pages and pages of unexplained tables, expecting the reader to unearth from them the same patterns that the researcher has observed. The report may contain technical terms such as *parameter estimate, F-distribution, statistical significance,*

Communication process
The process by which one person or source sends a message to an audience or receiver and then receives feedback about the message.

TOTHEPOINT

It is a luxury to be understood.

—Ralph Waldo Emerson

RESEARCHSNAPSHOT

Sloppy Numbers in the Crosshairs of Dow Jones Newspaper Fund's Director

As executive director of the Dow Jones Newspaper Fund, former *Wall Street Journal* editor Richard Holden has a mission to improve the quality of journalism education. His formal role emphasizes high school and college students, but Holden finds that even the professionals can use some education in reporting data. He has gathered examples of newspaper reports that present numbers in ways that are confusing, misleading, or even incorrect.

Consider the following examples, taken from a seminar Holden presented to journalists. See if you can identify the problem with each statement:

"Visa announced that its new credit card will carry an adjustable rate set monthly at four percent above the prime rate, in line with other variable-rate cards."

This is a common mistake: confusing *percentage* and *percentage points*. A rate set so slightly above the prime rate would be an

©BASSOULS SOPHIE/CORBIS SYGMA

unusually good bargain. For example, at the time of this writing, the prime rate is 7.5 percent; prime plus 4 percent would be just 7.8 percent, far below the rates charged for

most credit cards. The writer probably meant Visa would charge prime rate plus four percentage points, which in this example would be 11.5 percent.

"Battling Hunger, a food pantry, said it delivered 110,000 tons of food to Detroit last Thanksgiving. The food was delivered to help residents there overcome the effects of a severe economic slump, particularly in the automobile industry."

This example shows that it is important to check whether numbers themselves, including the units of measure, are logical. In this case, 110,000 tons equals 220 million pounds of food. Can that be reasonable? Even if the food pantry served a million people—all of Detroit plus some suburbanites—it would have distributed 220 pounds of food to each individual. Not likely. When numbers are this unrealistic, the writer should check the calculations, including the decimal point's location, and the units. Perhaps this writer meant 110,000 pounds or 110 tons.

Source: Based on Carl Bialik, "Monitoring Numbers in the News," The Wall Street Journal, January 20, 2006, http://online.wsj.com; Carl Bialik, "The Results Are In," The Wall Street Journal, January 27, 2006, http://online.wsj.com; and Dow Jones Newspaper Fund, "About DJNF," http://djnewspaperfund.dowjones.com, accessed March 29, 2006.

---

correlations, and *eigenvalue,* on the assumption that the reader will understand them. Another researcher may assume that the reader does not have a lot of background information and may go overboard explaining everything in the report in sixth-grade terms. Although the researcher's intent is to ensure that the reader will not get lost, this effort may insult the reader.

Usually when readers receive a report, they have not thought much about the project. They may not know anything about statistics and may have many other responsibilities. If they cannot understand the report quickly, they may put it on a stack of things to do someday.

Simply delivering a report to its audience is not sufficient to ensure that it gets attention. The report needs to be written so as to draw on the common experience of the researcher and the reader. And the person responsible for making sure that it does so is the writer—not the reader. Unless a report is really crucial, a busy reader will not spend time and effort struggling through an inadequate or difficult-to-read document.

The Report in Context

Research report
An oral presentation or written statement of research results, strategic recommendations, and/or other conclusions to a specific audience.

A **research report** is an oral presentation and/or written statement whose purpose is to communicate research results, strategic recommendations, and/or other conclusions to management or other specific audiences. Although this chapter deals primarily with the final *written* report required by an extensive research project, remember that the final report may not be the only kind prepared. For a small project, a short oral or written report on the results may be all that is needed. Extensive projects may involve many written documents, interim reports, a long final written report, and several oral presentations. In addition, technical materials may be posted on an organization's Intranet.

The chapter's emphasis on the final report should not be taken to mean that other communications, such as progress reports during the course of the project, are any less important to the project's eventual success. The chapter's suggestions can be easily adapted to apply to these additional communications and shorter, less formal reports.

Report Format

Although every research report is custom-made for the project it represents, some conventions of **report format** are universal. They represent a consensus about the parts necessary for a good research report and how they should be ordered. This consensus is not a law, however. Every book on report writing suggests the use of its own unique format, and every report writer has to pick and choose the section and order that will work best for the project at hand. Many companies and universities also have in-house report formats or writing guides for writers to follow. The format described in this section serves as a starting point from which a writer can shape his or her own appropriate format. It includes seven major elements:

Report format
The makeup or arrangement of parts necessary to a good research report.

1. Title page (sometimes preceded by a title fly page)
2. Letter of transmittal
3. Letter of authorization
4. Table of contents (and lists of figures and tables)
5. Executive Summary
   a. Objectives
   b. Results
   c. Conclusions
   d. Recommendations
6. Body
   a. Introduction
      1. Background
      2. Objectives
   b. Methodology
   c. Results
   d. Limitations
   e. Conclusions and recommendations
7. Appendix
   a. Data collection forms
   b. Detailed calculations
   c. General tables
   d. Bibliography
   e. Other support material

Tailoring the Format to the Project

The format of a research report may need to be adjusted for two reasons: (1) to obtain the proper level of formality and (2) to decrease the complexity of the report. The format given here is for the most formal type of report, such as one for a large project done within an organization or one done by a research agency for a client company. This type of report is usually bound in a permanent cover and may be hundreds of pages long.

In less formal reports, each part is shorter, and some parts are omitted. Exhibit 16.1 on the next page illustrates how the format is adapted to shorter, less formal reports. The situation may be compared to the way people's clothing varies according to the formality of the occasion. The most formal report is dressed, so to speak, in a tuxedo or long evening gown. It includes the full assortment of prefatory parts—title fly page, title page, letters of transmittal and authorization, and table of contents. Like changing into an everyday business suit, dropping down to the next level of formality involves eliminating parts of the prefatory material that are not needed in this situation and reducing the complexity of the report body. In general, as the report moves down through the sport coat and slacks and then blue jeans stages, more prefatory parts are dropped, and the complexity and length of the report body are reduced.

EXHIBIT 16.1 Adapting Report Format to Required Formality

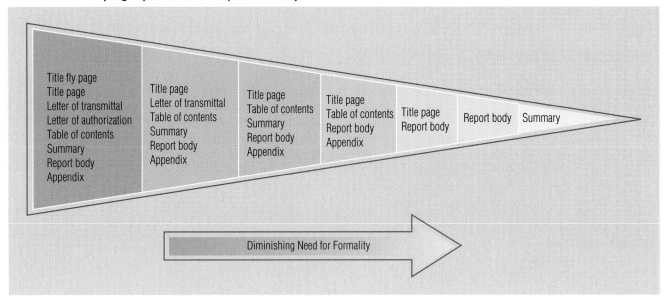

How does the researcher decide on the appropriate level of formality? The general rule is to include all the parts needed for effective communication in the particular circumstances—and no more. This depends on how far up in management the report is expected to go and how routine the matter is. A researcher's immediate supervisor does not need a 100-page, "black-tie" report on a routine project. However, the board of directors does not want a one-page "blue jeans" report on a big project that backs a major expansion program. The formal report to top management may later be stripped of some of the prefatory parts (and thus reduced in formality) for wider circulation within the company.

The Parts of the Report

The guidelines that call for each element of the research report also dictate the content of each part.

▤ TITLE PAGE

The *title page* should state the title of the report, for whom the report was prepared, by whom it was prepared, and the date of release or presentation. The title should give a brief but complete indication of the purpose of the research project. Addresses and titles of the preparer and recipient may also be included. On confidential reports, the title page may list the people to whom the report should be circulated. For the most formal reports, the title page is preceded by a title fly page, which contains only the report's title.

▤ LETTER OF TRANSMITTAL

Relatively formal and very formal reports include a *letter of transmittal.* Its purpose is to release or deliver the report to the recipient. It also serves to establish some rapport between the reader and the writer. This is the one part of the formal report in which a personal or even slightly informal tone should be used. The transmittal should not dive into the report findings except in the broadest terms.

Exhibit 16.2 presents a sample letter of transmittal. Note that the opening paragraph releases the report and briefly identifies the factors of authorization. The letter comments generally on findings and matters of interest regarding the research. The closing section expresses the writer's personal interest in the project just completed and in doing additional, related work.

EXHIBIT 16.2
Sample Letter of Transmittal

```
                SOFTPROOF LEATHER PRODUCTS COMPANY, INC.
                            KENT, OHIO 44240


                              December 1, 20XX


        Mr. Carl M. Wheeler
        Vice President for Marketing
        Home Office

        Subject:  Presentation of Report on Study of Small-Volume Customers

        Dear Mr. Wheeler:

        Here is my report on the study of small-volume customers.  This report, the
        subject of our conference today, was prepared according to your authorization
        memorandum dated April 21, 20XX.

        As we suspected would be the case when we started the study, the report
        recommends that we take a very careful new look at our present attitude toward
        serving customers whose volumes are less than $20,000 per year.  Some of the
        experienced salespeople whom we contacted in personal interviews gave us some
        excellent suggestions about what our new attitude should be.

        The returns from our mail survey of small-volume customers were not as high
        as we wanted them to be.  We do believe, though, that the questionnaires
        returned are representative of the customers involved in the study.  The
        follow-up survey of a sample of customers who did not return the first
        questionnaire was most reassuring on this point.

        As is perhaps typical of a research department, we discovered during this
        study another problem area which might bear investigation.  This area is
        that of redefining the boundaries of our sales territories.  We are now doing
        some preliminary thinking about this problem.  Should we decide research is
        warranted, we later will make our recommendations to you.

        We are grateful to you, Mr. Wheeler, for your cooperation in this important
        study.  Your keeping the president informally up to date on our progress
        should pave the way toward his accepting the recommendations made in the
        report.

                            Sincerely,

                            Harold M. Johnson

                            Harold M. Johnson
        Approved:           Associate Analyst
        December 1, 20XX    Sales Analysis Section


        T. T. Landham
        Director and Senior Analyst
        Sales Analysis Section
```

Source: Adapted from David M. Robinson, *Writing Reports for Management Decisions* (Columbus, OH: Merrill, 1969), p. 340. Reprinted with permission.

LETTER OF AUTHORIZATION

The *letter of authorization* is a letter to the researcher that approves the project, details who has responsibility for it, and describes the resources available to support it. Because the researcher would not write this letter personally, writing guidelines will not be discussed here. In many situations, simply referring to the authorization in the letter of transmittal is sufficient. If so, the letter of authorization need not be included in the report. In some cases, though, the reader may be unfamiliar with the authorization or may need detailed information about it. In such cases, the report should include this letter, preferably an exact copy of the original.

THE TABLE OF CONTENTS

A *table of contents* is essential to any report more than a few pages long. It should list the divisions and subdivisions of the report with page references. The table of contents is based on the final outline of the report, but it should include only the first-level subdivisions. For short reports it is sufficient to include only the main divisions. If the report includes many figures or tables, a list of these should immediately follow the table of contents.

THE SUMMARY

The *summary,* also known as executive summary, briefly explains why the research project was conducted, what aspects of the problem were considered, what the outcome was, and what should be done. It is a vital part of the report. Studies have indicated that nearly all managers read a report's summary, while only a minority read the rest of the report. Thus, the writer's only chance to produce an impact may be in the summary.

The summary should be written only after the rest of the report has been completed. It represents the essence of the report. It should be one page long (or, at most, two pages), so the writer must carefully sort out what is important enough to be included in it. Several pages of the full report may have to be condensed into one summarizing sentence. Some parts of the report may be condensed more than others; the number of words in the summary need not be in proportion to the length of the section being discussed. The summary should be written to be self-sufficient. In fact, the summary is often detached from the report and circulated by itself.

The summary contains four elements. First, it states the objectives of the report, including the most important background information and the specific purposes of the project. Second, it presents the methodology and the major results. Next come the conclusions. These are opinions based on the results and constitute an interpretation of the results. Finally come recommendations, or suggestions for action, based on the conclusions. In many cases, managers prefer not to have recommendations included in the report or summary. Whether or not recommendations are to be included should be clear from the particular context of the report.

THE BODY

Introduction section
The part of the body of a research report that discusses background information and the specific objectives of the research.

The *body* constitutes the bulk of the report. It begins with an **introduction section** setting out the background factors that made the project necessary as well as the objectives of the report. It continues with discussions of the methodology, results, and limitations of the study and finishes with conclusions and recommendations based on the results.

The introduction explains why the project was done and what it aimed to discover. It should include the basic authorization and submittal data. The relevant background comes next. Enough background should be included to explain why the project was worth doing, but unessential historical factors should be omitted. The question of how much is enough should be answered by referring to the needs of the audience. A government report that will be widely circulated requires more background than a company's internal report on customer satisfaction. The last part of the introduction explains exactly what the project tried to discover. It discusses the statement of the problem and research questions as they were stated in the research proposal. Each purpose presented here should have a corresponding entry in the results section later in the report.

Research methodology section
The part of the body of a report that presents the findings of the project. It includes tables, charts, and an organized narrative.

The second part of the body is the **research methodology section.** This part is a challenge to write because it must explain technical procedures in a manner appropriate for the audience. The material in this section may be supplemented with more detailed explanations in the appendix or a glossary of technical terms. This part of the report should address four topics:

1. *Research design.* Was the study exploratory, descriptive, or causal? Did the data come from primary or secondary sources? Were results collected by survey, observation, or experiment? A copy of the survey questionnaire or observation form should be included in the appendix. Why was this particular design suited to the study?
2. *Sample design.* What was the target population? What sampling frame was used? What sample units were used? How were they selected? How large was the sample? What was the response rate? Detailed computations to support these explanations should be saved for the appendix.
3. *Data collection and fieldwork.* How many and what types of fieldworkers were used? What training and supervision did they receive? Was the work verified? This section is important for establishing the degree of accuracy of the results.
4. *Analysis.* This section should outline the general statistical methods used in the study, but the information presented here should not overlap with what is presented in the results section.

Results section
The part of the body of a report that presents the findings of the project. It includes tables, charts, and an organized narrative.

The **results section** should make up the bulk of the report and should present, in some logical order, those findings of the project that bear on the objectives. The results should be organized as a continuous narrative, designed to be convincing but not to oversell the project. Summary tables and charts should be used to aid the discussion. These may serve as points of reference to the data being discussed and free the prose from excessive facts and figures. Comprehensive or detailed charts, however, should be saved for the appendix.

Because no research is perfect, its limitations should be indicated. If problems arose with nonresponse error or sampling procedures, these should be discussed. However, the discussion of limitations should avoid overemphasizing the weaknesses; its aim should be to provide a realistic basis for assessing the results.

The last part of the body is the **conclusions and recommendations section**. As mentioned earlier, conclusions are opinions based on the results, and recommendations are suggestions for action. The conclusions and recommendations should be presented in this section in more detail than in the summary, and the text should include justification as needed.

Conclusions and recommendations section
The part of the body of a report that provides opinions based on the results and suggestions for action.

THE APPENDIX

The *appendix* presents the "too . . . " material. Any material that is too technical or too detailed to go in the body should appear in the appendix. This includes materials of interest only to some readers or subsidiary materials not directly related to the objectives. Some examples of appendix materials are data collection forms, detailed calculations, discussions of highly technical questions, detailed or comprehensive tables of results, and a bibliography (if appropriate). Since the advent of company Intranets, much appendix material is posted on internal web pages.

The Oral Presentation

The conclusions and recommendations of most research reports are presented orally as well as in writing. The purpose of an **oral presentation** is to highlight the most important findings of a research project and provide clients or line managers with an opportunity to ask questions. The oral presentation may be as simple as a short video conference with a manager at the client organization's location or as formal as a report to the company board of directors.

In either situation, the key to effective presentation is preparation. Communication specialists often suggest that a person preparing an oral presentation begin at the end.[3] In other words, while preparing a presentation, a researcher should think about what he or she wants the client to know when it has been completed. The researcher should select the three or four most important findings for emphasis and rely on the written report for a full summary. The researcher also needs to be ready to defend the results of the research. This is not the same as being defensive; instead, the researcher should be prepared to deal in a confident, competent manner with the questions that arise. Remember that even the most reliable and valid research project is worthless if the managers who must act on its results are not convinced of its importance.

As with written reports, a key to effective oral presentation is adapting to the audience. Delivering an hour-long formal speech when a ten-minute discussion is called for (or vice versa) will reflect poorly on both the presenter and the report.

Lecturing or reading to the audience is sure to impede communication at any level of formality. The presenter should refrain from reading prepared text word for word. By relying on brief notes, familiarity with the subject, and as much rehearsal as the occasion calls for, the presenter will foster better communication. He or she should avoid research jargon and use short, familiar words. The presenter should maintain eye contact with the audience and repeat the main points. Because the audience cannot go back and replay what the speaker has said, an oral presentation often is organized around a standard format: "Tell them what you are going to tell them, tell them, and tell them what you just told them."

Graphic and other visual aids can be as useful in an oral presentation as in a written one. Presenters can choose from a variety of media. Slides, overhead-projector acetates, and on-screen computer-generated graphics are useful for larger audiences. For smaller audiences, the researcher may put the visual aids on posters or flip charts. Another possibility is to make copies of the charts for each participant, possibly as a supplement to one of the other forms of presentation.

Whatever medium is chosen, each visual aid should be designed to convey a simple, attention-getting message that supports a point on which the audience should focus its thinking. As they do

Oral presentation
A spoken summary of the major findings, conclusions, and recommendations, given to clients or line managers to provide them with the opportunity to clarify any ambiguous issues by asking questions.

RESEARCHSNAPSHOT

Noah's Law of Slide Presentations

During oral presentations of research reports, many presenters use slides that viewers in the back row cannot read. In fact, some presenters use slides that viewers in the front row cannot read.

All viewers would be much happier if all presenters were to follow Noah's Law of Slide Presentations. Noah's Law says, Never, ever, under any circumstances whatsoever, put more than forty words on a single slide. A number counts as a word. Noah's Law is called Noah's Law because when God made it rain for forty days and forty nights, He flooded the whole world, and no presenter should attempt that with one overhead.

Note that, in Noah's Law, forty is the absolute upper limit. Twenty is a good average. Seven is even better. If seven words look lonely, presenters can always MAKE THE LETTERS BIGGER.

Advertising legendary David Ogilvy was a devout follower of Noah's Law. He thought so highly of it that he invented and enforced Ogilvy's Corollary. Ogilvy's Corollary says, Never put anything on a slide that you don't intend to read out loud to your audience word for word. He reasoned that when one message comes in on the visual channel while another comes in on the auditory channel, the audience will probably neglect one message or the other.

©DAVID YOUNG-WOLFF/PHOTOEDIT

Source: Adapted with permission from William D. Wells, University of Minnesota, "Noah's Law of Overhead Transparencies," ACR Newsletter, June 1993, p. 10. Published by the Association for Consumer Research, Peter Bloch, 222 Middlebush Hall, University of Missouri, Columbia, MO 65211.

in written presentations, presenters should interpret graphics for the audience. The best slides are easy to read and interpret. Large typeface, multiple colors, bullets that highlight, and other artistic devices can enhance the readability of charts.

Using gestures during presentations also can help convey the message and make presentations more interesting. Here are some tips on how to gesture:[4]

- Open up your arms to embrace your audience. Keep your arms between your waist and shoulders.
- Drop your arms to your sides when not using them.
- Avoid quick and jerky gestures, which make you appear nervous. Hold gestures longer than you would in normal conversation.
- Vary gestures. Switch from hand to hand and at other times use both hands or no hands.
- Don't overuse gestures.

Some gestures are used to draw attention to points illustrated by visual aids. For these, gesturing with an open hand can seem more friendly and can even release tension related to nervousness. In contrast, a nervous speaker who uses a laser pointer may distract the audience as the pointer jumps around in the speaker's shaky hand.[5]

Reports on the Internet

Many clients want numerous employees to have access to research findings. One easy way to share data is to make executive summaries and reports available on a company Intranet. In addition, a company can use information technology on the Internet to design questionnaires, administer surveys, analyze data, and share the results in a presentation-ready format. Real-time data capture allows for beginning-to-end reporting. A number of companies offer fully web-based research management systems—for example, WebSurveyor's online solution for capturing and reporting research findings.

The Research Follow-Up

Research reports and oral presentations should communicate research findings so that managers can make business decisions. In many cases, the manager who receives the research report is unable to interpret the information and draw conclusions relevant to managerial decisions. For this reason,

RESEARCHSNAPSHOT

Online Reports: Easy to Get, Easy to Ignore

A variety of commercially available computer programs provide detailed data on website usage. Among these titles are ClickTracks Analytics, Fireclick, Sane Solutions, Urchin, WebSideStore, Web-trafficIQ, and WebTrends. These programs can gather details and generate reports about the behavior of various customer segments who visit a website (for example, new visitors, returning visitors, and subscribers to the company's e-mail newsletter). Behaviors that can be tracked include the links that visitors click on, the purchases they make, and the amount of time they spend at the website.

With reports so easy to obtain whenever they are needed or as frequently as every day, marketers can quickly accumulate mounds of data. But what do they do with the reports? Ideally, someone should be analyzing the reports and acting on the information. However, when reporters for *Network Computing*

recently asked two hundred web administrators about their use of web analytics software, the responses indicated a widespread lack of follow-up. Almost all the administrators used the software, but not a single one could think of a change they had made to their websites in response to information they obtained from the resulting reports.

Source: Based on Jeffrey Rubin and Ravind Budhiraja, "Intelligence Services," Network Computing, July 7, 2005, downloaded from Business & Company Resource Center, http://galenet.galegroup.com; Joshua Kaufman, "Practical Usability Testing," Digital Web, February 13, 2006, http://www.digital-web.com, accessed April 2, 2006.

©DAVID YOUNG-WOLFF/PHOTOEDIT

effective researchers do not treat the report as the end of the research process. They conduct a **research follow-up**, in which they recontact decision makers and/or clients after the latter have had a chance to read over the report. The purpose is to determine whether the researchers need to provide additional information or clarify issues of concern to management. Just as marketing research may help an organization learn about its customers' satisfaction, the research follow-up can help marketing research staffers ensure the satisfaction of their customers, marketing managers.

Research follow-up
Recontacting decision makers and/or clients after they have had a chance to read over a research report in order to determine whether additional information or clarification is necessary.

Summary

1. Discuss the research report from the perspective of the communications process. A research report is an oral or written presentation of research findings directed to a specific audience to accomplish a particular purpose. Report preparation is the final stage of the research project. It is important because the project can guide management decisions only if it is effectively communicated. The theory of communications emphasizes that the writer (communicator) must tailor the report (message) so that it will be understood by the manager (audience), who has a different field of experience.

2. Define the parts of a research report following a standard format. The consensus is that the format for a research report should include certain prefatory parts, the body of the report, and appended parts. The report format should be varied to suit the level of formality of the particular situation. The prefatory parts of a formal report include a title page, letters of transmittal and authorization, a table of contents, and a summary. The summary is the part of a report most often read and should include a brief statement of the objectives, results, conclusions, and (depending on the research situation) recommendations. The report body includes an introduction that gives the background and objectives, a statement of methodology, and a discussion of the results, their limitations, and appropriate conclusions and recommendations. The appendix includes various materials too specialized to appear in the body of the report.

3. Describe how to give an effective oral presentation. Most research projects are reported on orally as well as in writing, so the researcher needs to prepare an oral presentation. The presentation should defend the results without being defensive. The presentation must be tailored to the situation and the audience. The presenter should practice delivering the presentation in a natural way, without reading to the audience. Graphic aids are useful supplements when they are simple and easy to read. Gestures also add interest and emphasis.

4. Discuss the importance of Internet reporting and research follow-up. Posting a summary of results online gives clients ready access to that information. Some online survey software processes the data and displays results in a presentation-ready format. In the follow-up stage of a research project, the researchers recontact decision makers after submitting the report. This helps the researchers determine whether they need to provide further information or clarify any issues of concern to management.

Key Terms and Concepts

Communication process
Research report
Report format

Introduction section
Research methodology section
Results section

Conclusions and recommendations section
Oral presentation
Research follow-up

Questions for Review and Critical Thinking

1. Why is it important to think of the research report from a communications perspective?
2. As a manager, what degree of formality would you want from your research department?
3. What rules should be followed when preparing slides for computer-generated presentations?

4. **ETHICS** What ethical concerns arise when you prepare (or read) a report?
5. Go to your library and find some research reports. How do they meet the standards set forth in this chapter?
6. How does the oral presentation of research differ from the written research report?

Research Activity

1. **'NET** Go to the Business & Company Resource Center, which you can access through the publisher of this text (see www.thomsonedu.com/marketing/zikmund). Put "Starbucks" or "McDonald's" in the company search engine. Look at the news

and articles for that company. Limit the search by using the word "report." Find one of the articles that actually presents some research reports, such as consumer reactions to a new product. Evaluate the format of the online research report.

Case 16.1 Annenberg Public Policy Center

A recent study by the Annenberg Public Policy Center investigated one major area of marketing decisions: pricing practices.[6] Specifically, the study addressed consumer knowledge and attitudes about the practice of online retailers adjusting their prices according to customer characteristics, such as how frequently they buy from the retailer. For example, a website selling cameras charged different prices for the same model depending on whether the visitor to the site had previously visited sites that supply price comparisons. In general, charging different prices is called price discrimination and is legal unless it discriminates by race or sex or involves antitrust or price-fixing laws (such as two competitors agreeing to charge certain prices).

The Annenberg study consisted of telephone interviews conducted with a sample of 1,500 adults, screened to find persons who had used the Internet in the preceding thirty days. The questionnaire gathered demographic data and data about Internet usage. In addition, the interviewer read seventeen statements about

basic laws and practices related to price discrimination and the targeting of consumers according to their shopping behaviors. Respondents were asked whether each of these statements was true or false. Case Exhibits 16.1–1 through 16.1–4 summarize some of the results from this study.

Questions

1. The information provided here is not detailed enough for a formal report, but assume that you are making an informal report in a preliminary stage of the reporting process. Which of these findings do you want to emphasize as your main points? Why?
2. Prepare a written summary of the findings, using at least two types of tables or charts you learned about in Chapter 14.
3. Prepare two tables or charts that would be suitable to accompany an oral presentation of these results. Are they different from the visual aids you prepared for question 2? Why or why not?

CASE EXHIBIT 16.1-1 Selected Information about the Sample

Sex

Male	48%
Female	52%

Online Connection at Home

Dial-up connection only	31%
Cable modem (with/without dial-up)	18%
DSL (with/without dial-up)	25%
Cable or DSL with another method	13%
Don't know	4%
No connection at home	9%

Self-Ranked Expertise Navigating the Internet

Beginner	14%
Intermediate	40%
Advanced	34%
Expert	12%

Source: Joseph Turow, Lauren Feldman, and Kimberly Meltzer, "Open to Exploitation: American Shoppers Online and Offline," APPC report, June 2005, p. 15, downloaded at http://www.annenbergpublicpolicycenter.org.

CASE EXHIBIT 16.1-2 Responses to Selected Knowledge Questions

	Response*		
Statement	True	False	Don't Know
Companies today have the ability to follow my activity across many sites on the web.	**80%**	8%	12%
It is legal for an *online* store to charge different people different prices at the same time of day.	**38%**	29%	33%
By law, a site such as Expedia or Orbitz that compares prices on different airlines must include the lowest airline prices.	37%	**32%**	31%
It is legal for an *offline* store to charge different people different prices at the same time of day.	**29%**	42%	29%
When a website has a privacy policy, it means the site will not share my information with other websites or companies.	59%	**25%**	16%

*When the numbers do not add up to 100%, it is because of a rounding error. **Boldface** type indicates the correct answer.

Source: Joseph Turow, Lauren Feldman, and Kimberly Meltzer, "Open to Exploitation: American Shoppers Online and Offline," APPC report, June 2005, p. 20, downloaded at http://www.annenbergpublicpolicycenter.org. Accessed April 5, 2006.

CASE EXHIBIT 16.1-3 Responses to Selected Attitude Questions

	Response*			
Statement	Agree	Disagree	Neutral	Don't Know
It's okay if a store charges me a price based on what it knows about me.	8%	91%	—	1%
It's okay if an *online* store I use charges different people different prices for the same products during the same hour.	11%	87%	1%	1%
It would bother me to learn that other people pay less than I do for the same products.	76%	22%	1%	1%
It would bother me if websites I shop at keep detailed records of my buying behavior.	57%	41%	2%	1%
It's okay if a store I shop at frequently uses information it has about me to create a picture of me that improves the services it provides for me.	50%	47%	2%	1%

*When the numbers do not add up to 100%, it is because of a rounding error.

Source: Joseph Turow, Lauren Feldman, and Kimberly Meltzer, "Open to Exploitation: American Shoppers Online and Offline," APPC report, June 2005, p. 22, downloaded at http://www.annenbergpublicpolicycenter.org. Accessed April 7, 2006.

CASE EXHIBIT 16.1-4 Predicting Knowledge Score from Selected Demographics

	Unstandardized Regression Coefficient (B)	Standardized Regression Coefficient (β)
Education	0.630*	0.200
Income	0.383*	0.150
Self-perceived ability to navigate Internet	0.616*	0.149
Constant	2.687	
R^2	0.148	

*Significance <0.001 level.

Source: Joseph Turow, Lauren Feldman, and Kimberly Meltzer, "Open to Exploitation: American Shoppers Online and Offline," APPC report, June 2005, p. 29, downloaded at http://www.annenbergpublicpolicycenter.org. Accessed April 6, 2006.

Part 6
Comprehensive Cases with Computerized Databases

©MARK HARWOOD/ICONICA/GETTY IMAGES

CASE 1
Say It Ain't So! Is This the Real Thing?

CASE 2
TABH, INC., Automotive Consulting

COMPREHENSIVE CASES

Case 1: Say It Ain't So! Is This the Real Thing?

INTRODUCTION

David Ortega is the lead researcher for an upscale restaurant group hoping to add another chain that would compete directly with the upscale Smith and Wollensky restaurants (http://www.smithandwollensky.com). The average check for a customer at Smith and Wollensky is approximately $80 to $90.[1] Whenever a new venture of this type is planned, one has to wonder whether there are enough customers willing to pay premium prices given the large number of lesser priced alternatives. In fact, Smith and Wollensky is considering opening a lesser priced "Grill" that would be positioned so that the average customer check would be about half that of the original. What is it that people are willing to pay for and what sacrifices can be made to deliver a satisfying if not luxurious experience? How can he create a unique experience at a lower price? These are the questions facing David Ortega.

RESEARCH APPROACH

After considering how to study the issue, David decides a qualitative research approach will be useful. He hopes to develop a deep understanding of how the fine dining experience offers value—and perhaps some insights into what intangibles create value for consumers in general. After considering the different options, he decides on a phenomenological approach. The primary tool of investigation is conversational interviewing. David plans to enter into casual conversations with businesspeople in the lounge of the downtown Ritz Carlton. He begins the conversation by commenting on the wine he is sipping—something like, "It isn't bad, but it's hard to believe they get $14 for a glass of this stuff."

RESULTS

Two weeks later, David has conducted "conversations" with five consumers. He found them very willing and free to talk about the things they indulge in. He develops a field log of notes from the consumers' comments. The notes are recorded verbatim.[2] The following field notes are highlighted:

Respondent	Date/Time	Text
Joe, wm, 55, attorney	12/5/06 – 10:15 PM	Well, wine doesn't have to be expensive to be good. Beyond some basic price point . . . maybe $12 a bottle . . . I find a lot of good wines. But the wine has to fit the situation. It has to add something. A fake Rolex will tell time; but a real Rolex tells you about you. I don't mind paying for something that's unique—even though it might not be my cup of tea. Chateau Masur is like that. It's from Lebanon! It isn't always elegant or delicious, but it is always real. You always know it comes from some place very unique and is made under the most trying circumstances.

(continued)

[1] MacNealy, Jeremy (2006), "Smith and Wollensky on the Grill," The Motley Fool, http://www.fool.com/News/mft/2006/mft06040425.htm, accessed April 28, 2006.
[2] For more comments along this same line, see Beverland, M. (2006), "The Real Thing: Branding Authenticity in the Luxury Wine Trade," Journal of Business Research, 59 (Feb), 251–258; Beverland, M. (2005), "Crafting Brand Authenticity: The Case of Luxury Wines," Journal of Management Studies, 42 (July), 103–129; and Wolff, C. (2005), "Blending High Style and Authenticity," Lodging Hospitality, 61 (11/1), 72–76.

Respondent	Date/Time	Text	(continued)
Sally, hf, 45, medical sales	12/7/06 – 5:45 PM	We pay too much for a lot of stuff though. I like things to be genuine. When you ask for crab you get crab—not Krab with a "K." It's made of fish, you know!	
		. . .	
		I love old neighborhood Italian restaurants. They aren't always expensive. But they have character. I think that it is very easy to spoil. I might not want a checkered red and white table cloth at home, but the Italian restaurant has to have one. I have to smell the garlic from the parking lot. And, that cheap Chianti, the kind with the basket cradle—it had better be from Italy—it tastes sooo good there. You know, you could pay more, but a nice dinner there with a couple of friends is worth a lot.	
		You know, the people who make great wine or who have great restaurants kind of luck into it. I don't think they really ever sent out a survey asking what the restaurant or the wine should be like. I think they said I am going to make this the way that I want it to be . . . and it just happens to be right! They are so committed to the product that it works—no matter the price. But commitment like that costs a little more usually—although they aren't in it for the money.	
Hebert, wm, 40, oil executive	12/8/06 – 11:00 PM	How old is it? The older it is, the more it is worth—yeah! I like this French wine that has "depuis 1574," maybe its name is Hugel (trying to recall). Imagine the same family running that company for hundreds of years. I like to think about the family in the vineyards—the old man on a tractor with his sons running around the sides. Their kids are hanging around the barn.	
		. . .	
		You know, you can buy cheap things and get cheated too. We are free to be cheated at any price point! (laughter) I remember bringing home a bottle of "Louisiana Hot Sauce." Man, that stuff didn't have any heat to it at all. When I looked at the bottle, do you know where it was from? . . . Man, it was from Tennessee . . . can you believe that, Louisiana Hot Sauce from Tennessee!! What a scam.	
		. . . .	
		When I buy something nice, I want it to be real. Burgundy should be from Burgundy. Bordeaux should be from Bordeaux. Champagne should be from Champagne—not Texas or California! (laughter) Because I know in Champagne, they know how to make Champagne—sparkling wine. They have perfected the methods over hundreds of years. A good glass of Champagne is worth what you pay!	
Angela, bf, 60, insurance executive	12/9/06 – 6:45 PM	Look at this hotel . . . when you just look at the price you think "this is crazy!" But look at the attention to detail. Cleaning the floor is a production. Have you noticed the way they turn down your bed? Taking care of the plants is serious business to these people. I've stayed at a place like this in Florida—I loved it. At first, I couldn't put my finger on it. Then it hit me. The place smelled like Florida. They have a way of giving everything the smell of sweet grass and citrus. It's terrific. Another one in California smelled of sandalwood and cypress. You have to be willing to pay more for people that care so much about what they do. Maybe that's your wine? Those smells make me think of those special places. When I drink a wine, I think about where it comes from too.	
Burt, wm, 35, sales	12/9/06 – 9:30 PM	It's okay for something to be cheap . . . even fake! As long as I know it's fake. I've got three fake Rolexes. This one looks pretty good . . . looks genuine . . . but look at the way the second hand moves . . . it's jumping. A real one wouldn't do that!!	
		I ate with this guy the other night who sent back a bottle of wine after ordering it. When the waiter pulled the cork, it didn't have Domaine Mas Blanc written on it—that's the name of the wine. He said, "How do I know it is real?" You know, he was right. When you spend $80 for a bottle, you want the real stuff. But, if you spend $10 for a bottle of wine in a restaurant, who the hell cares?	

RESULTS

David decides to use a word count to try to identify the main themes. Hopefully, these themes can help clarify the business problem. Perhaps if the information can't answer the questions above, it will point him in the right direction. Whatever the case, David feels the project has helped him better understand the total value proposition offered by restaurants, wines, hotels, and other products.

Questions:

1. Comment on the research approach. Do you feel it was an appropriate choice?

2. **ETHICS** David did not inform these respondents that he was doing marketing research during these conversations. Why do you think he withheld this information and was appropriate to do so?

3. **'NET** Using the Internet, try to identify at least three restaurants that Smith and Wollensky competes with and three with whom the new S&W Grill may compete.

4. Try to interpret the discussions above. You may use one of the approaches discussed in the text. What themes should be coded? What themes occur most frequently? Can the different themes be linked together to form a unit of meaning?

5. What is the result of this research? What should David report back to the restaurant group?

Case 2: TABH, INC., Automotive Consulting

(Download the data sets for this case from http://www. thomsonedu.com/marketing/zikmund or request them from your instructor.) TABH consulting specializes in research for automobile dealers in the United States, Canada, Mexico, and Europe. Although much of their work is done on a pay-for fee basis with customers such as dealerships and dealership networks selling all major makes of automobiles, they also produce a monthly "white paper" that is sold via their website. This off-the-shelf research is purchased by other research firms and by companies within the auto industry itself. This month, they would like to produce a white paper analyzing the viability of college students attending schools located in small college towns as a potentially underserved market segment.

TABH management assigns a junior analyst named Michel Gonzalez to the project. Lacking time for a more comprehensive study, Michel decides to contact the traffic department at Cal Poly University in Pomona, California, and at Central Missouri State University in Warrensburg, Missouri. Michel wishes to obtain data from the students' automobile parking registration records. Although both schools are willing to provide anonymous data records for a limited number of students, Cal Poly offers Michel a chance to visit during the registration period, which just happens to be next week. As a result, not only can Michel get data from students' registration forms, but a small amount of primary data can be obtained by intercepting students near the registration window. In return, Michel is asked to purchase a booth at the Cal Poly career fair.

As a result, Michel obtains some basic information from students. The information results in a small data set consisting of the follow observations for 100 undergraduate college students in Pomona, California:

Variable	Description
Sex	Student's sex dummy coded with 1 = female and 0 = male
Color	Color of a student's car as listed on his or her registration form
Major	Student's major field of study (Business, Liberal Arts (LA), or Engineering (ENG))
Grade	Student's grade record reported as the mode (A, B, or C)
Finance	Whether the student financed the car he or she is driving or paid for it with cash coded 0 = cash payment and 1 = financed
Residence	Whether the student lives on campus or commutes to school coded 0 = commute and 1 = on campus
Animal	Michel asks each student to quickly draw a cartoon about the type of car they would like to purchase. Students are told to depict the car as an animal in the cartoon. Although Michel expects to interpret these cartoons more deeply when time allows, the initial coding specifies what type of animal was drawn by each respondent. When Michel was unsure of what animal was drawn, a second researcher was conferred with to determine what animal was depicted. Some students depicted the car as a dog, some as a cat, and some as a mule.

The purpose of the white paper is to offer car dealers considering new locations a comparison of the profile of a small town university with the primary market segments for their particular automobile. For instance, a company specializing in small pickup trucks appeals to a different market segment than does a company specializing in two-door economy sedans. Many small towns currently do not have dealerships, particularly beyond the "big 3." Although TABH cannot predict with certainty who may purchase the white paper, it particularly wants to appeal to companies with high sales growth in the United States, such as Kia (http://www.kia.com), Hyundai (http://www.hyundai.com), and potentially European auto dealerships currently without significant U.S. distribution, such as Smart (http://www.smart.com), among others. TABH also hopes the white paper may eventually lead to a customized project for one of these companies. Thus, the general research question is

What are the automobile market segment characteristics of students attending U.S. universities in small towns?

This question can be broken down into a series of more specific questions:

- What segments can be identified based on identifiable characteristics of students?

- How do different segments view a car?
- What types of automobiles would be most in demand?

Questions:

1. What types of tests can be performed using the data that may at least indirectly address the primary research question?
2. What do you think the primary conclusions of the white paper will be based on the data provided?
3. Assuming a small college town lacked an auto dealership (beyond Ford, GM, and Chrysler), what two companies should be most interested in this type of location? Use the Internet if necessary to perform some cursory research on different car companies.
4. What are the weaknesses in basing decisions on this type of research?
5. Are there key issues that may diminish the usefulness of this research?
6. What kinds of themes might emerge from the cartoon drawings?
7. Are there any ethical dilemmas presented in this case?

APPENDIX

APPENDIX

Statistical Tables

TABLE A.I **Random Digits**

37751	04998	66038	63480	98442	22245	83538	62351	74514	90497
50915	64152	82981	15796	27102	71635	34470	13608	26360	76285
99142	35021	01032	57907	80545	54112	15150	36856	03247	40392
70720	10033	25191	62358	03784	74377	88150	25567	87457	49512
18460	64947	32958	08752	96366	89092	23597	74308	00881	88976
65763	41133	60950	35372	06782	81451	78764	52645	19841	50083
83769	52570	60133	25211	87384	90182	84990	26400	39128	97043
58900	78420	98579	33665	10718	39342	46346	14401	13503	46525
54746	71115	78219	64314	11227	41702	54517	87676	14078	45317
56819	27340	07200	52663	57864	85159	15460	97564	29637	27742
34990	62122	38223	28526	37006	22774	46026	15981	87291	56946
02269	22795	87593	81830	95383	67823	20196	54850	46779	64519
43042	53600	45738	00261	31100	67239	02004	70698	53597	62617
92565	12211	06868	87786	59576	61382	33972	13161	47208	96604
67424	32620	60841	86848	85000	04835	48576	33884	10101	84129
04015	77148	09535	10743	97871	55919	45274	38304	93125	91847
85226	19763	46105	25289	26714	73253	85922	21785	42624	92741
03360	07457	75131	41209	50451	23472	07438	08375	29312	62264
72460	99682	27970	25632	34096	17656	12736	27476	21938	67305
66960	55780	71778	52629	51692	71442	36130	70425	39874	62035
14824	95631	00697	65462	24815	13930	02938	54619	28909	53950
34001	05618	41900	23303	19928	60755	61404	56947	91441	19299
77718	83830	29781	72917	10840	74182	08293	62588	99625	22088
60930	05091	35726	07414	49211	69586	20226	08274	28167	65279
94180	62151	08112	26646	07617	42954	22521	09395	43561	45692
81073	85543	47650	93830	07377	87995	35084	39386	93141	88309
18467	39689	60801	46828	38670	88243	89042	78452	08032	72566
60643	59399	79740	17295	50094	66436	92677	68345	24025	36489
73372	61697	85728	90779	13235	83114	70728	32093	74306	08325
18395	18482	83245	54942	51905	09534	70839	91073	42193	81199
07261	28720	71244	05064	84873	68020	39037	68981	00670	86291
61679	81529	83725	33269	45958	74265	87460	60525	42539	25605
11815	48679	00556	96871	39835	83055	84949	11681	51687	55896
99007	35050	86440	44280	20320	97527	28138	01088	49037	85430
06446	65608	79291	16624	06135	30622	56133	33998	32308	29434

A Million Random Digits with 100,000 Normal Deviates. Copyright 1955 by Rand Corporation. Reproduced with permission of Rand Corporation in the format Textbook via Copyright Clearance Center.

TABLE A.2 Area under the Normal Curve

z	.00	.01	.02	.03	.04	.05	.06	.07	.08	.09
0.0	.0000	.0040	.0080	.0120	.0160	.0199	.0239	.0279	.0319	.0359
0.1	.0398	.0438	.0478	.0517	.0557	.0596	.0636	.0675	.0714	.0753
0.2	.0793	.0832	.0871	.0910	.0948	.0987	.1026	.1064	.1103	.1141
0.3	.1179	.1217	.1255	.1293	.1331	.1368	.1406	.1443	.1480	.1517
0.4	.1554	.1591	.1628	.1664	.1700	.1736	.1772	.1808	.1844	.1879
0.5	.1915	.1950	.1985	.2019	.2054	.2088	.2123	.2157	.2190	.2224
0.6	.2257	.2291	.2324	.2357	.2389	.2422	.2454	.2486	.2518	.2549
0.7	.2580	.2612	.2642	.2673	.2704	.2734	.2764	.2794	.2823	.2852
0.8	.2881	.2910	.2939	.2967	.2995	.3023	.3051	.3078	.3106	.3133
0.9	.3159	.3186	.3212	.3238	.3264	.3289	.3315	.3340	.3365	.3389
1.0	.3413	.3438	.3461	.3485	.3508	.3531	.3554	.3577	.3599	.3621
1.1	.3643	.3665	.3686	.3708	.3729	.3749	.3770	.3790	.3810	.3830
1.2	.3849	.3869	.3888	.3907	.3925	.3944	.3962	.3980	.3997	.4015
1.3	.4032	.4049	.4066	.4082	.4099	.4115	.4131	.4147	.4162	.4177
1.4	.4192	.4207	.4222	.4236	.4251	.4265	.4279	.4292	.4306	.4319
1.5	.4332	.4345	.4357	.4370	.4382	.4394	.4406	.4418	.4429	.4441
1.6	.4452	.4463	.4474	.4484	.4495	.4505	.4515	.4525	.4535	.4545
1.7	.4554	.4564	.4573	.4582	.4591	.4599	.4608	.4616	.4625	.4633
1.8	.4641	.4649	.4656	.4664	.4671	.4678	.4686	.4693	.4699	.4706
1.9	.4713	.4719	.4726	.4732	.4738	.4744	.4750	.4756	.4761	.4767
2.0	.4772	.4778	.4783	.4788	.4793	.4798	.4803	.4808	.4812	.4817
2.1	.4821	.4826	.4830	.4834	.4838	.4842	.4846	.4850	.4854	.4857
2.2	.4861	.4864	.4868	.4871	.4875	.4878	.4881	.4884	.4887	.4890
2.3	.4893	.4896	.4898	.4901	.4904	.4906	.4909	.4911	.4913	.4916
2.4	.4918	.4920	.4922	.4925	.4927	.4929	.4931	.4932	.4934	.4936
2.5	.4938	.4940	.4941	.4943	.4945	.4946	.4948	.4949	.4951	.4952
2.6	.4953	.4955	.4956	.4957	.4959	.4960	.4961	.4962	.4963	.4964
2.7	.4965	.4966	.4967	.4968	.4969	.4970	.4971	.4972	.4973	.4974
2.8	.4974	.4975	.4976	.4977	.4977	.4978	.4979	.4979	.4980	.4981
2.9	.4981	.4982	.4982	.4983	.4984	.4984	.4985	.4985	.4986	.4986
3.0	.49865	.4987	.4987	.4988	.4988	.4989	.4989	.4989	.4990	.4990
4.0	.49997									

Chaiho Kim, *Statistical Analysis for Induction and Decision.* Copyright © 1973 by The Dryden Press, a division of Holt, Rinehart and Winston, Inc. Reprinted with permission of Holt, Rinehart and Winston.

TABLE A.3 Distribution of *t* for Given Probability Levels

d.f.	Level of Significance for One-Tailed Test					
	.10	.05	.025	.01	.005	.0005
	Level of Significance for Two-Tailed Test					
	.20	.10	.05	.02	.01	.001
1	3.078	6.314	12.706	31.821	63.657	636.619
2	1.886	2.920	4.303	6.965	9.925	31.598
3	1.638	2.353	3.182	4.541	5.841	12.941
4	1.533	2.132	2.776	3.747	4.604	8.610
5	1.476	2.015	2.571	3.365	4.032	6.859
6	1.440	1.943	2.447	3.143	3.707	5.959
7	1.415	1.895	2.365	2.998	3.499	5.405
8	1.397	1.860	2.306	2.896	3.355	5.041
9	1.383	1.833	2.262	2.821	3.250	4.781
10	1.372	1.812	2.228	2.764	3.169	4.587
11	1.363	1.796	2.201	2.718	3.106	4.437
12	1.356	1.782	2.179	2.681	3.055	4.318
13	1.350	1.771	2.160	2.650	3.012	4.221
14	1.345	1.761	2.145	2.624	2.977	4.140
15	1.341	1.753	2.131	2.602	2.947	4.073
16	1.337	1.746	2.120	2.583	2.921	4.015
17	1.333	1.740	2.110	2.567	2.898	3.965
18	1.330	1.734	2.101	2.552	2.878	3.922
19	1.328	1.729	2.093	2.539	2.861	3.883
20	1.325	1.725	2.086	2.528	2.845	3.850
21	1.323	1.721	2.080	2.518	2.831	3.819
22	1.321	1.717	2.074	2.508	2.819	3.792
23	1.319	1.714	2.069	2.500	2.807	3.767
24	1.318	1.711	2.064	2.492	2.797	3.745
25	1.316	1.708	2.060	2.485	2.787	3.725
26	1.315	1.706	2.056	2.479	2.779	3.707
27	1.314	1.703	2.052	2.473	2.771	3.690
28	1.313	1.701	2.048	2.467	2.763	3.674
29	1.311	1.699	2.045	2.462	2.756	3.659
30	1.310	1.697	2.042	2.457	2.750	3.646
40	1.303	1.684	2.021	2.423	2.704	3.551
60	1.296	1.671	2.000	2.390	2.660	3.460
120	1.289	1.658	1.980	2.358	2.617	3.373
∞	1.282	1.645	1.960	2.326	2.576	3.291

TABLE A.4 **Chi-Square Distribution**

Degrees of Freedom (d.f.)	Area in Shaded Right Tail (α)		
	.10	.05	.01
1	2.706	3.841	6.635
2	4.605	5.991	9.210
3	6.251	7.815	11.345
4	7.779	9.488	13.277
5	9.236	11.070	15.086
6	10.645	12.592	16.812
7	12.017	14.067	18.475
8	13.362	15.507	20.090
9	14.684	16.919	21.666
10	15.987	18.307	23.209
11	17.275	19.675	24.725
12	18.549	21.026	26.217
13	19.812	22.362	27.688
14	21.064	23.685	29.141
15	22.307	24.996	30.578
16	23.542	26.296	32.000
17	24.769	27.587	33.409
18	25.989	28.869	34.805
19	27.204	30.144	36.191
20	28.412	31.410	37.566
21	29.615	32.671	38.932
22	30.813	33.924	40.289
23	32.007	35.172	41.638
24	33.196	36.415	42.980
25	34.382	37.652	44.314
26	35.563	38.885	45.642
27	36.741	40.113	46.963
28	37.916	41.337	48.278
29	39.087	42.557	49.588
30	40.256	43.773	50.892

Example of how to use this table: In a chi-square distribution with 6 degrees of freedom (d.f.), the area to the right of a critical value of 12.592 — i.e., the α area — is .05.

TABLE A.5 **Critical Values of $F_{v_1 v_2}$ for $\alpha = .05$**

v_1 = Degrees of Freedom for Numerator

v_2	1	2	3	4	5	6	7	8	9	10	12	15	20	24	30	40	60	120	∞
1	161	200	216	225	230	234	237	239	241	242	244	246	248	249	250	251	252	253	254
2	18.5	19.0	19.2	19.2	19.3	19.3	19.4	19.4	19.4	19.4	19.4	19.4	19.5	19.5	19.5	19.5	19.5	19.5	19.5
3	10.1	9.55	9.28	9.12	9.01	8.94	8.89	8.85	8.81	8.79	8.74	8.70	8.66	8.64	8.62	8.59	8.57	8.55	8.53
4	7.71	6.94	6.59	6.39	6.26	6.16	6.09	6.04	6.00	5.96	5.91	5.86	5.80	5.77	5.75	5.72	5.69	5.66	5.63
5	6.61	5.79	5.41	5.19	5.05	4.95	4.88	4.82	4.77	4.74	4.68	4.62	4.56	4.53	4.50	4.46	4.43	4.40	4.37
6	5.99	5.14	4.76	4.53	4.39	4.28	4.21	4.15	4.10	4.06	4.00	3.94	3.87	3.84	3.81	3.77	3.74	3.70	3.67
7	5.59	4.74	4.35	4.12	3.97	3.87	3.79	3.73	3.68	3.64	3.57	3.51	3.44	3.41	3.38	3.34	3.30	3.27	3.23
8	5.32	4.46	4.07	3.84	3.69	3.58	3.50	3.44	3.39	3.35	3.28	3.22	3.15	3.12	3.08	3.04	3.01	2.97	2.93
9	5.12	4.26	3.86	3.63	3.48	3.37	3.29	3.23	3.18	3.14	3.07	3.01	2.94	2.90	2.86	2.83	2.79	2.75	2.71
10	4.96	4.10	3.71	3.48	3.33	3.22	3.14	3.07	3.02	2.98	2.91	2.85	2.77	2.74	2.70	2.66	2.62	2.58	2.54
11	4.84	3.98	3.59	3.36	3.20	3.09	3.01	2.95	2.90	2.85	2.79	2.72	2.65	2.61	2.57	2.53	2.49	2.45	2.40
12	4.75	3.89	3.49	3.26	3.11	3.00	2.91	2.85	2.80	2.75	2.69	2.62	2.54	2.51	2.47	2.43	2.38	2.34	2.30
13	4.67	3.81	3.41	3.18	3.03	2.92	2.83	2.77	2.71	2.67	2.60	2.53	2.46	2.42	2.38	2.34	2.30	2.25	2.21
14	4.60	3.74	3.34	3.11	2.96	2.85	2.76	2.70	2.65	2.60	2.53	2.46	2.39	2.35	2.31	2.27	2.22	2.18	2.13
15	4.54	3.68	3.29	3.06	2.90	2.79	2.71	2.64	2.59	2.54	2.48	2.40	2.33	2.29	2.25	2.20	2.16	2.11	2.07
16	4.49	3.63	3.24	3.01	2.85	2.74	2.66	2.59	2.54	2.49	2.42	2.35	2.28	2.24	2.19	2.15	2.11	2.06	2.01
17	4.45	3.59	3.20	2.96	2.81	2.70	2.61	2.55	2.49	2.45	2.38	2.31	2.23	2.19	2.15	2.10	2.06	2.01	1.96
18	4.41	3.55	3.16	2.93	2.77	2.66	2.58	2.51	2.46	2.41	2.34	2.27	2.19	2.15	2.11	2.06	2.02	1.97	1.92
19	4.38	3.52	3.13	2.90	2.74	2.63	2.54	2.48	2.42	2.38	2.31	2.23	2.16	2.11	2.07	2.03	1.98	1.93	1.88
20	4.35	3.49	3.10	2.87	2.71	2.60	2.51	2.45	2.39	2.35	2.28	2.20	2.12	2.08	2.04	1.99	1.95	1.90	1.84
21	4.32	3.47	3.07	2.84	2.68	2.57	2.49	2.42	2.37	2.32	2.25	2.18	2.10	2.05	2.01	1.96	1.92	1.87	1.81
22	4.30	3.44	3.05	2.82	2.66	2.55	2.46	2.40	2.34	2.30	2.23	2.15	2.07	2.03	1.98	1.94	1.89	1.84	1.78
23	4.28	3.42	3.03	2.80	2.64	2.53	2.44	2.37	2.32	2.27	2.20	2.13	2.05	2.01	1.96	1.91	1.86	1.81	1.76
24	4.26	3.40	3.01	2.78	2.62	2.51	2.42	2.36	2.30	2.25	2.18	2.11	2.03	1.98	1.94	1.89	1.84	1.79	1.73
25	4.24	3.39	2.99	2.76	2.60	2.49	2.40	2.34	2.28	2.24	2.16	2.09	2.01	1.96	1.92	1.87	1.82	1.77	1.71
30	4.17	3.32	2.92	2.69	2.53	2.42	2.33	2.27	2.21	2.16	2.09	2.01	1.93	1.89	1.84	1.79	1.74	1.68	1.62
40	4.08	3.23	2.84	2.61	2.45	2.34	2.25	2.18	2.12	2.08	2.00	1.92	1.84	1.79	1.74	1.69	1.64	1.58	1.51
60	4.00	3.15	2.76	2.53	2.37	2.25	2.17	2.10	2.04	1.99	1.92	1.84	1.75	1.70	1.65	1.59	1.53	1.47	1.39
120	3.92	3.07	2.68	2.45	2.29	2.18	2.09	2.02	1.96	1.91	1.83	1.75	1.66	1.61	1.55	1.50	1.43	1.35	1.25
∞	3.84	3.00	2.60	2.37	2.21	2.10	2.01	1.94	1.88	1.83	1.75	1.67	1.57	1.52	1.46	1.39	1.32	1.22	1.00

v_2 = Degrees of Freedom for Denominator

TABLE A.6 Critical Values of F_{v_1,v_2} for $\alpha = .01$

v_1 = Degrees of Freedom for Numerator

v_2	1	2	3	4	5	6	7	8	9	10	12	15	20	24	30	40	60	120	∞
1	4,052	5,000	5,403	5,625	5,764	5,859	5,928	5,982	6,023	6,056	6,106	6,157	6,209	6,235	6,261	6,287	6,313	6,339	6,366
2	98.5	99.0	99.2	99.2	99.3	99.3	99.4	99.4	99.4	99.4	99.4	99.4	99.4	99.5	99.5	99.5	99.5	99.5	99.5
3	34.1	30.8	29.5	28.7	28.2	27.9	27.7	27.5	27.3	27.2	27.1	26.9	26.7	26.6	26.5	26.4	26.3	26.2	26.1
4	21.2	18.0	16.7	16.0	15.5	15.2	15.0	14.8	14.7	14.5	14.4	14.2	14.0	13.9	13.8	13.7	13.7	13.6	13.5
5	16.3	13.3	12.1	11.4	11.0	10.7	10.5	10.3	10.2	10.1	9.89	9.72	9.55	9.47	9.38	9.29	9.20	9.11	9.02
6	13.7	10.9	9.78	9.15	8.75	8.47	8.26	8.10	7.98	7.87	7.72	7.56	7.40	7.31	7.23	7.14	7.06	6.97	6.88
7	12.2	9.55	8.45	7.85	7.46	7.19	6.99	6.84	6.72	6.62	6.47	6.31	6.16	6.07	5.99	5.91	5.82	5.74	5.65
8	11.3	8.65	7.59	7.01	6.63	6.37	6.18	6.03	5.91	5.81	5.67	5.52	5.36	5.28	5.20	5.12	5.03	4.95	4.86
9	10.6	8.02	6.99	6.42	6.06	5.80	5.61	5.47	5.35	5.26	5.11	4.96	4.81	4.73	4.65	4.57	4.48	4.40	4.31
10	10.0	7.56	6.55	5.99	5.64	5.39	5.20	5.06	4.94	4.85	4.71	4.56	4.41	4.33	4.25	4.17	4.08	4.00	3.91
11	9.65	7.21	6.22	5.67	5.32	5.07	4.89	4.74	4.63	4.54	4.40	4.25	4.10	4.02	3.94	3.86	3.78	3.69	3.60
12	9.33	6.93	5.95	5.41	5.06	4.82	4.64	4.50	4.39	4.30	4.16	4.01	3.86	3.78	3.70	3.62	3.54	3.45	3.36
13	9.07	6.70	5.74	5.21	4.86	4.62	4.44	4.30	4.19	4.10	3.96	3.82	3.66	3.59	3.51	3.43	3.34	3.25	3.17
14	8.86	6.51	5.56	5.04	4.70	4.46	4.28	4.14	4.03	3.94	3.80	3.66	3.51	3.43	3.35	3.27	3.18	3.09	3.00
15	8.68	6.36	5.42	4.89	4.56	4.32	4.14	4.00	3.89	3.80	3.67	3.52	3.37	3.29	3.21	3.13	3.05	2.96	2.87
16	8.53	6.23	5.29	4.77	4.44	4.20	4.03	3.89	3.78	3.69	3.55	3.41	3.26	3.18	3.10	3.02	2.93	2.84	2.75
17	8.40	6.11	5.19	4.67	4.34	4.10	3.93	3.79	3.68	3.59	3.46	3.31	3.16	3.08	3.00	2.92	2.83	2.75	2.65
18	8.29	6.01	5.09	4.58	4.25	4.01	3.84	3.71	3.60	3.51	3.37	3.23	3.08	3.00	2.92	2.84	2.75	2.66	2.57
19	8.19	5.93	5.01	4.50	4.17	3.94	3.77	3.63	3.52	3.43	3.30	3.15	3.00	2.92	2.84	2.76	2.67	2.58	2.49
20	8.10	5.85	4.94	4.43	4.10	3.87	3.70	3.56	3.46	3.37	3.23	3.09	2.94	2.86	2.78	2.69	2.61	2.52	2.42
21	8.02	5.78	4.87	4.37	4.04	3.81	3.64	3.51	3.40	3.31	3.17	3.03	2.88	2.80	2.72	2.64	2.55	2.46	2.36
22	7.96	5.72	4.82	4.31	3.99	3.76	3.59	3.45	3.35	3.26	3.12	2.98	2.83	2.75	2.67	2.58	2.50	2.40	2.31
23	7.88	5.66	4.76	4.26	3.94	3.71	3.54	3.41	3.30	3.21	3.07	2.93	2.78	2.70	2.62	2.54	2.45	2.35	2.26
24	7.82	5.61	4.72	4.22	3.90	3.67	3.50	3.36	3.26	3.17	3.03	2.89	2.74	2.66	2.58	2.49	2.40	2.31	2.21
25	7.77	5.57	4.68	4.18	3.86	3.63	3.46	3.32	3.22	3.13	2.99	2.85	2.70	2.62	2.53	2.45	2.36	2.27	2.17
30	7.58	5.39	4.51	4.02	3.70	3.47	3.30	3.17	3.07	2.98	2.84	2.70	2.55	2.47	2.39	2.30	2.21	2.11	2.01
40	7.31	5.18	4.31	3.83	3.51	3.29	3.12	2.99	2.89	2.80	2.66	2.52	2.37	2.29	2.20	2.11	2.02	1.92	1.80
60	7.08	4.98	4.13	3.65	3.34	3.12	2.95	2.82	2.72	2.63	2.50	2.35	2.20	2.12	2.03	1.94	1.84	1.73	1.60
120	6.85	4.79	3.95	3.48	3.17	2.96	2.79	2.66	2.56	2.47	2.34	2.19	2.03	1.95	1.86	1.76	1.66	1.53	1.38
∞	6.63	4.61	3.78	3.32	3.02	2.80	2.64	2.51	2.41	2.32	2.18	2.04	1.88	1.79	1.70	1.59	1.47	1.32	1.00

v_2 = Degrees of Freedom for Denominator

Glossary of FREQUENTLY USED SYMBOLS

Greek Letters

α (alpha)	level of significance or probability of a Type I error
β (beta)	probability of a Type II error or slope of the regression line
μ (mu)	population mean
ρ (rho)	population Pearson correlation coefficient
Σ (summation)	take the sum of
π (pi)	population proportion
σ (sigma)	population standard deviation
χ^2	chi-square statistic

English Letters

$d.f.$	number of degrees of freedom
F	F-statistic
n	sample size
p	sample proportion
Pr( )	probability of the outcome in the parentheses
r	sample Pearson correlation coefficient
r^2	coefficient of determination (squared correlation coefficient)
R^2	coefficient of determination (multiple regression)
S	sample standard deviation (inferential statistics)
$S_{\overline{X}}$	estimated standard error of the mean
S_p	estimated standard error of the proportion
S^2	sample variance (inferential statistics)
t	t-statistic
X	variable or any unspecified observation
$\overline{X}$	sample mean
Y	any unspecified observation on a second variable, usually the dependent variable
$\hat{Y}$	predicted dependent variable score
Z	standardized score (descriptive statistics) or Z-statistic

GLOSSARY
GLOSSARY

A

Acquiescence bias A tendency for respondents to agree with all or most questions asked of them in a survey.

Administrative error An error caused by the improper administration or execution of the research task.

Advocacy research Research undertaken to support a specific claim in a legal action or represent some advocacy group.

Alternative hypothesis A statement indicating the opposite of the null hypothesis.

Analysis of variance (ANOVA) Analysis involving the investigation of the effects of one treatment variable on an interval-scaled dependent variable; a hypothesis-testing technique to determine whether statistically significant differences on means occur among three or more groups.

Applied marketing research Research conducted to address a specific marketing decision for a specific firm or organization.

At-home scanning systems Systems that allow consumer panelists to perform their own scanning after taking home products, using handheld wands that read UPC symbols.

Attitude An enduring disposition to consistently respond in a given manner to various aspects of the world, composed of affective, cognitive, and behavioral components.

Attribute A single characteristic or fundamental feature of an object, person, situation, or issue.

B

Back translation Taking a questionnaire that has previously been translated into another language and having a second, independent translator translate it back to the original language.

Basic experimental design An experimental design in which only one variable is manipulated.

Basic marketing research Research conducted without a specific decision in mind that usually does not address the needs of a specific organization. It attempts to expand the limits of marketing knowledge in general and is not aimed at solving a particular pragmatic problem.

Behavioral differential A rating scale instrument similar to a semantic differential, developed to measure the behavioral intentions of subjects toward future actions.

Between-groups variance The sum of differences between the group mean and the grand mean summed overall groups for a given set of observations.

Bivariate analysis Tests of hypotheses involving two variables.

C

Callbacks Attempts to recontact individuals selected for a sample who were not available initially.

Case studies The documented history of a particular person, group, organization, or event.

Category scale A rating scale that consists of several response categories, often providing respondents with alternatives to indicate positions on a continuum.

Causal inference A conclusion that when one thing happens, another specific thing will follow.

Causal research Allows causal inferences to be made. That is, it seeks to identify cause-and-effect relationships. When something *causes* an effect, it means it brings it about or makes it happen. The effect is the outcome.

Census An investigation of all the individual elements that make up a population.

Central location interviewing Telephone interviews conducted from a central location using wats lines at fixed charges.

Central-limit theorem The theory that, as sample size increases, the distribution of sample means of size *n*, randomly selected, approaches a normal distribution.

Check boxes In an Internet questionnaire, small graphic boxes, next to answers, that a respondent clicks on to choose an answer; typically, a check mark or an **X** appears in the box when the respondent clicks on it.

Checklist question A fixed-alternative question that allows the respondent to provide multiple answers to a single question by checking off items.

Chi-square (χ^2) test A hypothesis test that allows for investigation of statistical significance in the analysis of a frequency distribution.

Choice A measurement task that identifies preferences by requiring respondents to choose between two or more alternatives.

Click-through rate Proportion of people who are exposed to an Internet ad who actually click on its hyperlink to enter the website; click-through rates are generally very low.

Cluster sampling An economically efficient sampling technique in which the primary sampling unit is not the individual element in the population but a large cluster of elements; clusters are selected randomly.

Coefficient alpha (α) The most commonly applied estimate of a multiple item scale's reliability. It represents the average of all possible split-half reliabilities for a construct.

Coefficient of determination (r^2) A measure obtained by squaring the correlation coefficient; that proportion of the total variance of a variable that is accounted for by knowing the value of another variable.

Cohort effect Refers to a change in the dependent variable that occurs because members of one experimental group experienced different historical situations than members of other experimental groups.

Communication process The process by which one person or source sends a message to an audience or receiver and then receives feedback about the message.

Composite measures Assign a value to an observation based on a mathematical derivation of multiple variables.

Composite scale A way of representing a latent construct by summing or averaging respondents' reactions to multiple items each assumed to indicate the latent construct.

Computer-assisted telephone interviewing (CATI) Technology that allows answers to telephone interviews to be entered directly into a computer for processing.

Concept A generalized idea that represents something of meaning.

Concept testing A frequently performed type of exploratory research representing many similar research procedures all having the same purpose: to screen new, revised, or repositioned ideas.

Conclusions and recommendations section The part of the body of a report that provides opinions based on the results and suggestions for action.

Concomitant variation One of three criteria for causality. It occurs when two events *covary,* meaning they vary systematically.

Confidence interval estimate A specified range of numbers within which a population mean is expected to lie; an estimate of the population mean based on the knowledge that it will be equal to the sample mean plus or minus a small sampling error.

Confidence level A percentage or decimal value that tells how confident a researcher can be about being correct; it states the long-run percentage of confidence intervals that will include the true population mean.

Confidentiality The information involved in a research will not be shared with others.

Conflict of interest Occurs when one researcher works for two competing companies.

Confound Means that there is an alternative explanation beyond the experimental variables for any observed differences in the dependent variable.

Constancy of conditions Means that subjects in all experimental groups are exposed to identical conditions except for the differing experimental treatments.

Constant-sum scale A measure of attitudes in which respondents are asked to divide a constant sum to indicate the relative importance of attributes; respondents often sort cards, but the task may also be a rating task.

Construct A term used to refer to concepts measured with multiple variables.

Construct validity Exists when a measure reliably measures and truthfully represents a unique concept; consists of several components including face validity, convergent validity, criterion validity, and discriminant validity.

Content analysis The systematic observation and quantitative description of the manifest content of communication.

Content providers Parties that furnish information on the World Wide Web.

Contingency table A data matrix that displays the frequency of some combination of possible responses to multiple variables; cross-tabulation results.

Contrived observation Observation in which the investigator creates an artificial environment in order to test a hypothesis.

Control group A group of subjects to whom no experimental treatment is administered.

Convenience sampling The sampling procedure of obtaining those people or units that are most conveniently available.

Convergent validity Another way of expressing internal consistency; highly reliable scales contain convergent validity.

Cookies Small computer files that a content provider can save onto the computer of someone who visits its website.

Correlation coefficient A statistical measure of the covariation, or association, between two variables.

Correspondence rules Indicate the way that a certain value on a scale corresponds to some true value of a concept.

Counterbalancing Attempts to eliminate the confounding effects of order of presentation by requiring that one fourth of the subjects be exposed to treatment A first, one fourth to treatment B first, one fourth to treatment C first, and finally one fourth to treatment D first.

Counterbiasing statement An introductory statement or preamble to a potentially embarrassing question that reduces a respondent's reluctance to answer by suggesting that certain behavior is not unusual.

Cover letter Letter that accompanies a questionnaire to induce the reader to complete and return the questionnaire.

Critical values The values that lie exactly on the boundary of the region of rejection.

Cross-checks The comparison of data from one source with data from another source to determine the similarity of independent projects.

Cross-functional teams Employee teams composed of individuals from various functional areas such as engineering, production, finance, and marketing who share a common purpose.

Cross-tabulation The appropriate technique for addressing research questions involving relationships among multiple less-than interval variables; results in a combined frequency table displaying one variable in rows and another in columns.

Cross-tabulation (contingency table) A joint frequency distribution of observations on two or more sets of variables.

Cross-validate To verify that the empirical findings from one culture also exist and behave similarly in another culture.

Custom research Research projects that are tailored specifically to a client's unique needs.

Customer discovery Involves mining data to look for patterns identifying who is likely to be a valuable customer.

Customer relationship management (CRM) Part of the DSS that addresses exchanges between the firm and its customers.

Customer-oriented Describes a firm in which all decisions are made with a conscious awareness of their effect on the consumer.

D

Data Facts or recorded measures of certain phenomena (things).

Data analysis The application of reasoning to understand the data that have been gathered.

Data conversion The process of changing the original form of the data to a format suitable to achieve the research objective; also called data transformation.

Data mining The use of powerful computers to dig through volumes of data to discover patterns about an organization's customers and products; applies to many different forms of analysis.

Data quality The degree to which data represent the true situation.

Data transformation Process of changing the data from their original form to a format suitable for performing a data analysis addressing research objectives.

Data warehouse The multitiered computer storehouse of current and historical data.

Data warehousing The process allowing important day-to-day operational data to be stored and organized for simplified access.

Data wholesalers Companies that put together consortia of data sources into packages that are offered to municipal, corporate, and university libraries for a fee.

Database A collection of raw data arranged logically and organized in a form that can be stored and processed by a computer.

Database marketing The use of customer databases to promote one-to-one relationships with customers and create precisely targeted promotions.

Data-processing error A category of administrative error that occurs because of incorrect data entry, incorrect computer programming, or other procedural errors during data analysis.

Debriefing The process of providing subjects with all pertinent facts about the nature and purpose of an experiment after its completion.

Decision support system (DSS) A computer-based system that helps decision makers confront problems through direct interaction with databases and analytical software programs.

Deliverables The term used often in consulting or applied market research to describe the objectives.

Demand characteristic Experimental design element or procedure that unintentionally provides subjects with hints about the research hypothesis.

Demand effect Occurs when demand characteristics actually affect the dependent variable.

Dependent variable The criterion by which the results of an experiment are judged; a variable expected to be dependent on the experimenter's manipulation of the independent variable.

Depth interview A one-on-one interview between a professional researcher and a research respondent conducted about some relevant business or social topic.

Descriptive analysis The elementary transformation of raw data in a way that describes the basic characteristics such as central tendency, distribution, and variability.

Descriptive research Describes characteristics of objects, people, groups, organizations, or environments. Descriptive research tries to "paint a picture" of a given situation.

Determinant-choice question A fixed-alternative question that requires the respondent to choose one response from among multiple alternatives.

Diagnostic analysis Seeks to diagnose reasons for market outcomes and focuses specifically on the beliefs and feelings consumers have about and toward competing products.

Dialog boxes Windows that open on a computer screen to prompt the user to enter information.

Direct observation A straightforward attempt to observe and record what naturally occurs; the investigator does not create an artificial situation.

Director of marketing research This person provides leadership in research efforts and integrates all staff-level research activities into one effort. The director plans, executes, and controls the firm's marketing research function.

Discussion guide A focus group outline that includes written introductory comments informing the group about the focus group purpose and rules and then outlines topics or questions to be addressed in the group session.

Do Not Call legislation Restricts any telemarketing effort from calling consumers who either register with a no-call list or who request not to be called.

Door-to-door interviews Personal interviews conducted at respondents' doorsteps in an effort to increase the participation rate in the survey.

Double-barreled question A question that may induce bias because it covers two issues at once.

Drop-down box In an Internet questionnaire, a space-saving device that reveals responses when they are needed but otherwise hides them from view.

Drop-off method A survey method that requires the interviewer to travel to the respondent's location to drop off questionnaires that will be picked up later.

E

Elaboration analysis An analysis of the basic cross-tabulation for each level of a variable not previously considered, such as subgroups of the sample.

Electronic data interchange (EDI) Type of exchange that occurs when one company's computer system is integrated with another company's system.

E-mail surveys Surveys distributed through electronic mail.

Empirical testing Means that something has been examined against reality using data. When the data are consistent with a hypothesis, we say the hypothesis is *supported*.

Environmental scanning Entails all information gathering designed to detect changes in the external operating environment of the firm.

Error trapping Using software to control the flow of an Internet questionnaire—for example, to prevent respondents from backing up or failing to answer a question.

Ethical dilemma Refers to a situation in which one chooses from alternative courses of actions, each with different ethical implications.

Experience survey An exploratory research technique in which individuals who are knowledgeable about a particular research problem are questioned.

Experimental group A group of subjects to whom an experimental treatment is administered.

Experimental treatment The term referring to the way an experimental variable is manipulated.

Exploratory research Conducted to clarify ambiguous situations or discover ideas that may be potential business opportunities.

External data Data created, recorded, or generated by an entity other than the researcher's organization.

External validity Is the accuracy with which experimental results can be generalized beyond the experimental subjects.

Extremity bias A category of response bias that results because some individuals tend to use extremes when responding to questions.

Eye-tracking monitor A mechanical device used to observe eye movements; some eye monitors use infrared light beams to measure unconscious eye movements.

F

Fax survey A survey that uses fax machines as a way for respondents to receive and return questionnaires.

Field experiments Research projects involving experimental manipulations that are implemented in a natural environment.

Field notes The researcher's descriptions of what actually happens in the field; these notes then become the text from which meaning is extracted.

Filter question A question that screens out respondents who are not qualified to answer a second question.

Fixed-alternative questions Questions in which respondents are given specific, limited-alternative responses and asked to choose the one closest to their own viewpoint.

Focus blog A type of informal, "continuous" focus group established as an Internet blog for the purpose of collecting qualitative data from participant comments.

Focus group A small group discussion about some research topic led by a moderator who guides discussion among the participants.

Focus group interview An unstructured, free-flowing interview with a small group of around six to ten people. Focus groups are led by a trained moderator who follows a flexible format encouraging dialogue among respondents.

Forced answering software Software that prevents respondents from continuing with an Internet questionnaire if they fail to answer a question.

Forecast analyst Employee who provides technical assistance such as running computer programs and manipulating data to generate a sales forecast.

Free-association techniques Record respondents' first (top-of-mind) cognitive reactions to some stimulus.

Frequency distribution A set of data organized by summarizing the number of times a particular value of a variable occurs.

Frequency table A table showing the different ways respondents answered a question.

Frequency-determination question A fixed-alternative question that asks for an answer about general frequency of occurrence.

F-test A procedure to determine whether there is more variability in the scores of one sample than in the scores of another sample.

Funnel technique Asking general questions before specific questions in order to obtain unbiased responses.

G

Geo-demographics Refers to information describing the demographic profile of consumers in a particular geographic region.

Global information system An organized collection of computer hardware, software, data, and personnel designed to capture, store, update, manipulate, analyze, and immediately display information about worldwide business activity.

Grand mean The mean over all observations.

Graphic rating scale A measure of attitude that allows respondents to rate an object by choosing any point along a graphic continuum.

Guinea pig effect An effect on the results of an experiment caused by subjects changing their normal behavior or attitudes to cooperate with an experimenter.

H

Hidden observation Observation in which the subject is unaware that observation is taking place.

Histogram A graphical way of showing a frequency distribution in which the height of a bar corresponds to the observed frequency of the category.

History effect Occurs when some change other than the experimental treatment occurs during the course of an experiment that affects the dependent variable.

Host Where the content for a particular website physically resides and is accessed.

Human subjects review committee Carefully reviews proposed research design to try to make sure that no harm can come to any research participant.

Hypothesis A formal statement explaining some outcome.

Hypothesis An empirically testable supposition that tentatively explains certain facts or phenomena; a proposition that is empirically testable.

Hypothetical constructs Variables that are not directly observable but are measurable through indirect indicators, such as verbal expression or overt behavior.

I

Idealism A term that reflects the degree to which one bases one's morality on moral standards.

Image profile A graphic representation of semantic differential data for competing brands, products, or stores to highlight comparisons.

Independent variable In an experimental design, a variable that can be manipulated, or altered, independently of any other variable.

Index measure An index assigns a value based on how much of the concept being measured is associated with an observation. Indexes often are formed by putting several variables together.

Index of retail saturation A calculation that describes the relationship between retail demand and supply.

Information Data formatted (structured) to support decision making or define the relationship between two facts.

Information completeness Having the right amount of information.

Informed consent When an individual understands what the researcher wants him or her to do and consents to the research study.

In-house research Research performed by employees of the company that will benefit from the research.

Instrumentation effect A nuisance that occurs when a change in the wording of questions, a change in interviewers, or a change in other procedures causes a change in the dependent variable.

Integrated marketing communication Means that all promotional efforts (advertising, public relations, personal selling, event marketing, and so forth) should be coordinated to communicate a consistent image.

Integrated marketing mix The effects of various combinations of marketing-mix elements on important outcomes.

Interactive help desk In an Internet questionnaire, a live, real-time support feature that solves problems or answers questions respondents may encounter in completing the questionnaire.

Interactive medium A medium, such as the internet, that a person can use to communicate with and interact with other users.

Internal and proprietary data Secondary data that originate inside the organization.

Internal validity Exists to the extent that an experimental variable is truly responsible for any variance in the dependent variable.

Internet A worldwide network of computers that allows users access to information from distant sources.

Internet survey A self-administered questionnaire posted on a website.

Interval scales Scales that have both nominal and ordinal properties, but that also capture information about differences in quantities of a concept from one observation to the next.

Interviewer bias A response bias that occurs because the presence of the interviewer influences respondents' answers.

Interviewer cheating The practice of filling in fake answers or falsifying questionnaires while working as an interviewer.

Interviewer error Mistakes made by interviewers failing to record survey responses correctly.

Intranet A company's private data network that uses Internet standards and technology.

Introduction section The part of the body of a research report that discusses background information and the specific objectives of the research.

Item nonresponse Failure of a respondent to provide an answer to a survey question.

J

Judgment (purposive) sampling A nonprobability sampling technique in which an experienced individual selects the sample based on personal judgment about some appropriate characteristic of the sample member.

K

Keyword search Takes place as the search engine searches through millions of web pages for documents containing the keywords.

L

Laboratory experiment The researcher has more complete control over the research setting and extraneous variables.

Laddering A particular approach to probing asking respondents to compare differences between brands at different levels that produces distinctions at the attribute level, the benefit level, and the value or motivation level.

Leading question A question that suggests or implies certain answers.

Likert scale A measure of attitudes designed to allow respondents to rate how strongly they agree or disagree with carefully constructed statements, ranging from very positive to very negative attitudes toward some object.

Literature review A directed search of published works, including periodicals and books, that discusses theory and presents empirical results relevant to the topic at hand.

Loaded question A question that suggests a socially desirable answer or is emotionally charged.

M

Mail survey A self-administered questionnaire sent to respondents through the mail.

Mall intercept interviews Personal interviews conducted in a shopping mall.

Manager of decision support systems Employee who supervises the collection and analysis of sales, inventory, and other periodic customer relationship management (CRM) data.

Manipulation check A validity test of an experimental manipulation to make sure that the manipulation does produce differences in the independent variable.

Marginals Row and column totals in a contingency table, which are shown in its margins.

Market intelligence The subset of data and information that actually has some explanatory power enabling effective decisions to be made.

Market tracking The observation and analysis of trends in industry volume and brand share over time.

Market-basket analysis A form of data mining that analyzes anonymous point-of-sale transaction databases to identify coinciding purchases or relationships between products purchased and other retail shopping information.

Marketing channel A network of interdependent institutions that perform the logistics necessary for consumption to occur.

Marketing concept A central idea in modern marketing thinking that focuses on how the firm provides value to customers more than on the physical product or production process.

Marketing ethics The application of morals to behavior related to the exchange environment.

Marketing metrics Quantitative ways of monitoring and measuring marketing performance.

Marketing orientation The corporate culture existing for firms adopting the marketing concept. It emphasizes customer orientation, long-term profitability over short-term profits, and a cross-functional perspective.

Marketing research The application of the scientific method in searching for the truth about marketing phenomena. These activities include defining marketing opportunities and problems, generating and evaluating marketing ideas, monitoring performance, and understanding the marketing process.

Matching A procedure for the assignment of subjects to groups that ensures that each group of respondents is matched on the basis of pertinent characteristics.

Maturation effects Effects that are a function of time and the naturally occurring events that coincide with growth and experience.

Mean A measure of central tendency; the arithmetic average.

Measurement The process of describing some property of a phenomenon of interest, usually by assigning numbers in a reliable and valid way.

Median A measure of central tendency that is the midpoint; the value below which half the values in a distribution fall.

Mixed-mode survey Study that employs any combination of survey methods.

Mode A measure of central tendency; the value that occurs most often.

Model building The use of secondary data to help specify relationships between two or more variables; can involve the development of descriptive or predictive equations.

Moderator A person who leads a focus group interview and ensures that everyone gets a chance to speak and contribute to the discussion.

Moderator variable A third variable that changes the nature of a relationship between the original independent and dependent variables.

Moral standards Principles that reflect beliefs about what is ethical and what is unethical.

Mortality effect (sample attrition) Occurs when some subjects withdraw from the experiment before it is completed.

Multiple regression analysis An analysis of association in which the effects of two or more independent variables on a single, interval-scaled dependent variable are investigated simultaneously.

Multiple-grid question Several similar questions arranged in a grid format.

Multistage area sampling Sampling that involves using a combination of two or more probability sampling techniques.

Multivariate data analysis A group of statistical techniques allowing for the simultaneous analysis of three or more variables.

Mystery shoppers Employees of a research firm that are paid to pretend to be actual shoppers.

N

Neural network A form of artificial intelligence in which a computer is programmed to mimic the way that human brains process information.

No contacts People who are not at home or who are otherwise inaccessible on the first and second contact.

Nominal scales Represent the most elementary level of measurement in which values are assigned to an object for identification or classification purposes only.

Nonprobability sampling A sampling technique in which units of the sample are selected on the basis of personal judgment or convenience; the probability of any particular member of the population being chosen is unknown.

Nonrespondents People who are not contacted or who refuse to cooperate in the research.

Nonresponse error The statistical differences between a survey that includes only those who responded and a perfect survey that would also include those who failed to respond.

Nonspurious association One of three criteria for causality. It means any covariation between a cause and an effect is true and not simply due to some other variable.

Normal distribution A symmetrical, bell-shaped distribution that describes the expected probability distribution of many chance occurrences.

Null hypothesis A statement about a status quo asserting that any change from what has been thought to be true will be due entirely to random sampling error.

Numerical scale An attitude rating scale similar to a semantic differential except that it uses numbers, instead of verbal descriptions, as response options to identify response positions.

O

Observation The systematic process of recording the behavioral patterns of people, objects, and occurrences as they are witnessed.

Observer bias A distortion of measurement resulting from the cognitive behavior or actions of a witnessing observer.

One-group pretest–posttest design A quasi-experimental design in which the subjects in the experimental group are measured before and after the treatment is administered, but there is no control group.

One-shot design An after-only design in which a single measure is recorded after the treatment is administered.

Online focus group A qualitative research effort in which a group of individuals provides unstructured comments by entering their remarks into an electronic Internet display board of some type.

Open-ended boxes In an Internet questionnaire, boxes where respondents can type in their own answers to open-ended questions.

Open-ended response questions Questions that pose some problem and ask respondents to answer in their own words.

Operationalization The process of identifying scales that correspond to variance in a concept to be involved in a research process.

Opt in To give permission to receive selected e-mail, such as questionnaires, from a company with an Internet presence.

Oral presentation A spoken summary of the major findings, conclusions, and recommendations, given to clients or line managers to provide them with the opportunity to clarify any ambiguous issues by asking questions.

Order bias Bias caused by the influence of earlier questions in a questionnaire or by an answer's position in a set of answers.

Ordinal scales Ranking scales allowing things to be arranged based on how much of some concept they possess.

Outside agency An independent research firm contracted by the company that actually will benefit from the research.

P

Paired comparison A measurement technique that involves presenting the respondent with two objects and asking the respondent to pick the preferred object; more than two objects may be presented, but comparisons are made in pairs.

Percentage distribution A frequency distribution organized into a table (or graph) that summarizes percentage values associated with particular values of a variable.

Performance-monitoring research Refers to research that regularly, sometimes routinely, provides feedback for evaluation and control of marketing activity.

Periodicity A problem that occurs in systematic sampling when the original list has a systematic pattern.

Personal interview Face-to-face communication in which an interviewer asks a respondent to answer questions.

Picture frustration A version of the TAT using a cartoon drawing in which the respondent suggests a dialogue in which the characters might engage.

Piggyback An interplay in which one respondent stimulates thought among the others; as this process continues, increasingly creative insights are possible.

Pilot study A collective term for any small-scale exploratory research project that uses sampling but does not apply rigorous standards.

Pilot study A small-scale research project that collects data from respondents similar to those to be used in the full study.

Pivot question A filter question used to determine which version of a second question will be asked.

Point estimate An estimate of the population mean in the form of a single value, usually the sample mean.

Population (universe) Any complete group of entities that share some common set of characteristics.

Population distribution A frequency distribution of the elements of a population.

Population element An individual member of a population.

Population parameters Variables in a population or measured characteristics of the population.

Pop-up boxes In an Internet questionnaire, boxes that appear at selected points and contain information or instructions for respondents.

Posttest–only control group design An after-only design in which the experimental group is tested after exposure to the treatment and the control group is tested at the same time without having been exposed to the treatment; no premeasure is taken. Random assignment of subjects and treatment occurs.

Preliminary tabulation A tabulation of the results of a pretest to help determine whether the questionnaire will meet the objectives of the research.

Pretest A small-scale study in which the results are only preliminary and intended only to assist in design of a subsequent study.

Pretesting Administering a questionnaire to a small group of respondents to detect ambiguity or bias in the questions or to iron out fundamental problems in the instructions or administrative procedures.

Pretesting Screening procedure that involves a trial run with a group of respondents to iron out fundamental problems in the survey design.

Pretest–posttest control group design A true experimental design in which the experimental group is tested before and after exposure to the treatment and the control group is tested at the same two times without being exposed to the experimental treatment.

Pricing Involves finding the amount of monetary sacrifice that best represents the value customers perceive in a product after considering various market constraints.

Primary sampling unit (PSU) A term used to designate a unit selected in the first stage of sampling.

Probability The long-run relative frequency with which an event will occur.

Probability sampling A sampling technique in which every member of the population has a known, nonzero probability of selection.

Production-oriented Describes a firm that prioritizes efficiency and effectiveness of the production processes in making decisions.

Product-oriented Describes a firm that prioritizes decision making in a way that emphasizes technical superiority in the product.

Projective technique An indirect means of questioning that enables a respondent to project beliefs and feelings onto a third party or an inanimate object or into a task situation.

Promotion The communication function of the firm responsible for informing and persuading buyers.

Promotion research Investigates the effectiveness of advertising, premiums, coupons, sampling, discounts, public relations, and other sales promotions.

Proportion The percentage of elements that meet some criterion.

Proprietary marketing research The gathering of new data to investigate specific problems.

Psychogalvanometer A device that measures galvanic skin response, a measure of involuntary changes in the electrical resistance of the skin.

Pull technology Consumers request information from a web page and the browser then determines a response; the consumer is essentially asking for the data.

Pupilometer A mechanical device used to observe and record changes in the diameter of a subject's pupils.

Push button In a dialog box on an Internet questionnaire, a small outlined area, such as a rectangle or an arrow, that the respondent clicks on to select an option or perform a function, such as submit.

Push technology Sends data to a user's computer without a request being made; software is used to guess what information might be interesting to consumers based on the pattern of previous responses.

Q

Qualitative data Data that are not characterized by numbers, and instead are textual, visual, or oral; focus is on stories, visual portrayals, meaningful characterizations, interpretations, and other expressive descriptions.

Qualitative marketing research Research that addresses marketing objectives through techniques that allow the researcher to provide elaborate interpretations of market phenomena without depending on numerical measurement; its focus is on discovering true inner meanings and new insights.

Quantitative data Represent phenomena by assigning numbers in an ordered and meaningful way.

Quantitative marketing research Marketing research that addresses research objectives through empirical assessments that involve numerical measurement and analysis.

Quasi-experimental designs Experimental designs that do not involve random allocation of subjects to treatment combinations.

Quota sampling A nonprobability sampling procedure that ensures that various subgroups of a population will be represented on pertinent characteristics to the exact extent that the investigator desires.

R

Radio button In an Internet questionnaire, a circular icon, resembling a button, that activates one response choice and deactivates others when a respondent clicks on it.

Random digit dialing Use of telephone exchanges and a table of random numbers to contact respondents with unlisted phone numbers.

Random sampling error A statistical fluctuation that occurs because of chance variation in the elements selected for a sample.

Random sampling error The difference between the sample result and the result of a census conducted using identical procedures.

Randomization The random assignment of subjects and treatments to groups; it is one device for equally distributing the effects of extraneous variables to all conditions.

Ranking A measurement task that requires respondents to rank order a small number of stores, brands, or objects on the basis of overall preference or some characteristic of the stimulus.

Rating A measurement task that requires respondents to estimate the magnitude of a characteristic or quality that a brand, store, or object possesses.

Ratio scales Represent the highest form of measurement in that they have all the properties of interval scales with the additional attribute of representing absolute quantities; characterized by a meaningful absolute zero.

Refusals People who are unwilling to participate in a research project.

Relationship marketing Communicates the idea that a major goal of marketing is to build long-term relationships with the customers contributing to their success.

Relativism A term that reflects the degree to which one rejects moral standards in favor of the acceptability of some action. This way of thinking rejects absolute principles in favor of situation-based evaluations.

Relevance The characteristics of data reflecting how pertinent these particular facts are to the situation at hand.

Reliability An indicator of a measure's internal consistency.

Repeated measures Experiments in which an individual subject is exposed to more than one level of an experimental treatment.

Replicable When the same conclusion is reached based on another researcher's interpretation.

Report format The makeup or arrangement of parts necessary to a good research report.

Research analyst A person responsible for client contact, project design, preparation of proposals, selection of research suppliers, and supervision of data collection, analysis, and reporting activities.

Research assistants Research employees who provide technical assistance with questionnaire design, data analyses, and similar activities.

Research design A master plan that specifies the methods and procedures for collecting and analyzing the needed information.

Research follow-up Recontacting decision makers and/or clients after they have had a chance to read over a research report in order to determine whether additional information or clarification is necessary.

Research methodology section The part of the body of a report that presents the findings of the project. It includes tables, charts, and an organized narrative.

Research objectives The goals to be achieved by conducting research.

Research program Numerous related studies that come together to address multiple, related research objectives.

Research project A single study that addresses one or a small number of research objectives.

Research report An oral presentation or written statement of research results, strategic recommendations, and/or other conclusions to a specific audience.

Research suppliers Commercial providers of marketing research services.

Researcher-dependent Research in which the researcher must extract meaning from unstructured responses such as text from a recorded interview or a collage representing the meaning of some experience.

Respondent error A category of sample bias resulting from some respondent action or inaction such as nonresponse or response bias.

Respondents People who verbally answer an interviewer's questions or provide answers to written questions.

Response bias A bias that occurs when respondents either consciously or unconsciously tend to answer questions with a certain slant that misrepresents the truth.

Response latency The amount of time it takes to make a choice between two alternatives; used as a measure of the strength of preference.

Response rate The number of questionnaires returned or completed divided by the number of eligible people who were asked to participate in the survey.

Results section The part of the body of a report that presents the findings of the project. It includes tables, charts, and an organized narrative.

Reverse directory A directory similar to a telephone directory except that listings are by city and street address or by phone number rather than alphabetical by last name.

Reverse recoding A method of making sure all the items forming a composite scale are scored in the same direction. Negative items can be recoded into the equivalent responses for a non-reverse coded item.

S

Sample A subset, or some part, of a larger population.

Sample bias A persistent tendency for the results of a sample to deviate in one direction from the true value of the population parameter.

Sample distribution A frequency distribution of a sample.

Sample selection error An administrative error caused by improper sample design or sampling procedure execution.

Sample statistics Variables in a sample or measures computed from sample data.

Sample survey A more formal term for a survey.

Sampling Involves any procedure that draws conclusions based on measurements of a portion of the population.

Sampling distribution A theoretical probability distribution of sample means for all possible samples of a certain size drawn from a particular population.

Sampling frame A list of elements from which a sample may be drawn; also called working population.

Sampling frame error An error that occurs when certain sample elements are not listed or are not accurately represented in a sampling frame.

Sampling unit A single element or group of elements subject to selection in the sample.

Scales A device providing a range of values that correspond to different values in a concept being measured.

Scanner data The accumulated records resulting from point of sale data recordings.

Scanner-based consumer panel A type of consumer panel in which participants' purchasing habits are recorded with a laser scanner rather than a purchase diary.

Scientific method, the The way researchers go about using knowledge and evidence to reach objective conclusions about the real world.

Search Engine A computerized directory that allows anyone to search the World Wide Web for information using a keyword search.

Secondary data Data that have been previously collected for some purpose other than the one at hand.

Secondary sampling unit A term used to designate a unit selected in the second stage of sampling.

Self-administered questionnaires Surveys in which the respondent takes the responsibility for reading and answering the questions.

Self-selection bias A bias that occurs because people who feel strongly about a subject are more likely to respond to survey questions than people who feel indifferent about it.

Semantic differential A measure of attitudes that consists of a series of seven-point rating scales that use bipolar adjectives to anchor the beginning and end of each scale.

Sensitivity A measurement instrument's ability to accurately measure variability in stimuli or responses.

Significance level The critical probability in choosing between the null and alternative hypotheses; the probability level that is too low to warrant support of the null hypothesis.

Simple linear regression A measure of linear association that investigates a straight-line relationship of the type $Y = a + \beta X$, where X is the independent variable and a and β are two constants to be estimated.

Simple random sampling A sampling procedure that assures each element in the population of an equal chance of being included in the sample.

Simple-dichotomy (dichotomous-alternative) question A fixed-alternative question that requires the respondent to choose one of two alternatives.

Single-source data Diverse types of data offered by a single company; usually integrated on the basis of a common variable such as geographic area or store.

Site analysis techniques Techniques that use secondary data to select the best location for retail or wholesale operations.

Smart agent software Software capable of learning an Internet user's preferences and automatically searching out information in selected websites and then distributing it.

Snowball sampling A sampling procedure in which initial respondents are selected by probability methods and additional respondents are obtained from information provided by the initial respondents.

Social desirability bias Bias in responses caused by respondents' desire, either conscious or unconscious, to gain prestige or appear in a different social role.

Sorting A measurement task that presents a respondent with several objects or product concepts and requires the respondent to arrange the objects into piles or classify the product concepts.

Split-ballot technique Using two alternative phrasings of the same question for respective halves of a sample to elicit a more accurate total response than would a single phrasing.

Spyware Software placed on a computer without consent or knowledge of the user.

Standard deviation A quantitative index of a distribution's spread, or variability; the square root of the variance for a distribution.

Standard error of the mean The standard deviation of the sampling distribution.

Standardized normal distribution A purely theoretical probability distribution that reflects a specific normal curve for the standardized value, z.

Standardized regression coefficient (β) The estimated coefficient indicating the strength of relationship between an independent variable and dependent variable expressed on a standardized scale where higher absolute values indicate stronger relationships (range is from 21 to 1).

Standardized research service Companies that develop a unique methodology for investigating a business specialty area.

Stapel scale A measure of attitudes that consists of a single adjective in the center of an even number of numerical values.

Static group design An after-only design in which subjects in the experimental group are measured after being exposed to the experimental treatment and the control group is measured without having been exposed to the experimental treatment; no premeasure is taken.

Statistical base The number of respondents or observations (in a row or column) used as a basis for computing percentages.

Status bar In an Internet questionnaire, a visual indicator that tells the respondent what portion of the survey he or she has completed.

Stratified sampling A probability sampling procedure in which simple random subsamples that are more or less equal on some characteristic are drawn from within each stratum of the population.

Streaming media Consist of multimedia content such as audio or video that is made available in real time over the Internet or a corporate Intranet.

Subjective Results are researcher-dependent, meaning different researchers may reach different conclusions based on the same interview.

Supply chain Another term for a channel of distribution, meaning the link between suppliers and customers.

Survey A research technique in which a sample is interviewed in some form or their behavior is observed and described in some way.

Syndicated service A marketing research supplier that provides standardized information for many clients in return for a fee.

Systematic (nonsampling) error Error resulting from factors not due to chance fluctuations, such as the nature of a study's design and imperfections in executions.

Systematic error Error resulting from some imperfect aspect of the research design that causes respondent error or from a mistake in the execution of the research.

Systematic or nonsampling error Occurs if the sampling units in an experimental cell are somehow different than the units in another cell, and this difference affects the dependent variable.

Systematic sampling A sampling procedure in which a starting point is selected by a random process and then every n^{th} number on the list is selected.

T

Tabulation The orderly arrangement of data in a table or other summary format showing the number of responses to each response category; tallying.

Tachistoscope Device that controls the amount of time a subject is exposed to a visual image.

Telephone interviews Personal interviews conducted by telephone, the mainstay of commercial survey research.

Television monitoring Computerized mechanical observation used to obtain television ratings.

Temporal sequence One of three criteria for causality. It deals with the time order of events. The cause must occur before the effect.

Tertiary sampling unit A term used to designate a unit selected in the third stage of sampling.

Test units The subjects or entities whose responses to the experimental treatment are measured or observed.

Testing effects A nuisance effect occurring when the initial measurement or test alerts or primes subjects in a way that affects their response to the experimental treatments.

Thematic apperception test (TAT) A test that presents subjects with an ambiguous picture(s) in which consumers and products are the center of attention; the investigator asks the subject to tell what is happening in the picture(s) now and what might happen next.

Theory A formal, logical explanation of some events that includes predictions of how things relate to one another.

Timeliness Means that the data are current enough to still be relevant.

Total value management Trying to manage and monitor the entire process by which consumers receive benefits from a company.

Total variability (SST) The sum of within-group variance and between-group variance. The sum of the differences between a set of observed values and the grand mean of all observations.

U

Uniform Resource Locator (URL) A website address that web browsers recognize.

Univariate analysis Tests of hypotheses involving only one variable.

Unobtrusive methods Methods in which research respondents do not have to be disturbed for data to be gathered.

V

Validity The accuracy of a measure or the extent to which a score truthfully represents a concept.

Variable piping software Software that allows variables to be inserted into an Internet questionnaire as a respondent is completing it.

Variance A measure of variability or dispersion. Its square root is the standard deviation.

Visible observation Observation in which the observer's presence is known to the subject.

Voice-pitch analysis A physiological measurement technique that records abnormal frequencies in the voice that are supposed to reflect emotional reactions to various stimuli.

W

Welcome screen The first web page in an internet survey, which introduces the survey and requests that the respondent enter a password or pin.

Within-group error or variance The sum of the differences between observed values and the group mean for a given set of observations; also known as total error variance.

World Wide Web (WWW) A portion of the Internet that is a system of computer servers that organize information into documents called web pages.

ENDNOTES

ENDNOTES

Chapter 1

1   Grapetime, Terry (2004), "Vote for Me," Marketing Research, 16 (Winter), 5; Best Review 2004), "AFLAC's Quacking Duck Selected One of America's Favorite Icons," 105 (October), 119; Gage, Jack (2005), "Waddling Through," Forbes, 176 (8/15), 90.

2   Keyo, Michelle (1996), "Web Site of the Week: Jelly Belly: Using Sampling to Build a Customer Database," Inc. Online, http://www.inc.com, December 9, 1996.

3   Penn, Catherine (2005), "New Drinks Include a Health Benefit for 05," Beverage Industry, 96 (January), 45–54.

4   Garvin, Andrew P. (2005), "Evolve Approach to Serve Complex Market," Marketing News (September 15), p. 22.

5   Thomas, Jerry W. (2002), "Skipping MR a Major Error," Marketing News (March 4), 50.

6   Gibson, Lawrence D. (2000), "Quo Vadis Marketing Research?" Marketing Research, 12 (Spring), 36–41.

7   Matthew, Arnold (2004), "FDA Delays DTC Draft Guidance to Study How Consumers Use Brief Summaries," Medical Marketing and Media, 39 (November), 10.

8   See, for example, Babin, Barry J., Chebat, J.C., and Richard Michon (2004), "Perceived Appropriateness and its Effect on Quality, Affect and Behavior," Journal of Retailing and Consumer Services, 11 (September), 287–298.

9   Leo Y. M. Sin, Alan C. B. Tse, Oliver H. M. Yau, Raymond P. M. Chow, Jenny S.Y. Lee, Lorett B.Y. Lau (2005), "Relationship Marketing Orientation: Scale Development and Cross-Cultural Validation," Journal of Business Research, 58 (February), 185–194; Nakata, Cheryl and K. Sivakumar (2001), "Instituting the Marketing Concept in a Multinational Setting: The Role of National Culture," Journal of the Academy of Marketing Science, 29 (Summer), 255–275; Day, George (1994), "The Capabilities of Market-Driven Organizations," Journal of Marketing, 58 (October), 37–52; Ward, James C., M. D. Hutt, and Peter H. Reingen (1994), "Evolving Patterns of Organizational Beliefs in the Formation of Strategy," Journal of Marketing, 58 (April), 96–110.

10 Reyes, Sonia (2000), "Ian Friendly: Groove Tube," Brandweek (October 16), M111–M116.

11 Gelb, Betsy D. and Gabriel M. Gelb (1991), "What Research Inside the Organization Can Accomplish," Marketing Research (December), 44.

12 Marketing News (1990), "Burger King Opens Customer Hot Line" (May 28), 7.

13 Professional Builder (2004), "David Weekley Homes Reign in Fort Worth Market," 69 (December), 31–34.

14 Professional Builder (2004), "Builder POV: David Weekley," 69 (January), 69, 31–32.

15 Sharman, G. K. (1997), "Sessions Challenge Status Quo," Marketing News (November 10), p. 18.

16 Schwartz, David, Concept Testing: How to Test Product Ideas Before You Go to Market (New York: AMACOM, 1987), p. 91.

17 Wyner, Gordon A. (2005), "Biz Problems Can Get Solved with Research," Marketing News (September 15), 33–34.

18 Benezra, Karen (1994), "Fritos Around the World," Brandweek (March 27), 32; USA Today, "Cheetos Make Debute in China But Lose Cheese in Translation" (September 2), B-1.

19 See Allenby, Greg M., Thomas S. Shively, Yang Sha, and Mark J. Garratt (2004), "A Choice Model for Packaged Goods: Dealing with Discrete Quantities and Quantity Discounts," Marketing Science, 23 (Winter), 14–21.

20 Mohn, N. Carroll (1995), "Pricing Research for Decision Making," Marketing Research (Winter), 11–12.

21 See Allenby, Greg M., Thomas S. Shively, Yang Sha, and Mark J. Garratt (2004), "A Choice Model for Packaged Goods: Dealing with Discrete Quantities and Quantity Discounts," Marketing Science, 23 (Winter), 14–21.

22 Mohn, N. Carroll (1995), "Pricing Research for Decision Making," Marketing Research (Winter), 11–12.

23 Ofir, Chezy (2004), "Reexamining Latitude of Price Acceptability and Price Thresholds: Predicting Basic Consumer Reaction to Price," Journal of Consumer Research, 30 (March), 612–621.

24 Bonamici, Kate (2004), "Big-Foot Dips Toe in Coffee," Fortune, 149 (January 26), 70.

25 Gardyn, Rebecca (2001), "Same Name, New Number: AT&T's Brand Image Gets a Needed Boost from a Well-Rounded Hero," American Demographics (March), 56.

26 Schneider, Lars-Peter and Bettina T. Cornwell (2005), "Cashing in on Crashes via Brand Placement in Computer Games," International Journal of Advertising, 24 (3), 321–342.

27 Low, George S. (2000), "Correlates of Integrated Marketing Communications," Journal of Advertising Research (May).

28 Hein, Kenneth (2004), "Best Buy Calls the 'Odd' Squad: Group of Tech 'Geeks' gets Spotlight in National Branding Spot," Brandweek, 45 (October 18), 11; DSN Retailing Today (2004), "Best Buy Turns On the Geek Appeal. (CE & Entertainment)," 42 (February 24), 22.

29 Garretson, Judith and Scot Burton (2005), "The Role of Spokescharacters as Advertisement and Package Cues in Integrated Marketing Communications," Journal of Marketing, 69 (October), 118–132.

30 Clancy, Kevin J. and Randy L. Stone (2005), "Don't Blame the Metrics," Harvard Business Review, 83 (June), 26–28.

31 Honomichl, Jack (2001), "Growth Stunt," Marketing News (June 4), 144.

32 Express Magazine, "You Say Tomato, I say Tomahto," (Spring), 19.

33 Information from Ben & Jerry's web page at http://www.benjerry.com; LearNet's Video Ben & Jerry's; and a press release from Ben & Jerry's, February 20, 1997.

Chapter 2

1   Collett, Stacy (2002), "External Business Intelligence Can Be a Powerful Addition to Your Data Warehouse, but Beware of Data Overload," Computerworld, (April 15), 34.

2   See Albers, Brad (2001), "Home Depot's Special Projects Support Team Powers Information Management for Business Needs," Journal of Organizational Excellence, 21 (Winter), 3–15; Songini, Marc L. (2002), "Home Depot's Next IT Project: Data Warehouse,"

Computerworld, 36
(October 7), 1–2.

3 LaBahn, Douglass W. and Robert
   Krapfel (2000), "Early Supplier
   Involvement in Customer
   New Product Development: A
   Contingency Model of Component
   Supplier Intentions," Journal of
   Busines Research, 47 (March),
   173–190.

4 DSN Retailing Today (2005),
   "Beneifts of RFID Becoming More
   Visible" (August 8), 22.

5 Hall, Mark (2002), "Seeding for Data
   Growth," Computerworld, 36
   (April 15), 52.

6 Angwein, J. and Delaney, K. J. (2005),
   "Top Web Sites Build Up Ad
   Backlog, Raise Rates," Wall Street
   Journal (November 16), A1.

7 Gale Annual Directory of Databases,
   Gale Research Inc.: Detroit.

8 Patrick A. Moore and Ronald
   Milliman (1995), "Application of the
   Internet in Marketing Education,"
   paper presented at the Southwest
   Marketing Association, Houston, Texas.

9 Business Week Online (2002), "A
   Better Web Through Higher Math"
   (January 22), http://www.
   businessweek.com (accessed
   November 12, 2005).

10 Rangaswamy, Arvind and G. Lilien
   (1997), "Software Tools for New
   Product Development," Journal of
   Marketing Research, 34 (February),
   177–184.

11 Desouza, Kevin and Yukika Awazu
   (2005), "Maintaining Knowledge
   Management Systems: A Strategic
   Imperative," Journal of the American
   Society for Information Science and
   Technology, 56 (May), 765–768.

12 Rangaswamy, Arvind and G. Lilien
   (1997).

13 Adopted with permission from
   deJony, Jennifer (1995), "View from
   the Top," Technology, 1, downloaded
   from the Internet July 3, 1998.

14 Excerpt reprinted with permission
   from http://houns54.clearlake.ibm.
   com/solutions/erp/erppub.nsf/
   detailcontacts/Stage_1_ERPLifecycle
   _Solution_Inquirywhat, downloaded
   June 21, 2001.

15 Wells, H.G. (1940), "The Brain:
   Organization of the Modern World."

Chapter 3

1 Zahay, Debra, Abbie Griffin, and Elisa
   Fredericks (2004), "Sources, Uses, and
   Forms of Data in the New Product
   Development Process," Industrial
   Marketing Management, 33
   (October), 658–666.

2 Hara, Yoshika (2002), "New Industry
   Awaits Human-Friendly Bipeds—
   'Personal Robots' Get Ready to Walk
   on the Human Side," Electronic
   Engineering Times (September 16),
   157–159.

3 Bocchi, Joe, Jacqueline K. Eastman,
   and Cathy Owens Swift (2004),

"Retaining the Online Learner:
Profile of Students in an Online
MBA Program and Implications for
Teaching Them," Journal of
Education for Business
(March/April), 245–253.

4 Janoff, Barry (2001), "Brands of the
   Land," Brandweek (April 20), 28.

5 Bocchi, Eastman, and Swift (2004);
   "Retaining the Online Learners";
   Carr, S. (2000), "As Distance
   Education Comes of Age, the
   Challenge Is Keeping the Students,"
   Chronicle of Higher Education, 23,
   A1.; Moskal and Dziuban (2001),
   "Present and Future Directions for
   Assessing Cybereducation: The
   Changing Research Paradigm," in
   Vandervert, L. R., L.V. Chavinina, and
   R. A. Cornell, Eds., Cybereducation:
   The Future of Long-Distance Learning,
   New York: Liebert, 157–184.

6 Einstein, A. and L. Infeld, The
   Evolution of Physics (New York: Simon
   and Schuster, 1942), p. 95.

7 Perdue, B.C. and J.O. Summers
   (1986), "Checking the Success
   of Manipulations in Marketing
   Experiments," Journal of
   Marketing Research, 23
   (November), 317–326.

8 See, for example, Kwok, S. and
   M. Uncles (2005), "Sales Promotion
   Effectiveness: The Impact of
   Consumer Differences at an Ethnic-
   Group level," Journal of Product
   and Brand Management, 14 (3),
   170–186.

9 Approximate currency rates as of
   September, 2006. See
   www.xrates.com for the latest rates.

10 Babin, B.J., D.M. Hardesty, and T.A.
   Suter (2003), "Color and Shopping
   Intentions: The Effect of Price
   Fairness and Perceived Affect,"
   Journal of Business Research, 56
   (July), 541–551.

11 Crowley, Michael (2004),
   "Conservatives (Finally) Rejoice,"
   New Republic, 231, 13–14.

Chapter 4

1 Wood, Charles M. and Tracy A. Suter
   (2004), "Making Marketing
   Principles Tangible: Online Auctions
   as Living Case Studies," Journal of
   Marketing Education, 26 (August),
   137–144; Weinberg, Bruce D. and
   Lenita Davis (2005), "Exploring the
   WOW in Online-Auction
   Feedback," Journal of Business
   Research, 58 (November),
   1609–1621.

2 Fellman, M.W. (1998), "Mesmerizing
   Method Gets Results," Marketing
   News, 32 (7/20), 1–38; McDonald,
   W. J. (1998), "Consumer Decision
   Making and Altered States of
   Consciousness: A Study of Dualities,"
   Journal of Business Research, 42
   (July), 287–294.

3 Handerson, Naomi R. (2005), "Good
   Research Tools Never Go out of Style

and Don't Shift in the Winds of
Whatever is New and Trendy,"
Marketing Research, 17 (Spring),
39–40.

4 Thomas C. Kinnear and Ann Root,
   Eds., Survey of Marketing Research
   (Chicago: American Marketing
   Association, 1994).

5 Kinnear and Root (1994).

6 See Izzo, G. Martin and Scott J. Vitell
   (2003), "Exploring the Effects of
   Professional Education on
   Salespeople: The Case of
   Autonomous Agents," Journal of
   Marketing Theory & Practice, 11
   (Fall), 26–38; Loe, Terry and William
   A. Weeks (2000), "An Empirical
   Investigation of Efforts to Improve
   Sales Students' Moral Reasoning,"
   Journal of Personal Selling and Sales
   Management, 20 (Fall), 243–252.

7 Barnett, Tim and Sean Valentino
   (2004), "Issue Contingencies and
   Marketers' Recognition of Ethical
   Issues, Ethical Judgments and
   Behavioral Intentions," Journal of
   Business Research, 57 (April),
   338–346.

8 Robin, D. P., R. E. Reidenbach, and
   B. J. Babin (1997), "The Nature,
   Measurement and Stability of Ethical
   Judgements in the Workplace,"
   Psychological Reports, 80, 563–580.

9 Gillin, Donna L. (2001), "The
   Evolution of Privacy Legislation:
   How Privacy Issues Are Changing
   Research," Marketing Research, 13
   (Winter), 6–7.

10 Gillin, Donna (2001).

11 Spangenberg, E., B. Grohmann, and
   D. E. Sprott (2005), "It's Beginning to
   Smell (and Sound) a Lot Like
   Christmas: The Interactive Effects of
   Ambient Scent and Music in a Retail
   Setting," The Journal of Business
   Research, 58 (November), 582–589;
   Michon, Richard, Jean-Charles
   Chebat, and L. W. Turley (2005),
   "Mall Atmospherics: The Interaction
   Effects of the Mall Environment on
   Shopping Behavior," Journal of
   Business Research, 58 (May),
   576–583.

12 Carrigan, M. and M. Kirkup (2001),
   "The Ethical Responsibilities of
   Marketers in Retail Observational
   Research: Protecting Stakeholders
   through the 'Ethical Research'
   Covenant," International Journal
   of Retail, Distribution and
   Consumer Research, 11 (October),
   411–435.

13 Marketing News (1995), "Marketers
   Value Honesty in Marketing
   Researchers," 29 (6/5), 27.

14 Brennan, M., S. Benson, and
   Z. Kearns (2005), "The Effect of
   Introductions on Telephone Survey
   Participation Rates," International
   Journal of Market Research, 47 (1),
   65–74.

15 Mack, Beth (2002), "Online Privacy
   Critical to Research Success,"
   Marketing News, 36 (11/25), 21.

Chapter 5

1 Cassidy, Hilary (2005), "Many Paths
   to Cool, But Big Gains for All,"
   Brandweek, 46 (June 20), S53.

2 Niemi, Wayne (2004), "Schoenfeld to
   Leave as Vans CEO; As Its Deal with
   VF Corp. Closes, the Skate Brand
   Gains a New President and a New
   Focus on Apparel," Footwear News
   (July 5), 2.

3 McLaughlin, Lisa (2004), "The New
   Roll Model," Time, 164 (7/26), 74.

4 Sayre, Shay, Qualitative Methods for
   Marketplace Research (Sage: Thousand
   Oaks, CA, 2001).

5 Sayre, Shay (2001); Morse, Janice M.
   and Lyn Richards, Readme First for a
   User's Guide to Qualitative Methods
   (Sage: Thousand Oaks, CA, 2002).

6 Semon, Thomas T. (2002), "You Get
   What You Pay for: It May Be Bad
   MR," Marketing News, 36
   (April 15), 7.

7 Hamel, G. and C. K. Prahalad (1991),
   "Corporate Imagination and
   Expeditioinary Marketing," Harvard
   Business Review (July–August), 85.

8 Martens, Claire (2004), "Sometimes a
   Great Notion Isn't Yet a Great
   Product," Harvard Management
   Update (March), 3–4.

9 Beverland, Michael (2005), "The
   Components of Prestige Brands,"
   Journal of Business Research,
   forthcoming. Beverland, Michael
   (2004), "Brand Value Convictions,
   Flexibility and New Zealand Wine,"
   Business Horizons, 47 (September/
   October), 53–64.

10 Heather, R. P. (1994), "Future Focus
   Groups," American Demographics,
   (January 1), 6.

11 Creamer, Mathew (2005), "Slowly,
   Marketers Learn How to Let Go and
   Let Blog," Advertising Age, 76
   (10/31), 1–35.

12 Fass, Allison (2005), "Collective
   Opinion," Forbes, 176 (11/28), 76–79.

13 O'Loughlin, Sandra (2005), "Real
   Women Have Lingerie," Brandweek,
   46 (11/14), 22–24.

14 See Palan, K. M. and R. E. Wilkes
   (1997), "Adolescent-Parent
   Interaction in Family Decision
   Making," Journal of Consumer
   Research, 24 (September), 159–170;
   Haytko, Diana L. and Julie Baker
   (2004), "It's All at the Mall: Exploring
   Adolescent Girls' Experiences,"
   Journal of Retailing, 80 (Spring),
   67–83.

15 Murphy, Ian (1996), "Aided by
   Research, Harley Goes Whole Hog,"
   Marketing News, 30 (12/02), 16–17.

16 Kotler, Philip "Behavioral Models for
   Analyzing Buyers," Journal of
   Marketing (October 1965), pp. 37–45.

17 Alsop, Ronald (1998), "Advertisers
   Put Consumers on the Couch," The
   Wall Street Journal (May 13), 19.

18 Grimm, Matthew (2002), "Wine Ads:
   A New Sobriety," American
   Demographics (February), 42–43.

Chapter 6

1 Joint Advertising, Market Research & Studies, "Market Research and Studies," JAMRS website, http://www.jamrs.org, accessed February 8, 2006; Arndorfer, James B., "Target Practice," Advertising Age, November 28, 2005, 76 (11/28), 1–41; Margolis, Emanuel, "Building a Database of Potential Soldiers," Connecticut Law Tribune, October 24, 2005, http://www.ctlawtribune.com; and James B. Arndorfer, "Army Looking for a Direct Hit," Advertising Age, July 11, 2005, 76 (7/11), 4–36.

2 "Breakfast Sandwich Boom," Chain Leader, November 2005, downloaded from InfoTrac at http://web2. infotrac.galegroup.com; and Perlik, Allison, "Fast Starts," Restaurants & Institutions, January 15, 2006, http:// web2.infotrac.galegroup.com.

3 Grow, Brian, "Yes, Ma'am, That Part Is in Stock," BusinessWeek, August 1, 2005, downloaded from InfoTrac at http://web2.infotrac.galegroup.com; and Servigistics, "Servigistics Pricing: Maximizing the Profitability of Your Service Network," http://www.servigistics.com, accessed February 7, 2006.

4 Prasso, Sheridan, "Battle for the Face of China," Fortune, December 12, 2005, downloaded from InfoTrac at http://web2.infotrac.galegroup.com.

5 Charles, Susan K., "Custom Content Delivery," Online, March–April 2004, downloaded from Business & Company Resource Center at http://galenet.galegroup.com; Fleming, Lee, "Digital Delivery: Pushing Content to the Desktop," Digital Information Group, January 31, 1997; and "How Smart Agents Will Change Selling," Forbes ASAP, August 28, 1995, p. 95.

6 "Seeking New Beer Drinkers in the High Andes," Global Agenda, July 20, 2005, downloaded from Business & Company Resource Center, http://galenet.galegroup.com; and "China Ranked Largest Beer Consumer in 2004," Kyodo News International, December 15, 2005, http://galenet.galegroup.com.

7 This section is based on Levy, Michael and Barton Weitz, Retail Management (Homewood, IL: Richard D. Irwin, 1992), pp. 357–358.

8 Data from the "About Us" section of the Capital One website, http://www.capitalone.com, accessed February 9, 2006.

9 Rao, Srikumar S., "Technology: The Hot Zone," Forbes, November 18, 1996.

10 IBM Business Intelligence Data Mining Product Discovery, http://www.ibm.com.

11 Wasserman, Todd, Gerry Khermouch, and Jeff Green, "Mining Everyone's Business," Brandweek, February 28, 2000, p. 34.

12 DataMind, "Clients: Case Studies," DataMind website, http://www.datamind.com, accessed February 6, 2006.

13 Totty, Michael, "Making Searches Work at Work," The Wall Street Journal, December 19, 2005, http://online.wsj.com.

14 "Hispanic-Owned Businesses: Growth Projections, 2004–2010," HispanicBusiness.com Store, http://www.hbinc.com, accessed February 7, 2006.

15 Neff, Jack, "Wal-Mart Takes Stock in RetailLink System," Advertising Age, May 21, 2001, p. 6.

16 See Federal Grants Wire, "National Trade Data Bank (NTDB)," http://www.federalgrantswire.com, accessed February 6, 2006; and STAT-USA, "What Information Is Available under GLOBUS and NTBD?" and "GLOBUS & NTDB," http://www.stat-usa.gov, accessed February 6, 2006.

17 Based on Brown, Warren, "Pain at the Pump Doesn't Faze New-Car Buyers," Washington Post, January 29, 2006, http://www.washingtonpost.com; Wells, Melanie, "Snowboarding Secrets," Forbes, February 14, 2005, downloaded from InfoTrac at http://web5.infotrac.galegroup.com; and Halliday, Jean, "Automakers Scrap SUVs, Tout Hybrids," Advertising Age, September 26, 2005, http://web5.infotrac.galegroup.com.

Chapter 7

1 Darlin, Damon, "The Only Question That Matters," Business 2.0, September 2005, downloaded from InfoTrac at http://web2.infotrac.galegroup.com; Kirkpatrick, David, "Throw It at the Wall and See if It Sticks," Fortune, December 12, 2005, http://web2.infotrac.galegroup.com; and McGregor, Jena, "Would You Recommend Us?" Business Week, January 30, 2006, http://web5.infotrac.galegroup.com.

2 Vascellaro, Jessica E. "Who'll Give Me $50 for This Purse from Nana?" The Wall Street Journal, December 28, 2005, http://online.wsj.com; and Survey.com, "Survey Reveals Majority of Americans Receive Unwanted Gifts," news release, December 19, 2005, http://www.survey.com.

3 Excerpts from Arlen, Michael J. Thirty Seconds (New York: Farrar, Straus and Giroux, Inc., 1979, 1980), pp. 185–186. This material first appeared in The New Yorker.

4 However, the popularity of marketing research has affected the willingness of respondents to participate in surveys. People are increasingly refusing to participate.

5 Tuckel, Peter and Harry O'Neill, "The Vanishing Respondent in Telephone Surveys," a paper presented at the 56th annual conference of the American Association of Public Opinion Research (AAPOR) in Montreal on May 17–20, 2001.

6 Cull, William L., Karen G. O'Connor, Sanford Sharp, and Suk-fong S. Tang, "Response Rates and Response Bias for 50 Surveys of Pediatricians," Health Services Research, February 2005, downloaded from Business & Company Resource Center, http://galenet.galegroup.com.

7 Lee, Eunkyu, Michael Y. Hu, and Rex S. Toh, "Respondent Non-cooperation in Surveys and Diaries: An Analysis of Item Non-response and Panel Attrition," International Journal of Market Research, Autumn 2004, downloaded from InfoTrac at http://web7.infotrac.galegroup.com.

8 For an interesting study of extremity bias, see Baumgartner, Hans and Jan-Benedict E. M. Steekamp, "Response Styles in Marketing Research: A Cross-National Investigation," Journal of Marketing Research, May 2001, pp. 143-156.

9 Turner, Charles F., Maria A. Villarroel, James R. Chromy, Elizabeth Eggleston, and Susan M. Rogers, "Same-Gender Sex among U.S. Adults: Trends across the Twentieth Century and during the 1990s," Public Opinion Quarterly, Fall 2005, downloaded from InfoTrac at http://web7.infotrac.galegroup.com.

10 Warwick, Donald T. and Charles A. Lininger, The Sample Survey: Theory and Practice (New York: McGraw-Hill, 1975), p. 2.

11 Lockley, L. C., "Notes on the History of Marketing Research," Journal of Marketing, April 1950, p. 733.

12 Hof, Robert D., "The Power of Us," BusinessWeek, June 20, 2005, downloaded from InfoTrac at http://web2.infotrac.galegroup.com.

13 For a complete discussion of conducting surveys in Hispanic neighborhoods, see Hernandes, Sigfredo A. and Carol J. Kaufman, "Marketing Research in Hispanic Barrios: A Guide to Survey Research," Marketing Research, March 1990, pp. 11–27.

14 Curtin, Richard, Stanley Presser, and Eleanor Singer, "Changes in Telephone Survey Nonresponse over the Past Quarter Century," Public Opinion Quarterly, Spring 2005, downloaded from InfoTrac at http://web3.infotrac.galegroup.com.

15 Cuneo, Alice Z. "Researchers Flail as Public Cuts the Cord," Advertising Age, November 15, 2004, downloaded from InfoTrac at http://web3.infotrac.galegroup.com.

16 See ibid.; and Jon Kamman, "Cell Phones Put Pollsters 'in a Muddle,'" USA Today, December 31, 2003, http://www.usatoday.com.

17 Hembroff, Larry A., Debra Rusz, Ann Rafferty, Harry McGee, and Nathaniel Ehrlich, "The Cost-Effectiveness of Alternative Advance Mailings in a Telephone Survey," Public Opinion Quarterly, Summer 2005, downloaded from InfoTrac at http://web3.infotrac.galegroup.com.

18 Brennan, Mike, Susan Benson, and Zane Kearns (2005), "The Effect of Introductions on Telephone Survey Participation Rates," International Journal of Market Research, 47 (1), 65–74.

19 Dillman, Don A. Mail and Internet Surveys: The Tailored Design Method (New York: John Wiley and Sons, 2000), p. 173.

20 Schaefer, David R. and Don A. Dillman, "Development of a Standard E-Mail Methodology: Results of an Experiment," Public Opinion Quarterly 62(3) (Fall 1998), p. 378.

21 Ibid.

22 For a complete discussion of fax surveys, see the excellent article by Dickson, John P. and Douglas L. Maclachlan, "Fax Surveys: Return Patterns and Comparison with Mail Surveys," Journal of Marketing Research, February 1996, pp. 108–113.

23 Merriman, Joyce A., "Your Feedback Is Requested," American Family Physician, October 1, 2005, downloaded from InfoTrac at http://web3.infotrac.galegroup.com.

24 Dillmann, D.A. (2000), Mail and Internet Surveys, The Tailored Design Method, NY: Wiley. pp. 369–372.

25 Göritz, Anja S. (2004), "Recruitment for On-Line Access Panels," International Journal of Market Research, 46 (4), 411–425.

26 Fricker, Scott, Mirta Galesic, Roger Tourangeau, and Ting Yan, "An Experimental Comparison of Web and Telephone Surveys," Public Opinion Quarterly, Fall 2005, downloaded from InfoTrac at http://web3.infotrac.galegroup.com.

27 See Nielsen, Jakob, "Keep Online Surveys Short," Alertbox, February 2, 2004, http://www.useit.com; "About Jakob Nielsen," http://www.useit.com, accessed February 21, 2006; and Nielsen Norman Group, "About Nielsen Norman Group," http://www.nngroup.com, accessed February 21, 2006.

28 Mary Lisbeth D'Amico, "Call Security," The Wall Street Journal, February 13, 2006, http://online.wsj.com.

29 For an interesting empirical study, see Akaah, Ishmael P. and Edward A. Riordan, "The Incidence of Unethical Practices in Marketing Research: An Empirical Investigation," Journal of the Academy of Marketing Sciences, Spring 1990, pp. 143–152.

30 Based on "Do-Not-Call List Reduces Telemarketing, Poll Finds," The Wall

Street Journal, January 12, 2006, http://online.wsj.com.

Chapter 8

1 Based on Thomas Mucha, "This Is Your Brain on Advertising," Business 2.0, August 2005, downloaded from InfoTrac at http://web2.infotrac.galegroup.com; and Peter Laybourne and David Lewis, "Neuromarketing: The Future of Consumer Research?" Admap, May 2005, pp. 28–30.

2 Selltiz, Claire, Lawrence S. Wrightsman, and Stuart W. Cook, *Research Methods in Social Relations* (New York: Holt, Rinehart and Winston, 1976), p. 251.

3 Campbell, Angus, Philip E. Converse, and Willard L. Rodgers, *The Quality of American Life* (New York: Russell Sage Foundation, 1976), p. 112. Although weather conditions did not correlate with perceived quality of life, the comfort variable did show a relationship with the index of well-being. This association might be confounded by the fact that ventilation and/or air-conditioning equipment is less common in less affluent homes. Income was previously found to correlate with quality of life.

4 Abrams, Bill, *The Observational Research Handbook* (Chicago: NTC Business Books, 2000), pp. 2, 105.

5 Adapted with permission from the April 30, 1980 issue of Advertising Age. Copyright © 1980 by Crain Communications, Inc.

6 Nielsen Media Research, "About Nielsen Media Research," http://www.nielsenmedia.com, accessed February 24, 2006.

7 Arbitron, "The Portable People Meter System," http://www.arbitron.com, accessed February 24, 2006.

8 PreTesting Company, "About the PreTesting Company" and "Television," http://www.pretesting.com, accessed February 24, 2006.

9 Kiley, David, "Google: Searching for an Edge in Ads," Business Week, January 30, 2006, downloaded from InfoTrac at http://web3.infotrac.galegroup.com. See also Pieter Sanders and Bram Lebo, "Click Tracking: A Fool's Paradise?" Brandweek, June 6, 2005, http://web3.infotrac.galegroup.com.

10 Neff, Jack, "Aging Population Brushes Off Coloring," Advertising Age, July 25, 2005, downloaded from InfoTrac at http://web5.infotrac.galegroup.com.

11 Stringer, Kortney, "Eye-Tracking Technology for Marketers," Detroit Free Press, August 1, 2005, downloaded from Business & Company Resource Center, http://galenet.galegroup.com.

12 Krugman's, Herbert B., statement as quoted in "Live, Simultaneous Study of Stimulus, Response Is

Physiological Measurement's Great Virtue," Marketing News, May 15, 1981, pp. 1, 20.

13 Based on "Mazda Turns to Eye-Tracking to Assist Revamp of European Site," New Media Age, November 3, 2005, downloaded from Business & Company Resource Center, http://galenet.galegroup.com; and "Persuasion Is the New Focus," Revolution, February 21, 2006, downloaded from the Media Coverage page of the Syzygy website, http://www.syzygy.co.uk.

14 Adapted with permission from Bruce Rayner, "Product Development, Now Hear This!" Electronic Business, August 1997.

Chapter 9

1 Like Dragnet, the story is true but the brand names are fictitious.

2 Shadish, William R., Thomas D. Cook, and Donald T. Campbell, *Experimental and Quasi Experimental Designs for Generalized Causal Inference.* (Geneva, IL: Houghton Mifflin, 2002).

3 Ellingstad, Vernon and Norman W. Heimstra, *Methods in the Study of Human Behavior* (Monterey, CA: Brooks/Cole, 1974).

4 Anderson, Barry F., *The Psychological Experiment: An Introduction to the Scientific Method.* (Belmont, CA: Brooks/Cole, 1971), p. 28, 42–44.

5 Reitter, Robert N. (2003), "Comment: American Media and the Smoking-Related Behaviors of Asian Adolescents," Journal of Advertising Research, 43 (March), 12–13.

6 Lach, Jennifer (2000), "Up in Smoke," American Demographics, 22 (March), 26.

7 Mitchell, Vincent-Wayne and Sarah Haggett (1997), "Sun-Sign Astrology in Market Segmentation: An Empirical Investigation," Journal of Consumer Marketing, 14 (2), 113–131.

8 Tybout, Alice M. and Gerald Zaltman (1974), "Ethics in Marketing Research: Their Practical Relevance," Journal of Marketing Research, 21 (November), 357–368.

9 Shadish, William R., Thomas D. Cook, and Donald T. Campbell (2002).

10 *Market Testing Consumer Products* (New York: National Industrial Conference Board, 1967), p. 13.

11 Riste, Christine (2002), La suprématie contée des prospectus, "Libre Service Actualité-LSA," (January 17), 1751.

12 Babin, B. J. and Adilson Borges (2005), "Product Category and Promotional Theme Congruency: Its Effect on Preference and Retail Store Image," in Development in Marketing Science, H. Spotts, Ed., Academy of Marketing Science, Coral Gables, FL.

13 Sally Scanlon (1979), "The True Test," Sales and Marketing Management, March, 57.

14 Pollack, Jodham (1996), "Price Issues Dog Frito Olean Tests," Advertising Age (November 25), 4.

15 Reprinted with permission from Martin, Geoffrey Lee, "Drinkers Get Court Call," Advertising Age, May 20, 1991. Copyright © 1991 Crain Communications, Inc.

Chapter 10

1 Babin, Barry J. and Jill Attaway (2000), "Atmospheric Affect as a Tool for Creating Value and Gaining Share of Customer," Journal of Business Research, 49 (August), 91–99; Verhoef, P.C. (2003), "Understanding the Effect of Customer Relationship Management Efforts on Customer Retention and Customer Share Development," Journal of Marketing 67 (October), 30–45.

2 Periatt, J. A., S. A. LeMay, and S. Chakrabarty (2004), "The Selling Orientation-Customer Orientation (SOCO) Scale: Cross-Validation of the Revised Version," Journal of Personal Selling and Sales Management," 24 (Winter), 49–54.

3 Anderson, Barry F., *The Psychology Experiment.* (Monterey, CA: Brooks/Cole, 1971), p. 26.

4 Kerlinger, Fred N., *Foundations of Behavioral Research.* (New York: Holt, Rinehart and Winston, 1973).

5 Cohen, Jacob (1990), "Things I Have Learned (So Far)," American Psychologist, 45 (December), 1304–1312.

6 Arnold, Catherine (2004), "Satisfaction's the Name of the Game," Marketing News, 38 (10/15), 39–45. Also, see http://www.theacsi.org.

7 In more advanced applications such as those involving structural equations analysis, a distinction can be made between reflective composites and formative indexes. See Hair, J. F., W. C. Black, B. J. Babin, R. Anderson, and R. Tatham, *Multivariate Data Analysis,* 6th Edition (Upper Saddle River, NJ: Prentice Hall, 2006).

8 Cox, Keith K. and Ben M. Enis, *The Marketing Research Process.* (Pacific Palisades, CA: Goodyear, 1972); Kerlinger, Fred N., *Foundations of Behavioral Research,* 3rd ed. (Ft. Worth: Holt, Rinehart and and Winston, 1986).

9 Breeden, Richard, "Owners, Executives Cite Small Firms' Advantages," The Wall Street Journal, January 3, 2006, http://online.wsj.com; and AllBusiness.com, "SMB State of the Union Study," Winter 2005, News and Press page, http://www.allbusiness.com/press/barometer.pdf.

10 Likert, Rensis "A Technique for the Measurement of Attitudes," Archives of Psychology 19 (1931), pp. 44–53.

11 Osgood, Charles, George Suci, and Percy Tannenbaum, *The Measurement of Meaning* (Urbana: University of Illinois Press, 1957). Seven-point scales were used in the original work; however, subsequent researchers have modified the scale to have five points, nine points, and so on.

12 Menezes, Dennis and Norbert F. Elbert, "Alternative Semantic Scaling Formats for Measuring Store Image: An Evaluation," Journal of Marketing Research, February 1979, pp. 80–87.

13 Costanzo, Chris "How Consumer Research Drives Web Site Design," American Banker, April 19, 2005, downloaded from Business & Company Resource Center, http://galenet.galegroup.com.

14 Headley, Dean E., Brent D. Bowen, and Jacqueline R. Liedtke. This case, originally titled "Navigating through Airline Quality," was reviewed and accepted for publication by the Society for Case Research.

Chapter 11

1 White, Joseph B., "The Price of Safety," The Wall Street Journal, December 5, 2005, http://online.wsj.com; and J. D. Power and Associates, "J. D. Power and Associates Reports: Premium Surround Sound Systems and HD Radio Garner High Consumer Interest Based on Their Market Price, while Consumers Prefer One-Time Fee over the Monthly Fee Associated with Satellite Radio," news release, http://www.jdpower.com, August 18, 2005.

2 Smith, Robert, David Olah, Bruce Hansen, and Dan Cumbo, "The Effect of Quesionnaire Length on Participant Response Rate: A Case Study in the U.S. Cabinet Industry," Forest Products Journal, November–December 2003, downloaded from Business & Company Resource Center, http://galenet.galegroup. com.

3 "Insurers Question Methods in U.S. Treasury Survey on Terror Backstop," A. M. Best Newswire, April 12, 2005, downloaded from Business & Company Resource Center, http://galenet.galegroup.com.

4 "Mothers Misunderstand Questions on Feeding Questionnaire," Medical Letter on the CDC and FDA, September 5, 2004, downloaded from Business & Company Resource Center, http://galenet.galegroup.com.

5 Donahue, Amy K. and Joanne M. Miller, "Citizen Preferences and Paying for Police," Journal of Urban Affairs 27(4) (2005): 419–35.

6 Nathan Weber, "Research: A Survey Shows How Media Influence Our Decorating and Cooking Choices," HFN, the Weekly Newspaper for the Home Furnishing Network, December 5, 2005, downloaded

from Business & Company Resource Center, http://galenet.galegroup.com.

7   Stanley L. Payne, *The Art of Asking Questions* (Princeton, NJ: Princeton University Press, 1951), p. 185. The reader who wants a more detailed account of question wording is referred to this classic book on that topic.

8   Roll, Charles W., Jr. and Albert H. Cantril, *Polls: Their Use and Misuse in Politics* (New York: Basic Books, 1972), pp. 106–7.

9   Other product attributes are relative advantage, compatibility, complexity, and communicability.

10 Payne, Stanley L. (1951), pp. 102–3.

11 Dillman, Don A., *Mail and Internet Surveys: The Tailored Design Method* (New York: John Wiley and Sons, 2000), pp. 357–61.

12 Young, Sarah J. and Craig M. Ross, "Web Questionnaires: A Glimpse of Survey Research in the Future," *Parks & Recreation*, Vol. 35, No. 6 (June 2000), p. 30.

13 Michel, Matt, "Controversy Redux," *CASRO Journal*, http://www.decisionanalyst.com/publ_art/contredux.htm, downloaded February 8, 2001.

14 Almekhlafi, Abdurrahman Ghaleb, "Preservice Teachers' Attitudes and Perceptions of the Utility of Web-Based Instruction in the United Arab Emirates," *International Journal of Instructional Media* 32(3) (2005): 269–84.

15 Harzing, Anne-Wil, "Does the Use of English-Language Questionnaires in Cross-National Research Obscure National Differences?" *International Journal of Cross Cultural Management* 5(2) (2005): 213–24.

16 Cateora, Philip R., *International Marketing* (Homewood, IL: Richard D. Irwin, 1990), pp. 387–89.

17 "Hospitals, Feds Design Survey to Identify Culture That Encourages Patient Safety," *Health Care Strategic Management*, February 2005, downloaded from Business & Company Resource Center, http://galenet.galegroup.com; and Agency for Healthcare Research and Quality, "Hospital Survey on Patient Safety Culture," accessed at http://www.ahrq.gov/qual/hospculture, March 7, 2006.

Chapter 12

1   Based on Deborah Ball, "As Chocolate Sags, Cadbury Gambles on a Piece of Gum," *The Wall Street Journal*, January 12, 2006, http://online.wsj.com; Cadbury Schweppes, "Products: Trident Splash," *Gumopolis*, http://www.tridentgum.com, accessed March 16, 2006; Cadbury Schweppes, "New Cadbury Schweppes Americas Confectionary Facility Holds Future Gum Innovation: New Jersey Based

Science & Technology Center to Meet Demands of Growing Gum Market," news release, http://www.cadburyschweppes.com, February 6, 2006.

2   Kinne, Susan and Tari D. Topolski, "Inclusion of People with Disabilities in Telephone Health Surveillance Surveys," *American Journal of Public Health* 95(3) (March 2005): 512–517.

3   Brock, Sabra E., "Marketing Research in Asia: Problems, Opportunities, and Lessons," *Marketing Research*, September 1989, p. 47.

4   Yeganeh, Hamid, Zhan Su, Elie Virgile, and M. Chrysostome, "A Critical Review of Epistemological and Methodological Issues in Cross-Cultural Research," *Journal of Comparative International Management*, December 2004, downloaded from InfoTrac at http://web2.infotrac.galegroup.com.

5   Sigenman, Lee, Steven A. Tuch, and Jack K. Martin, "What's in a Name? Preference for 'Black' versus 'African-American' among Americans of African Descent," *Public Opinion Quarterly*, Fall 2005, downloaded from InfoTrac at http://web2.infotrac.galegroup.com.

6   Rideout, Bruce E., Katherine Hushen, Dawn McGinty, Stephanie Perkins, and Jennifer Tate, "Endorsement of the New Ecological Paradigm in Systematic and E-Mail Samples of College Students," *Journal of Environmental Education*, Winter 2005, downloaded from InfoTrac at http://web2.infotrac.galegroup.com.

7   SurveySite, "What We Do: Quantitative Research," http://www.surveysite.com, accessed March 15, 2006.

8   Council of American Survey Research Organizations (CASRO), "Frequently Asked Questions about Conducting Online Research: New Methodologies for Traditional Techniques," 1998, http://www.casro.org.

9   Mellinger, Gloria, "Harris Interactive Inc.," *World Opinion Research Profiles*, July 18, 2000.

10 Ibid.

11 CASRO, "Frequently Asked Questions about Conducting Online Research."

12 Survey Sampling International, "Internet Sampling Solutions," http://www.ssisamples.com, accessed March 15, 2006.

13 Based on Gene Mueller, "It's Hard to Figure Number of Anglers," *Washington Times*, March 20, 2005, downloaded from InfoTrac at http://web3.infotrac.galegroup.com; Atlantic Coastal Cooperative Statistics Program, "About Us: Committees," http://www.accsp.org, accessed March 16, 2006; Atlantic States Marine Fisheries Commission, "About Us," http://www.asmfc.org, accessed March 16, 2006.

14 Material for this case is from *Scientific Telephone Samples User's Manual*, Scientific Telephone Samples, Santa Ana, CA.

Chapter 13

1   Based on Gerdes, Geoffrey R., Jack K. Walton II, May X. Liu, Darrel W. Parke, and Namirembe Mukasa, "Trends in the Use of Payment Instruments in the United States," *Federal Reserve Bulletin*, Spring 2005, downloaded from InfoTrac at http://web2.infotrac.galegroup.com.

2   Most of the statistical material in this book assumes that the population parameters are unknown, which is the typical situation in most applied research projects.

3   The reasons for this are related to the concept of degrees of freedom, which will be explained later. At this point, disregard the intuitive notion of division by n, because it produces a biased estimate of the population variance.

4   In practice, most survey researchers will not use this exact formula. A modification of the formula, $Z = (X - \mu)/S$, using the sample standard deviation in an adjusted form, is frequently used.

5   Hayes, William L., *Statistics* (New York: Holt, Rinehart and Winston, 1963), p. 193.

6   Wonnacott, Thomas H. and Ronald J. Wonnacott, *Introductory Statistics*, 2nd ed. (New York: Wiley, 1972), p. 125.

7   Note that the derivation of this formula is (1) $E = ZS_{\bar{X}}$; (2) $E = ZS/\sqrt{n}$; (3) $\sqrt{n}\ ZS/E$; (4) $(n) = (ZS/E)^2$.

8   Based on Bialik, Carl, "A Survey Probes the Back Seats of Taxis, with Dubious Results," *The Wall Street Journal*, January 28, 2005, http://online.wsj.com; and Pointsec Mobile Technologies, "Taxis Hailed as Black Hole for Lost Cell Phones and PDAs, as Confidential Data Gets Taken for a Ride," news release, January 24, 2005, http://www.pointsec.com.

Chapter 14

1   Dolliver, Mark (2005), Plow Under Your Hops and Plant Some Vines," *Adweek*, 46 (7/25), 36–38.

2   Ibid.

3   Kirsche, M.L. (2005), "Targeting Boomers Could Boost Fizzling Out Beer Sales," *Drug Store News*, 27 (6/6), 81.

4   Longo, Don (2005), "Drink Up," *Progressive Grocer*, 84 (10/15), 52–58.

5   *The Wall Street Journal* (2006), "Oprah Again Tops American's List of Favorite Personalities" (2/3), http://online.wsj.com/article_print/SB113889692780347.html, accessed February 2, 2006.

6   Ricklefs, Roger (1983), "Ethics in America," *The Wall Street Journal* (October 31), 33–42; November 1, 1983, p. 33; November 2, 1983, p. 33; November 3, 1983, 33–37.

7   See Dubinsky, Alan J., Rajan Nataraajan, and Wen-Yeh Huang (2005), "Consumers' Moral Philosophies: Identifying the Idealist and the Relativist," *Journal of Business Research*, 58 (December), 1690–1701. Deal, Ken (2005), "Deeper into the Trees," *Marketing Research*, 17 (Summer), 38–40.

8   The data analysis tool must be added to the conventional Excel install by unpacking the data tool. This can be done by clicking on tools and then clicking on ad-ins and following the instructions. See http://www.microsoft.com for more instructions on how to accomplish this.

9   Technically the t-distribution should be used when the population variance is unknown and the standard deviation is estimated from sample data. However, with large samples, it is convenient to use the z-distribution because the t-distribution approximates the z-distribution.

10 The reader with an extensive statistics background will recognize that there are a few rare cases in which the degrees of freedom do not equal $k - 1$. However, these cases will rarely be encountered by readers of this level of book, and to present them would only confuse the discussion here.

11 An example of how to use the chi-square table is given in Table 4 of the appendix.

12 Diamon, Sidney (1982), "Market Research Latest Target in Ad Claim," *Advertising Age* (January 25), 52. Reprinted with permission by Crain Communications, Inc.

13 Adapted with permission from Melvin Prince, *Consumer Research for Management Decisions* (New York: John Wiley and Sons, 1982), pp. 163–166.

Chapter 15

1   Murphy, Victoria (2003), "The Revolution That Wasn't," *Chain Store Age*, 172 (10/27), 210.

2   Tang, F.F. and X. Xing (2001), "Will the Growth of Multi-Channel Retailing Diminsh the Pricing Efficiency of the Web?," *Journal of Retailing*, 77, 319–333.

3   The formula is not shown here, but it can be found in most basic statistics books.

4   This is the "statistical alternative" hypothesis.

5   Recall that the mean for a standardized variable is equal to 0.

6   When the actual regression model is illustrated as an explanation of the actual dependent variable in a population, Y_i is used and an error

term (e_i) is included because the sample parameters cannot be expected to perfectly predict and explain the actual value of the dependent variable in the population. When we use a regression equation to represent its ability to predict sample values of the dependent variable from the estimated parameter coefficients, $\hat{Y}_i$ is used to represent predicted values of Y_i and no error term is included since the actual amount of error in any given observation is unknown.

7   School enrollment statistics can often be found using the Internet and either searching through government statistics or examining the website for the local school district or school board.

8   The constant term has disappeared since it is equal to 0 when the regression coefficients are standardized.

9   For more on this topic, see Hair, J. F., W. C. Black, B. J. Babin, R. Tathum, and R. Anderson (2006), *Multivariate Data Analysis*, 6th ed., Prentice Hall, Upper Saddle River, NJ.

10 Copyright © 1981, Dr. William J. Lundstrom; reprinted with permission.

Chapter 16

1   Based on Baker, Stephen, "Math Will Rock Your World," Business Week, January 23, 2006, downloaded from InfoTrac at http://web5. infotrac.galegroup.com; Natalie Canavor and Claire Meirowitz, "Good Corporate Writing: Why It Matters, and What to Do," Communication World, July–August 2005, http://web1.infotrac. galegroup.com; and National Commission on Writing, "Writing: A Ticket to Work . . . or a Ticket Out," September 2004, http://www. writingcommission.org.

2   The original version of this chapter was written by John Bush, Oklahoma State University, and appeared in William G. Zikmund, *Business Research Methods* (Hinsdale, IL: Dryden Press, 1984).

3   "A Speech Tip," Communication Briefings 14(2), p. 3.

4   These guidelines, adapted with permission from Marjorie Brody (President, Brody Communications, 1200 Melrose Ave., Melrose Park, PA 19126), appeared in "How to Gesture When Speaking," Communication Briefings 14(11), p. 4.

5   "Tips of the Month," Communication Briefings 24(7) (May 2005), p. 1.

6   Based on Bridis, Ted, "Study: Shoppers Naïve about Online Pricing," Information Week, June 1, 2005, downloaded from InfoTrac at http://web2.infotrac.galegroup.com; Annenberg Public Policy Center (APPC), "Annenberg Study Shows Americans Vulnerable to Exploitation in the Online and Offline Marketplace," news release, June 1, 2005, http://www. annenbergpublicpolicycenter.org; and Joseph Turow, Lauren Feldman, and Kimberly Meltzer, "Open to Exploitation: American Shoppers Online and Offline," APPC report, June 2005, downloaded at http:// www.annenbergpublicpolicy center.org.